Bob Hoover

GEORGE WASHINGTON

After the Athenæum Portrait by Gilbert Stuart

AN AMERICAN HISTORY

BY

DAVID SAVILLE MUZZEY
PROFESSOR OF HISTORY, COLUMBIA UNIVERSITY

... rerum cognoscere causas

REVISED EDITION

GINN AND COMPANY
BOSTON · NEW YORK · CHICAGO · LONDON
ATLANTA · DALLAS · COLUMBUS · SAN FRANCISCO

COPYRIGHT, 1933, BY DAVID SAVILLE MUZZEY
ENTERED AT STATIONERS' HALL
ALL RIGHTS RESERVED

PRINTED IN THE UNITED STATES OF AMERICA

F 335.10

COPYRIGHT, 1911, 1917, 1920, 1923, 1925, 1929, BY DAVID SAVILLE MUZZEY

The Athenæum Press
GINN AND COMPANY · PRO-
PRIETORS · BOSTON · U.S.A.

EDITORIAL PREFACE

The present volume represents the newer tendencies in historical writing. Its aim is not to tell over once more the old story in the old way, but to give the emphasis to those factors in our national development which appeal to us as most vital from the standpoint of today. However various may be the advantages of historical study, one of them, and perhaps the most unmistakable, is to explain prevailing conditions and institutions by showing how they have come about. This is our best way of understanding the present and of placing ourselves in a position to participate intelligently in the solution of the great problems of social and political betterment which it is the duty of all of us to face. Dr. Muzzey has not, therefore, tabulated a series of historical occurrences under successive presidential administrations, but has carefully selected the great phases in the development of our country and treated them in a coherent fashion. He has exhibited great skill in so ordering them that they form a continuous narrative which will secure and retain the interest of the student. There is no question at any point of the importance of the topics selected and their relation to our whole complex development. All minor, uncorrelated matters, such as the circumstances attending each colonial plantation, the tactics and casualties of military campaigns, the careers of men of slight influence in high office, are boldly omitted on the ground that they make no permanent impression on the student's mind and serve only to confuse and blur the larger issues.

Some special features of the book are its full discussion of the federal power in connection with the Constitution, its emphasis on the westward-moving frontier as the most constant and potent force in our history, and its recognition of the influence of economic factors on our sectional rivalries and political theories. It will be noted that from one fourth to one fifth of the volume deals with the history of our country since the Civil War and Reconstruction. Hitherto there has been a reluctance on the part of those who have prepared textbooks on our history to undertake the responsibility of treating those recent phases of our social, political, and industrial history which are really of chief concern to us. Dr. Muzzey has undertaken the arduous task of giving the great problems and preoccupations of today their indispensable historic setting. This I deem the very special merit of his work, and I am confident that it will meet with eager approbation from many who have long been dissatisfied with the conventional textbook, which leaves a great gap between the past and the present.

JAMES HARVEY ROBINSON

PREFATORY NOTE TO THE REVISED EDITION

Besides bringing the narrative down into the administration of President Hoover, the author has entirely recast that part of the book following the Spanish War and has made considerable changes in the preceding chapters. The changes are chiefly in the direction of added emphasis on social and economic factors in our history. New illustrative material has been added, the maps have been improved, and the bibliographical references have been brought down to date. The author takes this occasion to express his hearty thanks to many of his fellow teachers of American history throughout the country for their friendly criticisms and helpful suggestions.

DAVID SAVILLE MUZZEY

COLUMBIA UNIVERSITY

CONTENTS

CHAPTER	PAGE

PART I. THE ESTABLISHMENT OF THE ENGLISH

I. THE NEW WORLD

    The Discovery of America 3
    A Century of Exploration 11

II. THE ENGLISH COLONIES

    The Old Dominion 26
    The New England Settlements 33
    The Proprietary Colonies 45
    The Colonies in the Eighteenth Century 56

III. THE STRUGGLE WITH FRANCE FOR NORTH AMERICA

    The Rise of New France 70
    The Fall of New France 79

PART II. SEPARATION OF THE COLONIES FROM ENGLAND

IV. BRITISH RULE IN AMERICA

    The Authority of Parliament in the Colonies 90
    Taxation without Representation 94
    The Punishment of Massachusetts 102

V. THE BIRTH OF THE NATION

    The Declaration of Independence 110
    The Revolutionary War 116
    Peace 127

PART III. THE NEW REPUBLIC

VI. THE CONSTITUTION

    The Critical Period 135
    "A More Perfect Union" 141
    The Federal Power 146

CONTENTS

CHAPTER
VII. FEDERALISTS AND REPUBLICANS
    Launching the Government 155
    The Reign of Federalism 164
    The Jeffersonian Policies 174
    The War of 1812 180

PART IV. NATIONAL VERSUS SECTIONAL INTERESTS

VIII. THE GROWTH OF A NATIONAL CONSCIOUSNESS
    A New American Spirit 191
    The Monroe Doctrine 201

IX. SECTIONAL INTERESTS
    The Favorite Sons 210
    An Era of Hard Feelings 216

X. THE JACKSONIAN ERA
    Nullification 227
    The War on the Bank 231
    A New Party 237

PART V. SLAVERY AND THE WEST

XI. THE GATHERING CLOUD
    The Missouri Compromise 247
    The Abolitionists 255

XII. TEXAS
    Westward Expansion 264
    The " Reoccupation " of Oregon and the " Reannexation " of Texas 270
    The Mexican War 275

XIII. THE COMPROMISE OF 1850
    The New Territory 282
    The Omnibus Bill 287
    A Four Years' Truce 292

CONTENTS

PART VI. THE CRISIS OF DISUNION

XIV. APPROACHING THE CRISIS
- The Repeal of the Missouri Compromise and the Formation of the Republican Party 301
- "A House divided against Itself" 308

XV. SECESSION
- The Election of Abraham Lincoln 320
- The Southern Confederacy 326
- The Fall of Fort Sumter 331

XVI. THE CIVIL WAR
- The Opposing Forces 339
- From Bull Run to Gettysburg 344
- The Triumph of the North 358
- Emancipation 374

PART VII. THE POLITICAL AND INDUSTRIAL HISTORY OF THE REPUBLIC SINCE THE CIVIL WAR

XVII. TWENTY YEARS OF REPUBLICAN SUPREMACY
- Reconstruction 381
- The Aftermath of the War 390
- A New Industrial Age 402

XVIII. THE CLEVELAND DEMOCRACY
- A People's President 418
- A Billion-Dollar Country 427
- Problems of Cleveland's Second Term 437

XIX. ENTERING THE TWENTIETH CENTURY
- The Spanish War and the Philippines 451
- The Roosevelt Policies 464
- The Return of the Democrats 480

XX. THE WORLD WAR AND AFTER
- Neutrality 497
- Participation 510
- Problems of Peace 524
- The Coolidge and Hoover Administrations 541

CONTENTS

	PAGE
APPENDIX I. Declaration of Independence	i
APPENDIX II. Constitution of the United States	v
APPENDIX III. Members of the Supreme Court, 1933	xxii
APPENDIX IV. The States of the Union	xxiii
APPENDIX V. Presidents and Other High Officials	xxv
APPENDIX VI. Members of Recent Cabinets	xxviii
INDEX	xxxi

LIST OF FULL-PAGE ILLUSTRATIONS

	PAGE
George Washington (in colors)	Frontispiece
Types of Indian Dwellings, — the Pueblo, the Tepee, and the Long House	21
Pilgrim Monument at Provincetown	34
The Ambush of Braddock's Army	84
Franklin at the Court of France, 1778	118
Group of Famous Revolutionary Buildings	131
Lafayette	133
The Capitol	146
The White House	150
Alexander Hamilton	160
Washington's Home at Mount Vernon	163
John Adams	170
Thomas Jefferson	174
Henry Clay	214
Andrew Jackson	227
Webster's Reply to Hayne	230
Abraham Lincoln	332
Sherman's Army destroying the Railroads in Georgia	368
Woodrow Wilson	484
U. S. S. *New Mexico* in Gatun Locks, Panama Canal	492
The Bridge at Château-Thierry	520
Independence Day. American Soldiers saluting the Statue of Washington, Paris, July 4, 1918	522
The President and Mrs. Coolidge at the White House	539
Herbert C. Hoover	553
Hail and Farewell! President Hoover greets President-elect Roosevelt as they start for the Inauguration	565

LIST OF FULL-PAGE AND DOUBLE-PAGE MAPS

	PAGE
Voyages of Discovery in the Fifteenth and Sixteenth Centuries	9
Early Maps of America (Lenox, Finæus, Münster, Mercator)	16, 17
Exploration and Settlement in North America in the Sixteenth Century	23
Proprietary Grants made by the Stuart Kings	51
French Explorations of the Seventeenth Century about the Great Lakes and the Mississippi	76
Map of the French and Indian Wars	85
England's Acquisitions in America in the French Wars of 1689–1763	88
The Revolutionary War on the Atlantic Seaboard	121
The United States in 1783	126
The Louisiana Purchase Territory, with States subsequently made from it	178
The War on the Canadian Border	185
Routes to the West, 1815–1825	195
North America in 1815	202
The Acquisition of the Far West, 1845–1850	282
Canals and Railroads operated in 1850	295
The Status of Slavery, 1844–1854	306
The Presidential Election of 1860	326
Map of the Civil War	345
Territorial Growth of the United States	430
Map showing the Products of the United States	467
The Greater United States and the Panama Canal Routes	474
The Federal Reserve Districts	489
Air-Mail Routes	551

AN AMERICAN HISTORY

PART I. THE ESTABLISHMENT OF THE ENGLISH

CHAPTER I

THE NEW WORLD

THE DISCOVERY OF AMERICA

THE discovery of America was an accident. The brave sailors of the fifteenth century who turned the prows of their tiny vessels into the strange waters of the Atlantic were seeking a new way to the "Indies,"—a term vaguely used to denote not India alone but also China, Japan, and all the Far Eastern countries of Asia. From these lands western Europe had for centuries been getting many of its luxuries and comforts. Ever-lengthening traders' caravans brought oriental rugs, flowered silks, gems, spices, porcelains, damasks, dyes, drugs, perfumes, and precious woods across the plains and plateaus of middle Asia to the Persian Gulf and the Black Sea or crept along the hot borders of the Arabian peninsula to the headwaters of the Red Sea. At Constantinople and the seaports of Syria and Egypt the fleets of Genoa and Venice were waiting to carry the Indian merchandise to the distributing centers of southern Europe, whence it was conveyed over the Alpine passes or along the Rhone valley to the busy, prosperous towns of France, Germany, England, and the Netherlands.

1. The Shifting of Trade Routes. In the fifteenth century there occurred two events which were destined to change the routes of the Eastern traders from the Mediterranean to the ocean highways. The capture of Constantinople by the Osmanli Turks in 1453 ruined the trade of Genoa, which had special privileges in that great capital of the Byzantine, or eastern Roman, Empire. And in 1498 Portuguese mariners, sailing around the coast of Africa, reached India, whence they brought cargoes of spices to western Europe more cheaply than the Venetian traders, who depended on the long overland routes by caravan to the harbors of Syria and Egypt. By a series of wars, begun in the sixteenth century, the Turks drove the Franks (as they called all Europeans) from Syria and the islands of the Ægean Sea, and put an end to the Mediterranean trade with the East.

2. Maritime Science. The science of navigation was chiefly encouraged by Prince Henry of Portugal (1394–1460), whose sailors pushed out into the uncharted waters of the Atlantic and ventured more than one thousand miles down the western coast of Africa. Ships were designed to sail closer to the wind and to stand the buffeting of the high ocean waves. The compass and the astrolabe (for measuring latitude) were perfected. Six new editions of the "Geography" of Ptolemy[1] were published between 1472 and 1492. In 1486 Bartholomew Dias rounded the Cape of Good Hope, and had not his crew refused to go farther from home, he might have stood out across the Indian Ocean and reached the Spice Islands of the East and all the cities of the Chinese Empire.

3. Christopher Columbus. While Dias was making his way back to Portugal an Italian mariner from Genoa, named Cristoforo Colombo, better known by his Latinized name of Columbus, who had become interested in the search for "mainlands and islands" far out in the Atlantic (perhaps in reaching the "Indies"), was seeking aid for his project at the courts of Europe. He first applied to the king of Portugal, in whose service he had already made several voyages down the African coast. On being repulsed he transferred his request to Ferdinand and Isabella, the sovereigns of Spain, who finally granted him financial aid and created him admiral of all the lands and islands which he might find on his voyage. This was in April, 1492. By the following August, Columbus was ready to start from Palos, with three small ships and about a hundred sailors, on what proved to be the most momentous voyage in history.

Columbus was a student as well as a man of affairs. He shared with the best scholars of his day the long-established belief in the

---

[1] Claudius Ptolomæus, a Greek astronomer, wrote a "Geography" about the year A.D. 150, which remained the standard work on the shape and size of Europe, Asia, and Africa (the known world of the Middle Ages) until after the great voyages of the fifteenth century.

THE NEW WORLD

sphericity of the earth.[1] As a guide for his voyage he probably had charts or "portulani" which indicated the eastern coast of Asia lying far to the west of Europe. The so-called Toscanelli map, attributed to the Florentine astronomer, had calculated the size of the earth almost exactly, but the author, misled by the description of travelers to the Far East, had made the continent of Asia extend eastward almost all the way across the Pacific Ocean, so that Cipango (or Japan) on his

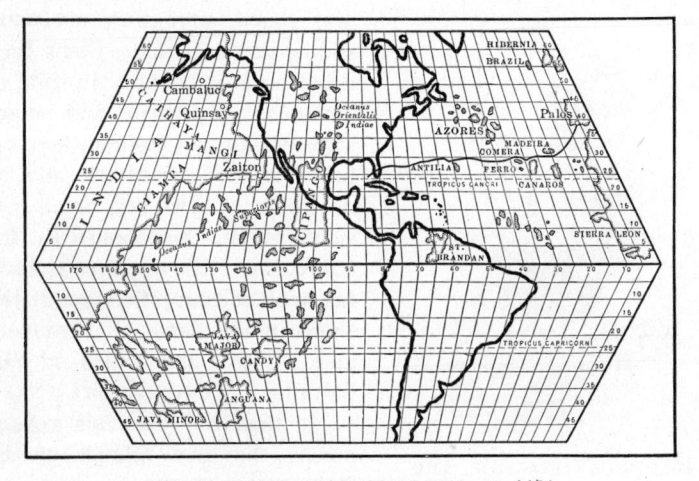

THE SO-CALLED TOSCANELLI MAP OF 1474

The actual position of the western continent is shown by the heavy black outline

map occupied the actual position of Mexico. Columbus, therefore, although not deceived as to the length of voyage necessary to reach land, was deceived to the day of his death as to the land he reached at the end of his voyage.

4. Columbus crosses the Atlantic. The trio of little vessels, favored by clear skies and a steady east wind, made the passage from the Canary Islands to the Bahamas in five weeks. No storms racked

---

[1] The popular idea that Columbus " discovered that the earth is round" is entirely false. More than eighteen hundred years before Columbus's day the Greek philosopher Aristotle demonstrated the sphericity of the earth from the altitude of the stars observed from various places. Roger Bacon, a Franciscan friar, in 1267 even collected passages from the writers of classical antiquity to prove that the ocean separating Spain from the eastern shore of Asia was not very wide.

the ships, but still it was a fearsome voyage over the quiet seas. To the trembling crews each mile westward was a further venture into the great mysterious "sea of darkness," where horrible monsters might be waiting to engulf them, where the fabled mountain of lodestone might draw the nails from their ships, or the dreaded boring worm puncture their wooden keels. The auspicious and unvarying east wind itself was a menace. How could they ever get home again in the face of it? And if it was really true that the world was round, were they not daily sliding down its slope, which they could never remount? In spite of ominous mutterings and overt signs of mutiny Columbus kept his prows headed westward, and at daybreak of October 12, 1492, sighted land. Surrounded by the naked awe-stricken natives, Columbus took solemn possession of the shore in the name of Ferdinand and Isabella and called it San Salvador ("Holy Saviour").

COLUMBUS'S FLAGSHIP, THE SANTA MARIA

He then continued his voyage among the small islands of the Bahamas, seeking the mainland of Cathay (China). When he reached the apparently interminable coast of Cuba he was sure that he was at the gates of the kingdom of the Great Khan, and that the cities of China with their fabulous wealth would soon hear the voice of his Arab interpreter presenting to the monarch of the East the greetings and gifts of the sovereigns of Spain. He was doomed to disappointment. The misfortunes which dogged his steps to the end of his life now began. Martin Pinzon, captain of the *Pinta*, deserted him on the coast of Cuba. His largest caravel, the *Santa Maria*, was wrecked a few weeks later on the coast of Haiti, which he mistook for the long-sought Cipango, and he hastened back to Spain in the remaining vessel, the tiny *Niña*. He was hailed with enthusiasm by the nation and loaded with honors by his sovereigns, who had no suspicion that he had failed to reach the islands lying off the coasts of the rich kingdoms of the East or that he had discovered still richer regions in the West.

5. Columbus's Later Voyages and Ill Fortune. Columbus made three more voyages to the "Indies" in 1493, 1498, and 1502. On the voyage of 1498 he discovered the mainland of South America, and in 1502 he sailed along the coast of Central America, vainly attempting to find a strait which would let him through to the main coast of Cathay. All the while the clouds of misfortune were gathering about him. His costly expeditions had so far brought no wealth to Spain. While his ships were skirting the pestilential coasts of South America

THE MAURA MEDAL (SPAIN), STRUCK TO COMMEMORATE THE FOUR-HUNDREDTH ANNIVERSARY OF COLUMBUS'S DISCOVERY OF AMERICA

the Portuguese Vasco da Gama had reached the real Indies by the Cape of Good Hope and brought back to Lisbon cargoes of spices, satins, damask, ivory, and gold (see map, p. 9). The Spanish sovereigns were jealous of the laurels of the Portuguese mariners. Mutiny, shipwreck, and fever were lighter evils for Columbus to contend with than the plots of his enemies and the envious disappointment of the grandees of Spain. One of the Spanish governors of Haiti sent him home in irons. His young sons, Diego and Ferdinand, who were pages in the queen's service, were jeered at as they passed through the courtyard of the Alhambra: "There go the sons of the Admiral of the Mosquitoes, who has discovered lands of vanity and delusion as the miserable graves of Castilian gentlemen." Returning from his fourth voyage, in 1504, he found his best friend at court,

Queen Isabella, on her deathbed, and, bowed with discouragement, illness, humiliation, and poverty, he followed her to the grave in 1506. So passed away in misery and obscurity a man whose service to mankind was beyond calculation. His wonderful voyage of 1492 had linked together the two hemispheres of our planet and "mingled the two streams of human life which had flowed for countless ages apart" (John Fiske).[1]

6. Pope Alexander VI's "Demarcation Line." Had Columbus and his fellow voyagers known that a solid barrier of land reaching from arctic to antarctic snows, and beyond that another ocean vaster than the one they had just crossed, lay between the islands they mistakenly called the Indies and the real Indies of the East, they would have probably abandoned the thought of a western route and returned to contest with Portugal the search for the Indies via the Cape of Good Hope. As it was, the Spanish sovereigns, confident that their pilots had reached the edge of Asia, asked of Pope Alexander VI a "bull" (or formal papal decree) admitting them to a share with Portugal in all lands and islands which should be discovered in the search for the Indies. The Pope, who was quite generally recognized in Europe as the arbiter of international disputes, acceded to the request, and in his bull of 1493 divided the undiscovered world between Spain and Portugal by a "demarcation line," which was fixed the next year by the Treaty of Tordesillas at three hundred and seventy leagues west of the Cape Verde Islands. All lands discovered west of this line were to belong to Spain; all east of it, to Portugal (see map, p. 9).

7. John Cabot's Voyage. The Pope's bull, however, did not deter the other nations of Europe from taking part in the search for the Indies by both the eastern and the western routes. The honor of being the first of the mariners of Columbus's time to reach the mainland of the western continent belongs to John Cabot, an Italian in the service of King Henry VII of England. In the summer of

---

[1] Columbus was by no means the first European to visit the shores of the western continent. There are records of a dozen or so pre-Columbian voyages across the Atlantic by Arabians, Japanese, Welshmen, Irishmen, and Frenchmen, besides the very detailed account in the Icelandic sagas, or stories of adventure, of the visit of the Norsemen to the shores of the western world in the year 1000. Under Leif the Lucky the Norsemen built booths or huts and remained for a winter on some spot along the coast of Labrador or New England. But these voyages of the Norsemen to America five hundred years before Columbus were not of importance, because they were not followed up by exploration and permanent settlement.

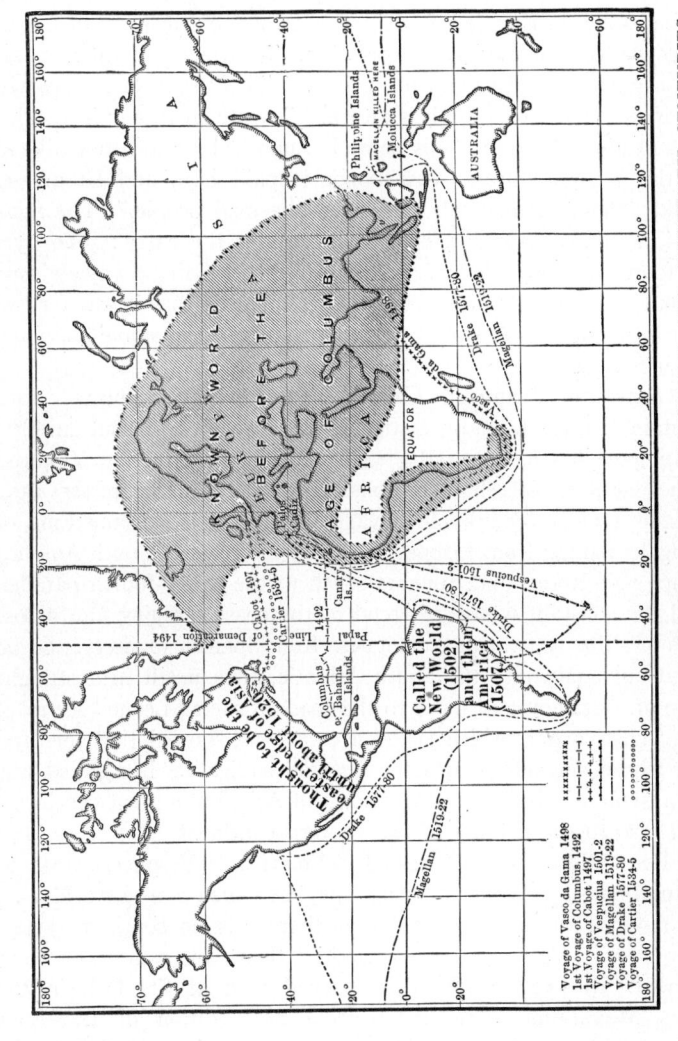

MAP SHOWING VOYAGES OF DISCOVERY IN THE FIFTEENTH AND SIXTEENTH CENTURIES

1497, while the Spanish navigators were still tarrying among the West Indies, Cabot sailed with one ship from Bristol, and after planting the banner of England probably somewhere on the coast of Labrador, returned to plan a larger expedition. The voyage of 1497 created great excitement in England for a time. "This Venetian of ours who went in search of new islands is returned," wrote an Italian in London to his brother at home; "his name is Zuan Cabot, and they all call him the great admiral. Vast honor is paid him, and he dresses in silk. These English run after him like mad people." The more prosaic account book of Henry VII contains the entry: "To hym that found the new isle 10£." But interest in Cabot's voyage soon died out. The importance of the voyage for us is that it was for two centuries made the basis of England's claims to the whole mainland of North America.

8. Amerigo Vespucci. Cabot's name is not connected with mountain, river, state, or town in the New World, but another Italian gave his name to the whole continent. Amerigo Vespucci was a Florentine merchant established at Cadiz in Spain. In 1501 he made a most remarkable voyage in the service of the king of Portugal. Sailing from Lisbon, he struck the coast of South America at Cape San Roque and, running south to the thirty-fourth parallel, found the constant westward trend of the coast carrying him across the Pope's line separating Portuguese from Spanish territory. So he steered out again into the South Atlantic, then north in a straight course of four thousand miles to the coast of Sierra Leone (see map, p. 9). This voyage, which lasted over a year, showed that the land along whose northern shores the Spanish navigators had sailed was not an island off the southeastern coast of Asia, but a great continent. It led also to the naming of the western continent.

9. The "New World" called "America." Vespucci wrote to Italian friends: "We found what may be called a new world ... since most of the ancients said that there was no continent below the equator." Vespucci's "new world," then, was a new *southern* continent. In 1507 a group of learned men at St. Dié, in the Vosges Mountains, were preparing a new edition of Ptolemy's "Geography." Martin Waldseemüller wrote an introduction to the edition, in which he included Vespucci's four letters and made the suggestion that since in addition to Europe, Asia, and Africa, "*another fourth part has been discovered by Americus Vespucius . . . I do not see what fairly hinders us from calling it Amerige or America, viz., the land of Americus.*" At the same time Waldseemüller made a map of the world on which he placed the new continent and named it America. This map was lost for centuries, and scholars were almost convinced that it never existed, when in the summer of 1901 an Austrian professor found it in the library of a castle in Württemberg. It had evidently circulated enough before its disappearance to fix the name "America" on the new southern continent, whence it spread to the land north of the Isthmus of Panama.[1]

10. Why the New World was not named for Columbus. The admirers of Columbus have protested against the injustice of the name "America" instead of "Columbia" for the New World, "as if the Sistine Madonna had been called not by Raphael's name, but by the name of the man who first framed it." But there was no injustice done, at least with intent. "America" was a name invented for what was thought to be a *new world south of the equator*, whereas Columbus and his associates believed that they had only found a *new way to the old world*. When it was realized that Columbus had really discovered the new world of which Vespucci wrote, it was too late to remedy the mistake in the name. So it came about that this continent was named by an obscure German professor in a French college for an Italian navigator in the service of the king of Portugal.

A Century of Exploration

11. The Explorers of the Sixteenth Century. From the death of Columbus (1506) to the planting of the first permanent English colony on the shores of America (1607) just a century elapsed,— a century filled with romantic voyages and thrilling tales of exploration and conquest in the New World. Nowadays men explore new countries for scientific study of the native races or the soil and its products, or to open up new markets for trade and develop the

---

[1] Although Waldseemüller himself dropped the name "America" when he realized that this was, after all, the land discovered by Columbus in 1498 and, in the same edition of Ptolemy for which he had written the Introduction, labeled South America *terra incognita* ("unknown land"), the name "America" soon reappeared and gradually spread to the northern continent. It appears on a map of the geographer Mercator in 1538 in designation of the whole mainland from Labrador to Patagonia.

hidden resources of the land; but in the romantic sixteenth century Spanish noblemen tramped through the swamps and tangles of Florida to find the fountain of perpetual youth, or toiled a thousand miles over the Western desert, lured by the dazzling gold of fabled cities of splendor. The sixteenth century was furthermore a century of intense religious belief; so we find a grim spirit of missionary zeal mingled with the thirst for gold. The cross was planted in the wilderness, and the soldiers knelt in thanksgiving on the ground stained by the blood of their heretical neighbors. Of course it was Asia with its fabulous wealth that was the real goal of European explorers. America was an obstacle. Until even far into the seventeenth century the mariners were searching the northern coast of America for a way *around* the continent, and hailing the broad mouth of each new river as a possible passage to the Indies.

12. Magellan's Ship sails around the World. With Columbus and Vespucci we must rank a third mariner, Ferdinand Magellan, a Portuguese in the service of the king of Spain. In September, 1519, Magellan with five ships and about three hundred men started on what proved to be the most romantic voyage in history. Reaching the Brazilian coast, he made his way south and, after quelling a dangerous mutiny in his winter quarters on the bleak coast of Patagonia, entered the narrow straits (since called by his name) at the extremity of South America. A stormy passage of five weeks through the tortuous narrows brought him out on the calm waters of an ocean to which, in grateful relief, he gave the name "Pacific."[1] Magellan met worse trials than storms, however, when he put out into the Pacific. Week after week he sailed westward across the smiling but apparently interminable sea, little dreaming that he had embarked on waters which cover nearly half the globe. Hunger grew to starvation, thirst to madness. Twice on the voyage of ten thousand miles land appeared to the eyes of the famished sailors, only to prove a barren, rocky island. At last the inhabited islands of Australasia were reached. Magellan himself was killed in a fight with the natives of the Philippine Islands, but his sole seaworthy ship, the *Victoria*, continued westward across the Indian Ocean and,

---

[1] Magellan was not the first European to see that great ocean. Several years earlier (1513) the Spaniard Balboa, with an exploring party from Haiti, had crossed the isthmus now named Panama and discovered the Pacific, to which he gave the name "South Sea."

rounding the Cape of Good Hope, reached Lisbon with a crew of eighteen "ghostlike men," September 6, 1522.

13. Significance of Magellan's Voyage. Magellan's ship had circumnavigated the globe. His wonderful voyage proved conclusively the sphericity of the earth, and showed the great preponderance of water over land. It demonstrated that America was not a group of islands off the Asiatic coast (as Columbus had thought), nor even a southern continent reaching down in a peninsula from the corner of China (see maps, pp. 16–17), but *a continent set off by itself*, and separated on the west from the old world of Cathay by a far greater expanse of water than on the east from the old world of Europe. It still required generations of explorers by land and sea to develop the true size and shape of the continent of America; but Magellan had located this continent at last in its relation to the known countries of the world.

14. Cortez's Conquest of Mexico. While Magellan's starving sailors were battling their way across the Pacific, stirring scenes were being enacted in Mexico. The Spaniards, starting from Haiti as a base, had conquered and colonized Porto Rico and Cuba (1508) and had sent expeditions to the Isthmus of Panama (Balboa, 1513) and north to Florida (Ponce de Leon, 1513). In 1519 Hernando Cortez, a Spanish adventurer of great courage and sagacity, was sent by the governor of Cuba to conquer and plunder the rich Indian kingdom which explorers had found to the north of the Isthmus. This was the Aztec confederacy of Indian tribes under an "emperor," Montezuma. The land was rich in silver and gold; the people were skilled in art and architecture. One of their religious legends told of a fair-haired god of the sky who had been driven out to sea, but who would return again to rule over them in peace and plenty. When the natives saw the Spaniard with his "white-winged towers" moving on the sea, they thought that the "fair god" had returned. Cortez was not slow to follow up this advantage. His belching cannon and armored knights increased the superstitious awe of the natives. He seized their ruler, Montezuma, captured their capital city, Mexico, and made their ancient and opulent realm a dependency of Spain (1521). It was the first sure footing of the Spaniards on the American continent and served as an important base for further exploration and conquest.

15. Spanish Pathfinders in America. The twenty years following Cortez's conquest of Mexico mark the height of Spanish exploration in America. From Kansas to Chile, and from the Carolinas to the Pacific, the flag and speech of Spain were carried. No feature of excitement and romance is absent from the vivid accounts which the heroes of these expeditions have left us. Now it is a survivor of shipwreck in the Mexican Gulf, making his way from tribe to tribe across the vast stretches of Texas and Mexico to the Gulf of California (Cabeza de Vaca, 1528–1536); now it is the ruffian captain Pizarro, repeating south of the Isthmus the conquest of Cortez and adding the untold wealth of the silver mines of Peru to the Spanish treasury (1531–1533); now it is the noble governor De Soto, with his train of six hundred knights in "doublets and cassocks of silk" and his priests in splendid vestments, with his Portuguese in shining armor, his horses, hounds, and hogs, all ready for a triumphal procession to kingdoms of gold and ivory, but doomed to toil, with his famished and ambushed host, through tangle and swamp from Georgia to Arkansas, and finally to leave his fever-stricken body at the bottom of the Mississippi, beneath the waters "alwaies muddie, down which there came continually manie trees and timber" (1539–1542); now it is Coronado and his three hundred followers, intent on finding the seven fabled cities of Cibola and chasing the golden mirage of the western desert from the Pacific coast of Mexico to the present state of Kansas (1540–1542). For all this vast expenditure of blood and treasure not a Spanish settlement existed north of the Gulf of Mexico in the middle of the sixteenth century. The Spaniards were gold seekers, not colonizers. They had found a few savages living in cane houses and mud pueblos, but the fountain of perpetual youth and the cities of gold they had not found. They could not, of course, foresee the wealth which one day would be derived from the rich lands through which they had so painfully struggled; and the survivors returned to the Mexican towns discouraged and disillusioned.

16. The Spanish Empire in America. South and west of the Gulf of Mexico, however, and in the islands of the West Indies the Spaniards had built up a huge empire. The discovery of gold in Haiti, and the conquest of the rich treasures of Mexico and Peru, brought thousands of adventurers and tens of thousands of negro slaves to tropical America. Spain governed the American lands despotically. Commerce and justice were exclusively regulated through the "India House" at Seville. Trade was restricted to certain ports. Heretics and their descendants to the third generation were excluded from the colonies. Many of the natives succumbed to the cruelty of the slave driver in the mines. The land was the property of the sovereign and by him was granted to nobles, who made their fiefs into great slave estates and treated both Indians and negroes with frightful severity. In spite of these evil features, however, Spanish colonization was a boon to the New World. The Spaniards introduced European methods of cultivation into the rich islands of Cuba, Porto Rico, Haiti, and Jamaica, and opened precious veins of gold and silver in Mexico and Peru. They built cities, dredged and fortified harbors, founded schools and universities, erected cathedrals and palaces. Spain, welded into a nation by the union of the crowns of Aragon and Castile (1469), her king elevated to the throne of the Holy Roman Empire in the person of Charles V (1519), was the most powerful state in Europe in the sixteenth century. Gold from the American mines enhanced the splendor of her throne, and her civilization, in turn, was reflected in her colonies in the New World. The decline of Spain's power began, however, with the wars which Charles's despotic son Philip II (1556–1598) waged to crush the liberty of his Dutch subjects, and the repulse which his great Armada met at the hands of Queen Elizabeth's seamen (1588). When the sixteenth century closed the vigor of Spanish colonization was gone.

CORNER OF FORT MARION, ST. AUGUSTINE, FLORIDA

Built by the Spaniards, 1656–1756

THE LENOX GLOBE (1510) SHOWING THE NEW WORLD AS AN
ISLAND OFF THE COAST OF ASIA

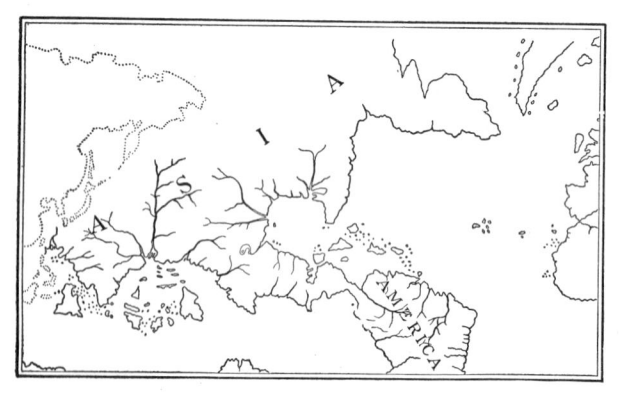

FINÆUS' MAP (1531) SHOWING THE NEW WORLD (AMERICA)
AS A PENINSULA ATTACHED TO ASIA

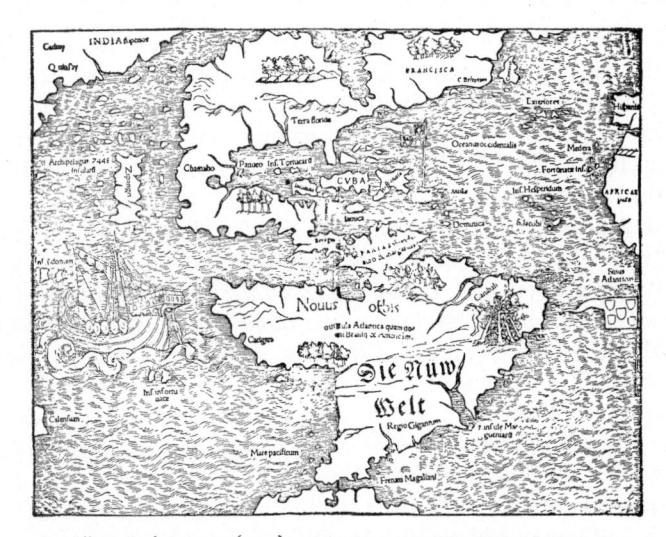

MÜNSTER'S MAP (1540) SHOWING LAND NORTH OF THE
ISTHMUS ATTACHED TO THE NEW WORLD

MERCATOR'S MAP (1541) SHOWING THE NAME "AMERICA" FOR
THE FIRST TIME APPLIED TO THE WHOLE CONTINENT

17. The French Explorers. The Spaniards were the chief, but not the only, explorers in America in the sixteenth century. In 1524 the king of France, scorning the papal bull of 1493, and jocosely asking to see old Adam's will bequeathing the world to Spain and Portugal, sent his Italian navigator, Verrazano, to seek the Indies by the western route. Verrazano sailed and charted the coast of North America from the Carolinas to Newfoundland, but did not find a route to Asia. Jacques Cartier sailed up the St. Lawrence River eleven years later to the Indian village on the site of Montreal. There his way to China was blocked by the rapids which were later named *Lachine* ("China") rapids. But wars, foreign and civil, absorbed the strength of France during the last half of the sixteenth century, and projects of colonization slept until the return of peace and the accession to the throne of the glorious King Henry of Navarre (1593).

18. The Elizabethan "Sea-Dogs." War, which was the death of French enterprise, was the very life of English colonial activity, which had languished since John Cabot's day. England and Spain became bitter rivals — religious, commercial, political — during Elizabeth's reign (1558-1603). Elizabeth had no army to attack Philip in his Spanish peninsula, but she struck at the very roots of his power by seizing his treasure-laden fleets from the Indies. England's dauntless seamen, Hawkins, Davis, Cavendish, and above all Sir Francis Drake, performed marvels of daring against the Spaniards, scouring the coasts of America and the high seas for their treasure ships, fighting single-handed against whole fleets, and even sailing into the harbors of Spain to "singe King Philip's beard" by burning his ships and docks. Sir Francis Drake circumnavigated the globe (1577-1580), plundering the Spanish ships on his voyage. When he returned to England with his enormous booty he was knighted by Queen Elizabeth on the quarter-deck of his vessel.

19. Gilbert and Raleigh. From capturing the Spanish gold on the seas to contending with Spain for the possession of the golden land was but a step; and we find the veteran soldier, Sir Humphrey Gilbert, receiving in 1578 a patent from Queen Elizabeth to "inhabit and possess all remote and heathen lands not in the actual possession of any Christian prince." Gilbert was unsuccessful in founding a colony on the bleak coast of Newfoundland, and his little ship foundered on her return voyage. His patent was handed on to his half brother, Sir Walter Raleigh, Elizabeth's favorite courtier. Raleigh's ships sought milder latitudes, and a colony was landed on Roanoke Island, off the coast of North Carolina (1585). The land, at Elizabeth's own suggestion, was named "Virginia," in honor of the "Virgin Queen." The colonists sought diligently for gold and explored the coasts and rivers for a passage to Cathay. But misfortune overtook them. Supplies failed to come from England on time, and the colony was abandoned. Three times Raleigh tried to found an enduring settlement (1585, 1586, 1587), but the struggle with Spain absorbed the attention of the nation, and the colonists preferred gold hunting to agriculture. Raleigh sank a private fortune equivalent to a million dollars in his enterprise and finally abandoned it with the optimistic prophecy to Lord Cecil: "I shall yet live to see it an Inglishe nation."

20. The Indians. Wherever the European visitors had struck the western continent, whether on the shores of Labrador or the tropical islands of the Caribbean Sea, on the wide plains of the southwest or the slopes of the Andes, they had found a scantily clad, coppercolored race of men with high cheek bones and straight black hair. Columbus, thinking he had reached the Indies, called the curious, friendly inhabitants who came running down to his ships *Indians*, and that inappropriate name has been used ever since to designate the natives of the Western Hemisphere. In Mexico, Central America, and South America the Spanish explorers and conquerors found a higher native development in art, industry, architecture, and agriculture than was later found among the Indians of the North. Even the germ of an organized state existed in the Aztec confederacy of Mexico. Huge pueblos, or communal houses, made of adobe (clay) were built around a square or semicircular court in rising tiers reached by ladders. A single pueblo sometimes housed a thousand persons. The Aztec and Inca chiefs in Mexico and Peru lived in elaborately decorated "palaces." Still the natives of these regions were by no means so highly civilized a race as the exaggerated accounts of the Spanish conquerors often imply. They had not invented such simple contrivances as stairs, chimneys, and wheeled vehicles. Their intellectual range is shown by the knotted strings which they used for mathematical calculations, and their moral degradation appears in the shocking human sacrifices of their barbarous religion.

21. The Northern Tribes. The Indian tribes north of the Gulf of Mexico had generally reached the stage of development called "lower barbarism," a stage of pottery making and rude agricultural science. Midway between the poor tepee, or skin tent, of the savage of the great plains and the imposing pueblo of Mexico was the ordinary "long house," or "round house," of the village Indians from Canada to Florida. The house was built of stout saplings, covered with bark or a rough mud plaster. Along a central aisle, or radiating from a central hearth, were ranged the separate family compartments, divided by thin walls. Forty or fifty families usually lived in the house, sharing their food of corn, beans, pumpkins, wild turkey, fish, bear, and buffalo meat in common. Only their clothing, ornaments, and weapons were personal property. The women of the tribe prepared the food, tended the children, made the utensils and ornaments of beads, feathers, and skins, and strung the polished shells, or "wampum," which the Indian used for money and for correspondence. The men were occupied with war, the hunt, and the council. In their leisure they repaired their bows, sharpened new arrowheads, or stretched the smooth bark of the birch tree over their canoe frames. They had a great variety of games and dances, solemn and gay; and they loved to bask idly in the sun.

22. Character and Fate of the Indians. In character the Indian showed the most astonishing extremes,—now immovable as a rock, now capricious as the April breeze. Around the council fire he was taciturn, dignified, thoughtful, but in the dance he broke into unrestrained and uncontrollable ecstasies. He bore with stoical fortitude the most horrible tortures at the stake, but howled in his wigwam over an injured finger. His powers of smell, sight, and hearing were incredibly keen on the hunt or the warpath, but at the same time he showed a stolid stupidity that no white man could match. The Indian seems to have been generally friendly to the European on their first meeting, and it was chiefly the fault of the white man's cruelty and treachery that the friendly curiosity of the red man was turned so often into malignant hatred instead of firm alliance.

There were probably never more than a few hundred thousand Indians in America. Their small number perhaps accounts for their lack of civilization. At any rate their development reached its highest point in the thickly settled funnel-shaped region south of the Mexican

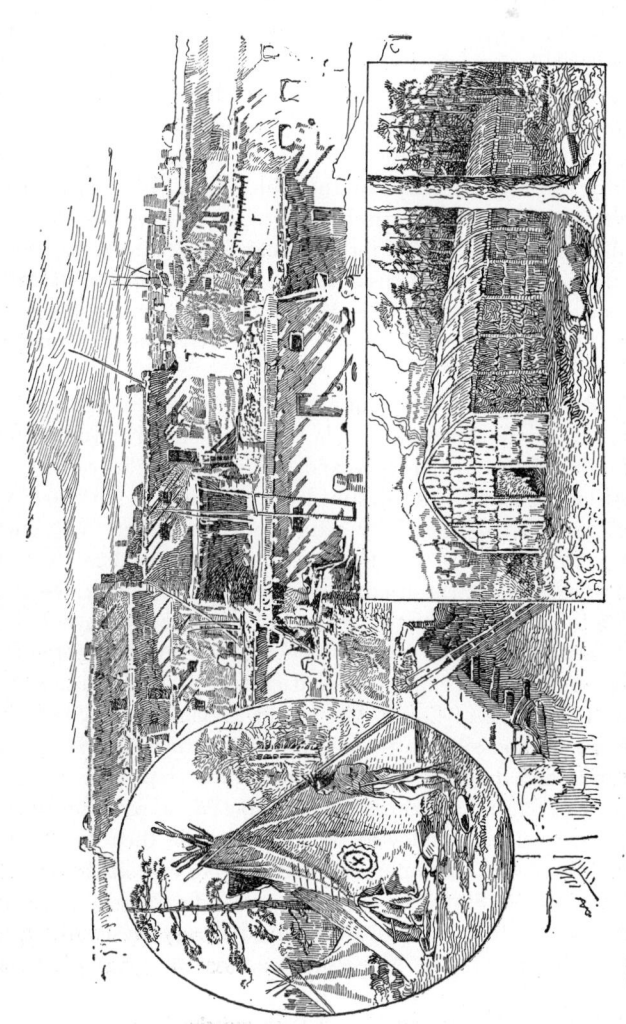

TYPES OF INDIAN DWELLINGS,—THE PUEBLO, THE TEPEE, AND THE LONG HOUSE

boundary, where it has been suggested that they were crowded by the advance of a glacial ice sheet from the north. There are now about 325,000 Indians in the United States, including the civilized tribes. Many tribes have died out; others have been almost completely exterminated or assimilated by the whites. The surviving Indians, on their Western reservations or in the government schools, are rapidly learning the ways of the white men. It is to be hoped that their education will be wisely fostered, and that instead of the billion dollars spent on the forty Indian wars of the nineteenth century a few hundred thousand dollars spent in the twentieth century on Indian schools like Hampton will forever divest the word "Indian" of its associations with the tomahawk, torture, and treachery.[1]

23. A Prophecy of our Country. The fairest portion of the continent of North America which the Spanish adventurers penetrated in the sixteenth century, and whose edges the explorers of other nations touched, was destined to become the United States of America. It was blessed by nature with a variety of climate, abundant rainfall east of the Rocky Mountains, wonderfully fertile soil, and priceless deposits of coal and metals. It was destined in the third decade of the twentieth century to produce a quarter of the world's wheat, one half of its coal, iron ore, and tobacco, three fifths of its copper, two thirds of its oil and cotton, and three quarters of its corn. The mines of South Africa and Mexico alone yield larger supplies of gold and silver. Some lands, like France and Italy, have for centuries had a highly civilized population, but have been relatively poor in natural resources; others, like Manchuria and Russia, have been marvelously endowed by nature, while their people have lacked the knowledge and enterprise necessary to exploit their wealth. But in the United States men and material have been admirably matched. As the tide of migration moved slowly westward, across the Alleghenies, across the Mississippi, across the great plains and

---

[1] The Indians, though always a subject of much curiosity, have only recently been studied scientifically. Our government, yielding to the entreaties of scholars who realized how fast the manners and customs of the natives were disappearing, established in 1879 a Bureau of Ethnology, for the careful study of the surviving vestiges of Indian life. To the reports of this bureau and to the researches of scholars and explorers connected with our various museums we are indebted for a great deal of valuable and fascinating information about the Indians.

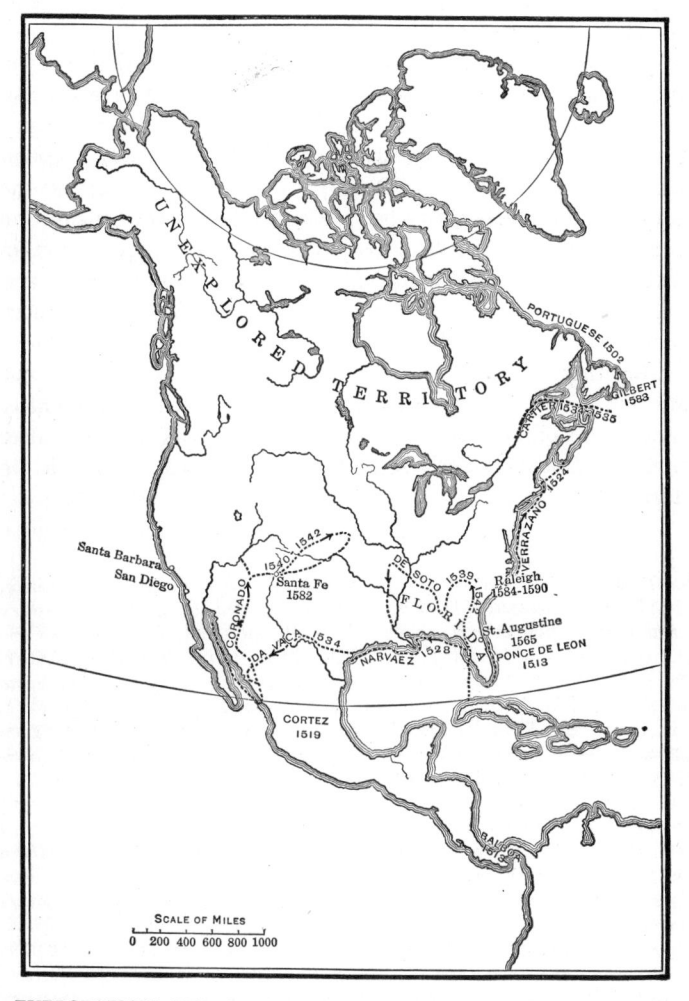

EXPLORATION AND SETTLEMENT IN NORTH AMERICA IN THE
SIXTEENTH CENTURY

the crests of the Rockies and the Sierras, an intelligent and energetic race of pioneers felled the forests, planted the rich river bottoms, and opened the veins of coal and iron.

The process was slow. The early explorers and settlers on the Atlantic coast had no idea, of course, of the vast continent which lay before them. Even beyond the middle of the seventeenth century the French explorers believed that the Mississippi River emptied into the South Sea (the Pacific Ocean). The English settlers on the Atlantic coast did not begin to cross the Alleghenies till far into the eighteenth century. The Rockies were discovered in 1743, and within the next fifty years our Pacific coast was charted by explorers and traders. Finally, in 1805, an expedition sent out by the president of the United States reached the mouth of the Columbia River, linking together for the first time by the feet of white men our Atlantic and Pacific shores. That was more than three centuries after the voyages of Columbus and almost exactly two hundred years after the first permanent English settlement in America, to which we now turn.

REFERENCES

The Discovery of America: JOHN FISKE, *The Discovery of America*, Vol. I; E. P. CHEYNEY, *The European Background of American History* (The American Nation Series), chaps. i–v; I. B. RICHMAN, *The Spanish Conquerors* (Chronicles of America, Vol. II), chaps. i, ii; ELROY M. AVERY, *History of the United States*, Vol. I, chaps. v, vii–xv; E. G. BOURNE, *Spain in America* (Am. Nation), chaps. i–vii; *Cambridge Modern History*, Vol. I, chap. i; OLSON and BOURNE, *The Northmen, Columbus, and Cabot* (Original Narratives of Early American History); JUSTIN WINSOR, *Narrative and Critical History of America*, Vol. I, chap. i; Vol. II, chaps. i–ii.

A Century of Exploration: FISKE, Vol. II; BOURNE, chaps. viii–xv; *Cambridge Modern History*, chap. ii; WINSOR, Vol. II, chaps. iv, vi, vii, ix; Vol. III, chaps. i–iii; HODGE and LEWIS, *Spanish Explorers in the Southern United States* (Orig. Narr.); H. S. BURRAGE, *Early English and French Voyagers* (Orig. Narr.); WM. WOOD, *The Elizabethan Sea Dogs* (Chronicles of America, Vol. III), chaps. i–xi; RICHMAN, chaps. iii–vi; A. B. HART, *American History told by Contemporaries*, Vol. I, Nos. 21–35; EDW. CHANNING, *History of the United States*, Vol. I, chaps. iii–v; L. FARRAND, *Basis of American History* (Am. Nation), chaps. v–xvii; ELLEN SEMPLE, *American History and its Geographical Conditions*, chaps. i, ii; ELLSWORTH HUNTINGTON, *The Red Man's Continent* (Chronicles of America, Vol. I); AVERY, chaps. ii, xvi–xxii.

Topics for Special Reports

1. **Geographical Knowledge before Columbus:** Winsor, Vol. I, pp. 1-33; Fiske, Vol. I, pp. 256-294; Cheyney, pp. 41-78; Avery, Vol. I, chap. v.

2. **Columbus's First Voyage:** Olson and Bourne (Orig. Narr.), pp. 89-258 (Columbus's Journal); Fiske, Vol. I, pp. 419-446; Old South Leaflets, Nos. 29 and 33 (descriptions of voyage by Columbus and by his son).

3. **De Soto's Journey to the Mississippi:** Hodge and Lewis (Orig. Narr.), pp. 129-272; Bourne, pp. 162-170; Winsor, Vol. II, pp. 244-254; W. Lowery, *Spanish Settlements*, pp. 213-252; E. G. Bourne, *De Soto* (Trail Makers Series).

4. **Raleigh's Attempts to found a Colony in Virginia:** Burrage (Orig. Narr.), pp. 225-323; Hart, No. 32; Winsor, Vol. III, pp. 105-116; Old South Leaflets, Nos. 92, 119; Wood, chap. xi.

5. **The American Indians:** Fiske, Vol. I, pp. 38-147; Farrand, pp. 195-271; Hart, Nos. 21, 60, 64, 91; Avery, Vol. I, pp. 338-368; Lowery, pp. 27-78.

CHAPTER II

THE ENGLISH COLONIES

The Old Dominion

24. European Conditions favoring Colonization. The gorgeous dreams of gold and empire which filled the minds of the explorers of the sixteenth century slowly faded into the sober realization of the hardships involved in settling the wild and distant regions of the New World. To the romantic age of discovery succeeded the practical age of colonization. The motives which led thousands of Europeans to leave their homes in the seventeenth century and brave the storms of the Atlantic to settle on the shores of the James and the Charles, the Hudson and the St. Lawrence, were those which have prompted migration in every age; namely, the desire to get a better living and the desire to enjoy a fuller freedom. Now it happened that both these desires were greatly stimulated by the events of the sixteenth century in Europe. In the first place, the masses of the people, who had lived as serfs on the great feudal estates of the nobles in the Middle Ages, were finding more and more diversified employment as citizens of national states — artisans and mechanics in the towns, free tenant farmers, merchants and traders. In other words, a middle class (a *bourgeoisie*) was emerging and was beginning to amass money. At the same time the military and civil expenses of the kings, whose responsibilities were growing with their states, made taxes high and land dear. The limitless virgin lands of the New World offered a tempting relief for the hard-pressed.

25. Protestant Revolt from Rome. In the second place, large parts of northern Europe had broken away from the ecclesiastical authority of the Roman Church in the sixteenth century, in the movement known as the Protestant Reformation. State churches were established in England, Germany, Scandinavia, and the Netherlands, with the rulers in authority instead of the Pope; and dissent from the doctrine of these established churches was treated not only as religious heresy but also as political treason. But the spirit of free inquiry and religious innovation which had destroyed the unity of the Roman Church could not be held in check by rulers. Men claimed individual freedom of belief and worship. A great variety of religious sects appeared. Kings and princes tried to reduce them to submission, and the persecutions in Europe sent many refugees as colonists to the New World.

26. England our "Motherland." From the seventeenth to the twentieth century the tide of immigration has flowed from Europe to America, until hardly more than one half the population of the United States are native-born with native-born parents. Yet these immigrants have not transported the political and social institutions of their own lands to the United States, but have themselves, with remarkable rapidity, adopted the speech, customs, and ideals of America. These are in their origin English. For although Spain and France held or claimed by far the largest part of North America, while the English settlements were still confined to a narrow strip along the Atlantic coast, nevertheless those English settlements absorbed all the rest in their spread to the Pacific and made the English civilization — English speech, English political ideals, English common law, English courts and local governments, English codes of manners and standards of culture — the basis of American life. We severed our political connection with England by the Revolution, but we could not lay aside the culture or destroy the institutions in which our forefathers had been trained for centuries. We still remained the daughter country, though we left the mother's roof and set up our own establishment.

27. The London and Plymouth Companies. Queen Elizabeth's long and glorious reign came to an end in 1603, when she was succeeded on the throne of England by James Stuart of Scotland.[1] In the year 1606 King James gave permission to "certain loving subjects to deduce and conduct two several colonies or plantations of settlers to America." The Stuart king had begun his reign with a pompous announcement of peace with all his European neighbors;

---

[1] Since all the English colonies along the Atlantic seaboard, with the exception of Georgia, were settled under the Stuart kings, whose names will occur constantly in the pages of this chapter, it will be convenient for the student to review the main facts of the rule of the Stuart dynasty in Cheyney's "Short History of England," chaps. xiv-xvi, or more briefly in Robinson's "History of Western Europe," chap. xxx.

28   THE ESTABLISHMENT OF THE ENGLISH

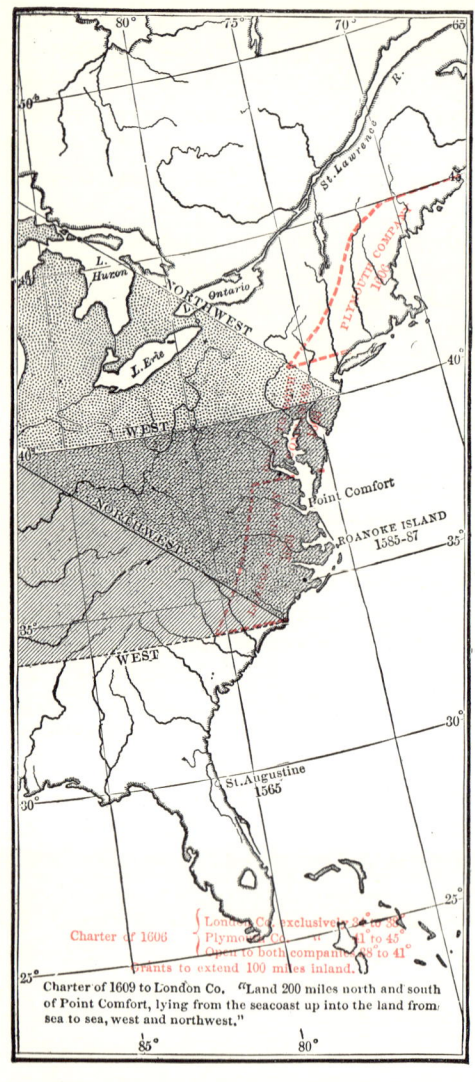

THE VIRGINIA GRANTS OF 1606 AND 1609

consequently, though England claimed all North America by virtue of Cabot's discovery of 1497, James limited the territory of his grant so as not to encroach on the Spanish settlements of Florida or on the French interests about the St. Lawrence. One group of "loving subjects," called the London Company, was to have exclusive right to settle between 34° and 38° of north latitude (see map); the other group, the Plymouth Company, was granted the equally broad region between 41° and 45°. The neutral belt from 38° to 41° was left open to both companies, with the proviso that neither should make any settlement within one hundred miles of the other. The grants extended one hundred miles inland. The powers of government bestowed on the new companies were as complicated as the grants of territory. The companies were to have a council of thirteen in England, appointed by the king and subject to his control. This English council was to appoint another council of thirteen members to reside in each colony, and, under the direction of a president, to manage its local affairs, subject always to the authority of the English council, which in turn was subject to the king.

28. The Settlement at Jamestown. In May, 1607, about a hundred colonists, sent out by the London Company, reached the shores of Virginia and, sailing some miles up a broad river, started a settlement on a low peninsula. River and settlement they named James and Jamestown in honor of the king. The colony did not thrive. By royal order the crops for five years were to be gathered into a common storehouse, and thence dispensed to the settlers, thus encouraging the idle and shiftless to live at the expense of the industrous. Authority was hard to enforce with the clumsy form of government, and the proprietors in England were too far away to consult the needs of the colonists. Exploring the land for gold and the rivers for a passage to Cathay proved more attractive to the settlers than planting corn. The unwholesome site of the town caused fever and malaria.

Had it not been for the almost superhuman efforts of one man, John Smith, the little colony could not have survived. Smith had come to Virginia after a romantic and world-wide career as a soldier of fortune. His masterful spirit at once assumed the direction of the colony in spite of president and council. His courage and tact with the Indians got corn for the starving settlers, and his indomitable energy inspired the good and cowed the lazy and the unjust. In his vivid narratives of early Virginia, the "Trewe Relaycion" (1608) and the "Generall Historie" (1624), he has done himself and his services to the colony full credit, for he was not a modest or retiring man. But his self-praise does not lessen the value of his services. In the summer of 1609 he was wounded by an explosion of gunpowder and returned to England. The winter following his departure was the awful "starving time." Of four hundred men in the colony in October but sixty were left in June. This feeble remnant, taking advantage of the arrival of ships from the Bermudas, determined to abandon the settlement. With but a fortnight's provisions, which they hoped would carry them to Newfoundland, bidding final farewell to the scene of their suffering, they dropped slowly down the broad James. But on reaching the mouth of the river they espied ships flying England's colors. It was the fleet of Lord de la Warre (Delaware), the new governor, bringing men and supplies. Thus narrowly did the Jamestown colony escape the fate of Raleigh's settlements.

29. Reorganization and Growth of the Colony. De la Warre brought more than food and recruits. The London Company had been reorganized in 1609, and a new charter granted by the king, which altered both the territory and the government of Virginia (see map, p. 28). Henceforth, as a large and rich corporation in

England, the company was to conduct its affairs without the intervention of the king. Virginia was to have a governor sent out by the company. Under the new régime the colony picked up. Order was enforced under the harsh but salutary rule of Deputy Governor Dale (1611-1616). The colonists, losing the gold fever, turned to agriculture and manufacture. Tobacco became the staple product of the colony, and experiments were made in producing soap, glass, silk, and wine. A better class of emigrants came over, and in 1619 a shipload of "respectable maidens" arrived, who were auctioned off to the bachelor planters for so many pounds of tobacco apiece. A little later the sharing of harvests in common was abandoned, and the settlers were given their lands in full ownership. In the words of one of the Virginia clergy of the period, "This plantation which the Divell hath so often troden downe is revived and daily groweth to more and hopeful successe."

The year 1619, which brought the Virginians wives and lands, is memorable also for two events of great significance for the later history of the colonies and the nation. In that year the first cargo of negro slaves was brought to the colony, and the first representative assembly convened on American soil. On July 30 two burgesses (citizens) from each plantation met with the governor and his six councilors in the little church at Jamestown. This tiny legislature of twenty-seven members, after enacting various laws for the colony, adjourned on August 4, "by reason of extreme heat both past and likely to ensue." Spanish, French, and Dutch settlements existed in America at the time of this first Virginia assembly of burgesses, but none of them either then had or copied later the system of representative government. *Democracy was England's gift to the New World.*

30. Virginia a Royal Province. The man to whom Virginia owed this great boon of self-government, and whose name should be known and honored by every American, was Sir Edwin Sandys, treasurer of the London Company. Sandys belonged to the country party in Parliament, who were making James I's life miserable by their resistance to his arbitrary government based on "divine right," or responsibility to God alone for his royal acts. Gondomar, the Spanish minister in London, whispered in James's ear that the meetings of the Company were "hotbeds of sedition." But James had let the London Company get out of his hands by the new charter, and when he tried to interfere in their election of a treasurer they rebuked him by choosing one of the most prominent of the country party (the Earl of Southampton, a friend of Shakespeare's). Not being able to dictate to the company, James resolved to destroy it. In a moment of great depression for the colony, after a horrible Indian massacre (1622) and a famine, James took the colony into his own hands and sent over men to govern it who were responsible only to his Privy Council. Virginia thus became a "royal province" (1624) and remained so for one hundred and fifty years, until the American Revolution. James intended to suppress the Virginia assembly (the House of Burgesses) too, and rule the colony by a committee of his courtiers. But he died before he had a chance to extinguish the liberties of Virginia, and his son, Charles I, hoping to get the monopoly of the tobacco trade in return for the favor, allowed the House of Burgesses to continue. So Virginia furnished the pattern which sooner or later nearly all the American colonies reproduced; namely, that of a governor (with a small council of Americans) appointed by the English king, and a legislature, or assembly, elected by the people of the colony.

IN CELEBRATION OF THE THREE-HUNDREDTH ANNIVERSARY OF THE SETTLEMENT OF JAMESTOWN

31. "The Old Dominion." The people of Virginia were very loyal to the Stuarts. When the quarrel between king and Parliament in England reached the stage of civil war (1642), and Charles I was driven from his throne and beheaded (1649), many of his supporters in England, who were called Cavaliers, emigrated to Virginia, giving the colony a decidedly aristocratic character. And when Charles II was restored to his father's throne in 1660, the Virginian burgesses recognized his authority so promptly and enthusiastically that he called them "the best of his distant children." He even elevated Virginia to the proud position of a "dominion,"

THE ENGLISH COLONIES 33

by quartering its arms (the old seal of the Virginia Company) on his royal shield with the arms of England, Scotland, and Ireland. The burgesses were very proud of this distinction and, remembering that they were the oldest as well as the most faithful of the Stuart settlements in America, adopted the name of "The Old Dominion."

32. Bacon's Rebellion. Though there were actually many occasions of dispute between the governors sent over by the king and the legislature elected by the people, only one incident of prime importance occurred to disturb the peaceful history of the Old Dominion under its royal masters. In 1675 the Susquehannock Indians were harassing the upper settlements of the colony, and Governor William Berkeley, who was profiting largely by his private interest in the fur trade, refused to send a force of militia to punish them. He was supported by an "old and rotten" House of Burgesses, which he had kept in office, doing his bidding, for fourteen years. A young and popular planter named Nathaniel Bacon, who had seen one of his overseers murdered by the Indians, put himself at the head of three hundred volunteers and demanded an officer's commission of Governor Berkeley. Berkeley refused, and Bacon marched against the Indians without any commission, utterly routing them and saving the colony from tomahawk and firebrand. The governor proclaimed Bacon a rebel and set a price upon his head. In the distressing civil war which followed, the governor was driven from his capital and Jamestown was burned by the "rebels." But Bacon died of fever (or poison) at the moment of his victory, and his party, being made up only of his personal following, fell to pieces. Berkeley returned and took grim vengeance on Bacon's supporters until the burgesses petitioned him to "spill no more blood." The rebellion forced the dissolution of the "old and rotten" assembly and the recall of Governor Berkeley. It showed that the people of the Old Dominion, though faithful to their king, would not tamely submit to despotic rule.

THE NEW ENGLAND SETTLEMENTS

33. Activities of Sir Ferdinando Gorges. While these things were going on in Virginia a very different history was being enacted in the northern regions granted to the Plymouth Company. This company sent out a colony in the very year that the London Company settled Jamestown (1607), but one winter in the little fort at the mouth of the Kennebec River, on the icebound coast of Maine, was enough to send the frozen settlers back to England. Sir Ferdinando Gorges, governor of Plymouth, was the moving spirit of the company, and, despite his losses in the expedition of 1607-1608, he showed a determination worthy of a Sir Walter Raleigh. In 1614 he sent John Smith to explore the coast of "northern Virginia," as the Plymouth grant was called. Smith made a map of the coast from Cape Cod to Nova Scotia and called the land "New England." In 1620 Gorges persuaded the king to make a new grant of this territory to a number of nobles and gentlemen about the court, who were designated as the Council for New England.

34. The Pilgrim Fathers. A few weeks after the formation of this new company there landed at Plymouth, from the little vessel *Mayflower* at anchor off Cape Cod, a group of one hundred men and women, known to later history as the "Pilgrims." They were not sent by the Council for New England or the London Company. Their object was neither to explore the country for gold nor to find a northwest passage to the Indies. They came of their own free will to found homes in the wilderness, where, unmolested, they might worship God according to their conscience. They were *Independents*, or *Separatists*, people who had separated from the Church of England because, when it broke away from the authority of the Pope in the reign of Henry VIII, it still retained in its worship many features of the Roman Catholic Church, such as vestments, altars, and ceremonies, which seemed to them "idolatrous." Three centuries ago religion was an affair of the state, not of private choice. Rulers enforced uniformity in creed and worship, in the belief that it was necessary to the preservation of their authority. If a subject could differ from the king in religious opinion, it was feared that it would not be long before he would presume to differ in political opinion, and then what would become of obedience and loyalty! For men who were too brave to conceal their convictions, and too honest to modify them at the command of the sovereign, only three courses were open — to submit to persecution and martyrdom, to rise in armed resistance, or to retire to a place beyond the reach of the king's arm. The history of the sixteenth, seventeenth, and eighteenth centuries is full of the story of cruel persecutions, civil wars, and exiles for conscience' sake. James I began his reign

MONUMENT AT PROVINCETOWN, MASSACHUSETTS, TO COMMEMORATE THE LANDING OF THE FIRST PARTY FROM THE *MAYFLOWER*

Dedicated by President Taft, August 8, 1910

by declaring that he would make his subjects conform in religion or "harry them out of the land." He "harried" the Separatist congregations of some little villages in the east of England until in 1608 they took refuge in Holland — the only country in Europe where complete religious toleration existed. Not content to be absorbed into the Dutch nation and have their children forget the customs and speech of England, the Separatists determined to migrate

FACSIMILE OF BRADFORD MS. HISTORY "OF PLIMOTH PLANTATION"

to the new land of America. They got permission from the London Company to settle in Virginia, but their pilot brought them to the shores of Cape Cod, where they landed December 21, 1620, although they had neither a right to the soil (a patent) nor power to establish a government (a charter).

35. The "*Mayflower* Compact" and the Plymouth Colony. Before landing, the Pilgrims gathered in the cabin of the *Mayflower* and pledged themselves to form a government and obey it. That was the first instance of complete self-government in our history, for the assembly which met at Jamestown the year before the Pilgrims landed was called together by orders from the Virginia

Company in England. The winter of 1620–1621 on the "stern and rock-bound coast" of New England went hard with the Pilgrims. "It pleased God," wrote Bradford, their governor for many years and their historian, "to vissite us with death dayly, and with so generall a disease that the living were scarce able to burie the dead." Yet when the *Mayflower* returned to England in the spring not one of the colonists went with her. Their home was in America. They had come to conquer the wilderness or die, and their determination was expressed in the brave words of one of their leaders: "It is not with us as with men whom small things can discourage." The little colony took its part bravely in the defense of the New England settlements against the Indians and saw half its towns destroyed in the terrible war set on foot by the Narragansett chief "King Philip" in 1675.[1] Finally, in 1691, it was annexed to the powerful neighboring colony of Massachusetts Bay.

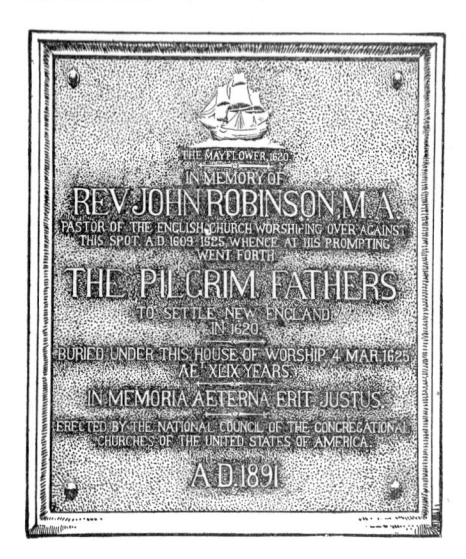

THE PILGRIM TABLET IN LEYDEN, HOLLAND

36. The Massachusetts Bay Company. In 1628 a company of Puritan[2] gentlemen secured a grant of land from the Council for New England and the next year obtained from Charles I a royal

---

[1] King Philip's War was only the fiercest of many Indian attacks on the westward-moving frontier of the English settlements in the seventeenth century. We have already noticed the attack of the Susquehannocks on the Virginian frontier in 1675–1676 (p. 33). King Philip's War, of the same years, in New England was crushed by a combination of troops from the Massachusetts, the Connecticut, and the Plymouth colonies, but not until half of the eighty or ninety towns of those colonies had been ravaged by fire, some hundred thousand pounds sterling of their treasure spent, and one out of every ten of their fighting men killed or captured.

[2] The Puritans got their name from their desire to purify the Anglican worship of forms which were retained from the Roman Church. They did not secede from the Church (like the Separatists), but tried to reform it.

charter constituting them a political body ruled by a governor, a deputy governor, and eighteen "assistants," all elected by the members of the company. In 1630 nearly two thousand emigrants sent out by the company arrived on the shores of Boston Harbor, the nucleus of the largest and most important of the English settlements in America — the Colony of Massachusetts Bay. The settlers carried their charter to Massachusetts, out of the reach of the king and his ministers. John Winthrop and John Cotton were the leading spirits of the colony in its first twenty years: the former, a cultivated gentleman from the south of England, serving almost continually as governor; the latter, a scholar and preacher of great power, acting as director of the Massachusetts conscience. The object of the Massachusetts Puritans was to establish a colony in which they could enjoy a worship purified of what they called "the idolatrous remnants of popery" in the English Church. They did not open a refuge for *freedom* of worship. To keep their community holy and undefiled they refused to admit as "freemen" (that is, participants in the government) any but members of their own church. Others might live in the colony so long as they did not resist the authorities, molest the ministers, or bring discredit on the Puritan system of worship and government; but they had to contribute to the support of the Church and submit to its controlling oversight of both public and private life. During the decade 1630–1640 the growing tyranny of King Charles and the persecutions of the zealous Archbishop Laud of Canterbury drove several thousands of refugees to the new colony. "God sifted a nation," wrote a Massachusetts governor a half century later, "in order that he might send choice grain to this wilderness"; but Archbishop Laud called the Puritans whom he drove into exile "swine which rooted out God's vineyard."

37. The Government of Massachusetts. The large emigration to Massachusetts brought about several important political results. It relieved the colony of immediate fear of attacks by the Indians;[1] it enabled the authorities easily to drive out various companies of

---

[1] It must be added that the danger to both the Plymouth and the Massachusetts colonies in their early years from Indian attacks was much lessened by a terrible plague which had swept over eastern New England three years before the Pilgrims landed, and destroyed perhaps one half of the Indians from Maine to Rhode Island.

settlers established by the agents of Gorges and other claimants to the Massachusetts lands under the grants of the Council for New England; and finally it led to a representative form of government. The freemen increased so rapidly that they could not come together in a body to make their laws; and after trying for a short time the experiment of leaving this power to the eighteen "assistants," the towns demanded the privilege of sending their own elected representatives to help the assistants make the laws (1634). The more liberal spirits of the colony protested against the narrowing of the suffrage to the "freemen" alone, but the Puritan leaders were firm in their determination to keep out of the government all who were suspected of heresy in belief or laxity in morals. "A democracy" (that is, the rule of all the people) "is no fit government either for Church or for commonwealth," declared Cotton; and even the tolerant John Winthrop defended the exclusive Puritan system in a letter to a protesting friend by the remark: "The best part is always the least, and of that best part the wiser part is always the lesser."

38. The Exile of Roger Williams. It was natural that this "Puritan aristocracy," which seemed so harsh to many colonists, should lead to both voluntary and enforced exile from the territory governed under the Massachusetts charter. Roger Williams, pastor of the church in Salem, taught doctrines very unacceptable to the Puritan governors of the colony. He said that the land on which they had settled belonged to the Indians, in spite of the king's charter, that the state had no control over a man's conscience, and that to make a man take the oath of citizenship was to encourage lying and hypocrisy. The civil authorities drove Williams from the colony in 1636. Making his difficult way southward in midwinter through the forests, from one Indian tribe to another, he arrived at the head of Narragansett Bay and, purchasing a tract of land from the Indians, began a settlement which he called, in recognition of God's guidance, "Providence."

39. The Rhode Island Colony. Other dissenters from Massachusetts followed, and soon four towns were established on the mainland about Narragansett Bay and on Rhode Island proper. In 1643 Williams secured recognition for his colony from the English Parliament, which the year before had driven King Charles from London. The little colony of "Rhode Island and Providence

THE ENGLISH COLONIES

Plantations" so established was remarkable for two things, — democracy and religious freedom. Election "by papers" (ballots) was introduced, and the government was "held by free and voluntary consent of all the free inhabitants." All men might "walk as their conscience persuaded them, every one in the name of his God." The scornful orthodox brethren in Massachusetts called Rhode Island's population "the Lord's débris," while the facetious said that "if a man had lost his religion, he would be sure to find it in some Rhode Island village." Massachusetts further showed her spite against the dissenting settlers by refusing to admit Rhode Island into the confederation of New England colonies, formed in 1643 for protection against the Indians; and it was not till the colony had received a royal charter from Charles II (1663), recognizing its boundaries and its self-elected government, that it was securely established. For his heroic devotion to principles of freedom, far in advance of his age, Roger Williams deserves to be honored as one of the noblest figures in our colonial history.

40. The Connecticut Settlements. The same year that Massachusetts drove Williams out of her jurisdiction the magistrates gave permission to "divers loving ffriends, neighbors, and ffreemen of Newetown (Cambridge), Dorchester, Watertown and other places, to transport themselves and their estates unto the Ryver of Conecticott, there to reside and inhabit." These emigrants were partly attracted by the glowing reports of the fertility of the Connecticut valley and partly repelled by the extreme rigor of the Massachusetts "aristocracy of righteousness," which made impossible honest expression of opinion. Led by their pastor, Thomas Hooker, they tramped across the wilderness between the Charles and the Connecticut, driving their cattle before them and carrying their household goods in wagons, — the first heralds of that mighty westward movement which was to continue through two centuries to the Pacific Ocean. The Connecticut emigrants founded the towns of Hartford, Windsor, and Wethersfield on the "long river." In 1639 they adopted their "Fundamental Orders," — the first constitution drawn up in America, and the first in modern history composed by the free founders of a state.[1] They

---

[1] The *Mayflower* agreement of 1620 was hardly a constitution, as it did not provide for a *form* of government, but only pledged its signers to obey the government which they should establish.

did not require a man to be a church member in order to vote, and their clergymen exercised far less influence over political life than those of the mother colony. Although they had trouble with Massachusetts, which still claimed that they were under her jurisdiction, and with the Dutch, who (as we shall see in the next section) had spread from the Hudson to the Connecticut, still the colonists of the river towns were strong enough to defend both their land

EMIGRANTS EN ROUTE FROM MASSACHUSETTS TO CONNECTICUT

and their government. After the extermination of the dangerous Pequot Indians in 1637 the colony enjoyed peace and prosperity. In 1662 it was granted a charter by Charles II, extending its territory westward to the South Sea (the Pacific).

41. The Puritan Colony of New Haven. John Davenport, a stern Puritan divine, founded a third seceding colony from Massachusetts when he took his congregation from Boston to the shores of Long Island Sound and started the settlement of New Haven (1638). The colony, which soon expanded into several towns, was even more strictly Puritan and "theocratic" (God-ruled) than Massachusetts. The founders hoped to add worldly prosperity to their piety by making

New Haven a great commercial port, but the proximity of the unrivaled harbor of New York (then called New Amsterdam) rendered any such hope vain from the beginning. Instead of becoming an independent commercial colony, New Haven and her sister towns found themselves, to their disgust, included in the limits of Connecticut by the royal charter of 1662. They protested valiantly against the consolidation, but were forced in the end to yield. Thus the New Haven colony ceased to exist in 1665.

42. Massachusetts annexes the Settlements of Gorges and Mason. With the process of radiation from Massachusetts of colonies to the south and west went a contrary process of absorption by Massachusetts of settlements to the north and east. Ferdinando Gorges was the father of these settlements. He was a deadly enemy of Massachusetts. As a courtier he opposed the reforming party in Parliament, and as a stanch Church of England man he hated the whole Puritan movement. He secured a royal charter in 1639 which made him proprietor of Maine and labored strenuously to have strong anti-Puritan settlers emigrate to his province and to New Hampshire, the neighboring province of his fellow courtier and fellow churchman, John Mason. Massachusetts, whose territory, by the charter of 1629, extended from three miles north of the Merrimac to three miles south of the Charles (see map, p. 42), laid claim to these settlements. She annexed the New Hampshire towns in 1641–1643 and, after a long quarrel over the Maine towns, finally bought the claims of Gorges's heirs for £1250 in 1677. Charles II was incensed at the transaction. In 1679 he separated New Hampshire from Massachusetts and gave it a royal governor; but Maine remained part of the Bay Colony and then of the Bay State until 1820.

43. The Spirit of the Massachusetts Colony. The domination of Massachusetts over the other New England colonies, at least up to the time when Connecticut and Rhode Island received their charters, was complete. She far surpassed them all in men and wealth. The New England Confederation, formed in 1643 by Massachusetts, Plymouth, Connecticut, and New Haven, chiefly for defense against the Indians and the Dutch, was theoretically a league of four equal states, each having two members with equal voice in the governing council. But the opposition of Massachusetts kept Rhode Island out of the confederation, and in the question of declaring war

42   THE ESTABLISHMENT OF THE ENGLISH

on the Dutch colony of New Netherland in 1653 the two Massachusetts councilors vetoed the unanimous vote of the other six. The second half of the seventeenth century exhibited the character of the colony in its most uncompromising and unlovely aspects. The

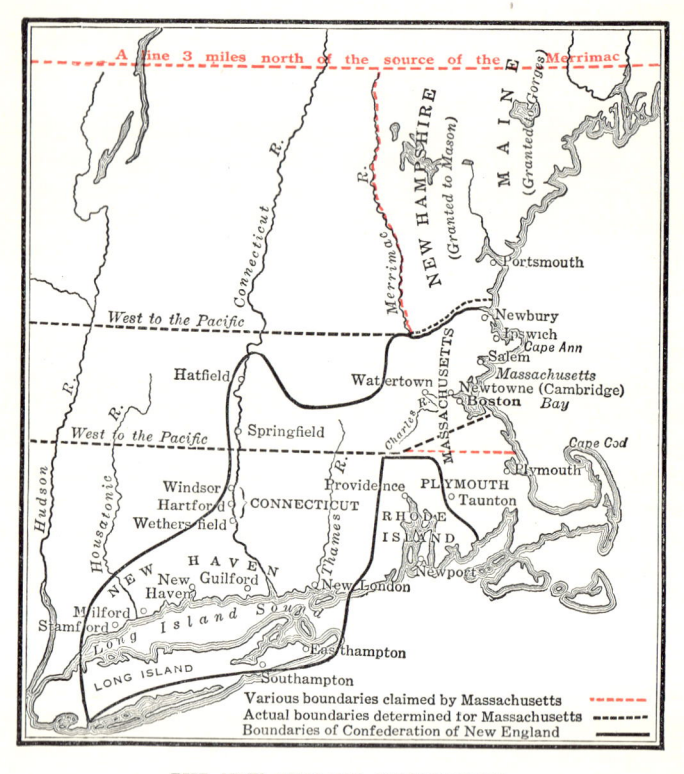

THE NEW ENGLAND SETTLEMENTS

large-minded, courteous Winthrop died in 1649, and was succeeded in the governorship by a harsh and bigoted Puritan "saint," John Endicott. Faithfulness to Puritan ideals reached a point of fanatic cruelty. Quakers were hanged in 1660 on Boston Common for the crime of testifying to the "inner light," or special divine revelation (which of course made Church and clergy superfluous). Again, in 1692, nineteen persons, mostly women, were hanged in

Salem village for witchcraft, or secret alliance with Satan, on the most unfair evidence of excited children and hysterical women.

On its political side the increasing power of the magistrates of Massachusetts aroused the angry suspicions of the king. The colony banished Episcopalians, coined money, omitted the king's name in its legal forms, and broke his laws for the regulation of their trade. When he sent commissioners in 1664 to investigate these conditions, they were insulted by a constable in a Boston tavern. Their chairman wrote back, "Our time is lost upon men puffed up with the spirit of independence." Edward Randolph, sent over a few years later as a collector of revenues, complained that "the king's letters are of no more account in Massachusetts than an old number of the London *Gazette*."[1] Finally, Charles II, provoked beyond patience, had the Massachusetts charter annulled in his court (1684), and the colony became a royal province.

THE PURITAN (BY AUGUSTUS ST. GAUDENS)

44. Edmund Andros in Boston. But before the great Puritan colony entered on its checkered career of the eighteenth century under royal governors, it bore a conspicuous part in the overthrow of that tyranny which the last Stuart king, James II, made unendurable for freeborn Englishmen. In 1686 James united New York, New Jersey, and all New England into one great province, which should be a solid bulwark against the danger of French and Indian invasion

---

[1] Randolph came at just the moment when Massachusetts was elated at having led the New England colonies victoriously through the severe war with King Philip, 1676 (see note, p. 36).

from the north, and when his governor should rule absolutely, unhampered by colonial charters or assemblies. He sent over Sir Edmund Andros as governor of this huge province extending from Delaware Bay to Nova Scotia. Andros was a faithful servant and an upright man, but a harsh, narrow, unbending governor, determined that the instructions of his royal master should be carried out to the letter. He attempted to seize the charters of Connecticut and Rhode Island, but was baffled by the local patriots in both colonies. Exasperated by resistance, Andros made his hand doubly heavy upon Massachusetts. He dismissed the assembly, abolished the colonial courts, dispensed justice himself, charging exorbitant fees, established a strict censorship of the press, introduced the Episcopal worship in Boston, denied the colonists fair and speedy trials, and levied a land tax on them without the consent of their deputies.

GOVERNOR EDMUND ANDROS

45. The "Glorious Revolution." The patience of the colony was about exhausted when the welcome news arrived, in April, 1689, that James II had been driven from the English throne. The inhabitants of Boston immediately responded by a popular rising against James's odious servant. Andros tried, like his master, to flee from the vengeance of the people he had so grievously provoked, but he was seized and imprisoned, and later sent back to England. The town meeting of Boston assumed the government, appointed a committee of safety, and sent envoys to London to learn the will of the new king, William of Orange. Thus the "Glorious Revolution" of 1689 in Massachusetts was truly a part of the English Revolution of 1688 and a foreshadowing of the greater Revolution begun eighty-six years later by the descendants of the men who expelled Andros in defense of the principles of the men who expelled James II.

THE ENGLISH COLONIES

46. The New Massachusetts Charter. King William granted a new charter to Massachusetts in 1691, while Connecticut and Rhode Island quietly resumed government under their old charters, retaining them as state constitutions well into the nineteenth century. The new Massachusetts charter provided for the union of Plymouth and Maine with the Bay colony under a royal governor and broke down the old Puritan régime by guaranteeing freedom of worship to all Protestant sects and making the possession of property instead of membership in the church the basis of political rights. Under this charter the Massachusetts colony lived until the American Revolution.

The Proprietary Colonies

47. The Nature of a Proprietary Province. Of the thirteen colonies which were later to unite to form the American nation, all except Virginia and the New England settlements were founded as *proprietorships*.[1] The Proprietorship was a sort of middle thing between the royal province and the self-governing colony. The king let the reins of government out of his own hands, but did not give them into the hands of the colonists. Between the king and the settlers stood the proprietor, a man or a small group of men, generally courtiers, to whom the king had granted the province. The proprietors appointed the governors, established courts, collected a land tax ("quitrent") from the inhabitants, offered bonuses to settlers, and in general managed their provinces like farms or any other business venture, subject always to the limitations imposed by the terms of their charter from the king and the opposition of their legislatures in the colonies.[2]

48. The Colony of Maryland. In 1632 George Calvert (Lord Baltimore), a Roman Catholic nobleman high in the favor of the court, obtained from Charles I the territory between the fortieth parallel of north latitude and the south bank of the Potomac,

---

[1] The proprietorship was not only the commonest form of colonial grant but it was also the earliest. Queen Elizabeth's patents to Gilbert and Raleigh were of this nature, and in the first half of the seventeenth century there were many attempts of proprietors, less heroically persistent than Sir Ferdinando Gorges, to found colonies on our shores.

[2] All the proprietors except the Duke of York, King Charles II's brother, forthwith granted their provinces assemblies elected by the people. They could not, in fact, get settlers on any other terms. In the royal provinces too the popularly elected assemblies were retained.

with a very liberal charter. The people of Maryland were to enjoy "all the privileges, franchises, and liberties" of English subjects; no tax was to be levied by the crown on persons or goods within the colony; laws were to be made "by the proprietor, with the advice ... of the freemen of the colony." George Calvert died before the king's great seal was affixed to the charter, but his son, Cecilius Calvert, sent a colony in 1634 to St. Marys, on the shores of Chesapeake Bay. The second Lord Baltimore needed all his tact, nobility, and courage to meet the difficulties with which he had to struggle. The tract of land granted to him by King Charles lay within the boundaries of the grant of King James to the Virginia Company (see map, p. 28). A Virginian fur trader named Claiborne was already established on Kent Island in Chesapeake Bay and refused either to retire or to give allegiance to the Catholic Lord Baltimore. It came to war with the Virginian Protestants before Claiborne was dislodged. Again, Lord Baltimore interpreted the words of his charter to mean that the proprietor was to frame the laws and the freemen to accept them; but the very first assembly of Maryland took the opposite view, insisting that the proprietor had only the right of approving or vetoing laws which they had passed. Baltimore tactfully yielded.

49. The Maryland Act of Toleration. Religious strife also played an important part in the troubled history of the Maryland settlement. Lord Baltimore had founded his colony chiefly as an asylum for the persecuted Roman Catholics of England, who were regarded as idolaters by both the New England Puritans and the Virginia Episcopalians. To have Mass celebrated at St. Marys was, in the eyes of the intolerant Protestants, to pollute the soil of America. As Baltimore tolerated all Christian sects in his province, the Protestants simply flooded out the Catholics of Maryland by immigration from Virginia, New England, and old England. Eight years after the establishment of the colony the Catholics formed less than 25 per cent of the inhabitants, and in 1649 the proprietor was obliged to protect his fellow religionists in Maryland by getting the assembly to pass the famous Toleration Act, providing that " no person in this province *professing to believe in Jesus Christ* shall be in any ways troubled, molested, or discountenanced for his or her religion ... so that they be not unfaithful to the lord proprietary or molest or conspire against the civil government established." Although this is the first act of religious toleration on the statute books of the American colonies, we should remember that Roger Williams, thirteen years earlier, had founded Rhode Island on principles of religious toleration more complete than those of the Maryland Act; for, by the italicized words of the latter, Jews or freethinkers would be excluded from Lord Baltimore's domain. By 1658 the fierce strife between Catholic and Protestant had been allayed, and Maryland settled down to a peaceful and prosperous development.

50. The Settlement and History of the Carolinas. Charles II, who took a great interest in the colonies in the early years of his reign, granted to a group of eight noblemen about his court, in 1663, the huge tract of land between Virginia and the Spanish settlement of Florida, extending westward to the "South Sea" (Pacific Ocean). The charter gave the proprietors powers as ample as Lord Baltimore's in Maryland. But the board of proprietors were not equal to Lord Baltimore in tact, energy, and devotion to the interests of the colony. Too many cooks spoiled the broth. The initial mistake was the attempt to enforce a ridiculously elaborate constitution, the "Grand Model," composed for the occasion by the celebrated English philosopher John Locke, and utterly unfit for a sparse and struggling settlement. A community grew up on the Chowan River (1670), founded by some malcontents from Virginia, and another on the shore of the Ashley River, three hundred miles to the south. The latter settlement was transferred ten years later (1680) to the site of the modern city of Charleston, South Carolina. These two widely separated settlements developed gradually into North and South Carolina respectively. The names are used as early as 1691, but the colony was not officially divided and provided with separate governors until 1711. There is little in the history of the Carolinas to detain us. It is a story of inefficient government, of wrangling and discord between people and governors, governors and proprietors, proprietors and king. North Carolina was described as "a sanctuary of runaways," where "everyone did what was right in his own eyes, paying tribute neither to God nor to Cæsar." The Spaniards incited the Indians to attack the colony from the south, and pirates swarmed in the harbors and creeks of the coast. Finally, the assembly of South Carolina, burdened by an enormous debt from the

48   THE ESTABLISHMENT OF THE ENGLISH

Spanish-Indian wars, offered the lands of the province for sale to settlers on its own terms. The proprietors vetoed this action, which invaded their chartered rights. Then the assembly renounced obedience to the proprietors' magistrates, and petitioned King George I to be taken under his protection as a royal province (1719). It was the only case in our colonial history of a proprietary government overthrown by its own assembly. Ten years later (1729) the proprietors sold their rights and interests in both Carolinas to the crown for the paltry sum of £50,000. So two more colonies were added to the growing list of royal provinces.

51. The Dutch on the Hudson. While the Carolina proprietors were inviting settlers to their new domain, an English fleet sent out by Charles II's brother, the Duke of York, sailed into New York harbor and demanded the surrender of the feebly garrisoned Dutch fort on Manhattan Island (September, 1664). The fort was commanded by Peter Stuyvesant, director general of the Dutch colony of New Netherland, which had been founded fifty years before and was governed by the Dutch West India Company. The company established fortified trading posts at New Amsterdam (New York) and Fort Orange (near Albany), but they did not make a success of the colony, although they offered tracts of land eight miles deep along both sides of the river to rich proprietors ("patroons"), with feudal privileges of trade and government, and in 1638 abolished all monopolies, opening trade and settlement to all nations and making liberal offers of land, stock, and implements to tempt farmers. Even the city of New Amsterdam, with its magnificent situation for commerce, reached a population of only sixteen hundred during the half century that it was under Dutch rule. The West India Company,

HENRY HUDSON'S VESSEL, THE *HALF MOON*, IN THE HUDSON

THE ENGLISH COLONIES

intent on the profits of the fur trade with the Indians of central New York, would not spend the money necessary for the development and defense of the colony. They sent over director generals who had little concern for the welfare of the people and refused to allow any popular assembly. If the settlers protested that they wanted a government like New England's, "where neither patroons, lords, nor princes were known, but only the people," they were met with the insulting threat of being "hanged on the tallest tree in the land." Furthermore, the Dutch magistrates were continually involved in territorial quarrels. When Henry Hudson sailed up the majestic river which bears his name (1609), he was trespassing on the territory granted by James I in 1606 to the Plymouth company. The Dutch disputed the right to the Connecticut valley with the emigrants from Massachusetts and claimed the land along the lower banks of the South River (the Delaware), from which they had driven out some Swedish settlers by force.[1] In 1653, when England was at war with Holland, New Netherland was saved from the attack of the New England colonies only by the veto of Massachusetts on the unanimous vote of the other members of the Confederation of New England.

52. New Amsterdam becomes New York. Every year the English realized more clearly the necessity of getting rid of this alien colony, which lay like a wedge between New England and the Southern plantations, controlling the valuable route of the Hudson and making the enforcement of the trade laws in America impossible. In 1664, therefore, Charles II, on the verge of a commercial war with Holland, granted to his brother, the Duke of York, the territory between the Connecticut and Delaware rivers as a proprietary province. The first the astonished burghers of New Amsterdam knew of this transaction was the appearance of the duke's fleet in the harbor, with the curt summons to surrender the fort. Director General Stuyvesant, the "valiant, weather-beaten, mettlesome, obstinate, leather-sided, lion-hearted old governor," as Diedrich

---

[1] Although without the shadow of a claim by discovery and exploration, the Swedish court imitated those of England, France, and Holland by giving to its subjects charters to establish settlements on the shores of the New World. Between 1638 and 1647 five or six Swedish trading posts were set up along the banks of the Delaware River, near its mouth, but the home government made no provision for their defense and they were easily captured by the Dutch in 1655.

Knickerbocker calls him, fumed and stormed, declaring that he would never surrender. But resistance was hopeless. The burghers persuaded the irate governor to yield, although his gunners had their fuses lighted. New Netherland fell without a blow, and the English flag waved over an unbroken coast from Canada to Carolina.

53. Absolute Rule in New York. There are still many traces in New York of its fifty years' occupancy by the Dutch. The names of the old Knickerbocker families remind us of the patroons' estates; and from the car windows one gets glimpses of the high Dutch stoops and quaint market places in the villages along the Hudson, or sees a group of men at sundown still rolling the favorite old Dutch game of bowls, which Rip van Winkle found the dwarfs playing in the Catskills. But a far more significant bequest of New Netherland to New York was the spirit of absolute government. Under the Dutch rule the people were without charter or popular assembly, and the new English proprietor was content to keep things as they were, publishing his own code of laws for the province (the "Duke's Laws"). It was not till 1683 that he yielded to pressure from his own colony and the neighbors in New England and Pennsylvania and granted an assembly. Two years later, on coming to the throne as James II, he revoked this grant and made New York the pattern of absolute government to which he tried to make all the English colonies north of Maryland conform. What success his viceroy Andros had in Massachusetts, Rhode Island, and Connecticut we have already seen (p. 44). In New York the deputy governor, Nicholson, deserted his post and sailed back to England.[1] When the new governor sent by King William III arrived in 1691, he brought orders to restore the popular assembly which James II had suppressed, and from that time on the colony enjoyed the privilege of self-government.

New York grew slowly. At the time of the foundation of our national government it was only one of the "small states" as

---

[1] The "revolution" in New York was headed by a fanatical demagogue, a German merchant named Jacob Leisler, who appropriated to himself the authority laid down by Nicholson and refused to surrender the fort on the Battery to King William's accredited agent before the arrival of the new governor. For this obstinate conduct Leisler was hanged as a traitor, although he protested that his only purpose in holding the reins of power was to prevent the Catholics in the colony from getting control of the government and betraying it to the French in Canada. He had done nothing more "treasonable" than had the leaders of the "glorious Revolution" in Massachusetts.

PROPRIETARY GRANTS MADE BY THE STUART KINGS

Showing how seven eighths of the Atlantic seaboard was granted to court favorites between 1632 and 1682 compared with Massachusetts, Virginia, and Pennsylvania. The immense Empire State of today, with its ten million inhabitants, is the growth of the last three generations. It began when the Erie Canal, and later the New York Central Railroad, made the Hudson and Mohawk valleys the main highway to the Great Lakes and the growing West.

54. The Colonial History of the Jerseys. Even before the Duke of York had ousted the Dutch magistrates from his new province he granted the lower part of it, from the Hudson to the Delaware, to two of his friends, who were also members of the Carolina board of proprietors, Lord Berkeley, brother of the irritable governor of Virginia, and Sir George Carteret, formerly governor of the island of Jersey in the English Channel. In honor of Carteret the region was named New Jersey (June, 1664). The proprietors of New Jersey immediately published "concessions" for their colony,—a liberal constitution granting full religious liberty and a popular assembly with control of taxation. In 1674 the proprietors divided their province into East and West Jersey, and from that date to the end of the century the Jerseys had a turbulent history, despite the fact that both parts of the colony, after various transfers of proprietorship, came under the control of the peace-loving sect of Friends, or Quakers.[1] New Jersey was put under the royal governor of New York in 1702 and separated again in 1738. There were constant quarrels between proprietors and governors, between governors and legislatures, until New Jersey revolted, with the rest of the American colonies, from the rule of Great Britain.

55. William Penn founds Pennsylvania. One of the Quaker proprietors of West Jersey in the early days was William Penn, a young man high in the favor of the Duke of York and his royal brother Charles, on account of the services of his father, Admiral Penn, to the Stuart cause. When the old admiral died he left a claim for

---

[1] The Friends, or Quakers, were a religious sect founded in England by George Fox in the middle of the seventeenth century. They believed that the "inner light," or the illumination of the Divine Spirit in each man's conscience, was a sufficient guide for conduct and worship. They were extreme "democrats," refusing to remove their hats in the presence of any magistrate. The Quakers had begun to come to America as early as 1653 to preach their doctrines of religious and political independence. We have already seen how cruelly they were persecuted by the Puritan authorities of Massachusetts (p. 42). In every colony except Rhode Island they were oppressed, until William Penn realized the dream of their founder and established a Quaker colony in the New World.

THE ENGLISH COLONIES

some sixteen thousand pounds against King Charles II, and William Penn, attracted by the idea of a Quaker settlement in the New World, accepted from the king a tract of land in payment of the debt. He was granted an immense region west of the Delaware River, which he named "Sylvania" (woodland), but which the king, in honor, he said, of the admiral, insisted on calling Pennsylvania (1681).[1] Charles II was in the midst of the quarrel with the stiff-necked colony of Massachusetts and was no longer willing to grant proprietors the almost unlimited powers which he had granted to Lord Baltimore and the Carolina proprietors. The Penn charter contained provisions that the colony must always keep an agent in London, that the Church of England must be tolerated, that the king might veto any act of the assembly within five years after its passage, and *that the English Parliament should have the right to tax the colony.* Disappointed that the charter of 1681 gave him no coast line, Penn persuaded the Duke of York in 1682 to release to him the land which Stuyvesant had wrested from the Swedes on the Delaware in 1655, and which, in spite of Baltimore's protests, had been held as a part of New York ever since the English "conquest" of 1664. This territory, called the "Three Lower Counties," Penn governed by a deputy. The Lower Counties were separated from Pennsylvania in 1702 and, under the name of the colony of Delaware, were given their own legislature; but they remained a part of the proprietary domain of the Penn family till the American Revolution.

56. The Prosperity of Penn's Colony. Penn offered attractive terms to settlers. Land was sold at ten dollars the hundred acres, complete religious freedom was allowed, a democratic assembly was summoned, and the Indians (Delawares), already humbled by their northern foes, the Iroquois, were rendered still less dangerous by Penn's fair dealing with them. Emigrants came in great numbers,

---

[1] According to the charter Penn's grant was bounded on the south "by a circle drawne at twelve miles distant from Newcastle, Northward and Westward unto the beginning of the 40th degree of Northern latitude." This confusing language is made all the more unintelligible by the fact that a circle drawn at a radius distance of twelve miles from Newcastle does not touch the fortieth parallel of latitude. Lord Baltimore's charter of 1632 gave him all the land "which lyeth under the 40th degree." The heirs of Penn and Baltimore quarreled over the boundary line for two full generations. Finally, in 1764–1767, two English surveyors, Mason and Dixon, ran the present boundary line (at 39° 43′ 26″), which was agreed on by both proprietors. For the disputed territory see map, p. 51.

especially the Protestants from the north of Ireland, who were annoyed by cruel landlords and oppressive trade laws, and the German Protestants of the Rhine country, against whom Louis XIV of France was waging a crusade. In the first half of the eighteenth century the population of Pennsylvania grew from twenty thousand to two hundred thousand. Philadelphia, the "city of brotherly love," which Penn had planned in 1683 "to resemble a green and open country town," soon outstripped New York in population, wealth, and culture and remained throughout the eighteenth century the leading city in the American colonies. Its neat brick houses, its paved and lighted streets, its printing presses, schools, hospital, and asylum, its library (1731), philosophical society (1743), and university (1749), all testified to the enlightenment and humanity of Penn's colony, and especially to the genius and industry of its leading citizen, the celebrated Benjamin Franklin (1706-1790).

PENN TREATING WITH THE INDIANS

From an old woodcut

57. The Character of William Penn. William Penn was the greatest of the founders of the American colonies. He had all the liberality of Roger Williams without his impetuousness, all the fervor of John Winthrop without a trace of intolerance, all the tact of Lord Baltimore with still greater industry and zeal. He was far in advance of his age in humanity. At a time when scores of offenses were punishable by death in England he made murder the only capital crime in his colony. Prisons generally were filthy dungeons, but Penn made his prisons workhouses for the education and correction of malefactors. His province was the first to raise its voice against slavery (in the Germantown protest of 1688), and his humane treatment of the Indians has passed into the legend of the spreading elm and the wampum belts familiar to every American school child. When Penn's firm hand was removed from the province (1712) disputes and wranglings increased between governor and assembly over taxes, land transfers, trade, and defense; but the colony remained in the possession of the Penn family throughout the American colonial period.

58. The Colony of Georgia. For the sake of completeness we must mention among these proprietorships the colony of Georgia, although it was founded long after the Stuart dynasty had given place to the House of Hanover on the English throne. In the year that George Washington was born (1732) James Oglethorpe obtained from the king a charter granting to a body of trustees for twenty-one years the government of that unsettled part of the old Carolina territory lying between the Savannah and Altamaha Rivers (see map, p. 51). Oglethorpe combined philanthropy and patriotism in his project. Horrified by the condition of poor debtors languishing in English prisons, he admitted many of them, after due examination, to his new colony, which he hoped would be a buffer against the Spanish power in Florida. The Church was anxious for the conversion of the Indians on the Carolina borders. Capitalists expected to make large profits out of the industries of silk and wine introduced into the province. And the government, drifting toward war with Spain, was glad to have the English frontier extended southward. So Parliament, the Society for the Propagation of the Gospel in Foreign Parts, the Bank of England, and many private citizens contributed toward the new colony, which was established on the banks of the Savannah in 1733 and named Georgia after the reigning king, George II. Slavery was forbidden in the new colony, also the traffic in rum. But the colony did not prosper. The industries started were unsuited to the land. Not wine and silk, but rice, indigo, and cotton, were destined to be the foundation of Georgia's prosperity. Oglethorpe battled manfully for his failing colony and defeated the Spaniards on land and sea, but the trustees had to surrender the government to the king in 1751. The founder of the last American colony lived to see the United States acknowledged by Great Britain and the other powers of Europe as an independent nation.

THE COLONIES IN THE EIGHTEENTH CENTURY

59. Royal Control in the Colonies. We have now traced the history of the establishment of the English colonies in America. It remains to devote a few pages to the economic and social condition

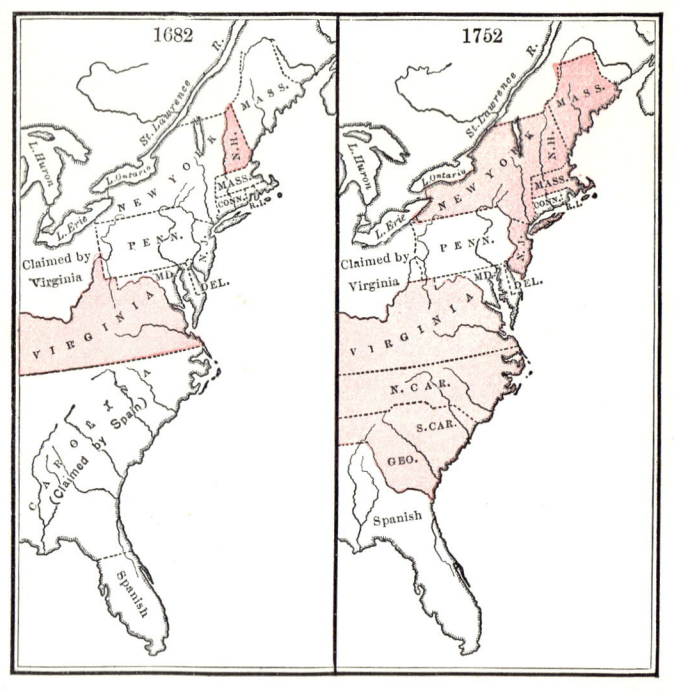

MAP ILLUSTRATING THE GROWTH IN THE NUMBER OF ROYAL PROVINCES FROM 1682 TO 1752

The royal provinces are colored red

of the colonies in their maturity in the eighteenth century. A glance at the accompanying map and table (pp. 56 and 58) will show how steady the tendency was for the colonies, especially those founded by proprietors, to become royal provinces. Only Connecticut and Rhode Island escaped at least a short period of the king's control; and repeated proposals were made in Parliament in the early years of the eighteenth century to suppress the few remaining colonial charters and unite all the colonies into one large province of the English crown, to be governed by the king's officers and provided with a provincial assembly. The causes for this tightening of royal control lay partly in the incompetency and selfishness of the proprietors, partly in the European politics,[1] partly in the need for protection against the French in Canada and their Indian allies. But the chief cause of the king's interference in colonial affairs was his desire to control their trade and manufactures for the profit of the mother country.

60. The Mercantile Theory of Commerce. The political economists of the seventeenth and eighteenth centuries quite commonly believed that a nation's wealth was measured not by the amount of desirable goods which it could produce and exchange but by the quantity of gold and silver which it could amass,—the miser's ideal. In accordance with this "mercantile" theory of commerce, as it was called, every nation tried to buy as little from others and sell as much to others as possible, so that the "favorable balance" of cash might come into its coffers. Naturally the European countries would look on their colonies, then, as places in which to sell goods. The colonies should furnish the raw materials—iron, wool, furs, hides—to the mother country, and then should buy back the finished products—steel, clothing, hats, shoes—from the mother country, paying the difference in coin. Where the money was to come from, when the colonies were forbidden either to manufacture goods themselves or to sell raw material to the other nations, does not seem greatly to have concerned the European statesmen. They believed that colonies existed for the advantage of the mother country, and that if they could not increase the flow of gold and silver into her treasury, they were useless.

61. The Navigation Acts. So Charles II's ministers were neither more nor less at fault than those of the European countries generally, when in 1660–1663 they fastened on the American colonies the Navigation Acts, or laws of trade. No goods could be carried into or out of the colonies except in ships built in the English domains

---

[1] With the accession of William of Orange, in 1689, England was involved in a long period of war with France and needed to concentrate all her resources. See Cheyney's "Short History of England," chap. xvii.

TABLE OF ENGLISH COLONIES

Name (the thirteen original states in italic)	Founded by	Date	Charter	Assembly	Made Royal	Status in 1775	Remarks
Virginia	London Company	1607	1606–1609 1612	1619	1624	Royal	
Plymouth	Separatists	1620		1639	1691	Royal	Merged with Massachusetts in 1691
Massachusetts	Puritans of the Mass. Bay Co.	1628	1629	1634	1684	Royal	Only royal colony to have its charter restored (1691)
Maryland	Lord Baltimore	1634	1632	1634		Proprietary	A royal province, 1690–1715
Rhode Island	Roger Williams	1636	1663	1647		Self-governing	Frustrated Andros's attempt to take away charters, 1686–1687
Connecticut	Emigrants from Massachusetts	1636	1662	1637		Self-governing	
New Haven	Emigrants from Massachusetts	1638		1643			Merged with Connecticut, 1662
Maine	F. Gorges	1641	1639				Bought by Massachusetts, 1677
North Carolina *South Carolina*	Eight nobles	1663	1663	1669	1691 N. 1729 S. 1719	Royal Royal	Informally separated, 1691; formally separated with different governors, 1711
New York	(Duke of York)	1664	1664	1683–1685	1685	Royal	Dutch colony of New Netherland, 1622–1664
New Hampshire	John Mason		1639	1680	1679	Royal	Towns absorbed by Massachusetts, 1641–1679
New Jersey	Berkeley and Carteret	1664		1664	1702	Royal	Under the governor of New York till 1738
Pennsylvania	William Penn	1681	1680	1681		Proprietary	A royal province, 1692–1694
Delaware	Swedes	1638		1702		Proprietary	Conquered by Dutch, 1655; by English, 1664 Merged with Pennsylvania, 1682 Separate governor (1691) and assembly (1702)
Georgia	Jas. Oglethorpe	1732	1732	1733	1752	Royal	

and manned by crews of which three fourths at least were English subjects. Certain "enumerated commodities," including tobacco, cotton-wool, and sugar (to which other articles, such as furs, rice, copper, naval stores, were added later), could not be exported from the colonies to any port outside the British domain. No European goods except salt and wine could be imported without first stopping in England to pay duties or be inspected. To be sure, England gave the enumerated colonial goods the preference, or even the monopoly, in her markets and, by a system of "drawbacks" or rebates, reduced the duties which the colonies had to pay on goods shipped through English ports. Nevertheless, it was a hindrance to the commercial prosperity of the colonies to be forbidden to sell directly in the markets of Europe, an inconvenience to be obliged to stop at England on all their return voyages, and a serious threat to their industrial life to be restricted in starting manufactures. It was like killing the goose that laid the golden eggs; for only by trading with the French and Spanish Indies, which wanted their lumber, fish, and grain, could the colonies get that coin which England demanded to maintain her "favorable balance." The fact that five sixths of the laws passed by Parliament from 1689 to 1760, touching the colonies, were for the regulation of trade and manufactures shows how serious was this policy of restricting the commerce and industry of America. But for all the laws of Parliament, illicit trade flourished and was the foundation of many a considerable colonial fortune. Probably 90 per cent of the tea, wine, fruit, sugar, and molasses consumed in the colonies was smuggled. "If the king of England," said James Otis, "were encamped on Boston Common with twenty thousand men, and had all his navy on our coast, he could not execute these laws."

FACSIMILE OF THE NAVIGATION ACT OF 1651

62. Why the Navigation Acts were not Enforced. Fortunately for the economic life of the colonies, the king's ministers did not devote their serious attention to the enforcement of the Navigation Acts until the eighteenth century was some sixty years old. War with Louis XIV of France began when William of Orange ascended the English throne in 1689 and lasted almost uninterruptedly to the Treaty of Utrecht (1713). During the years 1721-1742, England's great peace minister, Robert Walpole, directed the government, wisely overlooking the irregularities of colonial commerce so long as its prosperity contributed to England's wealth and quiet. Toward the middle of the century the war with France was renewed, and the decade 1750-1760 witnessed the culmination of the mighty struggle for the New World between France and England, which will be the subject of our next chapter. We shall see how the removal of the French from America affected the colonial policy of England. Our interest at present is in noting that the long period of England's "salutary neglect" permitted the colonies to develop their trade and manufactures to a considerable degree, in spite of the restrictions imposed by the Navigation Acts.

63. The Population of the Colonies. The American colonists numbered about 1,300,000 in the middle of the eighteenth century. They were mostly of English stock, though the Dutch were still numerous on the Hudson and the Delaware. French Huguenots had come in considerable numbers to the middle and lower colonies, Germans from the Rhine country had settled in Pennsylvania, and the Scotch-Irish, that sterling, hardy race of men which has given us some of the most distinguished names in our history, had come in great numbers to Pennsylvania and thence passed up the Shenandoah valley into Virginia and the Carolinas. Immigration practically ceased about 1730, not to be renewed on a large scale until the age of steamships a century later. There were between two and three hundred thousand negro slaves distributed through the colonies,— a few house servants and men of all work in the New England States, a greater number in the Middle States and Virginia, while farther south they even outnumbered the whites in some districts of South Carolina and Georgia. There were well-defined types of colonial society, due to circumstances of emigration from Europe, conditions of the soil, political institutions, and religious beliefs. These types were the more marked, as there were no adequate means of communication or routes of travel between the colonies.

64. The New England Type of Character. New England was inhabited by pure English stock and retained for many generations its Puritan character. The early immigrants had come in congregations and settled in compact groups, making little self-governing towns clustered about the church, the school, and the village green. Learning was more carefully nurtured and widely diffused in New

HARVARD COLLEGE IN 1726

England than anywhere else in the colonies.[1] Before 1650 public-school instruction had been made compulsory in all New England except Rhode Island, in order "that learning," in the noble words of the Massachusetts statute, "might not be buried in the graves of the fathers." Harvard College was established six years after Winthrop's landing, and "before the nightly howl of the wolf had ceased from the outskirts of their villages" the Massachusetts settlers had made provision whereby their young men might study the master

---

[1] The Puritan leaders of the New England settlements were highly educated men, who prized learning for the support it furnished to their independent religious ideas. Where the interpretation of Scripture depended, as it did in the Puritan system, on one's own enlightened mind, universal education was a necessity. The Massachusetts legislature, which voted £400 in 1636 "to found a college at Newtowne" (Cambridge), was "the first body in which the people by their representatives ever gave their own money to found a place of education" (Quincy, History of Harvard University, Vol. II, p. 654).

minds of the world. The excellent Earl of Bellomont, coming as royal governor to Massachusetts in 1700, wondered how so much learning could exist in the province side by side with so much fanaticism. The stony soil and rigorous climate of New England made the farmer's life a fit preparation for enduring the rough march or toiling on the rude fortifications against the Indians, whose war whoop so often interrupted his plowing and planting. The schools of bluefish, mackerel, and cod off the coast developed a race of hardy fishermen in the seaport towns; while the fleet sloops and cutters of the aristocratic merchants slipped by the customs patrol with the smuggled goods of the Indies. Until the rise of a class of brilliant young lawyers like Otis and the Adamses, on the eve of the Revolutionary War, the clergy were the undisputed leaders of society. Education was entirely in their hands, and the magistrates were controlled by a public opinion largely inspired from the pulpits of the Puritan divines. With the virtues of soberness, industry, scrupulous conscientiousness, and a high standard of private and public morality, Puritanism also unfortunately developed narrowness, self-righteousness, and unwholesome cultivation of the austere and joyless sides of life. The first play that ventured to invite the applause of a New England audience, "The Orphan," enacted in a Boston coffeehouse in 1750, was prohibited as "tending to discourage industry and frugality and greatly to increase impiety." At the same time New York, Baltimore, and cities to the south were centers of gayety.

65. Contrasts of Colonial Life. No greater contrast could be imagined than that of the hardy old Puritan divine, Samuel Emery, preaching interminable sermons in the arctic cold of a Maine meetinghouse without seats, windows, or plaster, on a salary of £45 a year, payable one half in farm truck and firewood, prepared every moment to seize his musket at the sound of the Indian war whoop, and fortified by inward grace against the still more redoubtable attacks of the tart tongues of "frightfully turbulent women" in his congregation; and the rich Carolina planter, wintering among the fashionable throng at Charleston, sipping costly wines at gay suppers, handing richly gowned women to their chariots with the grace of King Louis's courtiers, gaming, dueling, drinking, and remitting generous sums of his plantation profits to the son established in gentleman's quarters at Tory Oxford. Of course such a picture is not fair to the average life in the colonies, north and south. There were wealthy aristocrats among the Puritans of New England, as "Tory Row" in Cambridge testified; and there were numerous settlers of hardy Huguenot and Scotch-Irish stock in Virginia and the Carolinas. Nevertheless, the contrast between stern New England and the more aristocratic colonies south of the Potomac was marked.

A COLONIAL MANSION IN THE SOUTH

Thomas Jefferson's home at Monticello, Charlottesville, Va.

66. Colonial Society in the South. The rich soil of the South, with its staple crops of tobacco and rice, favored the plantation system and slave labor. Broad navigable rivers, reaching well up into the level lands, gave every planter his private wharf and made the huge plantations resemble feudal estates, with their stately manor houses dominating the stables, the storage sheds, and the clustering huts of the slave quarters. In Virginia, and perhaps to some extent in the Carolinas, these estates, by the laws of "primogeniture" and "entail," descended undivided to the eldest son of the family, while the younger sons either entered the ranks of the clergy and the professions of physicians and lawyers or sometimes became shiftless dependents and rovers. A public-school system was impossible when the white population was so scattered that a planter needed a field glass to see his neighbor's house. The slaves might be taught the elements of religion by a conscientious mistress, but "book learning" was no part of their equipment for the rice swamps, the kitchen, or the hunting stables. On court days the squires and rustics gathered at the county center, making a holiday with racing and speech making; but the tense and steady political interest of the New England town meeting was unknown.[1]

67. The Middle Colonies. The settlements between the Hudson and the Potomac were "middle colonies" in character as well as in situation,— between the puritanical, democratic type of New England, and the urbane, aristocratic, hospitable society of the South, so tenacious of rank and tradition. Politically these middle colonies combined some features of both the township government of the North and the county government of the South. They were (as they still are) cosmopolitan in population, and the region was most attractive to foreign immigration. A Jesuit missionary of Canada passing through New Amsterdam in 1643 found eighteen languages spoken among its four hundred inhabitants and noted an intense devotion to money making, which precluded much interest in education or religion. There were but two churches in the city when it was surrendered to the English in 1664.

68. Civilization developed Slowly in the Colonies. In lands so recently reclaimed from the virgin forest and the savage Indian as were the American colonies the progress of civilization was naturally slow. As late as the outbreak of the Revolutionary War, John Dickinson of Pennsylvania could write, "Some few towns excepted, we are all tillers of the soil from Nova Scotia to West Florida." Still Benjamin Franklin, already high in the estimation of Europeans for his scientific discoveries, when founding the first American Philosophical Society (1743), wrote: "The first drudgery of settling new colonies is pretty well over, and there were many in every colony in circumstances which set them at ease to cultivate the finer arts and improve the common stock of knowledge." An enterprising governor of New York, toward the end of the seventeenth century,

---

[1] In Virginia local courts were developed early in the seventeenth century, but in South Carolina every magistrate was appointed in Charleston and every court held there. Of county or township government there was no trace until after the Civil War.

started a monthly postal service between New York and Boston, over the New Haven-Hartford-Springfield route now followed by the railroad. In 1710 Parliament extended the British post office to America, with headquarters established at New York, and postal routes reaching from the Maine border on the north to Williamsburg,

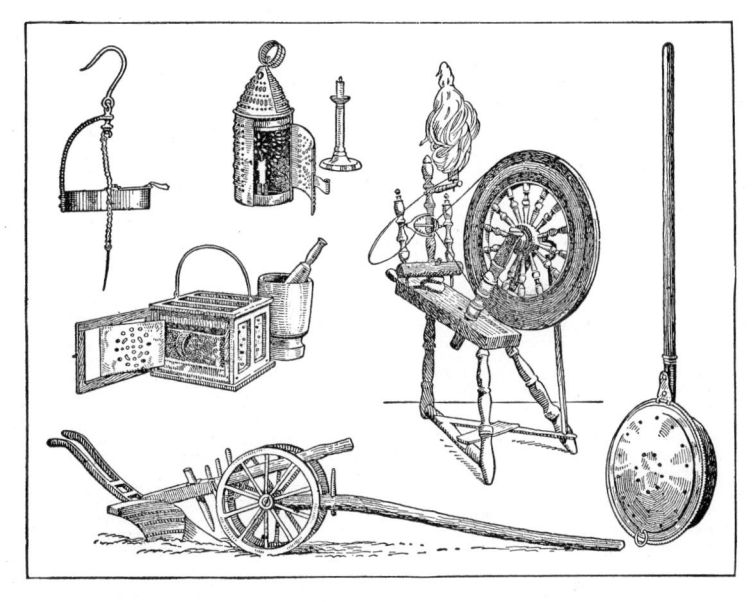

FARM AND HOUSEHOLD IMPLEMENTS OF COLONIAL DAYS

the capital of Virginia, on the south. Later Benjamin Franklin served for many years as postmaster-general of the colonies, and administered the office with great diligence and skill.

69. Education in the Colonies. Public schools existed from the first in New England, as we have seen, but were not established in the middle and southern colonies until the eighteenth century. For over half a century Harvard was the only college in America; then followed William and Mary in Virginia (1693), Yale in Connecticut (1701), Princeton in New Jersey (1746), Philadelphia (now the University of Pennsylvania) (1749), King's (now Columbia) in New York (1754), Rhode Island (now Brown University) (1764). The first medical treatise in America was published by Thomas Thacher in Boston in 1678, "to guide the common people of New England how to order themselves and theirs in the Small Pocks or Measels." But it was a full century before the first medical school was opened in Philadelphia, with lectures in anatomy, botany, and Lavoisier's discoveries in chemistry. Even then the science of medicine was crude and clumsy beyond belief. George Washington's life was sacrificed to medical ignorance in 1799. He was "bled" three times

FACSIMILE OF THE EARLIEST SUCCESSFUL NEWSPAPER IN AMERICA

by the leeches and then, after the loss of two quarts of blood, was "dosed to nausea and blistered to rawness." Even Washington's stout constitution could not stand this heroic treatment. His secretary, Tobias Lear, wrote sadly, "Every medical assistance was offered, but without the desired result."

70. Printing Presses and Newspapers. In 1638 the first font of type was brought from England, and in 1640 the Book of Psalms in meter (the old "Bay Psalm Book") was printed in Boston,— the first book printed in America north of the city of Mexico. On September 26, 1690, the first newspaper in America, *Publick Occurrences both Foreign and Domestic*, appeared in Boston; but it was promptly suppressed by the government "under high resentment."

However, in 1704 the *Boston News-Letter* had a kinder reception by the authorities, and became our first permanent newspaper. Within the next half century all the colonies except New Jersey, Delaware, and Georgia had *Gazettes* or *Chronicles*, and there were three or four respectable periodicals. But few books were produced in the colonies. The educated depended on England for their scientific works, and read with avidity the ponderous novels of the eighteenth century. The colonial presses were chiefly devoted to sermons and political "broadsides."

In 1734 a poor New York printer named Peter Zenger was tried for "seditious libel" in speaking freely of the government. He was defended by one of the ablest lawyers in the colonies, who offered his services gratis to "secure to ourselves and our posterity the liberty both of exposing and opposing arbitrary power by speaking and writing the truth." Zenger won his case, and the freedom of the press was thus early vindicated in our history.

71. Hindrances and Helps to Union among the Colonies. The observant Swedish traveler Kalm, visiting America in 1750, was astonished at the isolation of the colonies from one another, and it is said that the delegates who met from nine of them in a congress at New York fifteen years later regarded each other "like ambassadors from foreign nations, strange in face and action." It is not to be wondered at that the colonies knew little of one another in days when travel by stage, sloop, or saddle was laborious and expensive; nor that little love was lost between them when boundaries were constantly in dispute on account of the reckless grants of the Stuart charters, and when jealousies were rife over the appropriations of men and money for Indian defense. Yet, for all the diversity of type and disunion of sentiment in the colonies, there were some very fundamental bonds of union between them. They were all predominantly of English blood, with the inheritance of the English traditions of self-government. Popular assemblies insisted on the control of the public purse in every colony from New Hampshire to Georgia, often vexing the royal governors by doling out their salaries in niggardly fashion. The common law of England was universal. Trial by jury, liberty of speech and of the press, freedom from standing armies, absence of oppressive land taxes,— in short, the rights and privileges for which free-born Englishmen had contended from the days of Magna Carta to the overthrow of the Stuarts,—were possessed and prized by all the colonies. And when these guarantees of liberty were invaded by a headstrong king and a heedless Parliament, the people of the colonies forgot that they were Virginians or New Englanders, Episcopalians or Puritans, planters, traders, farmers, or fishermen, in the prouder, deeper consciousness that they were freemen.

REFERENCES

The Old Dominion: L. G. TYLER, *Narratives of Early Virginia, 1606–1625* (Original Narratives of Early American History); JOHN FISKE, *Old Virginia and her Neighbors*; JUSTIN WINSOR, *Narrative and Critical History of America*, Vol. III, chap. v; C. M. ANDREWS, *Colonial Self-Government* (Am. Nation), chaps. xiii, xiv; TYLER, *England in America* (Am. Nation), chaps. iii–vi; *Narratives of Early Virginia* (Orig. Narr.); MARY JOHNSTON, *Pioneers of the Old South* (Chronicles of America, Vol. V), chaps. i–viii, x–xiii, xv; E. M. AVERY, *History of the United States and its People*, Vol. II, chaps. iii, ix; EDW. CHANNING, *History of the United States*, Vol. I, pp. 143–236; J. A. DOYLE, *English Colonies in America*, Vol. I, chaps. vi–ix.

The New England Settlements: CHANNING, Vol. I, chaps. x–xv; Vol. II, chaps. vi, vii; FISKE, *The Beginnings of New England*; DOYLE, Vols. II and III; WINSOR, Vol. III, chaps. viii, ix; TYLER (Am. Nation), chaps. ix–xix; ANDREWS (Am. Nation), chaps. iii, iv, xvi, xvii; *The Fathers of New England* (Chronicles, Vol. VI); *Narratives of the Insurrections* (Orig. Narr.), pp. 165–297; W. T. DAVIS, *Bradford's History of Plymouth* (Orig. Narr.); J. K. HOSMER, *Winthrop's Journal* (Orig. Narr.); AVERY, Vol. II, chaps. v–viii, xv–xviii; A. B. HART, *American History told by Contemporaries*, Vol. I, Nos. 90–149.

The Proprietary Colonies: DOYLE, Vol. I, chaps. x–xii; Vol. IV, chaps. i–vii; J. F. JAMESON, *Narratives of New Netherland* (Orig. Narr.); FISKE, *Old Virginia and her Neighbors*, chaps. viii, ix, xiii, xiv; *The Dutch and Quaker Colonies in America*; MAUD W. GOODWIN, *Dutch and English on the Hudson* (Chronicles, Vol. VII); C. C. HALE, *Narratives of Early Maryland* (Orig. Narr.); GOODWIN, ROYCE, and PUTNAM, *Historic New York*; A. S. SALLEY, JR., *Narratives of Early Carolina* (Orig. Narr.); ANDREWS (Orig. Narr.), pp. 315–401; SYDNEY G. FISHER, *The Quaker Colonies* (Chronicles, Vol. VIII); AVERY, Vol. II, chap. x; Vol. III, chaps. i, iii–vi; CHANNING, Vol. I, chaps. xvi–xviii; Vol. II, chaps. ii, iv, xi, xii; TYLER (Am. Nation), chaps. vii, viii; ANDREWS (Am. Nation), chaps. v–xii, xv–xix; H. L. OSGOOD, *The American Colonies in the Seventeenth Century*, Vol. II; HART, Vol. I, Nos. 153–172; WINSOR, Vol. III, chaps. x–xiii; Vol. V, chaps. iii–vi.

The Colonies in the Eighteenth Century: DOYLE, Vol. V; E. B. GREENE, *Provincial America* (Am. Nation), chaps. i–vi, xi–xviii; R. G. THWAITES, *The Colonies*, pp. 265 ff.; HART, Vol. II, Nos. 1–108; CHANNING, Vol. II, chaps. xiii–xvii; *Cambridge Modern History*, Vol. VII, chap. ii; ANDREWS, *Colonial Folkways* (Chronicles, Vol. IX); *The Colonial Period* (Home University

THE ENGLISH COLONIES

Library); W. B. WEEDEN, *Economic and Social History of New England;*
P. A. BRUCE, *Economic History of Virginia*; E. L. BOGART, *Economic History
of the United States,* chaps. iii–vi; CARL BECKER, *The Beginnings of the
American People* (Riverside History), chaps. iv, v; G. L. BEER, *The Commercial Policy of England toward the American Colonies,* chaps. iv–viii.

TOPICS FOR SPECIAL REPORTS

1. **Bacon's Rebellion:** FISKE, *Old Virginia,* Vol. II, pp. 58–107; HART, Vol. I, No. 70; ANDREWS (Am. Nation), pp. 215–231; JOHNSTON, pp. 161–190; AVERY, Vol. III, pp. 28–45; OSGOOD, Vol. III, pp. 258–278.

2. **The Pilgrims in England and Holland:** M. DEXTER, *The Story of the Pilgrims,* pp. 1–150; CHANNING, Vol. I, pp. 293–304; HART, Vol. I, Nos. 49, 55, 97–104; W. E. GRIFFIS, *The Pilgrims in their Three Homes.*

3. **Dutch New York:** WINSOR, Vol. IV, pp. 395–499; CHANNING, Vol. I, pp. 438–483; HART, Vol. I, Nos. 150–155; FISKE, *Dutch and Quaker Colonies,* Vol. I, pp. 158–188.

4. **William Penn:** FISKE, *Dutch and Quaker Colonies,* Vol. II, pp. 109–139; WINSOR, Vol. III, pp. 469–495; CHANNING, Vol. II, pp. 94–126; DOYLE, Vol. IV, pp. 379–403; Old South Leaflets, Nos. 95, 171.

5. **Religion in New England:** WINSOR, Vol. II, pp. 219–244; DOYLE, Vol. II, pp. 85–120; Vol. V, pp. 166–193; OSGOOD, Vol. I, pp. 200–211; Old South Leaflets, No. 55.

CHAPTER III

THE STRUGGLE WITH FRANCE FOR NORTH AMERICA

The Rise of New France

72. European Claims in America in the Seventeenth Century. Three centuries ago the kings of Europe regarded as their own private property any distant lands or islands that mariners in their service might discover; and they granted these lands to settlers and trading companies with little regard for each other's claims. Immense tracts of land in America, extending from sea to sea, were given away by the Stuart kings, on the ground that John Cabot's discovery of the mainland of America in 1497 gave the New World to England. The States-General (parliament) of the Netherlands in 1621 granted to the Dutch West India Company exclusive privileges of trade "on the east coast of America from Newfoundland to the Strait of Magellan." Seven years later Richelieu, the powerful cardinal-minister who ruled the ruler of France, granted to the "Hundred Associates of Canada territory and trading rights, extending along the Atlantic coast from Florida to the Arctic circle." Even Sweden entered the ranks of the world-colonizing powers in 1632, with a charter to a company "for trade and settlement on the coasts of America, Africa, and Asia." The Swedes maintained their tiny posts on the Delaware River for less than twenty years, and the Dutch held the banks of the Hudson for about fifty years. Besides the English, only the French and Spanish came anywhere near making good, by settlement or exploration, their vast claims to territory in North America. With the French the English had to fight for the possession of the valleys of the St. Lawrence, the Ohio, and the Mississippi Rivers.

73. Early French Explorers. The French were early in the field of American exploration. Their traditions tell of the discovery of distant western shores by sailors of Dieppe more than a century before Columbus's birth. At any rate, the fishing vessels of the

STRUGGLE WITH FRANCE FOR NORTH AMERICA 71

Norman and Breton sea dogs were looming through the Newfoundland fogs soon after Columbus's death; and Verrazano had sailed the Atlantic coast from Florida to Nova Scotia for the French king sixty years before Sir Walter Raleigh opened the epoch of English settlement in Virginia. A long list of French names represent settlements attempted in Brazil, Carolina, Newfoundland, and Nova Scotia (Acadia) during the sixteenth century; but the only real discoverer among these French adventurers was Jacques Cartier, of St. Malo in Brittany.

74. Cartier on the St. Lawrence. In 1534 Cartier sailed into the Gulf of St. Lawrence, and on his next voyage (1535) discovered the broad mouth of the river. He made his way up the St. Lawrence, stopping to barter for furs at Indian villages on the magnificent sites where the cities of Quebec and Montreal now stand (see map, p. 23). Just beyond Montreal the way to the China Sea (the hope held out by every westward-reaching river or creek) was barred by the rapids whose name, *Lachine* ("China"), still tells of Cartier's disappointment in not reaching the East Indies. For several years Cartier labored in vain to establish a colony on the St. Lawrence, and one year his men actually wintered there. But the noble river of Canada was destined, like the lowlands of Virginia, to wait until the opening of a new century before its savage tribes were disturbed by the permanent presence of Europeans.

75. Champlain, the "Father of New France." The man who founded the French empire in Canada was Samuel de Champlain. Trained navigator, scientific student, intrepid explorer, earnest missionary, unwearied advocate of French expansion in the New World, Champlain established a trading post on the mighty rock of Quebec in 1608. The little colony, like the Pilgrim settlement at Plymouth twelve years later, barely survived its first winter. But an unfortunate circumstance in the summer of 1609 proved more disastrous to the French rule in America than many starving winters. Champlain was induced by the Algonquin Indians along the river to join them in an attack on their old enemies, the Iroquois, whose confederation of five powerful tribes stretched from the upper Hudson to Lake Erie. The expedition led Champlain's canoes into the sapphire waters of the Lake of the Iroquois, which now bears his name. A single volley from the French guns put to flight the astounded Indians gathered on the shore of the lake; but Champlain little dreamed of the far-reaching effect of those few shots that startled the virgin forest of the Lake of the Iroquois. On that very July day of 1609 Henry Hudson was off the New England coast on his way to discover the river which was to take him up to within a few miles of the lake. The defeat of the Iroquois by Champlain made that powerful league of tribes the allies of the Dutch (and later of the

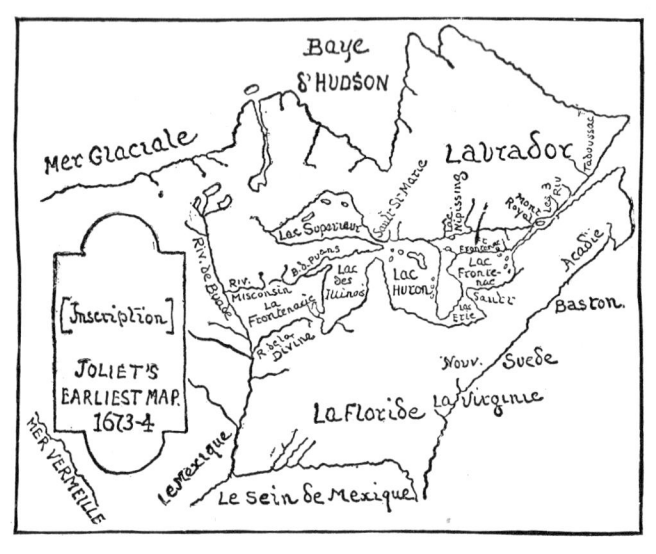

JOLIET'S MAP OF NEW FRANCE (FROM WINSOR'S "CARTIER TO FRONTENAC")

English) on the Hudson, and not of the French on the St. Lawrence. They massacred the French missionaries and exterminated the tribes that listened to their preaching. Their enmity forced the French explorers and traders to seek the interior of America by routes to the north of the Great Lakes.

76. French Ideas of Colonization. Had the French controlled the Ohio valley and the southern shores of Lakes Erie and Ontario (as they might have done with the Iroquois as allies), it is extremely likely that they would have succeeded in their long struggle to confine the English within the narrow strip of land between the

Allegheny Mountains and the Atlantic. Then the vast continent of America above the Gulf of Mexico would have developed under French instead of English institutions. What the French ideas of colonization were we see in the regulations made by Richelieu in 1627 to 1628 for the Hundred Associates of New France, and by the ministers of Louis XIV, when the colony became a province of the crown in 1663. None but Frenchmen and Roman Catholics were allowed in the colony. The land was all in the hands of great proprietors, who rented strips for cultivation along the river banks in exchange for labor on their big estates or payment in produce. The government was administered by the officers of the company or the crown, without the direction or even the advice of any representative assembly. There was no local government. Justice was dispensed by the magistrates without trial by jury. In place of the self-rule enjoyed by the English settlements on the Atlantic seaboard there prevailed in Canada the system known as "paternalism," which treated the inhabitants of the colony like irresponsible children under the firm, paternal hand of its governors. They were directed by the government not only what taxes to pay, with what ports to trade, what laws to obey, what worship to perform, but what tools to use, what seeds to plant, at what age to marry, and how large families to bring up. This absolute and paternal rule, while it promoted military efficiency, did not attract colonists. During the seventeenth century the English population along the Atlantic coast grew to over two hundred thousand, while the French in Canada barely reached eighteen thousand. The three chief posts of Quebec, Three Rivers, and Montreal were strung along the St. Lawrence at intervals of ninety miles. The sparseness of population permitted agriculture to be carried on only in the neighborhood of the forts which served to protect the settlers from the Indians.

77. *Coureurs de Bois* and Missionaries. Westward through the St. Lawrence valley and along the shores of the Great Lakes roamed the hunters and trappers and fur traders, the wood-rangers (*coureurs de bois*) who defied the trading laws of the king's governor at Quebec. These wild Frenchmen often sacrificed their native tongue, their religion, even their very civilization itself, and joined the aboriginal American tribes, marrying Indian squaws, eating boiled dog and mush, daubing their naked bodies with greasy war paint, and leading the hideous dance or the murderous raid. Missionaries, chiefly of the Jesuit order, penetrated the wilderness of Canada to convert the Indians to Christianity. In 1643 they were the pioneers to the savage lands of the Hurons about Georgian Bay, and during the whole of the seventeenth century they kept side by side with the explorer and the trader in their march westward. They have left us an account of their triumphs and martyrdoms in a series of annual reports sent home to the superior of their order in France during the years 1632 to 1675. These reports, called the "Jesuit Relations," have been edited in over seventy volumes by an American historian, Professor R. G. Thwaites. They form one of the most valuable sources for the study of the French in America.

78. French Explorers on the Great Lakes. Champlain had advocated westward expansion. He discovered Lake Ontario and Georgian Bay and explored the Ottawa valley. In 1634 he sent Jean Nicolet as far as the outlet of Lake Superior. A generation of explorers and traders followed in Nicolet's footsteps, penetrating the western wilderness to the upper waters of the Mississippi and even reaching the frozen shores of Hudson Bay. In 1671 St. Lusson, standing at Sault Ste. Marie, where the emerald flood of Lake Superior rushes to join the darker waters of Lake Huron, took possession, with great pomp and pageant, of the vast Northwest for his sovereign king, Louis XIV.

79. La Salle opens the Mississippi Valley. Already Robert Cavelier, the Sieur de la Salle, who was to repeat St. Lusson's ceremony eleven years later at the mouth of the Mississippi and so complete the dominion of France from the Lakes to the Gulf of Mexico, was pushing his way westward by the Lakes to reach the "Big Water" (*Mich sipi*) which the Indians said flowed southward for innumerable days. La Salle was a French nobleman, cultured, aristocratic, domineering; yet he sacrificed wealth and ease, bore with marvelous patience repeated and overwhelming misfortunes, endured physical hardship and forest travel which exhausted even his Indian guides, that he might accomplish his single purpose of extending the name and power of France in the New World. He labored twelve years in the face of jealousy and detraction at home, treachery in his own ranks, bankruptcy, shipwreck, and massacre, before he actually guided his canoes out of the Illinois into the long-desired stream of the Mississippi (February 6, 1682). The Jesuit priest Marquette and the trader Joliet had anticipated him by nine years, sailing down the great river as far as the mouth of the Arkansas, but returning when they had satisfied themselves that the river flowed into the Gulf of Mexico instead of the western sea. La Salle, however, was stimulated by a greater purpose than the discovery of a passage to China. He was adding a continent to the dominion of France. He planted the lilies of France on the shores of the Gulf of Mexico (April 9, 1682), naming the huge valley of the Mississippi "Louisiana" in honor of his sovereign, Louis XIV.

80. The Builders of New France. La Salle himself did not live to develop and govern the new domain of Louisiana.[1] But the line of posts down the Illinois and the Mississippi, which united the French possessions in Canada and Louisiana; the fortification of Detroit (1701), with its control of Lake Erie and the portages to the Ohio tributaries; the prosperous colony of seven thousand inhabitants in the lower Mississippi Valley, which grew up with New Orleans (founded, 1718) as its capital,—all were the outcome of La Salle's vast labors.

LA SALLE AT THE MOUTH OF THE MISSISSIPPI

---

[1] Returning to the New World from a visit to France, La Salle missed the mouth of the Mississippi and landed, perilously near being shipwrecked, on the Texan coast by Matagorda. He was treacherously assassinated by some of his own party while trying to reach Louisiana through swamp and jungle in 1687.

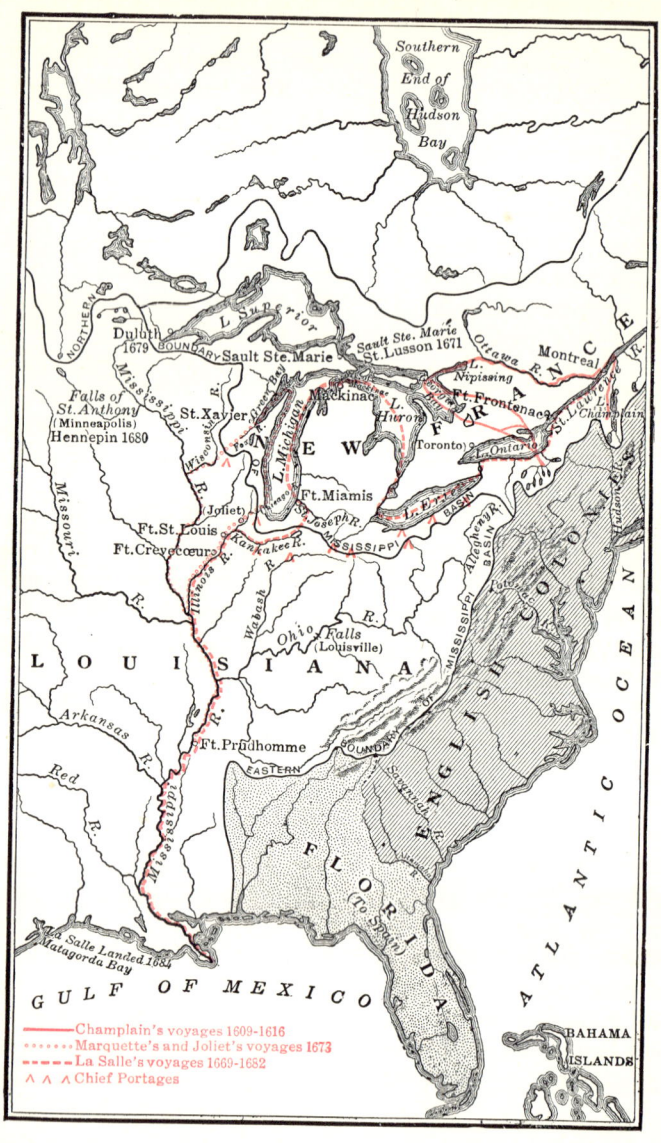

FRENCH EXPLORATIONS OF THE SEVENTEENTH CENTURY ABOUT THE GREAT LAKES AND THE MISSISSIPPI

STRUGGLE WITH FRANCE FOR NORTH AMERICA 77

If Champlain was the father of New France, La Salle was its elder brother. These two, together with the energetic, farseeing governor of Canada, the Count Frontenac (1672-1682, reappointed 1689-1698), form the trio who created the French power in the New World, and whose plan of empire building, had it not been thwarted by the narrow and bigoted policy of the court of Versailles, might have made not only the St. Lawrence and Mississippi valleys but all of America above the tropics an enduring colony of France.

81. How the English Colonies viewed French Expansion. The English colonies on the Atlantic seaboard, occupied with their own problems of developing their agricultural resources, building up their commerce, defending their precious rights of self-government against king and proprietor, were slow to realize the serious meaning of the French power which was gradually surrounding them in a long chain of posts from the mouth of the St. Lawrence to the mouth of the Mississippi. Though by their charters several of the colonies extended to the Pacific, the Allegheny Mountains, only a few score miles from the Atlantic coast, actually formed a western boundary which the colonists were over a century in reaching and another half century in crossing. When the Virginians were still defending their tide-swept peninsulas against the Susquehannock Indians, and the Carolinians were laying the foundations of their first city, what the French fur traders, missionaries, and explorers were doing at the head of the Great Lakes or along the Mississippi seemed too remote for notice. Only in Acadia (Nova Scotia), where the French had established their first permanent settlement, in 1604, and in the region of Hudson Bay, were there actual rivalry and armed conflict between French and English.

82. The Critical Situation of New York. New York differed from the other English colonies in this important respect: it was the only one not protected in the rear by the wall of the Alleghenies, and hence the only one that had direct and easy communication with the Iroquois south of the Great Lakes and with the French on the St. Lawrence. Furthermore, only the year before the Duke of York's fleet took New Netherland from the Dutch, Louis XIV, just come of age, had taken the colony of New France into his own hands (1663). His able minister, Colbert, reorganized the government, securing bounties for trade and large loans and gifts of money and stores from the king for the French colonies in Canada, the West Indies, South America, and Africa. A royal governor was sent to Canada, together with a military commander and a regiment of twelve hundred veterans of the European wars. The French frontier was pushed down to Lake Champlain, and the new governor was on his way south with five hundred men to chastise the Iroquois when he heard that the English had seized the Hudson. He "returned in great sylence and dilligence toward Canada, declaring that the king of England did grasp at all America." Still the commander wrote home to Colbert that it was necessary for the French to have New York. It would give them an ice-free entrance to Canada by the Hudson valley, would break up the English alliance with the Iroquois, and would divide the English colonies in America into a northern and a southern group. Under these circumstances it was not strange that New York should be the colony most concerned about the growth of the French power, and that it should be Dongan, the Duke of York's governor, who first urged upon his countrymen that to have the French "running all along from our lakes by the back of Virginia and Carolina to the Bay of Mexico" might be "very inconvenient to the English" (1683).

83. The Opening of a Century of Warfare with France. So long as the Stuarts occupied the English throne, however, their governors in New York or in any other American colony received little support against the French. The royal brothers Charles II and James II, who basely accepted millions of pounds from their cousin Louis XIV of France to combat their own parliaments in England, could not with very good grace attack King Louis's governors in America. But with the expulsion of the Stuarts and the accession of William of Orange to the English throne, in 1689, a great change came. William had for years been the deadly enemy of Louis XIV on account of the latter's shameful attack on the Netherlands in 1672.[1] Moreover, William, as the leading Protestant prince of Europe, was the champion of the reformed religion, which Louis was attempting to overthrow. England rallied to William's support against the absolute power of France. A mighty struggle

---

[1] William of Orange, when he was invited to the English throne in 1688, was serving his seventeenth year as Stadtholder (or President) of the Dutch Republic, the northern provinces of the Netherlands.

began between the two countries for the colonial and commercial supremacy of the world. In the century and a quarter that intervened between William's accession to the English throne and the defeat of Napoleon at Waterloo (1815), England and France fought seven wars, filling sixty years and covering lands and oceans from the forests of western Pennsylvania to the jungles of India, and from the Caribbean Sea to the mouth of the Nile.

THE FALL OF NEW FRANCE

84. Indian Attacks on the English Frontiers. Louis XIV's governor in Canada, the wily old Count Frontenac, was only waiting for an excuse to attack the English settlements in New England and New York. On learning of the outbreak of war between France and England (1689) he sent his bands of Indian allies against the frontier towns to pillage, burn, and massacre. Dover, in the present state of New Hampshire, and Schenectady, in the Mohawk valley, New York, were the scenes of frightful Indian atrocities. Even the conclusion of peace between the courts of London and Paris in 1697, and the death of Frontenac in the next year, brought only a lull in these savage raids.

85. The Treaty of Utrecht. In 1701 a new war broke out between the two great rival powers. Louis XIV, in defiance of all Europe, set his grandson on the vacant throne of Madrid, thinking by the combined strength of France and Spain to crush out Protestantism entirely, to control the wealth of the New World, and to destroy England's colonial empire and sweep her fleets from the ocean. The French king failed in his ambitious plans. After repeated defeats at the hands of Queen Anne's great general, the duke of Marlborough,[1] he was forced to conclude the humiliating Treaty of Utrecht (1713), which made England the foremost maritime power of the world. By the clauses of the treaty that referred to the New World, France surrendered to England the territories of Acadia (Nova Scotia), Newfoundland, and Hudson Bay. Statesmen in America urged that England should demand the whole St. Lawrence

---

[1] King William III died in 1702 and was succeeded by his sister-in-law, Anne, a Protestant daughter of James II. With England in this War of the Spanish Succession were allied the Netherlands, Savoy, and the Holy Roman Empire.

valley and free the colonies once for all from the danger of the French and Indians on the north. But the mother country was content for the moment to get a clear title to regions which had been in dispute for a hundred years and to secure the undisputed control of the Iroquois tribes in western New York. The French were destined to hold the great rivers of Canada for half a century more.

86. The Truce under Walpole and Fleuri. The Treaty of Utrecht was only a truce, after all, as far as America was concerned, for it decided nothing as to the possession of the vast territory west of the Alleghenies. But the truce was kept for many years on account of the death of the ambitious Louis XIV (1715) and the rise to power of the peacefully disposed ministers, Robert Walpole in England and Cardinal Fleuri in France. Till the middle of the eighteenth century, though Indian raids on the frontiers, promoted by the French, occurred at frequent intervals, only one real French war (King George's War, 1744–1748) disturbed the colonies.[1] A glorious exploit of the colonial troops in this war was the capture in 1745 of the imposing fortress of Louisburg on Cape Breton Island, guarding the mouth of the St. Lawrence. Colonel William Pepperrell of Maine was in command of the expedition, and his army consisted almost wholly of 4000 troops voted by the New England legislatures. The restoration of the fortress to France in the peace of 1748 created bitter feeling in the breasts of the New England yeomen, who thought that the mother country under-rated their sacrifices and courage.

87. The English Colonies wake to the Danger from the French. During the first half of the eighteenth century the English colonies grew more and more alive to the serious menace of the French occupation of the land beyond the mountains. The danger, which in the seventeenth century had seemed to threaten only the New England and the New York frontiers, extended to the Far South when the French governors of Louisiana warned English sailors away from the mouth of the Mississippi (1699) and the Spaniards instigated the Cherokee and Yamassee Indians against the Carolinas

---

[1] The names and dates of the actual French wars from the accession of William III to the middle of the eighteenth century were King William's War (1689–1697), Queen Anne's War (1702–1713), and King George's War (1744–1748). They were all parts of general European conflicts (see Robinson and Beard, Development of Modern Europe, Vol. I, pp. 28–33, 42–44, 60–68).

STRUGGLE WITH FRANCE FOR NORTH AMERICA 81

(1702). From Acadia to Florida came voices of entreaty to the English court. Governor Bellomont of New York urged the establishment of a line of posts along the northern frontier, since "to pursue the Indians again and again to the forests was as useless as chasing birds." From Governor Keith of Pennsylvania came the request (1721) "to fortify the passes on the back of Virginia," and build forts on the Lakes "to interrupt the French." Governor Burnet of New York actually fortified Oswego on Lake Ontario at his own expense (1727). A few years earlier Spotswood, the gallant governor of Virginia, had led a party of riders to the crest of the Blue Ridge, where, overlooking the beautiful Shenandoah valley, they drank the healths of the king and the royal household in costly wines and "fired a volley" after each bumper. From the Carolinas came anxious complaints about the new and growing colony of "Luciana [Louisiana] in Mississippi." And soon afterwards Oglethorpe's colony of Georgia was planted as a buffer state against the Spaniards in Florida and the French in the West Indies.

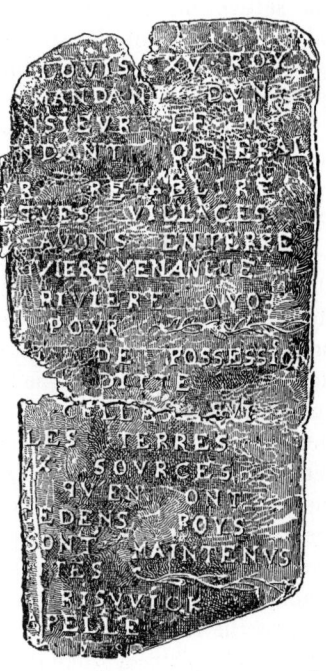

ONE OF CÉLERON DE BLAINVILLE'S LEAD PLATES, FOUND ON THE BANKS OF THE OHIO

88. The Rivalry in the Ohio Valley. The French too were active. They built forts at Crown Point and Niagara, put armed vessels on Lake Champlain, occupied Detroit for the control of Lake Erie and the portages to the Ohio streams, increased their posts along the Mississippi, and pushed forward the settlement of Louisiana. Both sides were waiting for the event which was to strike the spark of war. That event came when the French and the English at the same moment moved to seize the Ohio valley,— the French hoping to pen up the English colonies in the narrow strip of land east of the Alleghenies; the English to get elbowroom beyond the mountains and control the routes to the Mississippi. As Céleron de Bienville dropped down the Ohio (1749), nailing signs to the trees and burying lead plates by the river banks, proclaiming the land to be the domain of Louis XV of France, and Christopher Gist followed in his track (1750), selecting sites for the settlements of the Ohio Company of Virginia, they were the advance heralds of the struggle between France and England, not only for the valley of the Ohio but for the possession of the continent of North America.

89. Comparison of the French and English Colonies. The two powers brought thus face to face to contend for the mastery of America differed from each other in every respect. The one was Roman Catholic in religion, absolute in government, a people of magnificent but impracticable colonial enterprises; the other a Protestant, self-governing people, strongly attached to their homes, steadily developing compact communities. There was not a printing press or a public school in Canada, and plow and harrow were rarer than canoe and musket. The 80,000 inhabitants of New France were overwhelmingly outnumbered by the 1,300,000 English colonists. But two facts compensated the French for their inferiority in numbers: first, by their fortified positions along the St. Lawrence and the Great Lakes and at the head of the Ohio valley, they compelled the English, if they wished to pass the Alleghenies, to fight on French ground; secondly, the unified absolute government of New France enabled her to move all her forces quickly under a single command, whereas the English colonies, acting, as Governor Shirley of Massachusetts complained, "like discordant semirepublics," either insisted on dictating the disposition and command of the troops which they furnished, or long refused, like New Jersey and the colonies south of Virginia, to furnish any troops at all. To make matters worse, the generals sent over from England, with few exceptions, despised the colonial troops and snubbed their officers.

90. The Albany Plan of Colonial Union. Farseeing men like Governors Dinwiddie of Virginia and Shirley of Massachusetts tried to effect some sort of union of the colonies in the face of the imminent danger from the French. The very summer that the first shots of the war were fired (1754) a congress was sitting at Albany for the discussion of better intercolonial relations and the cementing of the Iroquois alliance. At that congress Benjamin Franklin, the foremost man in the colonies, proposed the scheme of union known as the Albany Plan. A grand council consisting of representatives from each colony was to meet annually to regulate Indian affairs, maintain a colonial army, control public lands, pass laws affecting the general good of the colonies, and levy taxes for the expenses of common undertakings. A president general chosen by the king was to have the executive powers of appointing high officials and of nominating the military commanders. He might also veto the acts of the council. Franklin's wise plan, however, found favor neither with the colonial legislatures nor with the royal governors. To each of them it seemed a sacrifice of their rightful authority; so the colonies were left without a central directing power, to coöperate or not with the king's officers, as selfish interests prompted.

91. George Washington opens the Great French War. The opening act of the contest for the Ohio valley is of special interest as introducing George Washington on the stage of American history. When the French began to construct a chain of forts to connect Lake Erie with the Ohio River, Governor Dinwiddie of Virginia sent Washington, a major in the Virginia militia, thoroughly familiar with the hardships of forest travel, to warn the French off of territory "so notoriously known to be the property of the crown of Great Britain." Washington faithfully delivered his message to the French commanders at Venango and Fort Le Bœuf in the wilds of northwestern Pennsylvania and was sent again the next year (1754) to anticipate the French in seizing the important position where the Allegheny and Monongahela Rivers join to form the Ohio. He clashed with a detachment of French and Indians at Great Meadows, and there the first shot was fired in the great war which was to disturb three continents.[1] The French had secured the "forks of the Ohio" with a strong fort (Duquesne), but Washington erected Fort Necessity close by to assert the claims of England to the region. His

---

[1] This war, called in Europe the Seven Years' War and in America the French and Indian War, was the most tremendous conflict of the eighteenth century. In Europe it assumed the form of a huge coalition of France, Austria, Spain, Russia, and minor countries against Frederick the Great of Prussia. England was Frederick's ally, and the war brought her into conflict with France for colonial supremacy in India and America (see Robinson and Beard, Development of Modern Europe, Vol. I, pp. 68, 71).

THE AMBUSH OF BRADDOCK'S ARMY

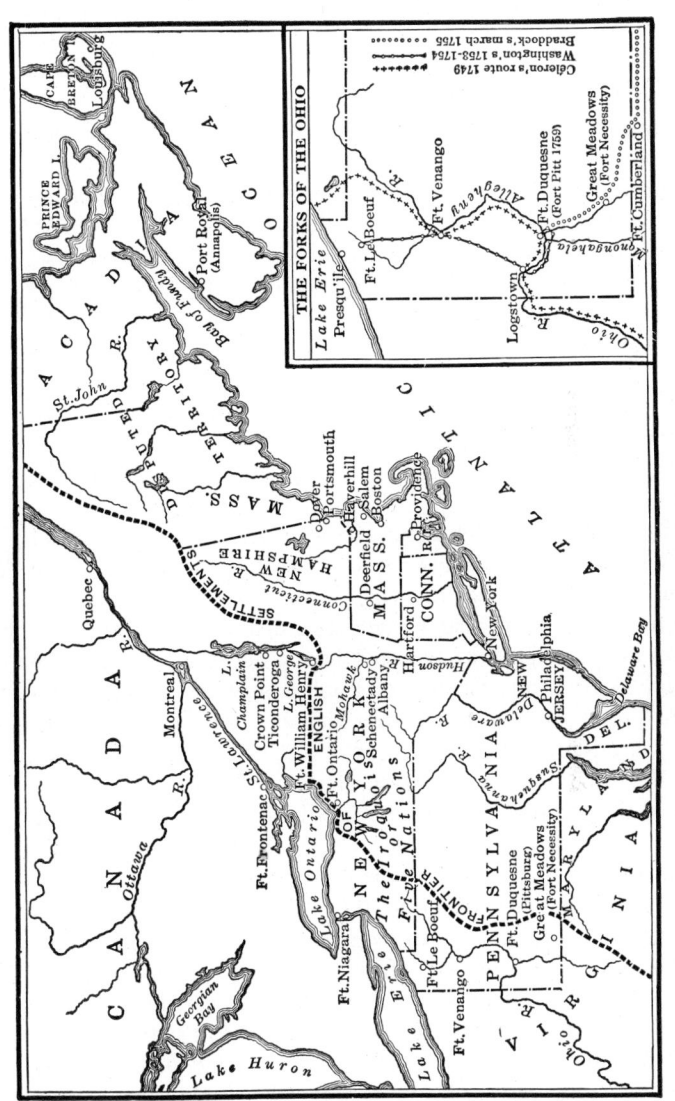

MAP OF FRENCH AND INDIAN WARS

garrison was not strong enough, however, to hold the fort, and he was forced to surrender on the Fourth of July,— a day which through his own devotion and courage, a quarter of a century later, was to become forever glorious in our history.

92. Braddock's Defeat. The war that opened with the skirmish at Great Meadows in 1754 went badly for the English in the early years. The first regular British troops sent over, under the command of the brave but rash General Braddock, to take Fort Duquesne, were surprised and almost annihilated in the Pennsylvania forests (July, 1755). Their French and Indian opponents fought behind rocks, trees, and bushes, in a kind of warfare utterly strange to the European veterans, who were used to beaten roads and wide fields of battle. In the awful confusion Braddock fell with nearly a thousand of his soldiers. It was only the gallant conduct of the young Washington, whose horse was shot under him twice and whose uniform was pierced with bullets, that saved the retreat from utter rout and panic.

93. William Pitt and the Turn of the War. Braddock's defeat exposed the whole line of frontier settlements from Pennsylvania to South Carolina to the savage raids of the Indians; while his papers, falling into the hands of the French, revealed and frustrated the whole plan of the English attack on Niagara and the forts of Lake Champlain. A frightful massacre of English prisoners at Fort William Henry on Lake George, by the Indian allies of the French, added to the miseries of the year 1757. That same year, however, William Pitt, the greatest English statesman of the eighteenth century and the greatest war minister in all England's history, came into power. Pitt was incorruptible and indefatigable, full of confidence in England's destiny as the supreme world power. He immediately infused new life into the British armies, and fleets spread over half the globe. Incompetent commanders were removed, discipline was stiffened, official thieving was stopped. An army of 22,000 Britishers was raised for the war in America, where the colonies, catching the infection of Pitt's tremendous energy, voted money and troops with lavish generosity. In all, about 50,000 troops were ready for the fourfold campaign of 1758 against the forts of Louisburg, Ticonderoga, Duquesne, and Niagara. Except for a bad defeat at Ticonderoga, the British and colonial troops were successful. In 1758 Louisburg was recaptured,

STRUGGLE WITH FRANCE FOR NORTH AMERICA 87

and Fort Duquesne was taken and rechristened Fort Pitt (Pittsburgh) in honor of the incomparable war minister. The next year Niagara and the lake ports fell.

94. The Fall of Quebec. Then came the crisis. Generals Wolfe and Amherst, the heroes of Louisburg, closed in upon the heart of New France, Wolfe leading a fleet up the St. Lawrence to attack Quebec, and Amherst approaching Montreal by the Hudson valley. After a summer of excruciating physical pain and apparent military failure, Wolfe conceived and executed a brilliant strategic movement. On September 12, 1759, under cover of a black midnight, he embarked about 3500 picked men in small boats and with muffled oars dropped down the river past the French sentries to a deserted spot on the bank a little above the city. Before dawn his men, in single file, were clambering up the wooded path of a ravine in the precipitous bank to the heights above the river, where they easily overpowered the feeble guard. When morning

THE WOLFE-MONTCALM MONUMENT [1]

broke, the astonished French commander, Marquis Montcalm, saw the red coats of the British soldiers moving on the Plains of Abraham

---

[1] In the governor's garden in Quebec stands the monument dedicated to these two noble commanders. The inscription which it bears is perhaps the most beautiful expression of commemorative sentiment in the world:

MORTEM VIRTUS COMMUNEM
FAMAM HISTORIA
MONUMENTUM POSTERITAS
DEDIT.
WOLFE   MONTCALM

("Valor gave them a common death, history a common fame, and posterity a common monument.")

in front of the city and hastened to the attack. Few battles in history have had more important results than the British victory on the Plains of Abraham; none has been invested with deeper pathos. The fall of Quebec was the doom of the French empire in America. But thoughts of victory and defeat are both lost in the common sacrifice of victor and vanquished on that day: Wolfe, young, brave, accomplished, tender, dropping his head in the moment of victory on the breast where he wore the miniature of his ladylove in far-away England; and the courteous, valorous Montcalm, turning a heart wrung with mortal pain and the anguish of defeat from the last longing for the chestnut groves of his beloved château in France to beg the new master of Canada to be the protector of its people, as he had been their father.

95. The Peace of Paris. Amherst took Montreal in 1760, and in the next two years English fleets completed the downfall of France and her ally Spain by seizing the rich sugar islands of the West Indies and capturing Havana in Cuba and Manila in the Philippines. Peace was signed at Paris in 1763. By its terms France ceded to England all of Canada and the region east of the Mississippi (except the Island of New Orleans), retaining only the two insignificant islands of St. Pierre and Miquelon (never to be fortified) on the coast of Newfoundland for drying their fish. To her ally Spain, France ceded New Orleans and the country west of the Mississippi. England gave back to France most of the islands of the West Indies; and, while retaining Florida, restored Havana and Manila to Spain, under whose authority they were destined to remain until the Spanish-American War of 1898.

96. Significance of the Peace of Paris. The Peace of Paris was of immense importance to France, England, and America. For France it meant (except for a brief revival in Napoleon's day) the abandonment of the idea of a colonial empire in North America. For England it marked the acme of colonial power and gave the promise of undisturbed empire in the New World. For Canada it meant the breaking of the unnatural alliance with savages and the eventual substitution of free institutions, trial by jury, religious toleration, and individual enterprise in place of the narrow, paternal absolutism of the Bourbons. Finally, for the American colonies it furnished the conditions for future greatness by removing the danger from organized Indian attack along the frontiers and opening the

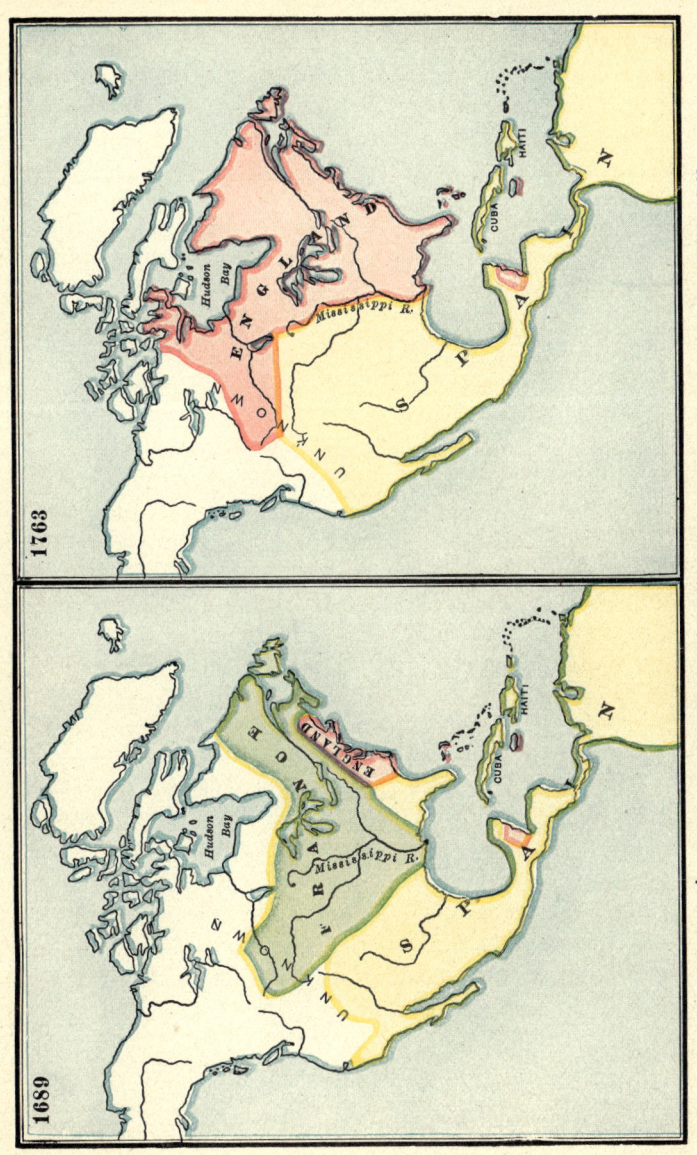

ENGLAND'S ACQUISITIONS IN AMERICA IN THE FRENCH WARS, 1689–1763

STRUGGLE WITH FRANCE FOR NORTH AMERICA

great territory west of the Alleghenies to the hardy pioneers and woodsmen who, from the crests of the mountains, were already gazing into the promised land.

REFERENCES

The Rise of New France: W. L. GRANT, *The Voyages of Samuel de Champlain* (Original Narratives of Early American History); FRANCIS PARKMAN, *The Pioneers of France in the New World; La Salle and the Discovery of the Great West; The Old Régime in Canada;* JUSTIN WINSOR, *Narrative and Critical History of America,* Vol. IV, chaps. iii–vii; *Cartier to Frontenac;* R. G. THWAITES, *France in America* (American Nation Series), chaps. i–v; WM. B. MUNRO, *Crusaders of New France* (Chronicles, Vol. IV); STEPHEN LEACOCK, *The Dawn of Canadian History; Canada and its Provinces,* Vol. I, *New France,* sects. i–iv; Vol. II; JAMES DOUGLAS, *Old France in the New World;* J. H. FINLEY, *The French in the Heart of America,* chaps. i–ix; E. M. AVERY, *History of the United States and its People,* Vol. II, chap. i; Vol. III, chaps. ix, xxii; *Cambridge Modern History,* Vol. VIII, chap. iii.

The Fall of New France: PARKMAN, *A Half Century of Conflict; Montcalm and Wolfe;* THWAITES, chaps. vi–xvii; G. M. WRONG, *The Conquest of New France* (Chronicles, Vol. X); *The Fall of Canada;* WM. WOOD, *The Passing of New France; Canada and its Provinces,* Vol. I, *New France,* sects. vi, vii; AVERY, Vol. IV; EDW. CHANNING, *History of the United States,* Vol. II, chaps. xvii–xix; WINSOR, *Narrative and Critical History of America,* Vol. V, chaps. vii, viii; *Cambridge Modern History,* Vol. VII, chap. iv; A. B. HART, *American History told by Contemporaries,* Vol. II, Nos. 117–129; JOHN FISKE, *Essays Historical and Literary,* Vol. II, chap. iii; J. A. DOYLE, *English Colonies in America,* Vol. V, chap. ix.

TOPICS FOR SPECIAL REPORTS

1. **The Albany Plan of Union:** Old South Leaflets, No. 9; THWAITES, pp. 168–172; WOODROW WILSON, *History of the American People,* Vol. II, pp. 342–356.

2. **George Washington's Embassy to the French Forts:** PARKMAN, *Montcalm and Wolfe,* Vol. I, pp. 128–161; WINSOR, Vol. V, pp. 490–494; THWAITES, pp. 157–165; Old South Leaflets, No. 187; A. B. HURLBURT, *Washington's Road* (Historic Highways Series), pp. 85–119.

3. **The Removal of the Acadians:** PARKMAN, *A Half Century of Conflict,* Vol. I, pp. 183–203; *Montcalm and Wolfe,* Vol. I, pp. 234–285; WRONG, pp. 164–177; AVERY, Vol. IV, pp. 93–112; HART, Vol. II, No. 126; WINSOR, Vol. V, pp. 415–418, 452–463.

4. **The French Explorers on the Great Lakes:** THWAITES, pp. 34–48; *Canada and its Provinces,* Vol. I, pp. 43–108; WINSOR, Vol. IV, pp. 163–196; PARKMAN, *La Salle and the Discovery of the Great West,* pp. 1–47.

5. **Paternal Government in Canada:** PARKMAN, *The Old Régime in Canada,* pp. 257–281; THWAITES, pp. 124–143; MUNRO, pp. 139–154, 180–227; *Cambridge Modern History,* Vol. VII, pp. 79–87, 102–109.

PART II. SEPARATION OF THE COLONIES FROM ENGLAND

CHAPTER IV

BRITISH RULE IN AMERICA

THE AUTHORITY OF PARLIAMENT IN THE COLONIES

97. The Origin of the American Revolution. The curtain had hardly fallen on the first act of American history—the establishment and triumph of the English race in the New World—when it rose on a second act, short but intense; namely, the American Revolution, which severed the colonies from England. This great event marked the entrance of the United States into the family of nations. It was the armed protest against the invasion by the British Parliament of rights long cherished by the American colonies—notably, the right of voting their own taxes in their own representative assemblies. The voices of Pitt, Burke, and Fox were raised in Parliament against the measures which drove the Americans to revolt, but these voices were powerless to stay the headstrong king and his subservient ministers in their policy of coercion. The colonies remonstrated in dignified petitions against the new policy of the British government. Parliament, however, would be satisfied with nothing less than the colonies' acknowledgment of its right to make laws binding upon them "in all cases whatsoever."

98. The "Immemorial Rights" of Englishmen. The first English emigrants to these shores brought with them, by the terms of their charters, for themselves and their posterity, "the same liberties, franchises, immunities . . . as if they had been abiding and born within this our realm of England or any other of our said dominions." Those liberties, for which their ancestors had been struggling for five hundred years, consisted in the right to protection of life and property, a fair trial and judgment by one's peers, participation in local self-government, freedom of movement, occupation, and trade, and, above all, the privilege, through the representatives of the people in Parliament, to grant the king the moneys needed for foreign war and the support of the state. In many a contest for those rights with headstrong kings and cruel or worthless ministers of state, the English nobles and commoners had won the victory. The American colonists cherished these "immemorial rights of Englishmen" with what Edmund Burke called a "fierce spirit of liberty." A goodly number of the colonists had come to these shores for the express purpose of enjoying political and religious liberty. They had created democratic governments in the New World, and the three thousand miles of ocean that rolled between them and the mother country necessarily increased their spirit of self-reliance. While acknowledging allegiance to the king of England, their actual relations with the English government were very slight. The attempt on the part of English ministers to make those relations closer revealed how far the colonies were separated from the mother country in spirit and led inevitably to their separation in fact.

99. Causes of Conflict: the Navigation Acts. At the bottom of the misunderstanding between the colonies and the mother country were two developments in English history which took place mainly in the eighteenth century. The first was the growth of the mercantile theory of trade. We have already noted (p. 57) how this theory caused the European nations to regard their colonies as mere sources of profit, and how the English Navigation Acts were passed to control the trade of America. A striking example of the harm done to colonial trade by this restrictive policy is the famous Sugar and Molasses Act of 1733. Barbados, Jamaica, San Domingo, and other islands of the West Indies, belonging to England, France, Holland, and Spain, produced immense quantities of sugar. The entire acreage of these islands was given over to sugar plantations, while all the necessities of life were imported. The American colonies, being near at hand, sent large supplies of fish, corn, wheat, flour, oil, soap, and lumber to the islands, and from this trade realized most of the money needed to pay the English manufacturers for goods imported from the mother country. Although the British West Indies alone did not begin to offer a sufficient market for the varied products of the colonial mainland, yet, in order to drive their French, Dutch, and Spanish rivals out of business, the English sugar planters of Barbados and Jamaica secured from Parliament an act imposing heavy duties on sugar, molasses, and rum imported from foreign colonies into the British-American colonies. This act, if strictly enforced, would have ruined the trade of New England and, by stripping the colonies of gold and silver, would have also deprived the manufacturers of Old England of their market in the New World.

The colonies were naturally aggrieved at such treatment. In spite of the fact that some of their products, like tobacco, were given favored treatment in the English market, they resented being restrained in their trade in order to make another part of the British Empire prosperous. Their sentiment was that expressed by a governor of Massachusetts in Charles II's time, when he was reproved for not enforcing the Navigation Acts: "The king can in reason do no less than let us enjoy our liberties and trade, for we have made this large plantation (colony) of our own charge, without any contribution from the crown." That a prosperous illicit trade flourished, and that English ministers like Walpole winked at the infringement of the Navigation Acts, was small comfort to the colonies. There the ugly laws stood on the statute book, and at any moment a minister might come into power who would think it good policy or his bounden duty to enforce them.

100. The Relation of the Colonies to Parliament. The second disturbing element in the relation of England to the colonies was the question of the supremacy of Parliament. The American colonies had all been settled under charters granted not by Parliament but by the English kings. The colonial assemblies passed laws, levied taxes, voted supplies, and raised troops for their own defense, just like the Parliament of England. They came to regard themselves, therefore, as filling the place of Parliament in America, and looked to the king as authority. But with the overthrow of the Stuarts in 1688 the position of king and Parliament was reversed. The king himself became practically a subject of Parliament, whose authority and sovereignty grew continually stronger as the eighteenth century advanced. The first kings of the Hanoverian dynasty, which succeeded the Stuarts on the English throne, recognized this change. For example, in 1624 the Stuart James I had snubbed Parliament when it attempted to interfere in the affairs of Virginia, telling the

House of Commons to attend to its own business and keep its hands off his domains; a century later (1720) the Hanoverian George I instructed his governor in Massachusetts to warn the inhabitants that in case of misbehavior their conduct *would be brought to the notice of Parliament*. Furthermore, Parliament extended the sphere of its interests in the colonies beyond the Acts of Trade, which had been its chief concern in the seventeenth century. It regulated the colonial currency, it made naturalization laws, it established a colonial post office. When the Stuart kings yielded to the power of Parliament, was it not useless for the colonies to plead the authority of their Stuart charters in opposition to that same Parliament? Clearly, unless the colonies were aiming at independence — a charge which they indignantly denied up to the very outbreak of the Revolutionary War — they were subject to the sovereign power of England; namely, the Parliament.

101. Other Causes of Friction. During the first half of the eighteenth century many colonial governors and high officials wished to see the authority of Parliament established beyond question in the American colonies. Such measures as the abolition of the New England charters, the union of several colonies under a single governor, the imposition of a direct tax by Parliament, and even the creation of an American nobility were recommended. But so long as the practical, peace-loving Walpole and the ardent patriot Pitt held the reins of government in England, no such irritation of the colonial spirit of independence was attempted. There were enough causes of friction, as it was, between the colonies and the mother country. Incompetent and arbitrary governors were often appointed, who quarreled continually with the colonial assemblies over salaries, fees, and appointments. The crown, although it had ceased at the beginning of the eighteenth century to veto acts of Parliament, continued to veto acts of the colonial legislatures. These vetoes were sometimes prompted by the most selfish and unworthy motives, as when statutes of Virginia in restraint of the slave trade were annulled by the crown because of the heavy profits which the English courtiers were reaping from that infamous business. The scornful treatment of colonial officers and troops by the British regulars, in the French wars; the increasing severity of the Navigation Acts; the persistent efforts of a group of high churchmen to establish the Anglican Church and an Anglican bishop in America,— all contributed to a spirit of wary self-defense and proud self-sufficiency, which observant men on both sides of the water said was developing into a desire for independence.

102. Apprehensions of Colonial Revolt. Samuel Adams in his commencement oration of 1743 at Harvard College, in the presence of the royal governor of Massachusetts and his retinue, dared to discuss the question of "whether it was lawful to resist rulers in time of oppression." The Swedish traveler Peter Kalm, who visited this country in 1748–1750, thought that the presence of the French in Canada was "the chief power that urged the colonies to submission." Many French statesmen comforted themselves for the loss of Canada by the thought that England "would repent having removed the only check on her colonies," which would "shake off dependence the moment Canada was ceded." There were even British statesmen who urged that England should keep Guadeloupe, in the West Indies, at the peace of 1763, and leave the French undisturbed in Canada, "in order to secure the dependence of the colonies on the mother country."

The existence of such sentiment before the enactment of a single coercive measure by the British Parliament, or any specific act of rebellion on the part of the American colonies, shows what a sorry business England had made of her colonial government in the eighteenth century and amply justifies the remark of Theodore Roosevelt, that the American Revolution was "a revolt against the whole mental attitude of Britain in regard to America, rather than against any one special act or set of acts."

Taxation without Representation

103. Grenville revives the Navigation Acts. "Special acts and sets of acts," however, came in abundance after the peace of 1763. Great Britain by her victories over the French in both hemispheres had become a great empire. But the cost had been great, too. The national debt had increased from £70,000,000 to £140,000,000. The British statesmen therefore began to devise plans for bringing the parts of the empire more closely together and making each contribute toward carrying the increased burden of colonial administration. Early in 1764 George Grenville, prime minister of England, got through Parliament a series of measures for the control of the trade of the American colonies. The Navigation Acts, especially the odious Sugar and Molasses Act of 1733, with its amendments, were to be strictly enforced, and all commanders of British frigates in American waters were to have the right of acting as customs officers, employing the hated Writs of Assistance,[1] or general warrants to search a man's premises for smuggled articles. The merchants of New England saw ruin staring them in the face if the Navigation Acts were enforced. Massachusetts alone had imported 15,000 hogsheads of molasses[2] from the French West Indies in 1763, and the hundreds of ships launched every year from the colonial yards were earning by their illegal foreign trade a large part of the millions which had to be paid yearly for imported British manufactured goods.

104. Grenville proposes to tax the Americans. At the same time that the Navigation Acts were renewed Grenville gave notice that he intended to lay a tax on the colonies to defray part of the expense of a small standing army in America. In justification of the proposed tax the ministry contended that English troops were necessary to protect the colonies against the Indians on their borders, although Benjamin Franklin testified before the House of Commons that the colonies had "defended themselves when they were but a handful" and were "very able" to take care of themselves now that they "had become so populous and so strong." Moreover, although the preamble to the tax act declared that all money collected was to be spent in America, the colonies raised the objection that when once they had paid the money they would have no means of preventing the British treasury from using it for whatever purpose it chose. Grenville professed his willingness to assess the tax in any manner acceptable to the Americans. He himself proposed a stamp tax, which required that all official and public documents, such as wills, deeds, mortgages, notes, newspapers, pamphlets, should be written on stamped paper or provided with stamps sold by the distributing agents of the British government; but at the same time he invited the colonial agents in London and influential men in the colonies to suggest any other form of taxation which appeared to

---

[1] Against these writs the Boston lawyer James Otis had pleaded so vehemently three years earlier that John Adams called his speech the opening act of the American Revolution.
[2] Destined for the most part, unfortunately, to be made into rum for the African negro.

them more suitable or acceptable, and announced that no definite action in the matter would be taken for a year.

105. Passage of the Stamp Act. No other plan was considered, and in March, 1765, the Stamp Act was passed with very little discussion, in a half-filled Parliament, by a vote of 205 to 49. Distributors of stamped paper were appointed for the colonies, Benjamin Franklin even soliciting the position in Pennsylvania for one of his friends. The British ministry anticipated no resistance to the act, which was to go into effect the first of November.

106. Patrick Henry's Resolutions. However, the Stamp Act met with an instant opposition in the colonies. A young lawyer named Patrick Henry rose from his seat in the Virginia House of Burgesses,[1] and in an impassioned speech which drew from some members of the House the cry of "treason!" presented and carried through the Assembly resolutions to the effect that "the General Assembly of this colony . . . have in their representative capacity the only exclusive right and power to lay taxes and imposts upon the inhabitants of this colony; and that every attempt to vest such power in any other person or persons . . . is illegal, unconstitutional, and unjust, and has a manifest tendency to destroy British as well as American liberty."

A BRITISH STAMP

107. Resistance to the Stamp Act. Henry's speech and resolutions stirred up great excitement in the colonies. James Otis of Massachusetts suggested a general meeting of committees from all the colonies to protest against this new and dangerous assault on colonial liberties. A writer in the New York *Gazette*, under the name of "Freeman," went so far as to suggest separation from the British Empire. When the stamp distributors were appointed late in the summer, they became the immediate objects of obloquy and persecution throughout the colonies; and before the first of November every one of them had been persuaded or forced to resign. There

---

[1] Henry had been elected as a reward for his speech against the king's veto of a law of the Virginia Assembly fixing the salaries of the clergy in tobacco at a very low price — the famous "Parsons' Cause."

was rioting in every New England colony as well as in New York and Pennsylvania. In Boston a mob hanged the distributor, Oliver, in effigy, destroyed the building which he had selected for his office, and wrecked the residence of Lieutenant Governor Hutchinson,[1] a high Tory, who four years earlier, as chief justice, had greatly offended the people of the province by his decision in favor of the legality of Writs of Assistance.

108. The Stamp Act Congress. The congress suggested by Otis met at New York in October, with twenty-seven members from

THE FUNERAL PROCESSION OF THE STAMP ACT

From an old print

nine colonies. It published a "declaration of rights and grievances," denied the legality of any taxes but those levied by their assemblies, and sent separate addresses to the king and both Houses of Parliament. These first state papers of the assembled colonies were dignified, able, cogent remonstrances against the disturbance of what they held to be sacred and long-enjoyed rights.

109. Why America Resisted. The British Parliament had, by the Stamp Act, undoubtedly struck at the most precious right of

[1] The library of Hutchinson was sacked and the books scattered in the street. The manuscript of his invaluable work on the History of the Massachusetts Bay Colony was rescued from the mud of the street. It is now in the historical museum in the Statehouse at Boston, the mud stains still visible on its rumpled edges.

the colonists, that of voting their own taxes. The act seemed to the Americans to have reduced their assemblies to impotent bodies and made their charters void. The chief safeguard of their liberties, the control of the purse strings of the province, was gone. It was right for Parliament to regulate their foreign commerce, they said; but *taxes* to men of English descent meant the free grant of money to the king by the representatives of the people in Parliament assembled. Their own colonial legislatures stood in the place of Parliament, since they had no part in the Parliament convened at Westminster. When the British statesmen argued that the colonies were "virtually represented" in Parliament, because all members of the House of Commons represented all the British subjects except the nobles and the clergy, the colonists failed to follow the reasoning. For them a "representative" meant a man of their own town, county, or hundred, elected by their own votes. As well tell a Virginian that he was "represented" in the assembly of New York as that he was represented in the British Parliament!

110. The Repeal of the Stamp Act. The violent and unexpected resistance to the Stamp Act in America woke in England some sense of the seriousness of the colonial problem. Grenville had been superseded (July, 1765) as prime minister by the Marquis of Rockingham, a liberal Whig statesman, opposed to the coercion of the American colonies. The Rockingham ministry moved the repeal of the Stamp Act early in 1766, and on the fourth of March, after the fiercest battle of the century in the halls of Parliament, the motion was carried.[1] The hated Stamp Act had been on the British statute book less than a year, and had been enforced in only a few American towns; yet its repeal was hailed in the colonies by as joyful a demonstration as could have greeted the deliverance from ages of cruel oppression. The British ministers might have learned from both the passionate protests of 1765 and the profuse gratitude of 1766 what a sensitive spirit of liberty they had to deal with in America. But less than a year after the repeal of the Stamp Act they began to set new mischief afoot.

---

[1] One of the reasons why the Whigs were more anxious than the Tories to conciliate the colonies was that the Whigs were the party of the great merchants, who feared their loss of trade if the Americans were driven by taxes to boycott British commerce through non-importation agreements. These merchants exerted considerable pressure on the House of Commons through delegations and petitions.

111. The Townshend Acts. In July, 1766, the Rockingham ministry fell. William Pitt (Earl of Chatham), the creator of England's colonial empire and the stanch friend of America, formed a cabinet of men of various shades of opinion, in order to restore harmony in the empire. But unfortunately Chatham himself, tormented by gout, retired to Bath, and the government was left without a firm guiding hand. The Chancellor of the Exchequer (or minister of finance) was Charles Townshend, a witty and persuasive orator, who was in favor of taxing America and had voted for the Stamp Act. Without the consent or even the knowledge of his fellow ministers, Townshend had the audacity, early in 1767, to introduce into Parliament new measures for raising revenue in America. Chatham was not there to protest, and the measures were carried. They provided that revenue cases in America should be tried in courts without a jury, declared Writs of Assistance valid, released colonial judges and governors from dependence on their assemblies for their salaries, provided for commissioners of customs to reside in the American ports, and, for the maintenance of this "American establishment," levied rather heavy duties on tea, glass, lead, paper, and painter's colors imported into the colonies.

WILLIAM PITT, EARL OF CHATHAM

112. Renewed Resistance of the Colonies. Again protest in America was immediate; the British Parliament must not lay any taxes on the colonies to raise a revenue. The town meeting of Boston declared against importing any English goods under the new duties. The ardent Samuel Adams, after preparing an address to the British ministry, to Chatham, and to Rockingham, drew up a circular letter to the other colonies, which elicited expressions of sympathy from New Hampshire, Virginia, New Jersey, Connecticut, and South Carolina. The British minister for the colonies ordered the Massachusetts legislature to rescind the circular letter, as being of a "dangerous and factious tendency," but the legislature flatly refused by a vote of ninety-two to seventeen. Whereupon two regiments of British troops were sent from Halifax to Boston and landed under the protection of the guns of the warships which had brought them (September 28, 1768). Virginia stood side by side with Massachusetts in resisting the Townshend Acts. George Washington and Patrick Henry were prominent in the adoption of resolutions by the Burgesses condemning the taxes and maintaining the right of the colonies to unite in petition to the crown. The boycott of English goods was effective, colonial importations falling off from £2,378,000 in 1768 to £1,634,000 in 1769. The Townshend duties, instead of yielding the £40,000 a year that their author boasted to Parliament they would, produced in three years only some £16,000, a sum which it cost the government £200,000 to collect.

113. The Boston Massacre. But the total failure of the Townshend legislation to produce a revenue was not its worst effect. The presence of British regiments in Boston, quartered upon the inhabitants of the town in time of peace and in violation of the Bill of Rights, was a just cause of exasperation to the people. On March 5, 1770, some British soldiers, provoked by taunts, fired upon a group of citizens, killing five and wounding several more. This Boston Massacre was the signal for the wildest excitement. A town meeting was called at once in Faneuil Hall, and Samuel Adams, proceeding as its delegate to the town house, demanded of acting Governor Hutchinson the immediate removal of both the regiments from the town. Hutchinson hesitated; but Adams, rising to his full height and extending a threatening arm toward the governor, cried: "There are three thousand people yonder in the town meeting, and the country is rising; night is coming on, and we must have our answer." The governor yielded.

114. The Boston Tea Party. Meanwhile the storm of protests from the colonies and the fervent petitions of English merchants, who were being ruined by the American boycott, led Parliament to repeal the Townshend duties as it had the Stamp Act. In January, 1770, Lord North became prime minister, and on the very day of the Boston Massacre moved to repeal all the duties except a trifling tax of threepence a pound on tea. King George III, in whose hands Lord North was a man of clay, insisted that the tax on tea be kept for the sake of asserting the right of Parliament to control the colonies. The king thought that by a smart trick he could ensnare the colonies into buying the tea and paying the tax. He got his compliant Parliament to allow the East India Company a monopoly to sell its tea in America without paying the heavy English duty. Thus relieved of duties, the Company offered its tea to the colonists at a lower

THE BOSTON MASSACRE

From Paul Revere's engraving

price, including the tax of threepence a pound, than they were paying for the same article smuggled from Holland. But the colonies were not to be bribed into an acknowledgment of the right of Parliament to levy even a threepenny tax. The cargoes of tea which the East India Company's ships brought over to American ports were rudely received. Philadelphia and New York refused to let the ships land. The authorities at Charleston held the tea in the customhouse, and later sold it. And in Boston, after vainly petitioning the governor to send the tea back to England, a committee of prominent citizens, disguised as American Indians, boarded the merchantmen on the evening of December 16, 1773, ripped open the chests of tea with their tomahawks, and dumped the costly contents into Boston Harbor.

The Punishment of Massachusetts

115. How Massachusetts irritated King George. In King George's eyes the "Boston Tea Party" was the last straw; the colonies had added insult to injury. The king called upon Parliament for severe measures of punishment. Massachusetts, especially Boston, must be made an example of the royal vengeance to the rest of the colonies; the province was an old offender. As early as 1646 the general court had assembled for the "discussion of the usurpation of Parliament," and a spirited member had declared that "if England should impose laws upon us we should lose the liberties of Englishmen indeed"; its attitude toward the Navigation Acts of Charles II has already been noticed (p. 92). Since the very first attempt of the British government after the French war to tighten its control of colonial commerce and raise a revenue in America, Massachusetts had taken the leading part in defiance. Letters, pamphlets, petitions, came in an uninterrupted stream from the Massachusetts patriots, Hancock, Warren, Otis, and the Adamses. It was in Boston that the chief resistance to the Stamp Act had been offered (1765); it was there also that the king had stationed his regiments of regulars (1768), and there that occurred the unfortunate "massacre" of the fifth of March (1770). "To George III's eyes the capital of Massachusetts was a center of vulgar sedition, strewn with brickbats and broken glass, where his enemies went about clothed in homespun and his friends in tar and feathers."

116. The "Intolerable Acts." When Parliament met in March, 1774, it passed a number of acts for the punishment of Massachusetts. The port of Boston was to be closed to trade until the tea destroyed should be paid for. Town meetings, which the king's ministers unjustly called "hotbeds of discussion and disobedience," were forbidden to convene without the governor's permission, except for the regular election of officers. Public buildings designated by the governor were to be used as barracks for the troops. The king's officials, if indicted for certain capital crimes, might be sent to England for trial. Up to this time the British government had not passed any measure of punishment or revenge. The Grenville legislation and the Townshend Acts, however unwelcome to the colonies, had not been designed for their chastisement, but only for their better coordination with the other parts of the British Empire. Parliament had blundered into legislation and backed out of it, pursuing a policy of alternate encroachment and concession,— as Edmund Burke said, "seeking fresh principles of action with every fresh mail from America," and "sneaking out of the difficulties into which they had so proudly strutted." But with the passage of the so-called Intolerable Acts of 1774 this shifting policy was at an end. There were no more repeals by Parliament. King George's "patience" was evidently exhausted.

117. The First Continental Congress. Expressions of sympathy now came to Massachusetts from all over the colonies. The Virginia Burgesses appointed the day on which the Intolerable Acts were to go into force as a day of fasting and prayer; and when they were dismissed by their royal governor for showing sympathy with "rebels," they promptly met again in the Raleigh tavern and proposed an annual congress of committees from all the colonies. The Virginia suggestion met with favor, and on September 5, 1774, the first Continental Congress met in Carpenter's Hall, Philadelphia, "to consult on the present state of the colonies ... and to deliberate and determine upon wise and proper measures ... for the recovery and establishment of their just rights and liberties ... and the restoration of union and harmony between Great Britain and the colonies, most ardently desired by all good men." All the colonies except Georgia were represented, and among that remarkable group of about half a hundred men were the leaders of the ten years' struggle against the British Parliament,— John and Samuel Adams of Massachusetts, Washington and Patrick Henry of Virginia, Stephen Hopkins of Rhode Island, John Dickinson of Pennsylvania, Roger Sherman of Connecticut, John Rutledge of South Carolina. They respectfully petitioned the king to put an end to their grievances, specifying thirteen acts of Parliament which they deemed "infringements and violations" of their rights. They urged on all the colonies the adoption of the "American Association" for

104 SEPARATION OF THE COLONIES FROM ENGLAND

the boycott of British trade, both import and export, and after a six weeks' session adjourned. Before separating, however, they voted to

COMMEMORATIVE OF THE BATTLE ON LEXINGTON GREEN

1, statue of a minuteman, by H. H. Kitson; 2, bowlder marking the line of Captain Parker's troops; 3, Major Pitcairn's pistols; 4, the oldest Revolutionary monument in America, 1799

reassemble on the tenth of the following May, unless the obnoxious legislation of Parliament were repealed before that day.

118. Armed Rebellion in Massachusetts. But before the second Continental Congress convened the British regulars and the rustic militia of Massachusetts had met on the field of battle. General Gage, who succeeded Hutchinson as governor of Massachusetts in the summer of 1774, tried to prevent the colonial legislature from meeting. But in spite of his prohibition they assembled at Salem and later at Cambridge and Concord. They appointed a Committee of Safety, began to collect powder and military stores, and assumed the government of the province outside the limits of Boston, where Gage had his regiments intrenched. Early in 1775 came news that Parliament, in spite of the repeated pleadings of Chatham, Burke, and Fox, had rejected the petition sent by the first Continental Congress and had declared that "rebellion existed in the American colonies."

119. The Battle of Lexington. On the night of the eighteenth of April Gage sent troops to seize the powder which the provincials had collected

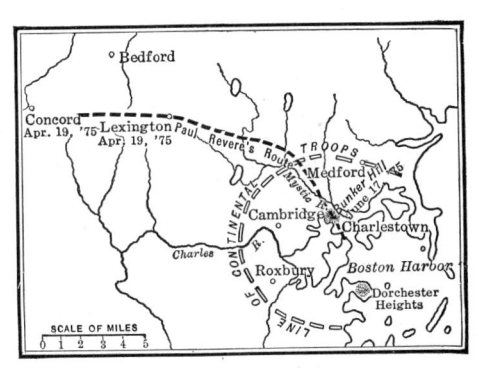

PAUL REVERE'S ROUTE, APRIL 19, 1775

at Concord and at the same time to arrest the "traitors" John Hancock and Samuel Adams, who had taken refuge with parson Jonas Clark of Lexington. But the ardent Boston patriot Paul Revere had learned of the expedition, and, galloping ahead of the British troops, he roused the farmers on the way and warned the refugees. When the van of the British column reached Lexington, they found a little company of "minutemen" (militia ready to fight at a minute's notice) drawn up on the village green under Captain Parker. The British major Pitcairn ordered "the rebels" to disperse. When the minutemen bravely stood their ground the British fired a volley of musket shots and marched on, leaving eight of the patriot band dead or dying on the green. Reaching Concord, Pitcairn's troops destroyed the powder which the natives had not yet hidden and soon began the long march back to Boston, harassed by a deadly fire from behind stone walls and apple trees. Lord Percy, with the main column, met the exhausted troops just below Lexington Green and conducted them safely within the British lines. The colonial militia, aroused for miles around, closed in upon Boston 16,000 strong and held Gage besieged in his capital.

120. The Colonists' View of their Rights. When we review, after a century and a half, the chain of events which changed the loyal British-Americans of 1763 into rebels in arms against their king in 1775, we see that the cause of the Revolution was a difference of opinion as to the nature of the British Empire. For the men

THE BATTLE OF LEXINGTON

From a drawing by an eyewitness

on this side of the Atlantic the Empire was a *federation* under a common sovereign. Each part of the federation was composed of groups of freemen who enjoyed all the "immemorial rights" of Englishmen,— a fair trial by one's peers, freedom of speech and assembly, and, above all, the right to vote money for the expenses of the king's government through their own representative bodies. These rights, they claimed, were guaranteed by their charters, which gave them all the privileges of Englishmen living in the realm. In theory they acknowledged the right of Parliament to regulate the commerce of the whole Empire, but in practice they had so long violated or evaded the Navigation Acts which they thought harmful to their own trade that the belated attempt of English ministers to enforce them seemed like a new "tyranny."

121. The British View. On the other side of the Atlantic the emphasis was on the *unity* of the British Empire. The great burden of debt incurred in the French wars, the desire to make America pay part of the expense for their own administration and defense, and, above all, the determination of King George and his Tory ministers to make the royal authority obeyed throughout the Empire, led to the new rigorous policy towards the colonies. With few exceptions, public men in England failed to see that the American colonies had any ground of complaint. If England controlled their trade, she also favored it, giving colonial goods preference in her markets and granting bounties on colonial products and drawbacks on colonial imports. It was universally agreed that no country of Europe had a more liberal colonial trade policy than England. As to the charters, they were royal favors creating corporations with certain powers of self-government (like a city charter), but not intended, of course, to exempt the grantees from the supreme authority of the state. That authority was the Parliament, in which the American subjects of his majesty were, like the great mass of English subjects, represented by the Commons.

122. Was Reconciliation Possible? Whether such widely separated theories as the federal empire of the colonial statesmen and the consolidated empire of the English statesmen could have been reconciled if the direction of affairs in England had been in the hands of wise men like Pitt, Burke, and Fox, we cannot say. Probably the colonies had already reached such a stage of economic self-sufficiency and political self-direction that their continued union with the British Empire could have been only on the basis of a virtual independence (like Canada's or Australia's today) such as not even a Pitt or a Burke would have tolerated in the eighteenth century.

123. The Responsibility of King George III. That the separation came when it did must be laid chiefly to the conduct of King George III. By lavish use of bribes ("golden pills"), places, and pensions he built up the powerful clique of the "King's Friends" in Parliament, who thwarted every move for broad and liberal statesmanship at Westminster. He gave his confidence to ministers of the type of Bute and Lord North, who made his will their law. He was determined to press the quarrel with the colonies to an issue; exclaiming with relief when the "Intolerable Acts" of 1774 were

108 SEPARATION OF THE COLONIES FROM ENGLAND

passed: "The die is now cast; the colonies must submit or triumph." This steady refusal of conciliation on his part added thousands to the followers of the irreconcilable spirits in the colonies, like Patrick Henry and the Adamses, and gave color to their impassioned warnings against being "reduced to slavery." We have the testimony of the best English historians of the nineteenth century that George III was the evil spirit of the British Empire. "He had rooted out courage, frankness, and independence from the councils of state, and put puppets in the place of men" (Trevelyan); "his tactics were fraught with danger to the liberties of the people" (May); "his acts were as criminal as any which led Charles I to the scaffold" (Lecky); "the shame of the darkest hour of England's history lies wholly at his door" (Green).

REFERENCES

The Authority of Parliament in the Colonies: G. E. HOWARD, *The Preliminaries of the Revolution* (American Nation Series), chaps. i–v; W. M. SLOANE, *The French War and the Revolution*, chap. x; J. A. WOODBURN, *Causes of the American Revolution* (Johns Hopkins Studies, Series X, No. 12); *Lecky's American Revolution*, chap. i, pp. 1–49; CARL BECKER, *The Beginnings of the American People*, chap. ii; EDWARD CHANNING, *History of the United States*, Vol. III, chap. i; WM. MACDONALD, *Select Charters of American History, 1606–1775*, Nos. 53–56; A. B. HART, *American History told by Contemporaries*, Vol. II, Nos. 45, 46, 88, 89; G. L. BEER, *British Colonial Policy, 1754–1765*; E. L. BOGART, *Industrial History of the United States*, chap. vii.

Taxation without Representation: BECKER, *The Eve of the Revolution* (Chronicles, Vol. XI), chaps. ii–iv; JUSTIN WINSOR, *Narrative and Critical History of America*, Vol. VI, chap. i; JOHN FISKE, *The American Revolution*, Vol. I, chaps. i, ii; M. C. TYLER, *Literary History of the American Revolution*, Vol. I; G. OTTO TREVELYAN, *The American Revolution*, Vol. I; HART, *Contemporaries*, Vol. II, Nos. 138–152; HOWARD, chaps. vi–xv; BOGART, chap. viii; CHANNING, Vol. III, chaps. ii–v; E. M. AVERY, *History of the United States and its People*, Vol. V, chaps. ii–ix; MACDONALD, Nos. 57–67.

The Punishment of Massachusetts: FISKE, chap. iii; TREVELYAN, chap. iii; HOWARD, chaps. xv–xvii; WINSOR, chap. ii; SLOANE, chaps. xiv, xv; BECKER (Chronicles), chaps. v–vi; CHANNING, Vol. III, chaps. v–vi; AVERY, Vol. V, chaps. xi–xiii.

TOPICS FOR SPECIAL REPORTS

1. **English Opinions of the American Cause:** (Dr. Samuel Johnson's) HART, Vol. II, No. 156; (Wm. Pitt's) HART, Vol. II, No. 142; Old South Leaflets, No. 199; (Edmund Burke's) Old South Leaflets, No. 200; WOODBURN, *Lecky's American Revolution*, pp. 154–165; TREVELYAN, Vol. I, pp. 28–44.

2. **The Navigation Acts:** HART, Vol. II, Nos. 45, 46, 67, 85, 87, 131; WINSOR, Vol. VI, pp. 5–12; G. L. BEER, *The Commercial Policy of England towards the American Colonies*, pp. 35–65; BOGART, pp. 90–103.

3. **The Conspiracy of Pontiac:** F. A. OGG, *The Old Northwest* (Chronicles, Vol. XIX), pp. 1–19; SLOANE, pp. 99–103; WINSOR, Vol. VI, pp. 688–701; PARKMAN, *The Conspiracy of Pontiac*, Vol. I, pp. 172–321; Vol. II, pp. 299–313; CHANNING and LANSING, *The Story of the Great Lakes*, pp. 113–134.

4. **The Boston Tea Party:** JOHN FISKE, *Essays Historical and Literary*, Vol. II, pp. 163–195; A. P. PEABODY, *Boston Mobs before the Revolution* (*Atlantic Monthly*, September, 1888); MACDONALD, Nos. 64–70; HART, Vol. II, No. 152; TYLER, Vol. I, pp. 246–266; TREVELYAN, Vol. I, pp. 135–139, 175–192; Old South Leaflets, No. 68.

5. **Thomas Hutchinson, the Last Royal Governor of Massachusetts:** SLOANE, pp. 163–170; HART, Vol. II, Nos. 139–148; FISKE, *Essays*, Vol. I, pp. 1–51; WINSOR, Vol. VI, pp. 49–58; J. H. STARK, *The Loyalists of Massachusetts*, pp. 145–174; BECKER (Chronicles), pp. 165–199.

CHAPTER V

THE BIRTH OF THE NATION

THE DECLARATION OF INDEPENDENCE

124. The Second Continental Congress. "The war has actually begun. The next gale that sweeps from the North will bring to our ears the clash of resounding arms. Our brethren are already in the field. Why stand we here idle? ... Is life so dear or peace so sweet as to be purchased at the price of chains and slavery? Forbid it, Almighty God! I know not what course others may take; but as for me, give me liberty or give me death!" These prophetic words were spoken by Patrick Henry at a convention in Richmond, Virginia, less than a month before the "clash of arms" at Lexington and Concord. Less than a month after that event the second Continental Congress met at Philadelphia (May 10, 1775). Events had moved rapidly since the adjournment of the previous October. George III had received the petition of Congress with the remark that the "New England Governments were in rebellion"; blood had been shed on both sides, not by irresponsible mobs or taunted soldiery, but by troops marshaled in battle; eastern Massachusetts had risen in arms and held its governor besieged in his capital of Boston; and on the very day when Congress assembled, Ethan Allen and his Green Mountain Boys surprised the British garrison in Fort Ticonderoga and turned them out "in the name of the Great Jehovah and the Continental Congress."

125. Bunker Hill and the Declaration of War. General Gage intended to occupy the heights (Bunker Hill and Breed's Hill) on the peninsula of Charlestown, which commanded the town of Boston. But the Americans anticipated him. Colonel William Prescott with 1200 men seized the position and toiled through the night of June 16, 1775, constructing a fortification of earthworks on Breed's Hill. At dawn the British warships in the harbor began to bombard the fortifications, but failed to dislodge the Americans. Then Gage ordered General Howe to storm the position by a frontal attack. Twice the British marched up the hill to within less than fifty yards of the

American line, and twice they were driven back by the deadly fire of the untrained militia who coolly stood their ground until they saw the whites of the enemy's eyes. At the third charge of the British regulars the Americans, their ammunition exhausted, were forced to abandon the intrenchments; but they retired in good order, leaving over 1000 of the redcoats killed or wounded. Among the 450 lost on the American side was Dr. Joseph Warren, one of the foremost patriot leaders in Massachusetts. The battle of Bunker (Breed's) Hill, though it was technically a defeat, was virtually an inspiring victory for the Americans. The men whom Gage sneeringly called "the rabble of New England" had faced more than double their number of the British regulars and had proved their marksmanship as well as their courage.

The second Continental Congress, meanwhile, with the tacit consent of the colonies, was assuming the powers of a regular government. It issued paper money, made trade regulations, sent agents abroad to win the favor of foreign courts, and advised the colonies to set up governments for themselves, regardless of the king's officials. It appointed George Washington commander of the Continental army, and, on July 6, 1775, made a formal declaration of war against Great Britain in these words: "Our cause is just. Our union is perfect. . . . Against violence we have taken up arms. We shall lay them down when hostilities cease on the part of our aggressors." In spite of the fact, however, that the appeal to arms had already been made, there was enough conservative sentiment in the Congress to support John Dickinson in his motion to send another appeal to the king to restore peace and harmony with his colonies in America.

126. American Protestations of Loyalty before 1775. Until this final petition of Congress was spurned, the leaders of the colonial resistance to Parliamentary taxation almost to a man protested their loyalty to King George III and the British Empire. "I have never heard from any person drunk or sober," said Benjamin Franklin to Lord Chatham in 1774, "the least expression of a wish for separation." Washington declared that even when he went to Cambridge to take command of the colonial army, the thought of independence was "abhorrent" to him. And John Adams said that he was avoided in the streets of Philadelphia in 1775 "like a man infected with leprosy" for his leanings toward "independency." To be sure, there were skeptical and ironical Tories in the colonies, who declared that the protestations of loyalty in the petitions of Congress and in the mouths of the patriots were only "the gold leaf to conceal the treason beneath"; but it is impossible to believe that men like Washington, Jefferson, Franklin, and Jay were insincere in their public utterances.

127. Events of 1775 which widened the Breach. However, by the end of 1775 the doctrine of the allegiance of the colonies to King George was so flatly contradicted by the facts of the situation that it became ridiculous. From month to month the breach between the colonies and the mother country had widened. In March, 1775, Benjamin Franklin, who for ten years had been the agent for several of the colonies in London, returned to America, thereby confessing that nothing more was to be accomplished by diplomacy. In April the Massachusetts minutemen had faced the British redcoats at Lexington Green. In May came Allen's bold capture of Fort Ticonderoga. In June followed Howe's costly victory at Bunker Hill and the firing of the adjacent town of Charlestown. In July Massachusetts set up a new government independent of the king, and George Washington took command of the colonial army which was besieging Gage in Boston. In August King George issued a proclamation calling on all loyal subjects to suppress the rebellion and sedition in North America. In September he hired 20,000 German soldiers from the princes of Hesse, Anhalt, and Brunswick, to reduce the colonies to submission. In October a British captain, without provocation, sailed into Falmouth harbor (Portland, Maine) and burned the town, rendering 1000 people homeless on the eve of a severe New England winter. In November two small American armies under Richard Montgomery and Benedict Arnold were invading Canada with the sanction of the Continental Congress. And on the last day of December, 1775, in a blinding snowstorm, the colonial troops made an attack on Quebec, in which Montgomery was killed and Arnold severely wounded. The news of the burning of Falmouth and the king's contract for German mercenaries reached Congress on the same day. The indignation of the assembly was extreme. "I am ready now, brother rebel," said a Southern member to Ward of Rhode Island, "to declare ourselves independent; we have had sufficient answer to our petition."

THE BIRTH OF THE NATION

128. Thomas Paine's "Common Sense." On the tenth of January, 1776, there came from a press in Philadelphia a pamphlet entitled "Common Sense," which made tens of thousands throughout the colonies ready also to declare themselves independent. The author was Thomas Paine, an Englishman of scanty fortune but liberal ideas, who had won Franklin's friendship in London and had come to the colonies in 1774 with what he later called "an aversion to monarchy, as debauching to the dignity of man." In "Common Sense" Paine argued with convincing clearness that the position of the colonies was thoroughly inconsistent,— in full rebellion against England, yet protesting loyalty to the king. He urged them to lay aside sentimental scruples, to realize that they were the nucleus of a great American nation destined to cover the continent and to be an example to the world of a people free from the servile traditions of monarchy and the low public morals of the Old World. It is doubtful whether any other printed work in all American history has had a greater influence than Paine's "Common Sense." Over 100,000 copies were sold, the equivalent of a circulation of 4,000,000 in our present population. Washington spoke enthusiastically of the "sound doctrine and unanswerable reasoning" of the pamphlet; and Edmund Randolph, the first attorney-general of the United States, said that the declaration of the independence of America was due, next to George III, to Thomas Paine.

129. The Declaration of Independence. When, therefore, the legislature of North Carolina ordered its representatives in Congress to advocate independence,[1] Virginia and all the New England colonies fell quickly into line. The Virginia delegation took the lead, its chairman, Richard Henry Lee, moving, on the seventh of June, that *these united colonies are and of right ought to be free and independent states, that they are absolved from all allegiance to the British Crown, and that all political connection between them and the state of Great Britain is and ought to be totally dissolved.* The vote on this

---

[1] The taxpayers of North Carolina had already resisted the king's troops in arms, in 1771, at Alamance, near the source of the Cape Fear River. They had been beaten and a number of them had been hanged as traitors. In May, 1775, some North Carolina patriots, of the county of Mecklenburg, had voted that "the king's civil and military commissions were all annulled and vacated." This vote was practically a declaration of independence by the patriots of Mecklenburg County, but no formal declaration was drawn up, and the North Carolina delegates failed to report the resolution to the Continental Congress.

momentous motion was postponed until the first of July, and a committee composed of Jefferson, Franklin, John Adams, Sherman, and Livingston was appointed to frame a fitting Declaration of Independence in case the motion was carried. Jefferson wrote the document in the fervor of spontaneous patriotism, "without reference to book or pamphlet," as he later declared. His draft was somewhat modified

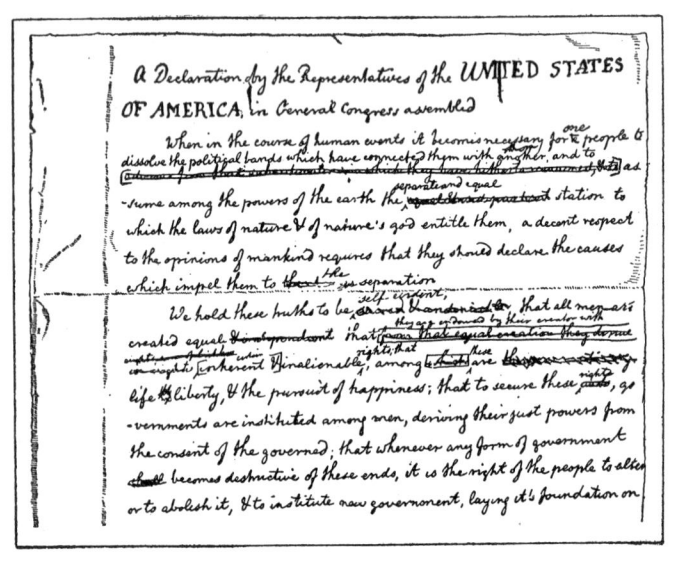

FACSIMILE OF THE OPENING LINES OF THE DECLARATION OF INDEPENDENCE

by the other members of the committee, especially Adams and Franklin. On the first day of July, Lee's motion was taken from the table for debate, and on the next day was passed by the vote of all the colonies except New York. Two days later (July 4) Jefferson's Declaration was adopted.[1] We celebrate the latter event in our national holiday, but the motion declaring our independence was carried the second of July.

[1] The Declaration was engrossed on parchment and signed a few weeks later by most members of the Congress. The original document, yellowed with age and hardly legible in spots, was transferred in 1921 by an executive order from the State Department to the Library of Congress, where it is now on exhibition, inclosed under glass with the Constitution, in a kind of little shrine.

130. Analysis of the Declaration. The Declaration of Independence was issued out of "a decent respect for the opinion of mankind." It asserted in the opening paragraph that all men are created equal and endowed with "certain unalienable rights," such as "life, liberty, and the pursuit of happiness," which it is the purpose of all governments to secure; and that "whenever any form of government becomes destructive of these ends, it is the right of the people to alter or to abolish it." The king of Great Britain, it declared, had violated those rights by a long train of abuses, and in proof there was submitted to a candid world a list of twenty-seven arbitrary and tyrannical acts aimed at the liberty of his American subjects. He had proved himself unfit to be the ruler of a free people. "We, therefore," concludes the Declaration, "the Representatives of the *United States of America*, in General Congress assembled, . . . solemnly publish and declare, that these United Colonies are, and of Right ought to be, *Free and Independent States*. . . . And for the support of this Declaration, with firm reliance on the protection of divine Providence, we mutually pledge to each other our Lives, our Fortunes, and our sacred Honor."

131. Effect of the Declaration. The Declaration of Independence put an end to the inconsistency of the colonial position. It made the troops of Washington, poor and meager as they were, a national army. It changed the struggle on the part of America from one of armed resistance to the unlawful acts of a sovereign still acknowledged, to a war against a foreign king and state. Until the Declaration was published the Tories or Loyalists, who numbered tens of thousands in the American colonies, were champions of one side of a much-debated question, namely, whether the abuses of the king's ministers justified armed resistance; but after the Declaration loyalty to the king of Great Britain became treason to their country. As traitors they were accordingly treated — their property confiscated, their utterances controlled, and their conduct regulated by severe laws in every one of the new states. In a general order of July 9, 1776, Washington communicated the Declaration to his army in New York, whither he had moved after compelling Howe to evacuate Boston (March 17, 1776). "The General hopes," read the order, "that this important event will serve as an incentive to every officer and soldier to act with fidelity and courage, as knowing that now the peace and safety of his country depend (under God) solely on the success of our arms; and that he is in the service of a state possessed of sufficient power to reward his merit and advance him to the highest honors of a free country."[1]

THE REVOLUTIONARY WAR

A detailed description of battles and campaigns is profitable only to experts in military science, whereas the causes that lead a country into war, especially into a war for independence, are most important stages in the evolution of a people's political and moral life. Therefore, after our rather full study of the preliminaries of the American Revolution, we shall dwell but briefly on the actual conflict.

132. Washington driven from New York and New Jersey. After Washington had compelled the British to evacuate Boston, the three major generals, Howe, Clinton, and Burgoyne, assumed the conduct of the war against the rebellious colonies (May, 1776). Washington tried to defend New York, but Howe's superior force of veterans drove his militia from Brooklyn Heights, Long Island, and compelled him to retreat step by step through the city of New York and up the Hudson, then across the river into New Jersey, and then across the state of New Jersey to a safe position on the western bank of the Delaware. With 3000 men left in the hands of the British as prisoners, and 7000 more under the command of the insubordinate and treacherous Charles Lee refusing to come to his aid, Washington wrote to his brother in December: "If every nerve is not strained to recruit a new army with all possible expedition, I think the game is pretty nearly up." A determined move by Howe from New York to the Delaware might easily have overwhelmed the remnants of Washington's army, some 2000 troops, and put an end then and there to the American Revolution. But fortunately for the patriot cause Howe was a lukewarm enemy. Surrounded by Tory flatterers, he believed that in chasing Washington from New York and New Jersey he had already given the American rebellion its deathblow, and that he had only to wait a few weeks before the penitent Congress at Philadelphia would be

---

[1] The troops and the citizens of New York celebrated this announcement by throwing down the leaden statue of George III, which stood on Bowling Green, and melting it into bullets for the colonial rifles.

THE BIRTH OF THE NATION

suing for the pardon George III had authorized him to grant when resistance to the royal will should cease.

133. The Recovery of New Jersey. But Washington with magnificent audacity recrossed the Delaware on Christmas night of 1776, surprised and overwhelmed a post of 1000 Hessians at Trenton, and a few days later defeated the British column under Mawhood at Princeton and drove it back to the neighborhood of New York. The courage and skill of Washington had saved the patriot cause. Enlistments increased; many loyalists in New Jersey swore allegiance to the United States; and our agents and emissaries in Europe took courage to urge our cause. Cornwallis himself, when complimenting Washington five years later on the skill with which the latter had forced him to the final surrender at Yorktown, added: "But after all, your Excellency's achievements in New Jersey were such that nothing could surpass them."

134. The British Plan for the Control of the Hudson. Disappointed in their hopes that the patriot cause would collapse of itself, the British ministry prepared an elaborate plan of attack for the campaign of 1777. Three armies were to invade New York. Burgoyne descending from Montreal via Lake Champlain and the upper Hudson, St. Leger marching eastward from Lake Ontario through the Mohawk valley, and Howe ascending the Hudson from New York City were to converge at Albany and so, by controlling the Hudson, were to shut New England off from the southern colonies. This ambitious scheme, with its total disregard of the conditions of travel in northern and western New York, showed how little the British War Department had learned from Braddock's defeat twenty years earlier.

135. Burgoyne's Surrender at Saratoga. St. Leger, toiling through the western wilderness, was defeated at Oriskany by the old Indian fighter General Herkimer long before he had got halfway to Albany; Howe's instructions to move up the river were tucked into a pigeonhole by the war minister, Lord George Germaine, who was anxious to get off to the country to shoot pheasants, and left there to gather the dust of years; while Burgoyne, fighting his way step by step against the dead resistance of the tangled and cluttered forests of northern New York and the live resistance of New England riflemen who gathered in swarms to harass his fatigued columns, was brought to bay near Saratoga, and by the dashing charges of Arnold's and Morgan's troops was obliged to surrender his total force of 6000 men and officers to General Horatio Gates, commander of the continental army on the Hudson (October 17, 1777).

136. The Turning Point of the War. Sir Edward Creasy has included Burgoyne's defeat at Saratoga among his "Fifteen Decisive Battles of the World." It was the turning point of the Revolution. The total failure of the Hudson River campaign left the British without a plan of war. To be sure, General Howe had sailed down from New York to the head of Chesapeake Bay, while he ought to have been marching up the Hudson to join Burgoyne, and seized and held the "rebel capital," Philadelphia, in spite of Washington's plucky opposition at Brandywine Creek and Germantown. But though the British officers with their Tory friends in Philadelphia were spending a gay winter at fêtes and balls while Washington's destitute fragment of an army was shivering and starving at Valley Forge close by, nevertheless the advantage of the winter of 1777–1778 was with the Americans. For the attempts of the British both to crush Washington's army and to sever the northern and southern colonies had failed. The impossibility of occupying the country back of the few seaport towns, such as New York, Newport, and Philadelphia, began to be apparent to the British ministry, as it had from the first been apparent to many British merchants, who had advised making the war a purely naval one, for the blockade of the American ports and the destruction of their commerce. The amiable Lord North, distressed as much by the prolongation of the war as by the disaster to Burgoyne, was allowed to send an embassy to the American Congress early in 1778, conceding to the colonies every right they had contended for since the days of the Stamp Act, if they would only lay down their arms and return to British allegiance.

137. The French Alliance. But Lord North's offer came too late. The victory at Saratoga had opened the eyes of another court and sovereign. Almost from the beginning of the Revolution unofficial aid had been granted to the colonies from sympathetic agencies in France, but the government of Louis XVI, uncertain of the outcome of the struggle, had been unwilling to commit itself to a formal alliance. The news of Saratoga removed this hesitation. In February, 1778, treaties of commerce and alliance were signed by the French

FRANKLIN AT THE COURT OF FRANCE, 1778

and American diplomats. The treaty of alliance (the only one ever made by the United States) pledged each nation to continue the war with England until the other was ready to make peace.

138. The War assumes a European Character. The French alliance was a great gain for the Americans. By it the independence of the United States was recognized by the strongest power of continental Europe. Men and money, both sorely needed, were furnished to the struggling states, and, above all, a fleet was sent over to deliver the American seaports from the British. John Paul Jones, the intrepid sea fighter, was fitted out with five vessels in France and, flying the new American flag from the masthead of the *Bonhomme Richard*, attacked the British frigates in their own waters. The war soon assumed a European aspect. Spain joined France (1779) not from any sympathy with the American cause, which she did nothing to aid, but only with the hope of regaining the island of Jamaica and the stronghold of Gibraltar, which she had lost to the British in former wars. The next year Holland, England's old commercial rival, also entered the war for the destruction of Britain's naval power and the overthrow of her empire. Thus the victory at Saratoga led directly to a coalition of three European powers against Great Britain.

LETTER OF FRANKLIN TO THE COUNT OF VERGENNES, — THE EARLIEST DIPLOMATIC CORRESPONDENCE OF THE AMERICAN CONGRESS

139. The British evacuate Philadelphia. Doubting their ability to defend the forts on the Delaware against a French fleet, the British evacuated Philadelphia in the summer of 1778, and fell back upon New York, escaping defeat at the hands of the American army on the way only by the treachery of General Charles Lee, who basely ordered a retreat at the battle of Monmouth. Washington arrived on the scene of action in time to save the day for the American cause, and sent Lee into long-merited disgrace.

140. The War in the South. At the close of 1778 the British transferred the seat of war to the South, with a view of detaching the states below the Potomac from the patriot cause. There was much British sentiment in Georgia and the Carolinas, where Sir Henry Clinton enrolled some 2000 Loyalist troops in his army. The fighting in the Carolinas, therefore, had some of the aspects of a civil war. The British had no systematic plan of campaign, but marched and countermarched in an irregular line between the coast and the interior, wherever the resistance was least and the hope of attracting soldiers to their banners greatest. All the while they were harassed by guerrilla bands of patriots under the brave leaders Marion, Sumter, and Pickens. In December, 1778, they captured Savannah and reëstablished the royal government in Georgia; and in 1780 they took Charleston, the other great Southern port. In the interior of the Carolinas they were generally successful, until General Nathanael Greene, next to Washington the ablest commander on the American side, was sent to replace Gates, the "hero of Saratoga," who had ignominiously fled from the field on his defeat at Camden, South Carolina (August, 1780).[1] By the victory at Cowpens (January, 1781) and the valiant stand at Guilford (March, 1781) Morgan and Greene retrieved the defeat of Gates and recovered the interior of the Carolinas.

141. King's Mountain. The most remarkable battle and the turning point of the war south of the Potomac River was the engagement at King's Mountain, on the border between North and South Carolina. Here about 1000 sturdy frontiersmen and Indian fighters recruited from the Carolinas, Virginia, Tennessee, and Georgia surrounded and captured a force of some 1200 Tory soldiers commanded by Colonel Ferguson, who had been sent by General

---

[1] Baron De Kalb, who, with Lafayette, had joined Washington's army during the famous campaign of 1776, was killed in this battle. Other distinguished foreigners who gave their services to the American cause were Baron Steuben, a veteran Prussian officer, and the Polish generals Kosciusko and Pulaski. The latter was mortally wounded in the attack on Savannah, October 9, 1779.

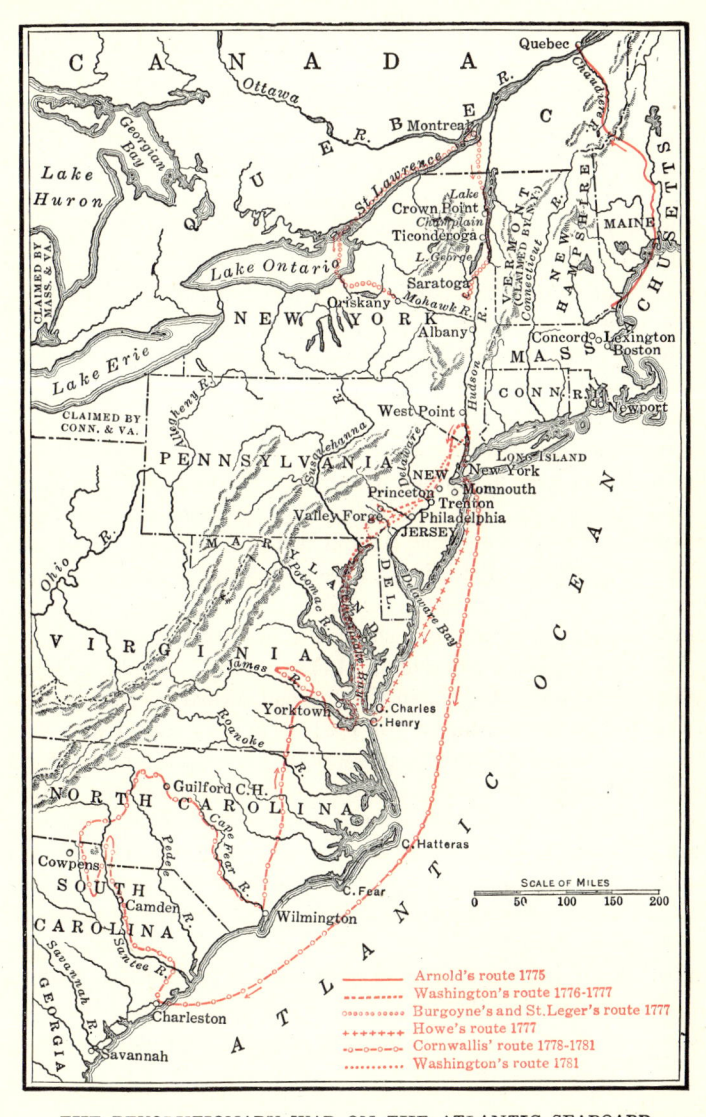

THE REVOLUTIONARY WAR ON THE ATLANTIC SEABOARD

122 SEPARATION OF THE COLONIES FROM ENGLAND

Cornwallis to clear the guerrillas out of the upland regions and make his march through the Carolinas easy.

142. The Treachery of Benedict Arnold. Meanwhile the most distressing incident of the war was taking place on the Hudson. Benedict Arnold, who had so signally distinguished himself for bravery at Quebec and Saratoga, had not been advanced so rapidly in the American army as he thought he deserved to be. Encouraged by his friends among the British officers, and by his wife, who had been a belle in the Tory circles of Philadelphia, he nursed his injured pride to a point where he determined to betray his country. He easily obtained from Washington the command of the important fortress of West Point on the Hudson, and forthwith opened negotiations with Sir Henry Clinton to hand the post over to the British. Major André, the British agent in the transaction, was caught inside the American lines at Tarrytown and the incriminating papers were found in his boots. He was hanged as a spy. Warned of Andre's capture in the nick of time, Arnold fled hastily from his breakfast table and reached a British war vessel lying in the Hudson. He was rewarded with a brigadier-generalship in Clinton's army, and assumed command of the British troops in Virginia.[1]

143. Cornwallis's Surrender at Yorktown. Arnold was joined by Lord Cornwallis (to whom Clinton had turned over his command in the South) in the summer of 1781. Their combined forces fortified a position at Yorktown, to await a British fleet bringing reënforcements from New York. Drawn northward across the Carolinas by the strategy of General Greene, Cornwallis began to harass the state of Virginia, which was protected only by a meager force under the gallant young Marquis de Lafayette, Washington's trusted friend, and the most devoted of the eleven foreign major generals who served in the American army. But the tables were turned on Cornwallis. While he was waiting in Yorktown, a French fleet under De Grasse, arriving off the mouth of Chesapeake Bay, defeated the British squadron which was bringing the reënforcements from New

---

[1] After the war Arnold went to England to live, where he had to endure at times insolent reminders of his treachery. He died, an old man, in London, June 14, 1801, dressed, by his own pathetic request, in his old colonial uniform with the epaulets and sword knot presented to him by Washington after the victory of Saratoga. In the great monument erected on the battlefield of Saratoga (1883) the niche which might have contained Arnold's statue is empty, while statues of Gates, Morgan, and Schuyler adorn the other three sides of the monument.

THE BIRTH OF THE NATION

York, and landed 3000 French troops on the peninsula in their stead. At the same moment Washington, always on the right spot at the right moment, conducted a brilliant march of four hundred miles from the Hudson to the York River, with 2000 Americans and 4000 Frenchmen, and, effecting a junction with Lafayette, penned Cornwallis up in the narrow peninsula between the York and the James. Cornwallis made a brave but vain effort to break the besieging lines. On the nineteenth of October, 1781, he surrendered his army of 7000 men and officers as prisoners of war. The British attempt to conquer the revolting colonies was over. North and south their armies had met with disaster. They abandoned the posts which they still held, with the exception of New York, and withdrew to the West Indies to triumph over France in a great naval battle and still preserve their ascendancy in that rich region of the western world.

144. The War in the West. While the American army on the Atlantic seaboard was successfully repelling the British invasion with the aid of the French fleet, a bold campaign was being conducted by the hardy frontiersmen of the West for the overthrow of England's authority beyond the Alleghenies.

145. The Proclamation Line of 1763. In the very year that the British took possession of the vast territory between the eastern mountains and the Mississippi, King George had issued a proclamation forbidding his governors in the American colonies to extend their authority or to permit settlement west of a line running along the crest of the Allegheny Mountains. The ostensible reason for drawing this "Proclamation Line" was to secure the allegiance and trade of the Indians so lately devoted to France, by giving them assurance that their hunting grounds would not be invaded by the white settlers from across the mountains; but the real reason was to curtail the power of the colonies, discredit their old "sea-to-sea" charters, and confine them to the narrow region along the Atlantic coast, where they could be within easier reach of the British authority.

146. The Westward March of the Pioneers. It was a bitter disappointment to the ambitious frontiersmen, after having defeated the French attempt to shut them in behind the mountains, to have the British king adopt the same policy. They felt that they were being kept out of a region destined for them by nature, and they resented being left exposed to danger from the fierce Indians

124 SEPARATION OF THE COLONIES FROM ENGLAND

who swept up and down the frontier in their intertribal raids and wars. Therefore the sturdy woodsmen and pioneers from the back counties of Pennsylvania, Virginia, and the Carolinas had pushed across the mountains into the densely wooded land of the Ohio, the Cumberland, and the Tennessee valleys. In 1769 Daniel Boone, the most celebrated of these pioneers, set out from his home in

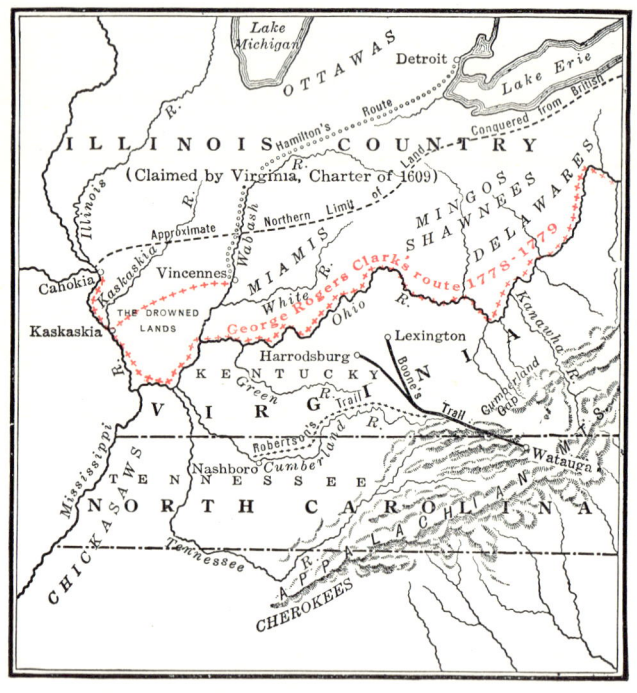

THE REVOLUTIONARY WAR IN THE WEST

North Carolina to seek "Kentucke" (the "dark and bloody ground"), which was stained by centuries of Indian feuds. In the next three years Virginia pioneers, led by James Robertson and John Sevier, had founded settlements on the Watauga River in the western mountains of North Carolina; and, like the early emigrants to the shores of New England, were devising a government even while they were clearing the soil and defending their rude homes against the attack of the savages.

THE BIRTH OF THE NATION

147. The Victories on the Kanawha and the Watauga. Though Pontiac's great conspiracy (p. 95) to keep the English out of the forts of the Northwest had been crushed (1765), and the Iroquois had abandoned their claims to the region south of the Ohio River (1768), nevertheless the savage tribes of Mingos, Shawnees, and Cherokees disputed with the white men every mile of the territory west of the Alleghenies. In October, 1774 (while the first Continental Congress was discussing methods of resistance to English taxation), a great victory of the Virginia backwoodsmen over Cornstalk, the Shawnee chieftain, at the mouth of the Kanawha River, had secured the rich lands of the present state of Kentucky against Indian domination. And in November, 1776 (while Washington's dwindling army was fleeing across the state of New Jersey), the decisive repulse of the Cherokees from the Watauga settlements opened to the pioneers the equally rich lands of Tennessee. The victories on the Kanawha and the Watauga, fought against the Indian foe, by men in the fringed hunting shirt of deerskin and by the rude tactics of Indian warfare, have often gone unmentioned, while unimportant skirmishes on the seaboard, between uniformed soldiers, commanded by officers in gold braid, have been described in detail. But in their effects on our country's history these Indian fights, with the later victories north of the Ohio to which they opened the way, deserve to rank with Saratoga and Yorktown. For if the latter victories decided that America should take her place among the nations of the world, the former proclaimed that the new nation would not be content to be shut up in a little strip of seacoast, but had set its face westward to possess the whole continent.

148. The Character of the Western Settlements. The settlers in Kentucky and Tennessee numbered only a few hundred at the outbreak of the American Revolution, but they were intensely democratic and patriotic. In May, 1775, delegates from four "stations" in Kentucky "met in a wide field of white clover, under the shade of a monstrous elm," and made wise laws for their infant colony. When a party of campers in the heart of Kentucky heard the news of the first battle of the Revolution, they enthusiastically christened their camp "Lexington." In the Watauga settlement the Tories were drummed out of camp several months before the Declaration of

Independence was adopted. Soon after that event Kentucky, though a county of Virginia, petitioned Congress to be received as the fourteenth state of the Union and sent a delegation to Patrick Henry, governor of Virginia, to offer that state the services of "a respectable body of prime riflemen."

149. George Rogers Clark wins the Northwestern Territory. One of these delegates was George Rogers Clark, a young Virginian scarcely past twenty, who had cast in his lot with the Kentucky settlers on the Ohio. Clark conceived and executed a plan of campaign which entitles him to be called the Washington of the West. Sending spies across the Ohio to the Illinois country, he learned that the Indians and French there were only lukewarm in their allegiance to their new English masters. He therefore determined to seize this huge territory for the patriot cause, and in the autumn of 1777 went to Williamsburg to lay his plans before Governor Patrick Henry. Henry, Jefferson, and other prominent Virginians approved Clark's bold scheme, but the utmost that the state could do for him was to authorize him to raise 350 men and advance him $1200 in depreciated currency. It was a poor start for the conquest of a region as large as New England, New York, and Pennsylvania combined, but Clark belonged to the men of genius who persist in accomplishing tasks which men of judgment pronounce impossible. He surprised the posts at Kaskaskia and Cahokia and, by intrepid assurance and skillful diplomacy, induced the French and Indians of the Mississippi Valley to transfer their allegiance from the British Empire to the new American republic. When he learned that Colonel Hamilton, the British commander at Detroit, had seized the fort of Vincennes on the Wabash, he immediately marched his men in midwinter over two hundred miles across the "drowned lands" of the Wabash, sometimes wading through icy water up to their chins, sometimes

GEORGE ROGERS CLARK

THE UNITED STATES
in 1783

Showing Western Land Claims of States and the Boundaries fixed by Treaty of 1783

Also the boundaries proposed by the French Court, Sept. 6, 1782

shivering supperless on some bleak knoll, but always courageous and confident, until he appeared before the post of Vincennes and summoned the wonderstricken Hamilton to an immediate and unconditional surrender (February, 1779). The capture of Vincennes was the deathblow of the British power north of the Ohio.

Peace

150. George III abandons the Struggle. When the news of Cornwallis's surrender at Yorktown reached Lord North, he threw up his hands and exclaimed, "My God! it is all over." The stubborn king was not so ready to read in Yorktown the doom of his tenacious policy of coercion. Always mistaking the satisfaction of his royal will for the salvation of the British Empire, he stormed against the rising sentiment for peace with America and wrote letters of petulant bombast to his prime minister, threatening to resign the British crown and retire to his ancestral domains in Germany. But threats and entreaties were of no avail. The nation was sick of the rule of the "King's Friends," and the early months of 1782 saw George III compelled to part with Lord North and receive into his service, if not into his confidence, the Whig statesmen. Lord Shelburne, the new prime minister, sent a diplomatic agent to Paris in April, 1782, to inform our minister, Benjamin Franklin, that England was ready to discuss terms of peace.

151. Complications in the Peace Negotiations. The situation was a very complicated one. The United States, by the treaty of alliance with France in 1778, had pledged itself not to make a separate peace with England. Then the French had drawn Spain into the war, with the promise of recovering for her the island of Jamaica in the West Indies (taken by Oliver Cromwell's fleet in 1655) and the rock fortress of Gibraltar (captured by the English in 1704). The Franco-American alliance had been successful, as we have seen, in defeating the British invasion of the Atlantic seaboard, thus assuring the independence of the United States. But the bolder Franco-Spanish design of destroying the naval supremacy of Great Britain and dividing up her colonial empire had entirely failed. It soon became evident to the American diplomats at Paris that France was planning to find consolation for her defeated ally, Spain, at the expense of her victorious ally, America. In fact, Vergennes, the French minister, had prepared a map on which the United States figured as the same old colonial strip between the Alleghenies and the sea, while the western region north of the Ohio was to be restored to England and that south of the Ohio to the Indians, partly under American and partly under Spanish protection (see map). Thus the new republic was to be robbed of the fruits of the labors of Boone, Sevier, Robertson, and Clark, and the Mississippi was to be a Spanish stream. "This court is interested in separating us from Great Britain," wrote Jay from Paris, "but it is not their interest that we should become a great and formidable people."

152. Our Great Debt to France. Yet we were greatly beholden to France. Her aid in men, ships, and money had been so timely and generous that it is almost certain that without it the American cause would have been lost. The Continental Congress, resorting to every possible device,— requisitions on the states, confiscation of Tory estates, domestic loans, even a national lottery,— could raise only a small fraction of the money needed to carry on the war. By 1778 it had issued $63,500,000 of paper money, which was rapidly coming to be worth hardly more than the paper on which it was printed. The bracing effect on our languishing finances of the arrival of 2,500,000 francs in French gold can easily be imagined. Our commissioners in Paris, therefore, were instructed by Congress not to proceed in the peace negotiations without the consent and concurrence of the French ministry.

153. The United States makes a Separate Treaty with England. John Jay, our minister to Spain, and John Adams, who had just secured the recognition of our independence by the Dutch government, joined Franklin in Paris to arrange the terms of peace. Owing to the complications of the French-Spanish alliance our commissioners found it necessary to exercise their own discretion and to negotiate with the English agents alone, with whom they agreed upon a preliminary treaty of peace on November 30, 1782, securing for the United States the whole eastern basin of the Mississippi. The French foreign minister, Vergennes, felt aggrieved by this action, but was persuaded by Franklin to accept the terms, which were embodied in the final treaty of September 3, 1783. Congress showed its full approval of the behavior of our commissioners by an enthusiastic ratification of their work.

154. Terms of the Peace. There were difficult points in the negotiations with England too, despite the desire of both sides to come to terms. The British ministry readily acknowledged the independence of the United States and made but slight protest against its extension westward to the Mississippi. England also conceded to the United States the valuable privilege of sharing the Newfoundland fisheries. But the questions of debts due to English merchants from the colonists before the war, and the treatment of the American Loyalists, or Tories, were very troublesome. The American Congress had no money of its own and had no authority to dispose of the funds of the states. It could not, therefore, give the British ministry any sufficient guarantee that the debts would be paid. John Adams might assure William Pitt with some asperity and indignation that the Americans had "no idea of cheating anybody," but the declaration looked to Pitt remarkably like Mr. Adams's private opinion merely. This matter of the debts might have frustrated the peace negotiations entirely, had not the British supplemented the American assurances of good will by the secret plan to hold on to the valuable fur-trading posts along the Great Lakes from Oswego to Mackinac until the debts were paid.

155. The Problem of the Loyalists. Still more delicate was the question of the treatment of the Loyalists. Tens of thousands of the American colonists had been opposed to the war with the mother country,— some out of prudent anxiety lest the war would entail business ruin and general disorder, others from an optimistic belief that in spite of "Grenville's well-meant blunder and Townshend's malicious challenge" the situation could be "rectified without the disruption of the Empire." The more ardent of these Loyalists denounced the Congress in unmeasured terms as a collection of quarrelsome, pettifogging lawyers and mechanics; and when the Declaration of Independence put them in the position of traitors, many of them entered the British armies. To abandon these allies, who, at the sacrifice of their property and reputation in America, had obeyed King George's call to all loyal citizens to aid in putting down rebellion, seemed to the British ministry an unpardonable injustice. It thought that the American Congress should restore to these Loyalists their confiscated estates (valued at some $20,000,000) or reimburse them with the territory north of the Ohio, which Clark had conquered.

156. The American View of the Tories. But in the breasts of the American patriots the thought of the Tories roused bitter memories. It was not alone their jibes and insults, their vilification of the character of Washington and his associates, their steady encouragement of desertion and mutiny in the American army, or their own appearance in the uniform of the king's troops. Congress remembered how, in the dark winter of 1776, when Washington was vainly imploring the farmers of New Jersey for food for his destitute soldiers, the Tory squires of the state were selling Lord Howe their rich harvests at good prices, to feed the British invaders; and how in the still darker winter that followed, while Washington's starving and shivering army at Valley Forge was losing more men by desertion daily than it was gaining by recruiting, the Tory drawing-rooms of Philadelphia were gay with festivities in honor of the British officers. It was hard that the new country, already burdened with a war debt of $50,000,000, with its political life to establish on a firm basis and its industries and commerce to organize anew, should be asked to recompense the men who had done their utmost to wreck the patriot cause,—men whom even the careful tongue of Washington called "detestable parricides!"

157. The Liberality of England's Terms. The British ministry finally accepted the assurance of the American commissioners that Congress would recommend to the states the restitution of the property of such Loyalists as had not borne arms against the United States and would put no obstacle in the way of the collection of debts due British subjects. The British government itself came to the aid of the "active" Loyalists, granting them liberal pensions and land in Canada. Europe was amazed at England's generosity. "The English buy the peace rather than make it," wrote Vergennes; "their concessions as to boundaries, the fisheries, the Loyalists, exceed everything I had thought possible." It was a complete if a tardy triumph of that feeling of sympathy for men of common blood, common language, traditions, and institutions, across the seas, which had been so long struggling to find a voice in the corrupt councils of the English court.

158. The Retirement of Washington. On the eighteenth of April, 1783, the eighth anniversary of the night when Paul Revere roused the minutemen of Lexington to meet the British regulars on the village green, Washington proclaimed hostilities at an end; and, by

GROUP OF FAMOUS REVOLUTIONARY BUILDINGS

Faneuil Hall, Boston; Old South Church, Boston; Independence Hall, Philadelphia; Old State House, Boston

132 SEPARATION OF THE COLONIES FROM ENGLAND

the splendid example of his single-minded patriotism, persuaded men and officers to go to their homes "without a farthing in their pockets," confident in the power and good will of their new government to reward them according to their deserts. The final articles of peace were signed September 3, 1783. On November 25 the last British regulars in America sailed out of New York harbor, and a few days later Washington bade his officers an affectionate farewell and retired to his home at Mount Vernon, there, as he hoped, "to glide gently down the stream of time until he rested with his fathers."

REFERENCES

The Declaration of Independence: C. H. VAN TYNE, *The American Revolution* (Am. Nation), chaps. iv-vi; JOHN FISKE, *The American Revolution*, Vol. I, chap. iv; JUSTIN WINSOR, *Narrative and Critical History of America*, Vol. VI, chap. iii; *Cambridge Modern History*, Vol. VII, chap. vi; G. OTTO TREVELYAN, *The American Revolution*, Vol. II, Part I, pp. 105-158; EDWARD CHANNING, *History of the United States*, Vol. III, chap. vii; E. M. AVERY, *History of the United States and its People*, Vol. V, chap. xxii; J. H. HAZELTON, *The Declaration of Independence*; A. B. HART, *American History told by Contemporaries*, Vol. II, Nos. 184-188.

The Revolutionary War: S. G. FISHER, *The Struggle for American Independence*; CHANNING, Vol. III, chaps. viii-xi; AVERY, Vol. V, chaps x, xiv-xxi; Vol. VI, chaps. i-xiv; VAN TYNE, chaps. vii-xvii; TREVELYAN, Vols. I-III (to 1777); FISKE, Vols. I, II; W. M. SLOANE, *The French War and the Revolution*, chaps. xx-xxviii; THEODORE ROOSEVELT, *The Winning of the West*, Vols. II, III; H. C. LODGE, *The Story of the Revolution*; G. M. WRONG, *Washington and his Comrades in Arms* (Chronicles, Vol. XII); WILLIAM H. ENGLISH, *The Conquest of the Country Northwest of the Ohio*; W. H. LECKY, *History of England in the Eighteenth Century* (ed. Woodburn), chap. ii; Old South Leaflets, Vol. IV, Nos. 5, 97, 98; G. S. CALLENDER, *Economic History of the United States*, chap. iv.

Peace: JOHN FISKE, *The Critical Period of American History*, chap. i; A. C. MCLAUGHLIN, *The Confederation and the Constitution* (Am. Nation), chaps. i-iii; CHANNING, Vol. III, chap. xii; AVERY, Vol. VI, chaps. xv-xvii; HART, Vol. II, Nos. 215-220; LECKY (ed. Woodburn), chap. iv; WINSOR, Vol. VII, chap. ii; WILLIAM MACDONALD, *Select Documents of United States History, 1776-1861*, No. 3 (for text of treaty).

TOPICS FOR SPECIAL REPORTS

1. **Thomas Paine's Contribution to American Independence:** TREVELYAN, Vol. II, Part I, pp. 147-155; HART, Vol. II, Nos. 159, 186; VAN TYNE, pp. 61-65, 129; M. C. TYLER, *Literary History of the American Revolution*, Vol. I, pp. 452-471; M. D. CONWAY, *Life of Thomas Paine* (use index).

LAFAYETTE

From a miniature portrait by La Perche, Courtesy of the Museum of Fine Arts, Boston

134 SEPARATION OF THE COLONIES FROM ENGLAND

2. **Lafayette in the American Revolution:** Old South Leaflets, Nos. 97, 98; FISKE, *The American Revolution*, Vol. II, pp. 43-46, 202-205, 231-233, 268-280 (Riverside Edition); SLOANE, pp. 264, 292, 324-344.

3. **The Tories:** TYLER, Vol. I, pp. 293-383; TREVELYAN, Vol. II, Part II, pp. 226-240; HART, Vol. II, Nos. 166-169; VAN TYNE, *The Loyalists in the American Revolution*, pp. 1-59; TYLER, *The Party of the Loyalists* (*American Historical Review*, Vol. I, pp. 24 ff.).

4. **Daniel Boone, a Pioneer to the West:** A. B. HURLBURT, *Boone's Wilderness Road*, pp. 1-47; H. A. BRUCE, *The Romance of American Expansion*, pp. 1-24; ROOSEVELT, Vol. I, pp. 134-136; J. R. SPEARS, *The History of the Mississippi Valley*, pp. 183-208; R. G. THWAITES, *Life of Daniel Boone*.

5. **Washington's Trials with the Army and Congress:** FISKE, *The American Revolution*, Vol. II, pp. 24-46, 62-72; *The Critical Period of American History*, pp. 101-119; HART, Vol. II, Nos. 174, 195, 198, 206; SLOANE, pp. 370-378; VAN TYNE, *The American Revolution*, pp. 236-247; Old South Leaflets, No. 47.

PART III. THE NEW REPUBLIC

CHAPTER VI

THE CONSTITUTION

The Critical Period

159. The End of the Colonial Period. With the Revolutionary War the first great epoch of American history, the colonial period, came to an end. The English colonies became an independent nation, and the political connections with the great British Empire were severed. Royal governors, councilors, judges, customs officers, and agents disappeared, and their places were taken by men chosen by the people of the new states,— public servants instead of public masters. Fortunately the break with Great Britain had not come before the serious and aggressive French rivals of the English in the New World had been subdued, and the country from the Atlantic to the Mississippi had been won for men of English speech, blood, tradition, and law. Two great facts, the separation of the colonies from England and the possession of a vast western territory to be settled and organized, determined the chief activities of the new republic. First of all, the United States, unless that name were to be a mere mockery, must devise a form of government to insure a national union ; and, in the second place, the national government must be extended westward as the new domain beyond the mountains developed. We have studied the winning of American Independence. We turn now to a study of the American Union.

160. The Nature and Authority of Congress. Thirteen years elapsed between the Declaration of Independence (1776) and the inauguration of George Washington as first president of the United States (1789). During those years our country was governed by a Congress, a group of delegates comprising from two to seven members from each state. Until a few months before the surrender of Cornwallis at Yorktown this Congress was without legal authority, or any written constitution defining its powers. Its members, acting on instructions from their states, or relying on the indorsement of their states, assumed very important functions of government. They raised and officered an army, assessed the states for its support, declared the colonies independent of England, borrowed money abroad on the credit of the new United States, rejected the British offer of reconciliation in 1778, and concluded treaties of commerce and alliance with France. But the Continental Congress could assume these vast powers of government without express authority only because the pressure of war united the colonies for the moment and made a central directing body an immediate necessity. For the Union to endure after the pressure of war was over, a regular national government had to be established.

161. The Articles of Confederation. About a year before the colonies declared their independence Benjamin Franklin, a lifelong advocate of colonial union, submitted to this Congress a draft of "Articles of Confederation and Perpetual Union" (July 21, 1775). But too many of the members of Congress still hoped for a peaceful settlement with England to make this plan acceptable. When independence was declared, however, the necessity of forming a government became obvious. A committee of thirteen, with John Dickinson of Pennsylvania as chairman, prepared Articles of Confederation, which were approved by Congress in November, 1777. But more than three years elapsed before the last of the states, Maryland, assented to the Articles and so made them the law of the land (March 1, 1781).

162. The Cession of Western Lands by the States. The delay of Maryland in accepting the Articles of Confederation was due to an important cause and resulted in a great benefit to the nation. The states of Massachusetts, Connecticut, Virginia, North and South Carolina, and Georgia claimed land between the Alleghenies and the Mississippi by virtue of their old colonial charters, which gave them indefinite westward extension. Virginia's claim, which overlapped that of both Massachusetts and Connecticut, was strengthened by the fact that George Rogers Clark had actually conquered the vast territory north of the Ohio under commission from the governor of Virginia. New York also maintained a claim to part of the same disputed territory on account of a treaty with the

Iroquois Indians, which had put those tribes under her protection (1768). The states whose western boundaries were fixed by their charters, like Maryland, New Jersey, and Pennsylvania, were at a disadvantage, since they had no Western lands with which to reward their veterans of the Revolution. Maryland, therefore, insisted, before accepting the Articles of Confederation, that the states with Western claims should surrender them to the United States, and that all the land between the Alleghenies and the Mississippi should be national domain. After some parleying, New York, in 1781, led the way in surrendering its claims. Virginia, with noble generosity, gave up her far better founded claims to the whole region north of the Ohio, in 1784. Massachusetts, Connecticut, and the Carolinas soon followed suit, although Georgia, partly on account of complications with Spain, maintained her claims as far west as the Mississippi until 1802. By these cessions the United States acquired an immense national domain (see map, p. 126), the sale of which could be applied to the payment of the Revolutionary War debt and from whose territory new states could be formed. It was the beginning of a truly national power, and honor is due to the state of Maryland for insisting on this fair and wise policy.

163. Criticism of the Articles of Confederation. The Articles of Confederation, though announcing a "perpetual union" and a "firm league of friendship" of the thirteen states, remained in force only eight years and failed utterly to bring strength or harmony into the Union. They had some merits, to be sure. They were the first definite formulation of a national government, in black on white, and the powers which they gave to Congress, had they only included the control of commerce and taxation, would have been ample to run the government. But the defects of the Articles may be summed up in a single clause: they failed to give the Congress of the United States enough authority to carry out the powers granted to it. At the very outset they declared that "each state retained its sovereignty, freedom, and independence," and all through them the unwillingness to force the states to part with any of their power is evident. For example, Congress pledged the faith of the United States to pay the war debt, yet it had neither the power to demand, nor the machinery to collect, a single penny from any citizen or state of the Union. It could only make "requisitions" on the states, and its repeated requests for money met with meager response. Gouverneur Morris called it a "government by supplication." The budget for 1781–1782 was $9,000,000. Of this, Congress negotiated for $4,000,000 by a foreign loan and assessed the states for the other $5,000,000. After a year's delay some $450,000 of the $5,000,000 asked for was paid in, and not a dollar came from Georgia, South Carolina, or Delaware. So, from year to year, the "government by supplication" worried along, asking millions and getting a few hundred thousands, in imminent danger of going bankrupt by failing to pay the interest on its debt, with scarcely enough revenue, as one statesman said with pardonable exaggeration, "to buy stationery for its clerks or pay the salary of a doorkeeper." The impotence of Congress in financial matters was only one example of the general inadequacy of the Articles of Confederation. They put on the central government certain grave responsibilities, such as defending the land from its foes, maintaining its credit, preserving order at home, and securing friendships abroad; and yet they gave the central government no means of enforcing obedience to its will. Congress had no executive power, no national courts of justice in which to condemn offenders against its laws, no control of commerce, no machinery of taxation, no check on the indiscriminate issue by the states of money of differing values, no efficient army or navy.

164. Our Government despised by the European Powers. It is no wonder that so weak a government failed to inspire respect abroad or obedience at home. England, in defiance of the treaty of 1783, still held the fur-trading posts of the Northwest and, confident that the thirteen states would not unite in a policy of retaliation, shut us out from the lucrative trade with her West Indies. The French ministers told Jefferson plainly in Paris that it was impossible to recognize the Congress as a government. The Spanish governor at New Orleans offered the Western frontiersmen the use of the Mississippi if they would renounce their allegiance to the United States and come under the flag of Spain. The thrifty merchants of Amsterdam were on tenterhooks for fear that the interest on their loans to the new republic would not be paid. And finally even the Mohammedan pirates of the Barbary States in northern Africa levied blackmail on our vessels which ventured into the Mediterranean. The government under the Articles of Confederation "had touched that lowest point of ignominy where it confessed its inability to protect the lives and property of its citizens."

165. The Threat of Anarchy at Home. At home anarchy was imminent. The glowing sentences in which patriots on the eve of the Revolution had declared themselves no longer Virginians or Carolinians, but henceforth Americans, were forgotten when peace was made. The states, with their conflicting commercial and agricultural interests, their diverse social and religious inheritances from early colonial days, their strong sense of local independence, nurtured by long defense against British officials and strengthened by the meagerness of intercolonial trade and travel, were jealous to preserve their individuality unimpaired. They indulged in petty tariff wars against one another, the defeated party often seeking a spiteful consolation in refusing to pay its contribution to Congress. Boundary disputes were frequent and fierce. The farmers of New York and New Hampshire fought over the region of Vermont like bands of Indians on the warpath, "with all the horrors of ambuscade and arson"; Pennsylvania allowed the Indians of the Wyoming valley to scalp New Englanders as "intruders." Congress was powerless to prevent states from plunging into the folly of issuing large sums of paper money to ease the debtor class. It looked on in distressed impotence while thriving towns like Newport were brought to the edge of ruin by wild financial legislation,[1] and the ancient and dignified commonwealth of Massachusetts had to subdue an armed mob of 1500 rebels of the debtor class, led by a captain of the Revolution named Daniel Shays, who closed the courts at Worcester and attacked the United States arsenal at Springfield (1786–1787).

166. The Apathy of Congress. As the weakness of Congress became more evident its dignity declined. The foremost statesmen preferred to serve their own states rather than to sit in a national assembly without power. Each state was entitled to seven representatives in Congress by the terms of the Articles, making a house of ninety-one members. But there were seldom more than a quarter

---

[1] A French visitor to America during this distressing period saw in Newport "groups of idle men standing with folded arms at the corners of the streets, houses falling to ruin, miserable shops with nothing but a few coarse stuffs, grass growing in the public square in front of the court of justice, and rags stuffed in the windows or hung on hideous women" (Brissot de Warville, Travels in America, Ed. of 1791, p. 145).

of that number in attendance. Some states went unrepresented for months at a time. Only twenty members were in session to receive George Washington and to express to him the country's gratitude for his invaluable services on the most solemn occasion of his surrender of the command of the American army in December, 1783. Only twenty-three assembled the next month to ratify the treaty of peace with England. Finally, the attendance dwindled away to a few scattering representatives, until from October, 1788, to April, 1789, not enough members assembled to make a quorum, and there was absolutely no United States government.

167. The Northwest Ordinance. It is a relief to be able to point to one piece of statesmanlike and constructive work done by the poor tottering government of the Confederation in these dismal years, fitly called "the critical period of American history." The large domain between the Great Lakes and the Ohio, which had become the property of the United States by the abandonment of the claims of the states of Massachusetts, Connecticut, New York, and Virginia, was organized by Congress into the Northwest Territory, July 13, 1787. The act of organization, called the Northwest Ordinance, placed the territory under a governor and three judges until the population should be large enough for real representative government. It also provided that the citizens of the territory should enjoy complete political and religious liberty, that a system of free public education should be introduced, that eventually from three to five new states should be carved out of the territory, and that slavery should forever be excluded from the domain.[1] Within a year colonists from Massachusetts, sent out by the Ohio Company, founded the town of Marietta in what is now southern Ohio, and, with the establishment of county government and courts, the Northwest Ordinance was put into operation (April, 1788). As the first law for the government of national territory, this ordinance declared that the extension of the power of the United States into the Western wilderness was to be at the same time the extension of the blessings of enlightenment, tolerance, and freedom. Daniel Webster, in a speech in the

---

[1] This territory was essentially the same as that reserved in Vergennes's plan of 1782 for further negotiations between England and the United States (see map, opposite p. 128). Out of it were formed later the states of Ohio, Indiana, Illinois, Michigan, and Wisconsin, with a small piece of Minnesota.

United States Senate forty years later, said, "I doubt whether any single law of any lawgiver ancient or modern has produced effects of more distinct and lasting character than the Ordinance of 1787."

"A More Perfect Union"

168. Proposals for a Stronger Government. The inadequacy of the Articles of Confederation was recognized from the beginning by some of the wisest of our statesmen. These Articles had been in operation (if one can speak of their "operating" at all) little more than a month when James Madison of Virginia proposed (April, 1781) that they should be amended so as to give the United States "full authority to employ force by sea as well as by land to compel any delinquent state to fulfill its federal obligations," or, in other words, to pay its share of the federal assessment. After the peace with England, two years later, Washington wrote in a circular letter to the governors of the states, "There should be lodged somewhere a supreme power to regulate the general concerns of the Confederated Republic, without which this Union cannot be of long duration." Again in 1784, he wrote, "I predict the worst consequences for a half-starved limping government, always moving on crutches, and tottering at every step." Finally, Congress itself officially proclaimed its inability to conduct the government under its meager powers, by supporting a proposal for a convention of delegates from all the states to revise the Articles of Confederation.

169. The Mount Vernon and Annapolis Conventions. The proposal had arisen out of an economic difficulty. Maryland and Virginia disputed the control of the Potomac River, and commissioners from these two states met as guests of Washington at Mount Vernon, in 1785, to settle the matter. In the course of the discussion it developed that the commercial interests of Pennsylvania and Delaware were also concerned, and the Virginia commissioners suggested that all the states be invited to send delegates to a convention at Annapolis, Maryland, the next year, to consider the commercial interests of the United States as a whole. But no sooner had the delegates of five states met at Annapolis in 1786 than they took a further important step. The New Jersey delegation had brought instructions to discuss the commercial question *and other important matters.*

Alexander Hamilton of New York, impressed by this phrase, proposed that still another convention of all the states be called at Philadelphia the next year for the general revision of the Articles of Confederation. Even before Congress sanctioned this proposal six of the states had appointed delegates, and after the approval of Congress was given six more states fell into line. Only little Rhode Island, fearing that her commerce would be ruined by national control and her representation overshadowed by the larger states in Congress, refused to send delegates to the convention.

170. The Constitutional Convention. It was an extraordinary array of political talent that was brought together in the convention which met in Independence Hall at Philadelphia in May, 1787, to devise a worthy government for the United States. John Adams and Thomas Jefferson were in Europe, as ministers to the courts of England and France respectively. John Jay was foreign secretary in Congress, and Patrick Henry and Samuel Adams, the foremost agitators of the American Revolution, were both opposed to strengthening the central government. But with these five exceptions the greatest men of the country were at the Philadelphia convention: Washington, Madison, Randolph, and Mason from Virginia; Franklin, Wilson, Robert and Gouverneur Morris from Pennsylvania; Roger Sherman and Oliver Ellsworth from Connecticut; Elbridge Gerry and Rufus King from Massachusetts; John Rutledge and Charles Pinckney from South Carolina; John Dickinson from Delaware; and Alexander Hamilton from New York. Washington was chosen president of the Convention. The sessions, which lasted from May 25 to September 17, were secret; but the methodical Madison took full notes of the debates, writing them out carefully every evening in the form of a journal. When he died fifty years later,— the last survivor of that remarkable gathering of men,— his widow sold the manuscript of this valuable journal, with other important Madison papers, to Congress for $30,000, and the journal was published at Washington in 1840.

171. The Virginia and New Jersey Plans. The Convention proceeded to give a very liberal interpretation to its instructions to "amend" the Articles of Confederation. The Virginia delegation brought in a plan for the entire remodeling of the government. There were to be three independent departments,— the legislative, the executive, and the judicial. The legislature was to consist of a House of Representatives elected by the people and a Senate elected by the House. The government, therefore, was to be *national*, deriving its power directly from the people of the nation at large, rather than a confederation, depending for its existence on the will of the various state legislatures. The small states, fearing that they would lose their individuality entirely in a national legislature elected in proportion to the population, supported a counter plan introduced by William Paterson of New Jersey. The New Jersey plan proposed to amend the Articles of Confederation, as did the Virginia plan, by the creation of executive and judicial departments and by giving Congress control of commerce and power to raise taxes. But the representatives in Congress were still to be representatives of the *states* and not of the *people* of the nation, and each state, large or small, was to have an equal number of delegates. In short, the existing confederation was to be perpetuated, with increased powers, to be sure, but still without the strength of a true *national* federation.

172. The Extremists. Then there were extremists on both sides. Some delegates, interpreting their instructions to "amend" the Articles very literally, left the Convention and went home when they saw that it was the intention of the members to change the nature of the government. On the other hand, Alexander Hamilton advocated a government in which the chief executive and the senators should hold office for life (like the English king and lords) and in which the executive should have power not only of vetoing state laws, as suggested in the Virginia plan, but also of appointing and removing the governors of the states, thus reducing the states to mere administrative departments of the national government, like the shires in England or the departments in France.

173. The "Great Compromise." The extremists found little following, however, in the Convention. The real struggle was between the Virginia and the New Jersey plan; that is, between a national federation and a mere confederacy of states. And on this question the Convention threatened to go to pieces, one party declaring that they would never consent to a government in which their states should be swallowed up, and the other with equal fervor declaring that they would not support a government in which the will of a large majority of the people of the United States could be thwarted by the selfish action of one or two small states, as it had been under the Articles of Confederation. Only the tact, patience, and persuasion of a few veteran statesmen like Benjamin Franklin, John Dickinson, and Roger Sherman, and the incomparable political wisdom and diligence in debate of James Madison, "the Father of the Constitution," finally succeeded in bringing about a series of compromises. The most important of these was on the form of the government. The states, large and small, were to preserve their equality of representation in the upper House of Congress (the Senate), while the members of the lower House (the House of Representatives) were to be elected by the people of the states, each state having a number of representatives in proportion to its population. As representatives of the people, the members of the lower House were to have control of the public purse, with the sole right to initiate legislation for the raising of revenue (taxation).

174. Further Compromises in the Constitution. When the great question of the general character of our government was settled by this first compromise, the other points of difference, most of which concerned the conflicting interests of the North and the South, were more easily adjusted. The Southern states demanded that their slaves (though they were not citizens) should be counted as population in the apportionment of representatives in Congress, that Congress should not interfere with the slave trade, and that a two-thirds vote of the House of Representatives should be necessary for passing tariff laws. Compromises were arrived at on all these questions. Three fifths of the slaves were to be included in making up the apportionment for Congress, so that a state with 100,000 white inhabitants and 50,000 slaves would be reckoned as having a population of 130,000. Congress was not to disturb the slave trade for twenty years, though it might levy a tax not exceeding ten dollars a head on slaves imported into the states. Finally, tariff laws were to be passed by a simple majority vote in the House, but no duties were to be levied on exports.

175. The Ratification of the Constitution. The Convention, after voting that the new Constitution should go into effect as soon as nine states had accepted it, sent the document to Congress, and Congress transmitted it to the several states for ratification. Delaware was the first to ratify the new Constitution, by a unanimous

THE CONSTITUTION

vote, December 7, 1787. By the twenty-first of the following June eight other states had ratified in the following order: Pennsylvania, New Jersey, Georgia, Connecticut, Massachusetts, Maryland, South Carolina, New Hampshire; and the Constitution thereupon became the supreme law for those states. Virginia and New York followed soon, ratifying by very narrow margins after bitter struggles in their conventions. North Carolina did not come under "the federal roof" until November, 1789, after Washington had been president for over six months. Rhode Island did not even send any delegates to the Constitutional Convention, and did not call any convention in the

The Ninth PILLAR erected !
"The Ratification of the Conventions of nine States, shall be sufficient for the establishment of this Constitution, between the States so ratifying the same." *Art.* vii.
INCIPIENT MAGNI PROCEDERE MENSES.

If it is not up it will rise.
The Attraction must be irresistible

DEL. PEN. N.JER. GEOR. CON. MASSA. MARY. S.CAROL NHAMP. VIRG. N.YORK

THE PROGRESS OF RATIFICATION
From an Old Chronicle

state to consider ratifying the Constitution, until the new Congress threatened to treat the state as a foreign nation and levy tariff duties on her commerce with the other states. Then she came to terms and entered the Union, May 29, 1790.

Some of the states (Delaware, New Jersey, Georgia) ratified the Constitution unanimously, but in others (Massachusetts, Virginia, Pennsylvania, New York) there was a severe struggle. A change of 10 votes in the Massachusetts convention of 355 members, or of 6 votes in the Virginia convention of 168, would have defeated the Constitution in these states. At Carlisle, Pennsylvania, shortly after the ratification of the Constitution there was rioting, with burning in effigy. After a long struggle in the convention at Poughkeepsie, New York, the Constitution was ratified by a vote of 30 to 27. The victory in New York was won only through the tireless advocacy of Alexander Hamilton, who loyally supported the Constitution, although, as we have seen, it did not satisfy him in some important respects. He made the campaign one of splendid political education through the anonymous publication (with the help of Madison and Jay) of a most remarkable set of essays called "The Federalist," explaining the nature of the new Constitution. In Virginia and Massachusetts such patriots as Richard Henry Lee, Patrick Henry, Samuel Adams, Elbridge Gerry, and John Hancock opposed the Constitution on the ground of its infringement on the powers of the states. Many of the farmer and debtor classes opposed it because of the unlimited power of taxation it gave to the central government. But when the ratification was finally assured, the American public forgot their differences and went wild with joy. Dinners, processions, illuminations, jollifications of every sort, followed each other in bewildering succession. Allegory was called to the aid of sober history. "The sloop *Anarchy*," declared one journal, "has gone ashore on the Union rock"; another said that "the old scow *Confederacy*, Imbecility master, had gone off to sea." "Federal punch" was a favorite brew in the taverns; "federal hats" were advertised in the shops; and "federal tobacco mixture" was smoked in patriot pipes.

176. The Constitution a Wonderful Achievement. By the adoption of the Constitution of the United States our country passed, without civil revolution or a military dictatorship, from anarchy to order, from weakness to strength, from death to life. Count Alexis de Tocqueville, our distinguished French visitor in 1833, and one of the keenest observers of our democratic institutions, wrote of this achievement: "It is new in the history of society to see a great people turn a calm and scrutinizing eye upon itself when apprized . . . that the wheels of its government are stopped; to see it carefully examine the extent of the evil and patiently wait two whole years until a remedy is discovered, to which it voluntarily submits without its costing a tear or a drop of blood from mankind."

The Federal Power[1]

177. The Constitution contrasted with the Articles of Confederation. This is the place to pause for a brief study of the wonderful instrument of government under which the United States has

[1] The text of the Constitution of the United States (Appendix II) should be carefully studied in connection with this section, which is virtually a commentary on it.

THE CAPITOL

lived for over a century and a quarter, and increased from a seaboard community of 4,000,000 to a continental nation numbering over 100,000,000. In contrast to the old government under the Articles of Confederation, the new Constitution was framed as a government "of the people, by the people, and for the people" of the United States. Whereas the members of the old Congress were appointed by their respective state legislatures, by whom they were recalled at pleasure, the members of the new House of Representatives, elected by the voters in congressional districts in every state, were to be servants of the nation, paid from its treasury to make laws for the good of the whole land. Whereas the president of the old Congress had been simply its presiding officer or moderator, the president of the United States under the new Constitution was given powers for the execution of the laws made by Congress,—powers extending into every corner of the land and greater than those enjoyed by most constitutional monarchs. And finally, whereas the old Congress provided for no permanent court to pronounce on the validity of its own laws or settle disputes at law between the various states, the new Constitution established a Supreme Court of the United States and gave Congress power to establish inferior national (or federal) courts throughout the Union.

178. The Three Departments of Government. The creation of these three independent departments of legislative, executive, and judicial power, reaching every citizen in every part of the land, was the fundamental achievement of the framers of the Constitution. The idea of the threefold division of power was not a new one, for the governments of the colonies had all consisted of lawmaking assemblies elected by the people, an executive appointed (except in Massachusetts, Connecticut, and Rhode Island) by king or proprietor, and courts of justice from which there was final appeal to the Privy Council of the king. But the task of adopting this triple plan of government on a national scale, while still preserving the individuality and even to a large extent the independence of the states, was a very difficult and delicate one.

179. The Legislative Department (Congress). The legislative department of our government is described in Article I of the Constitution, where the qualifications, length of term, method of election, duties and powers of the members of both Houses of Congress, are prescribed. The number of senators in every Congress is just twice the number of states in the Union, but the size of the House of Representatives is altered every ten years when a new census of the United States is taken. Congress then makes a new ratio of representation and a new apportionment of congressional districts for each state, according to its population. The present House (1920) contains 435 members, one for about every 212,000 of population. If the original ratio of 1 to 30,000 had been kept, the House would now contain about 2800 members.[1] A bill passed by both Houses of Congress becomes a law if the president signs it or if he lets ten days pass without signing or vetoing it. If the president vetoes a bill it still becomes a law if, on reconsideration, both Houses pass it by a two-thirds majority. If Congress passes a law which is not within its authority as granted by the Constitution (Art. I, sect. 8), the Supreme Court of the United States, when appealed to in any case to test that law, has the right and duty to declare the law void. The subjects on which Congress may legislate naturally include all those which concern the dignity and credit of the nation in the eyes of foreign powers, and its peace and security at home, namely: the regulation of commerce with foreign nations and between the states; the declaration of war and the direction of the military and naval forces of the country; the regulation of the currency and coinage; the control of territories and public lands; the care of the Indians, of rivers and harbors, lighthouses, coast survey, and all that pertains to shipping and defense. Moreover, the states are forbidden to exercise certain powers of sovereignty delegated to the national Congress. No state can make alliances, go to war, coin money, lay taxes on the commerce of another state, or make anything but gold and silver legal tender (lawful money) for the payment of debts.

180. The Powers left to the States. However, after deducting the powers delegated to Congress or expressly denied to the states, the latter have an immense field for legislation. Most of the things which especially interest the average citizen are affairs of the state government, namely: the protection of life and property; laws of marriage and inheritance; the chartering and control of business

---

[1] In the first House New York was allotted 6 representatives, Pennsylvania and Massachusetts 8 each, and Virginia 10. By the census of 1910 New York has 43 representatives, Pennsylvania 36, Massachusetts 16, and Virginia 10.

corporations, state banks, insurance and trust companies; the definition and punishment of crimes; the establishment of systems of public education; the creation of city, county, and town governments; and a host of other powers, political, moral, and social. Sometimes the field of jurisdiction between the national and the state power is hard to distinguish, but the decision of the Supreme Court is final in determining both the limits of the federal authority and the interpretation of the Constitution.

181. The Executive Department. The duty of putting into effect the laws of Congress is intrusted to the executive department of our government. Theoretically, the whole of this immense task falls on the president alone, who "shall take care that the laws be faithfully executed." Actually no man could do a hundredth part of the work of executing the hundreds of laws which Congress passes every session. To collect the duties and excises which Congress lays; to coin the money which it authorizes; to print and sell the bonds it issues; to command the armies it raises; to build and man the warships it votes; to appoint judges for the courts it erects; to handle the business of the post office; to carry into effect its agreements, political and economic, with the nations of the world; to govern its territories and dependencies in America, the West Indies, and the Pacific — all this calls for the labors of tens of thousands of secretaries, undersecretaries, and clerks in the various executive departments at Washington, and a host of federal officials in our seaports, our dockyards, our forts and arsenals, our islands and territories, and the capitals and chief commercial centers of foreign countries.

182. The Cabinet. Ten great executive departments have been created by Congress to perform these varied duties.[1] Every president, on coming into office, chooses the heads of these departments, and these ten secretaries form the president's "official family," or

---

[1] At the inauguration of the federal government there were but four departments: namely, State (Foreign Affairs), Treasury, War, and the Post Office. The following departments have been added as the business of government required them: Navy (1798), Interior (1849), Justice [the Attorney-General's department] (1870), Agriculture (1889), Commerce and Labor (1903), made into two separate departments (1913). The Attorney-General, or legal adviser of the president and prosecutor of suits brought by the United States, was a member of the president's cabinet from the inauguration of the government. On the other hand, though the Post-Office Department was organized in the colonial days, its head (the Postmaster-General) was not made a member of the cabinet until 1829.

cabinet. They are lieutenants of the president only, responsible to him alone, though they may be removed by the Senate if impeached and found guilty (Art. I, sect. 2, par. 5; Art. I, sect. 3, pars. 6, 7). Cabinet officers are not members of Congress (as ministers in Europe are), nor have they access to the floor of Congress. The president consults them in regular cabinet meetings as to the affairs of their departments, and, acting on their knowledge and advice, communicates with Congress by an annual message when the Houses assemble on the first Monday of each December, and by as many special messages during the session as he sees fit to send. Congress does not recognize the cabinet, but only the president. Laws on every subject go to him, not to the heads of departments, for signature. Appointments to executive and judicial offices, needing the consent of the Senate, are sent to that body not by the secretaries but by the president. He is the *only* executive officer recognized by the Constitution.

183. The Choice of a President. It was the intention of the framers of the Constitution to have the president, the most important servant of the government of the United States, chosen by a selected body of judicious men called "electors." Every state should choose, in the manner prescribed by its legislature, a number of men equal to that state's representation in Congress. The men so chosen were to assemble and vote for president and vice president.[1] Thus our chief executive was actually to be selected and elected by a small, carefully chosen body of men in each state. But the statesmen who planned this calm, judicious method of selecting a president did not foresee the intense party feeling that was to develop in the United States even before George Washington was out of the presidential chair. The party leaders began at once to select the candidates for president and vice president and have done so ever since.[2] The voters in each state still continue to cast their votes for presidential

[1] At first the electors did not vote for president and vice president separately, but simply marked two names on their ballots. The man who received the highest number of votes (if a majority of the whole number) became president, and the man with the next highest number vice president. Since this method of choice resulted in an embarrassing tie in the election of 1800, the Constitution was amended (Amendment XII) in 1804, so as to have each elector vote specifically for president and vice president.

[2] In the early years of the republic the candidates were selected by party caucuses in Congress or by the indorsement of the various state legislatures. About 1830 the national party "machines" were organized, and from that time great national conventions, engineered by these party machines, have met several months before each presidential election to nominate the candidates.

THE WHITE HOUSE

electors, but these electors do not *choose* the president. They simply register the vote of their state. In other words, each state, in choosing Republican or Democratic electors, simply *instructs those electors* to vote for the Republican or Democratic candidate who has been nominated months before by the national convention of the party. As soon, therefore, as the electors are voted for, in November, it is known which candidate has been elected president, without waiting for those electors to meet and cast their ballots the following January.

184. The Judicial Department. The judicial department of our government is the hardest to understand, because of the variety of courts and the double jurisdiction of national and state tribunals. Every citizen of the United States lives under two systems of law, national and state. For violation of national laws (the laws of Congress) he is tried in the federal (or national) courts; for violation of state laws he is tried in the state courts. The highest court in our judicial system is the United States Supreme Court, sitting at Washington, composed of a chief justice and eight associate justices, all appointed for life by the president, with the consent of the Senate, and removable only by the process of impeachment. This most dignified body in our government is invested with enormous power. Its decision is final in all cases brought to its jurisdiction from state or federal courts throughout the land.[1] It is the official interpreter and guardian of the Constitution. It has sole jurisdiction in cases affecting foreign ambassadors or ministers, and in cases between two states or between a state and the United States. But any case between corporations or individuals *involving the interpretation of a clause of the Constitution* may be appealed from the lower courts to its jurisdiction, and in the decision of such a case it has the right to nullify or declare void any law of Congress or of a state that it finds violating the Constitution.

185. The "Unwritten Laws" of the Constitution. There are many important features in the actual conduct of the government of the United States which are not mentioned in the Constitution at all. The president's cabinet, the national nominating conventions, and the instruction of electors to vote for the party's nominee for

---

[1] Congress has established federal courts in every state of the Union; and all the federal judges (now about one hundred in number) are appointed for life by the president, with the consent of the Senate. The judges of the state courts are either appointed by the governor (in a few of the older states) or elected by the people or the legislature for a term varying from two to twenty-one years.

president are examples that we have already noticed. Other customs which amount almost to "unwritten laws" of the Constitution are (1) the limitation of the president's office to two terms, an example set by Washington and never yet departed from; (2) "senatorial courtesy," which expects the president to follow the recommendation of the United States senators of his party in making federal appointments (judges, marshals, collectors of customs, important postmasters) in their respective states; (3) the power of the Speaker of the House of Representatives, who, by his influence in the choice of the committees and by "recognizing" on the floor of the House only such debaters as he chooses to, can exert considerable control over the legislation of Congress; (4) the transaction of practically all the business of Congress in committee rooms. In its earlier days Congress was a hall of debate in which national issues were threshed out by the greatest orators of the nation; but since the Civil War it has tended to become scarcely more than a great voting machine, run by the party in power. Few Americans have been in the habit of following the daily business of Congress as Englishmen follow the debates of their Parliament.

186. The Bill of Rights. Several of the states, notably Massachusetts, accepted the Constitution with the recommendation that amendments be added guaranteeing certain immemorial rights, such as liberty of speech and press, immunity from arbitrary arrest and cruel punishments, freedom of peaceable assembly, and the right to be tried by a jury of one's peers after a public hearing of witnesses on both sides. Ten amendments, constituting a Bill of Rights, were accordingly adopted by Congress and ratified by the states soon after the inauguration of the new government (November, 1791). The demand for these amendments shows that the states still regarded the central government with something of that jealous and cautious distrust with which they had viewed the officers of the British crown.

187. Amendments to the Constitution. Only nine amendments have been added to the Constitution since the passage of the Bill of Rights. Of these, two were slight revisions of clauses in the original articles, and three were occasioned by slavery and the Civil War. The Sixteenth Amendment (1913) gives Congress power to levy an income tax without regard to population; the Seventeenth (1913) provides for popular election of United States senators; the Eighteenth (1919) prescribes nation-wide prohibition; the Nineteenth

(1920) confers the suffrage throughout the country on women (who had already, in a campaign of seventy years, won the vote in about a score of states by state action). If the process of amending the Constitution were less complicated (see Art. V) we should probably have many more amendments, for proposals are constantly being agitated for changes in the Constitution, such as giving Congress the right to regulate corporations or to make laws governing marriage, divorce, and child labor, or providing for the election of the president for a single term or by a popular vote.

188. The "Implied Powers" of the Constitution. In the absence of specific amendments Congress is able to extend its authority pretty widely by stretching the so-called " elastic clause " of the Constitution, which, after the enumeration of specific powers of Congress, adds, " And to make all laws which shall be necessary and proper for carrying into execution the foregoing powers " (Art. I, sect. 8, par. 18). From the very earliest days of our government there have been parties with opposite views on the interpretation of this clause of the Constitution. The " strict constructionists " have held that the letter of the Constitution must be observed, and that Congress and the president must exercise only the powers *explicitly granted* to them in Articles I and II. On the other hand, the "loose constructionists," professing themselves equally devoted to the Constitution, have contended that the true interpretation of its spirit involves the assumption by the president and Congress of powers not explicitly granted, but evidently *intended* and *implied*. The recent industrial and commercial development of our country has made the question of the extent and power of the federal government a very vital one. For example, when the Constitution gives Congress the right to "regulate commerce among the several states" (Art. I, sect. 8, par. 3), does that power necessarily carry with it the regulation of the rates which railroads shall charge to carry goods from state to state, the regulation of the corporations which do a large business in and between many states, and even the regulation of the factories whose products go into all the states of the Union? Our rapid economic development has carried our great industries beyond the limits and control of the states. Can we respect the power of the states and still maintain the efficiency of our national government? That is the great question which today divides the advocates of federal extension and the critics of "federal usurpation."

References

The Critical Period: JOHN FISKE, *The Critical Period of American History*, chaps. ii–v; Old South Leaflets, Nos. 2 (The Articles of Confederation), 13, 127 (The Northwest Ordinance); A. C. MCLAUGHLIN, *The Confederation and the Constitution* (American Nation Series), chaps. iv–xi; J. B. MCMASTER, *History of the People of the United States*, Vol. I, chaps. i–v; EDWARD CHANNING, *History of the United States*, Vol. III, chaps. xiii–xv; E. M. AVERY, *History of the United States and its People*, Vol. VI, chap. xviii; A. B. HART, *American History told by Contemporaries*, Vol. III, Nos. 37–41, 46, 47, 52; THEODORE ROOSEVELT, *The Winning of the West*, Vol. III.

A More Perfect Union: FISKE, chaps. v–viii; MCLAUGHLIN, chaps. xii–xviii; *Cambridge Modern History*, Vol. VII, chap. viii; MAX FARRAND, *The Framing of the Constitution, Records of the Federal Convention*, and *The Fathers of the Constitution* (Chronicles, Vol. XIII); AVERY, Vol. VI, chap. xx; CHANNING, Vol. III, chap. xvi; C. A. BEARD, *Readings in American Government and Politics*, Nos. 14–21; Old South Leaflets, Nos. 70, 99, 186, 197; *The Federalist*, ed. PAUL LEICESTER FORD, Introduction, pp. vii–xxix, Nos. 2, 10, 15, 27, 85; HART, Vol. III, Nos. 60–75.

The Federal Power: B. MOSES, *The Government of the United States*, chaps. iv–vii; JAMES BRYCE, *The American Commonwealth* (abridged edition), chaps. iii–xxvi; R. L. ASHLEY, *The American Government*, pp. 204–355; S. E. FORMAN, *Advanced Civics*, pp. 115–161; *The Federalist*, Nos. 41–44, 52–82; BEARD, Nos. 55–158.

Topics for Special Reports

1. **The Northwest Ordinance:** WILLIAM MACDONALD, *Select Documents of American History, 1775–1861*, No. 4 (for text); FISKE, pp. 187–207; ROOSEVELT, Vol. III, pp. 231–276; Old South Leaflets, Nos. 13, 42; HART, Vol. III, Nos. 36, 42, 46; MCLAUGHLIN, pp. 108–122; B. A. HINSDALE, *The Old Northwest*, pp. 255–269; W. F. POOLE, in *The North American Review*, Vol. CXXII, pp. 229–265.

2. **The Opposition to the Constitution:** [in New York] *The Federalist*, Introduction, pp. xix–xxix; [in Massachusetts] S. B. HARDING, *Contest over Ratification in Massachusetts* (Harvard Historical Studies, 1896); [in general] HART, Vol. III, Nos. 70, 71, 73–75; MCLAUGHLIN, pp. 277–317; FISKE, pp. 306–345.

3. **The Powers of the Speaker of the House:** BEARD, Nos. 101–105; BRYCE, pp. 104–107; ANNA DAWES, *How we are Governed*, pp. 120–145; MARY FOLLETT, *The Speaker of the House*; HART, *Practical Essays in American Government*, No. 1; FRANKLIN PIERCE, *Federal Usurpation*, pp. 162–169.

4. **Our Foreign Relations under the Confederation:** MCLAUGHLIN, pp. 89–107; also *Western Posts and British Debts* (American Historical Association Report, 1894), pp. 413–444; MCMASTER, Vol. I, chaps. iii–iv; F. A. OGG, *The Opening of the Mississippi*, pp. 400–460; FISKE, pp. 131–144, 154–162.

CHAPTER VII

FEDERALISTS AND REPUBLICANS

Launching the Government

189. The United States in 1789. The United States which Washington was called upon to preside over in 1789, by the unanimous vote of the presidential electors, was a far different country from the United States of today. A free white population of 3,200,000, with 700,000 slaves,— considerably less altogether than the present population of New York City,— was scattered along the Atlantic seaboard from the rockbound coast of New England to the rice lands of Georgia. Philadelphia, the gay capital of the Confederation, had a population of 42,000. New York had about 32,000; Boston, Charleston, and Baltimore had passed the 10,000 mark. A small but steady immigration, chiefly of Scotch-Irish stock from Virginia and North Carolina, had followed Daniel Boone and John Sevier across the Alleghenies to found settlements in Kentucky and Tennessee. The census of 1790 estimated that 109,000 of these hardy frontiersmen were scattered through the rich valleys of the Ohio and Cumberland Rivers.

190. Industries and Commerce. What is now a land of factories and cities was then a land of forests and farms. Over 90 per cent of the inhabitants were tillers of the soil. Shipping and fishing were the only industries of importance. Manufactures, which, as we have seen, were discouraged by the mother country in colonial days, had made but little progress since the war. Our first Secretary of the Treasury, in a report on manufactures, two years after Washington's inauguration, could enumerate but seventeen industries which had reached a fair degree of development, chief among them being iron, leather, pottery, textiles, tools, and hardware. But money, capital, and free labor were scarce, while land was abundant and the foreign demand for foodstuffs constant. Moreover, England, by those inventions and improvements in spinning, weaving, mining, transportation, and the application of steam power to manufacture, which are known as the Industrial Revolution, had gained a prestige in industry which made her the workshop of the world. It was profitable for us to buy her manufactured goods with our agricultural products, and it fitted our habits as a people of farmers and traders. Our ships were already engaged in successful voyages to China, India, and the coast of Africa. Washington's first Congress passed laws favoring our commerce. A rebate of 10 per cent on the customs duties was allowed on goods imported in American ships, while the tonnage

EARLY RIVER STEAMBOAT

dues in our ports on foreign-owned vessels ranged from 30 to 50 cents a ton as against 6 cents a ton on American-owned vessels.

191. Travel and Transportation. Travel was infrequent in Washington's day. The roads were scarce and poor, and the inns crude and comfortless. The lumbering, springless stagecoach, with its stifling leathern curtains for protection against wind and rain, was the only means of transportation for those whose business prevented them from traveling by water, or whose health or circumstances made impossible the journey by horseback. In any case, the means of transportation at the end of the eighteenth century showed no essential improvement in comfort or speed over those of two thousand years earlier,— the horse, the sailboat, and the stage. The journey of a Roman official from Asia Minor to Italy in fourteen days, over the splendid roads of the Roman Empire, could not have been duplicated anywhere in America, or even in Europe, in the year 1800. Men were already experimenting with the propulsion of boats and wagons by steam, devising queer craft with paddling oars and vehicles with rattling chains, but it was to be some years still before the steamboat and the locomotive ushered in the age of rapid transit.

192. The Sale of Public Lands. A few years before Washington's inauguration Congress opened to sale the public domain west of the Alleghenies. The plan favored at first was the disposal of tracts reaching into millions of acres to land companies (the Ohio and Scioto) or to private speculators (the Symmes grant) who undertook to colonize the land with settlers from the states and from Europe. But the more successful method, suggested by Thomas Jefferson, was the laying out of townships six miles square, divided like a checkerboard into 36 sections of a square mile (or 640 acres) each. These sections were sold in Philadelphia at auction, at not less than $1 an acre. Later (1796, 1800) land offices were opened in Western towns, like Pittsburgh and Cincinnati; half sections were sold at $2 an acre, and purchasers were allowed liberal credit. Later still (1820) the price was reduced to $1.25 (cash) per acre, and parcels as small as 80 acres were sold. The government's encouragement of Western settlement was one of the most important facts in our history. We shall see in later chapters how the hardy, democratic people of the West influenced our political and social development.

193. Social Conditions. Society in the American cities jealously guarded the distinctions of high birth and good breeding. Powdered wigs, silver buckles, liveried footmen, stately courtesy of speech and manners, were the marks of the social aristocracy. But for all its brave show it was a harmless aristocracy. The wide gulf which today separates fabulous wealth from sordid poverty did not exist in the United States of 1789. Our visitors from Europe, especially the Frenchmen, were impressed with the general diffusion of moderate prosperity in America and were filled with prophetic hopes that this land would be forever a model of democracy to the "caste-ridden" countries of Europe.

194. The Inauguration of the Government. The first Wednesday in March (March 4), 1789, had been appointed by the old Congress of the Confederation as the day for the assembling of the new

Congress of the United States. On the third of March the guns of New York fired a parting salute to the old government, and on the next morning a welcoming salute to the new. But both salutes stirred only empty echoes; for the old Congress had ceased to meet some months before, and the new Congress was not ready to organize for nearly a month to come. Poor roads, uncertain conveyances, and the lateness of the elections had prevented more than half of the twenty-two senators[1] and three fourths of the fifty-nine congressmen from reaching New York City, the temporary capital, on the appointed day. It took the entire month of April for the Houses to organize, to count the electoral vote, notify Washington formally of his election, and witness the ceremony of his inauguration as first president of the United States (April 30). Washington's journey from his fine estate of Mount Vernon, on the Potomac, to the city of New York was one long ovation. The streets were strewn with flowers. Triumphal arches, dinners, speeches, cheers, and songs gave him the grateful assurance that his inestimable services in war and peace were appreciated by his countrymen. His characteristic response showed no elation of pride, but only a deepened sense of responsibility in his new office. "I walk on untrodden ground," he wrote; "there is scarcely any action the motive of which may not be subjected to a double interpretation; there is scarcely any part of my conduct that may not hereafter be drawn into precedent." All eyes were upon him. His task was immense. He had to create the democratic dignity of the president's office, to choose wise counselors, to appoint upright and able judges, to hold factions in check, to deal wisely with the representatives of foreign powers, to set a precedent for the relations of the executive to Congress, to preserve the due forms of official ceremony without offending republican principles; and it needed every particle of his wisdom, his tact, his patience, his zeal, to accomplish the task.

195. Thomas Jefferson, Secretary of State. After some entreaty Washington prevailed on Thomas Jefferson to give up his diplomatic position as minister to France and become Secretary of State in the first cabinet. Jefferson was a great statesman and scholar, with an intense faith in the sound common sense of the people, and an equally

---

[1] North Carolina and Rhode Island did not come into the Union until some months after Washington's inauguration.

strong distrust of a powerful executive government. Sometimes his enthusiasm led him to extreme statements, as, for example, that a revolution every twenty years or so was good for a nation; but his practice was more moderate than his theory, and he never actually encouraged or supported any revolution except the great one which made us an independent nation.

196. Alexander Hamilton, Secretary of the Treasury. For Secretary of the Treasury Washington chose Alexander Hamilton, a native of the British island of Nevis in the West Indies, who had come to New York for his education at King's (Columbia) College in 1769 and ardently embraced the American cause. He served as Washington's aid-de-camp during the Revolution, sat in the convention that framed the Constitution, and, by his brilliant essays in "The Federalist" and debates in the New York convention, secured almost single-handed the ratification of the Constitution by his state. He differed absolutely from Jefferson on every question of the interpretation of the Constitution and the policy of the government. The two men, each convinced of the justice and necessity of his own view, glared at each other across the cabinet table and even on occasions rose trembling with rage, ready to lay violent hands on each other. Each begged the President to choose between them and let the other resign. But Washington prevailed on them both to remain in the cabinet during his first administration.

197. The Business before Congress. An immense and varied mass of business confronted the first Congress of the United States in creating the departments of government (State, Treasury, War), establishing courts and post offices, subduing hostile Indians, sifting the proposed amendments to the Constitution (of which ten were adopted), taking the census, fixing salaries, and voting appropriations. But the most urgent business of all was the adjustment of the country's finances. Alexander Hamilton occupies the center of the stage in Washington's first administration. The brilliant young Secretary of the Treasury had two great problems to handle, namely, the establishment of the credit of the United States, and the providing of an adequate income to meet the expenses of the government. How well he solved these problems we may learn from the ornate eulogy bestowed on him forty years later by Daniel Webster: "He smote the rock of the national resources, and abundant streams of revenue gushed forth. He touched the dead corpse of Public Credit, and it sprang upon its feet."

198. The Debt of the United States. The debt of the United States in 1789 was $54,000,000. About $12,000,000 of this was owed to France and Holland, who had been our allies in the Revolutionary War; and the remainder was a domestic debt, mostly in the form of certificates of the government promising to pay the holder the amount named on the paper. Now everybody agreed that the good faith of the United States demanded that every dollar of the foreign debt should be paid. But Hamilton's proposal to pay the domestic debt as well, at its full face value, was strenuously resisted. During the weak administration of the Confederation the certificates, or the government's promises to pay, had fallen far below the value named on their face. Honest debtors had been forced to part with these government certificates at only a fraction of their value, and shrewd money changers had bought them up as a speculation. It was even hinted by Hamilton's enemies that he had given his friends and political supporters advance information that he was going to pay the full value of the certificates, and so enabled them to buy up the paper and make enormous profits out of the government. In spite of the fact that it enriched some rascals at the expense of the community at large, Hamilton insisted that the full faith of the United States be kept, and that the certificates be redeemed at their face value. It would be the only way, he argued, to prevent future holders from selling at a discount our government's pledges to pay. He was right. Since his day the credit of the United States has been so sound that its bonds, or promises to pay at a future date, have generally been as good as gold.

199. The "Assumption" of the Debts of the States. Besides paying the national debt in full, Hamilton insisted that the government should assume the debts (amounting to about $20,000,000) which the various states had incurred in the Revolutionary War. This policy of "assumption" was a very shrewd one, for, by making the national government responsible for the country's whole debt, it taught creditors both at home and abroad to regard the United States as a single political power, greater than the sum of its parts, the states. It made possible a uniform rate of interest and standard of security for all the public debt; and, as men are always interested

ALEXANDER HAMILTON

in the prosperity of those who owe them money, it rallied the rich investing classes to the support of the national government.

200. A Tariff Levied. To meet the interest on the $75,000,000 made by adding the state debts to the full face value and unpaid interest of the old national debt under the Confederation, an annual revenue of over $4,500,000 was needed. Hamilton proposed to raise this money by an excise tax on distilled liquors and by a tariff, or customs duties levied on imported goods. As our foreign trade was large, a tariff averaging less than 10 per cent was sufficient to meet the demand. Besides providing a revenue for running the government, the duties levied on imported goods would encourage native manufactures by "protecting" them against European competition. Our country would thus cease to be an almost purely agricultural community, with the limited outlook and interests of a farming people; cities would grow up, and the various fields of enterprise opened by manufacture and commerce would give employment to people of varied talents, would attract immigrants from foreign countries, and would promote inventiveness and alertness in our population.

201. A National Bank Chartered. The crowning feature of Hamilton's financial system was the establishment of a National Bank, chartered by Congress to act as the government's agent and medium in its money transactions. The Bank was to have the privilege of holding on deposit all the funds of the United States collected from customs duties, the sale of public lands, or other sources; $2,000,000 of the $10,000,000 of the Bank's capital was to be subscribed by the United States, and its notes were to be accepted in payment of all debts owed the United States. In return for these favors the Bank was to manage all the government loans, was to be ready in time of financial stress to furnish aid to the Treasury of the United States, and was to be subject to the general supervision of the national government through reports on its condition submitted not oftener than weekly to the Secretary of the Treasury.

202. Opposition to Hamilton's Policy. The whole financial program of Hamilton met with bitter antagonism. Assumption was opposed by states like Virginia and North Carolina, which through the sale of their Western lands had nearly paid off their debts. The excise was resented by the farmers, who found the most profitable and convenient disposition of their grain in its conversion into whisky. The tariff was opposed by the purely agricultural states of the South, which contended that the government had no business to encourage one form of industry (manufactures) in preference to another (farming). The Bank was opposed on the ground that Congress was nowhere in the Constitution given the power to create a corporation and to favor it with a monopoly of the government's financial business. In his famous reports and recommendations to Congress in the years 1790 and 1791 Hamilton argued his cause with such force and brilliancy that he overcame opposition and put his whole program through; although in some instances, as in the case of "assumption," only by the narrowest majorities.

203. The First Political Parties. The result of Hamilton's policy was the division of the cabinet, Congress, and the country at large into two well-defined parties, one led by himself (to which both Washington and the vice president, John Adams, inclined), the other led by Jefferson. Hamilton's followers were called Federalists, because they advocated a strong federal (central) government as opposed to the state governments. The Jeffersonian party took the name Democratic-Republican, from which they very soon dropped the "Democratic" part, as the word was brought into disrepute by extreme revolutionists in France. The Republican party of Jefferson's day (to be carefully distinguished from the present Republican party, which was organized in 1854 in opposition to the extension of negro slavery) had its chief following in the Southern states. It favored agriculture as against manufactures and commerce. It advocated the "strict construction" of the Constitution; that is, the rigid limitation of Congress to the exercise of those powers expressly granted to it by the Constitution. It opposed the perpetuation of a national debt which had to be supported by popular taxation. Finally, the Republicans had confidence in the people at large to conduct the greater part of the business of government in their local institutions of state, county, and town; whereas the Federalists believed that a part of the people, "the rich, the well-born, and the able," as John Adams wrote, should govern the rest.

204. Antagonism between Hamilton and Jefferson. Jefferson's ideal, in a word, was a government for the people and by the

WASHINGTON'S HOME AT MOUNT VERNON

people, while Hamilton's ideal was a government for the people by the trained statesmen allied with the great property holders. The former is the democratic ideal, the latter the aristocratic ideal. In varying degrees of intensity these two conceptions of government have been arrayed against each other through the entire history of our country. Party names have changed; men have called themselves Federalists, Republicans, Democrats, Whigs, Populists, Socialists; parties have emphasized scores of "paramount issues," such as a national bank, the tariff, state rights, curbing the trusts, the free coinage of silver, and the government ownership of the railroads. But underneath all these party issues lies the fundamental antagonism of the Jeffersonian and the Hamiltonian principles—the rule of the people or the rule of the chosen few; jealous limitation of the power of the central government or generous extension of it.

The Reign of Federalism

205. The Reëlection of Washington. As the election of 1792 approached, Washington wished to exchange the cares of the presidency for his beloved acres of Mount Vernon, on the banks of the Potomac. But he yielded to Hamilton's entreaty and became a candidate for a second term. The financial policy of the Secretary of the Treasury had aroused bitter antagonism, and was rapidly consolidating the opposition party of Republicans, headed by Thomas Jefferson. If the strong hand of Washington should be withdrawn from the government at this critical moment, the work of three years might be ruined by the strife of parties before it had had time to prove its worth. Washington was the only man above the party discord. His election was again unanimous, but the Republican party proved its strength throughout the country by electing a majority to the House of Representatives of the third Congress (1793–1795).

206. The French Revolution. Washington had scarcely taken the oath of office a second time when news came of events in France which were to plunge Europe into twenty years of incessant warfare, to color the politics of the United States during the whole period, and even to involve us in actual wars with both France and England. The French people accomplished a wonderful revolution in the years 1789–1791. They reformed State and Church by sweeping away many oppressive privileges and age-long abuses by the nobles and the clergy. But the enthusiasm for reform degenerated into a passion for destruction. Paris and the French government fell into the hands of a small group of ardent radicals, who overthrew the ancient monarchy, guillotined their king and queen, and inaugurated a "reign of terror" through the land by the execution of all those who were suspected of the slightest leanings toward aristocracy. The revolutionary French Republic undertook a defiant crusade against all the thrones of Europe, to spread the gospel of "liberty, equality, and fraternity." In the summer of 1793 it was at war with Prussia, Austria, England, and several minor kingdoms of western Europe.

207. Washington's Proclamation of Neutrality. Now France was our ally. Her government had been the first in Europe to recognize the independence of the United States, by the treaties of commerce and alliance of 1778. Her king had lent us large sums of money, and sent us men and ships, in the hope that he was contributing to the downfall of the British Empire. The treaty of alliance of 1778 pledged us to aid France in the defense of her possessions in the West Indies if they were attacked by a foreign foe, and to allow her the use of our ports for the ships she captured in war. But did the treaty with Louis XVI's government, made for mutual defense against England, pledge us, after both parties had made peace with England (1783), to support the French faction which had overthrown Louis XVI's government? The President thought not. Accordingly, with the unanimous assent of his cabinet, Washington issued on April 22, 1793, a proclamation of neutrality, which declared that it was the policy of the United States to keep aloof from the complicated hostilities of Europe.

208. Reasons for our Neutrality. The proclamation of neutrality was prompted by the state of our own country as well as by that of Europe. On our northwestern frontier the British were still in possession of a line of valuable fur posts extending along our side of the Great Lakes from Oswego to Mackinac, and were secretly encouraging the Indians to dispute the occupation of the Ohio valley with the emigrants from the Atlantic seaboard. To the south and southwest the Spaniards were inciting the Creeks and Cherokees of Florida against the inhabitants of Georgia and, by closing the mouth of the Mississippi to our western shipping, were tempting the pioneers of Kentucky and Tennessee from their allegiance to the United States. To have joined France in her war against England and Spain, therefore, would have been to let loose the horrors of Indian massacre on our borders,[1] to risk the permanent loss of our trading posts on the Great Lakes, and perhaps to throw the pioneer communities of the southwest into the arms of Spain, who offered them free use of the great river for the transportation of their hogs and grain. Neutrality was an absolute necessity for the maintenance of our territory and the amicable settlement of disputes then pending with our neighbors England and Spain.

209. "Citizen" Edmond Genêt. A few days before the proclamation of neutrality was issued "Citizen Genêt" arrived at Charleston, South Carolina, as minister of the French Republic to the United States. Genêt had no idea that America could remain neutral. He was coming quite frankly in order to use our ports as the base of naval war against the British West Indies, and to instruct this government in its proper conduct as the ally of the "sister republic" of France. His journey from Charleston to Philadelphia was a continuous ovation of feasting, oratory, and singing of the "Marseillaise" by the Republicans, who hated England as the source of the "aristocratic" ideas of Hamilton and the other Federalists. Genêt was vain and rash. His head was turned by Republican adulation. His conduct became outrageous for a diplomat. He issued his orders to the French consuls in America as if they were his paid agents and spies. He used the columns of the Republican press for frenzied appeals to faction. He scolded our President and secretaries for not learning from him the true meaning of democracy. He defied the proclamation of neutrality by openly bringing captured British ships into our ports and fitting them out as privateers to prey on English commerce in the West Indies. He even addressed his petulant letters to Washington, and when reminded by the Secretary of State

[1] The Indians south of Lake Erie, already excited over the immigration of the whites into Ohio, had ambushed a force of 1400 led by General St. Clair in 1791 and allowed but 50 to escape from the field uninjured. Lord Dorchester, governor of Canada, openly encouraged the Indian chiefs, telling them that war between England and America was imminent and that the Americans would be driven off the Indian lands. In the autumn of 1794 General Anthony Wayne defeated the Indians severely in the battle of the Fallen Timbers (sixty miles south of Detroit) and compelled them by the Treaty of Greenville (1795) to relinquish most of Ohio to the whites.

that the President did not communicate directly with ministers of foreign countries, he threatened to appeal to the people of the United States to judge between George Washington and himself. Such conduct was too impertinent for even the warmest Republican sympathizers with France to stand. At the request of the administration Genêt was dismissed. His behavior had brought discredit on the extreme Republicans and strengthened the hands of the Federalists.

210. Strained Relations with Great Britain. A more serious problem for the administration of Washington than the maintenance of neutrality was the preservation of peace with England. We have already seen how British garrisons still held fortified posts on our shores of the Great Lakes. The value of the fur trade at the posts was over $1,000,000 annually, and the excuse Great Britain gave for not surrendering them was that American merchants owed large debts in England at the time of the treaty of 1783, which our government had not compelled them to pay. We, on our side, complained that the British, on the evacuation of our seaports at the close of the Revolution, had carried off a number of our slaves in their ships; had closed the West Indian ports to our trade; had refused to send a minister to our country; and, at the outbreak of the war with France in 1793, had begun to stop our merchantmen on the high seas to search them for deserters from the British navy, and had actually "impressed" into British service many genuine American citizens. The exasperated merchants of New England joined with the Republican friends of France in demanding war with England. A bill to stop all trade with Great Britain (a "Nonintercourse Act") was defeated in the Senate only by the casting vote of Vice President Adams, who wrote that many in the country were "in a panic lest peace should continue." At a hint from Washington, Congress would have declared war on Great Britain.

211. The Jay Treaty. But Washington was determined to have peace. He nominated John Jay, Chief Justice of the Supreme Court, as special envoy to Great Britain to negotiate a new treaty. Jay sailed in May, 1794, and returned about a year later with the best terms he could obtain from the British ministry. England agreed to evacuate the fur posts by the first of June, 1796, and to submit to arbitration the questions of disputed boundaries, damages to

American shipping, and the debts due British merchants; but she refused to make any compensation for the stolen slaves, and made such slight concessions to our trade in the West Indies that the Senate threw out that clause of the treaty entirely. On one of the most important points, the forcible arrest and search of our vessels for the impressment of seamen, the treaty was silent. A storm of opposition greeted the treaty in America. Those who wanted Jay to fail in order that the war with England might be renewed and those who wanted him to succeed in securing advantageous terms from England were both disappointed. Jay, who was one of the purest statesmen in American history, was accused of selling his country for British gold and was burned in effigy from Massachusetts to Georgia. Hamilton was stoned in the streets of New York for speaking in favor of the treaty. Even Washington did not escape censure, abuse, and vilification. However, the President was persuaded that the terms of the treaty were the best that could be obtained, and his influence barely secured the necessary two-thirds vote of the Senate to ratify it (June 24, 1795).

JOHN JAY

212. The Pinckney Treaty with Spain. The same year that war with England was averted Thomas Pinckney was sent as special envoy to the court of Spain, and there negotiated an important treaty by which Spain recognized the thirty-first parallel as the boundary between Florida and the United States and granted us the free navigation of the Mississippi together with the "right of deposit" at New Orleans. This last provision meant that we could unload our river boats and transfer the cargoes to ocean-going vessels without payment of duty.

213. The End of Washington's Administration. Thus Washington closed the critical years of his second administration at peace with the world. In a Farewell Address to the people of America, published six months before his retirement from office, he warned the country against the spirit of faction at home and "permanent alliances with any part of the foreign world." He had attempted

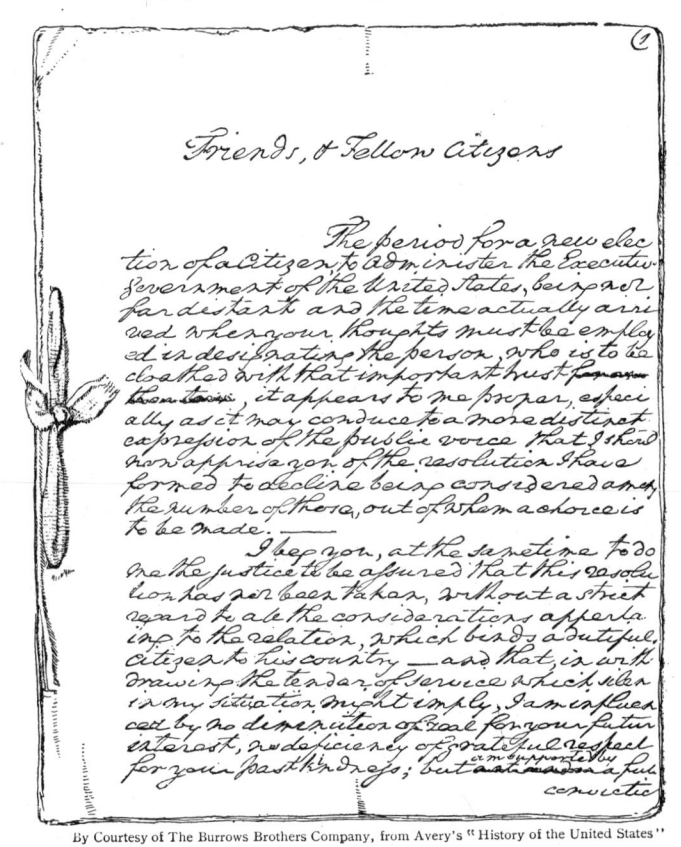

FACSIMILE OF THE FAREWELL ADDRESS

to give the country a nonpartisan administration, but during his second term he had inclined more and more to Federalist principles. Jefferson and Randolph, the two Republican members of his cabinet, had resigned, and their places had been taken by Federalists. Determined that the laws of Congress should be obeyed in every part of every state of the Union, the administration had summoned the militia of Pennsylvania, New Jersey, Maryland, and Virginia, fifteen thousand strong, to march against certain riotous counties in western Pennsylvania, where the taxes on whisky distilleries were resisted and the United States excise officers attacked.[1] The Republicans opposed the administration at every step. The press on both sides became coarse and abusive. Washington was reviled in language fit to characterize a Nero. "Tyrant," "dictator," and "despot" were some of the epithets hurled at him. He was called the "stepfather of his country," and the day was hailed with joy by the Republican press when this impostor should be "hurled from his throne." The election of 1796 was a bitter party struggle, in which the Federalist candidate, John Adams, won over Thomas Jefferson by only three electoral votes (71 to 68).

214. The "X Y Z Affair." A bitter quarrel with France filled Adams's administration. The Directory, as the government of the French Republic during the period 1795-1799 was called, resenting the refusal of their ally and "sister republic" of America to join in the war against aristocratic Britain and incensed by the Jay Treaty, declined to receive our minister C. C. Pinckney (December, 1796) and even ordered him to leave the soil of France. Adams addressed a special session of Congress in a message in which he declared that such conduct "ought to be repelled with a decision which should convince France and the world that we are not a degraded people, humiliated under a colonial spirit of fear." Still Adams desired peace, and, on a hint from Talleyrand, the French Minister of Foreign Affairs, that an embassy would be received to discuss the political and commercial disputes between the two countries, he appointed John Marshall of Virginia and Elbridge Gerry of Massachusetts to join Pinckney in negotiating a settlement with France. But the envoys were treated even worse than the minister had been. Talleyrand sent three private citizens to them as agents, demanding that before any negotiations were opened Adams should apologize to France for the language of his message to Congress, and that a large

---

[1] The "Whisky Rebellion" (1794) collapsed in the face of this prompt action by the government, and Washington, who had marched in person part of the way with the army, returned in relief to the capital. The Republicans alternately ridiculed the administration for its elaborate military preparations against a "few irate farmers," and censured it for being willing to shed the blood of American citizens over a few barrels of stolen whisky.

JOHN ADAMS

sum of money should be paid into the private purses of the directors. Two of the American commissioners then left Paris in disgust.[1]

215. A State of War with France. Adams sent a strong message to Congress, declaring that he had done everything in his power to preserve the peace. "I will never send another minister to France," he said, "without assurances that he will be received, respected, and honored as the representative of a great, free, powerful, and independent nation." The great majority of Americans heartily applauded the language of the President and joined in the new patriotic song "Hail, Columbia," with "huzzas for Adams and Liberty." Preparations for war were begun. Eighty thousand militia were held in readiness for service and George Washington was called to the chief command, with Hamilton and Knox as his major generals. The Navy Department was created and ships of war were laid down. Congress did not actually declare war on the French Republic, but it abrogated the treaties of 1778 and authorized our ships to prey upon French commerce. From midsummer of 1798 to the close of the following year a state of war with France existed, and several battles were fought at sea. Then Napoleon Bonaparte overthrew the Directory and made himself master of France. Napoleon desired peace with America; he had enemies enough in Europe. He signified his willingness to come to an agreement with the United States, and President Adams, to the great disappointment of the Federalists, who were bent on war, but to his own lasting honor as a patriot, accepted Napoleon's overtures and concluded a fair convention (treaty) with France in February, 1801. At the beginning of the new century we were again at peace with the world.

216. The Alien and Sedition Acts. But the government had already passed from the Federalists. In the heyday of their power, in the exciting summer of 1798, they had carried through Congress a set of laws designed to silence opposition to the administration. A Naturalization Act increased from five to fourteen years the term of residence in the United States necessary to make a foreigner a citizen. An Alien Act gave the president power for a term of two years "to order all such aliens as he should judge dangerous to the

---

[1] This insulting attempt to bribe the American commissioners is called the "X Y Z Affair," because the three French agents were designated by those letters, instead of by name, in the published dispatches of our State Department.

peace and safety of the United States . . . to depart out of the territory of the United States." A Sedition Act, to be valid till the close of Adams's administration, provided that anyone writing or publishing "any false, scandalous, and malicious writings" against the government, either House of Congress, or the president, "or exciting against them the hatred of the good people of the United States, to stir up sedition," should be punished by a fine not exceeding $2000 and by imprisonment not exceeding two years. These Alien and Sedition acts were opposed by John Marshall, Alexander Hamilton, and other clear-sighted Federalists; but in the hysterical war fever of 1798 any legislation directed against French immigrants and the unbridled insolence of the Republican press was sure to pass.

217. The Virginia and Kentucky Resolutions. The Republicans immediately took up the challenge of the Alien and Sedition acts. The legislatures of Kentucky and Virginia passed resolutions in November and December, 1798, prepared by Jefferson and Madison respectively. The former declared the Sedition Act "altogether void and of no effect"; and the latter characterized the acts as "alarming infractions of the Constitution," which guarantees freedom of speech and of the press (First Amendment). Kentucky and Virginia invited the other states to join with them in denouncing the acts and demanding their repeal at the next session of Congress. These resolutions are of great importance as the first assertion of the power of the states, through their legislatures, to judge whether the laws passed by Congress are valid (constitutional) or not.

218. The Downfall of the Federalists. The Alien and Sedition acts furnished fine campaign material for the Republicans, who could now change their poor rôle of champions of France for the popular cause of the defense of the Constitution and the dignity of the states. Aided by dissensions in the Federalist party between the followers of Hamilton and those of Adams, the Republicans carried the presidential election of 1800 for Jefferson and Burr, and secured a majority in the new Congress. The Federalists had bent the bow of authority too far, and it snapped. They never regained control of the government, although they continued to put a presidential candidate in the field and to poll a few votes until the election of 1816.

219. Attempt to keep Jefferson out of the Presidency. The last acts of the Federalists before their retirement on the fourth of

FEDERALISTS AND REPUBLICANS

March, 1801, showed a somewhat petty and tricky party spirit. Every Republican elector had written the names of Jefferson and Burr on his ballot, meaning, of course, that Jefferson should be president and Burr vice president. But as the Constitution then stood, the two men were technically tied for first place (see pages 150–151). Burr was an ambitious politician, and, though he knew that the electors did not intend to make him president, he would not withdraw in favor of Jefferson. The House of Representatives, with whom the choice lay (Constitution, Art. II, sect. 1, par. 2), was the Federalist House elected in the exciting year 1798. Many of the members voted for Burr, solely to keep the Republican leader out of the presidential chair. But after a long contest Jefferson finally won.

220. The "Midnight Judges." The Federalists, having lost control of the executive and legislative branches of the government by the elections of 1800, made a desperate attempt to hold the judicial branch at least. In its closing days the Federalist Congress created several new United States judgeships, many more than the judicial business of the country demanded, and the President filled the offices with stanch Federalists. These new officers were nicknamed the "midnight judges," because Adams was occupied until far into the evening of his last day of office (March 3, 1801) in signing their commissions. Early the next morning he left the White House without waiting to greet the incoming president.

221. Services of the Federalist Statesmen. In spite of their ungracious acts in the last days of their power, the Federalists had governed well. On the day of Jefferson's inauguration the *Columbian Centinel* of Boston, the leading Federalist paper in New England, published a long list of the benefits which that party had bestowed on the nation: peace secured with England, France, and Spain; credit restored abroad and the finances set in order at home; a navy created, domestic manufactures encouraged, and foreign trade stimulated. It pointed with just pride to the honest, able, courageous administrations of Washington and Adams; the constructive statesmanship of Hamilton and Gouverneur Morris; the diplomatic skill of Jay, Marshall, and the Pinckneys. The services of these men to the country were great and lasting.

THE JEFFERSONIAN POLICIES

222. The New Capital, Washington. The White House, which John Adams left so unceremoniously on the morning of the day Thomas Jefferson entered it, was a big, square, unfinished building, more like the quarters of a cavalry regiment than the residence of the chief executive of a nation. Thrifty Abigail Adams wrote to a friend that a retinue of thirty servants would be needed to run the house when it was finished; and meanwhile she dried the presidential washing in the unplastered East Room during stormy weather. The city of Washington, to which the seat of government had been moved from Philadelphia in the summer of 1800,[1] was itself as crude and unfinished as the president's mansion. A couple of executive buildings stood near the White House, and more than a mile to the eastward the masons were at work on the wings of the Capitol. Instead of the stately Pennsylvania Avenue which now connects the Capitol and the White House, there was a miry road running across a sluggish creek. The residential part of the city consisted of a few cheerless boarding houses for the accommodation of the members of Congress, exiled to these wastes from the gay city of Philadelphia. "We need nothing here," wrote Gouverneur Morris, "but houses, men, women, and other little trifles of the kind to make our city perfect."

223. Jefferson's Political Views. The new President, with his large, loose figure, his careless carriage, his ill-fitting and snuff-stained apparel, his profuse and informal hospitality, presented as great a contrast to the stately poise and ceremony of Washington and Adams as the crude city on the Potomac did to the settled colonial dignity of Philadelphia. Jefferson hated every appearance of "aristocracy." His confidence was in the plain people of America. He wanted to see them continue a plain agricultural people, governing themselves in their local assemblies. The national government at Washington should confine itself, he thought, to managing our dealings with foreign nations, a comparatively small task which

---

[1] The states of Maryland and Virginia presented the government a tract of land ten miles square on the Potomac. Congress named the tract the District of Columbia. The city of Washington was built on the northern side of the river on the Maryland cession, and the land to the south of the Potomac was retroceded to Virginia in 1846.

THOMAS JEFFERSON

could be performed by a few public servants. Army and navy were to be reduced, the public revenue was to be applied to paying the debt which the wicked war scares of the Federalists had rolled up, and the government was no longer, as Jefferson phrased it, to "waste the labors of the people under the pretense of taking care of them." Still Jefferson showed no desire to revolutionize the government, as some of the New England Federalists thought he would. In his inaugural address, which was couched in a dignified and conciliatory tone, he declared that Federalists and Republicans were one in common devotion to their country. He praised our government as a "successful experiment," and himself built on the foundations which the Federalists had laid. The Alien and Sedition laws expired with Adams's administration, and when the new Republican Congress had turned out the "midnight judges" by the repeal of the Judiciary Act, restored the five-year period for naturalization, and repealed the excise taxes, there was little to distinguish it from the Congresses of Washington's administration. The tariff was retained, and the Bank was not disturbed. But strict economy was introduced in the expenditures of the government by the new Secretary of the Treasury, Albert Gallatin of Pennsylvania, a naturalized Swiss, who is rated second only to Alexander Hamilton in the administration of the finances of our country. Gallatin introduced something like a budget with its specific appropriations for each item of national expense. Army and navy appropriations were more than cut in two, and about 70 per cent of the revenue, or over $7,000,000 a year, was devoted to paying off the national debt.

224. Napoleon Bonaparte acquires Louisiana. However, a piece of European diplomacy led President Jefferson, whose twin political doctrines were strict adherence to the letter of the Constitution and severe economy in the expenditures of the public moneys, himself to stretch the Constitution further than any Federalist had ever done, and to expend at a stroke $15,000,000 of the national revenue. In the year 1800 Napoleon Bonaparte, the new master of France, conceived the idea of establishing a colonial empire in the New World, in the valley of the great river which had been opened over a century before by the heroic labors of the French explorers Marquette, Hennepin, and La Salle. He induced Spain, by the secret treaty of San Ildefonso (1800), to cede to him the entire western basin of the Mississippi, called Louisiana.[1] When in the spring of the year 1802 Jefferson finally heard of this treaty of San Ildefonso, he was much disturbed by the prospect of having the control of the west bank and the mouth of the Mississippi pass from the feeble administration of Spain to the powerful and aggressive government of Napoleon. The settlers in the Northwest Territory, in Kentucky, and in Tennessee were completely isolated from the seaports of the East by the mountains. Their lumber, wheat, hogs, and tobacco had to seek a market by way of the Mississippi, with its tributaries, the Ohio, Cumberland, and the Tennessee Rivers. Three eighths of the commerce of the United States in 1800 passed through the mouth of the Mississippi to the Gulf of Mexico. It was therefore absolutely necessary to the life of our nation that the important city of New Orleans, which controlled the mouth of the river, should not be converted from a port of deposit for the commerce of the western states and territories into an armed base of war in the great duel between France and England. Much as he disliked England, Jefferson wrote to Robert R. Livingston, our minister in Paris, that "every eye in the United States was now turned to the affair of Louisiana," and that the moment Napoleon took possession of New Orleans we "must marry ourselves to the British fleet and nation."

225. Jefferson purchases Louisiana. The President's worst fears were realized when, in October, 1802, the Spanish government, probably at the bidding of Napoleon, to whom Louisiana was just about to be handed over, closed the mouth of the Mississippi by withdrawing the right of unloading and reshipping secured by Pinckney's treaty of 1795 (see page 168). Jefferson, knowing that it would be impossible to force Napoleon to open the river to our trade, secured an appropriation of $2,000,000 from Congress for the purpose of buying New Orleans and West Florida outright, and sent James Monroe to Paris to aid Livingston in the negotiation. At first Napoleon rejected any offer for New Orleans, but suddenly changed his mind and ordered his foreign minister, Talleyrand, to dispose of the whole province of Louisiana to the Americans. After the loss of

---

[1] The name "Louisiana," in honor of Louis XIV, was given to the whole Mississippi Valley by La Salle when he planted the cross at the mouth of the great river in 1682. In 1763 France had ceded the eastern basin to England and the western to Spain (p. 88).

an army under his brother-in-law Leclerc in the West Indies, Napoleon, with his characteristic caprice in shifting plans, had decided to abandon his colonial enterprise in the New World and confine his struggle with Great Britain in the Eastern Hemisphere. After much bargaining he accepted Livingston's offer of $15,000,000 for Louisiana, over $3,500,000 of which was to be paid back to our own citizens in the West for damage to their trade. The terms were agreed to April 30, 1803.

226. The Great Significance of the Louisiana Purchase. The purchase of Louisiana was the most important event of American history in the first half of the nineteenth century. It doubled the area of the United States and brought under our rule one of the most valuable tracts of land in the world. Fourteen states have been created wholly or in part out of the Louisiana territory. The population has grown from 50,000 in 1804, of whom half were slaves, to over 20,000,000. The cattle and timber of Montana, the wheat of Minnesota and the Dakotas, the corn of Iowa and Kansas, the sugar and cotton of Louisiana, have been the source of rapidly increasing wealth to our country. By the census of 1920 the value of the farm property alone in these fourteen states was $33,000,000,000, or over two thousand times what we paid for the territory.

227. The Lewis and Clark Expedition. Furthermore, the acquisition of Louisiana stimulated the interest of the government in the vast territory to the west of the Mississippi River. Less than two months after the cession of Louisiana to the United States, Jefferson commissioned Captain Meriwether Lewis, his private secretary, to head a scientific exploring party to the Far Northwest. It seems not to have troubled Jefferson that he was trespassing on Spanish territory. Lewis associated with him William Clark, younger brother of George Rogers Clark of Revolutionary fame. After wintering at the mouth of the Missouri River, the Lewis and Clark expedition started westward in the spring of 1804 with a company of thirty-five men. They ascended the Missouri to its source, crossed the Rockies, and descended the Columbia River to the sea, making important studies in their two and a half years' journey, of the natural features of the country and the habits of the Indian tribes. Their remarkable expedition was an important factor in our claim to the Oregon country in our dispute with England forty years later.

228. The Political Aspects of the Louisiana Purchase. The political consequences of the Louisiana Purchase were not less important than its geographical consequences. No clause of the Constitution of the United States could be found giving the president the right to purchase foreign territory by a treaty which promised (as the third article of the Louisiana treaty promised) that "the inhabitants of the ceded territory shall be incorporated in the Union of the United States, and admitted as soon as possible . . . to the enjoyment of all the rights, advantages, and immunities of citizens of the United States." Jefferson, somewhat disturbed by his departure from his own doctrine of the "strict construction" of the Constitution, contemplated at first having an amendment passed, giving the people's sanction to the purchase. But his friends in Congress persuaded him that it was both unnecessary and unwise,— unnecessary because the Constitution gives the president and Senate the right to conclude treaties, and unwise because during the long delay necessary to secure such an amendment Napoleon might again change his mind and deprive us of our fine bargain; or because Spain, hearing that Napoleon had broken the Treaty of San Ildefonso by the sale of the province to another power, might enter her protest at Washington. Jefferson acquiesced in the judgment of his friends and said nothing about the necessity for an amendment in his message to the new Congress which assembled in December, 1803.[1] That the vast province of Louisiana would ever be incorporated into the United States seemed questionable to Jefferson. He wrote in 1804, "Whether we remain one confederacy or fall into Atlantic and Mississippi confederacies I believe not very important to the happiness of either part." Meanwhile, however, by bringing within the jurisdiction of Congress a new territory which doubled the size of the United States, Jefferson enormously increased the authority of the central government,— an authority which in theory he combated.

229. Jefferson's Popularity. The country enthusiastically indorsed the purchase of Louisiana. President Jefferson was at the

[1] Congress established the extreme southern part of the Louisiana province as the territory of Orleans and provided for its administration by a governor, a secretary, and judges appointed by the president of the United States. For over a year there was no elected assembly in Orleans; there was not even the ancient civil right of trial by jury. The inhabitants of the territory were made subjects, not citizens, of the United States, and it was not until eight years later that they were admitted (as the state of Louisiana, 1812) to the "rights, advantages, and immunities" promised them in the treaty of 1803.

OREGON

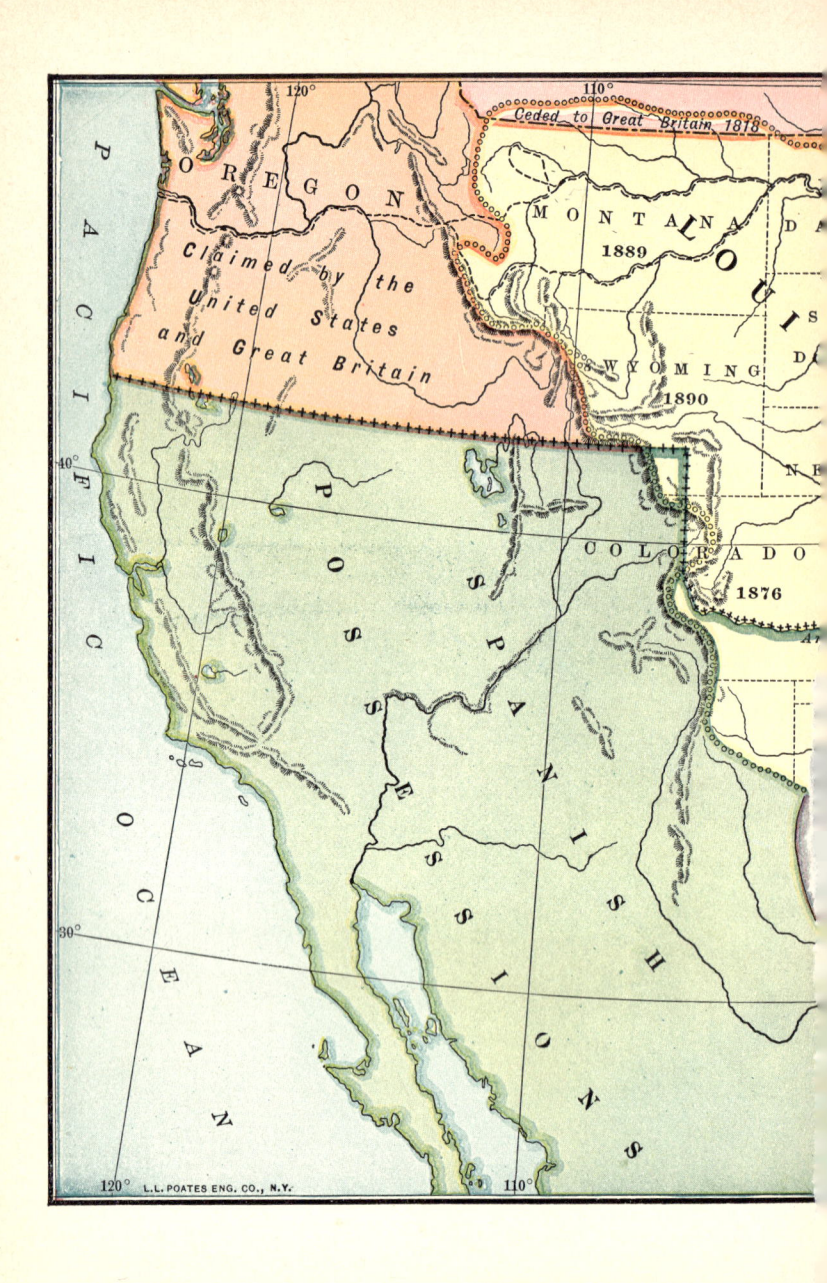

Claimed by the United States and Great Britain

Ceded to Great Britain 1818

MONTANA 1889

WYOMING 1890

COLORADO 1876

PACIFIC OCEAN

SPANISH POSSESSIONS

The Louisiana Purchase Territory with States subsequently made from it

- - - - Route of Lewis and Clark, 1804-1806
+++++ Western Boundary agreed on by Treaty with Spain, 1819

height of his popularity. In 1804 he was reëlected by 162 electoral votes to 14 for his Federalist opponent, C. C. Pinckney. At the same time with the election returns came the news of the success of the small American fleet in the Mediterranean Sea, under our commanders Barry, Preble, Bainbridge, and Decatur, in the war against the insolent pasha of Tripoli, who was attacking our commerce and levying blackmail on our government. Our diplomacy and arms successful abroad; our territory doubled at home; our debt reduced, in spite of the purchase of Louisiana; our people united, save for a few malcontents in New England and Delaware,— such was the record of the years 1801–1805.

230. The Conspiracy of Aaron Burr. But Jefferson's second term was filled with disappointment and chagrin. The country was distressed by the conspiracy of Aaron Burr. That brilliant but unprincipled politician, while still vice president, had offered himself as a candidate for governor of New York, and being defeated through the efforts of Alexander Hamilton, had challenged Hamilton to a duel and mortally wounded him at the first shot (July 11, 1804). After this dastardly act Burr conceived a desperate plan for retrieving his fortunes and reputation. Just what he intended to do is uncertain,— whether to establish an independent state in the Mississippi Valley, or to seize the city of New Orleans and carve an "empire for the Burr dynasty" out of Spanish territory to the southwest of the United States. At any rate, he threw the whole Western country into commotion for two years, until he was abandoned and betrayed by his treacherous accomplice, General James Wilkinson. In 1807 Burr was seized while trying to escape into Spanish Florida and brought to Richmond for trial. John Marshall, the Chief Justice of the Supreme Court, a Federalist appointed by President Adams, presided over the trial. Jefferson was extremely anxious to have Burr convicted; but the jury, under Marshall's charge, found no "overt act of treason" to justify a verdict of "guilty," and Burr was discharged, to spend the rest of his long life in obscurity and misery. But the Burr trial was of small account among Jefferson's troubles, when compared with the failure of his "peace policy," in the face of the devastating wars which raged in Europe.

The War of 1812

231. Napoleon Bonaparte the Tyrant of Europe. The unholy ambition of one man kept the civilized world in a turmoil during the first fifteen years of the nineteenth century and stirred war from the shores of Lake Erie to the steppes of Russia. Napoleon Bonaparte, made master of France by his sword at the age of thirty (1799), found France too small a theater for his genius and aimed at nothing less than the domination of the continent of Europe and the destruction of the British colonial empire. The latter object was frustrated when Admiral Nelson shattered the combined fleets of France and Spain off Cape Trafalgar, October 21, 1805. But a few weeks later, by his victory over the armies of Russia and Austria in the tremendous battle of Austerlitz, Napoleon began to realize his ambition of dominating the continent. Henceforth Britain was mistress of the ocean, but for ten years Napoleon was master of the land. Having failed to destroy Great Britain's fleet, Napoleon sought to kill her commerce. By decrees issued from Berlin and Milan in 1806 and 1807 he declared the continent closed to British goods and ordered the seizure of any vessel that had touched at a British port. Great Britain replied by Orders in Council, forbidding neutral vessels to trade with any countries under Napoleon's control (which meant all of Europe but Scandinavia, Russia, and Turkey), unless such vessels had touched at a British port. These decrees and orders, if strictly enforced, meant the utter ruin of neutral trade; for the English seized the merchant vessels that had not touched at British ports, and the French seized those that had.

232. The American Ocean Trade. It was the American trade that suffered especially. During the nine years' war between France and England (1793–1802) the United States had built up an immense volume of shipping. Her stanch, swift vessels, manned by alert tars, were the favorite carriers of the merchandise of South America, the West Indies, and the Far East to all the ports of Europe. Our own exports too — the fish and lumber of New England, the cotton and rice of the South, the wheat and live stock of the trans-Allegheny country — had increased nearly fivefold (from $20,000,000 to $95,500,000) since the inauguration of Washington. Our shipments of cotton alone, thanks to the invention, in 1793, of the cotton "gin" (engine) for separating the seed from the fiber, grew from 200,000 pounds in 1791 to over 50,000,000 pounds in 1805. In the latter year some 70,000 tons were added to our merchant marine, requiring the addition of 4200 seamen. Sailors' wages rose from $8 to $24 a month. Hundreds of foreigners became naturalized in order to enjoy the huge profits of American shipowners. Some idea of the volume of our foreign trade in proportion to the size and wealth of our country at the beginning of the nineteenth century, as compared with that at the close of the century, can be realized from the following figures: in 1900, when our population was almost 80,000,000 and our wealth $100,000,000,000, less than 10 per cent of our foreign trade (only 816,000 tons) was carried in American ships; in 1810 our population was less than 8,000,000 and our estimated wealth $2,000,000,000, but 91 per cent of our foreign trade (980,000 tons) was carried in our own vessels.

IMPRESSING AMERICAN SEAMEN

233. The Impressment of American Seamen. It was this immense foreign trade, the chief source of our country's wealth, that was threatened with ruin by Napoleon's decrees and the British Orders in Council. British frigates cruised along our shores from New England to Georgia, stopping our ships at will, boarding them, and taking off hundreds of sailors on the ground that they were British deserters. In her desperate struggle with Napoleon, Great Britain maintained that she could not afford to have her seamen desert her ships to take advantage of the high wages, good food, and humane treatment which they found aboard the American vessels. The British lieutenant conducted his examination of many an American crew in a summary fashion, and in violation of the rules of international law impressed not only thousands of Americans, but also citizens of other countries who were on board American ships and who could not possibly be mistaken for British citizens.

234. The *Chesapeake* Affair. The climax was reached when the British ship *Leopard* opened fire on the American frigate *Chesapeake* off the Virginia coast, June 22, 1807, because the American refused to stop to be searched for deserters. Three of the *Chesapeake's* men were killed and eighteen wounded before she surrendered. It was an act of war. The country was stirred as it had not been since the news of the battle of Lexington. Resolutions poured in upon the President pledging the signers to support the most rigorous measures of resistance.

235. The Embargo Act. But Jefferson had reduced our navy far below the point necessary to protect American commerce, and his only remedy was "peaceful coercion." By an Embargo Act of December 22, 1807, Congress forbade all ships to leave our harbors for foreign ports. The double purpose of the embargo was to starve Europe into showing a proper respect for our commerce and to prevent our ships from capture. The latter object the embargo certainly accomplished, for if the ships did not sail, they could hardly be taken. But the remedy was worse than the disease. The merchants of New England preferred risking the loss of a few men and vessels to seeing their ships tied idly to the wharves and their merchandise spoiling in warehouses. They even accused Jefferson of being willing to ruin their shipping in order to be avenged on the Federalists and to further his pet industry of agriculture. A storm of protest arose from the commercial classes of the country. It was evident that the continuance of the embargo would mean the overthrow of the Republican party, if not civil war; and the hated act, which cost New England merchants alone a loss of $8,000,000 in fifteen months, was repealed March 1, 1809, and a Nonintercourse Act with Great Britain and France passed in its stead. Three days later Jefferson turned over the government to his successor, James Madison.

236. President Madison's Diplomacy. Madison had rendered the country magnificent services a quarter of a century earlier in the convention which framed the Constitution of the United States, but he seemed to have lost all power of initiative. He neither prepared for war nor developed any effective policy of peace. He was singularly lacking in diplomatic judgment, allowing himself, in his anxiety for peace, to believe too readily the word of anyone who brought a welcome report. When the new British minister, Erskine, announced in 1809 that his country would withdraw the Orders in Council, Madison hastily reopened commerce with England, without waiting to see whether the British ministry would sanction Erskine's promise or not. To Madison's chagrin the promise was disavowed and the minister recalled. The next move of the administration was an attempt to get England and France to bid against each other for our trade. Congress repealed the Nonintercourse Act in 1810 and substituted for it Macon's bill, which provided that as soon as either France or England withdrew its decrees against our shipping the Nonintercourse Act should be revived against the other country. This was too good a chance for the wily Napoleon to let slip. He announced (August 5, 1810) that the Berlin and Milan Decrees were repealed, and called upon the American President to redeem his promise by prohibiting intercourse with Great Britain. Again Madison jumped at the chance of bringing Great Britain to terms by diplomacy. In spite of the British ministry's warning that Napoleon would not keep his word (a judgment amply proved by the facts), Madison issued a proclamation reviving the Nonintercourse Act against Great Britain if she should not have repealed her Orders in Council before February 2, 1811. The day passed without any word from the British ministry, and again Congress forbade all trade with Great Britain and her colonies.

237. New British Provocation. The year 1811 brought other fuel to feed the fires of anti-British sentiment. In May our frigate *President*, chasing a British cruiser which had impressed a citizen of Massachusetts, was fired upon by the British sloop of war *Little Belt*, which was forced by the American ship to strike her colors. In November, William Henry Harrison, governor of the Northwest, defeated the Indians at Tippecanoe Creek in the Indiana territory, and wrote home, "The Indians had an ample supply of the best British glazed powder, and some of their guns had been sent them so short a time before the action that they were not yet divested of the list coverings in which they are imported." The suspicions of our government, therefore, that the British had been inciting the Indians on our northwestern frontier since St. Clair's disastrous defeat twenty years before seemed to be confirmed.

238. Henry Clay urges War against England. The new Congress which met in the early winter of 1811 contained a group of energetic men, including Clay, Calhoun, Grundy, and Porter, who were determined that the independence and dignity of the United States should be respected. They were of the new generation that had grown up since the Revolutionary War, and their confidence in the greatness and future promise of the United States was unbounded. They demanded that the impotent diplomacy which had humiliated our government since the end of the first administration of Jefferson — the so-called "peaceful war" of embargo and nonintercourse — should be abandoned. The leader of the group was Henry Clay, a Virginian born, who had moved out to the new state of Kentucky as a young law student and had rapidly raised himself, by his great gifts of intellect and oratory, to be the first citizen of the state. Clay was elected Speaker of the House in the new Congress, and as he made up his committees it became evident that the war party was to direct the policy of the government. "The period has arrived," reported the Committee on Foreign Affairs, "when it is the sacred duty of Congress to call upon the patriotism and resources of the country." Clay descended from the chair and urged the war in such strains of oratory as had not been heard in Congress for twenty years. He held before the West the vision of the easy conquest of Canada, and defeated the proposal of the moderate members of the House to make one more effort for peace by sending a special envoy to England. President Madison was carried along by the war current.

239. Congress declares War on Great Britain. Madison sent a strong message to Congress, June 1, 1812, reviewing the hostile acts of Great Britain, and Congress responded on the 18th with a declaration of war. Had the special envoy been sent to England the war would have been averted; for, two days before Madison signed the declaration of war, the British ministry, sincerely anxious to preserve peace with the United States, decided to repeal the offensive Orders in Council. But there was no cable to bring the news at once, so the unfortunate war between the sister nations of the English tongue began just when Napoleon Bonaparte led his army of half a million men across the Russian frontier, hoping to crush the last great power of the European continent that dared to resist his despotic will.

240. Our Failures on the Canadian Frontier. The United States was woefully unprepared for war. Our regular army numbered less

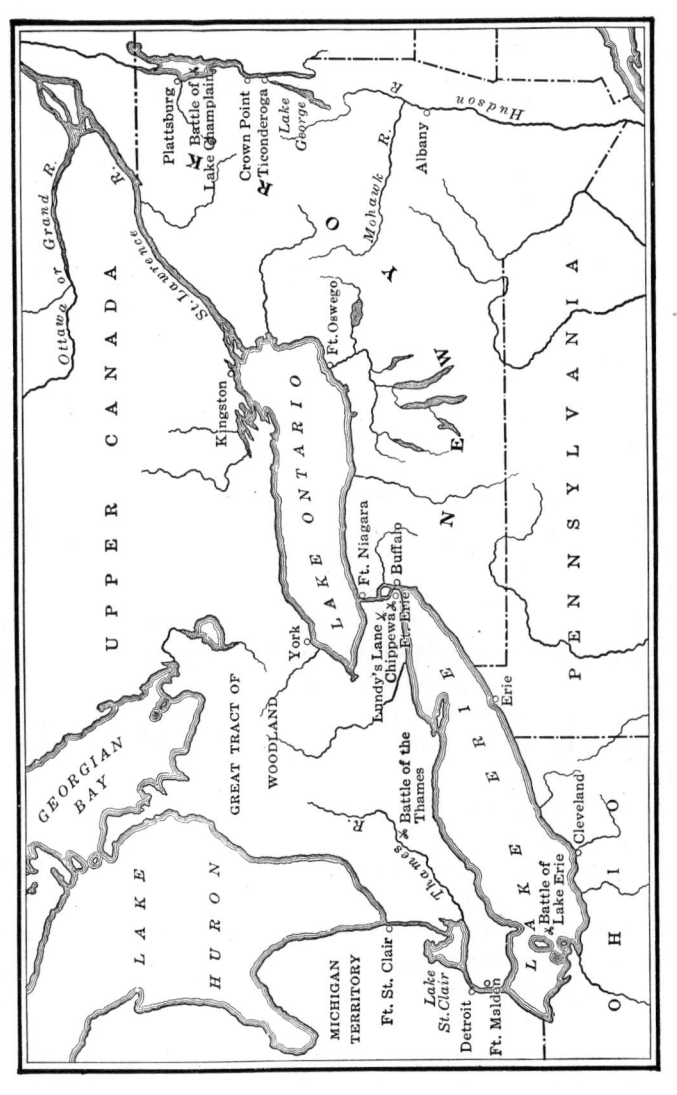

THE WAR ON THE CANADIAN BORDER

than 7000 soldiers, many of them raw recruits under untrained commanders. Our navy consisted of 15 ships to England's 1000. The New England States protested against "Mr. Madison's war" (which they would better have called "Mr. Clay's war"), and Vermont and Connecticut refused point-blank to furnish a man of their militia to invade Canada. The year 1812 saw our commander at Detroit, William Hull, court-martialed and sentenced to death for the cowardly abandonment of his post, and our generals at the other end of Lake Erie fighting duels with each other instead of advancing together against the enemy. The conquest of Canada, which Clay had boasted could be accomplished by the militia of Kentucky alone, showed little prospect of fulfillment in the campaign of 1812–1813. But for the victory of Oliver H. Perry's little fleet on Lake Erie (September 10, 1813) and Thomas MacDonough's deliverance of Lake Champlain (September 11, 1814), we could hardly have been saved from a British invasion from Canada, which would have cost us the Northwest Territory and the valley of the Hudson.

241. The Recapture of Detroit. Cheered by Perry's famous dispatch from Lake Erie, "We have met the enemy and they are ours," William Henry Harrison, who had succeeded Hull, was able to recapture Detroit and drive the British across the river, inflicting a severe defeat on them in the battle of the Thames (October 5, 1813). This was the nearest we came to a "conquest of Canada"; for at the eastern end of Lake Erie our last attempt at invasion, under General Jacob Brown, resulted only in the drawn battle of Lundy's Lane (July 25, 1814).

242. The British raid Washington. In August, 1814, a British force of about 5000 men sailed up the Patuxent and raided the city of Washington, after dispersing a force of 7000 untrained militia which had been hastily gathered at Bladensburg to defend the national capital. The British burned the White House, the Capitol, and some department buildings, and inflicted about $1,500,000 worth of wanton damage on the property of the city. They then departed for Baltimore, where a similar raid was frustrated by the alertness of the Maryland militia and the spirited defense of Fort McHenry (September 12, 1814). It was the sight of our flag still waving on the ramparts of Fort McHenry, after a night's bombardment, that inspired Francis Key's song, "The Star-Spangled Banner."

243. The War on the Sea. In sharp contrast with our disasters on land, the war on the ocean, despite the great inferiority of our navy in point of numbers, brought a number of surprising triumphs for the American ships. The exploits of our frigates *President*, *United States*, and *Constitution* ("Old Ironsides") kept the country in a fever of rejoicing. On all the lines of world commerce — in the Atlantic, the Pacific, and the Indian Oceans, off the coast of New England, among the Indies, in the English waters, and beyond the Cape of Good Hope — the privateers and merchantmen of both countries played the game of hide and seek. In the first seven months of the war over 500 British merchantmen were taken by the swift Yankee privateers, and before the war was over some 2000 prizes were captured, many of which were, however, retaken. The British had boasted at the beginning of the war that they would not let an American craft cross from New York to Staten Island, but before the war was over they were themselves paying 15 per cent insurance on vessels crossing the English Channel. However, in the end, the Americans were the worse sufferers by the war, their exports falling from $110,000,000 in 1807 to $7,000,000 in 1814. Eventually, too, our little navy, in spite of its exploits, had to yield to Great Britain's superiority in numbers. At the close of the war all our frigates but two were either captured, sunk, or interned in home ports.

244. The Treaty of Ghent. With the cessation of the long and severe commercial struggle between Napoleon and Great Britain, the causes of the war between Great Britain and the United States — impressments, right of search, blockades, embargoes, nonintercourse acts — were all removed. Peace was signed at Ghent in the Netherlands, on Christmas Eve, 1814, restoring the conditions before the war. The peace was silent on the questions of impressment and right of search. The settlement of boundary disputes between the United States and Canada was referred to commissioners.

245. Andrew Jackson's Victory at New Orleans. Before the news of the Treaty of Ghent reached New York, however (February 11, 1815), two events of importance took place in America. The British, failing in their attack on Baltimore, had sailed for the West Indies and there joined several thousand veteran troops under General Pakenham, just freed from service against Napoleon's armies in the Spanish peninsula. Their purpose was to seize New Orleans, paralyze the trade of the Mississippi Valley, and perhaps hold Louisiana for exchange at the close of the war for territory in the Northwest. But Andrew Jackson, a Tennessee frontiersman and Indian fighter of Scotch-Irish stock, who was in command of our small army in the Mississippi territory, was a man of different caliber from the generals on the northern frontier. Pressing every man and mule in the city of New Orleans into service, he constructed a hasty but effective line of fortifications below the city, and when the British veterans attacked with confidence, he drove them back with terrible slaughter, laying 2000 of their number on the field in a battle of twenty minutes' duration (January 8, 1815). Jackson, henceforth the "hero of New Orleans," was rewarded in the following years by the command against the Indians of Florida (1817), the governorship of the Florida territory (1821), a seat in the United States Senate (1823), and the presidency of the United States (1828). The battle of New Orleans, though fought several days after peace had been actually concluded at Ghent, was by no means "a wasted battle." It did much to restore the morale of the American army, which had suffered by repeated setbacks during the war, and it gave our diplomats abroad a new sense of the dignity of the nation and new courage in the negotiation of important treaties in the next decade.

246. Opposition of New England to the War. While Jackson was bringing the war to a victorious close for the American side in the far South, the discontent of the New England States with "Mr. Madison's war" was ripening into serious opposition to the administration. Every state north of Maryland with a seacoast had voted against Madison (that is, against the war) in the election of 1812. The sectional character of the war is strikingly shown by the fact that of the $11,000,000 loan authorized by Congress in 1812 New England, which was the richest section of the country, subscribed for less than $1,000,000. There were even those in New England who let their disgust with the policy of the administration carry them into treason and recouped the losses that Madison and Clay brought to their commerce by selling beef to the British army in Canada. By the end of 1813 about 250 vessels were lying idle at the docks of Boston alone. Petitions began to come in to the Massachusetts legislature from many towns, praying the state to take steps toward getting the Constitution of the United States amended in such a way as to "secure them from further evils."

247. The Hartford Convention. At the suggestion of Massachusetts delegates from the five New England States met in a convention at Hartford, Connecticut, December 15, 1814. These delegates, twenty-six in number, represented the remnant of the Federalist party. They denounced the "ruinous war" and proposed a number of amendments to the Constitution, designed to lessen the power of the slaveholding agricultural South, to secure the interests of commerce, to prevent the hasty admission of new Western states, and to check the succession of Virginia presidents. After a month's session they adjourned to the following June, and their messengers carried their demands to Washington. The messengers arrived only to find themselves in the midst of general rejoicing over the news of Jackson's victory at New Orleans and the tidings of the peace from Ghent, which reached Washington on the same day. The triumph of the Republicans was complete, and the crestfallen Hartford envoys returned to New England bearing the doom of the Federalist party. In the presidential election of the following year (1816) the Federalists for the last time put a candidate into the field, Rufus King of New York. But King got only 34 electoral votes to 183 for his Republican rival, James Monroe, Madison's Secretary of State, who continued for another eight years the "dynasty" of Virginia Republicans inaugurated by Thomas Jefferson in 1801.

REFERENCES

Launching the Government: J. B. MCMASTER, *History of the People of the United States*, Vol. I, chap. vi; HENRY ADAMS, *History of the United States of America during the Administrations of Jefferson and Madison*, Vol. I, chaps. i–vi; EDWARD CHANNING, *History of the United States*, Vol. IV, chaps. i–v; J. S. BASSETT, *The Federalist System* (American Nation Series), chaps. i–xiii; E. M. AVERY, *History of the United States*, Vol. VII, chaps. i–iv; D. R. DEWEY, *Financial History of the United States*, chaps. iii, iv; H. J. FORD, *Washington and his Colleagues* (Chronicles, Vol. XIV); biographies of George Washington by PAUL LEICESTER FORD, WOODROW WILSON, and HENRY CABOT LODGE; biographies of Alexander Hamilton by WILLIAM G. SUMNER, HENRY CABOT LODGE, and J. T. MORSE, JR.

The Reign of Federalism: BASSETT, chaps. xiv–xix; MCMASTER, Vol. II, chaps. x, xi; CHANNING, Vol. IV, chaps. v–viii; AVERY, Vol. VII, chaps. v–xiv; J. W. FOSTER, *A Century of Diplomacy*, chap. v; J. B. MOORE, *American Diplomacy*, chaps. ii, iii; EDWARD STANWOOD, *History of the Presidency*, chaps. iv, v; G. W. ALLEN, *The Barbary Wars*; A. B. HART, *American History told by Contemporaries*, Vol. III, Nos. 83–105; H. VON HOLST, *Constitutional History of the United States*, Vol. I, chaps. iii, iv.

The Jeffersonian Policies: EDWARD CHANNING, *The Jeffersonian System* (Am. Nation), chaps. i–xvii; *History of the United States*, Vol. IV, chaps. ix–xiii; R. G. THWAITES (ed.), *Original Journal of the Lewis and Clark Expedition*; MCMASTER, Vols. II, III; ADAMS, Vols. I–IV; HART, Vol. III, Nos. 106, 109, 115; AVERY, Vol. VII, chaps. xv–xx; F. A. OGG, *The Opening of the Mississippi*, chaps. x–xiv; W. F. MCCALEB, *The Aaron Burr Conspiracy*; biographies of Jefferson by PAUL LEICESTER FORD, J. T. MORSE, JR., H. C. MERWIN, and D. S. MUZZEY.

The War of 1812: CHANNING, *The Jeffersonian System*, chaps. xviii–xx; *History of the United States*, Vol. IV, chaps. xiii–xx; K. C. BABCOCK, *The Rise of American Nationality* (Am. Nation), chaps. i–xi; HART, Vol. III, Nos. 116–129; *Cambridge Modern History*, Vol. VII, chap. x; A. T. MAHAN, *The War of 1812*; RALPH D. PAINE, *The Old Merchant Marine* (Chronicles, Vol. XXXVI), chaps. vi, vii; *The Fight for a Free Sea* (Chronicles, Vol. XVII); THEODORE ROOSEVELT, *The Naval War of 1812*; CARL SCHURZ, *Henry Clay* (American Statesmen Series).

TOPICS FOR SPECIAL REPORTS

1. **The Condition of the Country at the Inauguration of Washington:** HART, Vol. III, Nos. 10–36; MCMASTER, Vol. I, pp. 1–101; Vol. II, pp. 1–24; BASSETT, pp. 163–177; CHANNING, *History of the United States*, Vol. IV, pp. 1–27; JUSTIN WINSOR, *The Westward Movement*, pp. 398–414.

2. **The Jay Treaty:** WINSOR, *The Westward Movement*, pp. 462–484; *Narrative and Critical History of America*, Vol. VII, pp. 463–471; GEORGE PELLEW, *John Jay* (Am. Statesmen), chaps. x, xi; HART, Vol. III, No. 97; BASSETT, pp. 125–135; MOORE, pp. 201–208; WILLIAM MACDONALD, *Select Documents*, No. 14 (for text of treaty).

3. **The French War of 1798–1799:** MCMASTER, Vol. II, pp. 370–388, 428–434; F. A. WALKER, *The Making of the Nation*, pp. 137–143; WINSOR, *Narrative and Critical History of America*, Vol. VII, pp. 361–368; A. J. WOODBURN, *American Political History*, Vol. I, pp. 162–179.

4. **The Lewis and Clark Expedition:** ROOSEVELT, *The Winning of the West*, Vol. IV, pp. 308–328; HART, Vol. III, No. 115; CHANNING, *The Jeffersonian System*, pp. 86–99; THWAITES, *Rocky Mountain Exploration*, pp. 92–187.

5. **The War Hawks in the Twelfth Congress:** MCMASTER, Vol. III, pp. 426–458; WALKER, pp. 220–227; BABCOCK, pp. 50–63; ADAMS, Vol. VII, pp. 113–175; SCHURZ, Vol. I, chap. v; JAMES SCHOULER, *History of the United States*, Vol. II, pp. 334–356.

6. **The Louisiana Purchase:** MCMASTER, Vol. II, pp. 620–635; CHANNING, *The Jeffersonian System*, pp. 47–72; *History of the United States*, Vol. V, pp. 298–335; ADAMS, Vol. II, pp. 116–134; WILLIAM M. SLOANE, in the *American Historical Review*, Vol. IV, pp. 439 ff.; ROOSEVELT, Vol. IV, pp. 258–282; HART, *Foundations of American Foreign Policy*, pp. 185–209; MACDONALD, No. 24 (for text of treaty).

PART IV. NATIONAL VERSUS SECTIONAL INTERESTS

CHAPTER VIII

THE GROWTH OF A NATIONAL CONSCIOUSNESS

A New American Spirit

248. The Completion of our Independence. The close of the second war with England (1815) marks an epoch in American history. During the quarter of a century which elapsed between the inauguration of George Washington and the conclusion of the treaty at Ghent, the United States was very largely influenced by European politics. Our independence was acknowledged but not respected. Neither the French republic nor the English monarchy accorded us the courtesies due to a sister power; neither Napoleon nor the ministers of George III heeded our protests against the violation of a neutral nation's rights. Foreign wars and rumors of war, treaties, protests, embassies, absorbed the energies of the administration at Washington. Many of our greatest statesmen were serving their country in foreign capitals. The eyes of our people were turned toward the Atlantic to welcome our swift packets bringing news from Paris, London, and Madrid. But with the "universal peace" of 1815 all this was changed. We turned our back on Europe and faced the problems of our own growing land. The development of the boundless resources of the United States invited the common effort of all sections of our country.

249. Hindrances to Western Development Removed. Many thousand pioneers had crossed the Alleghenies to the rich valleys of the Ohio and the Tennessee before the War of 1812, but the supply of both men and capital was too meager to develop the resources of the whole eastern basin of the Mississippi. The Indians, encouraged by England on the north and by Spain on the south, were a constant source of danger. Lack of roads was so serious a handicap that it was not profitable to raise wheat far from the banks of navigable rivers. The barrier of the Alleghenies made transportation between the Ohio valley and the seaboard so expensive that the wagon driver got the lion's share both of the money for which the Western farmer sold his wheat in Virginia and of the money which he paid for his plow in Ohio. If the pioneer floated his cargo of wheat, pork, or tobacco down the Mississippi to New Orleans in a flatboat, it was

CANAL BOATS CROSSING THE MOUNTAINS

more profitable to sell boat and all there and return home on horseback than to spend three months battling his way up against the current. But during the decade 1810–1820 these difficulties in the way of the development of the West were rapidly removed. William Henry Harrison by his victories over Tecumseh's braves at Tippecanoe Creek in Indiana territory (1811), and Andrew Jackson by his pacification of the Creeks and Seminoles in Florida (1813–1818), put an end to the danger from the Indians on our frontiers. In 1811 the steamboat (which many years of experiment by Fitch and Fulton, on the Delaware, the Seine, and the Hudson, had brought to efficiency) made its first appearance on the Ohio River. Henceforth the journey from Louisville to New Orleans and back could be made inside of a month, and the products of the Gulf region could be brought to the Northwest by the return voyage.

THE GROWTH OF A NATIONAL CONSCIOUSNESS 193

250. Renewed Westward Emigration. The interruption of our foreign commerce by embargo, nonintercourse, and war had sent thousands of families westward across the mountains, where better farm land could be bought from the government at two dollars an acre, with liberal credit, than could be had for ten times that price in cash on the seaboard. Moreover, a stream of immigrants of the hardy northern stocks of Europe began to pour into our country after the War of 1812, to swell the westward march to the farm

PICKING AND LOADING COTTON

lands of the Ohio valley. In the single year 1817, 22,000 Irish and Germans came over. A ceaseless procession passed along the Mohawk valley and over the mountain roads of Pennsylvania and Virginia. "The old America seems to be breaking up and moving westward," wrote an Englishman who migrated to Illinois in 1817. A gatekeeper on a Pennsylvania turnpike counted over 500 wagons with 3000 emigrants passing in a single month.

251. Extension of the Cotton Fields to the Mississippi. At the same time the cotton planters of the South were moving from the Carolinas and Georgia into the fertile Mississippi territory which the campaigns of Andrew Jackson had freed from the terror of the savage. The invention of machinery in England for the spinning and weaving of cotton had increased the demand for that article beyond the power of the planters to satisfy, even with the enormous increase of production effected by Eli Whitney's invention of the cotton gin[1] in 1793. How eagerly the planters turned to the virgin soil along the Gulf of Mexico may be seen from the following figures. In 1810 less than 5,000,000 pounds of cotton were grown west of the Alleghenies, out of a total crop of 80,000,000 pounds; ten years later the new Western states (Louisiana, Mississippi, Alabama) produced 60,000,000 pounds out of a total crop of 177,000,000 pounds; and five years later still, these same states raised over 150,000,000 pounds, or about one half the entire crop of the country.

252. Growth of the New West. With the attractions of cheap and fertile farm lands in the Northwest and virgin cotton soil in the Southwest, the trans-Allegheny country far outstripped the seaboard states in growth of population. While the census of 1820 showed an increase of only 35 per cent in the New England States, and 92 per cent in the Middle Atlantic States, over the population at the beginning of the nineteenth century, the western commonwealths of Ohio, Kentucky, and Tennessee increased 320 per cent in the same period. Six new Western states were added to the Union in the decade following the outbreak of the second war with England: Louisiana (1812), Indiana (1816), Mississippi (1817), Illinois (1818), Alabama (1819), Missouri (1821),—more than had been admitted since the formation of our government, and more than were to be admitted until the eve of the Civil War. The new West was rapidly coming to be a power to be reckoned with in national politics. By the apportionment of 1820, 47 of the 213 congressmen and 16 of the 46 senators came from beyond the Alleghenies,— the land which a generation before was, in the language of Daniel Webster, "a fresh, untouched, unbounded, magnificent wilderness."

253. The West calls for National Aid. The settlers of the new West had abundant courage but little capital. In order to connect their rapidly developing region with the Atlantic coast, that they might exchange their farm products for the manufactures of the eastern factories and the imports from the Old World, great outlays of money for roads and canals were needed. The national government

---

[1] The cotton gin (engine) was a machine for separating the cotton seed from the fiber. A man could clean about 300 pounds of cotton a day with the gin as against a single pound by hand. Whitney's invention was one of the most fateful in history, for it made the production of cotton so profitable that the slave system was fixed on the South. Less than 200,000 pounds of cotton were exported in 1791, but in 1807, on the eve of the embargo, the exports reached 63,000,000 pounds.

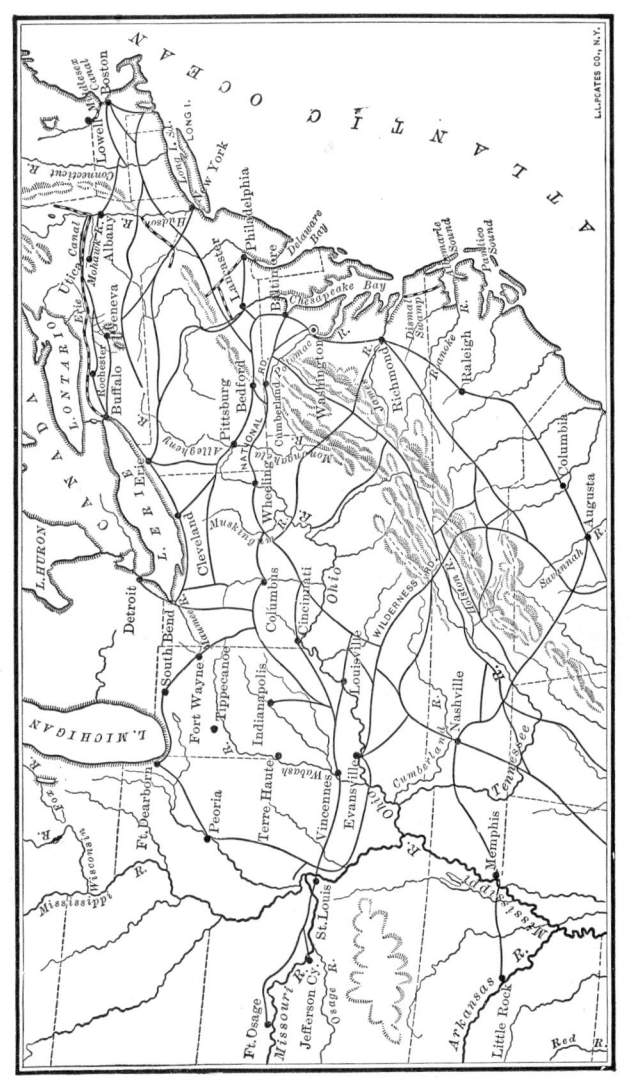

ROUTES TO THE WEST, 1815–1825

was asked to contribute to these improvements, which meant not the building up of one section of the country only, but the general diffusion of prosperity, the strengthening of a national sentiment, and the promise of a united people to resist foreign attack or domestic treachery. President Madison in his last annual message to Congress (December, 1816) urged that body to turn its particular attention to "effectuating a system of roads and canals such as would have the effect of drawing more closely together every part of our country."

VIEW OF CINCINNATI IN 1825

254. Calhoun's Bonus Bill. A few days later John C. Calhoun, an enthusiastic "expansionist" member from South Carolina, pushed a bill through Congress devoting to internal improvements the $1,500,000 which the government was to receive as a bonus for the establishment of a second National Bank, as well as all the dividends accruing to the government on its stock in the bank. Calhoun urged the need of good roads for transportation of our army and the movement of our commerce. "We are great, and rapidly (I was about to say, fearfully) growing," he cried; "the extent of our country exposes us to the greatest of all calamities next to the loss of liberty, *disunion*. . . . Let us bind the republic together with a perfect system of roads and canals. . . . Let us conquer space." But Calhoun's

THE GROWTH OF A NATIONAL CONSCIOUSNESS

Bonus Bill was vetoed by President Madison on his last day of office (March 3, 1817). Not that Madison was opposed to spending the nation's money for improving the means of communication with the West (as his message of the previous December shows), but because he thought that the Constitution needed amending in order to give Congress this power.

255. National Enthusiasm following the War. When Madison's successor, James Monroe, was inaugurated on the fourth of March, 1817, the country was already at the full tide of the enthusiasm for expansion which followed the conclusion of peace at Ghent. Our regular army had been thoroughly reorganized and raised to a peace footing of 10,000 men. The immense sum of $8,000,000 had been appropriated for a new navy. The tariff rates, which had been doubled in 1812 to provide a revenue for carrying on the war, were still kept up, and even slightly increased, by the tariff bill of 1816, whose object was to encourage and protect the rising manufactures which both North and South hoped would in a few years make us independent of Europe industrially, as the War of 1812 had made us independent of Europe politically. Every manifestation of a narrow sectional spirit, like that of the Hartford Convention (see page 189), was rebuked in Congress and the press as unpatriotic.

256. The "Era of Good Feeling." A few weeks after his inauguration Monroe made an extended tour through the New England States, New York, Pennsylvania, and Maryland, for the ostensible purpose of inspecting the national defenses. The real object of the journey was quite as much to strengthen the growing Republicanism of New England. In Boston, that same *Columbian Centinel* which on the day of the inauguration of the first Republican president, Thomas Jefferson, had published a bitter lament over the defeat of the glorious Federalist administration, now hailed the inauguration of Jefferson's bosom friend and political follower, James Monroe, as the promise of "an era of good feeling." The phrase took the popular fancy and pleased President Monroe, who spread it during his journey, and repeated it on the tour of the Southern states which he made in the autumn of the same year (1817).

257. The Second National Bank. Perhaps no act of Congress during the decade following the war shows more clearly how thoroughly the war had nationalized the Republican party than the establishment of a second National Bank in 1816. The Republican party had maintained a steady opposition to the Bank during the twenty years of its existence, and had refused to recharter it when its term expired in 1811. "The state banks," they said, "are the pillars of the nation." But during the War of 1812 the state banks had failed. There was no confidence in financial circles because there was no standard of currency. Notes of New York banks were at a discount in Boston, and notes of Baltimore banks at a discount in New York; while the paper of the "wildcat" banks of the West, unsupported by gold or silver, was practically worthless in the commercial centers of the Atlantic seaboard. The state banks, which had been "the pillars of the nation," had now become, said one senator, "the caterpillars of the nation." The same men who had denounced the National Bank in 1811 and refused to renew its charter now pleaded in favor of it. The same Republican press which had assailed Hamilton in 1791 now reprinted his arguments in favor of the Bank. And the same party which had feared the sinister influence on politics of a bank with $10,000,000 capital in 1811 now chartered a new National Bank with a capital stock of $35,000,000, of which the government was to hold $7,000,000. The effect of this was the return of confidence to the merchants and bankers of the country. The state banks were forced to keep their paper up to the standard set by the National Bank or retire from business. Secretary of the Treasury Dallas, who found the United States Treasury empty in the autumn of 1814, left a surplus of $20,000,000 to his successor, Crawford, three years later.

258. The Supreme Court under John Marshall. Another important sign of the growing national consciousness was the strengthening of the national government by several important decisions of the Supreme Court. John Marshall of Virginia, a moderate Federalist, who had served with distinction as an officer in the Revolution, and had later been special envoy to France, member of Congress, and for a brief period Secretary of State, was appointed Chief Justice of the Supreme Court by John Adams in January of 1801. Marshall held this highest judicial office in the country for thirty-four years, and, by his famous decisions interpreting the Constitution, made for himself the greatest name in the history of the American bench. When the peace of 1815 turned the attention of the country from

THE GROWTH OF A NATIONAL CONSCIOUSNESS 199

foreign negotiations to the development of the national domain, many questions arose as to the exact limits of the powers of the national government and of the various states. The people of the United States had given the national Congress certain powers enumerated in the Constitution, such as the power to lay taxes, to declare war, to raise and support armies, to regulate commerce, to coin money, and to make all laws which were "necessary and proper for carrying into execution" the powers granted. Marshall and his associates on the Supreme bench, in a number of important cases which came before them to test these powers, rendered decisions in support of the *national* authority against that of the states.

259. McCulloch vs. Maryland. For example, in 1819 the state of Maryland laid a tax on the business of the branch of the National Bank established in that state, claiming that the Constitution did not give Congress any right to establish a bank. Marshall wrote the decision of the Supreme Court in this case, justifying the right of Congress to establish a bank as a measure necessary and proper for carrying into execution the laws for raising a revenue and regulating the currency. The state was forbidden to tax the bank except for the ground and building it occupied.

CHIEF JUSTICE MARSHALL

The original is in the possession of the Law Association of Philadelphia. From a carbon by A. W. Elson & Co.

260. The Dartmouth College Case. In the same year, in the famous Dartmouth College case, the Supreme Court annulled a law of the legislature of New Hampshire, which altered the charter of the college against the will of the trustees. The charter, the court held, was a contract between the legislature and the trustees; and since the Constitution of the United States forbids any state to pass a law impairing the obligation of contracts (Art. I, sect. 10, par. 1), the law of the New Hampshire legislature was null and void. These decisions, with several others of like character, show how the judicial branch of our government contributed to the national feeling which we have already seen dominating the legislative branch (Congress) in the passage of the army and navy bills, the Bank bill, and the tariff bill (1816).

261. Changes in Social and Economic Conditions. Still further indications of a new national consciousness may be seen in our social and economic life. The movement and mingling of population in immigration from Europe and emigration to the West was rapidly breaking down the social privileges and prejudices of sections of our country. In New England, for example, the old Puritan dominion was yielding to democratic tendencies in politics and religion. Connecticut in her constitution of 1818 (the first new one since her colonial charter of 1662) did away with religious qualifications for office. New Hampshire passed a Toleration Act in 1819, and the next year the Massachusetts convention for framing a constitution was torn with dissensions between the new Unitarians and the old Orthodox believers. The Episcopal church in the Southern states also lost its predominance with the increase of Scotch-Irish Presbyterian immigrants and the growth of the Methodists and Baptists in the frontier communities. Distinctly popular movements looking toward the improvement of labor conditions, the establishment of public schools, the health and cleanliness of cities, began to be agitated in these years. Further westward emigration was encouraged by the reduction in 1820 of the price of public lands from $2 to $1.25 an acre, and the sale of 80-acre lots instead of the customary sections of 160 acres. In spite of the caution of Madison and Monroe, Congress passed ten acts before 1820, appropriating in all over $1,500,000 for roads and canals.

262. The Beginnings of an American Literature. Finally, the beginnings of a truly national literature fell within these years. The *North American Review*, our first creditable magazine, appeared in 1815. Two years later William Cullen Bryant published his "Thanatopsis." In 1819 appeared Washington Irving's "Sketch Book." James Fenimore Cooper began shortly afterward his famous series of novels dealing with Indian life. Hitherto the work of American writers, in all but political and religious subjects, had been but a feeble copy of the contemporary English models. In Bryant, Irving,

THE GROWTH OF A NATIONAL CONSCIOUSNESS

and Cooper, America produced her first distinctively native talent, which drew its inspiration from the natural beauties, the historical traditions, and the novel life of the western world.

263. The Reëlection of Monroe. When the election of 1820 approached there was no rival candidate to Monroe in the field. The Federalist party, with the exception of a few irreconcilables and immovables, who, in the witty language of one of their number, reminded themselves of the "melancholy state of a man who has remained sober when all his companions have become intoxicated," had been entirely merged with the nationalized Republicans in the "era of good feeling." Commerce was flourishing. Optimism prevailed. Only one disgruntled elector cast his ballot for John Quincy Adams and so deprived Monroe of sharing with George Washington the honor of being the unanimous choice of the American people.

The Monroe Doctrine

264. Our Neighbors in 1815. It was not alone in the development of our Western domain and the reënforcement of the federal power by acts of Congress and decisions of the Supreme Court that the spirit of the new Americanism manifested itself in the decade following the Treaty of Ghent. That generous glow of national enthusiasm cast its reflection over the whole Western Hemisphere. It must be borne in mind that the United States in 1815 occupied much less of the North American continent than it does today. Alaska, with its valuable furs and fisheries, belonged to the Russian Empire. Besides her present Dominion of Canada, Great Britain claimed the Oregon country, a huge region lying between the Rocky Mountains and the Pacific Ocean, extending from the northern boundary of the present state of California indefinitely toward the Alaskan shore. The possessions of Spain reached in an unbroken line from Cape Horn to a point three hundred miles north of San Francisco. They comprised not only all of South America (except Brazil and Guiana), Central America, Mexico, and the choicest islands of the West Indies, but also the immense region west of the Mississippi Valley, which now includes California, Nevada, Arizona, New Mexico, and Texas, with parts of Wyoming, Colorado, Kansas, and Oklahoma. Spain also owned what is now the state of Florida (then called East

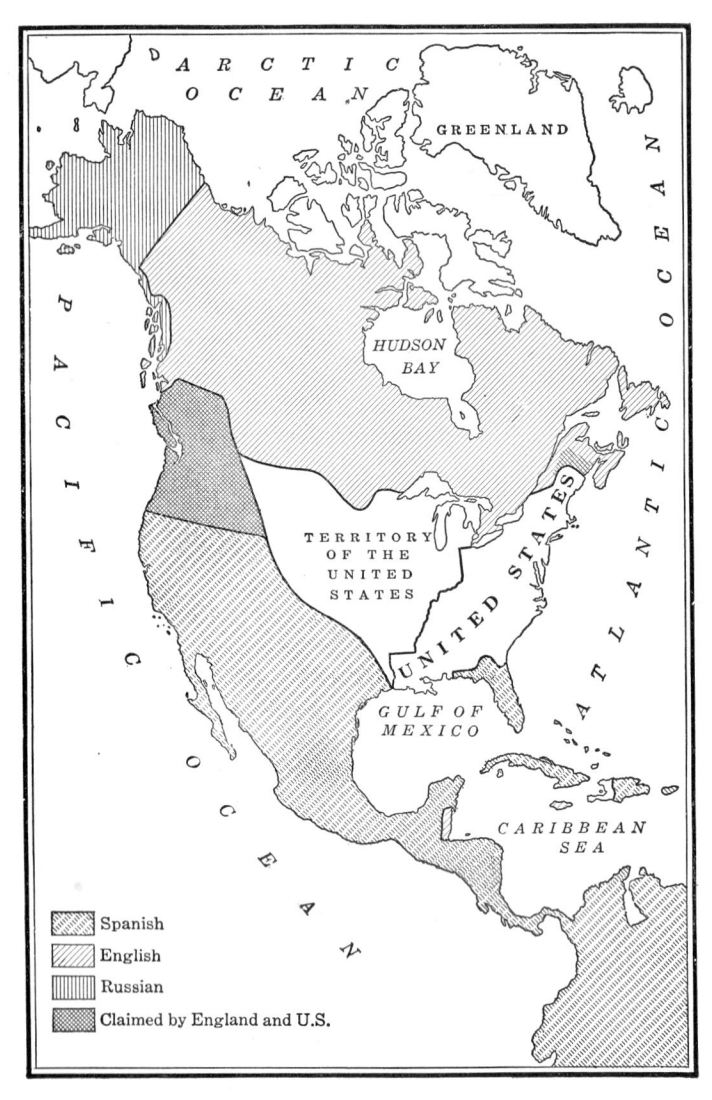

NORTH AMERICA IN 1815

THE GROWTH OF A NATIONAL CONSCIOUSNESS 203

Florida), and claimed a strip of land (called West Florida) extending along the shore of the Gulf of Mexico from Florida to the mouth of the Mississippi. This gave her practical control of the whole shore of the Gulf.

265. Our "Occupation" of West Florida. We disputed the claim of Spain to West Florida, however. According to the interpretation of our State Department at Washington, this territory formed part of the original French tract of Louisiana (1682–1763), and hence was included in the transfer from Spain to Napoleon in 1800, and in Napoleon's sale of Louisiana to the United States three years later. Spain, with better reason, maintained that the boundaries of the old French Louisiana had nothing to do with the transactions between Napoleon and the United States at the opening of the nineteenth century; that she had received West Florida by the treaty of 1783, and that she had not parted with it since. We wanted the Florida strip along the Gulf of Mexico for many reasons. It was the refuge of Indians, runaway slaves, fugitives from justice, pirates, and robbers, who terrorized the South and prevented the development of Georgia and the Mississippi territory. It offered in the fine harbors of Mobile and Pensacola an outlet for the commerce of the new cotton region. Besides, the Gulf of Mexico was the "natural boundary" of the United States on the south. President Madison, therefore, in October, 1810, ordered Governor Claiborne of the Orleans territory to take possession of West Florida as far as the Perdido River. Early the next year Congress by a secret act authorized the President to occupy East Florida also. If the occupation of West Florida by the United States was of very doubtful legality, the attempted seizure of East Florida was downright robbery. Great Britain protested so strongly that Madison prudently disavowed the acts of his agents in the latter province and withdrew the American troops in 1813.

266. Jackson's Conquest of East Florida. But the Floridas continued to be a source of annoyance to the United States. They even furnished a base for England in the War of 1812. Spain was too weak to maintain her authority there and miserably failed to redeem her pledge in the treaty of 1795, to prevent the Indians of Florida from attacking citizens of the United States. Finally, the Seminole Indians grew so dangerous that President Monroe ordered

General Andrew Jackson, the "hero of New Orleans," to pursue them even into Spanish territory (December, 1817). Jackson was a man who needed no second invitation for an Indian hunt. "Let it be signified to me through any channel," he wrote Monroe, "that the possession of the Floridas would be desirable to the United States, and in sixty days it will be accomplished." Jackson did not even wait for a reply to his letter. He swept across East Florida, reducing the Spanish strongholds of Gadsden, St. Marks, and Pensacola, executed by court-martial two British subjects who were inciting the negroes

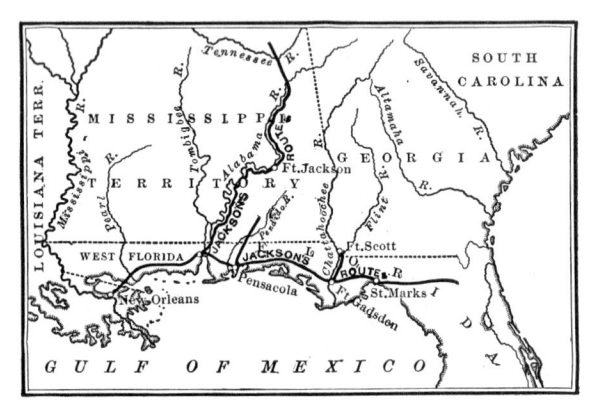

JACKSON IN FLORIDA

and Indians to murder and pillage, and by the end of May, 1818, was on his way back to Tennessee, leaving Florida a conquered province.

267. Our Ultimatum to Spain. Jackson's campaign brought the Florida question to a crisis. The administration at Washington was in a dilemma. If it indorsed his course, it would have to go further and put the responsibility for war in Florida on the shoulders of Spain. On the other hand, if it should repudiate Jackson's course, it would strengthen the position of Spain in Florida and make it more difficult to acquire that desirable province. John C. Calhoun, the Secretary of War, was for censuring Jackson for exceeding his instructions; but John Quincy Adams, Secretary of State, persuaded the President to uphold Jackson and put on a bold front. "We shall hear no more apologies from Spanish governors and commandants of their inability to perform the solemn contracts of their country," he wrote to Minister Erving at Madrid. ". . . The duty of this government to protect the persons and property of our fellow citizens on the borders of the United States is imperative — it *must* be discharged."

268. Spain surrenders Florida to the United States. But Spain was in no condition in 1818 to perform her "solemn contracts." Her colonies in South and Central America, taking advantage of the overthrow of her dynasty by Napoleon (1808), had revolted and established themselves as independent republics. Embarrassed by these difficulties, the Spanish court decided to abandon Florida to the United States. The treaty was signed at Washington, February 22, 1819. The United States assumed about $5,000,000 of claims of its citizens against Spain, for damages to our commerce in the Napoleonic wars, and in return received the whole of Florida. At the same time the western boundary of the Louisiana Purchase territory was fixed by a line running from the Sabine River in a stairlike formation north and west to the forty-second parallel of latitude, and thence west to the Pacific Ocean.[1]

269. Our Interest in Spanish America. Meanwhile we were watching with great interest the progress of the revolution in the Spanish colonies of South America. As early as 1811 President Madison had called the attention of Congress to "the scenes developing among the great communities which occupy the southern portion of our hemisphere." During the years 1811–1817 the United States maintained "consuls," who were really government spies, at Buenos Aires, Caracas, and other centers of the revolt. Henry Clay tried to force President Monroe into a hasty recognition of the South American republics. But the Secretary of State, John Quincy Adams, was more cautious. He had little confidence that the new republics would be able to maintain their independence, and he furthermore feared that interference by the United States in the affairs of the "rebellious colonies" of South America would offend the Spanish court and so endanger the success of the negotiations for the acquisition of Florida.

[1] The line ran up the Sabine River to 32°, thence due north to the Red River; thence west along the Red River to the one-hundredth meridian of west longitude; thence north to the Arkansas River; thence west along the Arkansas to its source; thence north to the forty-second parallel of latitude; thence due west to the Pacific Ocean (see map, opposite page 178).

270. Our Recognition of the Spanish American Republics. However, in the year 1821 there occurred four events which determined the administration to change its policy in regard to the recognition of the South American republics. First, the final ratifications of the treaty of 1819 were signed, and Florida was ours; secondly, the House, by a vote of 86 to 68, resolved to support the President as soon as he saw fit to recognize the independence of the South American states; thirdly, the Czar of Russia issued a *ukase* (decree) forbidding the vessels of any other nation to approach within one hundred miles of the western coast of North America, above the fifty-first parallel of latitude, claimed by Russia as the southern boundary of her colony of Alaska; and fourthly, the allied powers of Russia, Prussia, Austria, and France, having pledged themselves by the "Holy Alliance" to the restoration of the power and the possessions of all the "legitimate thrones" which the Napoleonic wars had overthrown, began to listen to Spain's request to subdue revolts in Madrid and restore the rebellious colonies in South America. On May 4, 1822, President Monroe took the first step in the protection of the South American republics, by recognizing their independence; and Congress immediately made provision for the dispatch of ministers to their capitals.

271. The Monroe Doctrine. Neither Great Britain nor the United States could view with indifference the intervention of the allied powers of Europe to reduce the South American republics to submission to Spain. These republics had naturally thrown off the commercial restrictions of Spain with her political authority. They had already, by 1822, built up a trade of $3,000,000 a year with Great Britain, and their market was too valuable a one to lose. Our own government was distressed by the rumors that France would take Mexico, and Russia would seize California, with perhaps Chile and Peru to boot, as a reward for their part in crushing the rebellious governments. Accordingly the English premier, George Canning, suggested to Richard Rush, our minister in London, that the United States join Great Britain in making a declaration to the allied powers to keep their hands off the new South American states. Monroe was anxious to act on Canning's suggestion, and the two ex-presidents, Madison and the aged Jefferson, replied to his request for advice by letters of hearty approval. Secretary Adams declared we ought not to follow England's lead, trailing "like a cockboat to a British man-of-war," but rather assume full and sole responsibility ourselves for the protection of the republics on the American continent. He therefore advised President Monroe to incorporate in his annual message to Congress of December 2, 1823, the famous statement of the policy of the United States toward the territory and government of the rest of the American continent, which has ever since been celebrated as the Monroe Doctrine.

272. Analysis of the Doctrine. The message declared that the continents of the Western Hemisphere were "henceforth not to be considered as subjects for future colonization by any European powers,"—this to prevent the encroachments of Russia on the Pacific coast, and the designs of France on Mexico. Further, it announced the determination of the United States neither to meddle with the European systems of government nor to disturb the existing possessions of European powers in the New World. "But," it continued, "we owe it to candor and to the amicable relations existing between the United States and those powers to declare that we should consider any attempt on their part to extend their system [of the Holy Alliance] to any portion of this hemisphere as dangerous to our peace and safety." In other words, the South American republics, whose independence we had, "on great consideration and on just principles, acknowledged," were no longer existing possessions of Spain; and any attempt to impose upon them the absolutism of the Spanish court by the powers of continental Europe would be "viewed as the manifestation of an unfriendly disposition toward the United States." From the acknowledgment of the South American republics, then, in 1822, the United States advanced in 1823 to the defense of their territory and of their republican form of government against European interference.

273. Interpretations of the Doctrine. The Monroe Doctrine has been called "the cornerstone of American foreign policy." It goes back for its basal idea to George Washington's warning against "entangling our peace and prosperity in the toils of European ambitions and rivalries," in his Farewell Address of 1796; and it has been ardently defended whenever there is a question of settling a boundary or collecting a debt in the Spanish-American states. Our statesmen have gradually stretched the doctrine far beyond its original declaration of the protection of the territory and the government of the republics of Central and South America. It has even been invoked as

208 NATIONAL VERSUS SECTIONAL INTERESTS

a reason for annexing territory to the United States in order to prevent the seizure of the same territory by some European power. With the entrance of the United States into the great World War, in April, 1917, and the conspicuous participation of our President in the adjustment of complicated world problems at the Peace Conference at Paris (1918–1919), that part of the Monroe Doctrine which regards the world as divided into two separate and remote halves has been rendered obsolete. If we still maintain that our interests are "paramount" in the Western Hemisphere, we no longer refrain from interfering in the political and territorial questions of the Eastern Hemisphere.

REFERENCES

A New American Spirit: E. E. SPARKS, *The Expansion of the American People*, chaps. xii, xiii, xx, xxii, xxiii; ELLEN SEMPLE, *American History and its Geographical Conditions*, chaps. ix, xiii; E. L. BOGART, *Economic History of the United States*, chaps. xiii, xiv; K. C. BABCOCK, *The Rise of American Nationality* (American Nation), chaps. xii–xv; HENRY ADAMS, *History of the United States of America during the Administrations of Jefferson and Madison*, Vol. IX; J. B. MCMASTER, *History of the People of the United States*, Vol. IV, chaps. xxxiii, xxxvi; J. W. BURGESS, *The Middle Period*, chap. i; D. C. GILMAN, *James Monroe* (American Statesmen); E. S. CORWIN, *John Marshall and the Constitution* (Chronicles, Vol. XVI), chaps. v–viii.

The Monroe Doctrine: MCMASTER, Vol. V, chap. xli; BURGESS, chaps. ii, v; BABCOCK, chap. xvii; F. J. TURNER, *The Rise of the New West* (American Nation), chap. xii; F. L. PAXSON, *The Independence of the South American Republics*; C. R. FISH, *The Path of Empire* (Chronicles, Vol. XLVI), chap. i; J. H. LATANÉ, *The Diplomatic Relations of the United States and Spanish America*; W. C. FORD, *John Quincy Adams; his Connection with the Monroe Doctrine* (American Historical Review, Vol. VII, pp. 676–696; Vol. VIII, pp. 28–52); W. F. REDDAWAY, *The Monroe Doctrine*.

TOPICS FOR SPECIAL REPORTS

1. **The Development of Canals and Roads:** KATHERINE COMAN, *Industrial History of the United States*, pp. 202–211; BABCOCK, pp. 243–258; MCMASTER, Vol. IV, pp. 381–429; SPARKS, pp. 264–269; R. T. STEVENS, *The Growth of the Nation, 1809–1837*, pp. 145–174.

2. **John Marshall and the Supreme Court:** A. B. HART, *The Formation of the Union*, pp. 234–236; H. C. LODGE, *Daniel Webster* (American Statesmen), chap. iii; A. B. MAGRUDER, *John Marshall* (American Statesmen), chap. x; BABCOCK, pp. 290–308; C. A. BEARD, *Readings in American Government and Politics*, Nos. 27, 112–114, 118.

3. **The Holy Alliance:** HART, *American History told by Contemporaries*, Vol. III, No. 142; BURGESS, pp. 123–126; MCMASTER, Vol. V, pp. 30–41;

C. A. FYFFE, *History of Modern Europe*, Vol. II, chap. i; M. E. G. DUFF, *Studies in European Politics*, chap. ii.

4. **Modern Interpretations of the Monroe Doctrine:** J. B. MOORE, *American Diplomacy*, pp. 152-167; also in *Harper's Magazine*, Vol. CIX, pp. 857 ff.; HART, *Foundations of American Foreign Policy*, pp. 211-240; A. C. COOLIDGE, *The United States as a World Power*, pp. 95-110; LATANÉ, *America as a World Power* (American Nation), pp. 255-268.

5. **American Literature a Century Ago:** MCMASTER, Vol. V, pp. 268-306; ADAMS, Vol. IX, pp. 198-214; W. E. SIMONDS, *Student History of American Literature*, pp. 94-146.

CHAPTER IX

SECTIONAL INTERESTS

The Favorite Sons

274. The Development of Sectional Rivalry. If we contrast the decade which preceded the announcement of the Monroe Doctrine with the decade which followed it, this remarkable fact stands out, that every single act and policy of the earlier period in support of nationalism—the increase of the army and navy, the recharter of the Bank, the sale of public lands on liberal terms, the expenditure of money from the public treasury for internal improvements, the increased authority of the Supreme Court, the high tariff, and even the Monroe Doctrine itself—became the subject of violent sectional controversies in the later period. The rivalry of the sections first showed itself in the fight for the presidency in 1824. It was not a contest of parties; for since the fall of the Federalists in 1816 the nationalized Republican party had stood without a rival in the field. Monroe's reëlection in 1820 was practically unanimous. But in 1824 there was no single candidate acceptable to East, West, and South. Instead, there was a group of remarkably able statesmen who, in spite of their own desire to cherish the broad national spirit of the second decade of the century, found themselves drawn year by year into the more exclusive service of their sections.

275. John Quincy Adams, 1767–1848. New England was represented in this group by John Quincy Adams and Daniel Webster. The former was one of the best-trained statesmen in all our history. He was the son of the distinguished patriot and Federalist president, John Adams. As a boy of eleven he had accompanied his father on a diplomatic mission to Paris (1778), and during the next forty years had served his country in the capacity of secretary, minister, or special envoy at the courts of Russia, Prussia, the Netherlands, Sweden, France, and England. He served as United States senator from Massachusetts from 1803 to 1808, and President Monroe called him, in 1817, to the first place in his cabinet, a position which he filled with great success during the eight years of Monroe's administration. For all his cosmopolitan experience, Adams remained a New England Puritan, and preserved to the end of his career the noble austerities and repelling virtues of the Puritan,—unswerving conscientiousness, unsparing self-judgment, unflagging industry, unbending dignity, unyielding devotion to duty. He rose before daylight, read his Bible with the regularity of an orthodox clergyman, and in his closely written diary of a dozen volumes recorded the affairs of his soul as faithfully as the affairs of state.

276. Daniel Webster, 1782–1852. Daniel Webster, fifteen years Adams's junior, had by no means reached the latter's level as a statesman at the close of Monroe's administration. He had neither been a member of the cabinet nor filled a diplomatic post. The son of a sturdy New Hampshire farmer, he had secured a college education at Dartmouth, at some sacrifice to his family, and had amply justified their faith in his promise by a brilliant legal career. In 1813 he had been sent to Washington as congressman from a New Hampshire district. A few years later he moved his law office to Boston, and from 1823 to the middle of the century continued almost uninterruptedly to represent the people of Massachusetts in the national House and Senate. By his famous plea in the Dartmouth College case, his Plymouth oration on the two-hundredth anniversary of the landing of the Pilgrims (1820), and his speeches in Congress, he had already won a national reputation as an orator before the close of Monroe's administration. When it was known that Webster was to speak, the gallery and floor of the Senate chamber would be crowded with a throng eager to sit or stand for hours under the spell of his sonorous and majestic voice. Like Adams, Webster inherited and appreciated New England's traditions of learning, and took just

JOHN QUINCY ADAMS

pride in the contribution of its Puritan stock to the mental and moral standard of our country; but he was not a Puritan in temper and habits, like Adams, who wrote himself down in his diary as "a man of cold, austere, and forbidding manners." When Webster erred it was rather on the side of conviviality than of austerity.

277. Albert Gallatin, 1761–1849. The Middle Atlantic region had two or three statesmen of first rank, besides scores of politicians who were contending for political influence. Albert Gallatin of Pennsylvania, a Swiss by birth, had been Secretary of the Treasury under Jefferson and Madison (1801–1813), had been with Adams and Clay on the commission which negotiated the peace with England in 1814, and was serving as minister to France when he was persuaded to come home to take part in the campaign of 1824.

278. Rufus King, 1755–1827. Rufus King, senator from New York, had, in his younger days, been one of the Massachusetts delegates to the Constitutional Convention of 1787. Three times since 1800 he had been candidate for president or vice president on the Federalist ticket. At the time of Monroe's presidency he was one of the most eloquent antislavery orators in Congress.

279. De Witt Clinton, 1769–1828. De Witt Clinton had been governor of New York for two terms, and in 1812, as candidate of the Federalist party, he had seriously contested Madison's reëlection. His monument is the great Erie Canal (opened in 1825), which runs through the Mohawk valley and, connecting with the Hudson, unites the waters of the Great Lakes with those of the Atlantic Ocean. But none of these men was an "available" candidate in 1824. Gallatin was a nationalized foreigner, King had been standard bearer of the Federalists in their humiliating defeat of 1816, and Clinton, besides the handicap of his old Federalist connections, was too much engrossed in the strife of factions in New York state to emerge as a national figure.

280. William H. Crawford, 1772–1834. Among the brilliant group of orators and statesmen from the South, William H. Crawford of Georgia and John C. Calhoun of South Carolina stood preëminent. Crawford had a powerful mind in a powerful body. He entered the United States Senate in 1807, at the age of thirty-five, was made minister to France in 1813, and was in the cabinet continuously as Secretary of War and of the Treasury from 1815 to 1825. A most accomplished politician, he came very near defeating Monroe for the Republican nomination for the presidency in 1816, despite the latter's hearty support by Madison. Crawford was retained by Monroe as the head of the Treasury Department, where he won from so high an authority as Gallatin the praise of having "a most correct judgment and inflexible integrity."

281. John C. Calhoun, 1782–1850. John C. Calhoun probably has even today but one rival in the hearts of Southern patriots,— the gallant warrior-gentleman, Robert E. Lee. Calhoun, just past thirty, was one of the brilliant group of "new men" in the Twelfth Congress, who in their national enthusiasm forced Madison to declare war on England in 1812, and followed the successful conclusion of the war with the liberal legislation on army, bank, tariff, and internal improvements which we have studied in the preceding chapter. Monroe offered Calhoun the War portfolio in 1817, and, like Adams and Crawford, the South Carolinian remained in the cabinet during both of Monroe's terms. Some of Calhoun's contemporaries feared that "the lightning glances of his mind" and his passion for national expansion sometimes disturbed his solid judgment in these early years; but Adams, who sat for eight years at the same council board with him, described Calhoun in his diary as "fair and candid, of clear and quick understanding, cool self-possession, enlarged philosophical views, and ardent patriotism."

JOHN C. CALHOUN

282. Thomas H. Benton, 1782–1858. The West boasted of three men of national reputation in Benton, Clay, and Jackson, all of whom had emigrated from the South Atlantic States. Thomas Hart Benton, born in North Carolina in 1782, had gone west in early life to help build up the commonwealth of Tennessee; and, following the impulse of the pioneer, had continued farther to the trans-Mississippi frontier. In 1821 he was sent by the new state of Missouri to the

Senate, where he continued for thirty years to plead the cause of westward expansion with an almost savage enthusiasm. He denounced the "surrender of Texas"[1] to Spain in the treaty of 1819 with all the zeal of an ancient prophet, and foretold the day when the valley of the Columbia River should be the granary of China and Japan.

283. Henry Clay, 1777-1852. The name of Henry Clay has already appeared frequently on these pages, for no account of the War of 1812 and the system of national development which followed could be written without giving Clay the most conspicuous place. He was a born leader of men, adapting his genial personality to the humblest and roughest frontiersman without a sign of condescension, and meeting the lofty demeanor of an Adams with an easy charm of manner. When still a young law student of nineteen Clay had migrated from Virginia, in 1796, to the new state of Kentucky, where his great gifts of leadership and marvelous oratory obtained for him in 1806 a seat in the United States Senate before the legal age of thirty years. In 1811 he entered the House, and as Speaker of the Twelfth Congress began a career of leadership in American politics which was to extend over four decades to his death in 1852. If Webster's voice was the most convincing that ever sounded in the halls of Congress, Henry Clay's was the most winning. He spoke to the hearts of men. He was not merely the "choice" of his supporters; he was their idol. And when he was defeated for the high office of president, it is said men wept like children.

284. Andrew Jackson, 1767-1845. Finally, in Andrew Jackson of Tennessee the Southwest had a hero of the pure American democracy. Jackson was born of Scotch-Irish parentage in the western uplands on the border of the Carolinas in 1767. He joined the tide of emigration to Tennessee, where his energy, pluck, and hard sense gained for him a foremost place in local politics, while his prowess as an Indian fighter won him a generalship in the War of 1812. The victory of New Orleans (1815) made Jackson the most conspicuous soldier of the republic, and the "conquest of Florida" in the Seminole War, three years later, brought him before the cabinet at Washington

---

[1] When the boundary treaty of 1819 was concluded (see page 205) some of our statesmen claimed, but without right, that Texas, being a part of the Louisiana Purchase territory, was "sacrificed" or "surrendered" to Spain.

Courtesy of the Long Island Historical Society

HENRY CLAY

and the court of Madrid as the decisive factor in the long negotiations over the Florida territory. Jackson was a man of action, not words. His bitter rival, Henry Clay, never tired of calling him a mere "military chieftain." Away back in Washington's administration Jackson had entered Congress from the new state of Tennessee (1796) in his backwoodsman's dress, "a tall, lank, uncouth-looking personage, with long locks of hair hanging over his face, and a cue down his back tied in an eelskin." Jefferson, who was president of the Senate when Jackson was a member of that body, in 1797–1798, said that he had often seen this violent member from Tennessee struggling in vain to speak on the floor, his voice completely choked by rage. But Jackson left the halls of Congress in 1798, not to return for a full quarter of a century,—and then crowned with the laurels of his great victories and already the choice of the legislature of his state for president.

285. The Election of 1824. Four of these "favorite sons" of the various sections of the country were rivals for the presidency in 1824, —General Jackson, Henry Clay, and Monroe's cabinet officers Adams and Crawford. During the whole of Monroe's second term these men were laying their plans to gain the coveted honor. Crawford secured the support of the congressional caucus,[1] but candidates of the other sections were enthusiastically nominated by state legislatures and mass meetings. It was the first popular presidential campaign in our history, abounding in personalities, cartoons, emblems, banners, songs, speeches, and dinners. "Old hickory" clubs were formed for Jackson, and men wore black silk vests with his portrait stamped upon them. The support of the New England States was pledged to Adams; Tennessee, Alabama, and Pennsylvania declared for Jackson; and Clay secured the legislatures of Kentucky, Missouri, Ohio, and Louisiana. In New York there was a battle royal, resulting in the distribution of the 36 electoral votes of the state among the four candidates. When the vote was formally counted it was found that Jackson had 99 votes, Adams 84, Crawford 41, and Clay 37.

[1] Since John Adams's day it had been customary for the members of each party to meet in a caucus, or conference, and select the candidates of their party for president and vice president. But by 1824 the increasing democratic sentiment of the country made this exclusive method of selecting presidential candidates unpopular.

286. Adams chosen by the House. As no candidate had received the majority (more than half) of the electoral votes required by the Constitution for the choice of a president, the House of Representatives had to select from the three highest names on the list (Twelfth Amendment). Clay, being out of the race, decided quite naturally to throw his influence on the side of Adams, who was not, like Jackson, his rival in the West, and whose political views were much closer to his own on such questions as internal improvements, the tariff, the Bank, and other points of the "American System," than were those of the "military chieftain" Jackson. Adams was chosen by the House, and immediately offered Clay the first place in his cabinet. The Jackson supporters were furious. The "will of the people" had been defeated, they said. The House was morally bound, they claimed, to choose the man who had the greatest number of electoral and popular votes. They declared that the aristocratic Adams and Henry Clay, "the Judas of the West," had entered into a "corrupt bargain" to keep the old hero of New Orleans out of the honors which the nation had clearly voted him. Jackson appealed from Congress to the people. He resigned his seat in the Senate, and with an able corps of managers in every section of the country began a four years' campaign against Adams, Clay, and the whole "dynasty of secretaries," to restore the government of the American republic to the ideals of its founders and to servants of the people's choice.

An Era of Hard Feelings

287. The Sections of our Country. With our present rapid means of transportation and communication by the railroad and the airplane, the telegraph and the telephone; with our tremendous interstate commerce binding section to section; with our network of banks and brokerage houses maintaining financial equilibrium between the different parts of our country, we find it hard to realize the isolation and the consequent antagonism of the various geographical sections in the early years of the nineteenth century. The wonder really is that our country held together as well as it did, and not that it tended to separate into sections. For in spite of the temporary unifying effect of the second war with Great Britain, it was not until the crisis of the great Civil War that the United

States became an assured Union. We shall better appreciate the United States of 1825 if we think of it as a huge geographical framework containing several distinct communities with widely differing social and industrial interests.

288. New England. New England, with its two full centuries of Puritan history behind it, though at last outgrowing its religious narrowness, was still a very conservative region socially and politically. It had been the last stronghold of Federalism, which stood, in John Adams's phrase, for government by "the rich, the well born, and the able." It had never made the ballot common or office cheap. As its farming population was attracted westward to the rich lands of the Ohio valley,[1] power was even more consolidated in the hands of the rich merchant and manufacturing classes on the seaboard. New York, New Jersey, and eastern Pennsylvania, without sharing the religious prejudices of New England, were generally allied with that region in their industrial and mercantile interests.

289. The "Planter Aristocracy" in the South. To New England's aristocracy of merchants the South opposed an aristocracy of planters. The cultivation of cotton, increasing as we have seen at a marvelous rate in the early years of the nineteenth century, was rapidly fixing on the South an institution which was fraught with the gravest consequences for our country's history,— the institution of negro slavery. We shall discuss the political and ethical consequences of slavery in later chapters. Here we note simply the economic fact that the increase of negro slave labor in the South made free white labor impracticable, and with it shut out the possibility of the development of manufactures, which, since the second war with England, had been thriving in the Northern states.

290. The Pioneer Community of the West. A third distinct section of our country, growing every year more conscious of its peculiar temper and its peculiar needs, was the West. To the merchant aristocracy of the East and the planter aristocracy of the South, the West opposed the rugged democracy of a pioneer community. Men were scarce in Ohio, Indiana, Kentucky, Tennessee, and the Mississippi territory in the early days, and every man

---

[1] The influence of New England on the West may be seen in the fact that in 1830 thirty-one members of Congress were natives of Connecticut, though the state itself sent but five members.

counted. The artificial distinctions of name and education weighed but little compared with the natural distinctions of brawn and wit. The pioneer was rough, hardy, and self-reliant. He made his way with knife and gun. A convention at Knoxville for framing the constitution of Tennessee adopted the rule that any man who digressed from the discussion "in order to fall upon the person of another member" should be suppressed by the chair. Justice was summary. The feud and the duel often replaced the tedious processes of the courts. The test of a man was what he could *do*, not how much he *knew*. If he could manage a wild horse, drive an ax deep, and repel an Indian raid, he was the right kind of American; and his vote and opinion were worth as much in this democratic country as those of any merchant in Boston.

291. The New Democracy. The people of the Atlantic seaboard had all inherited European ideas of rank. They had, to be sure, developed a political democracy, but not a social one. They believed in a government *for* the people and perhaps *of* the people — but not *by* the people. In Washington's day only some 120,000 out of a population of nearly 4,000,000 had the right to vote, and religious or property qualifications were attached to the offices of government in almost all the states. But the new states of the West were all for manhood suffrage, without regard to birth, profession, or wealth. The time had now come when these states, with their immense growth in population, were conscious of their influence over the national government. In the words of Senator Benton of Missouri, they demanded "some share in the destinies of this republic."

292. The Difficult Position of President Adams. The events of the period which we are studying can be understood only in the light of this sectional rivalry. The upright Adams met with opposition all through his term because he was unable to see or unwilling to encourage such rivalry. While his opponents were busy building up their party machine, Adams steadily refused to use his high position for such a purpose. He would not remove a man from office for voting against the administration; he would not appoint a man to office as a reward for services to the party. He declined to exchange the responsibilities of the statesman for the intrigues of the politician. He held to the policy of a strong national government controlling all parts of the country, just at the moment when these various parts were coming more and more keenly to realize their conflicting sectional interests.

293. The Panama Congress. The affair of the Panama Congress is an excellent illustration of the frustration of the national ideas of Adams and Clay by sectional interests. The newly liberated republics of Mexico, Colombia, and Central America, whose independence the United States had guaranteed in the Monroe Doctrine, decided to hold a congress on the Isthmus of Panama for the purpose of forming a league to oppose the aggressions of Spain or any other European nation. A courteous invitation was sent to the United States in the autumn of 1825 to participate in this congress. But the slaveholding states of the South saw in it a grave danger. The revolt of the Spanish colonies had been accompanied by a movement in favor of slave emancipation. If Cuba and Porto Rico were added to the new group of republics, it would mean the liberation of the slaves of those islands. If Haiti, already a free negro republic, were admitted to the congress, we should be logically forced to welcome its ministers to our country. "The peace of eleven states of this Union," said a Southern member of Congress, "will not permit black consuls and ambassadors to establish themselves in our cities and parade through our country, and give their fellow blacks in the United States proof in hand of the honors which await them for a like successful insurrection on their part." After a long and bitter debate the names of the two envoys whom Adams had appointed to represent us at the Panama Congress were confirmed in the Senate by the close vote of 24 to 19. But it was a fruitless victory. One of the envoys died on the way to Panama, and the other reached his destination only to find the congress adjourned.

294. The Failure of the "American Policy." The Adams-Clay policy of internal improvements at national expense met the same sectional opposition. The President praised the spirit of New York State in completing the Erie Canal (1825) and tried to stimulate Congress by this example to the "accomplishment of works important to the whole country, to which neither the authority nor the resources of any one state could be adequate." But the tide of opinion was running strongly against him. The West replied, Let the government give us the lands which are now being bought up by Eastern speculators, and we will take care of our own development. And the

South said, Let the government reduce the tariff duties which are enriching the Northern merchants at our expense, and it will not have so much money to spend "in charity" on roads and canals.[1]

295. Georgia defies the Administration. Even a single state defied the national policy of the administration. Georgia had for several years been hindered in its development by the presence of the large and powerful nations of Creek and Cherokee Indians on its fertile soil. The United States had promised as early as 1802 to remove these Indians, but they were still there when Adams became president in 1825. Clay negotiated a treaty with the Indians, giving them the occupancy of the land till 1827. But Governor Troup of Georgia had already begun to survey the lands as state property. Adams warned the governor against interfering with "the faith of the nation" toward the Indians; but Troup replied that Georgia was "sovereign on her own soil" and notified the Secretary of War that he would "resist by force the first act of hostility on the part of the United States, the unblushing ally of the savages." To Adams's chagrin the Senate refused to support him in forcing Georgia to obedience, and Governor Troup proceeded with his surveys.

296. Our Manufacturing Interests. These examples of the Panama fiasco, the failure of the policy of internal improvements, and the successful defiance of the government by the state of Georgia show how rapidly sectional interests were replacing the national enthusiasm of the two previous administrations. But the most striking example of all was the quarrel over the tariff. When we were drawn into the struggle between Napoleon and Great Britain, and our shipping was destroyed by embargoes, nonintercourse, and war

---

[1] The failure of the so-called "American policy" of government aid for improvements in transportation is seen in its true significance when we remember that it was just at this epoch that the great railway systems of our country were begun. The Mohawk and Hudson Railway (parent of the New York Central) was started in 1825, the Boston and Albany and the Pennsylvania in 1827, and the Baltimore and Ohio in 1828. These railways soon superseded the canals as routes of transportation and have now grown into several vast systems of trunk lines and branches, with 250,000 miles of track,— enough to circle the earth ten times. They are owned and until the entrance of the United States into the World War were managed by private corporations, chartered by the state governments. The Pennsylvania system, for example, has between thirty and forty charters granted by a dozen states. Who can calculate the effect on the economic and political history of our country if the construction and management of railways had been adopted as part of the national government's business in John Quincy Adams's administration, and if Congress had maintained the same control over the steel lines of land transportation that it has over the rivers and harbors of the United States!

(1807–1815), the merchants of the country began to put their capital into manufactures. Cotton, woolen, and paper mills, tanneries, furniture factories, iron forges, glass and pottery works, sprang up. At the close of the war with England (1815) there was close to $100,000,000 invested in manufacturing industries in this country, giving employment to 200,000 workers. Just at the same moment the return of universal peace in Europe found Great Britain with an immense amount of manufactured goods on her hands, which had accumulated while the ports of the Continent were closed to her commerce by Napoleon's decrees (p. 180). These goods Great Britain proceeded to "dump" on the United States at low prices, to glut our markets and, as Lord Brougham put it, "to stifle in the cradle those rising manufactures in the United States which the war had forced into existence." In the single year of 1816, $90,000,000 worth of goods were sent over to this country.

297. The Tariff of 1816. Hatred of England and patriotic pride in our own new industries, confidence in our destiny as a great manufacturing people, the self-interest of the manufacturers, and the conviction that "to be independent for the comforts of life," as Thomas Jefferson said, "we must fabricate them ourselves, putting manufactures by the side of agriculture,"— all combined to cause the passage in 1816 of a tariff bill which not only continued the high duties levied for the extraordinary war expenses in 1812 but even increased the rates by 15 or 20 per cent. All sections of our country contributed to the passage of this bill (see map, p. 223), for, although less than 5 per cent of the manufactures of the country were in the states south of Virginia in 1816, nevertheless these states hoped to build up mills and factories like those of the North.

298. The Protective Tariff of 1824. But the tariff of 1816 did not stop the flood of importations from England, and the manufacturers in the Northern states begged Congress to save them from ruin by laying still higher duties. Tariff bills increasing the rates were introduced into the House in 1820, 1821, and 1823, but it was not till 1824 that a new tariff passed the House by the narrow majority of 107 to 102 votes, and the Senate by a vote of 25 to 22. The tariff of 1824 raised the average duty from 20 per cent to 36 per cent. Since our revenues from the tariff of 1816 were more than ample for running the government, and a large surplus was piling up in the treasury, this additional tariff of 1824 was purely "protective"; that is, to protect the prices of our goods against competition from England, where labor was cheaper and more abundant, and the processes of manufacture were more advanced.

299. Antitariff Sentiment in the South. Moreover, the tariff of 1824 was purely sectional, only three votes being cast for it south of the Potomac and Cumberland Rivers. For the South had discovered in the years since 1816 that it was not destined to become a manufacturing region and thus to share in the benefits of a protective tariff. The extension of the cotton area to Alabama, Mississippi, and Louisiana, and the immense leap in cotton exportation from 60,000,000 pounds in 1816 to 200,000,000 pounds in 1824, made it certain that the South would continue to devote itself to the production of this agricultural staple by slave labor. Without manufactures, then, or hope of manufactures, the South saw itself taxed by the tariff to support the mills and factories of the North. The price of raw cotton was constantly falling, owing to the great increase of the crop, and the cost of manufactured goods for which the South exchanged its cotton was constantly rising, owing to the increasing tariff. The planter had to buy food and clothing for his slaves, and the tariff raised the price of these necessities so high that John Randolph wittily said that unless the rates were lowered in a short time, instead of the masters advertising for fugitive slaves, the South would see the slaves searching for their fugitive masters. Under this economic pressure the South, in spite of its votes for the tariff of 1816, now challenged the right of Congress to levy a protective tariff at all. The Constitution gave Congress the right to raise a revenue, the objectors said, but not to levy a tax on the industries of one part of the country to protect the industries of another part. The North, with its system of free labor and small farms, inviting industry at home and immigration from abroad, was rapidly outgrowing the South in population. Hence its majority was constantly increasing in the House of Representatives. If the Northern majority in Congress were to be allowed to pass measure after measure for the benefit of their own section, the South would be "reduced to the condition of a subject province."

300. The "Tariff of Abominations." When a still higher protective tariff was demanded by the Northern woolen and iron manufacturers in 1827, the South protested. Thomas Cooper, president of South Carolina College, declared in a fiery speech that when the "Massachusetts lords of the spinning jenny and peers of the loom" presumed by virtue of their majority in Congress to tax the South, it was "high time to calculate the value of the Union." The Southerners were not strong enough to keep a new high tariff bill out of Congress in 1828, but they resorted to a shrewd trick to defeat it. Instead of seeking to lower the tariff rates proposed, they joined with the

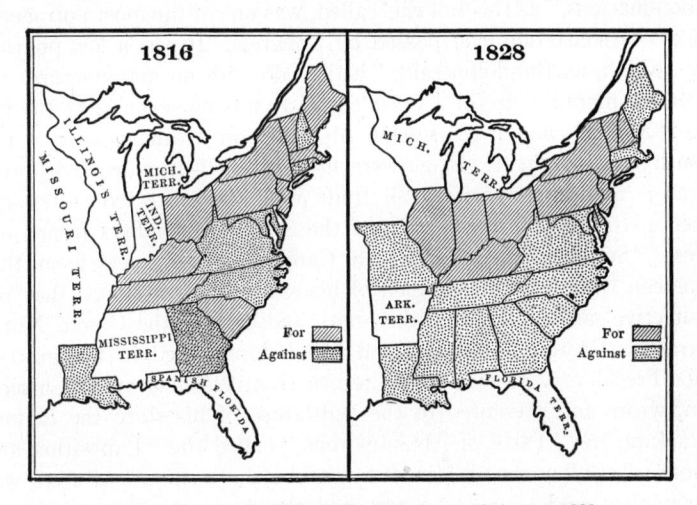

THE VOTE ON THE TARIFF BILLS OF 1816 AND 1828

Western farmers in greatly increasing them. A presidential election was approaching, and the South appealed to the large anti-Adams sentiment to frame a tariff bill so preposterous that New England would reject it, and so bring dishonor and defeat upon Adams's cause. For example, New England wanted a high duty on manufactured woolens to exclude English goods, but at the same time it wanted cheap raw wool for its factories. It wanted a high duty on cordage to protect its shipbuilding industries, but it wanted cheap raw hemp for its ropewalks. It wanted a high duty on iron manufactures, but cheap pig iron for its forges. All New England's demands for protection to manufactures were granted in the bill, but their benefits were largely neutralized by the addition of high duties on raw wool to please the sheep raisers of Ohio, on hemp to satisfy the farmers of Kentucky, and on pig iron to conciliate the miners of Pennsylvania. In spite of this shrewd plan of the South to match the West against New England, and thus to please nobody by pleasing everybody, the fantastic bill passed the House by a vote of 105 to 94, the Senate by a vote of 26 to 21, and became a law by President Adams's signature (May 19, 1828).

301. Calhoun's "Exposition and Protest." The "Tariff of Abominations," as this bill was called, was one of the most outrageous pieces of legislation ever passed by Congress. It was a low political job, which, as Randolph said, "had to do with no manufactures except the manufacture of a president." It was not even (like the bill of 1824) the honest expression of a section of the country. The South was indignant. Flags were flown at half-mast in Charleston. Orators advised boycotting all trade with the protected states and even advocated the resignation of the Southern members from Congress. Senator Hayne of South Carolina wrote to Jackson that nineteen twentieths of the men of his state were convinced that the protective tariff would ruin the South and destroy the Union. North Carolina, Georgia, Alabama, and Mississippi joined in the protest. Vice President Calhoun, on his return from Washington to Charleston, wrote and presented to the legislature of his state the famous attack on the "Tariff of Abominations," called the "Exposition and Protest." Calhoun maintained, first, that the tariff act of 1828 was unconstitutional, since Congress had the power to lay taxes only for a revenue; secondly, that the act was sectional, since by it the South, which had but one third of the votes in the House (76 out of 213), paid over two thirds of the customs duties; and thirdly, that, as our government was an agreement or compact between the states, the national government created by that compact could not be superior to the states in sovereignty and could not be itself the judge of what its proper powers were. The states, which had bestowed on Congress its powers, were the ultimate judges of whether or not Congress was overstepping those powers. And hence, at any time, a state might challenge an act of Congress and appeal to its sister states for the verdict. Congress must then secure the votes of three fourths of the states in ratification of an amendment giving it the express power in dispute.

SECTIONAL INTERESTS

302. The Election of Andrew Jackson. The presidential election of 1828 took place a few weeks before Calhoun presented his "Exposition." The Republican party was still the only one in the field, but its two wings had drawn so far apart that new names were necessary to denote them. The supporters of the policy of Adams and Clay (high tariff, national improvements, strong central government) were called National-Republicans; while the opposition forces, led by Calhoun, Crawford, and Jackson, revived the original party name of Democratic-Republicans. Jackson's victory over Adams in the election of 1828 was overwhelming; he carried every state west of the Alleghenies and south of Maryland, besides Pennsylvania and the majority of the votes of New York. His victory was hailed as the triumph of democratic principles, an assertion of "the people's right to govern themselves."

303. A Truce on the Tariff. Calhoun advised South Carolina to wait, before taking any radical steps, to see what Jackson would do. A Southerner and a slaveholder, the recipient of their unanimous vote for the presidency, he must, thought the men of the South, reverse the iniquitous tariff policy of his predecessor. So the commercial North and the agricultural South stood facing each other in a hostile truce, while "the people" invaded the White House on inauguration day, standing with muddy cowhide boots on the damask-covered chairs, spilling orange punch on the carpets, and almost suffocating the old "Hero of New Orleans" as they pressed round him to shake his hand and declare that his inauguration was the inauguration of the rule of American democracy pure and undefiled.

REFERENCES

The Favorite Sons: E. E. SPARKS, *The Men who made the Nation*, chaps. viii–x; J. B. MCMASTER, *History of the People of the United States*, Vol. V, chap. xlii; EDWARD STANWOOD, *History of the Presidency*, chap. xi; J. W. BURGESS, *The Middle Period*, chap. vi; F. J. TURNER, *The Rise of the New West* (American Nation), chaps. xi, xv; also *The Frontier in American History* (in *American Historical Association Reports*, Vol. III, pp. 197–227); ALLEN JOHNSON, *Union and Democracy* (Riverside History of U. S., Vol. II), chap. xvii; biographies of John Quincy Adams (by MORSE), Benton (by ROOSEVELT), Webster (by LODGE), Gallatin (by STEVENS), Clay (by SCHURZ), Jackson (by SUMNER), and Calhoun (by VON HOLST), in the American Statesmen Series.

An Era of Hard Feelings: MCMASTER, Vol. V, chaps. xlvi, li–liii; TURNER, chaps. xviii, xix; BURGESS, chaps. vii, viii; WOODROW WILSON, *Division and*

Reunion, chap. i; JOHNSON, chap. xviii; H. VON HOLST, *Constitutional History of the United States*, Vol. I, chap. xi; D. R. DEWEY, *Financial History of the United States*, chap. viii; F. W. TAUSSIG, *Tariff History of the United States*, chap. ii; STANWOOD, *American Tariff Controversies*, chap. viii; J. F. RHODES, *History of the United States from the Compromise of 1850*, Vol. I, pp. 40-53; *Cambridge Modern History*, Vol. VII, pp. 374-380; WILLIAM MACDONALD, *Select Documents of United States History, 1776-1861*, Nos. 44, 45 (for text of tariff protests).

TOPICS FOR SPECIAL REPORTS

1. **Thomas H. Benton's Prophecies of Western Growth:** MCMASTER, Vol. V, pp. 24-27; W. M. MEIGS, *Life of Thomas Hart Benton*, pp. 90-103; THEODORE ROOSEVELT, *Thomas Hart Benton*, pp. 50-58; THOMAS H. BENTON. *Thirty Years' View*, Vol. I, pp. 13, 14; H. A. BRUCE, *Romance of American Expansion*, pp. 106-122.

2. **The Selection of a Presidential Candidate:** F. W. DALLINGER, *Nominations for Elective Office*, pp. 13-48; MCMASTER, Vol. V, pp. 55-67; M. I. OSTROGORSKI, *Democracy and the Party System in the United States*, pp. 3-16; STANWOOD, *History of the Presidency*, pp. 125-132; J. A. WOODBURN, *Political Parties and Party Problems in the United States*, pp. 165-196; JAMES BRYCE, *The American Commonwealth* (abridged edition), pp. 465-485; C. A. BEARD, *Readings in American Government and Politics*, Nos. 46-50.

3. **The Panama Congress:** BURGESS, pp. 147-155; VON HOLST, Vol. I, pp. 409-433; J. D. RICHARDSON, *Messages and Papers of the Presidents*, Vol. II, pp. 318-329; MCMASTER, Vol. V, pp. 433-459; A. B. HART, *Contemporaries*, Vol. III, No. 150; BENTON, Vol. I, pp. 65-69.

4. **The Arguments for a Protective Tariff:** DEWEY, pp. 191-196; TAUSSIG, pp. 1-67; W. M. GROSVENOR, *Does Protection Protect?* pp. 176-201; HENRY GEORGE, *Protection or Free Trade*, pp. 88-120, 154-230; EDWARD TAYLOR, *Is Protection a Benefit?* pp. 96-173, 206-232; A. MAURICE LOW, *Protection in the United States*, pp. 40-59, 94-119; H. R. SEAGER, *Introduction to Economics*, pp. 371-383; also article "Protection," in the New International Encyclopædia.

Andrew Jackson

CHAPTER X

THE JACKSONIAN ERA

Nullification

304. Jackson's Conception of the Presidency. The fathers of the American Revolution in their long contest against the royal governors in the colonies had come to regard a strong executive as the greatest menace to freedom. Therefore in the first form of government that they devised (the Articles of Confederation) they created no executive department at all. The improved Constitution of 1787 made provision for a president, but gave Congress, especially the Senate, a very considerable control over his policies. During the first forty years of our national history our presidents had respected the spirit of the framers of the Constitution and regarded themselves as the agents chosen by the people to execute the will of the people's representatives in Congress. But with Andrew Jackson a new type of president appeared. Jackson considered himself in no way bound to defer to Congress. He thought of himself rather as the champion of the great mass of the American people. Congress and the courts, he feared, had become corrupted by association with the moneyed men of the country and by too long a tenure of power. The favorite historical analogy of Jackson and his supporters was the Roman tribune, an officer chosen by the common folk of Rome to protect them from oppressive legislation by the rich and high-born patricians.

305. His Absolutism of Character. Jackson interpreted his election in 1828 as a rebuke to the "corrupt" manipulation of Congress, which had seated Adams in the presidential chair in 1825. He came into the office with the vindictive elation of a man who had been kept out of his rightful inheritance for four years. His strong will, doubly steeled by long years of military command, refused to bend to entreaty or threat. From his own intense devotion to his country he drew the hasty and unwarranted conclusion that all who were opposed to him were enemies of that country. He was seldom without a personal quarrel, and, like all combative natures, he often lacked the judgment to know what causes were worth a controversy and what were not. His partisan temperament acted like a strong chemical reagent, bringing out the political color of every mind with which it came into contact. Everybody had to take sides for or against Andrew Jackson. Least of all our presidents—less even than Lincoln or Roosevelt—did he sink his personality in his office. He dominated the office and even scouted its traditions. He made it Jacksonian. Although he declaimed against the "effete dynasties" and "pampered minions" of Europe, his political enemies declared that he was wont to conduct himself more like an absolute ruler than like the sworn defender of a democratic constitution, and spoke of his presidency as "the reign of Andrew Jackson."

306. His Lack of Consistency. A will so absolute as Jackson's could have little regard for consistency. In 1816 he had written to President-elect Monroe that party spirit was a monstrous thing, unworthy of a great and free nation; yet when he himself came into office in 1829 he showed himself the most partisan president our country has ever had. Between his inauguration in March and the meeting of his first Congress in December he removed over a thousand government officials in order to make places for men who had supported his campaign, whereas all the previous presidents had together made less than a hundred political removals. He had protested vigorously against allowing any member of Congress to be appointed to an executive office, yet he himself chose four out of the six members of his first cabinet from Congress. In each of his annual messages he advised against a second term, yet he allowed himself, after his first year of office, to be announced through the administration newspapers at Washington and elsewhere as a candidate for reëlection in 1832. He poured out his wrath on the leaders of the preceding administration for "crooked politics," "corrupt bargains," jobbery, and underhand methods; yet he himself carried on his government almost exclusively with the help of shrewd newspaper editors and devoted partisans in minor public offices. Even the official cabinet, with the exception of Van Buren, was ignored in favor of a group of unofficial advisers called the kitchen cabinet.

307. His Indifference to the Tariff. As for the antitariff men of the South, they got small comfort from Jackson. In his first message he scarcely mentioned the tariff, and in his next one (December, 1830), while admitting that the tariff was "too high on some of the comforts of life," he nevertheless declared both that Congress had the right to levy a protective tariff and that the policy of protection was desirable. Meanwhile an event had occurred in the United States Senate which greatly inflamed the hostile feelings of North and South and hastened South Carolina into a policy of defiance.

308. The Debate on the Public Lands. The sale of public lands in the West was an important source of income to the national government. The low price of these lands tempted speculators to buy them up and hold them for a rise in price. Accordingly Senator Foote of Connecticut, in December, 1829, proposed a resolution to the effect that no more public land should be put on the market for a time. The Southern and Western members of Congress attributed this motion to the selfish spirit of the Eastern merchants, who, they said, wanted to stop migration to the West in order to keep a mass of cheap laborers for their factories, just as they wanted high duties to protect the output of those factories. During the debate Robert Hayne of South Carolina left the specific subject under discussion, namely, the land sales, to rebuke the attitude of the North in general and of Massachusetts in particular. He accused the Bay State of having shown a narrow, selfish, sectional spirit from the earliest days of the republic. He declared that the only way to preserve the Union of free republics, which the "fathers" wished this country to be, was to resist the economic tyranny of the manufacturing states, which had got control of Congress. The proper method of resistance had already been set forth by Calhoun in his "Exposition."

309. Daniel Webster's Reply to Hayne. Daniel Webster replied to Hayne in an oration which is considered the greatest speech ever delivered in the halls of Congress (January 26–27, 1830). After defending Massachusetts against the charge of sectionalism, Webster went on to develop the theory of the national government as opposed to the mere league of states which the Southern orators advocated. Not the states, he claimed, but the *people* of the nation had made the Union. "It is, sir, the people's Constitution, the people's government, made for the people, made by the people, answerable to the people." If Congress exceeded its powers, there was an arbiter appointed by the Constitution itself, namely, the Supreme Court, which had the authority to declare laws null and void. This authority could not be vested in a state or a group of states. Pennsylvania would annul one law, Alabama another, Virginia a third, and so on. Our national legislature would then become a mockery, and our Constitution, instead of a strong instrument of government, would be a mere collection of topics for endless dispute between the sections of our country. The Union would fall apart. The states would return to the frightful condition of anarchy which followed the Revolutionary War, and our flag, "stained with the blood of fratricidal war," would float over "the dismembered fragments of our once glorious empire."

310. Jackson defends the Union. The echoes of Webster's speech were still ringing through the land when President Jackson gave a public and unmistakable expression of his view of nullification. At a dinner in celebration of Jefferson's birthday (April 13), Jackson responded to a call for a toast with the sentiment, "Our federal Union—it *must* be preserved!" The vice president, Calhoun, immediately responded with the toast, "Liberty dearer than Union!" Feeling was intense. For the party of Hayne and Calhoun the Union had become a menace to liberty; for the party of Jackson and Webster it was the only condition and guarantee of liberty. When the advocates of nullification in South Carolina were warned by the Union men that their course might bring war, they contemptuously asked these "submission men" whether the "descendants of the heroes of 1776 should be afraid of war!"

311. South Carolina annuls the Tariff Acts. In the summer of 1832 a new tariff bill was passed by Congress. Its rates were somewhat lower than those of the "Tariff of Abominations," but still it was highly protective. The Southern members of Congress wrote home from Washington that no help was to be expected from that quarter. A convention met at Columbia in November, 1832, and by the decisive vote of 136 to 26 declared the tariff acts of 1828 and 1832 "null, void, and no law." The people of the state were ordered to pay no duties under these laws after February 1, 1833. At the same time the convention declared that any attempt by Congress to enforce the tariff law in South Carolina, to close her ports or destroy her commerce, would be a just cause for the secession of the state from

WEBSTER'S REPLY TO HAYNE

the Union. Governor Hamilton called for 10,000 volunteer troops to defend the state. Jackson answered in a strong proclamation. "I consider the power to annul a law of the United States, assumed by one state, incompatible with the existence of the Union, . . . inconsistent with every principle on which the Constitution was founded, and destructive of the great object for which it was formed." To Poinsett, collector of the port of Charleston, he wrote, "In forty days I will have 40,000 men in the state of South Carolina to enforce the law."

312. Clay's Compromise Tariff. Calhoun, who had resigned the vice presidency to enter the Senate, now called on Clay to help in reconciling South Carolina's claims with the preservation of the Union. Clay, who had little desire to see the "military chieftain" in the White House directing 40,000 men against South Carolina, worked out a compromise tariff, by which the duties were to be reduced gradually, until in 1842 they should reach approximately the level of the tariff act of 1816. Clay's compromise tariff passed both Houses of Congress and was signed by Jackson, March 2, 1833, at the same moment with a "Force Bill," which gave the President the right to employ the army and navy of the United States to collect the duties in South Carolina.

313. Civil Strife Averted. The protesting state accepted the compromise tariff, and by a vote of 153 to 4 the convention rescinded the ordinance of nullification (March 15, 1833). Each side claimed the victory,—South Carolina for having compelled Congress to lower the tariff, and the United States for having forced South Carolina to retract the ordinance of nullification. Jackson's strong hand had preserved the Union, but his words had not restored unity between the warring sections. The language of nullification was not forgotten in South Carolina. Twenty-eight years later it was revived and intensified in a struggle far more serious than that over tariff rates, — the great slavery controversy which precipitated the Civil War.

The War on the Bank

314. The Second National Bank. Two days after signing the compromise tariff of 1833 Jackson was inaugurated president a second time. He had defeated Clay, the National-Republican candidate, in a campaign fought on the recharter of the National Bank. The Bank of the United States was very prosperous at the beginning of Jackson's administration. In addition to $8,000,000 of the public money, it held some $6,000,000 in deposits of private persons. It made a profit of $3,000,000 a year, from which it paid handsome dividends to its stockholders. Its shares of $100 par value sold frequently as high as $140 each. "Besides the parent bank at Philadelphia, with its marble palace and hundreds of clerks," says Parton in his "Life of Andrew Jackson," "there were twenty-five branches in the towns and cities of the Union, each of which had its president, cashier, and board of directors. The employees of the Bank were more than five hundred in number, all men of standing and influence, and liberally salaried. In every county of the Union, in every nation on the globe, were stockholders of the Bank of the United States. . . . One fourth of its stock was held by women, orphans, and trustees of charity funds—so high and unquestioned was its credit." Its notes passed as gold, not only in every part of the Union but in the distant cities of London, St. Petersburg, Cairo, and Calcutta as well.

315. Opposition to the Bank. The opponents of the Bank saw how great a hold such an institution could get on the government by showing it financial favors in time of stress, and what an influence it could wield in politics by contributions from its vast wealth to the election of candidates favorable to its interests.[1] That the government should charter such an institution, they said, was contrary to the principles of democracy. It was encouraging corruption in public life by favoring the rich, instead of standing for equal rights and equal protection for all. Jackson was naturally a bitter opponent of the Bank. In his first message to Congress (December, 1829), although the charter of the Bank had still seven years to run, he spoke disparagingly of it. "Both the constitutionality and the expediency of the law creating this Bank," he wrote, "are well questioned by a large portion of our fellow citizens." Jackson's suspicions of the political corruption exercised by the Bank were much strengthened by the fact that most of the officers of that institution were his political opponents. The hostility of President Jackson injured the credit of the Bank. Its stocks fell in price, and its

---

[1] The managers of the Bank actually confessed that they spent $58,000 of its funds in the campaign to elect Henry Clay in 1832. This was after Jackson had vetoed the bill for the Bank's recharter, however.

managers began to fear that its business would be ruined. Therefore its president, Nicholas Biddle, acting on the advice of Clay, Webster, and other friends, applied to Congress early in 1832 for a renewal of the charter. The bill passed the House by a vote of 107 to 86.

316. Jackson vetoes the Bank Bill. It was the year of the presidential election. Clay, who was Jackson's opponent, urged the application for a recharter of the Bank in order to make campaign material. He thought that Jackson would not dare to veto the bill for fear of losing his support in the Northern states, where the Bank was in favor. But Clay was mistaken in thinking that Jackson would not dare to do what he had determined to do, whether he gained the presidency or not. Jackson promptly sent back the bill with a veto message which, as Clay wrote to Biddle, had "all the fury of a chained panther biting the bars of his cage." In his veto Jackson denounced the Bank as a dangerous monopoly, managed by a "favored class of opulent citizens," interfering with the free exercise of the people's will and bending the government to its selfish purposes. Furthermore, the Bank was keeping the West poor by concentrating the money of the country in the Eastern cities. The Supreme Court had declared, in the case of McCulloch *vs.* Maryland (p. 199), that Congress had the right to charter the Bank. Jackson made short work of this argument by the astonishing statement that the president's opinion of what was constitutional was as good as the Supreme Court's. "Each public officer," he wrote, "who takes an oath to support the Constitution swears that he will support it as he understands it. The opinion of the judges has no more authority over Congress than the opinion of Congress has over the judges, and on that point the President is independent of both."

317. The Removal of the Deposits. Clay was never more mistaken than when he appealed to the people to defeat Andrew Jackson on the issue of the National Bank. Jackson was overwhelmingly elected in November, 1832, with 219 electoral votes to Clay's 49. Even Pennsylvania gave her 30 electoral votes to Jackson, though only one of the Pennsylvania congressmen had voted against the bill for rechartering the Bank. Interpreting his reëlection as a mandate from the American people to destroy the Bank, Jackson began his attack on the institution. A special committee appointed to examine the financial condition of the Bank reported it sound, and both Houses of Congress voted their confidence in the institution. But this only increased the President's determination to destroy it. Taking advantage of a clause in the charter of the Bank which gave the Secretary of the Treasury the right to discontinue the government deposits in the Bank, if he gave his reasons to Congress, Jackson instructed Secretary Taney[1] to issue the order that after October 1, 1833, the government should no longer use the Bank of the United States for its deposits, but would place its revenues in certain state banks (called from this order the "pet banks") in various parts of the country.

318. Jackson censured by Senate. All this happened during the recess of Congress. When the Senate met, it voted that the reasons given by Taney for removing the deposits from the Bank of the United States were "unsatisfactory and insufficient," and refused to confirm the appointment of Taney as Secretary of the Treasury. Furthermore, by a vote of 26 to 20, it spread upon its journal a formal censure of Andrew Jackson, to the effect that "the President, in the late executive proceedings in relation to the public revenue [had] assumed upon himself authority and power not conferred by the Constitution and the laws, but in derogation of both." The censure was unmerited, for the President had not exceeded his power in dismissing a cabinet officer, neither had the Secretary of the Treasury, in ceasing to make government deposits in the Bank. The censure was also illegal, for the only way the Senate can condemn the president is to convict him in a regular trial after he has been impeached by the House of Representatives. Jackson with perfect right protested against the censure; but it was only after a hard fight of three years that his champion in the Senate, Thomas H. Benton, succeeded in getting the offensive vote expunged from the journal.

319. A Critical Moment in our Economic History. Jackson's overthrow of the Bank of the United States was undoubtedly approved by the majority of American citizens as the removal of a dangerous influence in our political life. The act would probably have had little effect on the business of the country had it not come at a critical moment in our industrial development. The period just

---

[1] Jackson removed one Secretary of the Treasury (McLane) by promoting him to the State Department, and accepted the resignation of another (Duane), before he found in Taney a Secretary willing to carry out his order.

following Jackson's second election was one of overconfidence in our country's growth. Our foreign trade was large. The country was out of debt, and the customs duties were bringing a large surplus into the Treasury every year. The recent introduction of the steam engine running on iron rails promised to revolutionize the whole system of slow transportation by river, cart, and canal. Individuals, stock companies, and state governments were anxious to borrow large sums of money to invest in land, labor, and building and transportation supplies, believing that we were on the eve of a marvelous "boom" in real estate and commerce.

320. The Fever of Speculation in Western Lands. The new Western states vied with each other in patriotic projects of extension. For example, Indiana, whose population in 1836 was only about 500,000, undertook to build 1200 miles of railroad through her forests and farm lands, thereby contracting a debt of $20 a head for every man, woman, and child in the state. Banks multiplied in the West, facilitating rash investments by lending on easy terms.[1] These "wildcat" banks, as they were called, issued notes far beyond the legitimate business needs of the country and far beyond their real capital in gold and silver. This great increase of the amount of currency put into circulation was mistaken for an increase in the country's wealth. The fever of speculation reached its height in the purchase of Western lands. In 1834 less than $5,000,000 worth of land was sold by the United States government. Next year the sales jumped to $14,000,000, and the following year to $24,000,000.

321. The Specie Circular. The purchasers paid for their lands in the paper money of the unreliable Western banks, and the United States Treasury was soon overflowing with this depreciating currency. In the summer of 1836 Jackson issued his famous Specie Circular, forbidding the officers of the Treasury of the United States to accept any money but gold and silver (specie) in payment for further sales of public land.

322. The Panic of 1837. The Specie Circular was the needle that pricked the bubble of speculation. The "wildcat" banks did not have the gold and silver to pay for the notes they had issued.

---

[1] In 1829 there were 329 of these state banks in the West, and by 1837 the number had reached 788. The hope of getting a share of the United States funds denied to the National Bank was a great stimulus to the state banking business.

Speculators could not borrow "hard money" on such easy terms as they had borrowed paper; and the "boom" of the West collapsed.[1] Land sales dropped to less than $900,000 for the year 1837. Building operations ceased. Long lines of rails were left to rust in the Western forests. Thousands of laborers were thrown out of employment. The New York *Era* reported nine tenths of the factories in the Eastern states closed by September, 1837. The distress of industrial depression following this financial panic was increased by the general failure of the crops in the summers of 1836 and 1837. The Hessian fly ravaged the wheat fields of Maryland, Virginia, and Pennsylvania, and the price of flour rose to $12 a barrel. The starving populace of New York and Philadelphia rioted. Mobs broke into the warehouses where the flour was stored and threw the precious barrels into the street. Over 600 banks went down in failure, including nearly all the "pet banks" that held the government's deposits. Our credit abroad was almost ruined. Foreign trade languished. At the close of the period of depression the Treasury showed a deficit of over $10,000,000.

323. The Independent-Treasury System. Five or six years passed before the country fully recovered from the panic of 1837 and confidence returned to merchants, bankers, and investors. The government did not again intrust its funds to either a National Bank or the "pet banks" of the states. The former had been condemned as a political menace; the latter had proved themselves financially unsound. A system of government deposit was adopted under Jackson's successor, Van Buren (1840), which completely separated the public funds from the banking business in any form. This was called the Independent-Treasury or the Subtreasury system. The government constructed vaults in several of the larger cities of the country — New York, Philadelphia, Boston, St. Louis, Charleston, New Orleans — and stored its revenues in these vaults. It was not until the Civil War that our government, under the stress of enormous expenses, was again obliged to appeal to the financial institutions of the country. It then devised the present system of national banks, to which we shall refer in a later chapter.

[1] The citizens of Louisville, Kentucky, presented a memorial to the Senate in which they said: "Had a large invading army passed triumphantly through our country it could not have so completely marred our prosperity. The countenances of our citizens are more gloomy and desponding than when the dread cholera was amongst us."

A New Party

324. Important Events of the Jacksonian Era. Although the contest with South Carolina over nullification and the war on the United States Bank were the two most important events in Jackson's administrations, both illustrating vividly the domineering character of the man, they were by no means the only matters of importance in his administrations. We shall have occasion later to revert to this period when dealing with the abolition of slavery, the acquisition of Texas, and the extension of our settlements into the great region beyond the Mississippi and the Missouri Rivers. The decade 1830–1840 was, in fine, a new era in our history. It was a period of epoch-making inventions and discoveries in the industrial world, of far-reaching innovations in politics, of ardent social reforms and humanitarian projects.

325. New Inventions and Discoveries. We are accustomed to think of battles and treaties as the exciting events which have brought the changes in a nation's life — and it is true that some few "decisive battles" have altered the course of history. But the steady, silent work of the head and hands of a people engaged in invention and industry has done more to shape the course of history than all the array of armies with bugle and sword. The invention in 1834 of the McCormick reaper was the prophecy that our great wheat and corn fields of the West would some day produce enough to feed half the world. The utilization of the immense anthracite-coal deposits of Pennsylvania in the process of iron smelting in 1836 foreshadowed this mighty age of steel which has superseded our fathers' age of wood. The appliance of the screw propeller to ocean steamers in 1839 opened the way for the *Leviathan*. And, chief of all, the appearance in 1830 of a steam locomotive on the new 23-mile track of the Baltimore and Ohio Railway gave promise of the network of nearly 250,000 miles of railroad track which covers our country today, bringing the Pacific coast within five days of New York City. It is an interesting coincidence that while the steam locomotive was being tested, and its advocates were laboring to overcome the foolish prejudices against its adoption,[1] statesmen in Congress were ridiculing

---

[1] The locomotive, it was said, would spoil the farms by its soot and ignite barns and dwellings by its sparks. Its noise would frighten the animals so that hens would not lay and cows would refuse to give their milk.

the idea of our taking any interest in the Oregon region beyond the Rockies, on the ground that it would take a representative from that country a year to make the journey to Washington and back.

326. Effect of the Railroads on Economic Development. By the end of the decade the 23 miles of railroad had increased almost a hundredfold, and steam trains were running in all the Atlantic states from New York to Georgia. This improvement in transportation over wagon and canal stimulated business in every direction. The demand for the products of American farms and factories increased with the extension of the means of transportation. As the

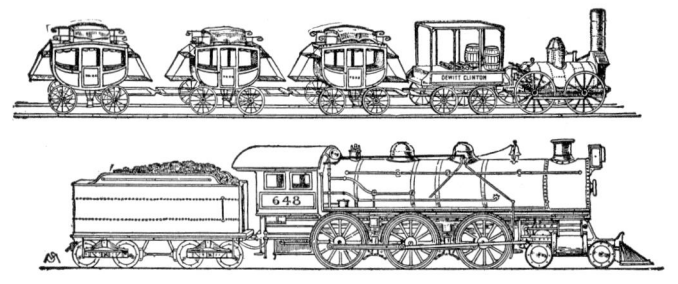

A RAILROAD TRAIN OF 1830 COMPARED WITH A MODERN LOCOMOTIVE

volume of freight traffic grew, cities began to develop rapidly at certain distributing or terminal points. Large sums of money were concentrated in these cities in business schemes or invested in the stocks and bonds of the new railroads. With the gathering of population and capital in the cities, and the enlargement of the small local business concerns into joint-stock companies employing hundreds of workmen, the conditions of the laboring class and the relations of labor to capital began to claim serious attention.

327. Labor Agitation. In 1833 a Labor party held its first national convention at Philadelphia and formulated demands for higher wages, shorter hours of work, and more sanitary conditions in shops and factories. Trade unions began to be formed — the workers banding together both to keep unskilled laborers out of the trades and to enforce their demands for higher wages and shorter hours of labor. There were strikes in various cities because the employers refused the workmen's demands. The laborers also sought relief from the state legislatures. They asked to have "mechanics' lien laws" passed, giving them a claim upon the buildings which they constructed and thus assuring them of pay for their labor in case the contractors failed. They protested against the competition of goods made in prisons by convict labor, demanded free schools for their children, and denounced the laws which every year sent 75,000 men to jail for debt.[1]

328. The Democratic Revolution. Besides these social and industrial reforms, far-reaching political changes were in progress in the decade 1830–1840.[2] It is hardly an exaggeration to say that America became a democracy in that decade, which was the first to see all classes of her people participating actively in the government. In Washington's day only some 120,000 persons in a population of 4,000,000 had a right to vote — about one in seven of the adult male population. The other six sevenths were excluded from the franchise by high property qualifications or religious tests inherited from colonial days. As late as the election of 1828 Rhode Island, with a population of 97,000, cast only 3575 votes. But in the Jacksonian period the democratic ideal of manhood suffrage was transforming the political aspect of the whole country. States which had not altered their constitutions since their establishment (Tennessee, Mississippi), or even since colonial days (Rhode Island, North Carolina), now undertook extensive revisions. They extended the right of suffrage, shortened the terms of officers, and transferred the choice of many executive officials and judges from the governor to the people.

329. The "Spoils System." This democratic revolution had its evil side. Clever political managers, or "bosses," began to build up party machines in every state by organizing the great masses of voters and using the victory of their party for the strengthening of the machine. Appointments to public offices in the gift of the successful candidates were made as rewards to the men who had done most to win the elections, quite irrespective often of their fitness for the offices. Faithful and able officials and clerks of many years' service were removed simply to make room for men of the victorious party, who were clamoring for their places. This use of government offices,

---

[1] It is hard to imagine a more stupid form of punishment than sending a man to jail for debt, forcing him into idleness for a fault which only diligence and industry can cure. Yet this custom prevailed on both sides of the Atlantic well into the nineteenth century. Charles Dickens portrays its evil effects in "Little Dorrit."

[2] For the contemporary reforms in England of the poor laws, the penal laws, the factory laws, and the labor laws, see Cheyney's "Short History of England," chap. xix.

from the cabinet portfolios down to the humblest clerkships, as prizes of war to be fought for at the polls was vindicated in classic language by a New York politician named Marcy, who declared that "to the victor belong the spoils." We have seen how Jackson, by his wholesale removals from office, extended the "spoils system" to the national government.

330. The National Nominating Conventions. Another important feature of the democratic revolution of the decade 1830–1840 was the development of the national conventions for nominating the candidates of each party for president and vice president and for publishing a declaration, or "platform," of the principles of the party. In 1831 and 1832 three such conventions were held, all at Baltimore. The Antimasons (a small party formed to combat the secret order of the Masons)[1] were first in the field (September, 1831), with William Wirt of Maryland as candidate for president. The National Republicans followed in December, nominating Henry Clay of Kentucky; and the Jackson men, now calling themselves Democrats,[2] met in May, 1832, and indorsed the ticket, Jackson

---

[1] Since the foundation of our government two great parties have generally been opposed to each other (Federalists and Republicans, 1790–1816; Whigs and Democrats, 1834–1852; Republicans and Democrats, 1854 to the present). However, many minor parties (or "third parties"), formed on various issues, have appeared in our politics since 1830, but so serried have been the party ranks that only twice since the Civil War, namely, in the elections of 1892 and 1912, have third parties had sufficient strength to carry states and so appear in the electoral column.

[2] The political parties are rather difficult to keep clearly distinguished, owing to the various uses of the names "Republican" and "Democrat" at different times in our history. The following chart will aid the student:

DATE			PAGE
1791–1792	FEDERALISTS (for strong national government)	vs. DEMOCRATIC REPUBLICANS (for strictly limited national government)	
1793		dropped the name Democratic and became simply the Republicans.	162
1816 cir.	died out, leaving only the		
1820 cir.		REPUBLICANS ("era of good feeling") who split on the question of "internal improvements," such as national aid for the construction of canals and roads, and the charter of the National Bank, into two wings:	197
			225
1825–1830	NATIONAL REPUBLICANS the nucleus of a new party which, in opposition to Jackson, took the name of	vs. DEMOCRATIC REPUBLICANS who dropped the name Republican and became simply	241
1834	WHIGS	vs. (Jacksonian) DEMOCRATS On the great question of slavery the Whig party went to pieces soon after 1850, and the present Republican party was organized,	307

and Van Buren. At first each state had one vote in the selection of the candidates, irrespective of the number of delegates it sent to the convention; but soon the plan was adopted, which still prevails, of having each state represented by a number of delegates twice as large as its representation in Congress.[1] All our presidents and vice presidents since 1832 have been nominated by national conventions.

331. The New Whig Party. Jackson had not been in office many months before his autocratic conduct made him many public opponents and private enemies. When he issued his famous proclamation against the nullifiers in South Carolina, in December, 1832, the Charleston *Mercury* came out with a flamboyant article against him, in which it declared: "An infuriated administration has been driven to the use of brute force. . . . If this Republic has found a master, let us not live his subjects!" Recalling the Revolutionary days, when our forefathers fought against the "tyrant King George the Third," it recommended that the opponents of "King Andrew" adopt the old name of *Whigs*, which in the eighteenth century stood for the foes of executive tyranny. As the war on the United States Bank and the removal of the government's deposits in 1833 made the President enemies in the North as well as in the South, the anti-Jackson men became sufficiently numerous to form the new Whig party. The nucleus of the Whig party was the faithful group of National Republicans, led by Henry Clay, with their devotion to a high tariff, the National Bank, and internal improvements at the cost of the government — the so-called "American System." To these were added now the Southerners, whom Jackson had offended by his attack on the rights of the states, and people from all sections

CARTOON OF THE CAMPAIGN OF 1832

---

[1] The Democrats have always required a two-thirds vote of their convention to nominate a candidate, while a simple majority vote has nominated the Republican candidate.

of the country who were opposed to his financial policy, his "personal" conduct of the government through a group of favorites, and his adoption of the odious spoils system. It was essentially an anti-Jackson party.

332. Election of Van Buren. The Whigs were not quite strong enough in 1836 to defeat Jackson's chief lieutenant and personal choice for the presidency, Martin Van Buren of New York. Van Buren had been vice president during Jackson's second term, and it was a great triumph for the old hero of New Orleans over the Senate, which had passed a vote of censure on him, when he saw Van Buren, whom the Senate had formerly rejected as minister to England, sworn into the presidency by Chief Justice Taney, whom it had likewise formerly refused to confirm as Secretary of the Treasury.

333. Van Buren's Unpopularity. Van Buren, although he was one of the most adroit and able politicians in our history and had come into office pledged to "tread in the footsteps of his illustrious predecessor," failed to hold the Democratic party together and to lead it to victory in 1840. Both public and private causes conspired to his defeat. The financial panic of 1837, which followed Jackson's issue of the Specie Circular, came in Van Buren's administration, and quite naturally he was blamed for it by the unthinking majority. Moreover, Van Buren was an aristocratic New Yorker, a rich widower, who, according to campaign orators, lived in solitary splendor at the White House, eating off golden plates and drinking costly wines from silver coolers. The reputation for such conduct, however exaggerated the details, was little likely to win for Van Buren the support which the "unspoiled West" had given to the rough old hero, Andrew Jackson. And it is not strange that when the Whigs nominated William Henry Harrison of Ohio—like Jackson a frontiersman and Indian fighter, a hero of the War of 1812, and a plain, rugged, honest man of the people—the West flocked to his banner and carried him triumphantly into the presidency in a second "democratic revolution."

334. Why Clay was not Nominated in 1840. The presidential campaign of 1840 was most exciting and spectacular. Henry Clay, the towering genius of the Whig party, should have been the candidate and confidently expected the nomination. But Clay's **very prominence was against him.** He had been badly beaten in the election of 1832 for his mistake in forcing the Bank charter into politics to defeat Jackson. Many old Jackson men, disgusted with Van Buren, could be counted on to vote for any other Whig nominee than Jackson's lifelong enemy, Clay. And finally the growing antislavery sentiment of the North made it desirable for the Whigs to oppose to Van Buren (himself an antislavery man from a free state) not the slaveholder Henry Clay, but a representative of the free North who could also appeal to the frontier enthusiasm of the new West.

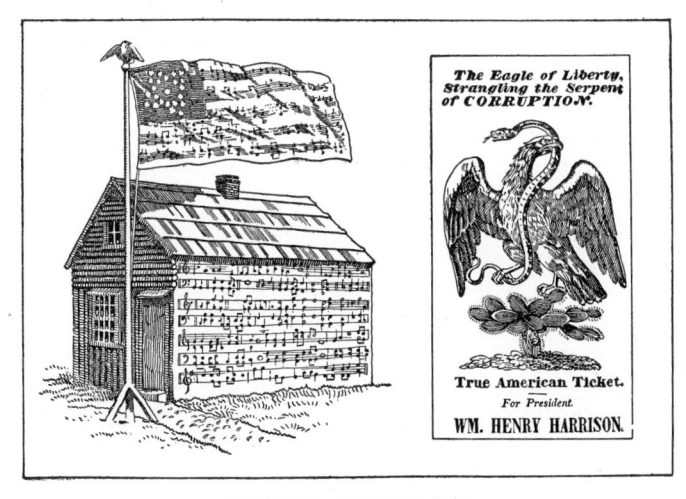

CAMPAIGN EMBLEMS, 1840

335. The Triumph of Harrison. A Democratic paper in Baltimore made the sneering comment on the choice of Harrison: "Give him a barrel of hard cider and settle $2000 a year on him, and ... he will sit the remainder of his days in his Log Cabin ... by the side of his fire studying moral philosophy." The Whigs immediately took up the challenge and made the homely virtues and simple tastes of the old hero, who had spent his nearly seventy years in the defense and service of his country, the chief issue of the campaign. "Yes, he has lived long enough in the Log Cabin," they said, "and we intend to give him rent-free after March 4, 1841, the great White House at Washington." Hard cider was the beverage on tap at the Whig rallies all over the country. The feature of every Whig procession was its Log Cabin, with the latchstring out and the coonskin nailed to the door, wheeled along to the uproarious shouts of "Tippecanoe[1] and Tyler too," and "Van, Van is a used-up man!" The Whig ticket swept the country. Harrison got 234 electoral votes to 60 for Van Buren. The Whigs secured both branches of Congress too, with a majority of seven in the Senate and forty-four in the House.

336. The Close of the Jacksonian Epoch. Harrison's decisive victory marks the end of the "reign of Andrew Jackson." The date also marks the moment when the different sections of our country had become fully conscious of their conflicting interests. Two irreconcilable forms of civilization had been developing during the quarter of a century which followed the War of 1812. In the North the democratic, diversified life of manufacture and commerce was attended by rapid growth of population through natural increase and immigration from Europe. In the South a more stationary and aristocratic civilization was founded on the wealth of the cotton fields, which were cultivated by an army of 2,000,000 negro slaves. The conflict of these two forms of civilization, with their utterly opposite economic needs, their diverging political views of the relative rights of the states and the Union, their jealousy of each other's extension into the West, and their deepening disagreement as to the moral right of one man to hold another man in bondage, began about 1840 to overshadow all the other questions of the period which we have been studying,— the Bank, the tariff, the public lands, and internal improvements. Not a national election was held from 1840 to the Civil War that did not turn chiefly or wholly on the slavery issue. At the close of his term of office Jackson had written to Congress, "Unless agitation on this point [slavery] cease, it will divide the Union." And in fact the systems of North and South were becoming "too unlike to exist in the same nation." What would the outcome be? Should the Union be divided, or should the institution of slavery be abolished?

References

Nullification: WILLIAM MACDONALD, *Jacksonian Democracy* (American Nation Series), chaps. iv–vi; *Select Documents of United States History, 1776–1861*, Nos. 53, 55, 56; F. A. OGG, *The Reign of Andrew Jackson* (Chronicles, Vol. XX), chaps. vi–viii; D. F. HOUSTON, *A Critical Study of Nullification in*

---

[1] In reference to Harrison's victory over Tecumseh at Tippecanoe Creek, in 1811 (see above, p. 192).

THE JACKSONIAN ERA

South Carolina (Harvard Historical Studies, Vol. III); J. W. Burgess, *The Middle Period*, chap. x; J. B. McMaster, *History of the People of the United States*, Vol. VI, pp. 148-177; H. von Holst, *Constitutional History of the United States*, Vol. I, chap. xii; Edward Stanwood, *American Tariff Controversies of the Nineteenth Century*, chap. ix; C. H. Peck, *The Jacksonian Epoch*, chap. v; J. S. Bassett, *Andrew Jackson*, chap. xxvi.

The War on the Bank: McMaster, Vol. VI, chap. lix; MacDonald, *Jacksonian Democracy*, chaps. vii, xiii; *Select Documents*, Nos. 46, 50, 51, 52, 54, 57-62; Woodrow Wilson, *History of the American People*, Vol. IV, chap. ii; Ralph H. Catterall, *The Second Bank of the United States*; Burgess, chaps. ix, xii; Ogg, chap. ix; D. R. Dewey, *Financial History of the United States*, chap. ix.; Bassett, chaps. xxvii, xxviii.

A New Party: MacDonald, *Jacksonian Democracy*, chaps. xi, xiv, xvii; S. P. Orth, *The Boss and the Machine* (Chronicles, Vol. XLIII), chaps. i, ii; J. A. Woodburn, *Political Parties and Party Problems in the United States*, chap. iv; McMaster, Vol. VI, chap. lxix; Ogg, chap. xi; Stanwood, *History of the Presidency*, chaps. xv, xvi; E. E. Sparks, *The Men who made the Nation*, chap. ix; E. L. Bogart, *Economic History of the United States*, chaps. xvi, xvii, xx; Peck, chap. xi; biographies of Jackson by W. G. Brown (very brief), William G. Sumner (American Statesmen Series), A. C. Buell (2 vols.), and J. S. Bassett (2 vols.).

Topics for Special Reports

1. **Foreign Affairs in Jackson's Administration:** J. D. Richardson, *Messages and Papers of the Presidents*, Vol. II, pp. 437 ff.; Von Holst, Vol. II, pp. 553-570; McMaster, Vol. VI, pp. 236-242, 299-303, 421-446; J. W. Foster, *A Century of American Diplomacy*, pp. 273-281; Bassett, pp. 656-683; MacDonald, *Jacksonian Democracy*, pp. 200-218.

2. **The Webster-Hayne Debate:** Edward Everett, in *North American Review*, Vol. XXXI, pp. 462-546; McMaster, in *Century Magazine*, Vol. LXII, pp. 228-246; MacDonald, *Select Documents*, Nos. 47-49; Alexander Johnston (ed. Woodburn), *American Orations*, Vol. I, pp. 231-302.

3. **Coercing South Carolina:** Bassett, pp. 552-583; T. H. Benton, *Thirty Years' View*, Vol. I, chaps. lxxx-lxxxvi; E. P. Powell, *Nullification and Secession in the United States*, pp. 262-288, and Appendix, pp. 298-324; MacDonald, *Select Documents*, No. 56; Houston, pp. 106-133; T. D. Jervey, *Robert Y. Hayne and his Times*, pp. 297-356.

4. **Jackson the Autocrat:** A. B. Hart, *American History told by Contemporaries*, Vol. III, Nos. 158, 160; MacDonald, *Select Documents*, Nos. 64, 68; Carl R. Fish, *The Civil Service and the Patronage*, pp. 105-133; Von Holst, Vol. II, pp. 1-39; Buell, Vol. II, pp. 383-412; C. A. Davis, *Major Jack Dowling's Letters* (a satire on Jackson); Higginson and MacDonald, *History of the United States*, pp. 411-428.

5. **Travel and Transportation in Jackson's Day:** Hart, *Slavery and Abolition* (American Nation Series), pp. 33-48; *American History told by Contemporaries*, Vol. III, Nos. 165-168; Josiah Quincy, *Figures of the Past*, pp. 188-208; McMaster, Vol. VI, pp. 77-95; MacDonald, *Jacksonian Democracy*, pp. 136-147; Bogart, pp. 208-219; Charles Dickens, *American Notes* (ed. of 1842).

PART V. SLAVERY AND THE WEST

CHAPTER XI

THE GATHERING CLOUD

The Missouri Compromise

337. Slavery in the Colonies. Up to this point we have mentioned only incidentally and occasionally the institution of negro slavery, which led to the greatest crisis in our country's history — disunion and civil war. In the year 1619 a Dutch trading vessel brought twenty slaves from the West Indies to the Virginia colony at Jamestown, and during the century which followed about 25,000 negroes were landed on our shores to work in the tobacco and rice fields of the South or to become household servants in the wealthier families of the middle and northern colonies. The eighteenth century, however, saw a great increase in the importation of slaves into the colonies, when Great Britain, victorious in a long war with France and Spain (1702-1713), demanded as one of the terms of peace the monopoly of carrying negroes from the African coast to the New World. Reputable business firms, high nobles, even Queen Anne herself and her courtiers, had large sums of money invested in the slave trade, from which the dividends sometimes mounted to fortunes.

338. The Horrors of the Slave Trade. The slave hunters kidnaped the negroes in Africa, chained them together in gangs, and packed them closely into the stifling holds of their narrow wooden ships, to suffer torments on the tropical voyage from the African coast to the West Indies. This awful journey was called the "middle passage," because it was the second leg of a triangular voyage from which the British and colonial captains derived large profits. They took rum from the New England distilleries to Africa to debauch the innocent natives, whom they seized and brought to the West Indies to exchange for sugar and for molasses, which went to New England to make more rum. So rum, negroes, and molasses made the endless chain of this disgraceful traffic. The horrors of the middle passage moved the colonists at times to pass bills prohibiting the slave trade. But the British crown vetoed the bills.[1] We must remember in all our study and judgment of the problems which the presence of the negro in the South has forced upon our country, that it was not so much the colonists as the merchant traders and capitalists who were responsible for the slave traffic in the eighteenth century; and that the New England rum distillers were responsible for bringing thousands of negroes from Africa to sell as slaves in the West Indies.

339. The Increase of Slavery in the South. As the different types of colonial industry developed,—shipping, fishing, farming in the North, and the cultivation of the large tobacco, cotton, and rice plantations in the South,— it became evident that the home of the negro was to be that part of our land whose climate fitted his physique and whose labor fitted his intellect. As early as 1715 the negroes comprised 25 per cent of the population of the colonies south of the Potomac River, in comparison with 9 per cent in the middle colonies and less than 3 per cent in New England. South Carolina already had, as she has had ever since, a larger negro than white population. Before the close of the eighteenth century every state north of Maryland except New Jersey had provided for the immediate or gradual abolition of slavery, while Whitney's invention of the cotton gin in 1793 had fixed the institution firmly upon the

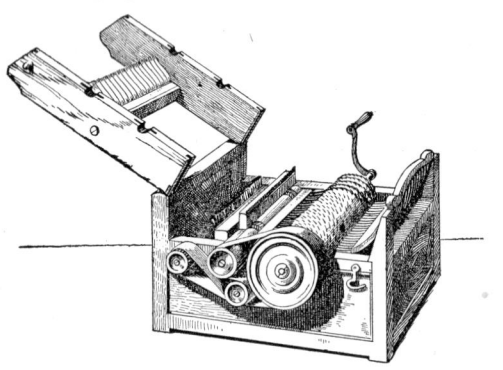

WHITNEY'S COTTON GIN

---

[1] One of the charges brought against George III by Thomas Jefferson in the original draft of the Declaration of Independence was that he had encouraged the slave trade, "violating the most sacred rights of life and liberty in the persons of a distant people [the Africans] who never offended him, captivating and carrying them into slavery in another hemisphere, or to incur miserable death in their transportation thither." The Friends of Germantown, Pennsylvania, protested against the practice of slavery as early as 1688.

South. The English colonies in America, therefore, were not a free land which was gradually encroached upon by slavery, but a land in all of whose extent slavery was at first recognized by law, and only later excluded from those portions where it was economically unprofitable.

340. Humanitarian Views of Southern Slave Owners. A small number of plantation owners, like Washington, Jefferson, Madison, and Randolph, influenced no doubt by the spirit of humanity and philanthropy which was abroad in the later years of the eighteenth century, had misgivings as to the justice of holding slaves.[1] Thomas Jefferson, for example, the most pronounced of the antislavery slaveholders suggested in his "Notes on Virginia" (1784) that the slaves be purchased by the state and sent to form a colony in the West Indies. He also, the same year, tried in vain to persuade Congress to exclude slavery from all the territory west of the Alleghenies. But however much the enlightened men of the South deplored the existence of slavery from the point of view of ethics and humanity, they found themselves part of an industrial system which seemed to demand the negro slave for its very existence.

341. Slavery recognized by the Constitution. When the Constitution was framed, therefore, the slaveholding states of the South secured recognition of their institution and indulgence for it. Three fifths of the slaves were counted in the population in making up the census for the House of Representatives, and Congress was forbidden to prohibit the slave trade for twenty years — a period sufficiently long to supply the South with enough slaves to insure the indefinite continuance of the institution.

342. Legislation Favorable to Slavery, 1790–1819. A little group of antislavery people in the North had from the first been dissatisfied with the tolerant attitude of the Constitution toward slavery. In Washington's first administration (1790) they began a series of petitions to Congress for the abolition of slavery in the United States, which were continued for three quarters of a century, to the Civil War. Congress returned to the first petition of 1790

---

[1] Jefferson, in discussing slavery, said, " I tremble for my country when I reflect that God is just." Washington wrote to his secretary, Tobias Lear, that he was anxious to " dispose of a certain kind of property [negro slaves] as soon as possible." John Randolph (who liberated his slaves) declared that " all other misfortunes of life were small compared with being born a master of slaves."

the same answer that it gave to all the later ones; namely, that slavery, being a "domestic institution," was subject to the laws of the states, not to those of the national government. Even the repeated attempts to get Congress to impose a tax of $10 a head on imported slaves, which was authorized by the Constitution, all failed. On the other hand, the favors which slavery received from Congress during this period were many. In 1792 Kentucky was admitted to the Union with a constitution which sanctioned slavery. In 1793 Congress passed a fugitive-slave law, allowing a slave owner to reclaim a runaway negro in any state in the Union by a mere decision of the local judge, without jury trial. In 1796 Congress accepted North Carolina's cession of land west of the Alleghenies, promising not to prohibit slavery therein; and immediately Tennessee, which lay within this territory, was admitted as a slaveholding state. In 1798 the territory of Mississippi was organized, and only 12 votes were cast in Congress in favor of excluding slavery from its borders. In 1803 the immense territory of Louisiana was purchased from Napoleon under terms which protected slavery wherever it already existed in the territory. In 1805 Congress, by a vote of 77 to 31, defeated a bill to emancipate the slaves in the national domain of the District of Columbia. In 1812 the lower end of the Louisiana territory was admitted to the Union as the state of Louisiana, with slavery—the third slave state to be admitted since the organization of the government, as against the two free states of Vermont (1791) and Ohio (1803).

ADVERTISEMENT FOR A RUNAWAY SLAVE

343. The Missouri Bill. It is no wonder, in view of such generous recognition of the slavery interests, that the Southerners were taken by surprise at the serious opposition aroused in Congress when the slaveholding territory of Missouri[1] applied for admission to the Union as a state in the autumn of 1818. The bill for the

---

[1] When the state of Louisiana was formed in 1811, the name of the Louisiana territory above 33° was changed to the "territory of Missouri."

admission of Missouri was laid before the House of Representatives for debate on February 13, 1819. The same day James Tallmadge of New York moved as an amendment to the bill, "That the further introduction of slavery or involuntary servitude be prohibited . . . and that all children born within the said state after admission thereof into the Union shall be free at the age of twenty-five years." The amendment passed the House by a narrow margin, but was promptly and decisively rejected by the Senate (31 to 7); and the Congressional session of 1818–1819 came to an end with Missouri's application for statehood still pending. During the summer of 1819 excitement over the Missouri question was aroused throughout the country. Mass meetings were held in the Northern states condemning the extension of slavery and in the Southern states demanding the rights of the slave owners under the Constitution. The legislatures of Pennsylvania, New York, New Jersey, Ohio, and even slaveholding Delaware passed resolutions against the admission of Missouri to the Union with slavery. When Congress met in December, 1819, it was overwhelmed with petitions for and against the Tallmadge amendment.

344. Importance of the Missouri Question. There were several important points involved in the admission of Missouri. In the first place, there were an equal number of free and slave states (eleven each) in the Union at the close of the year 1819, which made an even balance between the two sections in the Senate. Secondly, Missouri was to be the first state wholly west of the Mississippi River created out of territory acquired since the formation of the Union, and it was felt that if the first state formed from this territory were opened to slavery, a precedent would thereby be established for admitting all future states on the same basis. Furthermore, by the third article of the treaty by which the territory was acquired from Napoleon the inhabitants were guaranteed "protection of their liberty, property, and religion." Many planters had taken their slaves into the Missouri territory, relying on this guarantee. Could Congress now fairly deprive them of their "property" by emancipating all negroes born in the new state?

345. Can Congress impose Restrictions on a State? But the most serious question involved touched the power of Congress under the Constitution to pass the Tallmadge amendment. Congress had the express power to "admit new states to this Union." But did it have the right to impose restrictions on new states as a condition of admission? The Tallmadge men argued that the power to *admit* necessarily implied the power to *refuse to admit*, and hence the power to make conditions on which it *would admit* new states to the Union. They cited the case of the admission of Ohio, Indiana, and Illinois, which had been required to frame antislavery constitutions. On the other hand, the opponents of the amendment declared that Ohio, Indiana, and Illinois might legally have insisted, when they became states, on determining for themselves the nature of their "domestic institutions," which had been prescribed for them by Congress so long as they were a part of the Northwest Territory. For Congress to determine on what terms a state should come into the Union, they argued, would be to substitute for our federal Union of equal states a centralized despotism; for could not Congress, with such power, reduce a state to the most abject position of dependence! The "Union" then would be a union between a giant Congress and pigmy states, between absolutism and impotence. The states which Congress should admit to the Union must have the same powers and privileges as the states which originally united to form the Union.

346. Arguments for the Extension of Slavery. Confident that their constitutional arguments for slavery were sound, the Southern orators proceeded to show not only that the institution was legal but that its extension into the new West was desirable. Granted that slavery was a moral evil, would it not be better, they said, to diminish the evil by spreading it? Would not the black cloud be lightened by diffusion? Since not another negro slave was to be brought to America, would not the evils arising from those already here be lessened the more widely the slaves were scattered?

347. A Compromise Measure passed. Early in the session of 1819–1820 an event occurred which enabled the proslavery Senate and the antislavery House to come to an agreement on the Missouri question. The province of Maine, which since 1677 had been a part of Massachusetts (see page 42), got the consent of Massachusetts to separate from it and apply to Congress for statehood. Accordingly, in December, 1819, Maine, with an antislavery constitution already prepared, asked for admission into the Union. By way of compromise, to end the debate, the Senate combined the Maine and

Missouri bills and added to them, in the place of the Tallmadge amendment, one by Senator Thomas of Illinois, which prohibited slavery in all the Louisiana Purchase territory lying above 36° 30′ north latitude, except the proposed state of Missouri. The Maine-Missouri-Thomas compromise bill was then sent to the House. In return for the admission of the free state of Maine, and for the exclusion of slavery from five sixths of the Louisiana Purchase territory, the House by a vote of 90 to 87 dropped the Tallmadge

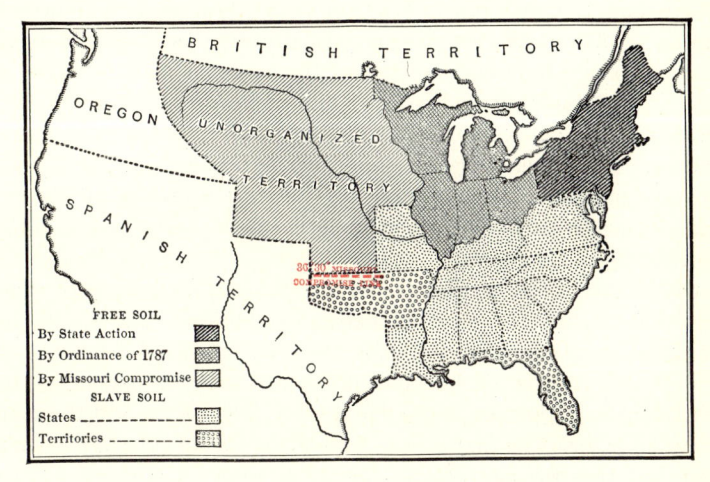

STATUS OF SLAVERY BY THE MISSOURI COMPROMISE

amendment and, to keep the balance in the Senate, let Missouri enter the Union as a slave state. President Monroe signed the bills for the admission of Maine and Missouri on the third and sixth of March, 1820, after being assured by every member of his cabinet except John Quincy Adams that the prohibition of slavery in the great Louisiana tract north of 36° 30′ applied to the region only so long as it was under *territorial* government.[1]

[1] As a matter of fact Missouri, owing to her incorporation of a clause in the new constitution, prohibiting free negroes from entering the state, was not admitted until August, 1821, while Maine, whose constitution was already framed when she applied for statehood, was admitted in 1820. It is important to note here, in view of a later controversy, that Congress, by this compromise bill, *excluded slavery from territory of the United States,* and that all of the 75 votes in the House from the states south of Pennsylvania were cast in favor of the bill.

348. Significance of the Missouri Compromise. The Missouri Compromise was one of the most important measures ever passed in our history. First of all, it connected the question of slavery with westward expansion and revealed to farsighted men, both North and South, the fact that the development of our national domain was to be marked by a struggle between freedom and slavery. Furthermore, the South saw for the first time, in the Missouri debates, how determined antislavery sentiment was growing in the North and resented the attacks on their institution by Northern orators. Then, again, the Missouri debates were an important factor in that change from the national to the sectional point of view, on the part of Calhoun and other Southern leaders, which we have already studied in connection with the tariff agitation (pp. 220 f., 230 f.). These men saw how dangerous such powers as those which the Tallmadge amendment gave to Congress would be to slavery, and consequently they grew more insistent on the doctrine of the sovereignty of the states.

349. Slavery as a Moral Issue. Finally, and perhaps most significant of all, the Missouri debates emphasized the ethical side of the slavery question as it had not been emphasized before. To answer the stronger legal argument of their Southern opponents, the Northern men appealed to the moral sense of Congress and the country at large, insisting that a slave population was an enfeebled population, and that the existence of human bondage in our country was an outrage to the sublime principles of the Declaration of Independence. To meet the moral objections of the North the Southerners now began to defend as a blessing to the negro the system which they had earlier been inclined to deplore as a necessary evil. Hard feeling began to develop between the two sections. The North accused the South of the sin of willfully maintaining an inhuman and barbarous institution, and the South charged the North with overlooking all the social and economic arguments for slavery and only encouraging discontented negroes to rise and massacre their masters. The aged Jefferson wrote of the Missouri Compromise: "This momentous question, like a fire bell in the night, awakened me and filled me with terror. I considered it at once as the knell of the Union." The echoes of this alarm bell rang through North and South, growing louder and louder each decade, till they drowned all other issues of

THE GATHERING CLOUD

the century in their clamor,— the Bank, the tariff, public lands, the currency, internal improvements, foreign negotiations, and domestic expansion. The slavery question invaded our pulpits and pervaded our literature. It seized on press and platform. It disturbed our industries and commerce. And finally it precipitated the mighty strife of the Civil War.

The Abolitionists

350. The Rise of Abolitionist Sentiment. In the year in which Missouri was finally admitted to the Union, Benjamin Lundy, a New Jersey Quaker, began to publish in Ohio the *Genius of Universal Emancipation*, a weekly periodical devoted to the cause of the abolition of slavery. Lundy was the first American to embrace the cause of negro emancipation as a life mission, advocating the establishment of colonies of liberated slaves on the island of Haiti. He traveled thousands of miles, often on foot, through nearly every state of the Union, addressing meetings, appealing to churches and colleges, and forming antislavery societies wherever he went. Previous to the bitter Missouri debates the slaveholding states were as promising a field for emancipation activity as the free North. Antislavery societies existed in Kentucky, Delaware, Tennessee, North Carolina, Maryland, and Virginia before a single one was formed in New England.[1] But the rapid extension of cotton cultivation after the second war with England and the feeling aroused by the Missouri debates produced a great change in the attitude of the South toward slavery. After the Missouri Compromise was passed, free discussion of the evils of slavery began to die out in the South, being branded by the political and social leaders as treason to the interests of their section of the country. On the other hand, the little group of Northern abolitionists began to redouble their efforts.

351. William Lloyd Garrison. On a visit to Boston in 1828 Benjamin Lundy met a young man of twenty-two, named William Lloyd Garrison, who was earning a bare living by doing compositor's

---

[1] For example, the plan to get rid of slavery by purchasing the negroes and establishing them in a colony on the African coast was almost exclusively a Southern measure. Between 1820 and 1860 the Colonization Society spent $1,806,000 and colonized but 10,500 negroes,— fewer than the increase by births in *one month*. Obviously, trying to remove the negroes from the South by colonization was like trying to bail out the sea with a dipper.

work in various printing offices. Garrison was immediately won to the cause of abolition and a year later joined Lundy at Baltimore in the editorship of the *Genius of Universal Emancipation*. Garrison announced in his first article that all slaves were "entitled to immediate and complete emancipation." This position was too radical for Lundy, who, with some regard for the property of the slaveholders, advocated a gradual emancipation. So the partnership was dissolved and Garrison set up his own press in Boston, from which on New Year's Day, 1831, he issued the first number of *The Liberator*. He had neither capital nor influence. His office was "an obscure hole," which the police had difficulty in finding. He had but one man and a negro boy to help him in composition and presswork. He himself was editor, typesetter, proofreader, printer, and distributor of *The Liberator*, and the very paper on which the first number was printed was bought on credit.

> In a small chamber, friendless and unseen,
>   Toiled o'er his types one poor, unlearned young man.
> The place was dark, unfurnitured, and mean,
>   Yet there the freedom of a race began.[1]

352. Garrison's Antislavery Manifesto. Garrison was of the stern, unyielding, undaunted race of the ancient Hebrew prophets. He saw, and wished to see, only one truth, namely, that slavery was sin. "On this subject," he wrote in his first announcement in *The Liberator*, "I do not wish to think, or speak, or write with moderation. No! no! Tell a man whose house is on fire to give a moderate alarm, ... tell the mother to gradually extricate the babe from the fire into which it has fallen — but urge me not to use moderation in a cause like the present. ... I will be as harsh as truth and as uncompromising as justice. ... I am in earnest — I will not equivocate — I will not excuse — I will not retreat a single inch — AND I WILL BE HEARD! The apathy of the people is enough to make every statue leap from its pedestal, and to hasten the resurrection of the dead."

353. Nat Turner's Insurrection. A horrible massacre, by negroes, of over sixty white people (mostly women and children) occurred in Southampton County, Virginia, in the late summer of the same

---

[1] James Russell Lowell's "To William Lloyd Garrison."

year that *The Liberator* was started. Nat Turner, the slave who led the insurrection, was a fanatical lay preacher who could read and write. The Southerners laid the dreadful deed to the influence of *The Liberator* and other abolitionist literature that was being sent into the slave states. They demanded that the legislatures of the free states should silence all antislavery agitation by a strict censorship of the press and of the public platform. They increased the severity of their own laws in restraint of negroes, both slave and free. In Delaware the assembling of more than six negroes was forbidden. In Virginia thirty-nine lashes were given a slave who was found with a gun in his possession. A law of Tennessee provided that no slave "dying

FACSIMILE OF THE HEADING OF *THE LIBERATOR*

under moderate correction" (that is, the slave driver's lash) could be held by the courts to have been "murdered." A wave of apprehension ran through the South lest the Southampton horror should be repeated.

354. Northern Hostility to the Abolitionists. The majority of the business and professional men of the North were scarcely less hostile to the abolitionists of the Garrison type than were the slaveholders themselves. In fact, Garrison declared that he found "contempt more bitter, opposition more active, detraction more relentless, prejudice more stubborn," in New England than in the South. It was not in Charleston or Richmond but in Boston that he was dragged through the streets, with a rope around his neck, by a "mob of respectable citizens," to be tarred and feathered on the Common, and was with difficulty rescued by the police and lodged in the city jail for his safety. As a rebuke to the abolitionists the free negroes in many cities of the North were treated with contemptuous discrimination; they were ejected from cars and coaches, assigned to corners in the churches, and excluded from the schools. Daniel Webster assured an anxious Southern correspondent in 1833 that "the North entertained no hostile designs toward slavery," and Charles Sumner (who twenty-five years later nearly paid with his life for his advocacy of free soil) declared that "an omnibus load of Boston abolitionists had done more to harm the antislavery cause than all its enemies."

355. Contrast between Antislavery Men and Abolitionists. We must distinguish carefully between the antislavery men, like Webster and Sumner, on the one hand, and the Garrison abolitionists on the other. The former recognized that the slavery question was exceedingly complicated, involving considerations of property, of social rank, of the rights of the states, and of the established industrial system of the South, as well as the moral issue. But the Garrison abolitionists saw only that slavery was sin, the violation of the Christian principle of the brotherhood of man. When therefore the moderate emancipators said that slavery was "the calamity of the South and not its crime," the abolitionist replied that it was a calamity *because* it was a crime. When the moderates suggested that the nation should assume the burden of emancipation by appropriating to it the revenues from the sale of the public lands, the abolitionists declared for immediate, unconditional, and uncompensated emancipation. The antislavery men were willing to proceed according to the methods recognized by the Constitution; that is, to confine their demands to emancipation in the District of Columbia (which was national territory) or to petition for an amendment to the Constitution giving Congress the power to abolish slavery in the states. But Garrison denounced the Constitution as "a covenant with death and an agreement with hell" and burned a copy of it publicly to show his horror of its recognition of slavery. He proclaimed as his motto "No union with slaveholders!" and forbade his followers to vote or hold office or even take the oath of allegiance to a constitution which supported slavery.

356. The South makes Abolitionists. As the abolitionists were very active in organizing societies in every town and flooding the South with literature, while the more moderate antislavery men refrained from speaking their mind for the sake of preserving as much harmony as possible between the two sections of the country, it was only natural that the South should believe the extreme abolitionist sentiment to be much more widespread in the North than it really was. In fact, the abolitionists might have long remained a small sect of extremists had not the Southerners themselves driven thousands into their ranks by trying to muzzle the liberty of petition and debate in Congress, thus identifying the cause of slavery with the denial of free speech.

357. The Abolition Controversy enters Congress. The introduction of abolitionism into Congress marks an important epoch in the slavery question. During the early years of Garrison's activity (1829–1833) Congress was busy with the agitation over the "Tariff of Abominations," the renewal of the Bank charter, the great Webster-Hayne debates on sectionalism, and the crisis of nullification. The slavery issue was kept in the background, being confined to the lecture hall and the abolitionist journals. But from the session of 1834–1835 on, numerous petitions for the restriction or abolition of slavery were presented in both Houses of Congress.[1] The attitude of the Southern members toward such petitions was shown when Wise of Virginia declared in the House (February, 1835) : "Sir, slavery, interwoven with our very political existence, is guaranteed by our Constitution. You cannot attack the institution of slavery without attacking the institutions of our country." And Calhoun in the Senate called a mild petition from the Pennsylvania Friends for the abolition of slavery in the District of Columbia (1836) "a foul slander on nearly one half the states of the Union."

358. The "Gag Resolution." The first amendment to the Constitution forbids Congress to make any law abridging "the right of the people to petition the government for redress of grievances." Up to the days of the abolitionist excitement Congress had respected this amendment and received all petitions. But in May, 1836, the enemies of abolition, North and South, united in the following resolution in the House: "That all petitions . . . relating in any way to the subject of slavery or the abolition of slavery, shall, without being either printed or referred [to a committee], be laid upon the

[1] The American Antislavery Society had been organized by the abolitionists at Philadelphia in 1833 and had added 200 branch societies by 1835. Before this epoch only the Friends had taken an interest in petitioning Congress for the destruction of slavery.

table, and that no further action shall be had thereon." This "gag resolution" furthered the abolitionist cause more than all the published numbers of *The Liberator.* John Quincy Adams, no friend of abolition before,[1] answered, when his name was called on the vote, "I hold the resolution to be a direct violation of the Constitution of the United States, of the rules of this House, and of the rights of my constituents." The gag resolution passed, however, by a vote of 117 to 68 and, in spite of Adams's valiant opposition, was renewed in succeeding sessions, and in 1840 was made a "standing" or permanent rule of the House.[2]

359. The Slaveholders' Demands. Meanwhile the Senate, although it did not pass any similar resolution, rejected the abolitionist petitions decisively. In the course of the debates the Southern members, led by Calhoun, formulated the full demands of the slave interests; namely, that the government should protect slavery in the Southern states, that the people of the North should cease to attack or even discuss the institution, and that there should be no agitation for the abolition of slavery in the District of Columbia or the territory of Florida.[3]

360. Attempt to exclude Abolitionist Matter from the Mails. Furthermore, the executive department of the government had been drawn into the abolitionist struggle. The people of the South objected to the distribution of abolitionist literature through their mails. One night in the summer of 1835 a number of leading citizens of Charleston, South Carolina, broke into the post office, seized a mail sack full of abolitionist documents, and publicly burned them. Appeal was made to the Postmaster-General, Amos Kendall, himself a slaveholder, to refuse the abolitionists the use of the United States mails. Kendall declared that he would not compel any postmaster to deliver abolitionist mail, but a clause was introduced into the post-office bill of July 2, 1836, punishing with dismissal, fine, and

---

[1] In 1807 he had voted in the Senate against the law to prohibit the slave trade, and in 1814, as peace commissioner at Ghent, he had insisted that the British pay for the slaves they had stolen in the United States.

[2] It was not till December, 1844, that Adams, after an eight years' fight, during which an attempt was made to censure him publicly, was able to get the gag resolution repealed by a vote of 108 to 80.

[3] Arkansas, the only territory of the Louisiana Purchase tract left open to slavery after the Missouri Compromise, was admitted as a slave state in 1836. This left Florida the only territory in which slavery legally existed.

imprisonment any postmaster who intentionally detained mail matter from reaching the person to whom it was addressed.

361. The Abolitionists Victims of Violence. These events of the years 1835–1837 in Congress woke the people of the land to realization of the tremendous problem they had on their hands. The antislavery men of the North drew closer to the abolitionist position when they saw how little chance there was of friendly cooperation with the South for the removal of slavery. Deeds of mob violence still further inflamed the antislavery spirit. In 1836 the office of *The Philanthropist*, an abolitionist paper published in Cincinnati by James G. Birney, a former Alabama planter who had come North and been converted to the abolitionist cause, was sacked by a mob, and Birney was obliged to flee for his life. The next year Elijah Lovejoy, after his printing press had been wrecked three times, was deliberately shot by a mob in Alton, Illinois, for insisting on publishing an abolitionist paper.

362. The Liberty Party. Although Garrison and his New England followers condemned any participation in politics under a constitution which recognized slavery, the more practical abolitionists of the Middle and Western border states, Pennsylvania, Ohio, Indiana, and Illinois, formed a political party. In 1838 they elected Joshua R. Giddings to Congress, and in the presidential campaign of 1840 they cast over 7000 votes for James G. Birney. We shall see in the next chapter what a great influence this Liberty party exercised in the decade 1840–1850. In spite of Garrison's opposition to the party, it was nevertheless the natural and logical outcome of the abolitionist movement and the true foundation of the new Republican party which twenty years later triumphed in the election of Abraham Lincoln.

363. The Southern Apology for Slavery. The failure of the South to get rid of slavery in the early decades of the nineteenth century must be set down to the domination of a class of rich, aristocratic planters, who found slavery both economically profitable and the basis of a social order in which they enjoyed a comfortable and commanding position. Their slaves excluded the competition of free labor and kept the poorer whites from attaining the industrial development which would have given them a share in the commercial wealth and the political power of the South. Calhoun, in a conversation with Horace Binney, a Northern friend, in 1834, boasted of the superiority of slave labor over free labor in a democracy. Of the Northern laborers he said: "The poor and uneducated are increasing. There is no power in representative government to suppress them. Their numbers and disorderly tempers will make them in the end the enemies of the men of property. They have the right to vote, and will finally control your elections, invade your houses, and drive you out of doors. . . . They will increase till they overturn your institutions. Slavery cuts off this evil at its roots. . . . There cannot be a durable republic without slavery."

364. The Failure of the Moral Argument. The moral argument of the abolitionists had less and less weight as this caste system hardened. "By what moral suasion," asked an apologist for slavery in the South, "do you imagine you can prevail on us to give up a thousand millions of dollars in the value of our slaves and a thousand millions more in the depreciation of our lands?" Had the South been willing, there is little doubt that a plan of gradual emancipation could have been found. Other nations had got rid of slavery without revolution or bloodshed, and the example of England, which purchased and set free the slaves in her West Indian colonies in 1833, was before the eyes of the world. But under the provocation of the abolitionists' attacks the legislatures of the Southern states, instead of devising plans of emancipation, passed laws to fix the status of slavery on the negroes forever.

References

The Missouri Compromise: W. E. B. DuBois, *The Suppression of the African Slave Trade*, chaps. i–iii; A. B. Hart, *American History told by Contemporaries*, Vol. I, Nos. 86, 87; Vol. II, Nos. 42, 102–108; F. J. Turner, *Rise of the New West* (Am. Nation), chap. x; John Quincy Adams, *Memoirs*, Vols. IV, V; J. A. Woodburn, *Historical Significance of the Missouri Compromise*, in *American History Association Report*, 1893, pp. 249–298; J. W. Burgess, *The Middle Period*, chap. iv; J. B. McMaster, *History of the People of the United States*, Vol. IV, chap. xxxix; J. F. Rhodes, *History of the United States from the Compromise of 1850*, Vol. I, pp. 29–39; Carl Schurz, *Henry Clay*, Vol. I, chap. viii.

The Abolitionists: Hart, *Contemporaries*, Vol. III, Nos. 174–181, 186; *Slavery and Abolition* (Am. Nation), chaps. vii–xviii; W. P. and F. J. Garrison, *Life of William Lloyd Garrison*; McMaster, Vol. VI, chap. lxi; Higginson and MacDonald, *History of the United States*, chap. xix; Jesse Macy, *The*

Anti-Slavery Crusade (Chronicles, Vol. XXVIII), chaps. ii–v; WILLIAM MAC-DONALD, *Select Documents of United States History, 1776–1861*, Nos. 63–69; T. C. SMITH, *The Liberty and Free-Soil Parties in the Northwest*, chaps. ii, iii; BURGESS, chap. xi; RHODES, Vol. I, pp. 53–75; BOOKER T. WASHINGTON, *The Story of the Negro*, chap. xiv.

TOPICS FOR SPECIAL REPORTS

1. **Antislavery Sentiment in the Eighteenth Century**: HENRY WILSON, *The Rise and Fall of the Slave Power*, Vol. I, pp. 1–30; THOMAS JEFFERSON, *Notes on Virginia*; WILLIAM BIRNEY, *James G. Birney, His Life and Times*, Appendix C; JOHN WOOLMAN, *Considerations on the Keeping of Negroes*; HART, *Contemporaries*, Vol. II, Nos. 102, 103, 106; GAILLARD HUNT, *Life of James Madison*, pp. 70–76.

2. **Slavery in the Constitution of the United States**: WILSON, Vol. I, pp. 39–56; DUBOIS, pp. 53–69; JONATHAN ELLIOT, *Debates on the Adoption of the Federal Constitution*, Vol. V; J. R. BRACKETT, *The Status of Slavery, 1775–1789* (in J. F. JAMESON's *Essays in Constitutional History*), pp. 263–311; H. V. AMES, *Slavery and the Constitution*.

3. **The "Gag Resolution"**: J. Q. ADAMS, *Memoirs*, Vol. VIII, pp. 434–481; Vol. IX, pp. 267–286; HART, *Contemporaries*, Vol. III, No. 184; C. H. PECK, *The Jacksonian Epoch*, pp. 273–279, 373–392; J. T. MORSE, JR., *John Quincy Adams*, pp. 243–262; JOSIAH QUINCY, *Memoir of John Quincy Adams*, pp. 251–262; HART, *Slavery and Abolition* (Am. Nation), pp. 256–275.

4. **Abolitionist Literature in the United States Mail**: HART, *Contemporaries*, Vol. III, No. 180; *Slavery and Abolition*, pp. 286–288; J. D. RICHARDSON, *Messages and Papers of the Presidents*, Vol. III, pp. 175 ff.; AMOS KENDALL, *Autobiography*, pp. 645 ff.

5. **James G. Birney**: WILLIAM BIRNEY, *James G. Birney, His Life and Times*; SAMUEL J. MAY, *Recollections of the Antislavery Conflict*, pp. 203–211; HART, *Contemporaries*, Vol. III, No. 177; WILSON, Vol. I (use index).

CHAPTER XII

TEXAS

Westward Expansion

365. The Freedom of the New World. One of the chief traits of the American people has been their restless activity. The settlers who came to our shores in the seventeenth and eighteenth centuries came in search of an ampler life than they found in the Old World. They wanted elbow room. They demanded freedom — freedom from religious persecution, social oppression, and commercial restriction. For the sake of living untrammeled lives and working out their own destinies they accepted the privations and hardships of the New World. Their descendants, increased by new thousands of adventurous immigrants, tended constantly westward, making the extension of our frontier to the Pacific the most important influence in American history.

366. Waves of Westward Migration. The westward movement is characterized by successive waves of migration. The first great wave followed the expulsion of the French from North America in 1763. Through the passes of the Alleghenies, "the arteries of the West," a stream of pioneers led by Boone, Sevier, Robertson, Harrod, and our other early "empire builders"[1] poured into the forest lands of the Ohio, the Tennessee, and the Cumberland valleys; while George Rogers Clark, during the American Revolution, won for Virginia and the Union the magnificent territory between the Ohio and the Great Lakes, extending westward to the Mississippi. A second wave of westward migration followed the War of 1812, filling Indiana and Illinois Territories on the north and Mississippi and Missouri Territories to the south and bringing five new Western states (Indiana, Mississippi, Illinois, Alabama, Missouri) into the Union

---

[1] "A roughened race, embrowned in the sun, loving the rude woods and the crack of the rifle, delicate in nothing but the touch of the trigger, leaving cities in their track as if by accident rather than by design. . . . Settled life and wild life side by side; civilization frayed at the edges; Europe frontiered!" Woodrow Wilson, in *The Forum*, Vol. XIX, p. 544.

in as many years (1816–1821). The third and most wonderful era of westward expansion (1835–1848) carried our boundary across the Rockies and the Sierras to the Pacific Ocean. It is this third period which we are to study in the present chapter. The chapter is entitled "Texas," because the annexation of that great commonwealth to the Union, and the disposition of the land that was acquired in the war with Mexico which followed the annexation, determined the whole policy of our government toward the West during the decade 1840–1850.

367. The Opposition of the East. The path of westward expansion was never smooth. Besides the dangers of the wilderness,

AN EMIGRANT TRAIN ON THE WAY TO THE WEST

the pioneer communities had to contend with opposition from the older states. Up to the time of the Missouri Compromise this opposition arose from the apprehension of the original states that the burden of the defense and the development of the new communities would fall upon their shoulders, and from the jealousy of the political power which the new communities would wrest from them. When the bill to admit Louisiana to the Union was proposed in 1811 Josiah Quincy of Massachusetts declared on the floor of Congress: "If this bill passes, it is my deliberate opinion that it is virtually a dissolution of the Union.... Do you suppose the people of the Northern and Atlantic states will, or ought to, look on with patience and see representatives and senators from the Red River and the Missouri pouring themselves on this floor, managing the concerns of a seaboard 1500 miles, at least, from their residence?"

368. Slavery and the West. This narrow and selfish opposition of the East to the expansion of the West was broken down by the democratic revolution of the third decade of the nineteenth century, which put Andrew Jackson into the presidential chair. But a still more serious complication arose with the debates over the Missouri Compromise and the abolitionist agitation. Then the question of the growth of the West became connected with the question of the extension of slavery. After the bitter struggle of the years 1835-1837 in Congress over the antislavery petitions and the use of the United States mails for antislavery propaganda, no movement for the acquisition of new territory or the admission of new states could arise without immediately starting the strife between the friends and the foes of slavery. Senator Benton of Missouri likened the slavery question to the plague of frogs sent on the Egyptians. "We can see nothing, touch nothing, have no measures proposed," he said, "without having this pestilence thrust before us." It would be impossible to overestimate the importance of this connection between westward expansion and slavery. The slavery issue came to a crisis not as a struggle between North and South, but as a struggle of North and South *for the West*. The sentiment of expansion, so deeply implanted in the breasts of Northerners and Southerners alike, and the glory of carrying the American flag to the Pacific Ocean impelled our fathers to take possession of the Western land and trust to future compromises to settle the question of freedom or slavery within its borders. The history of those compromises we shall trace in a later chapter. First we must see how the Western land was won.

369. Claims to the Oregon Region. It will be remembered that the treaty of 1819 with Spain fixed our western boundary as far north as the forty-second parallel. We had just concluded (1818) a treaty with Great Britain by which we agreed to share with that power for ten years the great Oregon region lying beyond the Rocky Mountains (between 42° and 54° 40′ north latitude). The agreement was fair, for both countries had claims on Oregon, based upon exploration and settlement. For the Americans, a Boston sea captain named Gray had sailed into the mouth of the Columbia River in 1792; the famous Lewis and Clark expedition had traversed the region to the Pacific in 1804-1806; and John Jacob Astor had established the fur post of Astoria near the mouth of the Columbia in

1811. For the English, the Hudson's Bay Company had established several trading posts north of the Columbia River. Some of our Western statesmen, led by Senator Benton, who realized the importance of our extension to the Pacific, urged a settlement of the Oregon question which should give the United States full title to the land at least as far north as the forty-ninth parallel (our northern boundary east of the Rockies). But public opinion was not yet sufficiently aroused to the value of Oregon; and the agreement of 1818 was renewed, in 1827, for an indefinite period, either party having a right to terminate it on a year's notice to the other.

370. The Settlement of Oregon. In spite of the indifference of the government and the people at large, a few enthusiasts labored hard during the Jacksonian period to secure settlers for the Oregon region. A group of about 50 colonists went out in the summer of 1832, under Nathaniel Wyeth of Massachusetts, but only 11 reached Fort Vancouver. Two years later the Methodists sent out Daniel and Jason Lee as missionaries to the Flathead Indians in the region, and other denominations followed their lead. Dr. Marcus Whitman of New York, a missionary sent by the American Board of Missions, was a most indefatigable worker for the settlement of Oregon. He went out in 1835, came back the next year for helpers, then returned to Oregon with his newly married wife and another missionary couple. When there was some danger that the Board would discontinue its stations in Oregon, Whitman again came East, making the trip of nearly 4000 miles alone on horseback, to plead for the maintenance of the missions. On his return journey he was of great service to a group of several hundred emigrants from the Middle West to the Columbia valley. By this time (1843) the settlers in Oregon had increased to about 1000. Their presence was henceforth our strongest claim to the region.

371. The Condition of Texas about 1830. While Oregon was thus being opened for American settlement, a most exciting incident in the great drama of expansion was being enacted on our southern borders, in Texas. Two years after the treaty of 1819 with Spain, which fixed our southwestern boundary at the Sabine River, Mexico joined the long list of Spanish-American colonies which had established their independence of the mother country. The government of the new republic of Mexico was very weak, however, especially in the provinces lying at a distance from the capital. Texas formed one of these provinces and for several reasons chafed under the control of Mexico. In the first place, since the beginning of the nineteenth century Americans[1] had been crossing the Sabine into Texas, until by 1830 there were nearly 20,000 of them in the province. The Americans at first had been welcomed and given large tracts of land by the Mexicans, partly in return for the aid they furnished the latter in their revolt from Spain. But when the number of Americans increased to the point where they threatened to rule the province, the Mexican president, Bustamante, issued an edict (1830)

CONVENT AND GROUNDS OF THE ALAMO

forbidding all further immigration from the United States into Texas.[2] Furthermore, the Mexican government had subjected Texas, with its predominating Protestant population and its democratic ideals imported from America, to the Roman Catholic Spanish officials of the smaller province of Coahuila. When Texas petitioned

[1] The term "American," of course, in its literal sense means an inhabitant or citizen of America — North, South, or Central. But, as we have no single word to denote an inhabitant or citizen of the United States, we quite commonly use the term "American" for that purpose, calling the other "Americans" Canadians, Mexicans, Brazilians, etc.

[2] Alexis de Tocqueville, our most distinguished foreign critic in the first half of the nineteenth century, wrote shortly after 1830: "In the course of the last few years, the Anglo-Americans have penetrated into this province [Texas], which is still thinly peopled. They purchase land, they produce the commodities of the country, and supplant the original population. It may be easily foreseen that if Mexico takes no step to check this change, the province of Texas will soon cease to belong to her" (Democracy in America, Vol. I, p. 448). In a hundred years Spain had brought less than 3000 white colonists to Texas, while in the single decade 1817–1827 about 12,000 Americans crossed the borders into the province.

for a separation from Coahuila the Mexican government sent troops into the province to maintain order and dispatched a warship to patrol the Texan coast.

372. Texas wins its Independence. Incensed by this treatment and encouraged by their American neighbors across the Sabine, the Texans, on the second of March, 1836, declared their independence and drove the Mexican troops across their border. Santa Anna, the new Mexican president, a man of perfidious and cruel character, led an army in person to punish the rebellious province. His march was marked with horrible atrocities. At the Alamo, a mission building in San Antonio, a garrison of 166 Texans was absolutely exterminated, even to the sick in the hospital ward; and a little further on, at Goliad, the defenders were massacred in cold blood after their surrender. Santa Anna with some 1200 troops was met at the San Jacinto River (April 21, 1836) by a force of about 750 Texan volunteers under General Sam Houston, a veteran of the War of 1812 and an ex-governor of Tennessee. The Mexican army was utterly routed

SAM HOUSTON, PRESIDENT OF THE REPUBLIC OF TEXAS

and Santa Anna himself fell into Houston's hands as a prisoner of war. The independence of Texas was won. A republic was set up with Houston as president, and a constitution was adopted patterned after those of the American commonwealths. Slavery was legitimized in the new republic, but the importation of slaves from any place except the United States was forbidden. Some 50,000 out of the 68,000 inhabitants of Texas were Americans, and the sentiment of President Houston, the legislature, and the people at large was overwhelmingly in favor of annexation to the United States.

373. The Question of the Annexation of Texas. The administration at Washington was also in favor of the annexation of Texas, and had been ever since Mexico had secured its independence from

Spain. In 1827 President John Quincy Adams had offered Mexico $1,000,000 for Texas; and President Jackson had twice tried to purchase the province (1829, 1835), raising Adams's offer to $5,000,000. Nevertheless, Jackson refused to conclude a treaty of annexation with Texas against the will of Mexico, even after both Houses of Congress had recognized the independence of the province by large majorities. We were at peace with Mexico, even if on bad terms with her on account of claims for damages to American property in Texas and to American commerce in the Gulf. Mexico still claimed Texas as a dependency. The revolt was still too recent to make the Texan republic an assured fact. Under these circumstances, for the United States to take Texas without the consent of Mexico would have been a breach of the law of nations and would probably have brought on war between the two countries. Moreover, it was a most inauspicious moment for the attempt to add the immense slave area of Texas to the Union. The abolitionist struggle in Congress was at its height. Jackson's successor, Van Buren, was a New Yorker and had little desire for extending the domain of slavery. He refused to consider any proposition for the annexation of Texas and even came to an agreement with Mexico (which that country soon broke) for the settlement of the American claims. So the whole matter slumbered through Van Buren's administration and played no part at all in the turbulent election of 1840, in which the new Whig party overthrew the Jackson machine.

The "Reoccupation" of Oregon and the "Reannexation" of Texas

374. President Tyler and the Whigs. The triumph of the Whigs in 1840 was short-lived. President Harrison, the old hero of Tippecanoe, died a month after his inauguration, and Vice President Tyler succeeded to his place. Tyler was a Virginian and a Democrat. He had been put on the Whig ticket with Harrison in order to win votes in the South. The only bond of union between him and men like Adams, Clay, Harrison, and Webster was his enmity for Andrew Jackson, which had been strong enough to drive him into the Whig party. On the great questions of public policy, such as a strong central government, internal improvements, the tariff, and the Bank of the United States, he was opposed to the Whig leaders. When, therefore, Tyler vetoed a bill passed by the Whig Congress in 1841 for the recharter of the National Bank, he was "read out" of the Whig party, and every member of his cabinet resigned except Daniel Webster.

375. The Webster-Ashburton Treaty. Webster retained his office of Secretary of State because of an important diplomatic negotiation with England. Ever since the treaty of peace of 1783 the extreme northeastern boundary of the United States (between Maine and New Brunswick) had been unsettled, due to a disagreement over the exact location and meaning of "the Highlands," or watershed, which divided the St. Lawrence valley from the Atlantic coast. British and American lumbermen quarreled over the disputed region. In the late thirties the authorities of New Brunswick and Maine were at the point of war. An exchange of correspondence on the subject between Washington and London resulted in Lord Ashburton's being sent over here in the summer of 1842 to arrange a settlement. Ashburton was a friend of Webster's, and the negotiations between them proceeded with all the courtesy and smoothness possible. The Webster-Ashburton treaty was concluded in August, 1842, dividing the disputed territory almost equally between the claimants.

376. Plan for the Annexation of Texas revived. The next spring Daniel Webster retired from the cabinet and was replaced by Upshur of Virginia. Webster was a strong antislavery Whig, who had put himself on record against the acquisition of Texas in a speech made in New York City, on his way home from the congressional session of 1836-1837. "Texas is likely to be a slaveholding country," he said, "and I frankly avow my entire unwillingness to do anything that shall extend the slavery of the African race on this continent, or add other slaveholding states to the Union." Upshur, on the other hand, was an ardent advocate of the annexation of Texas. With the cabinet thus reorganized, and all the men of Harrison's choice replaced by men of Tyler's views, the project for annexation was revived.

377. The Annexationists demand Both Oregon and Texas. It was just at this time that popular interest in the distant region of Oregon was aroused. This interest furnished the annexationists with fine political capital. By combining the demand for Oregon with the demand for Texas they could appeal to the people of the United States on a platform which emphasized the expansion of American territory rather than the extension of the area of slavery. With Oregon they might win the Northern expansionists who were opposed to annexing Texas on account of slavery. Thus Oregon was used as a makeweight for Texas.

378. Growth of the Expansionist Sentiment. As the year 1843 passed, the policy of both Great Britain and Mexico strengthened the expansionist sentiment in the United States. The British ministry rejected the offer of our government to divide Oregon by running the boundary line of 49° north latitude to the Pacific; and Mexico, besides breaking the agreement made with Van Buren for the adjustment of American claims, notified our State Department that any move to annex Texas would be regarded as an act of war. Moreover, there were fears that Great Britain was using her influence to keep us out of Texas. Mexico owed about $50,000,000 to British capitalists, for which her lands to the north and west of the Rio Grande were mortgaged. An independent state of Texas under British protection would furnish England plentiful supplies of cotton, and a market for her manufactures unhampered by the tariff of the United States. Our minister to Paris wrote home in 1845, "There is scarcely any sacrifice England would not make to prevent Texas from coming into our possession."

379. Calhoun's Treaty of Annexation rejected. Calhoun, who had succeeded Upshur in the State Department, concluded a treaty for the annexation of Texas in April, 1844. But the Senate refused by a large majority to ratify it. Besides the antislavery men of the North, many Southerners voted against the treaty for various reasons: because our chargé in Texas had promised that men and ships would be sent to protect Texas from Mexican interference while the treaty was under discussion; because they saw in the treaty a bid on Calhoun's part for the presidency; because they thought that Calhoun deliberately misrepresented Great Britain's attitude in order to hasten annexation; because they knew that many speculators in Texan lands were trying to influence senators in the lobbies of Congress to vote for the treaty; because they were not ready to invite war with Mexico; because they doubted that the

Constitution gave power to the president and Senate to annex an independent foreign state to our Union by treaty.

380. The National Conventions of 1844. While Calhoun's treaty was being discussed in the Senate, the Whig and Democratic conventions met to select their candidates for the presidential campaign. The Whigs unanimously nominated Henry Clay. On the subject of expansion their platform was silent. They relied entirely on the record and the popularity of their candidate. In the Democratic convention the friends of annexation carried the day after a hard battle. Van Buren was rejected, and James K. Polk of Tennessee was nominated on the ninth ballot. Polk was an ardent annexationist. He had been a member of Congress from 1825 to 1839 and Speaker of the House during the stormy days of the abolitionist debates. From 1839 to 1841 he served as governor of Tennessee. Although by no means an obscure man, Polk had not been regarded as a presidential possibility before the convention met. He is the first example of the "dark horse"[1] in the national convention; and it is a significant fact that from this time to the choice of Abraham Lincoln in 1860, the men of first rank (like Clay, Calhoun, Webster, and Douglas) were passed over for more "available" (compromise) candidates. It is the most striking proof of the influence of the slavery question in our politics; for no other issue since the establishment of our government had been strong enough to keep from the highest offices the statesmen of conspicuous genius.

381. Polk defeats Clay at the Polls. The Democrats went into the campaign of 1844 with a frank appeal to the expansionist sentiment of the country. Their platform was the *re*-occupation of Oregon and the *re*-annexation of Texas. The prefix *re* in this confident declaration implied that Oregon was already ours by discovery, settlement, and treaty; and that Texas had been really purchased with Louisiana in 1803 but had been weakly surrendered to Spain in the treaty of 1819. Clay tried to "straddle" the issue of annexation, publishing opinions both for it and against it, and concluding in the end that "the subject of slavery ought not to affect the question one way or the other." Disgusted with Clay's instability, enough

---

[1] A term borrowed from the language of the race track to denote a horse of whose qualities and speed nothing is known; then used in politics of an obscure candidate who "comes up from behind" and wins the race.

Whigs in New York and Michigan cast their votes for the abolitionist James G. Birney, the candidate of the Liberty party, to give those two states, and therewith the election, to Polk.

382. The Annexation of Texas. Tyler interpreted the election of Polk as the indorsement by the American people of the policy of the immediate annexation of Texas. He therefore suggested to Congress that it might admit Texas under the clause of the Constitution which gives it the right to "admit new states into this Union." In February, 1845, both branches of Congress passed a resolution in favor of annexing Texas, the House by a vote of 132 to 76, the Senate by the close vote of 27 to 25. President Tyler signed the resolution on the first of March, three days before his retirement from office. The people of Texas welcomed the resolution of Congress with a rejoicing almost as tumultuous as that which had greeted the news of the victory of San Jacinto. Late in the year 1845 the republic of Texas became a state of the Union on generous terms. She left to the United States government the adjustment of her boundaries with Mexico; handed over to the United States her ports and harbors as well as her fortifications, arsenals, and public buildings, keeping, however, her public lands and her debt; and agreed to the prohibition of slavery in that part of the state north of the Missouri Compromise line of 36° 30′. With her consent four additional states might be made out of her territory.

383. Settlement of the Oregon Boundary. Texas being safely in the Union, the new President began to redeem his campaign pledge for the "reoccupation" of Oregon. In his first message to Congress (December, 1845) he asserted the claims of the United States to the whole of the Oregon region from the Spanish-Mexican boundary on the south (42°) to the Russian boundary on the north (54° 40′). Great Britain must retire from the whole of Oregon, back to the Hudson Bay territory. "Fifty-four forty or fight" was the popular war cry in which the victorious Democrats voiced their preposterous claims to the whole of Oregon. However, as Mexico began to make preparations for carrying out her threats of war, the administration at Washington grew more moderate in its claims to Oregon. Neither Polk nor Congress had any intention, at such a crisis, of going to war with England over a difference of five degrees of latitude on our northwestern boundary. So, after a rather amusing campaign of correspondence, in which the President and the Senate each tried to throw on the other the responsibility of deserting the blustering platform of "Fifty-four forty or fight," a treaty was made with Great Britain (June, 1846) continuing the parallel of 49°, from the Rockies to the Pacific, as the northern boundary of the United States.

The Mexican War

384. Mexico refuses to recognize the Annexation of Texas. The annexation of Texas was a perfectly fair transaction. For nine years, since the victory of San Jacinto in 1836, Texas had been an independent republic, whose reconquest Mexico had not the slightest chance of effecting. In fact, at the very moment of annexation, the Mexican government, at the suggestion of England, had agreed to recognize the independence of Texas, on condition that the republic should not join itself to the United States. We were not taking Mexican territory, then, in annexing Texas. The new state had come into the Union claiming the Rio Grande as her southern and western boundary. By the terms of annexation all boundary disputes with Mexico were referred by Texas to the government of the United States. President Polk sent John Slidell of Louisiana to Mexico in the autumn of 1845 to adjust any differences over the Texan claims. But though Slidell labored for months to get a hearing, two successive presidents of revolution-torn Mexico refused to recognize him, and he was dismissed from the country in August, 1846.

385. Taylor attacked on the Rio Grande. The massing of Mexican troops on the southern bank of the Rio Grande, coupled with the refusal of the Mexican government to receive Slidell, led President Polk to order General Zachary Taylor to move to the borders. Taylor marched to the Rio Grande and fortified a position on the northern bank. The Mexican and the American troops were thus facing each other across the river. When Taylor refused to retreat to the Nueces, the Mexican commander crossed the Rio Grande, ambushed a scouting force of 63 Americans, and killed or wounded 16 of them (April 25, 1846).

386. The United States accepts War with Mexico. When the news of this attack reached Washington early in May, Polk sent a special message to Congress, concluding with these words: "We have tried every effort at reconciliation. . . . But now, after reiterated menaces, Mexico has passed the boundary of the United States [the Rio Grande], has invaded our territory and shed American blood upon the American soil. She has proclaimed that hostilities have commenced, and that the two nations are at war. As war exists, and, notwithstanding all our efforts to avoid it, exists by the act of Mexico herself, we are called upon by every consideration of duty and patriotism to vindicate with decision the honor, the rights, and the interests of our country." The House and the Senate, by very large majorities (174 to 14, and 40 to 2), voted 50,000 men and $10,000,000 for the prosecution of the war.

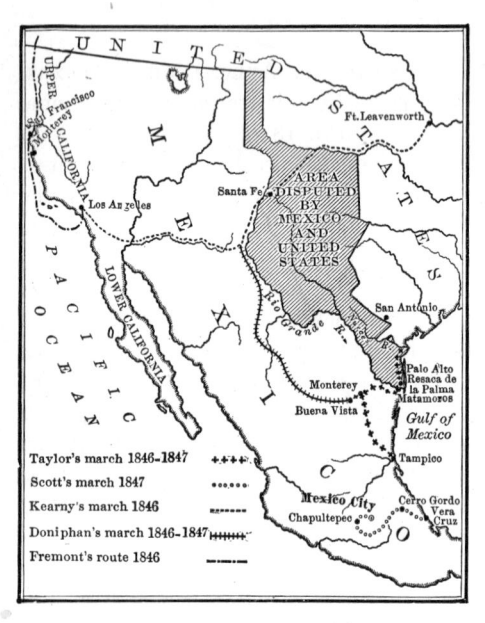

THE CAMPAIGNS OF THE MEXICAN WAR

387. Taylor invades Mexico. Meanwhile, General Taylor had driven the Mexicans back to the south bank of the Rio Grande in the battles of Palo Alto and Resaca de la Palma. Six days after the vote of Congress sanctioning the war, he crossed the Rio Grande and occupied the Mexican frontier town of Matamoros, whence he proceeded during the summer and autumn of 1846 to capture the capitals of three of the Mexican provinces.

388. The Occupation of California and New Mexico. As soon as hostilities began, Commodore Sloat, in command of our squadron in the Pacific, was ordered to seize California, and General Kearny was sent to invade New Mexico. The occupation of California was practically undisputed. Mexico had only the faintest shadow of authority in the province, and the 6000 white inhabitants made no objection to seeing the flag of the United States raised over their forts. Kearny started with 1800 men from Fort Leavenworth, Kansas, in June, and on the eighteenth of August defeated the force of 4000 Mexicans and Indians which disputed his occupation of Santa Fé. After garrisoning this important post he detached Colonel Doniphan with 850 men to march through the northern provinces of Mexico and effect a juncture with General Taylor at Monterey, while he himself with only 100 men continued his long journey of 1500 miles to San Diego, California, where he joined Sloat's successor, Stockton.

389. Taylor's Victory at Buena Vista. After these decided victories and uninterrupted marches of Taylor, Kearny, Sloat, Stockton, and Doniphan, the Mexican government was offered a fair chance to treat for peace, which it refused. Then President Polk decided, with the unanimous consent of his cabinet, to strike at the heart of Mexico. General Winfield Scott, a hero of the War of 1812, was put in command of an army of about 12,000 men, to land at Vera Cruz and fight his way up the mountains to the capital city of Mexico. Santa Anna, who, by the rapid shift of revolutions, was again dictator in Mexico, heard of this plan to attack the capital and hastened north with 20,000 troops to surprise and destroy Taylor's army before Scott should have time to take Vera Cruz. But Taylor, with an army one fourth the size of Santa Anna's, drove the Mexicans back in the hotly contested battle of Buena Vista (February 23, 1847), securing the Californian and New Mexican conquests. Santa Anna hastened southward to the defense of the city of Mexico.

390. Scott takes the city of Mexico. Scott took Vera Cruz in March and worked his way slowly but surely, against forces always superior to his own, up to the very gates of Mexico (August, 1847). Here he paused, by the President's orders, to allow the Mexicans another chance to accept the terms of peace which the United States offered,— the cession by Mexico of New Mexico and California in return for a large payment of money. The Mexican commissioners, however, insisted on having both banks of the Rio Grande and all of California up to the neighborhood of San Francisco, besides receiving damages for injuries inflicted by the American troops in their invasions. These claims were preposterous, coming from a conquered country, and there was nothing left for Scott to do but to resume military operations. Santa Anna defended the capital with a force of 30,000 men, but the Mexicans were no match for the American soldiers. Scott stormed the fortified hill of Chapultepec and advanced to the gates of the city. On the thirteenth of September his troops entered the Mexican capital and raised the Stars and Stripes over "the palace of the Montezumas."

WINFIELD SCOTT   ZACHARY TAYLOR

The heroes of the Mexican War

391. Polk's Efforts to secure Peace. From the beginning of the war Polk had been negotiating for peace. He had kept Slidell in Mexico long after the opening of hostilities and had sent Nicholas Trist as special peace commissioner to join Scott's army at Vera Cruz and to offer Mexico terms of peace at the earliest possible moment. He had allowed Santa Anna to return to Mexico from his exile in Cuba in the summer of 1846, because that wily and treacherous dictator held out false promises of effecting a reconciliation between Mexico and the United States. He had asked Congress for an appropriation of $2,000,000 for peace negotiations when General Taylor was still near the Rio Grande, ten days before General Kearny had taken Santa Fé and the province of New Mexico, and before General Scott's campaign had been thought of.

392. The Treaty of Guadalupe-Hidalgo. When the Mexican commissioners made advances for peace at the beginning of the year 1848, they were given terms almost as liberal as those offered them before Scott had stormed and occupied their capital. By the treaty concluded at Guadalupe-Hidalgo, February 2, 1848, Mexico was required to cede California and New Mexico to the United States and to recognize the Rio Grande as the southern and western boundary of Texas. In return, the United States paid Mexico $15,000,000 cash and assumed some $3,250,000 more in claims of American citizens on the Mexican government. Considering the facts that California was scarcely under Mexican control at all and might have been taken at any moment by Great Britain, France, or Russia; that New Mexico was still the almost undisturbed home of Indian tribes; that the land from the Nueces to the Rio Grande was almost a desert; and that the American troops were in possession of the Mexican capital, the terms offered Mexico were very generous. Polk was urged by many to annex the whole country of Mexico to the United States, but he refused to consider such a proposal.

393. The Justice of the Mexican War. The Mexican War has generally been condemned by American historians as "the foulest blot on our national honor," a war forced upon Mexico by slaveholders greedy for new territory, a perfect illustration of La Fontaine's fable of the wolf picking a quarrel with the lamb solely for an excuse to devour him. But Mexico had insulted our flag, plundered our commerce, imprisoned our citizens, lied to our representatives, and spurned our envoys. As early as 1837 President Jackson said that Mexico's offenses "would justify in the eyes of all nations immediate war." To be sure we were a strong nation and Mexico a weak one. But weakness should not give immunity to continued and open insolence. We had a right to annex Texas after that republic had maintained its independence for nine years; yet Mexico made annexation a cause of war. We were willing to discuss the boundaries of Texas with Mexico; but our accredited envoy was rejected by two successive Mexican presidents, who were afraid to oppose the war spirit of their country. We even refrained from taking Texas into the Union until Great Britain had interfered so far as to persuade Mexico to recognize the independence of Texas if she would refuse to join the United States.

394. The Moral Aspect of the Annexation of Texas. If there was anything disgraceful in the expansionist program of the decade 1840–1850, it was not the Mexican War, but the annexation of Texas. The position of the abolitionists on this question was clear and logical. They condemned the annexation of Texas as a wicked extension of the slavery area, notwithstanding all arguments about "fulfilling our manifest destiny" or "attaining our natural boundaries." To annex Texas might be legally right, they said, but it was morally wrong. James Russell Lowell, in his magnificent poem "The Present Crisis" (1844), warned the annexationists that "They enslave their children's children who make compromise with sin." We certainly assumed a great moral responsibility when we annexed Texas. However, it was not to Mexico that we were answerable, but to the enlightened conscience of the nation.

395. Completion of the Program of Expansion. With our acquisition of the Oregon territory to the forty-ninth parallel by the treaty of 1846 with Great Britain, and the cession of California and New Mexico by the treaty of Guadalupe-Hidalgo in 1848, the boundaries of the United States reached practically their present limits.[1] The work of westward extension was done. Expansion, the watchword of the decade 1840–1850, was dropped from our vocabulary for fifty years, and the immense energies of the nation were directed toward finding a plan on which the new territory could be organized in harmony with the conflicting interests of the free and slave sections of our country.

REFERENCES

Westward Expansion: G. P. GARRISON, *Westward Extension* (American Nation Series), chaps. i, ii, vi, vii; F. J. TURNER, *Rise of the New West* (Am. Nation), chaps. v–viii; E. E. SPARKS, *The Expansion of the American People*, chap. xxv; ELLEN SEMPLE, *American History and its Geographical Conditions*, chaps. x–xii; FRANCIS PARKMAN, *The Oregon Trail*, chaps. xix–xxi; W. E. DODD, *Expansion and Conflict* (Riverside History, Vol. III), chap. vii; J. W. BURGESS, *The Middle Period*, chaps. xiii, xiv; J. B. MCMASTER, *History of the People*

---

[1] A small strip south of the Gila River (southern Arizona) was bought from Mexico, through Mr. Gadsden, in 1853, for $10,000,000. The large sum paid for the Gadsden Purchase has been called by the critics of the Mexican War "conscience money" paid to Mexico for the provinces of which we "robbed" her.

of the United States, Vol. V, chap. liii; Vol. VI, chap. lx; J. F. RHODES, *History of the United States since the Compromise of 1850*, Vol. I, pp. 75-85; GARRISON, *The First Stage of the Movement for the Annexation of Texas* (*American Historical Review*, Vol. X, pp. 72-96).

The "Reoccupation" of Oregon and the "Reannexation" of Texas: SPARKS, chaps. xxv-xxvii; BURGESS, chap. xv; L. G. TYLER, *Letters and Times of the Tylers*, Vol. II, chaps. ix-xii, xv; WILLIAM MACDONALD, *Select Documents of United States History, 1776-1861*, No. 71; JUSTIN H. SMITH, *The Annexation of Texas*; A. B. HART, *American History told by Contemporaries*, Vol. III, Nos. 185-189; H. VON HOLST, *John C. Calhoun*, chap. viii; HORACE GREELEY, *The American Conflict*, Vol. I, chap. xii; GARRISON, *Texas*, chaps. x-xx; *Westward Extension*, chaps. viii-xi; J. W. FOSTER, *A Century of American Diplomacy*, chap. viii.

The Mexican War: HART, Vol. IV, Nos. 8-14; MACDONALD, Nos. 72-74, 76; BURGESS, chap. xvi; DODD, chap. viii; RHODES, Vol. I, pp. 86-98; GREELEY, Vol. I, chap. xiv; VON HOLST, chap. ix; GARRISON, *Westward Extension*, chaps. xiii-xv; *Texas*, chaps. xxi-xxii; JAMES SCHOULER, *History of the United States*, Vol. V, chap. xviii; *President Polk's Administration* (*Atlantic Monthly*, Vol. LXXVI, pp. 371-380); *Polk's Diary*, ed. M. M. QUAIF; U. S. GRANT, *Personal Memoirs*, Vol. I, chaps. iii-xiii; CHARLES H. OWEN, *The Justice of the Mexican War*; E. G. BOURNE, *The United States and Mexico, 1847-1848* (*American Historical Review*, Vol. V, pp. 491-502); J. S. REEVES, *The Treaty of Guadalupe-Hidalgo* (*American Historical Review*, Vol. X, pp. 309-324).

TOPICS FOR SPECIAL REPORTS

1. The Legend of Marcus Whitman: BOURNE, *The Legend of Marcus Whitman* (*American Historical Review*, Vol. VI, pp. 276-300); WILLIAM BARROWS, *Oregon*, pp. 160-254; SCHOULER, Vol. IV, pp. 504-514.

2. American Pioneers in Texas: H. ADDINGTON BRUCE, *The Romance of American Expansion*, pp. 78-105; GARRISON, *Texas*, pp. 137-169; HART, Vol. III, No. 185; MCMASTER, Vol. VI, pp. 251-266; HENRY BRUCE, *Samuel Houston*, pp. 64-156; SARAH B. ELLIOTT, *Samuel Houston*, pp. 31-72.

3. The Conquest of California: SPARKS, pp. 324-335; JOSIAH ROYCE, *California*, pp. 48-150; GARRISON, *Westward Extension*, pp. 230-243; JOHN BIDWELL, *Frémont and the Conquest of California* (*The Century*, Vol. XIX, pp. 518-525).

4. The Webster-Ashburton Treaty: MACDONALD, No. 70 (for text); G. T. CURTIS, *Life of Daniel Webster*, Vol. II, pp. 94-107, 130-172; H. C. LODGE, *Daniel Webster*, pp. 241-263; TYLER, Vol. II, pp. 216-243; T. H. BENTON, *Thirty Years' View*, Vol. II, pp. 420-452; SCHOULER, Vol. IV, pp. 403-406; JARED SPARKS, *The Webster-Ashburton Treaty* (*The North American Review*, Vol. LVI, pp. 452 ff.); FOSTER, pp. 281-286.

5. Henry Clay's Letters of 1844 on the Admission of Texas: HART, Vol. III, No. 187; CARL SCHURZ, *Henry Clay*, Vol. II, pp. 242-268; GARRISON, *Westward Extension*, pp. 135-140; EDWARD STANWOOD, *History of the Presidency*, pp. 209-225.

CHAPTER XIII

THE COMPROMISE OF 1850

The New Territory

396. The New Far West. An area larger than the original territory ceded to the United States by Great Britain at the close of the War of Independence in 1783, and larger than the vast Louisiana region purchased from Napoleon in 1803, was added to the United States between 1845 and 1848 by the annexation of Texas, the Oregon treaty, and the Mexican cession of California and New Mexico.[1] The land varied in value. Between the rich cotton areas of Texas and the smiling valleys of California were the arid plateaus and majestic cañons of the Rockies. In Oregon fine timber and farm lands were awaiting the settler. The sudden acquisition of the Pacific coast, in an unbroken line of more than a thousand miles from Puget Sound to San Diego, opened our view upon the great western ocean and made us neighbors of China and Japan. The new region, although sparsely populated by white men, was still not entirely unknown. Ever since the days of the Lewis and Clark expedition there had been adventurous explorers beating into wagon roads the Indian trails to Oregon, California, and Santa Fé, and reporting to the government at Washington what rivers and mountains, what rocks and soils and plants and peoples they found on their journeys. The most noted of these Western explorers was John C. Frémont, "the Pathfinder,"[2] who made four wonderful expeditions to Oregon and California in the years 1842–1848 (see map). He was in California in 1846, and his little "army" coöperated with Sloat and Stockton in occupying the country.

[1] Area of U. S. before 1845

	Sq. miles
Original area, 1783 . . .	(about) 830,000
Louisiana Purchase, 1803 . .	" 875,000
Florida Purchase, 1819 . .	" 65,000
	1,770,000

Additions, 1845–1848

	Sq. miles
Texas, 1845	(about) 390,000
Oregon, 1846	" 290,000
Mexican Cession, 1848 . .	" 520,000
	1,200,000

[2] The account of Frémont's journey over the Sierra Nevada mountains to the valley of San Joaquin, in 1844, reads like the romantic adventures of an explorer of the sixteenth

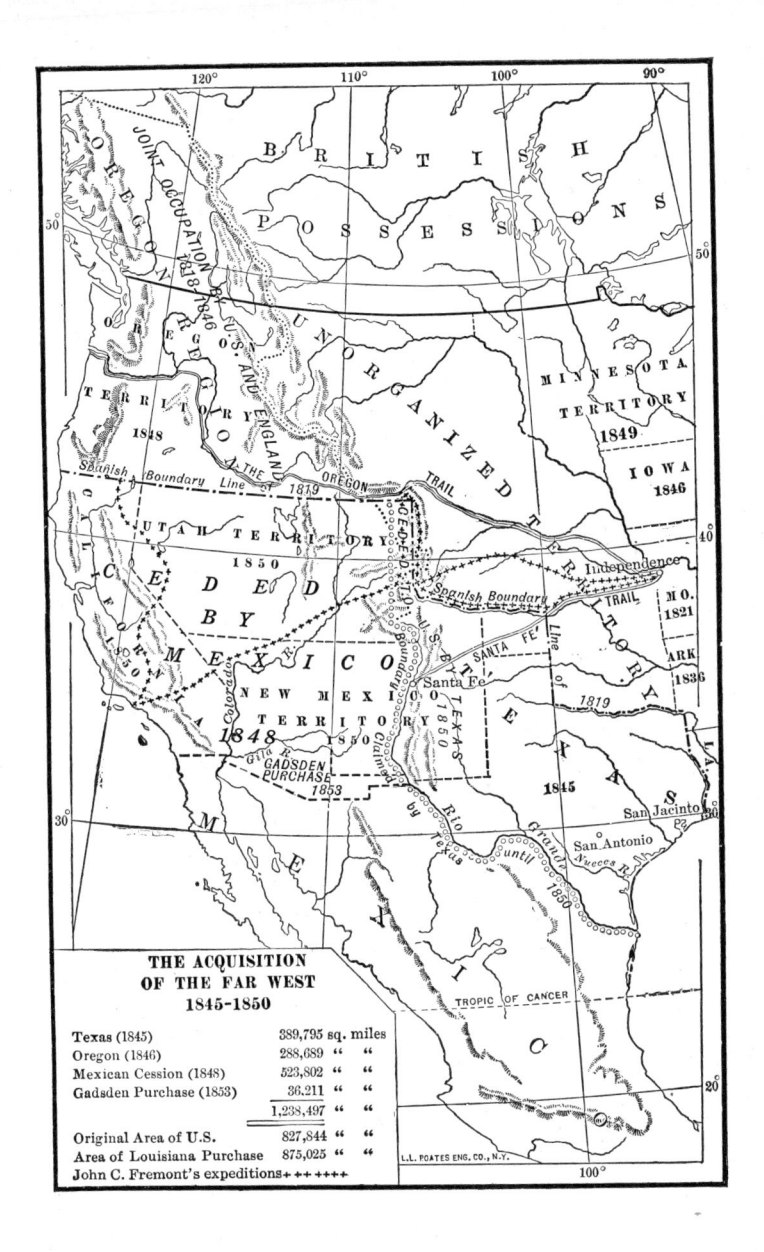

**THE ACQUISITION
OF THE FAR WEST
1845-1850**

Texas (1845)	389,795 sq. miles
Oregon (1846)	288,689 " "
Mexican Cession (1848)	523,802 " "
Gadsden Purchase (1853)	36,211 " "
	1,238,497 " "
Original Area of U.S.	827,844 " "
Area of Louisiana Purchase	875,025 " "
John C. Fremont's expeditions	+·+·++++

397. The Wilmot Proviso. Even before the Mexican War was over, it was evident that the United States would demand the cession of California and New Mexico in its terms of peace. It was evident also that the great question in the acquisition and organization of the new territory would be the status of slavery in it. On the very day the bill asking for an appropriation to meet the expenses of the peace negotiations was introduced into the House, David Wilmot of Pennsylvania offered an amendment providing that "neither slavery nor involuntary servitude ... should ever exist *in any part*" of any territory acquired from the republic of Mexico. The Wilmot Proviso was carried in the House, but defeated in the Senate, where, since the admission of Florida and Texas in 1845, the slave states were in the majority. However, the Wilmot Proviso was not dropped. It was passed again and again by the House and was before the country as the official demand of the antislavery men in the organization of the new territory.

398. The Organization of Oregon. The Oregon region was naturally the first to be organized, being acquired nearly two years before the Mexican lands. As there was no chance for the cultivation of cotton, sugar, or rice in this region, the controversy over slavery need not have entered into the Oregon bill at all. But the radical leaders of the South were not willing to let Wilmot's challenge go unanswered. So Jefferson Davis of Mississippi, a disciple of Calhoun and destined in a few years to become his successor as the champion of the interests of the slave states, introduced an amendment into the Oregon bill to the effect that "nothing should authorize the prohibition of slavery in Oregon so long as it was a territory of the United States." Davis's amendment, like Wilmot's, was defeated, and Oregon was organized as a territory without slavery in August, 1848. But the significant thing in the debates of 1846-1848 was that both the antislavery and the proslavery leaders were dissatisfied with the Missouri Compromise made a quarter of a century earlier. The former now demanded the exclusion of slavery from territory below the 36° 30' line (New Mexico), the latter its admission into territory above the 36° 30' line (Oregon).

century. For eleven months his difficult path lay alternately over the icy crests of the mountains and through valleys parched with tropical heat. Orders had been sent from Washington to hold him at St. Louis, for fear his proposed expedition would give offense to Mexico. But his wife (Senator Benton's daughter) held the message until he was fairly started on his way.

399. The Question of Slavery in the Mexican Cession. When therefore Polk, in his special message of July, 1848, urged Congress to proceed to the immediate organization of California and New Mexico, which had been under military régime since their conquest in 1846, there were several possible ways of dealing with the question of slavery in the territories under discussion. The Wilmot Proviso might be adopted, excluding slavery from the whole region; the Calhoun-Davis theory[1] might be accepted, opening the whole region to slavery; the principle of the Missouri Compromise might be applied, dividing California and New Mexico into free and slave sections by a parallel of latitude running to the Pacific coast; or the question of freedom or slavery might be left to the settlers of the territory themselves.

400. The Doctrine of "Squatter Sovereignty." This last solution was proposed by Lewis Cass of Michigan and is known as the doctrine of "popular sovereignty," or, more familiarly, "squatter sovereignty." The new territories should be open to settlers, or "squatters," from free states and slave states on equal terms. Those territories which were suitable for slave labor would naturally attract slaveholders and would eventually apply for admission to the Union as slave states; while the others would naturally be filled up with a free population and come in with state constitutions prohibiting slavery.

401. The Campaign of 1848. Both of the great political parties tried to keep in favor with both sections of the country in the presidential campaign of 1848. The Democrats nominated Cass, a Northern man opposed to the Wilmot Proviso. The Whigs nominated General Zachary Taylor, the hero of Buena Vista, a Southerner who repudiated the extreme proslavery doctrine of Calhoun and Davis. Taylor was a Louisiana sugar planter and the owner of several hundred slaves. But he had not manifested any interest in the extension of slavery. He had had no experience in political affairs and for years had not even voted. The Whigs nominated him for his brilliant record in the Mexican War, hoping that he would repeat

---

[1] That theory was, briefly, as follows: slaves were private property; private property was subject to state laws, not national law; the territories were the common property of the states, held in trust by the nation; hence Congress could not pass any law excluding from the territories property whose possession was legal in the states. This theory made the Missouri Compromise unconstitutional.

the sweeping victory of General Harrison in 1840. "Old Rough and Ready" was the campaign cry, recalling the "Tippecanoe and Tyler too" of eight years before.

402. The New Free-Soil Party. In striking contrast to the evasive attitude of both Whigs and Democrats on the slavery question was the platform of a new party, the Free-Soilers, who declared that it was "the settled policy of the nation not to extend, nationalize, or encourage slavery, but to limit, localize, and discourage it." They nominated Van Buren, who had been passed over by the Democrats in 1844 to make room for a candidate in favor of annexing Texas, and inscribed on their banner, "Free soil, free speech, free labor, free men." The new party differed from the Garrison abolitionists in that it prized the Union and accepted the Constitution with all its compromises on slavery. It even differed in a most important respect from the Liberty party, which it largely absorbed. For the Liberty party of 1844 wished to abolish slavery in the Southern states, where it was protected by the Constitution, whereas the Free-Soilers demanded only its exclusion from the territories of the United States. The Liberty men denounced the *existence of slavery* in any part of the Union; the Free-Soilers opposed the *extension of slavery* to the trans-Mississippi territories of the Union. This distinction is of great importance, because it was the Free-Soil doctrine and not the abolitionist doctrine that was made the basis a few years later of the new Republican party, which finally overthrew slavery.

403. The Election of Taylor. The Free-Soilers did not carry any states, but they elected enough congressmen to hold the balance between Whigs and Democrats in the sessions of 1849–1851, and took enough votes from Cass in New York to give that state, and consequently the election, to Taylor, by an electoral vote of 163 to 127.

404. Gold discovered in California. President Polk's term expired March 4, 1849, without any step having been taken by Congress toward the organization of New Mexico and California, acquired over a year before. The proslavery men demanded that their institution should be admitted into the new territory and be legalized there by a definite statute. Their opponents declared that "no power in the world would make them vote to establish slavery where it did not exist." But while Congress was thus deadlocked, events occurred on the Pacific coast which gave a new aspect to the question. Just as the final negotiations for peace with Mexico were begun (January, 1848), gold was discovered in the Sacramento valley in California. As the news of the richness of the deposits spread, a wild rush into the gold fields began. Merchants, farmers, physicians, lawyers, artisans, shopkeepers, and servants abandoned their business to stake out claims in the gold valleys, from which thousands took their fortunes in a few weeks.[1] The fever extended even to the Atlantic coast. Men started on the nine months' sail around Cape Horn or, crossing the pestilence-laden Isthmus of Panama, fought like wild animals for a passage on the infrequent ships sailing up to the Californian coast. Others went "overland," making their way slowly across the Western deserts and mountains in their unwieldy "prairie schooners," the monotonous dread of famine and thirst varied only by the excitement of Indian attacks. The immigration by sea and land in the single year 1849 raised the population of California from 6000 to over 85,000 souls.

GOLD DISCOVERED AT SUTTER'S MILL, CALIFORNIA

405. California draws up a "Free" Constitution. The "Forty-niners," as these gold seekers were called, came almost wholly from the free states of the North. Migration across hundreds of miles of desert country did not tempt the plantation owner with his slaves. Consequently, when delegates from the new Californian immigrants met at Monterey, in September, 1849, to devise a government, they drew up a constitution excluding slavery by a unanimous vote. When Congress met in December, 1849, therefore, California was no longer waiting to be organized as a territory, but was ready for admission to the Union as a state with a free constitution.

[1] The product of the California mines and washings was fabulous. The country was hailed as a modern El Dorado. Five years after the discovery, the gold yield was $65,000,000 in a single year. In fifty years over $2,000,000,000 was taken from the mines.

406. Congress faces a Crisis. With the example of California before them, the people of New Mexico were already taking steps to form a government for themselves. It was evident, therefore, that the Congress of 1849-1851 would be forced to deal with the organization of the new territory. In spite of Taylor's first message of December, 1849, advising Congress to "abstain from the introduction of those exciting topics of a sectional character which have hitherto produced painful apprehensions in the public mind,"—in plain words, not to quarrel about slavery,—Congress and the country at large believed that the acquisition of the new Western lands had brought the crisis which must now be faced.

The Omnibus Bill

407. The Thirty-first Congress. Probably no other gathering of public men in our history, except the convention which met at Philadelphia in 1787 to frame the Constitution of the United States, contained so many political geniuses of the first rank as the Senate which assembled in December, 1849. There met, for the last time, the great triumvirate of American statesmen, Clay, Webster, and Calhoun,—all three born during the Revolutionary War, and all so identified with every public question for a generation that to write the biography of any one of them would be to write the history of our country during that period. With them came a number of brilliant men whose names appear often on these pages,—Benton, Cass, Bell, Douglas, Davis, Seward, Chase, and Hale, the last three being the first pronounced antislavery delegation in the Senate. In the House, Democrats and Whigs were so evenly matched (112 to 105) that the 13 Free-Soilers held the balance of power. The temper of Congress was shown at the very beginning of the session, when in a fierce struggle for the speakership, a fiery proslavery member from Georgia, Robert Toombs, declared amid hisses and applause that if the North sought to drive the slaveholder from New Mexico and California—land "purchased by the common blood and treasure of the nation"—and thereby "to fix a national degradation on half the states of the Confederacy," he was *ready for disunion.*

408. Henry Clay introduces the Omnibus Bill. In this critical situation the aged Henry Clay, whose voice had been raised for moderation and conciliation ever since the days of the Missouri

Compromise thirty years before, again came forward with measures calculated to reconcile the opposing sections (January 29, 1850). Clay proposed that (1) California should be admitted as a free state; (2) the rest of the Mexican cession should be divided by the thirty-seventh parallel of latitude into the territories of Utah on the north and New Mexico on the south, both organized on the "squatter-sovereignty" principle[1]; (3) the boundaries of the slaveholding state of Texas should be cut down from 379,000 to 264,000 square miles, but in return Texas should receive $10,000,000 from the government to pay her war debt contracted before 1845; (4) the slave trade (but not slavery) should be prohibited in the District of Columbia; (5) a new fugitive-slave law should be enacted, making the recovery of runaway negroes much easier than under the old law of 1793. This proposal of Clay's was called the Omnibus Bill, on account of the number of provisions which it included.[2]

409. Conflicting Demands of North and South. We can see what a difficult task Clay had undertaken when we compare the demands of the radical leaders, North and South, on these questions. On the

Question of	The South demanded	The North demanded
(1) California	organization as a territory, admitting slavery	immediate admission as a free state
(2) New Mexico	legalization of slavery by Congress (at least below 36° 30′)	the application of the Wilmot Proviso
(3) Texas	the same boundaries as the Texan republic claimed in 1836	a reduction in the size of Texas without any money compensation
(4) District of Columbia	no interference with slavery by Congress	abolition of slavery
(5) Fugitive slaves	a strict law enforced by national authority, with no jury trial for negroes	jury trial for every negro claimed as a fugitive slave

410. Debates on Clay's Compromise Bill. The debates on the compromise measures called forth some of the finest speeches ever

---

[1] This division of New Mexico was in reality the extension of the Missouri Compromise to the new territory. It was expected that slavery would enter New Mexico, but not the northern territory of Utah.

[2] Strictly speaking, only the clauses referring to California, New Mexico, and Texas were called the Omnibus Bill. But the other two propositions (4 and 5) were so intimately connected with them, both in time and purpose, that the whole legislation may be considered together.

THE COMPROMISE OF 1850

made in the Senate. Clay's fervid plea for harmony, in introducing his bills, was enhanced by the fact that the venerable statesman, now in his seventy-third year, had left the quiet of his well-earned retirement to make this supreme effort for the preservation of the Union, whose welfare and glory had been his chief pride since his boyhood's recollection of the inauguration of his great Virginia neighbor, George Washington.

411. Calhoun's Speech. Calhoun was to speak on the fourth of March, 1850. But he was too enfeebled by the ravages of consumption to deliver his carefully prepared speech. He was borne to his place in the Senate chamber, where he sat, alive only in the great deep eyes which still flashed beneath his heavy brows, while his colleague, Senator Mason, read his speech. It was a message of despair. The encroachments of the North on the constitutional rights of the slaveholders had already proceeded so far, he said, that the great Kentuckian's plan of compromise was futile. The North was the aggressor. *Her* institutions were not attacked, *her* property was not threatened, *her* rights were not invaded. She must cease all agitation against slavery, return the fugitive slaves willingly, and restore to the South her equal rights in all parts of the Union and all acquired territory. Otherwise, the cords which had bound the states together for two generations would every one be broken, and our Republic would be dissolved into warring sections. It was Calhoun's last word. Before the month closed, he had passed beyond all earthly strife.

412. Webster's Seventh-of-March Speech. Daniel Webster spoke on the seventh of March. Webster had put himself squarely on record against the extension of slavery into new territory. Besides his New York speech of 1837, already quoted (p. 271), he had said in the Oregon debates that his objections to slavery were "irrespective of lines and latitudes, taking in the whole country and the whole question." The antislavery men of the North, therefore, to many of whom Webster was almost an idol, were bitterly disappointed when he spoke in favor of Clay's compromise measures. His love of the Union, and his desire to see peace reëstablished between the two sections, proved stronger than his hatred of slavery. He maintained that there was no danger that New Mexico would become slave territory, because the physical geography of the region forever excluded the cotton planter from its deserts and high plateaus.

"I would not take pains," he said, "uselessly to reaffirm an ordinance of nature nor to reënact the will of God. I would put in no Wilmot Proviso for the mere purpose of a taunt or a reproach." He spoke in behalf of the fugitive-slave law, because such a law had always been on the statute books of the country. He denounced the abolitionists as men who had no right to set up their conscience in opposition to the law. In a fine peroration he implored his countrymen of the South to dismiss the awful thought of secession and cherish the Union forever. The Free-Soilers said that the great man's ambition to be the next president tempted him to forsake his principles in the seventh-of-March speech. But his sincere, though mistaken, belief that the Union could be saved by compromise is sufficient to account for his support of Clay's measures, without attributing base motives to him.

413. Seward pleads for the Higher Law. Webster was answered a few days later by William H. Seward, the new Whig senator from New York. Seward thought the compromise vicious because it surrendered principles. The law might stand on the statute books, but the conscience of the people would condemn it and repudiate it. The Constitution might tolerate slavery, but there was "a higher law than the Constitution," namely, the moral law. Seward's appeal to the "higher law" was in line with the abolitionists' doctrine that the evil of slavery far outweighed all political, legal, or economic considerations.

414. Chase's Speech. Salmon P. Chase of Ohio, a Democrat converted to the Free-Soil doctrine, denounced the compromise as a weak surrender to the slaveholders' interests. In answer to Calhoun he declared that not the North but the South had been the aggressor ever since the days when threats and intimidation had forced upon the framers of the Constitution concessions to slavery.

415. The Passage of the Omnibus Bill. The great debate on the compromise seemed no nearer its end in July than it had been in January. Senator Seward's influence over the President was so strong that any bill favoring the extension of slavery was likely to be vetoed. But when President Taylor died suddenly, July 9, 1850, the whole aspect of the question was changed. Vice President Fillmore, who succeeded him, was in favor of the compromise, and with the help of the administration the bills were passed through the

Senate and the House by fair majorities, and signed by the President in August and September. The chief gain for the North in the compromise measures of 1850 was the admission of California as a free state.[1] The prohibition of the slave trade in the tiny District of Columbia had no practical effect on the domestic slave trade, which was amply supplied by Maryland, Virginia, and Kentucky. The South, on the other hand, secured the opening of the whole of the Mexican cession east of California to slavery. The reduction of

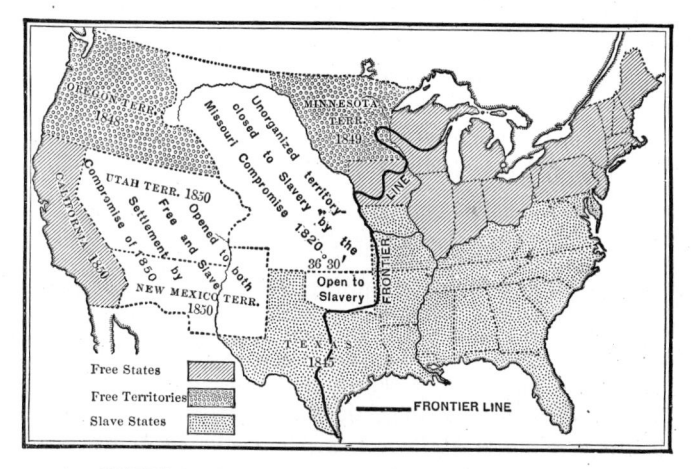

STATUS OF SLAVERY BY THE COMPROMISE OF 1850

the boundaries of Texas was no disadvantage to the slave cause, since slavery was not forbidden in the territory transferred from Texas to New Mexico, while the payment of $10,000,000 to Texas set that state on the path to prosperity, which made it a powerful aid to the Confederate cause in the great struggle of the Civil War ten years later.

416. The New Fugitive-Slave Law. Finally, the new fugitive-slave law brought the whole machinery of the United States into play, if necessary, to recover a runaway negro. The fugitive was not allowed a trial, either in the state where he was seized or in the

---

[1] Since there were fifteen free and fifteen slave states at the beginning of 1850, the admission of California gave the Senate a majority for the North. After 1850 no new slave states were admitted.

state from which he had fled. The magistrate's fee was twice as large when he handed the negro over to the claimant as when he declared the negro free. The alleged fugitive was not allowed to testify in his own behalf. The United States marshals were heavily fined if they let the reclaimed fugitive escape. At the call of the marshals all good citizens of any state must aid in the seizure of the runaway negro, and persons willfully preventing his arrest or helping his escape were subject to a fine of $1000, or six months' imprisonment, in addition to damages to the owner, up to $1000, for the value of the slave. The new fugitive-slave law, therefore, sought to guarantee the protection of slave property in every part of the United States by making every man and woman of a free state a partner in the business of restoring to his master the fugitive who had followed the Northern Star to the "land of freedom."

A Four Years' Truce

417. The Finality of the Compromise of 1850. The Compromise Measures of 1850 were regarded by the vast majority of the people of the United States as a final settlement of the sectional disputes over slavery. The status of slavery was now fixed in every square mile of our domain from the Atlantic to the Pacific. Henry Clay was hailed as "the great Pacificator," and the foremost statesmen of both parties devoted their best talents to proving that the Compromise of 1850 was the just and sole basis on which the Union could be preserved. The agitation over slavery in the new Western territory had caused much talk of disunion in the South. A convention was assembled at Nashville, Tennessee, in the early summer of 1850, to decide on what terms the cotton states would still remain in the Union. But the passage of the Compromise Measures quieted the disunion movement. The Unionists were triumphant in the elections of 1851 in every Southern state but South Carolina.

418. The "Underground Railroad." In the Northern states it was harder to make the people accept the Compromise of 1850. In spite of the efforts of such persuasive advocates as Webster and Choate in the East, and Douglas and Cass in the West, the pulpit, press, and platform would not cease in their condemnation of the new fugitive-slave law. A public meeting in Indiana declared its "absolute refusal to obey the inhuman and diabolical provisions" of the law, and the declaration was indorsed by hundreds of mass meetings from Boston to Chicago. For several years there had been in operation in New York, Pennsylvania, and all along the northern bank of the Ohio River a system called the "underground railroad," whose object was to give food, shelter, and pecuniary aid to the negro escaping across the line into the free states. Prominent citizens were engaged in this work, offering their barns and sheds, and even their houses, as "stations" on the "underground." The fugitive was

CHIEF ROUTES OF THE UNDERGROUND RAILROAD

passed on from station to station with remarkable secrecy and dispatch until he reached the shores of Lake Erie and took ship for Canada. The people of the free states felt fairly secure in breaking the old fugitive-slave law of 1793, because that law depended on the state authorities for its execution, and in a notable case (Prigg *vs.* Pennsylvania), in 1842, the Supreme Court of the United States had decided that the Constitution did not compel the officers of a state to assist in restoring fugitive slaves. The new law of 1850, however, if strictly enforced, would have closed every station on the "underground" and made the soil of Ohio as dangerous for the escaping negro as the canebrakes of Louisiana or the swamps of Virginia.

419. The Democratic Victory of 1852. In the presidential campaign of 1852 the Democrats nominated General Franklin Pierce of New Hampshire, a man of winning personality, with a creditable but not brilliant record as a legislator and soldier. The Whigs, with both their great leaders gone,[1] made a desperate attempt to win the presidency with their third military candidate, General Winfield Scott, "the hero of Lundy's Lane and Chapultepec." Pierce won a sweeping victory, carrying all the states of the Union but four. He announced in his inaugural address that a "sense of repose and security had been restored throughout the country," and expressed the "fervent hope that no sectional or fanatical excitement might again threaten the durability of our institutions or obscure the light of our prosperity."

420. The Prosperity of the Country. When Pierce mentioned "the light of our prosperity," he struck the real note of the truce of 1850-1854. It was a business man's peace. The commercial and industrial classes were tired of the agitation over slavery. They were glad to have Congress stop discussing the Missouri Compromise and the Wilmot Proviso, and attend to the business interests of the country. An era of great prosperity was opening. The discovery of immense deposits of gold and silver in California; the extension of the wheat fields into Wisconsin, Iowa, and Minnesota; the great increase in the products of the Northern mills and factories; and the growing fleet of our merchant marine, were all signs of rapidly increasing wealth. The railroad mileage of the country up to the year 1848 was less than 6000, but during the next ten years over 16,500 miles of new track were laid. Between 1850 and 1855 the important railroads of the Atlantic coast (the New York Central, the Erie, the Pennsylvania, the Baltimore and Ohio) were all connected with the Great Lakes or the Ohio River.[2] Thus the immense northern basin of the Mississippi, which, as part of the Louisiana Purchase, had been connected with the Gulf of Mexico, through the highway of the great river, now began to be joined with the Eastern states and to send its growing trade through the Great Lakes and over the Atlantic-seaboard railroads.

---

[1] Clay died in June, 1852, carrying to his grave the Whig party which he had called into existence twenty years before, when he forced through Congress the bill for the recharter of the Bank (1832) and rallied to his standard the forces of opposition to Andrew Jackson. Webster followed Clay to the grave in October, 1852.

[2] An interesting result of this new connection was shown in the immense growth of the Lake cities, Chicago, Buffalo, Detroit, Cleveland, and Milwaukee, in the decade 1850-1860.

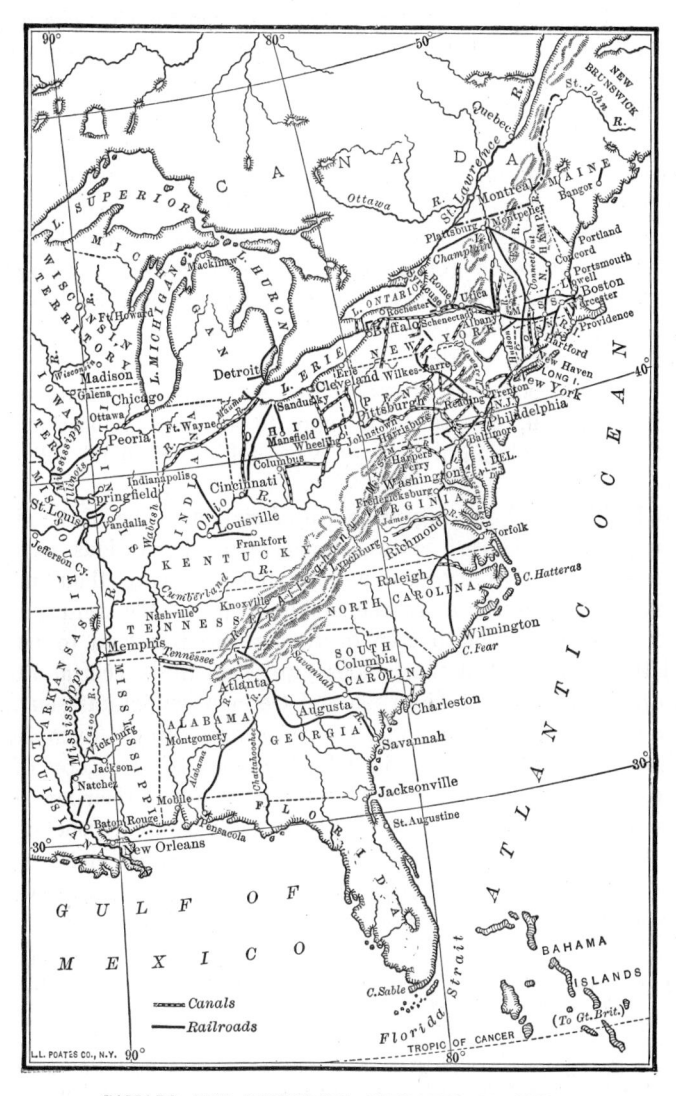

CANALS AND RAILROADS OPERATED IN 1850

421. The Reign of "King Cotton" in the South. The wealth of the South seemed even more firm in its foundations and more rapid in its increase. An apparently limitless demand for cotton by the mills of America and Europe encouraged the cultivation of that staple to the neglect of every other form of industry. By 1850 the value of the cotton crop was over $100,000,000 annually, while the rice and sugar crops combined yielded less than $16,000,000. In the same year, of the total of $235,000,000 of exports from the United States, $112,000,000 (or 48 per cent) was in cotton, as against $21,000,000 (or 9 per cent) in grain and provisions. Such a trade naturally led the Southerners to believe that slavery was the basis of the prosperity of the country. "Cotton is king!" they said. "In the 3,000,000 bags of cotton that slave labor annually throws upon the world, we are doing more to advance civilization than all the canting philanthropists of New and Old England will do in a century."[1]

422. Increased Immigration to America. The demand for laborers in the United States, supplemented by various forms of distress in Europe, caused the migration of many thousands of foreigners to our shores in the middle years of the century. The utter ruin of the potato crop in 1845 reduced Ireland to famine, and the revolutions of the famous year 1848 threw central Europe into political turmoil. The Irish and German immigrants sought in America a land of plenty and a refuge for democracy.[2] Even distant China, disturbed by war and rebellion, sent some 25,000 of her poverty-stricken laborers to our Pacific coast, where their low standards of living and their strange oriental habits caused economic and social friction. The Germans tended to move westward and helped to

---

[1] The Southern writers were guilty of two serious errors in their economics: first, in mistaking the great wealth of a few planters for general prosperity; secondly, in thinking that free negro labor was impossible. There were about 75,000 large planters in the South in 1850, out of a population of 5,000,000 whites. Their prosperity was that of "a dominant minority," and was not diffused through all classes as in the North. Again, while the value of the cotton crop in 1850 with slave labor was $105,000,000, in 1880 under free negro labor it was $275,000,000, and in 1910 over $700,000,000. Slave labor produced 2,200,000 bales of cotton in 1850; free labor produced 10,650,000 bales in 1910.

[2] American sympathy for the Hungarians, who were fighting for independence from oppressive Austria, was freely expressed. When Austria protested, Daniel Webster, our Secretary of State, in 1850, wrote a defiant letter to the Austrian chargé at Washington, declaring "the right of the American people to sympathize with the efforts of any nation to acquire liberty." Louis Kossuth, the great Hungarian patriot, visited America as the nation's guest in 1851-1852, but failed to get substantial help for his cause.

develop the agricultural regions of our country, while the Irish for the most part were content to remain in the cities of the Atlantic coast. From 84,066 in 1840, the immigrants increased to 427,833 in 1854.

423. The Clayton-Bulwer Treaty. It seemed as though no decade of our history could pass without some new cause for ill feeling toward Great Britain. To the perpetual quarrel over the rights of our fishermen off the Newfoundland coast, and the disputes over our northern boundaries, there was added in the middle of the nineteenth century an important controversy in Central America. We had looked forward for years to building a canal cutting the isthmus which connects the two great continents of the Western Hemisphere, and had even made a treaty in 1846 with the Spanish-American republic of New Granada (now Colombia), in which we agreed to keep open to all nations, on the same terms, any canal or railroad built across the Isthmus of Panama. The discovery of gold in California shortly afterwards (1848) set American capitalists, headed by Cornelius Vanderbilt, actively to planning transportation routes across the Isthmus. Here they came into collision with the British, who had a colony in Central America, and were attempting to extend their "protectorate" over miles of the coast. After long negotiations Clayton, our Secretary of State under President Taylor, came to an agreement with the British minister, Sir Henry Lytton Bulwer, in 1850. The Clayton-Bulwer Treaty, which remained in force until the end of the nineteenth century, provided that the United States and Great Britain should jointly guarantee the neutrality of any canal built across the Isthmus. Each government pledged itself not to seek exclusive control over the canal, never to erect any fortifications upon it, or to acquire any colonies in Central America. Each promised that it would extend its protection to any company that should undertake the work of building a canal, and would use its influence with the governments of Central America to give their aid to such a project.

424. Our Interest in Cuba. The most critical incident in our mid-century diplomacy, however, concerned Cuba. That rich island possession of Spain, lying just off our coast, had always been regarded with especial interest by our statesmen. Expansionists had wanted it for the United States: others had been afraid that it might pass into the hands of a strong power like England or France. When President Polk offered Spain $120,000,000 for the island (eight times the price paid for the great Louisiana territory) the ministers at Madrid replied that they "had rather see Cuba sunk in the ocean than transferred to any power." Still, Spanish government was oppressive in Cuba, and the island was in a chronic state of revolt. In 1851 about fifty American citizens, some of them young men belonging to the best families of New Orleans, joined a noted adventurer, named Lopez, in a desperate attempt to seize Cuba. When the men were captured on the Cuban coast and promptly shot, a mob at New Orleans sacked the Spanish consulate, tore down the ensign of Castile, and defaced the portrait of Queen Isabella. Daniel Webster apologized for this insult to Spain, but a little later Webster's successor in the State Department, William L. Marcy, was asking the ministry at Madrid to apologize to the United States for the unjust seizure and condemnation of the American steamer *Black Warrior* by the authorities at Havana. Relations between the United States and Spain were severely strained.

425. The Ostend Manifesto. During Pierce's administration (1853–1857) the influence of the South was strong at Washington; and the South wanted Cuba for the extension of its slave area. Pierce sent as minister to Spain Pierre Soulé of Louisiana, the most ardent annexationist in the country. Soulé met Mason, our minister to France, and Buchanan, our minister to England, at the Belgian town of Ostend in the summer of 1854, and there the three ministers issued the famous Ostend Manifesto, which declared that the possession of Cuba was necessary to the peace of the United States. If, "actuated by stubborn pride and a false sense of honor," Spain should refuse to sell Cuba, then we were "justified by every law, human and divine," in wresting the island from her by force. There was, as a matter of fact, no law, human or divine, that could justify the language of the Ostend Manifesto or the deed of pure robbery which it proposed. The cautious Marcy disowned the Manifesto and a few months later accepted Spain's tardy apology for the *Black Warrior* affair. It was reserved for a far greater disaster to another American vessel forty-four years later — the destruction of the *Maine* in Havana harbor — to precipitate the war which cost Spain "the Pearl of the Antilles."

THE COMPROMISE OF 1850

REFERENCES

The New Territory: G. P. GARRISON, *Westward Extension* (American Nation Series), chaps. xvi, xvii, xix; EDWARD STANWOOD, *History of the Presidency*, chap. xviii; NICOLAY and HAY, *Abraham Lincoln, a History*, Vol. I, chaps. xv–xviii; T. C. SMITH, *The Liberty and Free-Soil Parties in the Northwest* (Harvard Historical Studies, Vol. VI); J. R. LOWELL, *The Biglow Papers* (First Series); STEWART EDWARD WHITE, *The Forty-Niners* (Chronicles, Vol. XXV); E. L. BOGART, *Industrial History of the United States*, chaps. xviii–xx; J. B. MCMASTER, *History of the People of the United States*, Vol. VII, chap. lxxxiii; JESSE MACY, *The Anti-Slavery Crusade* (Chronicles, Vol. XXVIII), chaps. vi–viii; A. B. HART, *American History told by Contemporaries*, Vol. IV, Nos. 15–18; *Salmon P. Chase*, chap. v.

The Omnibus Bill: HART, Vol. IV, Nos. 19–22; GARRISON, chap. xx; WILLIAM MACDONALD, *Select Documents of United States History, 1776–1861*, Nos. 78–83; G. T. CURTIS, *Life of Daniel Webster*, Vol. II, chaps. xxxvi, xxxvii; CARL SCHURZ, *Henry Clay*, Vol. II, chap. xxvi; JEFFERSON DAVIS, *Rise and Fall of the Confederate Government*, Vol. I, chaps. ii, iii; J. F. RHODES, *History of the United States from the Compromise of 1850*, Vol. I, pp. 119–198; J. W. BURGESS, *The Middle Period*, chaps. xvii, xviii.

A Four Years' Truce: SMITH, *Parties and Slavery* (Am. Nation), chaps. i–vi; W. E. DODD, *Expansion and Conflict* (Riverside History, Vol. III), chap. x; STANWOOD, chap. xix; RHODES, Vol. I, chap. iii; MACDONALD, No. 77; Old South Leaflets, No. 111; A. T. HADLEY, *Railroad Transportation, its History and its Laws*, chaps. i, ii; D. R. DEWEY, *Financial History of the United States*, chaps. x, xi; GARRISON, chap. xviii; I. D. TRAVIS, *The History of the Clayton-Bulwer Treaty* (Michigan Political Science Publications, Vol. II, No. 8); J. H. LATANÉ, *The Diplomacy of the United States in Regard to Cuba* (*American Historical Association Report*, 1897, pp. 217–277); JAMES SCHOULER, *History of the United States*, Vol. V, chaps. xx, xxi.

TOPICS FOR SPECIAL REPORTS

1. **John C. Frémont's Explorations:** Old South Leaflets, No. 45; R. G. THWAITES, *Rocky Mountain Exploration*, pp. 228–243; J. C. FRÉMONT, *Report of Exploring Expedition to the Rocky Mountains in the Year 1842, and to Oregon and North Carolina in the Years 1843–1844*; JESSIE B. FRÉMONT, *Souvenirs of my Time*, pp. 189–209; *Century Magazine*, Vol. XIX, pp. 759–780 (with interesting illustrations).

2. **Daniel Webster and the Slavery Question:** MCMASTER, *Life of Webster*, pp. 241–254, 303–324; RHODES, Vol. I, pp. 137–161; ALEXANDER JOHNSTON, *American Orations*, Vol. II, pp. 161–201; H. C. LODGE, *Daniel Webster*, pp. 301–332; HART, Vol. IV, Nos. 20, 21; J. G. WHITTIER, *Ichabod*; W. C. WILKINSON, *Daniel Webster and the Compromise of 1850* (*Scribner's*, Vol. XII, pp. 411–425).

3. **The Underground Railway:** HART, Vol. III, Nos. 172, 183; Vol. IV, Nos. 29–32; W. H. SIEBERT, *The Underground Railway*, pp. 18–76; B. T.

Washington, *The Story of the Negro*, Vol. I, pp. 215-250; McMaster, Vol. VII, pp. 240-257; Hart, *Salmon P. Chase*, pp. 28-53; Alexander Johnston (ed. J. A. Woodburn), *American Political History, 1763-1876*, Vol. II, pp. 127-140.

4. **Gold and Politics in California, 1849-1850:** Josiah Royce, *California*, pp. 220-246, 278-356; E. E. Sparks, *The Expansion of the American People*, pp. 336-350; Rhodes, Vol. I, pp. 111-116; Schouler, Vol. V, pp. 130-146; J. S. Hittell, *The Discovery of Gold in California* (*Century Magazine*, Vol. XIX, pp. 525-536); McMaster, Vol. VII, pp. 585-614; Bayard Taylor, *El Dorado*.

5. **Mid-Century Plans for a Canal across the Isthmus:** McMaster, Vol. VII, pp. 552-577; Latané, *Diplomatic Relations of the United States and Spanish America*, pp. 176-195; T. J. Lawrence, *Disputed Questions in Modern International Law*, pp. 89-142; W. F. Johnson, *Four Centuries of the Panama Canal*, pp. 51-77; Henry Huberich, *The Trans-Isthmian Canal*, pp. 6-15.

PART VI. THE CRISIS OF DISUNION

CHAPTER XIV

APPROACHING THE CRISIS

The Repeal of the Missouri Compromise and the Formation of the Republican Party

426. The Louisiana Purchase Territory in 1850. By the terms of the Missouri Compromise of 1820 all the Louisiana Purchase territory north of the line 36° 30′, except the state of Missouri itself, was closed to slavery. It was an immense region of over half a million square miles, larger than all the free states east of the Mississippi River combined. While the attention of the country had been fixed on the annexation of Texas, the acquisition of the territory of Oregon in the Far West, the Mexican War, and the organization of the vast Mexican cession of California and New Mexico, this Louisiana territory had remained almost unnoticed. Up to the middle of the nineteenth century only the single state of Iowa (1846) and the single territory of Minnesota (1849) had been formed out of it. The rest of the region, extending from the Missouri River to the Rockies, was unorganized Indian territory in 1850, with less than 1000 white inhabitants. The addition to our domain, however, of the land west of the Rockies at once made the organization of the middle part of the Louisiana region (then known as Nebraska) important as a link between the Mississippi Valley and the Pacific. Thousands of emigrants were passing through the country on their way to the gold fields of California, and the settlers of Missouri and Iowa, with the irrepressible American frontier spirit, were eager to drive the Indians from their borders and to press westward into the rich valleys of the Kansas and Missouri Rivers.

427. The Kansas-Nebraska Bill. Stephen A. Douglas of Illinois was chairman of the Senate Committee on Territories. He was a self-made man of tremendous energy, a masterful politician, and an unrivaled debater, who had come from a Vermont farm to the new Western country as a very young man and had risen rapidly through minor offices to a judgeship in the supreme court of Illinois. He was sent to the House of Representatives in 1843 and to the Senate in 1846. Although then but thirty-three years of age, Douglas immediately assumed an important place in the Senate through his brilliant powers of debate. He was soon recognized as the leader of the Democratic party in the North, and after the death of Calhoun, Clay, and Webster he became the foremost figure in American public life. On January 4, 1854, Douglas reported a bill for the organization of the territory west of Missouri (Nebraska) on the principle of "squatter sovereignty" as set forth in the Compromise of 1850.

Douglas did not mention the Missouri Compromise in this bill, but some days later, on the advice of the Southern senators, and with the approval of President Pierce, he substituted for it a new bill which expressly repealed the Missouri Compromise and divided the territory into two parts by the parallel of 40° north latitude,—Kansas to the south (into which it was expected slavery would enter) and Nebraska to the north (which would probably be free soil).

STEPHEN A. DOUGLAS

428. Effect of the Bill on the North. The indignation of the North over the proposed annulment of the Missouri Compromise was instantaneous and strong. The day after the Kansas-Nebraska Bill was reported, the Free-Soil men in Congress, led by Senator Chase of Ohio, issued a spirited protest entitled "The Appeal of the Independent Democrats." They denounced the bill as "a gross violation of a sacred pledge" and called upon all good citizens to protest by every means possible against "this enormous crime." Hundreds of mass meetings were held in the North to denounce the bill. The legislatures of Maine, Massachusetts, Rhode Island, New York, and Wisconsin sent their protests to Congress. Senator Seward of New

York wrote, "The storm that is rising is such a one as this country has never yet seen." Douglas was denounced as a turncoat, a traitor, a Judas, a Benedict Arnold, who had sold himself to the South for the presidential nomination. He was burned in effigy so frequently that he himself said he could travel from Boston to Chicago by the light of the fires.

429. Motives for Douglas's Action. Douglas had voted in the House for the 36° 30' line at the time of the annexation of Texas in 1845, and declared in a speech in the Senate four years later that the Missouri Compromise was "canonized in the hearts of the American people as a thing which no ruthless hand would ever be reckless enough to disturb." Yet he now maintained that by the Compromise of 1850 the American people had substituted for the principle of a *line dividing free territory from slave territory* the new principle of the *choice of the people of the territory themselves*, and that he acquiesced gladly in that change of principle. Douglas's motive for thus shifting his ground is not wholly clear. It is true that he could not hope to win the Democratic nomination for president without the favor of the South, and that the men who in all probability would be his rivals for the nomination in 1856 were all, in one way or another, courting the favor of the South in 1854.[1] It is true also that he was heavily interested in railway projects for opening up the Far West. But all this does not prove that Douglas, with his hearty confidence in the ability of the people of a locality to manage their own affairs, was not perfectly honest in preferring the "popular-sovereignty" principle of 1850 to the Missouri-Compromise principle of 1820.

430. The Kansas-Nebraska Bill passed. In the debate on the Kansas-Nebraska Bill Douglas proved himself the master of all his opponents. Alone he faced the fire of Wade, Chase, Seward, Sumner, and Everett,—all masterly speakers,—meeting their attacks at every point with a vigor and tact which won even from his adversaries expressions of admiration. On March 4, 1854, after a continuous session of seventeen hours, Douglas carried the bill through the Senate by a vote of 37 to 14. It passed the House on May 22 by

---

[1] These men were President Pierce, who was almost slavishly following the guidance of his Secretary of War, Jefferson Davis; Secretary of State Marcy, who advocated the annexation of Cuba; and our minister to England, Buchanan, who signed the Ostend Manifesto.

the close vote of 113 to 100 and was signed by Pierce. Thus the Missouri Compromise, for thirty-four years "canonized in the hearts of the American people," was repealed, and 485,000 square miles of territory that had been "forever" dedicated to freedom were opened to the slaveholder. Mr. James Ford Rhodes, the foremost historian of this period, says that the Kansas-Nebraska Act was "the most

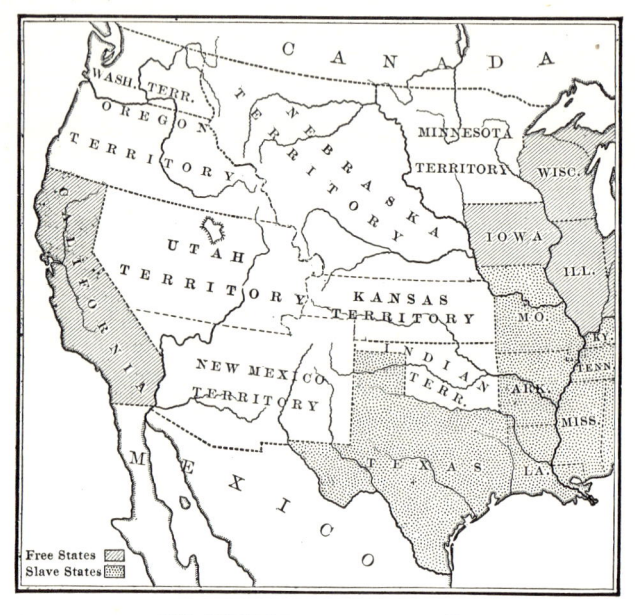

OUR WESTERN TERRITORIES, 1854

momentous measure that passed Congress from the day that the Senators and Representatives first met to the outbreak of the Civil War." It was the end of compromise on the slavery question. It was the declaration on the part of the South that no more lines of latitude or acts of Congress could debar slavery from the territories of the United States. It suddenly woke the North to the realization that nothing would satisfy the slaveholder short of the recognition of slavery as a national institution.

431. Growth of Abolitionist Sentiment. The first effect of the bill was a great accession to the antislavery ranks in the North.

Horace Greeley, editor of the New York *Tribune,* the most influential newspaper in the country at this period, wrote, "Pierce and Douglas have made more abolitionists in three months than Garrison and Phillips could have done in half a century." Deprived of the free territory of the West, the abolitionists determined that henceforth there should be no quarter given to slavery in the free states of the North. They began again to resist the Fugitive-Slave Law of 1850, now not a "band of fanatics," but a great company of men of culture, rank, and wealth.[1]

432. The Personal-Liberty Acts. Ten states of the North passed Personal-Liberty acts forbidding their officers to aid in the seizure of fugitive slaves, denying the use of their jails for the detention or imprisonment of fugitives, ordering their courts to provide jury trials for all negroes seized in the state, and generally annulling the provisions of the Fugitive-Slave Law of 1850. When the fugitive Anthony Burns was arrested in Boston in 1854, a "mob," in which were some of the most prominent authors, preachers, and philanthropists of the city, attempted to rescue him by battering down the doors of the jail. He had to be escorted to the wharf by battalions of United States artillery and marines, through streets cleared by the cavalry and lined with 50,000 hooting, hissing, jeering, groaning men, under windows draped in mourning and hung with the American flag bordered with black. It cost the United States government $40,000 to return Anthony Burns to his Virginia master.

433. The Break-up of the Whig Party. The political effect of the repeal of the Missouri Compromise was no less remarkable than the moral effect, for it led directly to the formation of a new and powerful party. The Whigs, although badly beaten by Pierce in the election of 1852, had nevertheless sent over 60 members to Congress. A majority of the Southern Whigs voted for the Kansas-Nebraska Bill, while every single one of the 45 Northern Whigs voted against it. This vote showed that the old Whig party was hopelessly split by the slavery issue into a Northern and a Southern wing. The

---

[1] The Abolitionist movement was greatly stimulated by Mrs. Harriet Beecher Stowe's novel, "Uncle Tom's Cabin" (1852), a pathetic but exaggerated portrayal of the cruelties practiced by the inhuman slave driver. The author implored "the Christian and humane people of the North" not to acquiesce in the new Fugitive-Slave Law. Her novel, selling by the hundreds of thousands of copies, so influenced public opinion in the North that President Lincoln, meeting her later in the White House, greeted her as "the woman who brought on the Civil War."

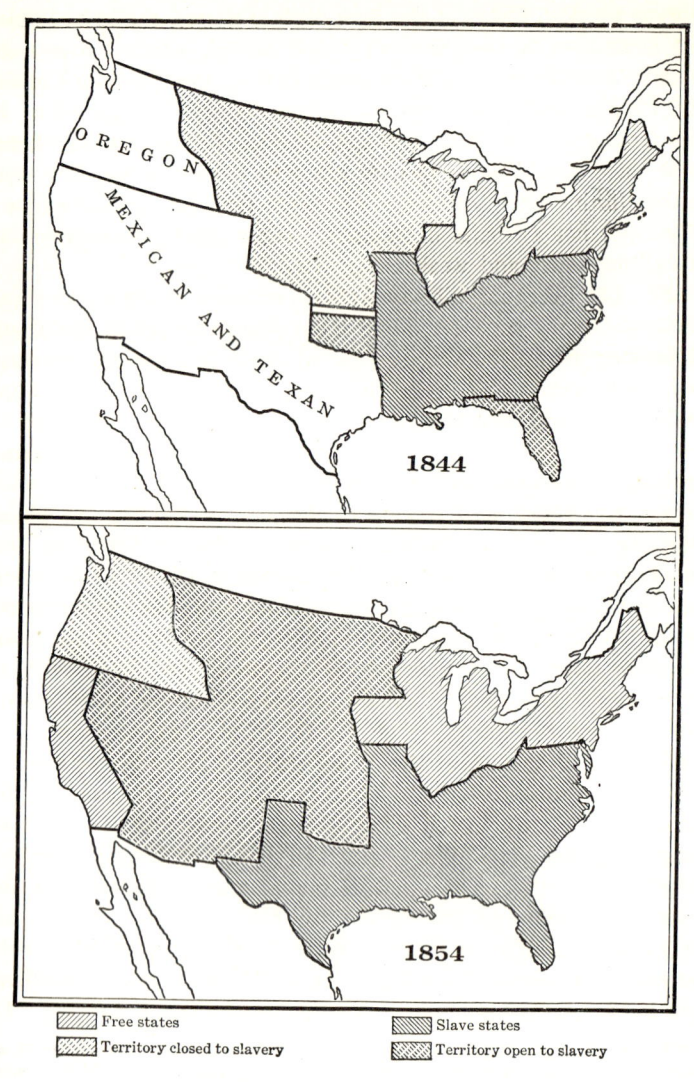

THE STATUS OF SLAVERY, 1844-1854

proslavery Whigs of the South gradually went over to the Democratic party until, by the end of 1855, there were only the mere remnants of the once powerful Whig party south of the Potomac.[1] In the North the Whigs were stronger, but the Northern Whigs alone could not hope either to control Congress or to elect a president. They hoped that the other Anti-Nebraska men of the North — the Free-Soilers, the Know-Nothings,[2] and the Anti-Nebraska Democrats — would join them in making a great new Whig-Unionist party. But they were mistaken. Most of the Northern Democrats were skillfully rallied to the party standards by the incomparable activity of Douglas; while the Free-Soil men had no intention of subordinating their one great issue of slavery to the questions of tariff, finance, or any other part of the Whig platform. If the Anti-Nebraska Whigs wished to see a united North, they themselves would be forced to come into the new party which was already gathering the determined antislavery men out of every political camp.

434. Formation of the New Republican Party. This new party was formed at Jackson, Michigan, a few weeks after the passage of the Kansas-Nebraska Bill, in response to a call for a state mass meeting of all men opposed to the extension of slavery (July 6, 1854). No hall was large enough to hold the immense gathering, which adjourned to a grove of oaks on the outskirts of the town. Amid great enthusiasm the meeting declared that slavery was a great "moral, social, and political evil," demanded the repeal of the Kansas-Nebraska Act and of the Fugitive-Slave Law of 1850, and resolved that "postponing all differences with regard to political economy or administrative policy," they would "act cordially and faithfully in unison" until the contest with slavery was ended. They adopted the name "Republican,"[3] nominated an entire state ticket,

---

[1] The process of the dissolution of the Whig party in the South began when thousands deserted Scott for Pierce in the presidential election of 1852, fearing that Scott was "tinged with Free-Soil principles." The vote on the Kansas-Nebraska Bill completed the process.

[2] The Know-Nothing party was the most curious development in our political life. It originated in 1852 as a protest against foreign influence in our politics. It was more like a lodge, or secret order, than a political party. The chaos in the old Whig and Democratic parties produced by the Kansas-Nebraska agitation drove thousands into the ranks of the Know-Nothings simply because they had no other place to go to. Thus that queer secret society actually carried several states in the elections of 1854 and 1855 and gained a momentary political significance far beyond its real importance.

[3] The organization and the name had both been suggested by an antislavery meeting at Ripon, Wisconsin, before the Kansas-Nebraska Bill had passed.

and invited other states to follow them. State after state responded, organizing the Anti-Nebraska forces into the Republican party, until at the close of 1855 the chairmen of the Republican committees in nine states of the Union issued a call for a national Republican convention to be held at Pittsburgh on February 22, 1856, for the purpose of organizing a national Republican party and appointing a time and place for nominating a presidential candidate. From this convention the Republican party issued full-grown.

435. The Mistake of Douglas. The formation of the Republican party was a direct result of the repeal of the Missouri Compromise. The party was really called into existence by Stephen A. Douglas, who later had cause bitterly to regret his blunder in consolidating the antislavery spirit of the North. There was no good reason in the year 1854 for disturbing the compromise agreed on in 1850. On the basis of that compromise the Democratic party had achieved an overwhelming success at the polls in 1852 and the Southern states had declared their adherence to the Union. Prosperity was general; the country seemed calm. One might have prophesied at the opening of the year 1854 a long and undisturbed tenure of power for the Democratic party. At the end of that year the country was in a ferment. The Democratic majority of 84 in the House had been changed to a minority of 75. A new party had been formed which in a few years was to defeat the Democrats both of the North and of the South and give the death blow to the institution of slavery, to which the Kansas-Nebraska Act had seemed to open new and promising territory.

"A House divided against Itself"

436. The Colonization of Kansas. When the Kansas-Nebraska Bill became law, Douglas boasted that "the struggle over slavery was forever banished from the halls of Congress to the Western plains." He was mistaken about its being banished from the halls of Congress, but right about its reaching the Western plains. While the bill was still pending, a group of determined Free-Soilers in Massachusetts resolved that if the question of slavery was to be left to the settlers of Kansas, then Kansas should be settled by anti-slavery men. Accordingly, at the suggestion of Eli Thayer of

APPROACHING THE CRISIS 309

Worcester, they formed the New England Emigrant Aid Society, whose object was to conduct companies of emigrants to the new territories and help them with loans for the erection of houses and the cultivation of farms. The first colony, some thirty men and women, arrived in Kansas in the summer of 1854. By March, 1855, several hundred emigrants had come and were busy building the town of Lawrence,[1] on the Kansas River. In less than three months over fifty dwellings were built, a hotel and public buildings were started, and Lawrence had taken on the aspect of a thriving New England town.

437. The Missourians "invade" Kansas. The attempt to "abolitionize Kansas" exasperated the South and, above all, the neighboring state of Missouri. The Missourians called the New England emigrants "an army of hirelings," "reckless and desperate fanatics," who "had none of the purpose of the real pioneers," but were clothed and fed, as they were transported, by abolitionist "meddlers" of the North, who wanted to prevent a fair and natural settlement of Kansas. Large bands of armed men (the "border ruffians") from Missouri swarmed into the Kansas territory whenever elections were held. In the spring of 1855 their thousands of fraudulent votes elected a territorial legislature, which removed its meeting place to a point near the Missouri border and proceeded to enact a code of laws in which the severest penalties were decreed against anyone who attempted to aid slaves to escape or even spoke or wrote of slavery as illegal. Companies of volunteers from Alabama, Florida, South Carolina, and Georgia marched to Kansas to join the Missourians in the battle "for slavery and the South."

438. Civil War in Kansas. The Free-Soil emigrants in Kansas, who now numbered over 3000, refused to recognize the legislature elected by the "border ruffians" from Missouri. Their delegates met at Topeka, organized an antislavery government, and, following the example of California six years earlier, applied to Congress for immediate admission to the Union as a free state. In the spring of

---

[1] The town was named after A. A. Lawrence, a noted merchant and philanthropist of Boston, who was one of the chief supporters of the Emigrant Aid Society. John Greenleaf Whittier, the abolitionist poet, gave the colonists their marching song:

We cross the prairie as of old the pilgrims crossed the sea,
To make the West, as they the East, the homestead of the free!

1856, then, there were two hostile governments facing each other in Kansas, each charging the other with fraud and violence. The Free-Soil party was determined that Kansas should not be sacrificed to the slave interests of Missouri. "If slavery in Missouri is impossible with freedom in Kansas," said their leader, Robinson, "then slavery in Missouri must die that freedom in Kansas may live." The proslavery men, on the other hand, declared that they would win Kansas though they had to wade in blood to their knees. It was inevitable that deeds of violence should occur under such circumstances.

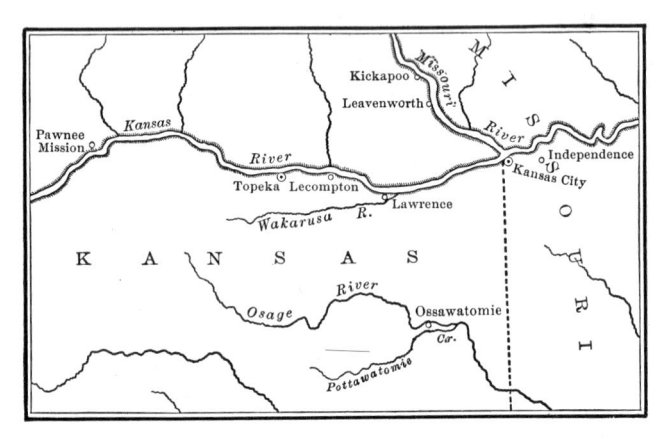

CIVIL WAR IN KANSAS, 1855-1857

On May 21, 1856, the Missourians attacked the Free-Soil town of Lawrence, destroying the public buildings, breaking up the abolitionist presses, and burning private dwellings. The sack of Lawrence was frightfully avenged three days later. John Brown, an old man of the stock of the Puritans, with the Puritan idea that he was appointed by God to smite His enemies, led a small band of men (including his four sons) to a proslavery settlement on the banks of Pottawatomie Creek and there dragging five men from their beds at dead of night, massacred them in cold blood. Thenceforward there was war in "Bleeding Kansas" when Free-Soilers met proslavery men. "Bitter remembrances filled each man's mind," wrote an English visitor to Kansas, "and impelled to daily acts of hostility and not infrequent bloodshed."

439. How President Pierce dealt with the situation. President Pierce ignored the situation as long as he could, declaring in his message of December, 1855, that there had been disorderly acts in Kansas, but that nothing had occurred as yet "to justify the interposition of the federal executive." The next month, however, Pierce sent a special message to Congress, in which he took sides squarely with the proslavery party in Kansas. He did not deny that there might have been "irregularities" in the election of the territorial legislature, but he recognized that legislature as the lawful one and declared his intention of supporting it with all the authority of the United States. The message plainly shows the hand of the Secretary of War, Jefferson Davis of Mississippi, who controlled the administration of President Pierce.

440. Brooks's Assault on Sumner. On the twentieth of May Charles Sumner of Massachusetts delivered a speech in the Senate on "The Crime against Kansas," which was the most unsparing philippic ever pronounced in Congress. Sumner lashed the slaveholders with a tongue of venom. He spared neither coarse abuse nor scathing sarcasm. Among the senators especially singled out for Sumner's shafts was A. P. Butler of South Carolina, who was ill and absent from Washington at the time of the speech. Two days later Preston Brooks, a representative from South Carolina and a relative of Senator Butler, entered the Senate chamber late in the afternoon, when Sumner was bending over his desk at work, and beat him almost to death with a heavy gutta-percha cane.[1]

441. The First Republican Convention. Sumner's speech, the attack of Brooks, the sack of Lawrence, and the massacre on the Pottawatomie all occurred within the five days May 20-24, 1856. These events were a sad commentary on "popular sovereignty" in Kansas and a sinister omen for the approaching presidential campaign. The Republican nominating convention arranged for at Pittsburgh (see page 308) met at Philadelphia, June 17. The platform adopted declared that it was "both the right and the duty of Congress" to prohibit slavery in the territories. It condemned the

---

[1] Sumner's speech had been outrageous, but Brooks's attack was unspeakably base and cowardly. The motion to expel Brooks from Congress failed of the necessary two-thirds vote, and when he resigned shortly afterwards, he was immediately reëlected by the almost unanimous voice of his district in South Carolina.

policy of the administration in Kansas, denounced the Ostend Manifesto, and demanded the immediate admission of Kansas as a free state. Chase and Seward, the leading men of the party, were both passed over on account of their former prominence in the Democratic and the Whig party respectively; and John C. Frémont, of California, "the Pathfinder," renowned for his explorations and his military services in the Far West (see page 282), was nominated for president, with Dayton of New Jersey for vice president.

442. Threats of Secession. The selection of both of the candidates from free states was in the eyes of the South a proof of the sectional character of the Republican party — the "Black Republicans," as the Southerners called them on account of their interest in the negro. From all over the South came threats that Frémont's election would mean the end of the Union. "The Southern states," wrote Governor Wise of Virginia, "will not submit to a sectional election of a Free-Soiler or Black Republican. . . . If Frémont is elected this Union will not last one year from November next. . . . The country was never in such danger."

443. The Election of Buchanan. The Democrats too passed over their great leader, Stephen A. Douglas, and nominated James Buchanan of Pennsylvania, a dignified, formal, mediocre gentleman, who was especially "available" because he had been absent in England as minister during the Kansas struggle. The Democrats realized that the pacification of Kansas was the most important element of their success in the approaching election. Every fresh deed of violence reported from the territory was making thousands of Republican converts. Pierce sent out a new governor (the third in two years), Geary of Pennsylvania, with authority to use the United States troops to restore order. Geary drove the Missourian invaders out and stanched the wounds of bleeding Kansas (September, 1856). The election was saved for the Democrats. Buchanan carried all the slave states (except Maryland), besides New Jersey, Pennsylvania, Indiana, Illinois, and California. His electoral vote was 174 to 114 for Frémont. Still the new Republican party, in its first presidential campaign, with a comparatively weak candidate at that, had made a remarkable fight. It had carried eleven states and polled 1,341,264 votes to 1,838,169 for Buchanan. With an enthusiasm as great as that with which, in the summer's campaign, they had shouted, "Free

APPROACHING THE CRISIS

speech, free press, free soil, *Fré*-mont and Victory!" the Republicans now closed their ranks and entered on the next four years' campaign with the battle song of Whittier ringing in their ears:

> Then sound again the bugles,
> Call the muster-roll anew;
> If months have well-nigh won the field,
> What may not four years do?

444. The Political Situation in 1856. The whole conservative element of the country was relieved by the election of 1856. Buchanan was deemed a "safe" man, while the erratic, popular Frémont, urged by the abolitionists, might have precipitated a crisis. The country was at the flood tide of material prosperity. The national debt, which stood at $68,000,000 in 1850, had been reduced to less than $30,000,000. The Walker tariff of 1846, though moderate, was bringing into the Treasury so large a surplus that a new tariff bill was passed without opposition in the last month of Pierce's term (February, 1857), reducing the rates to the lowest levels since the War of 1812. Buchanan declared in his inaugural address that he owed his election "to the inherent love for the Constitution and the Union which still animates the hearts of the American people" and expressed the hope that the long agitation on slavery was now "approaching its end." But before the echoes of the inaugural speech had died away, an event occurred which again roused the indignation of the antislavery men of the North and won thousands more to the conviction that the sections of our country could not dwell together in harmony until slavery was either banished from our soil or extended to every part of the Union. This event was the Dred Scott decision of the Supreme Court, delivered March 6, 1857.

445. The Dred Scott Decision. Dred Scott, a negro slave belonging to a man in Missouri, had been taken by his master into free territory in the Northwest and brought back again to Missouri. Some years later he sued his master's widow for his freedom, on the ground that residence in a free territory had emancipated him. The case reached the highest court of Missouri, which denied that Scott was a "citizen," with the right to institute a suit. Meanwhile Scott had come into the possession of a New Yorker named Sandford and again sued for his freedom in the United States circuit court of

Missouri.[1] The federal court rendered the same decision as the state court, and Dred's patrons appealed the case to the Supreme Court of the United States. The Supreme Court decided that the federal court of Missouri had no jurisdiction in the case: the status of Dred Scott was fixed by the decision of the state court of Missouri. The matter should have ended there, but the Chief Justice of the Supreme Court, Roger B. Taney of Maryland (who had been appointed by President Jackson on the death of John Marshall in 1835), went on to deliver a long opinion[2] on the status of the negro. The negro was not a citizen, he declared, in the eyes of the Constitution of the United States. That Constitution was made for white men only. The blacks, at the time of its adoption, were regarded as "so far inferior that they had no rights which the white man was bound to respect." Not being a citizen, the negro could not sue in a court of the United States. The slave was the *property* of his owner, and the national government was nowhere given power over the property of the inhabitants of the states of the Union. Furthermore, the Missouri Compromise of 1820 was declared unconstitutional.

446. Importance of the Decision. The Southerners were jubilant. At last the extreme proslavery doctrine of Calhoun and Davis (note, p. 284) was recognized by the federal power at Washington, and by the most august branch of that power, the Supreme Court of the United States. "The nation has achieved a triumph; sectionalism has been rebuked and abolitionism has been staggered and stunned," said a Richmond paper. But the Northern press spoke of "sullied ermine" and "judicial robes polluted in the filth of proslavery politics." "The people of the United States," cried Seward, "never can and never will accept principles so abhorrent." Of course, the effect of the decision was greatly to strengthen the Republican party, which maintained that Congress had the power (as exercised in the Missouri Compromise bill) to exclude slavery from the territories. The issue was clear cut now between the Republican doctrine

---

[1] When a citizen of one state sues a citizen of another state, the case is tried in a federal, or United States, court. Of course the negro slave Dred Scott did not initiate this case himself. It was managed by antislavery men in Missouri who wished to test the position of the courts on the subject of slavery.

[2] An opinion expressed by a judge beyond what is called for in the actual case is called *obiter dictum*, a Latin phrase meaning literally "spoken by the way." It was improper for the court to render this most important part of its decision on a matter which was not before it at all.

and the Dred Scott doctrine, leaving no middle ground for Douglas and his doctrine of popular sovereignty to stand upon.

447. The Lecompton Constitution. Six months after the Dred Scott decision another crisis occurred in Kansas. A convention met at Lecompton, in September, 1857, to frame a constitution for the territory. The Free-Soil men refused to attend the convention, remembering the frauds of the earlier elections, but they were persuaded by Governor Walker's good faith to take part in the elections for a territorial legislature in October and succeeded in returning a majority of Free-Soil members. When the proslavery convention in session at Lecompton saw that the Free-Soil men would control the legislature of the territory, they drew up a constitution in which the protection of all the *existing* slave property in Kansas was guaranteed and then submitted to the vote of the people only the question of adopting this constitution *with slavery* or *without slavery*. Whichever way the people voted there would be slavery in Kansas; for a vote for the constitution "without slavery" simply meant that no *more* slaveholders would be admitted. The Free-Soil men denounced the fraud and demanded that the vote should be simply *Yes* or *No* on the whole Lecompton Constitution. They stayed away from the polls, and the proslavery people adopted the "constitution with slavery," casting in all 6226 votes (December 21, 1857). Two weeks later the Free-Soil legislature put the Lecompton Constitution *as a whole* before the people and the Free-Soil citizens rejected it by a vote of over 10,000. It was clear enough that the majority of the inhabitants of Kansas did not want slavery.

448. Douglas rebukes the Lecompton Fraud. When the Lecompton Constitution came before Congress, in December, 1857, Douglas immediately protested against the fraud as a violation of the principle of popular sovereignty, on which the territory was organized. The people of Kansas, he insisted, must be allowed to vote fairly on the question of slavery or no slavery in the territory. A new convention must be called, and a new constitution submitted. But President Buchanan, in spite of the Free-Soil vote of 10,000 against it, sent the Lecompton Constitution to Congress with the recommendation that Kansas be admitted as a state under its provisions. Douglas was firm. He defied the administration, rebuked President Buchanan to his face, and labored with might and main to defeat the bill. The South assailed him as a "traitor" and a "renegade" and a "Judas,"— the very epithets with which he had been branded in the North four years earlier. In spite of his efforts, the bill was passed by the Senate. The House, however, defeated the bill; and when the Lecompton Constitution was submitted again to the people of the territory, they again rejected it by the decisive vote of 11,000 to 2000.[1]

449. Douglas and Lincoln Compared. Douglas's second term in the United States Senate was about to expire, and he returned to Illinois in the summer of 1858 to make the canvass for his reëlection, in disgrace with the administration and in some private embarrassment.[2] His Republican rival for the senatorship was Abraham Lincoln. The two men had known each other for twenty years. They were both alike in being poor farmers' sons, who had come into the growing state of Illinois as young men and had engaged there in the practice of law. They were alike too in their intense ambition to make a name for themselves in politics. But here the resemblance ceased. While Douglas had been a national figure in the United States Senate for over a decade and twice a serious competitor for the Democratic presidential nomination, Lincoln's national honors had been limited to one inconspicuous term as a Whig member of Congress. In appearance, temper, and character the two men were exact opposites: Lincoln very tall and lanky, awkward, reflective, and slow in speech and motion; Douglas scarcely five feet in height, thickset, agile, volcanic in utterance, impetuous in gesture; Lincoln undeviatingly honest in thought, making his speech always the servant of his reason; Douglas, in his brilliancy of rhetoric, often confusing the moral principle for the sake of making the legal point.

450. Lincoln's Position on Slavery. Somewhat disheartened by his lack of success, Lincoln was losing interest in politics, when the repeal of the Missouri Compromise again roused him. In a speech at Peoria, Illinois, in October, 1854, he warned Douglas that his doctrine would "bring Yankees and Missourians into clash over slavery in Kansas" and with prophetic vision asked, "Will not the first drop of blood so shed be the knell of the Union?" He joined

---

[1] In 1861 Kansas was admitted to the Union as a free state.

[2] A great part of Douglas's fortune had been swept away by a severe financial panic which came upon the country in 1857, as the result of overconfidence in the prosperity of the early fifties and too sanguine investments in Western farms and railways.

the new Republican party and soon rose to be its recognized leader in Illinois. When the Republican state convention nominated him for the senatorship in June, 1858, he addressed the delegates in a memorable speech: "In my opinion it [the slavery agitation] will not cease until a crisis shall have been reached and passed. 'A house divided against itself cannot stand.' I believe this government cannot endure permanently half slave and half free. I do not expect the Union to be dissolved; I do not expect the house to fall; but I do expect it will cease to be divided. It will become all one thing or all the other. Either the opponents of slavery will arrest the further spread of it . . . or its advocates will push it forward till it shall become alike lawful in all the states."

451. The Lincoln-Douglas Debates. Lincoln challenged Douglas to a series of debates before the people of Illinois on the respective merits of the Democratic doctrine of popular sovereignty in the territories and the Republican doctrine of the control of slavery in the territories by Congress. Douglas accepted, and seven remarkable debates took place in various parts of the state. The immediate object of the debates was to influence the people of the state in the election of the legislature which was to choose the United States senator. But the contest was not merely over a seat in the Senate. It was a great struggle watched with interest by the whole country. The point at issue was, Does the Constitution give Congress the right to exclude slavery from the territories?

452. The "Freeport Doctrine." The Dred Scott decision declared it unconstitutional for the national government to exclude slavery from the territories; but at the same time the Kansas-Nebraska Bill, with its doctrine of popular sovereignty, conferred on a territory the right to exclude slavery for itself. Douglas supported both these positions. But, asked Lincoln in the debate at Freeport, how can a territory forbid slavery when Congress cannot? The territory is the creation of Congress. Does it have more power than the Congress which creates it? Can water rise above its source? The question brought the answer Lincoln wanted. Douglas maintained that legislation hostile to slavery by the *people of the territory* would make the territory free soil in spite of the Dred Scott decision. "It matters not," he said, "what way the Supreme Court may hereafter decide as to the abstract question whether slavery may or may not go into a territory under the Constitution; the people have the lawful means to introduce it or exclude it, as they please, for the reason that slavery cannot exist a day or an hour anywhere unless it is supported by local police regulations." This was the celebrated "Freeport Doctrine."[1]

453. The Southern Radicals repudiate Douglas. Douglas won the senatorship by the narrow margin of eight votes. But his admission that the people of a territory might exclude slavery by "hostile legislation" cost him the presidency two years later. The Southern radicals had reached the point where they demanded that Congress should interfere *positively* to protect slavery in the territories, even against the hostile legislation of the territory itself. "Would you have Congress protect slaves any more than any other property in the territories?" asked Douglas of Jefferson Davis. "Yes," replied Davis, "because slaves are the only property the North will try to take from us in the territories." "You will not carry a state north of the Ohio River on such a platform," cried Douglas. "And you could not get the vote of Mississippi on yours," answered Davis. The Democratic party was hopelessly divided. Douglas had railed at the "abolitionist" Republican party as "sectional." Now he and his followers were accused of the same fault by the Southern leaders. He woke finally to the realization that his efforts to hold the Northern and Southern wings of the Democratic party together on the compromise doctrine of popular sovereignty were vain. Every concession to the slaveholders was only the basis of a new demand. Lincoln was right. The house was divided against itself.

References

The Repeal of the Missouri Compromise and the Formation of the Republican Party: T. C. SMITH, *Parties and Slavery* (American Nation), chaps. vii, viii; JESSE MACY, *The Anti-Slavery Crusade* (Chronicles, Vol. XXVIII), chaps. x–xiii; W. E. DODD, *Expansion and Conflict* (Riverside History), chap. xii; J. G. NICOLAY, *Life of Lincoln*, chap. vii; HENRY WILSON, *Rise and Fall of the Slave Power*, Vol. II, chaps. xxx, xxxi; J. B. MCMASTER, *History of the People of the United States*, Vol. VIII, chaps. lxxxvi, lxxxix, xc; J. F. RHODES,

---

[1] Lincoln neatly paraphrased this "Freeport Doctrine" of Douglas in a speech at Columbus a year later: "Then a thing may be legally driven away from a place where it has a legal right to be."

APPROACHING THE CRISIS

History of the United States from the Compromise of 1850, Vol. I, chap. v; Vol. II, chap. vii; J. W. BURGESS, *The Middle Period*, chap. xix; A. B. HART, *American History told by Contemporaries*, Vol. IV, Nos. 34, 35; Old South Leaflets, No. 82; WILLIAM MACDONALD, *Select Documents of United States History, 1776–1861*, Nos. 85–88; EDWARD STANWOOD, *History of the Presidency*, chap. xx; ALLEN JOHNSON, *Stephen Arnold Douglas*, chaps. xi–xiv.

"A House divided against Itself": SMITH, chaps. ix–xvii; MCMASTER, Vol. VIII, chaps. xci, xciii; BURGESS, chaps. xx–xxii; JOHNSON, chaps. xv–xvii; HART, Vol. IV, Nos. 36–45; Old South Leaflets, Nos. 83–85; MACY, chaps. xx; RHODES, Vol. II, chap. ix; NICOLAY, chaps. viii, ix; CHARLES ROBINSON, *The Kansas Conflict*, chaps. v–xvii; OSWALD G. VILLARD, *John Brown*, chaps. v–vii; J. T. MORSE, JR., *Abraham Lincoln*, Vol. I, chap. v; A. ROTHSCHILD, *Lincoln, Master of Men*, chap. iii; N. W. STEPHENSON, *Abraham Lincoln and the Union* (Chronicles, Vol. XXIX), chaps. i–iii; C. E. MERRIAM, *American Political Theories*, chap. vi; MACDONALD, Nos. 91, 93; SAMUEL TYLER, *Memoir of Roger B. Taney*, chap. v.

TOPICS FOR SPECIAL REPORTS

1. **The Birth of the Republican Party:** G. W. JULIAN, *Personal Recollections*, pp. 134–150; STANWOOD, pp. 258–278; T. K. LOTHROP, *William H. Seward*, pp. 142–161; RHODES, Vol. II, pp. 45–50, 177–185; A. C. MCLAUGHLIN, *Lewis Cass*, pp. 293–321; FRANCIS CURTIS, *The Republican Party*, Vol. I, pp. 172–234; JOHNSON, pp. 260–280.

2. **Industrial Prosperity in the Fifties:** SMITH, pp. 59–74; E. L. BOGART, *Economic History of the United States*, pp. 206–215, 222–226, 238–249; D. R. DEWEY, *Financial History of the United States*, pp. 248–274; C. D. WRIGHT, *Industrial Evolution of the United States*, pp. 133–142; EDWARD INGLE, *Southern Sidelights*, pp. 55–66, 88–94; W. G. BROWN, *The Lower South in American History*, pp. 32–49; RHODES, Vol. III, pp. 1–56; G. S. CALLENDER, *Readings in the Economic History of the United States*, pp. 738–793.

3. **The Personal-Liberty Laws:** HART, Vol. IV, No. 33; WILSON, Vol. II, pp. 50–60; MARION G. MACDOUGALL, *Fugitive Slaves* (Fay House Monographs); T. W. HIGGINSON, *Cheerful Yesterdays*, pp. 132–166; NICOLAY and HAY, *Abraham Lincoln, a History*, Vol. III, pp. 17–34; J. J. LALOR, *Cyclopædia of Political Science*, Vol. III, pp. 162–163.

4. **Criticisms of the Dred Scott Decision:** HART, Vol. IV, No. 43; TYLER, pp. 373–400; RHODES, Vol. II, pp. 257–270; G. T. CURTIS, *Memoir of B. R. Curtis*, Vol. I, pp. 211–251; J. G. BLAINE, *Twenty Years of Congress*, Vol. I, pp. 131–137; MACY, pp. 190–199; LALOR, Vol. I, pp. 838–841.

5. **Antislavery Poems:** LUCY LARCOM, *Call to Kanzas* (HART, Vol. IV, No. 37); WILLIAM CULLEN BRYANT, *The Prairies, The Call to Arms*; JAMES RUSSELL LOWELL, *The Present Crisis, The Biglow Papers*; JOHN GREENLEAF WHITTIER, *Expostulation, The Farewell, Massachusetts to Virginia, The Kansas Emigrants, Burial of Barber, The Panorama, Brown of Ossawatomie*.

CHAPTER XV

SECESSION

THE ELECTION OF ABRAHAM LINCOLN

454. The Outlook in 1860. When the presidential year 1860 opened, the antislavery cause seemed to be defeated at every point. Congress, which in 1820 had excluded slavery from the larger part of the Western territory of the United States by the Missouri Compromise, had by the Compromise of 1850 substituted the principle of noninterference with slavery in the territories, and by the Kansas-Nebraska Act of 1854 repealed the Missouri Compromise outright. A stringent fugitive-slave law had been enacted by Congress (1850). The Supreme Court, in the Dred Scott decision, had declared that Congress had no power to exclude the property (that is, the slaves) of the citizens of any of the states from any territories of the Union (1857). Finally, the executive branch of the government, since the inauguration of Pierce, in 1853, had been conspicuously under the influence of Jefferson Davis and the other radical proslavery leaders.

455. Slavery fixed on the South. In the Southern states the institution of slavery seemed fixed beyond any power to disturb it. The slaves had increased from 2,000,000 in 1820 to nearly 4,000,000 in 1860; yet the constantly increasing demand for cotton in the mills of England and the North made the supply of slaves inadequate. The same quality of negro that sold for $400 in 1820 brought $1200 to $1500 in 1860. Why pay $1500 apiece in Virginia for slaves that could be bought for $600 in Cuba and for less than $100 in Africa? said the Mississippi planter. A convention of the cotton-raising states at Vicksburg, in May, 1859, passed a resolution that "all laws, state or federal, prohibiting the African slave trade ought to be repealed." Cargoes of slaves were landed at Southern ports in almost open defiance of the law of 1807 prohibiting the foreign slave trade.[1]

---

[1] In 1859 the yacht *Wanderer* landed 300 slaves, brought direct from the African coast at Brunswick, Georgia. They were distributed as far as Memphis, Tennessee. The owner

SECESSION

456. John Brown's Raid. John Brown, whose fanatical deed of murder in Kansas we have already described (p. 310), felt that he was commissioned by God to free the slaves in the South. He conceived the wild plan of posting in the fastnesses of the Appalachian Mountains small bodies of armed men, who should make descents into the plains, seize negroes, and conduct them back to his "camps

THE MARINES STORM THE ARSENAL AT HARPER'S FERRY

of freedom." He made a beginning at the little Virginia town of Harpers Ferry, at the junction of the Potomac and Shenandoah Rivers, where with only eighteen men he seized the United States arsenal and, raiding the houses of a few of the neighboring planters, forcibly freed about thirty of their slaves. They were huddled

and the captain of the vessel were indicted on a charge of breaking the federal law of 1807, but no Southern jury could be found to convict them, and they went free. Douglas said that 15,000 slaves were imported in the last years of the decade 1850–1860. What a contrast to the attitude of Thomas Jefferson, who wrote in his presidential message of December, 1806, "I congratulate you, fellow citizens, on the approach of the period at which you may [prohibit] all further violations of human rights, which have so long been continued on the unoffending inhabitant of Africa, and which the morality, the reputation, and the best interests of our country have long been eager to proscribe."

together with his men in the arsenal, rather bewildered, and more like captives than newly baptized freemen, when a detachment of United States marines (under the command of Robert E. Lee) arrived on the scene, battered down the doors of the arsenal, and easily made captives of Brown's band (October 18, 1859). Brown, severely wounded, was tried for treason by the laws of Virginia. He pleaded only his divine commission in his defense and was speedily condemned and hanged. When Brown was hailed as a martyr by many antislavery men in the North, who were jubilant to see a blow struck for freedom, even if it were a murderous blow,[1] thousands in the South were persuaded that the "Black Republicans" were determined to let loose upon their wives and children the horrors of negro massacre.

457. The Davis Resolutions. Early in February, 1860, Jefferson Davis brought into the Senate a set of resolutions containing the demands of the South. Douglas's doctrine of popular sovereignty was entirely repudiated. Congress must protect slavery in every part of the territory of the United States. The Northern states must repeal their Personal-Liberty laws and cease to interfere with the thoroughgoing execution of the Fugitive-Slave Law of 1850. The Dred Scott decision must be respected. These extreme proslavery resolutions, which demanded everything but the actual introduction of slavery into the free states of the North, were intended as a platform for the Democratic party in the approaching convention for the choice of a presidential candidate.

458. Lincoln's Cooper Union Speech. At the close of the same month of February, 1860, Abraham Lincoln, at the invitation of the Republicans of the Eastern states, delivered a notable speech in the hall of the Cooper Union, New York City. Since the debates with Douglas in 1858 Lincoln had been recognized in the West as the leading man of the Republican party, but before the Cooper Union speech the East did not accord him a place beside Seward and Sumner. His clothes were ill-fitting, his voice was high and thin, his gestures were awkward as he stood before the cultured audience

---

[1] The tense feeling in the North led many men of note to indorse John Brown's deed in words of extravagant praise. Theodore Parker declared that his chances for earthly immortality were double those of any other man of the century, and Ralph Waldo Emerson even compared the hanging of John Brown with the crucifixion of Jesus Christ. The funds and firearms for Brown's expedition of course came from the North, but the men who contributed them (with perhaps one or two exceptions) thought they were to be used in Kansas and not for a raid in the state of Virginia. John Brown's deed at Harpers Ferry, like his deed at the Pottawatomie, deserves only condemnation.

of New York; but all these things were forgotten as he proceeded with accurate historical knowledge, keen argument, lucid exposition, and great charity to expound the position of the Republican party on the issue of slavery. He showed that a majority of the fathers of the Constitution believed that the Federal government had the power to restrict slavery; that Congress had repeatedly legislated to control slavery in the territories, and that the South had accepted and even voted for such laws; that no particle of proof could be adduced to show that the Republican party or any member of it had anything to do with John Brown's raid at Harpers Ferry; that the talk of the Southerners about the disasters which the election of a Republican president would bring upon them was the product of their own imagination; and that the threats of the South to break up the Union in case of such an election were simply the argument of the highway robber. He concluded by a ringing appeal to the men of the North to stand by their principles in the belief that right makes might. The speech served as a reply to Davis's resolutions and made Lincoln a serious candidate for the Republican nomination for president.

459. The Split in the Democratic Party. The great conventions of 1860, which were to nominate candidates for the most important presidential election in our history, began with the meeting of the Democratic delegates at Charleston, South Carolina, April 23. There was a struggle between the Douglas men and the supporters of the Davis resolutions. The Douglas platform won by a margin of about thirty votes, whereupon the Alabama delegation, led by William L. Yancey (for ten years an ardent advocate of secession), marched out of the hall, followed by the delegates of five other cotton states. The convention reassembled at Baltimore (without the Charleston "bolters") and again divided. The "regulars" nominated Douglas; the seceders, John C. Breckinridge of Kentucky. Thus the extreme proslavery men of the South deliberately split the Democratic party and made probable the election of the Republican candidate. It was the defiant deed of men who were determined to listen to no further discussion of their demands for the full protection of slavery by the national government. Alexander Stephens of Georgia, perhaps the ablest statesman of the South, said that within a twelvemonth of the disruption of the Democratic convention at Charleston the nation would be engaged in a bloody civil war. And so it was.

460. The Republican Convention at Chicago. Meanwhile the Republican convention had met at Chicago (May 16) in a huge structure called the Wigwam. Ten thousand people packed the building, while outside tens of thousands more were breathlessly waiting in hopes to hear that the favorite son of the West, "honest Abe" Lincoln, the "rail-splitter," had been chosen to lead the party to victory. The delegates adopted a platform asserting the right and duty of Congress to prohibit the further spread of slavery into the territories of the United States. They condemned Buchanan's administration for its encouragement of the Lecompton fraud, demanded the immediate admission of Kansas as a free state, and denounced the opinion of Taney in the Dred Scott case.

461. The Nomination of Abraham Lincoln. When the convention met, Senator Seward of New York was considered the leading candidate for the Republican nomination, which he himself confidently expected. Other aspirants for the honor were Chase of Ohio, Bates of Missouri, Cameron of Pennsylvania, Smith of Indiana, and Lincoln of Illinois. Seward led on the first ballot, but he could not command the 233 votes necessary for nomination. He was suspected in some states of being intimately allied with the abolitionists, and in others of being too closely connected with the political machine in New York State. His vote remained nearly stationary, while delegation after delegation went over to Lincoln. On the third ballot Lincoln was nominated and the convention went wild. Pandemonium reigned within the hall, while cannon boomed without. Men shouted and danced and marched and sang. They hugged and kissed each other, they wept, they fainted for joy. Seward, although his friends were stunned with disappointment, showed his nobility of character and his devotion to the Republican cause by an instant and hearty support of Abraham Lincoln.[1]

462. The Constitutional Union Party. There was a fourth ticket in the field, headed by John Bell of Tennessee and Edward Everett of Massachusetts, supported by the old Whigs and Union men in the South, especially in the border states. Their platform ignored

---

[1] Seward's disappointment is expressed in a letter to his wife, written May 30, 1860, " I am a leader deposed by my own party in the hour of organization for decisive battle." Lincoln recognized Seward's valuable support and great gifts when he bestowed on him the office of Secretary of State. The other aspirants for the nomination, Chase, Smith, Bates, and Cameron, also received places in Lincoln's first cabinet.

the subject of slavery, simply declaring "for the maintenance of the Union and the Constitution and the enforcement of the laws."

463. Lincoln's Election. In the election on the sixth of November Lincoln carried all the Northern states except New Jersey, receiving 180 electoral votes. Douglas got only 12 electoral votes, from Missouri and New Jersey. Bell carried Kentucky, Tennessee, and Virginia, with 39 votes. And Breckinridge got the 72 votes of the rest of the Southern states. But the electoral vote does not tell the story of the election. Douglas polled a very large vote (1,370,000) in the states of the North (see map); and had he received the united support of the Southern Democrats, his popular vote would have been considerably larger than Lincoln's. He was repudiated by the administration of Buchanan and by the radical slavery leaders of the South, yet he received nearly twice as many votes (1,370,000 to 850,000) as their candidate, Breckinridge. It was a wonderful testimony to his personal and political hold on his countrymen. Again, although Lincoln received 180 electoral votes to 123 for Douglas, Bell, and Breckinridge combined, his popular vote was only 1,860,000 as against 2,810,000 cast for his opponents.[1] He was the choice of exactly 40 per cent of the voters of the country. Finally, the election showed that the South *as a whole* was not in favor of secession in 1860.

FACSIMILE OF THE ORDINANCE OF SECESSION

---

[1] The electoral system of choice of president may fail to show the popular choice. The candidate who receives most votes (a plurality) in any state gets *all* the electoral votes of that state, though his opponents *combined* may poll more than double his vote, as Lincoln's opponents did in California and Oregon.

For Douglas and Bell, both stanch Union men, polled 115,000 votes more than Breckinridge in the slave states.

464. The Secession of South Carolina. When the legislature of South Carolina, which had met to choose the presidential electors for the state,[1] got the news of Lincoln's election, it immediately called a convention to carry out its threat of secession. On the twentieth of December the convention met at Charleston and carried, by the unanimous vote of its 169 members, the resolution that "the Union now subsisting between South Carolina and the other states, under the name of the *United States of America,* is hereby dissolved." The ordinance of secession was met with demonstrations of joy by the people of South Carolina. The city of Charleston was decked with the palmetto flag of the state. Salvos of artillery were fired, houses were draped with blue bunting, and the bells were rung in a hundred churches. The ancient commonwealth of South Carolina, after many threats and warnings, had at last "resumed" its position as a free and independent state.

SECESSION BANNER

Displayed in the South Carolina Convention

THE SOUTHERN CONFEDERACY

465. The Southern Confederacy. Within six weeks after the secession of South Carolina the states of Mississippi, Florida, Alabama, Louisiana, Georgia, and Texas had severed their connection with the Union. Delegates from six of these seven "sovereign states"

---

[1] South Carolina was the only state in 1860 that continued the custom, common in the early days of our history to most of the states, of choosing presidential electors by vote of the legislature. In all the other states they had come to be chosen by vote of the people.

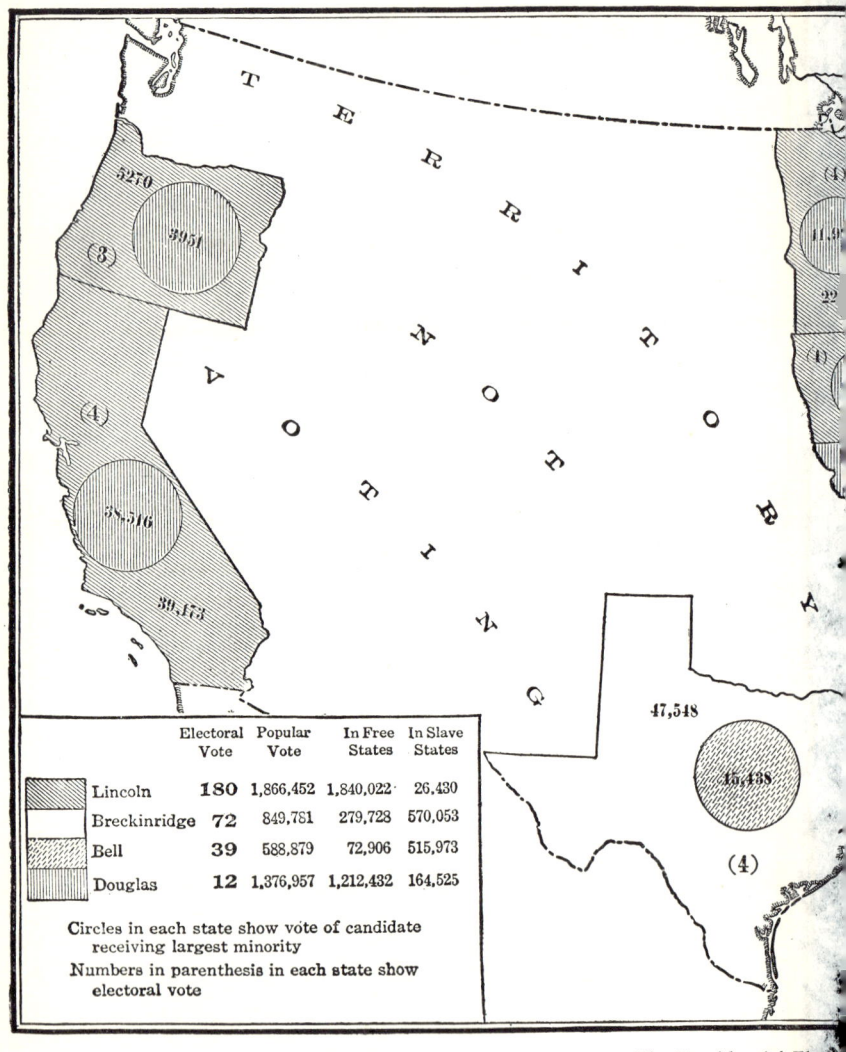

	Electoral Vote	Popular Vote	In Free States	In Slave States
Lincoln	180	1,866,452	1,840,022	26,430
Breckinridge	72	849,781	279,728	570,053
Bell	39	588,879	72,906	515,973
Douglas	12	1,376,957	1,212,432	164,525

Circles in each state show vote of candidate receiving largest minority

Numbers in parenthesis in each state show electoral vote

The Presidential Elec

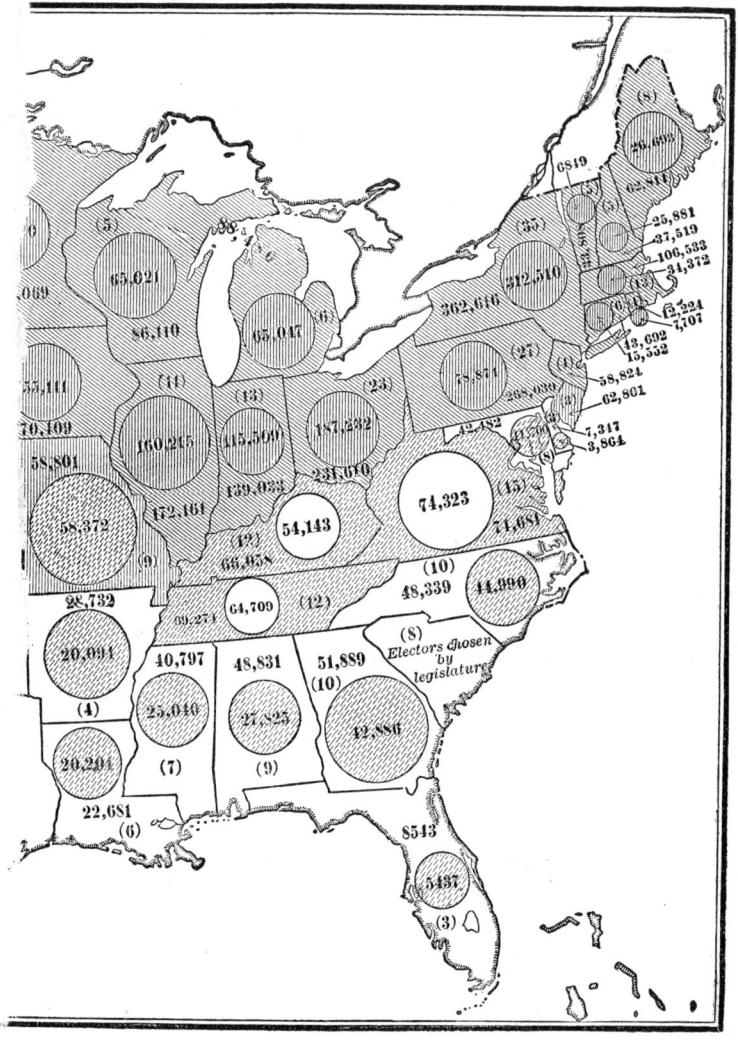

...tion of 1860

met at Montgomery, Alabama, February 4, 1861, and organized a new Confederacy. Jefferson Davis of Mississippi was chosen president, and Alexander H. Stephens of Georgia vice president. A constitution was drawn up and submitted to the several states of the Confederacy for ratification. This constitution was very similar to the Constitution of the United States, except that slavery was expressly sanctioned, Congress was forbidden to levy protective duties, the president was elected for a term of six years without eligibility for reëlection, and the members of the cabinet were given the right to speak on the floor of Congress.[1] A Confederate flag, the "stars and bars," was adopted. A tax of one eighth of a cent a pound on exported cotton was levied. President Davis was authorized to raise an army of 100,000 men and secure a loan of $15,000,000, and a committee of three, with the impetuous Yancey of Alabama as chairman, was sent abroad to secure the friendship and alliance of European courts. Both Davis and Stephens believed that the South would have to fight "a long and bloody war" to establish its independence.

JEFFERSON DAVIS

466. Lincoln's Election no Cause for Secession. The Southern leaders spoke much of the "tyranny" of the North and compared themselves to the Revolutionary fathers of 1776, who wrested their independence from Great Britain. But the simple facts of the case warranted no such language. A perfectly fair election in November had resulted in the choice of a Republican for president. Abraham Lincoln, although he believed that slavery must ultimately disappear from the United States, had given repeated assurances to the men of the South that he would not disturb the institution in their states

---

[1] The Confederate constitution is printed in parallel columns with the Constitution of the United States in Wilson's "History of the American People," Vol. IV, Appendix. Of course, the Confederate constitution never had a chance to go into fair operation, as the Southern Confederacy was overthrown in the great Civil War, which followed immediately upon its adoption.

and that he was even in favor of the execution of the Fugitive-Slave Law of 1850, the violation of which by the Personal-Liberty acts of the Northern states was the one real grievance of the South. Southern statesmen all knew that Abraham Lincoln's plighted word was good.[1] Besides, as Stephens pointed out in the speech by which he endeavored to restrain Georgia from secession, the Republicans were in the minority in both branches of Congress, and the President, even if inclined to "invade the rights of the South," could do nothing without the support of Congress.

467. Buchanan's Weakness. The conduct of President Buchanan certainly was anything but "tyrannical." In his annual message of December 4, 1860, when it was almost certain that South Carolina would secede, he declared that no state had a right to leave the Union. Yet at the same time he gave the secessionists comfort by adding that the government of the United States had no legal means of compelling a state to remain in the Union. He made no attempt to restrain the seceding states when they seized the property of the United States within their borders (public buildings, forts, arsenals, arms, money) for the use of the Confederacy. He was so anxious to avert war, or at least to ward it off until he should have surrendered the reins of government into the hands of Abraham Lincoln on the fourth of March, 1861, that he lost the respect even of the secessionists. They called him an imbecile and boasted of "tying his hands." Had it not been for the presence in the

THE STARS AND BARS

---

[1] Lincoln asked the senators from the cotton states to advise their people to wait before seceding until "some act deemed violative of their rights was done by the incoming administration." To his friend, Alexander H. Stephens of Georgia, he wrote (December 22, 1860): "Do the people of the South really entertain fears that a Republican administration would directly or indirectly interfere with their slaves . . . ? If they do, I wish to assure you . . . that there is no cause for such fears. The South would be in no more danger in this respect than it was in the days of Washington." It was a grave fault in Stephens that he did not publish this letter until after Lincoln's assassination, though even this assurance would probably not have held the Southern states back from secession.

cabinet of a trio of stanch Unionists (Black, Holt, and Stanton), President Buchanan probably would have yielded to the demands of a commission sent to Washington by South Carolina and recognized that state as independent and "sovereign."[1]

468. The Crittenden Amendments. The behavior of the Congress which sat in the winter of 1860-1861 gave the South as little provocation for secession as did the words of Lincoln or the deeds of Buchanan. Instead of preparing for war, Congress bent its whole effort to devising a plan of compromise which should keep the Union intact. The venerable Senator J. J. Crittenden of Kentucky, the successor of Henry Clay, proposed a series of "unamendable amendments" to the Constitution (December 18, 1860), restoring the Missouri-Compromise line of 36° 30' as the boundary between slave territory and free territory, pledging the United States government to pay Southern owners for all runaway slaves they lost through non-enforcement of the Fugitive-Slave Law in the free states, and forbidding Congress ever to interfere with the domestic slave trade or with slavery in the states where it was established by law.[2] A select committee of thirteen in the Senate, including the leaders of public opinion in the North and the South (Seward, Douglas, and Davis), was appointed to consider the Crittenden amendments. At the same time a committee of thirty-three in the House was chosen to work also at the problem of reconciliation.

469. Why Compromise failed. But the committees accomplished nothing. The Republican members refused to accept the line 36° 30' or any other line dividing slaveholding territories from free territories. Their platform called for the prohibition by Congress of slavery in *all* the territories of the United States; and their position was supported by President-elect Lincoln, who wrote to Mr. Kellogg, the Illinois member of the House committee, "Entertain no proposition for the extension of slavery." On the other side, it was precisely the unrestricted extension of slavery in the territories, and its unqualified recognition by the government, for which the

---

[1] The men of the North who remembered the days of 1832 were crying, "O for one hour of Andrew Jackson!" Strangely enough, it was to Buchanan himself (then minister to Russia) that Jackson sent the message, in 1832, "I have met nullification at the threshold."

[2] This last provision was actually passed in the form of an amendment to the Constitution by the necessary two-thirds vote in each House (February 28, 1861). But it was then too late for compromise. Only two states ratified the proposed amendment.

South was contending. The "tyranny" which drove the seven cotton states into secession was the election of Abraham Lincoln on a platform which declared that the spread of slavery must stop,—that slavery was sectional and freedom national. James Russell Lowell summed the whole matter up in a single sentence, when he wrote in the January (1861) number of the *Atlantic Monthly*, "The crime of the North is the census of 1860." Steadily and rapidly the North had been growing in numbers and in the sentiment of freedom during the decades 1840-1860, until it contained enough liberty men to elect a president on a Free-Soil platform.[1]

470. Slavery the Cause of the Civil War. Both Davis and Stephens in their accounts of the Southern Confederacy, written after the Civil War, asserted that not slavery but the denial to the South of her rights under the Constitution was the cause of secession and of the war which followed. But the only "right" for which the South was contending in 1860 was the right to have the institution of slavery recognized and protected in all the territory of the United States. Whether or not the Constitution gave the South this right was exactly the point of dispute. It was not a case of the North's refusing to *give* the South its constitutional right but of the North's denying that such *was* the constitutional right of the South. It was a conflict in the interpretation of the Constitution; and slavery *alone* was the cause of that conflict.

471. The Argument for Secession. Whether or not the Southern states had a right to secede from the Union and form a new Confederacy, for the cause of slavery or anything else, is another question. The Supreme Court of the United States in one of its decisions says, "Such words as 'right' are a constant solicitation to fallacy." A people has always been its own judge as to whether its grievances at any moment were sufficient to cause it to revolt against the government which it has heretofore acknowledged. If a revolt is successful, it is called a revolution and marks the birth of a new civil society or

---

[1] The following table shows the increase of the Liberty, Free-Soil, and Republican vote between the years 1840 and 1860:

1840	James G. Birney	received	7000 votes
1844	James G. Birney	received	62,000 votes
1848	Martin Van Buren	received	290,000 votes
1852	John P. Hale	received	156,000 votes
1856	John C. Frémont	received	1,340,000 votes
1860	Abraham Lincoln	received	1,860,000 votes

state. There has never been a revolution the "right" of which has been acknowledged by both sides. With frequent appeals to the example of the Revolutionary patriots the South proclaimed its right to independence in 1860–1861, believing that its grievances justified secession. That view the North, convinced of the sacredness of the Union, could not accept. So the matter passed beyond argument to the dread arbitrament of war.

472. Conduct of the Southern Leaders at Washington. A number of Southerners remained at Washington, in Congress or in executive positions, long after they had become hostile to the national government. Two members of the cabinet, Floyd of Virginia and Thompson of Mississippi, used their high positions to encourage disunion. The senators from six of the cotton states met in a committee room of the Senate, January 5, 1861, and advised their states to secede immediately. Even then these senators did not resign their seats, but waited until they heard that their states had actually passed secession ordinances. This conduct of the Southern statesmen was resented in the North as a violation of their oath to support the Constitution of the United States.

The Fall of Fort Sumter

473. Lincoln faces a Crisis. It was a serious condition of affairs that confronted Abraham Lincoln when he was sworn into the office of president on March 4, 1861. A rival government in the South had been in operation for a full month. All the military property, except one or two forts, in the seven states which composed the Southern Confederacy had been seized by the secessionist government. From Congress and the executive departments at Washington, from federal offices all through the North, and from army and navy posts, Southern men were departing daily in order to join the fortunes of their states. Many voices in the North were bidding them farewell and godspeed. And, most serious of all, brave Major Robert Anderson, with a little garrison of 83 men in Fort Sumter in Charleston harbor, was writing to the War Department that his stores of flour and bacon were almost exhausted.

474. The Inaugural Address. Lincoln's inaugural address was a reassertion of his kindly feeling toward the South and a plea for calm deliberation before any acts of violence. The new President declared his purpose of holding the forts and property belonging to the government of the United States and of collecting the duties and imposts. But beyond what was necessary to execute the laws according to his oath of office, he disclaimed any intention of using force or of "invading" the South. He appealed to the common memories of the North and the South, which, like "mystic cords, stretched from every battlefield and patriot grave to every living heart . . . over this broad land." Turning to the South he said: "In *your* hands, my dissatisfied fellow countrymen, and not in *mine* is the momentous issue of civil war. The government will not assail you. You can have no conflict without yourselves being the aggressors. *You* have no oath registered in heaven to destroy the government, while *I* shall have the most solemn one to preserve, protect, and defend it."[1]

475. The Situation in Charleston Harbor. A few days after his inauguration President Lincoln called the members of his cabinet[2] together, and laid before them the critical situation at Charleston. In the previous December Buchanan had promised the representatives of South Carolina in Congress not to make any move to provision or reënforce the forts in Charleston harbor so long as the state refrained from attacking them. The next month, however, Buchanan had been spurred by the Unionists in his cabinet to send the transport *Star of the West* with provisions for Major Anderson's garrison in Fort Sumter. The guns of Morris Island opened fire on the transport and compelled her to turn back (January 9, 1861). In spite of this attack upon the flag, Buchanan parleyed and excused, praying for the arrival of the day which should release him from the responsibilities of his high office. That day had now arrived. But meanwhile the South Carolinians had strengthened the batteries that bore upon Fort Sumter, until Major Anderson reported that reënforcements of 20,000 men would be necessary to maintain his position.

[1] The entire inaugural address should be read by every student. It is one of the finest state papers in our history. It can be found in full in Nicolay and Hay's "Abraham Lincoln, a History," Vol. III, p. 327.

[2] The cabinet was composed of the following men: State, William H. Seward; Treasury, Salmon P. Chase; War, Simon Cameron; Navy, Gideon Welles; Interior, Caleb Smith; Attorney-General, Edwin Bates; Postmaster-General, Montgomery Blair. Edwin M. Stanton succeeded Cameron in the War Department early in 1862.

From the bust by Louis Mayer (Copyright, 1916)

ABRAHAM LINCOLN

476. Lincoln determines to provision Fort Sumter. It was a critical moment. To send reënforcements to Major Anderson would probably precipitate war. There was a widespread feeling in the North that if the Southern states wished to secede in peace, they should be allowed to do so. Horace Greeley, editor of the New York *Tribune*, next to Lincoln and Seward the most influential man in the Republican party, wrote: "If the cotton states shall decide that they can do better out of the Union than in it, we insist on letting them go in peace.... We hope never to live in a republic whereof one section is pinned to the residue by bayonets." Lincoln himself hated the thought of war, but his oath of office would not allow him to parley with disunion. On the eighth of April, therefore, he notified Governor Pickens of South Carolina that an attempt would be made to supply Fort Sumter with provisions, but that no men or ammunition would be thrown into the fort except in case of resistance on the part of the state.

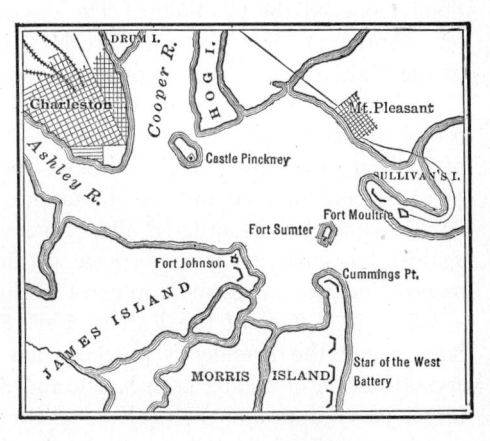

CHARLESTON HARBOR

Showing Fort Sumter and the battery which fired on the *Star of the West*

477. The Bombardment of Fort Sumter. When the Confederate government at Montgomery heard of Lincoln's intentions, it ordered General Beauregard, who was in command of some 7000 troops at Charleston, to demand the immediate surrender of the fort. Major Anderson refused to abandon his post, and General Beauregard, following orders from Montgomery, made ready to reduce Fort Sumter by cannon. Before dawn, on the twelfth of April, 1861, a shell rose from the mortars of Fort Johnson and, screaming over the harbor, burst just above the fort. It was the signal for a general bombardment. In a few minutes, from the batteries of Sullivan's,

Morris, and James Islands, east and south and west, fifty cannons were pouring shot and shell upon Fort Sumter. Anderson stood the terrific bombardment for two whole days, while Northern steamers lay rolling in the heavy weather outside the bar, unable to come to his relief. Finally, when the fort had been battered to ruins and was afire from red-hot shot, Anderson surrendered, saluting the tattered flag as he marched his half-suffocated garrison to the boats.

478. Lincoln's Call for Troops. The bombardment of Fort Sumter opened the Civil War. The day after the surrender of the fort (April 15) Lincoln issued a proclamation declaring that the laws of the United States were opposed in the states of South Carolina, Georgia, Alabama, Florida, Mississippi, Louisiana, and Texas "by combinations too powerful to be suppressed by the ordinary course of judicial proceeding" and called on the states of the Union for 75,000 troops of their militia "to suppress the said combinations." At the same time he ordered all persons concerned in this uprising against the government to disperse within twenty days and summoned Congress to assemble in extra session on the fourth of July.

479. The Effect of the Fall of Fort Sumter. The fall of Fort Sumter and the President's proclamation meant the instantaneous crystallization of feeling both North and South. In the North men forgot party lines and political animosities. Douglas, the leader of a million and a half Democrats, hastened to the White House to grasp Lincoln's hand and pledge him his utmost support in defending the Union. Ex-Presidents Pierce and Buchanan, hitherto ruled by Southern sympathies, came over to the Union cause. Editors like Horace Greeley, preachers like Henry Ward Beecher, statesmen like Edward Everett, who had lately found the idea of forcing the Southern states to remain in the Union abhorrent, now joined in the call to arms. One thing only filled men's thoughts,— the American flag had been fired on by order of the secessionist government at Montgomery. The South was rejoicing over the fall of Fort Sumter. Walker, the Confederate Secretary of War, predicted that by the first of May the Confederate flag would float over the dome of the Capitol at Washington. Lincoln's call for troops, which to the North meant the preservation of the Union, was looked on by the South as a wicked threat to invade the sacred soil of sovereign states and subjugate a peaceful people who asked only "to be let alone," to live under their own institutions. The Confederate Congress met "Mr. Lincoln's declaration of war on the South" by raising an army of 100,000 men and securing a loan of $50,000,000.

480. The Confederacy Enlarged. There were eight slaveholding states which had not joined the Southern Confederacy before the attack on Fort Sumter. Lincoln's call for troops drove four of these

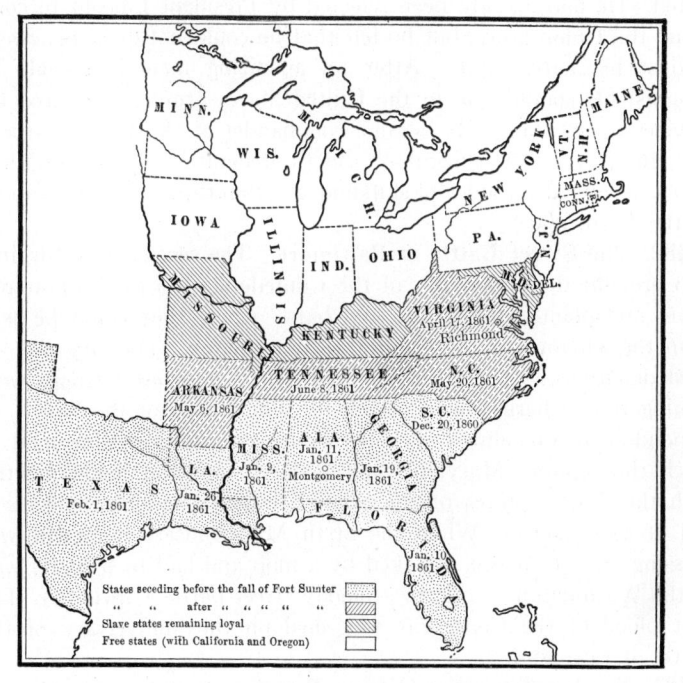

HOW THE SOUTHERN CONFEDERACY WAS ENLARGED AFTER THE FALL OF FORT SUMTER

states (Virginia, North Carolina, Arkansas, and Tennessee) into the Confederacy; while Kentucky and Missouri, whose governors also had refused to furnish their militia for the purpose of "subjugating their sister states of the South," were kept in the Union only with great difficulty. In Missouri it actually came to civil war, the Unionist troops of Captain Lyon driving the supporters of Governor Jackson (secessionist) out of the capital.

336   THE CRISIS OF DISUNION

481. General Robert E. Lee. The secession of Virginia two days after Lincoln's call for troops was an event of prime importance. It gave the South her greatest general, Robert E. Lee. General Lee was the son of a distinguished Revolutionary general, belonging to one of the first families of Virginia, and was himself a gentleman of spotless purity of character,— noble, generous, sincere, brave, and gifted. He had already been selected by President Lincoln to command the Union army, but he felt that he could not draw his sword against his native state. After an agonizing mental struggle he resigned his commission in the United States army and offered his services to his state. He became commander of the Virginia troops and, in May, 1862, general of the Confederate army in Virginia, which he led with wonderful skill and devotion through the remainder of the Civil War.[1]

482. The Street Battle in Baltimore. The secession of Virginia also brought the boundaries of the Confederacy up to the Potomac River and planted the "stars and bars" where they could be seen from the windows of the Capitol at Washington. The city was almost defenseless. There were rumors that Beauregard's troops were coming from Charleston to attack it. The troops of the North, in responding to Lincoln's call, had to cross the state of Maryland to reach the capital. Maryland was a slave state and her sympathy with the "sister states of the South" was strong. Baltimore was full of secessionists. While the Sixth Massachusetts regiment was crossing the city it was attacked by a mob and had to fight its way to the Washington station in a bloody street battle (April 19). The first blood of the Civil War was shed on the anniversary of the battle of Lexington.

483. Washington relieved from Danger. President Lincoln was in great distress for the safety of the capital.[2] In a panic, men were leaving Washington by hundreds, fleeing as from a doomed city. Governor Hicks of Maryland, swept along by the secessionist

---

[1] It was not till near the close of the war (1865) that President Davis, who never very cordially recognized Lee's greatness, was forced by public opinion to make him general in chief of the Confederate forces in the field.

[2] Nicolay and Hay (Vol. IV, p. 152) tell how President Lincoln paced the floor of his office in the White House for hours on the twenty-third of April, gazing out of the windows that looked down the Potomac, where he expected any moment to see the Confederate gunboats appear, and calling out audibly, in his anxiety, for the Union troops to hasten to the relief of the city.

sentiment at Baltimore, telegraphed President Lincoln, begging him to send no more troops through the city (April 22), and mobs tore up railroads and destroyed bridges. The telegraph wires were cut and the government was shut off from communication with the loyal states, while the officials and citizens of the capital were in a panic lest Beauregard should appear on the southern bank of the Potomac with his victorious troops from Charleston. But plucky regiments from Massachusetts and New York ("the dandy Seventh") reached Annapolis by the waters of Chesapeake Bay, and relaying the track and rebuilding the bridges as they marched, came into the city of Washington on the twenty-fifth of April. As they marched up Pennsylvania Avenue, with colors flying and bands playing, the anxious gloom which had lain on the city since the fall of Fort Sumter was changed to rejoicing. The national capital was safe.

REFERENCES

The Election of Abraham Lincoln: EDWARD STANWOOD, *History of the Presidency*, chap. xxi; F. E. CHADWICK, *Causes of the Civil War* (American Nation), chaps. i–ix; NICOLAY and HAY, *Works of Abraham Lincoln*, Vol. VI; ALLEN JOHNSON, *Stephen Arnold Douglas*, chap. xviii; WILLIAM MACDONALD, *Select Documents of United States History, 1776–1861*, No. 94; J. F. RHODES, *History of the United States from the Compromise of 1850*, Vol. II, chaps. x, xi; Vol. III, chap. xiii; J. B. MCMASTER, *History of the People of the United States*, Vol. VIII, chap. xcvi; N. W. STEPHENSON, *Abraham Lincoln and the Union* (Chronicles, Vol. XXIX), chaps. iv, v; A. B. HART, *Contemporaries*, Vol. IV, Nos. 49–61; J. W. BURGESS, *The Civil War and the Constitution*, Vol. I, chaps. iii, iv.

The Southern Confederacy: RHODES, Vol. III, chap. xiv; MACDONALD, Nos. 95–97; HART, Vol. IV, Nos. 62–69; BURGESS, Vol. I, chaps. iv–vi; CHADWICK, chaps. ix–xi; HORACE GREELEY, *The American Conflict*, Vol. I, chaps. xxvi, xxvii; J. S. WISE, *The End of an Era*, chaps. x, xi; NICOLAY and HAY, *Abraham Lincoln, a History*, Vol. III, chap. i; JEFFERSON DAVIS, *Rise and Fall of the Confederacy*, Vol. I, part iii; G. T. CURTIS, *James Buchanan*, Vol. II, chap. xv.

The Fall of Fort Sumter: RHODES, Vol. III, chap. xiv; MCMASTER, Vol. VIII, chap. xcvii; STEPHENSON (Chronicles), chap. vi; HART, Vol. IV, Nos. 70–74; BURGESS, Vol. I, chap. vii; GREELEY, Vol. I, chaps. xxviii, xxix; W. E. DODD, *Expansion and Conflict* (Riverside History, Vol. IV), chap. xiii; CHADWICK, chaps. xii–xix; S. W. CRAWFORD, *The Genesis of the Civil War*; ABNER DOUBLEDAY, *Reminiscences of Forts Sumter and Moultrie*; C. E. MERRIAM, *American Political Theories*, chap. vi; J. G. NICOLAY, *The Outbreak of the War*, chaps. ii, iii; DAVIS, Vol. I, part iv; J. B. MOORE, *Works of James Buchanan*, Vol. XI (use complete table of contents).

Topics for Special Reports

1. **The Republican Convention of 1860 at Chicago:** Rhodes, Vol. II, pp. 456–473; Burgess, Vol. I, pp. 58–67; Hart, Vol. IV, No. 50; Stanwood, pp. 290–297; James Schouler, *History of the United States*, Vol. V, pp. 457–461; Nicolay and Hay, *Abraham Lincoln, a History*, Vol. II, pp. 255–278.

2. **Alexander H. Stephens, a Southern Antisecessionist:** Nicolay and Hay, Vol. III, pp. 266–275; Johnston and Browne, *Alexander H. Stephens*, pp. 357–387; Louis Pendleton, *Alexander H. Stephens*, pp. 153–170; Hart, Vol. IV, No. 53; Henry Cleveland, *Letters and Speeches of Alexander H. Stephens*, pp. 694–713; A. H. Stephens, *A Constitutional View of the Late War between the States*, Vol. II, p. 299 ff.

3. **Efforts at Compromise, 1860-1861:** Chadwick, pp. 166–183; Hart, Vol. IV, Nos. 63, 65, 68, 69; Nicolay and Hay, Vol. III, pp. 214–238; Greeley, Vol. I, pp. 351–406; W. G. Brown, *The Lower South in American History*, pp. 83–112; MacDonald, Nos. 93, 95, 96; Curtis, Vol. II, pp. 439–444; Mrs. Chapman Coleman, *Life of John J. Crittenden*, Vol. II, pp. 224–260.

4. **The Struggle to keep Missouri in the Union:** Burgess, Vol. I, pp. 186–191; Lucien Carr, *Missouri*, pp. 267–341; Greeley, Vol. I, pp. 488–492; S. B. Harding, *Missouri Party Struggles in the Civil War (American Historical Association Reports*, Vol. VII, pp. 85–103); Schouler, Vol. VI, pp. 186–192; Nicolay and Hay, Vol. IV, pp. 206–226; T. L. Snead, *The Fight for Missouri*.

5. **John Brown, Apostle:** T. W. Higginson, *Cheerful Yesterdays*, pp. 199–234, 258–262; O. P. Anderson, *A Voice from Harpers Ferry*; Hart, Vol. IV, Nos. 47, 48; Chadwick, pp. 67–89; Rhodes, Vol. II, pp. 401–416; J. G. Whittier, *Brown of Ossawatomie*; M. J. Wright, *The Trial and Execution of John Brown (American Historical Association Reports*, Vol. IV, pp. 111–126); O. G. Villard, *John Brown, An Autobiography Fifty Years After*, pp. 558–589.

CHAPTER XVI

THE CIVIL WAR

The Opposing Forces

484. North and South Embattled. So the men of the North and the sons of Dixie[1] were mustering to arms in the spring of 1861. Each side doubted whether the other really meant to fight; each believed that, if they fought, its own victory would be short and decisive. Each was absolutely convinced of the righteousness of its own cause. "War has been forced upon us by the folly and fanaticism of the Northern abolitionists," said an Atlanta paper; "we fight for our liberties, our altars, our firesides. . . . Surely 8,000,000 people armed in the holy cause of liberty . . . are invincible by any force the North can send against them." On the other side of Mason and Dixon's line Northern mass meetings resolved that "this infamous, hell-born rebellion against the mildest, the most beneficent government ever vouchsafed to men" should be speedily put down, and "our glorious Constitution restored in every part of our country." Thirty years of gathering bitterness had made it absolutely impossible for the men of the North and of the South to understand each other. As early even as 1832 our distinguished French visitor and critic De Tocqueville had prophesied the "inevitable separation" of the two sections.[2]

485. The Resources of the Two Sections: Population. North and South were unequally matched for the great struggle that was

[1] The boundary line which was run in 1764-1767 between the colonies of Pennsylvania and Maryland, by the surveyors Mason and Dixon (p. 53, note 1), became the dividing line between free and slave soil. The Southerners called their side of Mason and Dixon's line "Dixie land" or "Dixie."

[2] It was apparently the honest conviction of Northerners that every man south of Mason and Dixon's line was a Preston Brooks, and of Southerners that every man north of the line was a John Brown. Mr. Russell, the correspondent of the London *Times*, found that on one side of the Ohio River he was among "abolitionists, cutthroats, Lincolnite mercenaries, invaders, assassins," and on the other side among "rebels, robbers, conspirators, wretches bent on destroying the most perfect government on the face of the earth." He testified that there was "certainly less vehemence and bitterness among the Northerners," but no less determination.

before them. Although the seceding and the loyal states were about equal in territory, the resources of the North far exceeded those of the South. Of the 31,000,000 inhabitants of the United States by the census of 1860, there were 19,000,000 in the eighteen free states of the North, 3,000,000 in the four loyal slave states of Delaware, Maryland, Kentucky, and Missouri, and 9,000,000 in the eleven states of the Southern Confederacy. But of the last 9,000,000, nearly one half (3,600,000) were negro slaves. For military service the North could furnish 5,000,000 men between the ages of eighteen and sixty, to about 1,500,000 in the South. Furthermore the population of the North was increasing very rapidly (41 per cent in the decade 1850–1860), whereas in most of the states of the South it was almost stationary. During the decade 1850–1860 immigrants (mostly Irish and Germans) had come into the United States in numbers equal to the entire slave population of the seceding states and had all gone into the free North to increase the wealth produced by the mills, the forges, and the wheat fields.[1]

486. Industries. Because cotton formed two thirds of the exports of the United States in 1860 ($125,000,000 out of $197,000,000), the South was deceived into thinking that it was the most prosperous part of the country and that its slave labor was making New England rich. But the South overlooked the fact that a country's wealth consists not in the amount of its exports but in its ability to distribute the necessities and comforts and luxuries of life to a growing population. Measured by this standard of wealth, the South was poor in 1860 in spite of its $235,000,000 crop of cotton. For while a few thousand rich planters were selling this crop and investing their profits in more negroes and more land, a majority of the white inhabitants of the South were in comparative poverty and idleness, seeing the land absorbed by the cotton plantations and the labor market filled with negro slaves.

487. Social Progress. Manufactures, railroad mileage, the growth of cities, the diffusion of knowledge, progress in art and

[1] There was no result of the Compromise of 1850 more favorable to the North than its postponement of the great Civil War for ten years. During that decade the states of the Northwest were filled up with a hardy, loyal population, who furnished immense strength to the Northern side during the war. Wisconsin, for example, gained 475,000 inhabitants, and Michigan over 650,000, in the decade. Discerning Southerners since Calhoun's day had seen the advantage of fighting soon if they fought at all.

letters, are all signs of a country's prosperity. The South had hardly any manufactures in 1860.[1] She spun and wove but 2½ per cent of the cotton she raised, and only one fourth of the 31,000 miles of railroad track in the United States was laid on her soil. While the free states of the North abounded in thriving cities, equipped with gas and water systems, tramways, public schools and libraries, hospitals, banks, and churches, the census of 1860 found only six

A GROUP OF WAR ENVELOPES

"cities" in Alabama with a population of 1000 or over, four in Louisiana, and one in Arkansas.[2] The public-school system was but meagerly developed before the war. Fifteen per cent of the adult male white population of Virginia (in addition of course to practically all the negroes) were unable to read or write, according to the census of 1850, while only two fifths of one per cent of the adult males of Massachusetts were illiterate.

[1] The North turned out manufactures in 1860 valued at $1,730,330,000, compared with an output valued at $155,000,000 for the South, a ratio of 12 to 1. Governor Wise of Virginia said to the people of his state in 1859: "Commerce has long since spread her sails and sailed away from you.... You have not as yet dug more than enough coal to warm yourselves at your own hearths ... you have not yet spun coarse cotton enough to clothe your own slaves." As against a cotton crop worth $235,000,000 raised by the South, the North produced wheat and corn valued at $845,000,000.

[2] Zachary Taylor of Louisiana, while on a Northern visit as President-elect, in 1848–1849, looked from a height near Springfield, Massachusetts, on a group of thriving towns and remarked, "You cannot see any such sight as that in a Southern state!"

488. Slavery the Bane of the South. The cause of the backward social and industrial condition in the South was the plantation system founded on negro slavery, which developed a "caste" of some 380,000 aristocratic planters at the expense of over 5,000,000 non-slaveholding whites. Whatever relieving touches there are in the picture of the slave plantation,—the devoted Southern woman nursing her sick negroes with her own hands, and the strong and tender attachment of the children of the household to the old black "mammy" in whose arms they had been sung to sleep since infancy, —the system of slavery was a blight on industry and a constant menace to the character of the slaveholder. That the men of the South, in defending what they believed to be their rights under a government of "liberty and equality," were pledged to perpetuate such an institution was a misfortune which is deplored by none more heartily than by the descendants of those men today.[1]

489. Helper's "Impending Crisis." We may wonder why the millions of citizens in the South, who had no slaves and no interest in slavery, should have fought through four years with desperate gallantry for the maintenance of a system which meant for them only disadvantage. One of their number, Hinton R. Helper of North Carolina, had published a book in 1857, entitled "The Impending Crisis," in which he showed with a merciless array of figures the economic burden which slavery entailed upon the South. Helper called the slaveholding aristocracy no better than the basest "ruffians, outlaws, and criminals" and advised "no coöperation with them in religion, no affiliation with them in society." The poorer whites were not able to read and understand the figures and arguments of Helper's book. They believed that the "Black Republicans" of the North meant to subjugate them and turn their land over to the negro. They rose in a mass to defend a civilization which, had they but realized it, was the worst enemy of their interests.

490. Military Advantages of the South. The leaders of the South knew, of course, that the North was superior in resources, but they counted on several real advantages and several anticipated

---

[1] Louis Pendleton of Georgia, in his biography of Alexander H. Stephens, writes (1904), "Reflecting Southern men today are filled with sadness as they read their grandfathers' eulogies of an institution which wrought the ruin of the fairest portion of the United States."

developments to give them the victory. First, and most important of all, they would be fighting on their own soil, whereas the North, in order to "put down the rebellion" would have to invade Southern territory. The men who fight on the defensive are always at an advantage. They know the lay of the land; they have their base of supplies close at hand; they are inspired by the thought that they are defending their homes. Then, too, the Southerners, by nature and training, were better fitted for war than the mechanics, clerks, and farmers of the North. The Southern temper was more ardent. The men of the South commonly carried firearms. They were accustomed from boyhood to the saddle. In the Mexican War many more Southern than Northern officers had been trained for the great civil contest.

491. The South disappointed in its Expectations. Besides her actual military advantages the South counted on help in three directions. She expected that foreign nations, especially Great Britain and France, dependent on her for their supply of raw cotton, would lend their aid to establish an independent cotton-raising South, which would levy no duties on their manufactures. She thought too that the first move in behalf of a new republic whose corner stone was slavery would bring all the other slaveholding states into the Confederacy. And she looked to the Democrats of the North, who had cast 1,370,000 votes against Abraham Lincoln and whose leaders had repeatedly shown signs of Southern leanings, to defeat any attempt of the Republicans to "subjugate the South." We have seen how completely deceived the South was in the last expectation, when the shot fired on Fort Sumter roused the North as one man to pledge President Lincoln its aid in defending the Union.[1] We have seen also how only four of the eight slaveholding states north of the cotton states joined the Confederacy on Lincoln's call for troops (p. 335). The South was equally disappointed in the hope of foreign intervention and aid. Queen Victoria issued a proclamation of strict neutrality a month after the fall of Fort Sumter; and Emperor Napoleon III, although expressing to Mr. Slidell, the Confederate

---

[1] The Southern press was very bitter over the " desertion " of the Democrats of the North: "Where are Messrs. Cushing, Van Buren, Pierce, Buchanan, Douglas *et id omne genus*, — where are they in the bloody crusade proposed by President Lincoln against the South? . . . Hounding on the fanatic warfare! . . . The Northern politicians have all left us. Let them fly — all, false thanes!"

envoy to France, his personal sympathy for the South, was careful to avoid any official breach with the government at Washington.

492. The State of West Virginia. Moreover, large portions even of some of the seceding states remained faithful to the Union, especially the mountain districts in western Virginia and North Carolina and in eastern Tennessee. Over forty counties in western Virginia broke away from the state and formed a loyal government, which was recognized by President Lincoln and later received into the Union (1863) as the state of West Virginia. A striking proof of the divergent views of loyalty in North and South is the fact that the wise and moderate Robert E. Lee called the people of West Virginia "traitors" for leaving their state to adhere to the Union.

So the men of the North and the sons of Dixie were arrayed against each other, in the spring of 1861, for a contest which none dreamed would be the most prolonged and bloody since Napoleon's rash attempt, at the beginning of the century, to subjugate the continent of Europe.

From Bull Run to Gettysburg

493. The Importance of the Civil War. The work entitled "The Official Records of the Union and Confederate Armies and Navies in the War of the Rebellion," published by the government at Washington, fills more than 130 bulky volumes, and chronicles over 2000 engagements, of which about 150 are important enough to be called "battles." A mere list of the titles of historic biographies and memoirs relating to the Civil War would fill hundreds of pages. Such a list prepared only a year after the close of the war (Bartlett's "Literature of the Rebellion," 1866) contains 6073 such titles. This immense mass of literature pertaining to the Civil War is a proof of the significance of that event in our country's history. Except for the critical years 1775–1789, in which our nation was formed, no other period in our history can compare in importance with the great Civil War of 1861–1865, which determined that the nation which the fathers had founded should endure one and undivided, and removed from it the ugly institution of negro slavery, which for decades had cursed its soil, embroiled its politics, and outraged the conscience of half its people.

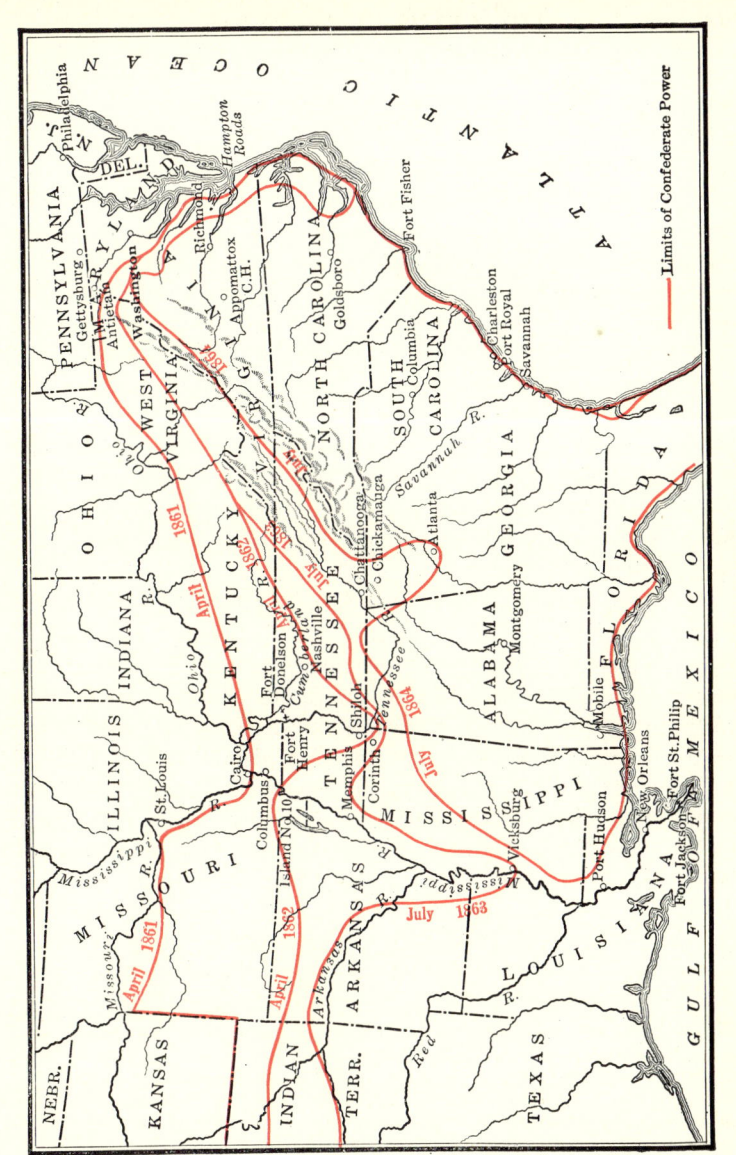

MAP OF THE CIVIL WAR

494. How we shall study the War. We need not go into the military details of the Civil War in order to appreciate its importance. Military history is useful only for the special student of the science of war. The marching and countermarching of the 2,500,000[1] men who fought the battles of the Civil War, the disposition of artillery, cavalry, and infantry by thousands of officers in hundreds of important engagements, the countless deeds of heroism on both sides, on land and sea, we must pass over, only to sketch in outline the few great campaigns on which the fortunes of the republic hung. Two things we must constantly bear in mind: first, the superior resources of the North in men and wealth, which told with increasing emphasis as the war progressed; and secondly, the advantage that the South had in fighting on her own soil against the invading armies of the North.[2] Had the South possessed the resources of the North, she could never have been beaten; had she attempted to invade the North, her armies would have been repulsed at the borders.

495. "On to Richmond!" We turn now to the field of battle. When Virginia seceded, the capital of the Confederacy was changed from Montgomery, Alabama, to Richmond, and the Confederate Congress was called to meet at the new capital, July 20, 1861. The North, in the first flush of its enthusiastic response to Lincoln's call for troops, was determined that the Confederate Congress should not meet. "On to Richmond!" was the cry that rang through the North. The raw troops were not properly organized or drilled, and the quartermaster's and commissariat departments[3] were not prepared for a campaign. But President Lincoln and General Scott yielded to the popular demand for a move on Richmond, especially

---

[1] Livermore, in his "Numbers and Losses in the Civil War" (1901), our best authority, gives the total numbers on each side, on the basis of an enlistment for three years,— Union, 1,556,678; Confederate, 1,082,119.

[2] Strictly speaking, it was not a "civil war." That term refers to a struggle between two opposing factions or parties (religious or political) living on the same soil. In the war of 1861–1865 a united South, claiming to be an independent country, was invaded by the armies of a (less) united North. Compare the actual "civil war" in Kansas in 1855–1856, where free-state men and slave-state men were fighting for control of their common territory. Alexander H. Stephens more accurately calls the war of 1861–1865 the *War between the States*. A still better title would be the *War of Secession*.

[3] The quartermaster's department has charge of the transportation of all the baggage, food, clothing, and blankets of the army, and the provision of all supplies except food and munitions. The commissariat department's business is to provide the supplies of food for the soldiers.

as the term of service of the militia, who had enlisted in April for only three months, was about to expire.

496. The Battle of Bull Run (or Manassas). General Beauregard, with 22,000 troops, was at Manassas Junction, a town near the little stream called Bull Run, about thirty-five miles southwest of Washington. In the Shenandoah valley, across the Blue Ridge, were 9000 more men under General Joseph E. Johnston, who was to become, next to Lee, the greatest commander of the South. General Patterson, a veteran of the War of 1812, was to hold Johnston in the valley, while General McDowell, with an army of 30,000, attacked General Beauregard at Manassas. McDowell's "grand army" set out in high spirits, July 16, accompanied by many of the congressmen and officials in Washington, who went to see the "rebellion crushed by a single blow." The battle (on the twenty-first) was well planned and bravely fought. Up to early afternoon the advantage was with the Union troops,[1] but at the critical moment Johnston's army, which had eluded Patterson and joined Beauregard on the twentieth with 6000 troops, appeared on the field and turned the Union victory into a rout. The undisciplined soldiers of McDowell, wearied with the day's fighting, threw down their muskets and fled to the Potomac. For two days they straggled into Washington, and the capital was in a panic for fear Beauregard and Johnston would come on their heels.

497. McClellan in Command of the Union Army. The disaster at Bull Run sobered the overconfident enthusiasm of the Northerners, but did not destroy their determination. They set to work in earnest to prepare for the long, severe struggle that was before them. George B. McClellan, a young general who had done brilliant work in holding West Virginia for the Union in May and June, was now put in command of the army on the Potomac. McClellan was a magnificent organizer and drillmaster, and by the autumn of 1861 he had the 180,000 men who poured into his camp in response to Lincoln's call organized into a splendid army nearly three times the size of the opposing forces under Lee and Johnston. The aged General Scott resigned on the last day of October, and McClellan was made general in chief of the forces of the United States.

---

[1] Jefferson Davis, who came in person from Richmond to the battlefield in the afternoon, was met by fleeing Confederate soldiers, who told him that the battle was lost.

498. The Peninsular Campaign.

McClellan could and should have taken Richmond in the autumn of 1861, but he was cautious to the point of timidity. Personally brave, he feared for the magnificent army under his command. He magnified the enemy's forces to three times their actual number and looked on the loss of a brigade from his own army as a great calamity. He berated Lincoln and Stanton for not sending him more reënforcements.[1] It was not until well into the spring of 1862 that McClellan, after repeated orders from Washington to advance, began to move up the peninsula between the York and James Rivers (see map, p. 364). Even then the Peninsular campaign, which should have been a steady triumphal march to the Confederate capital, like Scott's march from Vera Cruz up to the city of Mexico in 1847, was a slow, guarded approach of many weeks' duration, as if against an enemy vastly superior in forces. Once, within four miles of Richmond, and already within sight of its church spires, McClellan decided to shift his base to the James River because Lincoln detained McDowell's division of 40,000 men to protect Washington.[2] Lee and Johnston were quick to seize the moment of the deliverance of Richmond to follow up the Army of the Potomac. McClellan, always masterly on the defensive, won several engagements from his pursuers, finally routing them decisively at Malvern Hill (July 1, 1862) in one of the severest battles of the war. Richmond again seemed to be within his grasp, but instead of advancing he led his army back to Harrisons Landing on the James River within reach of the Union gunboats. The famous Peninsular campaign was ended. Richmond was still undisturbed. President Lincoln removed McClellan from the command of the armies of the United States, July 11, 1862.

[1] McClellan took it upon himself to criticize the administration at Washington unsparingly, spoke of the "insane folly" of Stanton and Chase, and constantly prated about "saving the country." To Stanton, who had assumed the War portfolio in January, 1862, displacing Cameron, he wrote: "You must send me large reënforcements, and send them at once. . . . If I save this army now, I tell you plainly that I owe no thanks to you or to any other persons in Washington [President Lincoln]. You have done your best to sacrifice this army." Remarkable language for a commander with an army already more than double the strength of his adversaries to use to his superiors in Washington!

[2] The cause of the detention of McDowell's troops was the campaign of General Thomas J. Jackson in the Shenandoah valley. This wonderful commander (a third great Virginian, with Lee and Johnston) with an army of 17,000 men had defeated and outwitted 50,000 Union troops in the valley and threatened the capital so effectively that the eyes of the administration were drawn off the Army of the Potomac. It was Jackson who saved Richmond. Jackson was a rare combination of fighter and religious fanatic, not unlike

THE CIVIL WAR

499. The *Trent* Affair. A year had passed since the battle of Bull Run, yet the Union arms had made no progress in Virginia. But the United States navy, under the efficient management of Secretary Welles, had accomplished important results. First, it had established so effective a blockade along the 3000 miles of the Confederate coast that the exports of cotton dropped in value from $125,000,000 in 1860 to $4,000,000 in 1862. The Southerners, especially after their victory at Bull Run, could not believe that Great Britain would stand by quietly and allow the North to shut off her cotton supply by a blockade. Their expectations of British intervention were heightened almost to a certainty when, in November, 1861, Captain Wilkes of the Union war sloop *San Jacinto* stopped the British mail steamer *Trent* as she was sailing from Havana, forcibly removed from her deck the Confederate commissioners to Great Britain and France, Messrs. Mason and Slidell, and took them as prisoners to Fort Warren in Boston harbor. The deed was hailed with rejoicing in the North. The Navy Department congratulated Wilkes, and the House of Representatives gave him a formal vote of thanks. The South was in high hopes that this insult to the British flag would involve the administration at Washington in a war with England, and the Queen's government began, in fact, to send troops to Canada. But the sober sense of Lincoln, Seward, and Sumner[1] realized that Wilkes's act, however gratifying to public sentiment in the North, was a high-handed outrage of the principle of the inviolability of vessels of neutral nations, for the defense of which we had gone to war with Great Britain in 1812. Consequently, Seward informed the British minister, Lord Lyons, on December 26, that the prisoners in Fort Warren would be "cheerfully liberated." Mason and Slidell were given up, the British government was satisfied, and the blockade of the Southern ports continued undisturbed.

500. The *Virginia* and the *Monitor*. The Northern navy won a notable victory in a strange kind of battle that took place in

---

Oliver Cromwell. At the battle of Bull Run one of his fellow generals said to his troops, " Look at Jackson standing there firm as a stone wall! " From this remark the general got the name " Stonewall " Jackson.

[1] Charles Sumner of Massachusetts was the chairman of the Senate committee on foreign relations. He did a great deal to win the reluctant sympathy of the English people for the Northern cause.

Hampton Roads, Virginia, March 9, 1862. The Confederates had raised the sunken hull of the *Merrimac* at the Norfolk navy yards and, covering her with a sloping roof of iron rails smeared with plumbago and tallow, had made of her the first "ironclad" in the history of naval warfare. This formidable craft, rechristened the *Virginia*, easily destroyed two of the finest ships of our wooden navy in Hampton Roads, on March 8, and waited only for the morrow to destroy the rest of the fleet and then sail up the Potomac to shell the city of Washington. But that same night there arrived at Hampton Roads from New York a war vessel stranger even than the *Virginia*. This was the *Monitor* (invented by Captain Ericsson), a small iron craft shaped like a torpedo boat, her decks flush with the water, and having amidships a revolving gun turret rising only a few feet. A witty observer called the boat "a cheese box on a raft." The *Monitor* placed herself between the *Virginia* and the wooden ships of the federal navy, and after an all-day fight the dreaded Confederate ram steamed back to the Virginia shore. The wooden ships were saved, but at the same time they were made forever obsolete. This first battle in history between ironclads announced that henceforth the world's navies were to be ships of steel.

THE *VIRGINIA* DESTROYING THE *CUMBERLAND* IN HAMPTON ROADS

501. The War in the West. While the wearisome and futile Peninsular campaign was dragging through the spring months of 1862, relieved only by the victory of the *Monitor*, the Union arms were making splendid progress in the West. Of equal importance to the Union cause with the blockade of the Southern ports and the hoped-for capture of Richmond was the opening of the Mississippi River, which the Confederates held from its junction with the Ohio down to its mouth. The possession of the river would bring the Unionists the double advantage of freeing an outlet for the commerce of the Northwestern states and cutting off the states of Arkansas, Louisiana, and Texas from the rest of the Confederacy. The credit for accomplishing this great work belongs, more than to all others, to General Ulysses S. Grant and Captain David G. Farragut.

GENERAL ULYSSES S. GRANT

502. Grant's Victories on the Mississippi. Grant (born in Ohio in 1822) was a graduate of West Point. He had served creditably in the Mexican War, but since its close had remained in complete obscurity. The outbreak of the Civil War found him, at the age of thirty-nine, working in his father's leather and hardware store in Galena, Illinois, and earning only a precarious support for his wife and family. But the call to war transformed the poor business man into a military genius of the highest order. In February, 1862, with the consent of General H. W. Halleck, who commanded the Union armies of the West, Grant seized the very important forts Henry and Donelson,[1] on the lower Tennessee and Cumberland Rivers, and carried his victorious army up the Tennessee River, 100 miles across the state of Tennessee, to Pittsburg Landing. While waiting here for the arrival of General Buell's army, which Halleck had ordered to join him from Nashville, Grant was attacked by a superior force under General Albert S. Johnston, the best Confederate general in the West. The terrific battle of Shiloh (or Pittsburg Landing) lasted two days (April 6–7, 1862). At nightfall of the first day the Union troops had been driven back to the bluffs along the river; but before morning Buell's army arrived, and the second day's fighting was a triumph for the Union side. The Confederates fell back to Corinth, Mississippi. They had lost 10,000 men, but could better have spared 10,000 more than lose their gallant commander, General Johnston, who was killed on the field. The capture of Forts Henry and Donelson and the victory of Shiloh cleared western Tennessee of Confederate troops,[2] while General John Pope and Commodore Foote in a parallel campaign brought their gunboats down the Mississippi and secured the river as far south as the high bluffs of Vicksburg.

503. Farragut captures New Orleans. Meanwhile the great river was being opened from the southern end. New Orleans, which lies some 110 miles up the river, was protected by the strong forts Jackson and St. Philip and by a heavy "boom" of chained and

---

[1] These forts, built at points where the two great rivers were but twelve miles apart, both secured the navigation of the rivers and strengthened the Confederate line of defense, which extended from Columbus, Kentucky, on the Mississippi, eastward across the state (see map, p. 345). Grant captured 17,000 troops, with large quantities of supplies, at Donelson. To the request of the Confederate general as to the terms of capitulation, Grant replied, "Unconditional surrender." The phrase stuck to him, and U. S. Grant became in popular language "Unconditional Surrender" Grant.

[2] Except for Memphis, which surrendered in June. President Lincoln immediately began the "reconstruction" of Tennessee by appointing Andrew Johnson of that state as military governor. Johnson was a man of great energy and ambition, who had worked his way up from a tailor's bench to the United States Senate. He belonged to the "poor white" class of the South and was an intensely loyal Union man.

anchored hulks stretching a quarter of a mile across the current between the forts. On the night of the twenty-third of April, 1862, Captain David G. Farragut, in a most spectacular battle, broke the boom and ran the gantlet of the fire of the forts. New Orleans was left defenseless. The small Confederate army withdrew, and General B. F. Butler entered the city, which he ruled for over six months under military régime. The capture of New Orleans opened the river as far north as Port Hudson. Thus, by midsummer of 1862, only the high bluffs of Vicksburg and Port Hudson, with the 150 defenseless miles of river bank between, were left to the Confederacy.[1]

504. Failure of the Army of the Potomac. The successes in the West contrasted strikingly with the delays and disappointments of the army in the East, and when McClellan was relieved of his command in July it was natural that a Western general

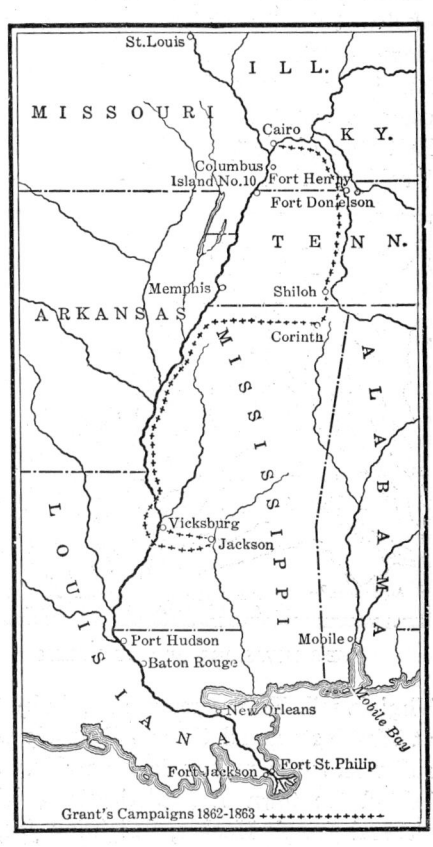

THE WAR IN THE MISSISSIPPI VALLEY

should succeed him. Halleck, under whose command the brilliant operations in Tennessee had been conducted, was called to Washington, July 11, 1862, as general in chief of the armies of the United States, to advise the President and the Secretary of War; while General Pope

---

[1] These 150 miles, however, were very important as a "bridge," over which came immense stores of Louisiana sugar and Texas beef and grain for the armies of the Confederacy.

was given command of a new "Army of Virginia," independent of McClellan's diminished Army of the Potomac. The ten months that followed, from August, 1862, to June, 1863, present a dreary record of defeat for the Union cause in Virginia. General Lee, with his magnificent corps of lieutenants,—"Stonewall" Jackson, Longstreet, Ewell, the Hills, and Stuart,—outwitted and outfought the Union commanders at every turn. Pope was beaten at a second battle of Bull Run (August, 1862) and his entire army forced to retreat on Washington.[1] In spite of the protests of Stanton and Halleck, McClellan was restored to command and hailed with joy by his old soldiers. He stopped Lee's invasion of Maryland in the bloodiest single day's battle of the war, at Sharpsburg on the Antietam Creek (September 17, 1862); but with his old reluctance to follow up a victory by crushing the foe he let the shattered Confederate army get back across the Potomac to Virginia soil. He was removed again by the distressed administration at Washington, and General Burnside was put in his place, only to suffer an awful repulse in his reckless assault on Marye's Heights behind the town of Fredericksburg (December 13, 1862). Then General Joseph Hooker, "Fighting Joe," who succeeded Burnside, was routed in the three days' fight at Chancellorsville (May 1–4, 1863).[2]

LEE'S INVASIONS OF THE NORTH

---

[1] An especially humiliating feature of Pope's defeat was the capture of all his stores and his own headquarters by a brilliant move of "Stonewall" Jackson. The stores, filling a train of cars two miles long, were burned after the Confederates had taken all the plunder they could carry, and the light of the costly bonfire could be seen even from Washington.

[2] After a day's fighting at Chancellorsville, "Stonewall" Jackson, riding back in the twilight with his staff from a reconnoissance, was mistaken by Confederate sharpshooters for a Union officer and fatally shot. The loss of Jackson was one of the severest blows to the Confederate cause.

THE CIVIL WAR

505. The Lowest Point in the Union Fortunes. The early months of 1863 mark the lowest ebb of the fortunes of the Union cause. For nearly two years the superior Federal forces in Virginia had been trying to take Richmond, but they had not been able even to hold their own position south of the Rappahannock. General Lee was planning another invasion of the North. Union soldiers were deserting at the rate of a thousand a week, and hundreds of officers

From the " Photographic History of the Civil War." Copyright by Patriot Publishing Company

THE ARMY OF THE POTOMAC IN CAMP

were finding excuses to leave the army for "vacations." The attempts to draft new recruits into the army were met with serious resistance in many states. In New York City the draft riots of July, 1863, resulted in the destruction of $1,500,000 worth of property and the loss of 1000 lives. The cost of the war was enormous; the debt was increasing at the rate of $2,500,000 a day. The Secretary of the Treasury was having difficulty in borrowing enough money to keep the army in the field. A widespread conviction that Lincoln's administration was a failure was shown by the triumph of the Democrats, in the elections of 1862, in such important states as New York, New Jersey, Pennsylvania, Ohio, Indiana, Illinois, and Wisconsin. Clement Vallandigham of Ohio declared in a speech in the House early in the year 1863: "You have not conquered the South. You never will. . . . Money you have expended without limit, and blood poured out like water. . . . Defeat, debt, taxation, and sepulchers,—these are your only trophies."[1] But the darkest hour is the hour before the dawn. In June, 1863, the Southern hopes were high. In the West the great fortress of Vicksburg, which Grant and Sherman had been manœuvering against for months, still blockaded the lower Mississippi to the Union fleets; and in the East, General Lee, at the height of his power and popularity, was crossing the Potomac northward with a magnificent army of 75,000 veterans. But on the fourth of July, Lee was leading his defeated army back to the Potomac after the tremendous fight at Gettysburg, while General Grant was entering Vicksburg in triumph.

506. The Battle of Gettysburg. The battle of Gettysburg (July 1–3, 1863) was the most important battle of the war and the only one fought on the free soil of the North.[2] Knowing the widespread discouragement in the Northern states and the dissatisfaction in many quarters with Lincoln's conduct of the war, Lee hoped that a brilliant stroke as near New York as he could get might terrify the Northern bankers and lead them to compel the administration to stop the war for lack of funds and recognize the Southern Confederacy. General George G. Meade, who had just succeeded Hooker (June 27) in the command of the Army of the Potomac, met Lee's attack with a fine army of over 80,000 men securely posted on the heights of Round Top and Cemetery Ridge, south of the town of Gettysburg. The first and second days' fighting (July 1, 2) was favorable to the Confederates, but reënforcements kept pouring in for the Army of the Potomac, and, in spite of heavy losses, the Federal position was being strengthened from hour to hour. At the beginning of the third day of the fight General Meade had over 90,000 men posted on the heights above and around Gettysburg.

---

[1] Vallandigham was afterwards arrested by General Burnside and court-martialed for treason. Lincoln, as a grim sort of joke, made his punishment exile into the lines of the Confederacy. Edward Everett Hale's famous story "The Man without a Country," appearing in the *Atlantic Monthly* for December, 1863, was written to show the sad failure of such unpatriotic conduct as Vallandigham's.

[2] There were several "raids" into Northern territory—in Ohio, Indiana, and Pennsylvania—by the renowned "irregular" cavalry rangers of Morgan, Mosby, and Stuart. But these raids succeeded only in terrorizing a few villages and plundering such booty as the flying horsemen could take with them. They were a foolish, unproductive kind of warfare.

507. Pickett's Charge. Lee, fagged with his immense labors and desperate in his demand for victory, now failed for once in generalship. Disregarding the almost tearful remonstrances of General Longstreet, he sent General Pickett with 15,000 men, the flower of the Confederate infantry, to carry by storm the impregnable position of the Union troops, under General W. S. Hancock, on Cemetery Ridge. It was the most dramatic moment of the war, as Pickett's splendid division, in perfect order, swept across the wide plain which separated the two armies and dashed up the opposite slope in the face of the withering fire of the Union guns. The men went down like grain before a hailstorm, but still there was no pause. A hundred led by Armistead pierced the Union line and planted the flag of the Confederacy on the ridge — the "high-water mark of the Rebellion." But no human bravery could stand against the blasting wall of fire that closed in upon Pickett's gallant men. The line wavered, then stopped, then bent slowly backward, and broke. The day, the battle, and the Southern cause were lost!

ROBERT E. LEE

508. The Fall of Vicksburg. The next day, the "glorious fourth" of July, at evening, while the North was celebrating the great victory of Gettysburg, General Lee began his slow retreat to the Potomac through a heavy, dismal storm of rain. Lee's grief and chagrin would have been doubled had he known that, on that same dismal fourth of July, General Pemberton, after a valiant defense of six months against the superior strategy and numbers of Grant and Sherman, had surrendered the stronghold of Vicksburg, with 170 cannon and 50,000 rifles, and had delivered over his starving garrison of 30,000 men as prisoners of war.[1] Five days after the fall of Vicksburg, Port Hudson yielded, and the Mississippi was again a Union stream from source to mouth. "The Father of Waters," wrote Lincoln exultantly, "goes again unvexed to the sea."

The Triumph of the North

509. The Turning Point of the War. The victories at Gettysburg and Vicksburg were the turning point of the war. Not that the South as yet acknowledged defeat or even distress. On the contrary, the tone of her press and the utterances of her public men were more confident than ever. Newspapers in Richmond and Charleston actually hailed Gettysburg as a Confederate victory, presumably because Lee had been allowed to withdraw his shattered army across the Potomac without molestation.[2] But to men who did not let their zeal blind them to facts the disasters which overtook the Confederacy at Gettysburg and Vicksburg appeared to be almost beyond repair. It was not alone the loss of 60,000 soldiers from armies in which every man was sorely needed that made those midsummer days of 1863 so calamitous to the South. It was even more the change which they brought in the public sentiment of the North, in the attitude of Great Britain toward the Confederacy, and in the plan of campaign of the Union commanders.

510. Financial Condition of the North. In the North the bankers, whose cash vaults Lee hoped to close tightly by his invasion of Pennsylvania, now lent to the government freely, and private individuals bought millions of dollars' worth of the "coupon bonds"

---

[1] The siege of Vicksburg was the only protracted siege of the war. The shelling of the city by Grant's mortars was so severe that many of the people lived in underground caves, and the inhabitants and garrison were compelled to eat mules, rats, and even shoe leather to keep from starvation. Pemberton held out as long as he did in the constant hope that Johnston might break through Grant's lines and come to his relief.

[2] Lincoln was much distressed that Meade did not follow Lee up after Gettysburg and crush his army before it could get back over the Potomac. "We had them in our grasp," he said; "we had only to stretch forth our hands and they were ours." Still Meade was not relieved of his command. His army slowly followed Lee into Virginia and, after some unimportant skirmishing, went into winter quarters at Culpeper, about 75 miles northwest of Richmond.

issued to support the war. Secretary Chase had been obliged to pay 7.3 per cent interest on money loaned the government in 1861, when the public debt was less than $100,000,000; now, however, he could borrow all he wanted at 6 per cent, although the debt had risen to over $1,000,000,000. The rate of interest at which a country can borrow money is generally an index of the confidence the people have in the stability of the government. President Lincoln, in his annual message to Congress, December, 1863, could say: "All the demands on the Treasury, including the pay of the army and navy, have been promptly met and fully satisfied. . . . By no people were the burdens incident to a great war ever more cheerfully borne."

511. How the Government financed the War. The government raised about $667,000,000 by taxation during the war and borrowed $2,620,000,000 more. The taxes were both "direct" and "indirect": the former consisting of an income tax of 3 per cent on incomes under $10,000 and 5 per cent on those over $10,000; the latter consisting of greatly increased tariff duties and internal revenue taxes on almost every article of consumption except one's daily bread. The government borrowed in two ways: it issued "notes" (or certificates of indebtedness) in payment of its obligations, and it sold "bonds" (or promises to pay back the amount borrowed with interest, at the end of a term of years). Secretary Chase, early in 1863, devised a very effective method of selling these bonds, by the creation of the national-bank system. Any group of five men, furnishing a specified capital, might be granted a charter by the national government to organize a banking business, if they purchased United States bonds and deposited them at Washington. They were then allowed to issue notes ("bank bills") up to the value of 90 per cent (since 1900, up to the full value) of the bonds, and the government assumed the responsibility for paying these notes if the bank failed. The bankers, of course, besides receiving the interest from their bonds on deposit, made a profit by lending their notes (or credit) to their customers at a fair rate of interest. The national-bank system was a benefit to all parties concerned. It enabled the government to sell its bonds readily; it gave the banking capitalists of the country a chance to make a profit on their loans; and it gave the borrowing public a currency which was "protected" by the government, whether the bank issuing it succeeded or failed. There were in 1917 over 7600 national banks in the United States, with an aggregate capital of over $1,000,000,000. These national banks are not to be confused with the National Bank of 1791-1811, 1816-1836. They are private institutions and enjoy none of the government's favors such as are described on page 161. They are called "national" simply because they are chartered and inspected by the national government.

512. Change of Sentiment in England. In England, though the *Trent* affair had been satisfactorily adjusted, the sympathy of the higher classes of society and of most of the government officials was decidedly in favor of the South. The long series of Federal reverses in 1862 had strengthened their belief that President Lincoln's government would fail to restore the Union. Men in high positions in the British government openly expressed their confidence in the Southern cause. Mr. Gladstone, then a cabinet minister, said in a speech at Newcastle, October 7, 1862: "There is no doubt that Jefferson Davis and other leaders of the South have made an army; they are making, it appears, a navy; and they have made what is more than either,—a nation. . . . We may anticipate with certainty the success of the Southern states so far as their separation from the North is concerned." British capitalists bought $10,000,000 worth of Confederate bonds offered them at the beginning of 1863, when the Southern cause looked brightest. The fall of Vicksburg sent the bonds down 20 per cent in value. The British people woke with a shock from their dream of an "invincible South," and all hope of aid from Great Britain, as President Davis sorrowfully acknowledged in his next message to the Confederate Congress, was lost.[1]

513. No Union Plan of Campaign before Gettysburg. The effect of the victories at Gettysburg and Vicksburg on the conduct of the war was also important. Up to the middle of the year 1863

---

[1] While Mason was trying to get help in England for the Confederacy, Slidell was busy on the same errand in France. At a meeting with Emperor Napoleon III, in July, 1862, Slidell made the offer of 100,000 bales of cotton (worth $12,500,000) if Napoleon would send a fleet to break the blockade of the Southern ports. Napoleon made efforts to get Great Britain and Russia to join him in demanding from the administration at Washington the independence of the South, but with no success. After Gettysburg all such efforts were stopped.

there had been no coöperation between the Union armies. The Army of the Potomac, in Virginia, had been battling in vain to break through Lee's defense of Richmond. The army on the Mississippi had been slowly accomplishing its great task of opening the river. Meanwhile a third army under Buell (succeeded later by Rosecrans) had with difficulty been defending central Kentucky and Tennessee from the advance of the Confederate general Braxton Bragg.

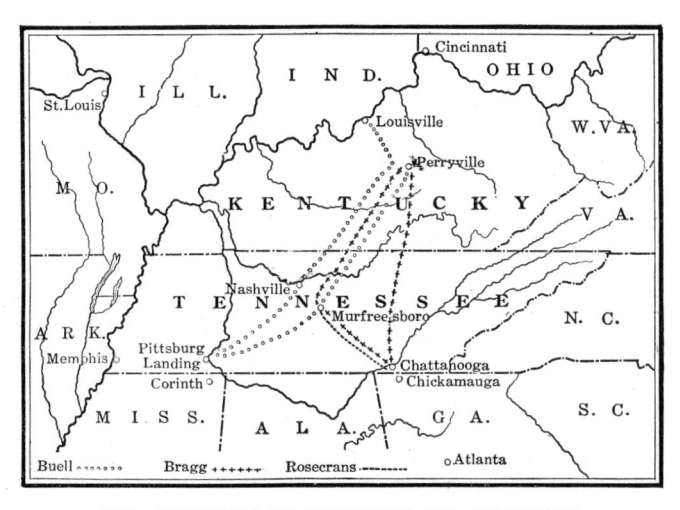

THE CAMPAIGNS IN KENTUCKY AND TENNESSEE

514. Bragg driven from Kentucky. Simultaneously with Lee's invasion of Maryland in September, 1862, Bragg had invaded Kentucky, appealing to the proslavery and states-rights sentiment in the state with the confident manifesto, "Kentuckians, I offer you the opportunity to free yourselves from the tyranny of a despotic ruler." Bragg brought 15,000 stands of arms for the Kentuckians, but they did not join his army. Buell turned him back from Kentucky in the battle of Perryville (October 8, 1862), and Rosecrans, after a tremendous three days' fight at Murfreesboro, Tennessee (December 31–January 2), compelled him to retire to Chattanooga.[1]

[1] The acquisition of eastern Tennessee was especially desired by Lincoln, on account of the great number of Union men in that part of the state. We have already seen how, after Grant's victories at Forts Henry and Donelson, Lincoln had appointed Andrew Johnson as military governor of Tennessee (p. 352, note 2).

515. The "Anaconda Policy." The fall of Vicksburg left the troops of Grant and Sherman free to move eastward across Mississippi and Alabama, driving Johnston's inferior forces before them, and to join with Rosecrans at Chattanooga and push the Confederate armies across the lower end of the Appalachian range into Georgia. While this great flanking movement was going on from the West, the Army of the Potomac was to press down on Lee from northern Virginia. So the forces of the Confederacy would be crushed between the two great Union armies in Virginia and Georgia. This plan of wrapping the Union armies about the Confederacy and squeezing the life out of it was called the "anaconda policy." It was in view of this coöperation of all the Union forces in 1863 that General Sherman later wrote, "The war did not begin professionally until after Gettysburg and Vicksburg."

516. The Battle of Chickamauga. Next to Richmond and Vicksburg the most important military position in the Confederacy was Chattanooga. This city, protected by the deep and wide Tennessee River on the north and the high ridges of the Appalachian Mountains on the south, guarded the passes into the rich state of Georgia, the "keystone of the Confederacy." Rosecrans, as we have seen, confronted Bragg at Chattanooga in the autumn of 1863. Bragg retired before his opponent across the Tennessee River into the mountains of the northeastern corner of Georgia, then suddenly turned on him at Chickamauga Creek, where Rosecrans had hastily concentrated his forces. The battle of Chickamauga, which followed Rosecrans's frantic effort to get his army together (September 19–20, 1863), would have been as complete a disaster for the Union cause as Bull Run, had it not been for the intrepid conduct of one man, General George H. Thomas. Rosecrans had given a blundering order which left a wide gap in the Union lines. Into this gap the Confederate regiments poured, driving the entire right wing of Rosecrans's army off the field in a panic and sweeping Rosecrans with his men back to Chattanooga, where he telegraphed Halleck that his army was "overwhelmed by the enemy." But General Thomas on the left, with only 25,000 men, refused to leave the field. Forming his men into a convex front like a horseshoe, he stood firm against the furious onslaught of 60,000 Confederate troops, from half past three in the afternoon till the deep twilight four hours later. It was the most magnificent defensive fighting of the war. It almost turned defeat into victory. It earned for General Thomas the proud title of the "Rock of Chickamauga" and justified his promotion by Grant to the command of the Army of the Cumberland in place of Rosecrans. After his dearly bought victory at Chickamauga, General Bragg proceeded to lay siege to Chattanooga.

517. The Fighting around Chattanooga. General Grant, who had been put in command of the armies of the West as a reward for his capture of Vicksburg, now dispatched the Army of the Tennessee (as the Vicksburg army was henceforth called), under General Sherman, to join Thomas at Chattanooga and, by the middle of November, was ready with the combined armies to begin operations against Bragg and Johnston. The three days' battle around Chattanooga (November 23-25) was a fitting climax to Grant's splendid achievements of the year 1863. The enthusiasm his presence inspired in the Union army was unbounded. On the twenty-fourth of November Hooker seized the top of Lookout Mountain in the "Battle above the Clouds." On the twenty-fifth General Thomas's troops were ordered to seize the Confederate rifle pits at the foot of Missionary Ridge. They seized the pits and then, without waiting for further orders, stormed up the steep and crumbling sides of the mountain in the face of a deadly fire from thirty cannon trained on every path and drove the astounded Bragg, with his staff and his choicest infantry, from the crest of the hill.[1] The

GENERAL PHILIP H. SHERIDAN

[1] This impetuous charge of 20,000 Union troops up the sides of Missionary Ridge was as dramatic and courageous as the famous charge of Pickett's division at Gettysburg. The leader of the charge was "Phil" Sheridan, a young Irish general who had distinguished himself for bravery in the battles of Perryville and Murfreesboro and who later became the most famous cavalry commander in the Union army. The battle of Chattanooga was the only one of the war in which the four greatest Union generals — Grant, Sherman, Sheridan, and Thomas — took part.

Confederate general withdrew southward into Georgia with his army of 35,000 men, burning his depots and bridges behind him.

518. Grant raised to the Command of the Army. On the first day of the session of Congress, which assembled a fortnight after the battle of Chattanooga, Representative Washburne of Illinois introduced a bill to revive the rank of lieutenant general, which had not been held by any general in the field since George Washington. Everybody knew that the new honor was intended for General Grant. The bill was passed February 29, 1864, and immediately Grant was summoned to Washington by the President and in the presence of the cabinet and a few invited guests was formally invested with the rank of lieutenant general and the command, under the President, of all the armies of the United States (March 9, 1864). Grant made his dear friend and companion in arms, General William T. Sherman, his successor in the command of the armies of the West, while he established his own headquarters with the Army of the Potomac.

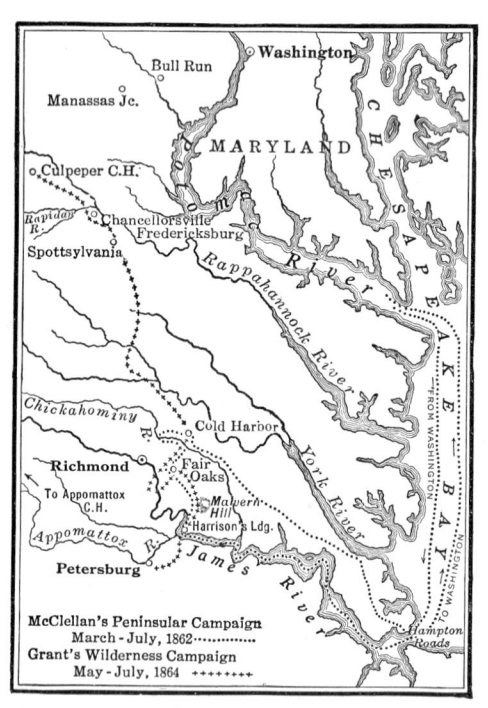

SEAT OF WAR IN EASTERN VIRGINIA 1861-1865

519. Plans of Grant and Sherman, 1864. The plan of campaign was now very simple. Sherman, with the armies of the Ohio (General Schofield), the Cumberland (General Thomas), and the Tennessee (General McPherson), 100,000 strong, was to advance from

Chattanooga to Atlanta against Joseph E. Johnston, who had succeeded Bragg. Grant, with the Army of the Potomac (General Meade still nominally in command), was to resume the campaign against Richmond, in which McClellan, Pope, Burnside, and Hooker had all failed. Both Grant and Sherman greatly outnumbered their opponents, Lee and Johnston: but the advantage was not so overwhelming as the size of their armies would indicate, for Sherman was to move through a hostile country, with his base of supplies at Louisville, Kentucky, hundreds of miles away, and leaving an ever-lengthening line of posts to be guarded in his rear; while Grant was assuming the offensive on soil which he had never trodden before, but every inch of which was familiar to Lee's veterans of the Army of Northern Virginia.

520. The Wilderness Campaign. On the fourth of May, 1864, Grant's army crossed the Rapidan and began to fight its way through the Wilderness, where Hooker had been defeated in the battle of Chancellorsville just a year earlier. Though his losses were heavy (17,500 men in the Wilderness fights), Grant turned his face steadily toward Richmond. "I propose to fight it out on this line," he wrote Halleck, "if it takes all summer."[1] At Cold Harbor (June 3) he attacked Lee's strongly fortified position in front and lost 7000 men in an hour, in an assault almost as rash as Burnside's at Fredericksburg.[2] After this awful battle, Grant led the Army of the Potomac down to the James River to renew the attack on Richmond from the south. In the Wilderness campaign of forty days, from the Rapidan to the James, Grant had lost 55,000 men (almost as many

---

[1] His men were with him, too, keyed to the highest pitch of enthusiasm. The writer has heard from the lips of one of the members of Company A of the Twelfth Massachusetts regiment the thrilling story of the resumption of the march southward after the terrible losses in the Wilderness. The orders to move came one stormy evening, just as the heavy clouds were parting, and the soldiers were uncertain whether the column was headed northward in retreat or southward for Richmond. As they came out upon an open road and were greeted by the stars, the shout came from the head of the column, "Boys, we are leaving the North Star behind us!" "I have heard the army cheer after victory," said the veteran, "but I have never heard cheering like that which swept down the marching column then."

[2] Horace Porter, an aid-de-camp of General Grant, tells in the *Century Magazine* for March, 1897, how the Union soldiers were seen the night before the terrible assault at Cold Harbor quietly pinning on the backs of their coats slips of paper with their name and address, so that their bodies might be taken back to their families in the North. Grant himself confesses in his "Memoirs," written nearly twenty years after the battle, that "no advantage whatever was gained to compensate for the heavy loss which we sustained." The attack at Cold Harbor was a serious mistake on Grant's part.

as Lee had in his entire army), but he had at least shown Lee the novel sight of a Union commander who did not retreat when he was repulsed or rest when he was victorious.

521. Sherman takes Atlanta. Sherman left Chattanooga two days after Grant crossed the Rapidan (May 6). Mile by mile he forced Johnston back until by the middle of July he was in sight of Atlanta. Jefferson Davis replaced Johnston by Hood, but

From the "Photographic History of the Civil War." Copyright by Patriot Publishing Company
THE CONFEDERATE TRENCHES BEFORE ATLANTA

it was of no avail. Sherman beat Hood in several engagements before Atlanta and entered the city on the third of September, 1864.

522. The Presidential Campaign of 1864. While Grant was fighting his way through the Wilderness, and Sherman was slowly advancing on Atlanta, the national conventions met to nominate candidates for the presidential election of 1864. Secretary Chase was ambitious for the Republican nomination. When a circular recommending his candidacy appeared in the press, he confessed his ambition to Lincoln, who generously refused to consider it a reason for removing Chase from the head of the Treasury Department.

Chase was a very able man,—"about one and a half times bigger than any other man I've known," Lincoln said once,—but he was also very pompous and conceited and needed little persuasion to believe that he was indispensable to the country's salvation. His surprise and chagrin were, therefore, great when his canvass fell flat. He withdrew in February, and on June 8 Lincoln was nominated by the convention at Baltimore.[1] The Democrats met at

ADMIRAL FARRAGUT ATTACKING THE FORTS IN MOBILE HARBOR

Chicago (August 29) and nominated General McClellan, recommending in their platform that "after four years of failure to restore the Union by the experiment of war . . . immediate efforts be made for the cessation of hostilities . . . and peace be restored on the basis of the federal union of the states."[2]

[1] Chase harbored some ill will toward the administration and on June 29 resigned his secretaryship rather petulantly. Lincoln accepted the resignation, but showed his utter magnanimity by nominating Chase to the position of Chief Justice of the Supreme Court (December 6, 1864), made vacant by the death of the aged Roger B. Taney. This gracious act drew from Chase a beautiful letter of gratitude.

[2] It is only fair to say that McClellan did not consent to the platform which declared the war a "failure." Nevertheless it is little credit to him, who was once in command of the United States armies and supported by Lincoln to the utmost of the President's ability, to be now associated with a party that was trying to discredit the war and "push Lincoln from his throne."

523. The Reëlection of Lincoln. All through the summer of 1864 there was doubt and discouragement in the Republican ranks. Grant's Wilderness campaign brought no comfort to the administration. Lincoln himself at one period had no hope of being reëlected. But the autumn brought changes in the Unionist fortunes. In August, Admiral Farragut sailed into the harbor of Mobile, Alabama, by an exploit as daring as the running of the New Orleans forts, and deprived the Confederacy of its last stronghold on the Gulf of Mexico. In September, Sherman entered Atlanta after a four months' campaign against Johnston and Hood. And in October, Sheridan, by his wonderful ride up the Shenandoah valley, "from Winchester twenty miles away," literally turned defeat into victory and saved Washington from the raid of General Early's forces. These Union victories were the most powerful campaign arguments for the Republican cause. "Sherman and Farragut," cried Seward, "have knocked the bottom out of the Chicago platform." Lincoln was reëlected in November by an electoral vote of 212 to 21 and a popular majority of nearly 500,000. The election meant the indorsement by the people of the North of Lincoln's policy of continuing the war until the South recognized the supremacy throughout the United States of the national government at Washington.

GENERAL WILLIAM T. SHERMAN

524. Sherman's March to the Sea. When Atlanta fell, Hood, thinking to draw Sherman back from further invasion of Georgia, and at the same time to regain Tennessee, made a dash northward against Thomas, who had been left to protect Nashville and Chattanooga. Sherman trusted the reliable Thomas to take care of Tennessee and, boldly severing all connection with his base of supplies, started on his famous march "from Atlanta to the sea," 300 miles across the state of Georgia. He met with no resistance. The march through Georgia was more like a continuous picnic of three months for his 60,000 troops than like a campaign. They lived on the fat

SHERMAN'S ARMY DESTROYING THE RAILROADS IN GEORGIA

After an engraving by Darley

of the land,— the newly gathered harvests of corn and grain, abundance of chickens, turkeys, ducks, pigs, and sweet potatoes. Sherman entered on the march with a grim determination to make the state of Georgia "an example to rebels," and he carried out his threat. Railroads were torn up, public buildings, depots, and machine shops burned, stores of cotton destroyed, 10,000 mules and horses taken, and the military resources of the state damaged beyond repair.[1] Reaching the coast in December, Sherman easily broke through the weak defenses of Savannah, and on Christmas evening President Lincoln read a telegram from him announcing "as a Christmas gift the city of Savannah, with 150 heavy guns, plenty of ammunition, and about 25,000 bales of cotton."

525. Thomas's Victory at Nashville. Meanwhile the complete success of Sherman's campaign was insured by the failure of Hood's plan to dislodge Thomas from Nashville. For had Hood retaken Tennessee and driven Thomas back into Kentucky, he might have turned eastward rapidly and, summoning the Carolinas to his banners, have confronted Sherman with a most formidable army barring his march north from Savannah. But Thomas was equal to the occasion. On the fifteenth of December, before Nashville, he almost annihilated Hood's army and drove the remnants out of Tennessee. The battle of Nashville was the deathblow of the Confederacy west of the Alleghenies. Virginia and the Carolinas alone were left to be subdued.

526. The Hampton Roads Conference. Before the campaign of 1865 opened, there was an attempt to close the war by diplomacy. Vice President Stephens of the Confederacy, with two other commissioners, met Lincoln and Seward on board a United States vessel, at Hampton Roads (February 3) to discuss terms of peace. But as Lincoln would listen to no terms whatever except on the basis of a reunited country, the conference came to naught.

---

[1] Sherman has been execrated by Southern writers for the "barbarity" of his soldiers during this march through Georgia; and it is certain that much irregular plundering and thieving were done, such as taking jewelry from women, burning private houses, and wantonly insulting the feelings of the inhabitants. Sherman's chief of cavalry, Kilpatrick, was a coarse and brutal man, who was responsible for much of the damage. Then a crowd of "bummers" followed the army, out of the reach of Sherman's officers. Although Sherman was severe in this march, it must be said to his credit that he gave orders to have private property respected, and there is no complaint of his soldiers' treating defenseless women as the armies of European conquerors were accustomed to do.

527. The Fall of Richmond. In March, 1865, the Army of the Potomac renewed its operations against Richmond. The stronghold of Petersburg, to the south of the city, fell on Sunday, April 2. Jefferson Davis was at worship in St. Paul's church in Richmond when news was brought to his pew, by a messenger from the War Department, that the city could no longer be held. Hastily collecting his papers, he left Richmond for Danville at eleven o'clock the same night, with his cabinet and several of his staff officers. On the third of April the Union troops entered the city, followed the next day by President Lincoln, who spoke only words of conciliation and kindness in "the enemy's capital." Lee, with his dwindling army, moved westward toward the mountains, but Grant followed him hard, while Sheridan's cavalry encircled his forces. On the seventh of April, the Union commander wrote to Lee: "General — The result of the last week must convince you of the hopelessness of further resistance on the part of the Army of Northern Virginia." Brought to a standstill, Lee consented to listen to Grant's terms for surrender.

528. Lee's Surrender at Appomattox. The two great generals met in a farmhouse at Appomattox, on the ninth of April, 1865. After a few minutes of courteous conversation recalling the days of their old comradeship in arms in the Mexican War, Grant wrote out the terms of surrender. They were generous, as befitted the reconciliation of brother Americans. The Army of Northern Virginia was to lay down its arms, but the officers were to retain their horses and side arms, and even the cavalrymen and artillerymen were to be allowed to keep their horses. "They will need them for the spring plowing," said Grant, with his wonderful simplicity. Lee accepted the terms with sorrowing gratitude and surrendered his army of 26,765 men.[1] When the Union soldiers heard the good news they began to fire salutes, but Grant stopped them, saying, "The war is over; the rebels are our countrymen again." Lee had hinted that his men were hungry, and Grant immediately ordered the distribution of 25,000 rations to the Confederate army.

---

[1] As Lee rode back to his army after the conference with Grant, the soldiers crowded around him, blessing him. Tears came to his eyes as he made his farewell address of three brief sentences: "We have fought through the war together. I have done the best I could for you. My heart is too full to say more." At the close of the war this noble and heroic man accepted the presidency of Washington College in Virginia, which he served with devotion for the five years of life that remained to him.

7 - Apl /65

Genl

I have rec'd your note of this date. Though not entertaining the opinion you express of the hopelessness of further resistance on the part of the Army of N. Va. I reciprocate your desire to avoid useless effusion of blood, & therefore before considering your proposition ask the terms you will offer on condition of its surrender

Very respt your Obt Srvt
R E Lee
Genl

Lt Genl U. S. Grant
Comd'g Armies of the U. States

LEE'S LETTER TO GRANT RESPECTING THE SURRENDER OF THE CONFEDERATE ARMY OF NORTHERN VIRGINIA

529. The Collapse of the Confederacy. With the fall of Richmond and the surrender of Lee's army the Confederacy collapsed.[1] It is a marvel that it fought through the last year of the war. For the South was brought to the point of actual destitution. The paper money which the Confederacy issued had depreciated so much that it took $1000 to buy a barrel of flour and $30 to buy a pound of tea. Its credit was dead in Europe and its bonds were worthless. When the blockade of their ports stopped the export of cotton, the Southerners planted their fields with corn and grain. But the lack of means of transportation made it almost impossible to distribute the products of the farms to the soldiers at the front. While Sherman's army was reveling in the abundance of the farms and harvests of central Georgia, the knapsacks found on the poor fellows who fell in the defense of Richmond contained only scanty rations of corn bread and bacon. The women of the South, accustomed to handsome dress and dainty fare, wore homespun gowns and cheap rough boots and cheerfully ate porridge and drank "coffee" made of roasted sweet potatoes. They knew no hardships but the failure of fathers and brothers and sons in battle; they were visited by no calamities except the presence of the "Yankee" soldier. It is impossible for

THE HOUSE IN WHICH ABRAHAM LINCOLN DIED

Now used as a Lincoln Museum

---

[1] Joseph E. Johnston surrendered his army of 37,000 men to Sherman near Durham, North Carolina, on April 26; Generals Taylor in Alabama and Kirby Smith in Arkansas turned over the armies under their command to the Union officers in the South and Southwest. In all 174,000 Confederate soldiers laid down their arms at the close of the war. Jefferson Davis was captured on May 10 at Irwinville, Georgia, and imprisoned two years at Fortress Monroe. After his release he lived quietly in the South till his death, December 6, 1889.

the student of history today to feel otherwise than that the victory of the South in 1861-1865 would have been a calamity for every section of our country. But the indomitable valor and utter self-sacrifice with which the South defended her cause both at home and in the field must always arouse our admiration.

Friday, the fourteenth of April, 1865, was a memorable day in our history. It was the fourth anniversary of the surrender of Fort Sumter. A great celebration was held at Charleston, and General Robert Anderson raised above the fort the selfsame tattered flag which he had hauled down after Beauregard's bombardment in 1861. William Lloyd Garrison was present. Flowers were strewn in his path by the liberated slaves. He spoke at the banquet held that evening in Charleston, and the echoes of his voice reached a grave over which stood a marble stone engraved with the single word "Calhoun."

530. The Assassination of President Lincoln. On the evening of the same day President Lincoln was sitting in a box at Ford's theater in Washington, with his wife and two guests, when a miserable, half-crazy actor named Wilkes Booth stepped into the box and shot the President in the back of the head.[1] Lincoln was carried unconscious to a private house across the street and medical aid was summoned. But the precious life, the most precious of the land and of the century, was ebbing fast. Early in the morning of the fifteenth of April, surrounded by his prostrated family and official friends, Abraham Lincoln died. He had brought the storm-tossed ship of state safely into port. The exultant shores were ringing with the people's shouts of praise and rejoicing. But in the hour of victory the great Captain lay upon the deck—"fallen cold and dead."[2]

Words have no power to tell the worth of Abraham Lincoln. His name, linked with the immortal Washington's, is forever enshrined in the hearts of the American people, for he was the savior of our country as Washington was its founder and father.

---

[1] The assassination of Lincoln was part of a deep-laid plot to kill several of the high officers of the Union. Secretary Seward, who was abed suffering from injuries received in a runaway accident, was stabbed severely the same night, and his son Frederick was injured while defending his father's life. Both men recovered. Grant was proscribed also, but the assassin lost courage apparently after gazing into the general's carriage window. The wretch Booth fell to the stage in trying to escape, and broke his leg. He was soon caught in a barn in Virginia and was shot after the barn had been set on fire.

[2] Every student should learn by heart Walt Whitman's superb elegy on Lincoln, "O Captain! my Captain!" See Muzzey's "Readings in American History," p. 445.

> Our children shall behold his fame,
> The kindly-earnest, brave, foreseeing man,
> Sagacious, patient, dreading praise, not blame,
> New birth of our new soil, the first American.[1]

Stanton, the great Secretary of War, pronounced Abraham Lincoln's best eulogy, when he stood with streaming eyes by the bedside of the martyred President and murmured with choking voice, "Now he belongs to the ages."

EMANCIPATION

531. The Purpose of the War. Although slavery was the cause of the Civil War, both the North and the South insisted that the war was not begun on account of slavery. The South declared that it was fighting for its constitutional rights, denied by a hostile majority in Congress and destroyed by the election of a purely sectional president; while the North, with equal emphasis, insisted that it took up arms not to free the slaves but to preserve the Union. Lincoln thought slavery a great moral, social, and political evil, and never hesitated to say so; but he repeatedly declared that neither the president nor Congress had any right to interfere with slavery in those states where it was established by law, and assured the South that he would not attack their institution so long as it was confined to those states. The day after the disaster at Bull Run (July 21, 1861), both branches of Congress passed a resolution to the effect that "this war is not waged . . . in any spirit of oppression, or for any purpose of conquest or subjugation, or of overthrowing or interfering with the rights or established institutions of those [seceding] states, but to defend and maintain the supremacy of the Constitution."

532. Slaves treated as "Contraband." It soon became evident that the slaves were a valuable war asset to the South, and Congress began to treat them as "property" which could be confiscated. In a series of acts beginning in August, 1861, Congress declared that all negroes employed in a military capacity by the South, as workers on forts or trenches or in the transportation of stores or ammunition, should be liberated; that slaves of "rebel"

---

[1] James Russell Lowell's "Commemoration Ode," read at the memorial services for Harvard men who fell in the war (July 21, 1865).

owners escaping to the Union lines should not be returned; and that all slaves in places conquered and held by the Union armies should be free. Two generals in the field went even further than Congress. Frémont in Missouri and Hunter in South Carolina, on their own responsibility, issued military proclamations emancipating slaves in the districts subject to their authority.

533. Lincoln's Views on Emancipation. President Lincoln signed the Confiscation Acts of Congress with reluctance and immediately disavowed and annulled the proclamations of Frémont and Hunter, to the great disappointment of thousands of radical antislavery men of the North. To preserve and cherish the Union sentiment in the loyal slaveholding states of Kentucky, Missouri, and Maryland seemed to him the most immediate duty of his administration. If he could get these border states to lead the way in the peaceful emancipation of their slaves, he was in hopes that their example would prevail with the states in secession further south. At any rate, he was sure that any hasty measures for negro emancipation, either by Congress or by the military authorities, would drive these border slave states into the Confederacy and make more difficult the task of preserving the Union. Accordingly the President, in a special message to Congress, March 6, 1862, recommended that a law be passed pledging the United States government to *coöperate* with any state in the emancipation of its slaves by compensating the owners of the slaves for their loss. He invited the congressmen of the border states to a conference and urged them to contribute their valuable aid toward preserving the Union by the acceptance of this plan of "compensated emancipation." But they hung back, doubting the power or the will of the government to deal fairly with them. Lincoln got little support, either from his cabinet or from Congress, in spite of repeated efforts, and he sorrowfully gave up the realization of this wise and humane policy of emancipation (July, 1862).[1]

---

[1] It is doubtful in the extreme if the adoption of Lincoln's plan by the border states would have had any effect on the seceding states or shortened the war a day. The failure of the plan, however, was about the keenest political disappointment in Lincoln's life. The slaves in the four border states of Delaware, Maryland, Kentucky, and Missouri numbered 430,000, and at $400 apiece their emancipation would have cost the government about $175,000,000, or the cost of eighty-seven days of war. Lincoln had no doubt that the emancipation of these slaves would shorten the war by more than eighty-seven days, but one sees no ground for such confidence.

534. Slavery abolished in the Territories. Meanwhile Congress had passed an act in April abolishing slavery in the District of Columbia, with a compensation to the owner of $300 for each slave liberated; and two months later fulfilled the pledges of the platform on which Lincoln was elected, by prohibiting slavery in all the territories of the United States and in all territory which might be acquired by the United States in the future (June 19, 1862).

535. Pressure exerted on Lincoln to free the Slaves. After the failure of the border states to accept the compensated-emancipation scheme, the President grew more favorable to the idea of military emancipation. The pressure brought to bear on him to liberate the slaves was enormous. The radical antislavery men of the North wanted to know how long the evil which had brought on the war was to be tolerated,[1] and our ministers abroad were writing home that the sympathy of Europe could not be expected by the North until it was clear that the war was for the extermination of slavery and not for the subjugation of the South. At the cabinet meeting of July 22, 1862, therefore, President Lincoln read a paper announcing his intention of declaring free, on the first of the following January, the slaves of all people then in rebellion against the authority of the United States. The members of the cabinet approved the paper, but Seward suggested that the moment was inopportune for its publication. McClellan had just been removed from his command after the futile Peninsular campaign, and the new generals, Halleck and Pope, were as yet untried in the East. Would it not be better to wait for a Union victory before publishing the proclamation? Lincoln agreed with Seward and put the paper in his desk.

536. The Emancipation Proclamation. The dark days of the second Bull Run and Pope's retreat followed (August, 1862); but when McClellan repulsed Lee's invasion of Maryland at Antietam Creek (September 16), Lincoln thought that the favorable moment had come. Accordingly he published the warning announcement,

---

[1] Horace Greeley, editor of the influential New York *Tribune*, wrote an editorial in August, 1862, which he called the Prayer of Twenty Millions, taking the President severely to task for his "mistaken deference to rebel slavery" and calling on him to execute the Confiscation Acts immediately. Lincoln replied in a famous letter, in which he declared that he was acting as seemed best to him for the preservation of the Union. That was his "paramount object." "If I could save the Union without freeing any slave, I would do it; and if I could save it by freeing all the slaves, I would do it. ... What I do about slavery and the colored race, I do because I believe it helps to save the Union."

September 22, 1862, and on New Year's Day, 1863, issued the famous Emancipation Proclamation, designating the states and parts of states in which rebellion against the authority and government of the United States then existed and declaring, by virtue of the power vested in him as commander in chief of the army and navy of the United States, that "all persons held as slaves within said

> And by virtue of the power and for the purpose aforesaid, I do order and declare that all persons held as slaves within said designated States, and parts of States, are, and henceforward shall be free;
>
> And upon this act, sincerely believed to be an act of justice, warranted by the Constitution upon military necessity, I invoke the considerate judgment of mankind, and the gracious favor of Almighty God.
>
> (L.S.) Independence of the United States of America the eighty-seventh.
>
> Abraham Lincoln

FACSIMILE OF THE CLOSING WORDS OF THE EMANCIPATION PROCLAMATION

designated States, and parts of States, are, and henceforward shall be free." This immortal proclamation is one of the landmarks of universal history. It announced the liberation of three and a half million slaves. It changed the status of nearly one eighth of the inhabitants of this country from that of chattels who could be bought and sold in the auction market to that of men and women endowed with the right to "life, liberty, and the pursuit of happiness"—the right to labor, like other human beings, for employers whom they chose and under terms to which they agreed.

537. The Proclamation a War Measure. But splendid as this proclamation was, it was nevertheless only a *war measure*. While the President as commander in chief of the army could confiscate the "property" of men in rebellion against the government, by declaring their slaves free, neither he nor Congress could permanently alter the constitutions of the states. Slavery was legally established in the states south of Mason and Dixon's line, and the only way it could be permanently abolished in those states was either by the

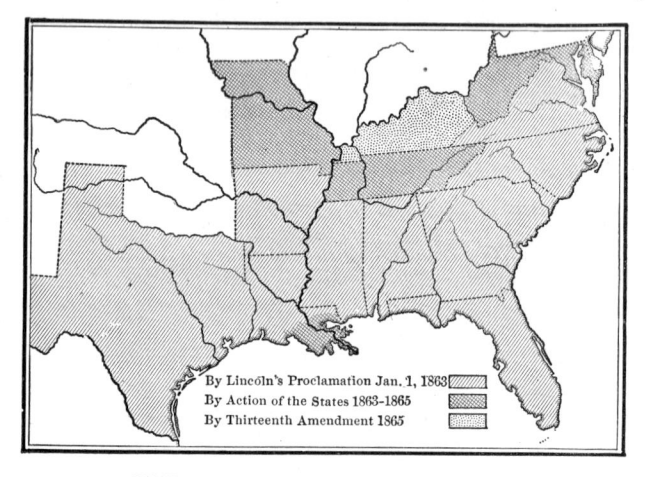

HOW THE SLAVES WERE EMANCIPATED

action of the states themselves or by an amendment to the Constitution of the United States. Lincoln's proclamation did not free a single slave in the *loyal* slaveholding states of Kentucky, Missouri, Maryland, and Delaware. And when the seceded states should cease to be "in rebellion against the authority of the United States," there was nothing to hinder their legislatures from passing laws to re-enslave the negroes. In order to have emancipation permanent, then, the Constitution must be amended so as to prohibit slavery in the whole of the United States.

538. The Thirteenth Amendment. An amendment providing that "neither slavery nor involuntary servitude, except as a punishment for crime, whereof the party shall have been duly convicted, shall exist within the United States or any place subject to their

THE CIVIL WAR

jurisdiction,"[1] was passed through Congress on January 31, 1865, by the necessary two-thirds vote, amid great enthusiasm, and the House adjourned "in honor of the immortal and sublime event." The amendment was duly ratified by three fourths of the states, including eight of the states of the late Confederacy, and on December 18, 1865, was proclaimed part of the Constitution of the United States, the supreme law of the land. Whether slavery could have been removed from our land without war is a question no one can answer. Certain it is that before the war, in spite of political compromises of forty years, in spite of the labors of the greatest statesmen and orators to preserve concord between the North and the South, in spite of the mobs that assaulted the abolitionists in Boston and the voices that rebuked the "fire eaters" in Charleston, the argument over slavery grew more and more bitter each year. When we consider that the thirteenth amendment to our Constitution might have been the prohibition of Congress ever to disturb slavery in the Southern states,[2] instead of the eternal banishment of slavery from our land, we may say that the awful sacrifices of the Civil War were not made in vain.

References

The Opposing Forces: J. K. HOSMER, *The Appeal to Arms* (American Nation Series), chaps. i–iii; T. A. DODGE, *A Bird's-eye View of the Civil War*, chaps. ii, xxv; J. C. ROPES, *Story of the Civil War*, Vol. I, chaps. vii, viii; W. E. DODD, *The Cotton Kingdom* (Chronicles, Vol. XXVII); F. L. PAXSON, *The Civil War*, chap iv; A. B. HART, *American History told by Contemporaries*, Vol. IV, Nos. 75–83; J. W. DRAPER, *The Civil War in America*, Vol. II, chaps. xxxvii–xxxix; JEFFERSON DAVIS, *Rise and Fall of the Confederacy*, Vol. I, part iv, chaps. i–iv.

From Bull Run to Gettysburg: HOSMER, chaps. iv–xiii, xv–xix; DODGE, chaps. iv–xxvi; ROPES, Vol. I, chaps. ix–xii; Vol. II, chaps. i–vii; DRAPER,

---

[1] Of course the exception in the middle of the amendment refers to the labor of convicts in prisons or workhouses. The amendment was violated when we acquired the Philippine Islands in 1898, for slavery existed on some of those islands, though they were "under the jurisdiction" of the United States. But it was a condition which we inherited with the Islands and which we have largely remedied since.

[2] The student will remember that Congress, in the last hope of preventing the war, actually passed an amendment, February 28, 1861, to the effect that Congress should never have "the power to abolish or interfere within any state with the domestic institutions thereof, *including that of persons held to labor or service by the laws of said state*" (see page 329, note 2). Before the amendment had a fair chance to secure ratification by the states the war had broken out.

Vol. II, chaps. xlix–lix; PAXSON, chaps. v–viii; U. S. GRANT, *Personal Memoirs*, Vol. I, chaps. xx–xxxix; J. W. BURGESS, *The Civil War and the Constitution*, Vol. I, chaps. viii–xi; Vol. II, chaps. xii–xxv; J. F. RHODES, *History of the Civil War*, chaps. i–v; NICOLAY and HAY, *Abraham Lincoln, a History*, Vols. III–VII.

The Triumph of the North: N. W. STEPHENSON, *The Day of the Confederacy* (Chronicles, Vol. XXX), chaps. v–xii; NICOLAY and HAY, Vols. VIII–X; HOSMER, chaps. i–xiii, xvii; PAXSON, chaps. ix–xii; RHODES, chaps. vi–xiv; BURGESS, Vol. II, chaps. xxvi–xxxii; DODGE, chaps. xxvii–xl; DRAPER, Vol. III; GRANT, Vol. II.

Emancipation: NICOLAY and HAY, Vol. IV, chaps. xxii, xxiv; Vol. VI, chaps. v, vi, viii, xix; Vol. X, chap. iv; HOSMER, chap. xiv; DAVIS, Vol. II, part iv, chaps. xxv, xxvi; HART, *Salmon P. Chase*, chap. x; *Contemporaries*, Vol. IV, Nos. 124–131; BURGESS, Vol. II, chaps. xvi, xviii, xx; DRAPER, Vol. II, chap. lxiv; J. G. BLAINE, *Twenty Years of Congress*, Vol. I, chap. xx; HORACE GREELEY, *The American Conflict*, Vol. II, chaps. xi, xii.

TOPICS FOR SPECIAL REPORTS

1. **The Blockade of the Southern Coast:** NICOLAY and HAY, Vol. V, pp. 1–20; HART, *Contemporaries*, Vol. IV, No. 116; E. S. MACLAY, *History of the United States Navy*, Vol. II, pp. 225–281; J. R. SOLEY, *The Blockade and the Cruisers*; H. L. WAIT, *The Blockade of the Confederacy* (*Century Magazine*, Vol. XXXIV, pp. 914–928).

2. **Great Britain's Attitude during the War:** RHODES, pp. 261–286; T. K. LOTHROP, *William H. Seward*, pp. 271–287, 320–336; C. F. ADAMS, *Charles Francis Adams*, pp. 147–344; HART, *Contemporaries*, Vol. IV, No. 98; HOSMER, *The Appeal to Arms*, pp. 306–319; MONTAGUE BERNARD, *The Neutrality of Great Britain*.

3. **Vicksburg during the Siege:** HART, Vol. IV, No. 119; NICOLAY and HAY, Vol. VIII, pp. 282–310; RHODES, *History of the United States from the Compromise of 1850*, Vol. IV, pp. 312–318; *My Cave Life in Vicksburg*, by a Lady (New York, 1864).

4. **The Draft Riots in New York:** NICOLAY and HAY, Vol. VII, pp. 1–27; RHODES, Vol. IV, pp. 320–332; GREELEY, Vol. II, pp. 500–508; HART, Vol. IV, No. 121; *Harper's Magazine*, Vol. XXVII, pp. 559–560; J. B. FRYE, *New York and the Conscription of 1863*.

5. **The Economic and Social Condition of the South during the War:** HART, Vol. IV, Nos. 141–144; *Cambridge Modern History*, Vol. VII, pp. 603–621; DRAPER, Vol. III, pp. 480–496; STEPHENSON, pp. 99–111; WOODROW WILSON, *History of the American People*, Vol. IV, pp. 290–312; DAVIS, Vol. I, pp. 471–504; DAVID DODGE, *The Cave Dwellers of the Confederacy* (*Atlantic Monthly*, Vol. LVIII, pp. 514–521).

6. **Prisons, North and South:** NICOLAY and HAY, Vol. VII, pp. 444–472; RHODES, Vol. V, pp. 483–515; DRAPER, Vol. III, pp. 498–520; HOSMER, *The Outcome of the War*, pp. 240–248; A. B. ISHAM, *Prisoners of War and Military Prisons*; J. V. HADLEY, *Seven Months a Prisoner*.

PART VII. THE POLITICAL AND INDUSTRIAL HISTORY OF THE REPUBLIC SINCE THE CIVIL WAR

CHAPTER XVII

TWENTY YEARS OF REPUBLICAN SUPREMACY

RECONSTRUCTION

539. Andrew Johnson President. A few hours after Lincoln's death, Andrew Johnson of Tennessee took the oath of office as president of the United States (April 15, 1865). Johnson had been given the second place on the Republican ticket in 1864 not by reason of any fitness to occupy high office, but partly to reward him for his fidelity to the Union cause in the seceding state of Tennessee (p. 352, note 2) and partly to save the Republican party from the reproach of being called "sectional" in again choosing both its candidates from Northern states, as it had done in 1856 and 1860. But the selection of Johnson was most unfortunate. He was coarse, violent, egotistical, obstinate, and vindictive. Of Lincoln's splendid array of statesmanlike virtues he possessed only two, honesty and patriotism. Tact, wisdom, magnanimity, deference to the opinion of others, patience, kindness, humor—all these qualities he lacked; and he lacked them at a crisis in our history when they were sorely needed.

540. The Problem of Reconstruction. Armed resistance in the South was at an end. But the great question remained of how the North should use its victory. Except for a momentary wave of desire to avenge Lincoln's murder by the execution of prominent "rebels," there was no thought of inflicting on the Southern leaders the extreme punishment of traitors;[1] but there was the difficult problem of

---

[1] Jefferson Davis was brought from his prison at Fortress Monroe to the federal court at Richmond to answer the charge of treason. But he was released on bail, and the case was never pressed.

restoring the states of the secession to their proper place in the Union. What was their condition? Were they still states of the Union, in spite of their four years' struggle to break away from it? Or had they lost the rights of states and become territories of the United States, subject to such governments as might be provided for them by the authorities at Washington? Or was the South merely a "conquered province," which had forfeited even the right to be considered a part of the country and which might be made to submit to such terms as the conquering North saw fit to impose?

541. Lincoln's 10 Per Cent Plan. Long before the close of the war President Lincoln had answered these questions according to the theory he had held consistently from the day of the assault on Fort Sumter; namely, that not the states themselves, but combinations of individuals in the states, too powerful to be dealt with by the ordinary process of the courts, had resisted the authority of the United States. He had therefore welcomed and nursed every manifestation of loyalty in the Southern states. He had recognized the representatives of the small Unionist population of Virginia, assembled at Alexandria within the Federal lines, as the true government of the state. He had immediately established a military government in Tennessee on the success of the Union arms there in the spring of 1862. He had declared by a proclamation in December, 1863, that as soon as 10 per cent of the voters of 1860 in any of the seceded states should form a loyal government and accept the legislation of Congress and the proclamations of the President on the subject of slavery, he would recognize that government as legal. And such governments had actually been set up in Tennessee, Arkansas, and Louisiana. True, Lincoln had not come to an agreement with Congress as to the final method of restoring the Southern states to their place in the Union.[1] That question waited till the close of the war; and the pity is that when it came Abraham Lincoln was no longer alive.

---

[1] Congress admitted only two representatives from Louisiana from these "Lincoln governments" and in 1864 passed the Wade-Davis bill prescribing conditions on which the seceding states should be readmitted to the Union. Lincoln, unwilling to have so weighty a question decided hastily, allowed the Congress of 1864 to expire without giving the bill his signature. Wade and Davis protested against this "usurpation of authority" by the executive; and there is no doubt that, if Lincoln had been spared to serve his second term, he would have had to use all his tact and patience in finding a fair ground of agreement between the President and Congress in the reconstruction of the Southern states.

542. The "Johnson Governments." During the summer and autumn of 1865, when Congress was not in session, President Johnson proceeded to apply Lincoln's plan to the states of the South. He appointed military governors in North and South Carolina, Georgia, Florida, Alabama, Mississippi, and Texas. He ordered conventions to be held in those states, which repealed the ordinances of secession and framed new constitutions. State officers were elected. Legislatures were chosen, which repudiated the debts incurred during the war (except in South Carolina) and ratified the Thirteenth Amendment abolishing slavery (except in Mississippi). When Congress met in December, 1865, senators and representatives from all the states of the secession (except Florida and Texas[1]) were waiting at the doors of the Capitol for admission to their seats. But Congress was opposed to the recognition of the Johnson governments. In the first place, the President had arrogated to himself, during the recess of Congress, the sole right to determine on what terms the seceded states should be restored to the Union, as if it were simply a question of the exercise of his power of pardon; whereas, Congress maintained that the relation of states to the Union was a question for it to decide itself.

543. The "Black Codes." Furthermore, the conduct of the Johnson governments in the autumn and winter of 1865–1866 was offensive to the North. Although they accepted the Thirteenth Amendment, they passed "vagrancy" laws imposing a fine on negroes who were wandering about without a domicile, and allowing the man who paid the fine to take the negro and compel him to work out his debt; and "apprentice" laws assigning young negroes to "guardians" (often their former owners), for whom they should work without wages in return for their board and clothing. The North regarded these laws as a defiant determination to thrust the negro back into slavery. But to the Southerners they were only the necessary protection of the white population against the deeds of crime and violence to which a large, wandering, unemployed body of negroes might be tempted. Nearly 4,000,000 slaves had been suddenly liberated. Very few of them had any sense of responsibility or any capacity or capital for beginning a life of industrial freedom. Their emotional nature led

---

[1] The Johnson government in Texas did not get organized until 1866, and the Florida legislature had not met to choose the senators from that state.

them to believe that miraculous prosperity was to be bestowed upon them without their effort; that the plantations of their late masters were to be divided among them as Christmas and New Year's gifts, and that every negro was to have "forty acres and a mule." They were unfortunately encouraged in these ideas by many low-minded adventurers and rascally, broken-down politicians, who came from the North and posed as the guides and protectors of the colored race,[1] poisoning the minds of the negroes against the only people who could really help them begin their new life of freedom well, — their old masters.

544. The South sends its Leaders to Congress. A further offense in the eyes of the North was the sort of men whom the Southern states sent up to Washington in the winter of 1865 to take their places in Congress. They were mostly prominent secessionists. Some had served as members of the Confederate Congress at Richmond; some as brigadier generals in the Confederate army. Alexander H. Stephens, vice president of the Confederacy, was sent by the legislature of Georgia to serve in the United States Senate. To the Southerners it seemed perfectly natural to send their best talent to Congress. They would have searched in vain to find statesmen who had not been active in the Confederate cause. But to the North the appearance of these men in Washington seemed a piece of defiance and bravado on the part of the South; a boast that they had nothing to repent of, and that they had forfeited no privilege of leadership. Furthermore, these men were almost all Democrats, and as hostile to the "Black Republican" party as they had been in 1856 and 1860. Combined with the Democrats and "copperheads" of the North, who had opposed the war, they might prove numerous enough to oust the Republicans from power. The party which had saved the country must rule it, said the Republican orators.

[1] These men were called "carpetbaggers," because they were popularly said to have brought all their property with them in the cheap kind of valise which in those days was made of carpet material; and the Southerners who acted with them in their attempt to raise the negro above his former master in society and politics were called "scalawags." The carpetbaggers and scalawags were of course working for their own profit and political advancement. They must not be confused with the many good men and women who went South to work solely for the education, protection, and uplift of the negro. Before the close of the war Congress had established a Freedman's Bureau in the War Department (March 3, 1865), whose duty it was to look after the interests of the emancipated blacks, securing them labor contracts, settling their disputes, aiding them to build cottages, etc. The carpetbaggers tempted the negroes away from industrial pursuits into politics.

545. Johnson quarrels with Congress. Moved by these reasons Congress, instead of admitting the Southern members, appointed a committee of fifteen to investigate the condition of the late seceded states and to recommend on what terms they should be restored to their full privileges in the Union. Naturally, Johnson was offended that Congress should ignore or undo his work; and he immediately assumed a tone of hostility to the leaders of Congress. He had the coarseness, when making a speech from the balcony of the White House on Washington's birthday, 1866, to attack Sumner, Phillips, and Stevens[1] by name, accusing them of seeking to destroy the rights of the Southern states and to rob the President of his legal powers under the Constitution, and even to encourage his assassination. When Congress, in the early months of 1866, passed bills[2] to protect the negroes against the hostile legislation of the Southern states, Johnson vetoed the bills. But Congress was strong enough to pass them over his veto. The battle was then fairly joined between the President and Congress, and it boded ill for the prospects of peace and order in the South.

546. The Fourteenth Amendment. On April 30, 1866, the committee of fifteen reported. It recommended a new amendment to the Constitution (the fourteenth) which defined as "citizens of the United States and of the State wherein they reside," "all persons born or naturalized in the United States and subject to the jurisdiction thereof," and guaranteed these citizens full protection in their civil rights.[3] Furthermore, the amendment reduced the representation in Congress of any state which refused to let the negro vote, and disqualified the leaders of the Confederacy from holding federal or

---

[1] Thaddeus Stevens of Pennsylvania (not to be confused with Stephens of Georgia) was the chairman of the Committee on Appropriations in Congress, a bitter enemy of the South, and leader of the "radical" Republicans, who were determined to punish the "rebels" severely. Stevens ruled Congress as no other politician in our history had done.

[2] To wit, the Freedman's Bureau Bill, continuing and enlarging the power of that bureau of the War Department (p. 384, note), and the Civil Rights Bill, protecting the negro in his life, property, and freedom of movement and occupation.

[3] Civil rights (see note 2) are distinguished from political rights. The former are the rights that every citizen (*civis*) has; the latter are the privileges of voting and holding office. Women and children, for example, have full civil rights, that is, the *protection of the government*; but until the ratification of the Nineteenth Amendment, the women of the country as a whole did not have the political right of *taking part in the government*. By the grant of citizenship to the negro, the Fourteenth Amendment overruled Chief Justice Taney's decision in the Dred Scott case (see p. 313).

state office.[1] This last provision, which deprived the Southern leaders of their political rights, was harsh and unkind, assuming as it did that these men were not reconciled to the Union. But the rest of the Fourteenth Amendment was a fair basis for the reconstruction of the Southern states. Congress passed the amendment June 13, 1866, and Secretary Seward sent it to the states for ratification. Tennessee ratified in July, 1866, and was promptly restored to its full privileges in the Union. The other states of the secession might well have followed the lead of Tennessee; but every one of them, indignant at the disqualifying clause, overwhelmingly rejected the amendment. It thus failed to secure the votes of three fourths of the states of the Union, necessary for its ratification.

547. The Reconstruction Act. Congress angered by the South's rejection of the amendment and backed by the decisive victory of the anti-Johnson forces in the autumn elections of 1866, determined to apply severe measures. By the Reconstruction Act of March 2, 1867, the whole area occupied by the ten recalcitrant states was divided into five military districts, and a major general of the Union army was put in command of each district. The Johnson governments of 1865 were swept away, and in their place new governments were established under the supervision of the major generals and their detachments of United States troops.[2] The Reconstruction Act provided that negroes should be allowed to participate both in framing the new constitutions and in running the new governments, while at the same time their former masters were in large numbers disqualified by the third section of the Fourteenth Amendment. The act further provided that, when the new state government should have ratified the Fourteenth Amendment and that amendment should have become part of the Constitution of the United States, these states should be restored to their place in the Union.

548. Negro Suffrage forced on the South. Thus by the Reconstruction Acts[3] of 1867 Congress deliberately forced negro suffrage

[1] The Fourteenth Amendment must be carefully studied and mastered. It is printed in full in Appendix II.
[2] In October, 1867, there were 19,320 United States soldiers distributed at 134 posts in the South. At Richmond and New Orleans there were over 1000 troops; at other posts less than 500. They had charge of the registering of voters and supervised the polling.
[3] Two acts supplementary to the one of March 2 prescribed the method for conducting elections in the South (March 23) and made the military authorities in control of the districts of the South responsible to the general of the army (Grant) and not to the President (July 19).

on the South at the point of the bayonet. The negroes enrolled under the acts outnumbered the whites in the states of South Carolina, Alabama, Florida, Louisiana, and Mississippi. They were, with few exceptions, utterly unfit for the exercise of political rights. Even the colored men of the North, far in advance of their Southern brothers who labored in the cotton fields, were allowed the suffrage in only six states, where they counted as the tiniest fraction of the population. Ohio, in the very year Congress was forcing negro

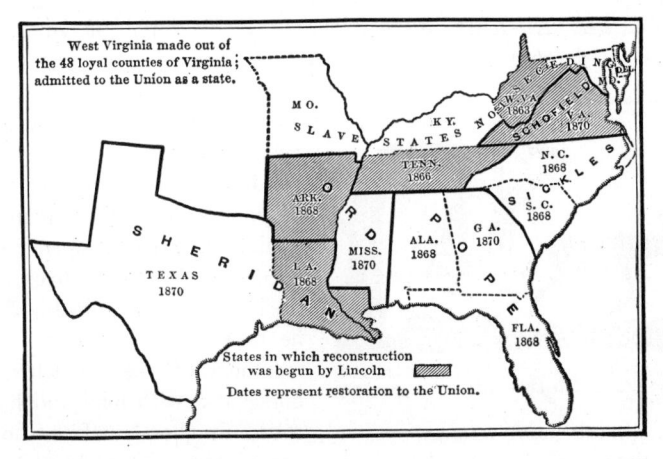

THE MILITARY DISTRICTS OF THE RECONSTRUCTION ACT OF 1867

suffrage on the South (1867), rejected by over 50,000 votes the proposition to give the ballot to the few negroes of that state. To reverse the relative position of the races in the South, setting the ignorant black man in power over his former master, was no way to insure either the protection of the negro's right or the stability and peace of the Southern states.[1]

549. Character of the Reconstruction Governments. The Reconstruction governments of the South were sorry affairs. For the exhausted states, already amply "punished" by the desolation of

[1] Lincoln had suggested to the military governor of Louisiana during the war that the most capable negroes and those who had shown their devotion to the Union by fighting in the Federal armies *might* be given the right to vote. But he had no idea of *forcing* the South to give a single former slave political rights. Johnson also had earnestly advised the Mississippi convention of 1865 to give a vote to negroes who possessed $250 worth of property.

war, the rule of the negro and his unscrupulous carpetbagger patron was an indescribable orgy of extravagance, fraud, and disgusting incompetence,— a travesty on government. Instead of seeking to build up the shattered resources of the South by economy and industry, the new legislatures plunged the states further and further into debt by voting themselves enormous salaries and by spending lavish sums of money on railroads, canals, and public buildings and works, for which they reaped hundreds of thousands of dollars in "graft."[1]

550. The Ku-Klux Klans. Deprived by force of any legal means of defense against this iniquitous kind of government, the South resorted to intimidation and persecution of the negro. Secret organizations, called the Ku-Klux Klans, made up mostly of young men, took advantage of the black man's superstitious nature to force him back into the humble social position which he held before the war. The members of the Ku-Klux on horseback, with man and horse robed in ghostly white sheets, spread terror at night through the negro quarters and posted on trees and fences horrible warnings to the carpetbaggers and scalawags to leave the country soon if they wished to live. Inevitably there was violence done in this reign of terror inaugurated by the Ku-Klux riders. Negroes were beaten; scalawags were shot. Of course these deeds of violence were greatly exaggerated by the carpetbag officials, who reported them to Washington and asked more troops for their

A KU-KLUX WARNING

---

[1] The economic evils and social humiliation brought on the South by the Reconstruction governments are almost beyond description. South Carolina, for example, had a legislature in which 98 of the 155 members were negroes. Nearly half of the members paid no taxes; yet this legislature spent the people's money by millions. The debt of the state was $5,000,000 in 1868; by 1872 it had been increased to $18,000,000; in one year $200,000 was spent in furnishing the state capitol with costly plate-glass mirrors, lounges, desks, armchairs, and other luxurious appointments, including a free bar, for the use of the negro and scalawag legislators. It took the Southern states from two to nine years to get rid of these governments.

protection. It came to actual fighting in the streets of New Orleans, and the trenches outside Vicksburg, which were used in 1863 by the Union sharpshooters, were the scene, ten years later, of a disgraceful race conflict between blacks and whites. Thus long after the war was over, the prostrate South, which should have been well on the way to industrial and commercial recovery, under the leadership of its own best genius, still presented in many parts a spectacle of anarchy, violence, and fraud,— its legislatures and offices in the grasp of low political adventurers, its resources squandered or stolen, its people divided into two bitterly hostile races.

551. The "Crime of Reconstruction." Why did the North put upon the South the unbearable burden of negro rule supported by the bayonet? For various reasons. Some men, desiring justice above all things, believed that the only way to secure the negro in his civil rights was to put the ballot into his hands immediately, regardless of his ability to use his political privileges wisely. The partisan politicians welcomed negro suffrage as a means of assuring and retaining Republican majorities in the Southern states.[1] And finally, there were thousands of men in the North who wished to punish the South for the defiant attitude of the Johnson governments in passing the "black codes," in sending Confederate brigadier generals up to Congress, and in rejecting the Fourteenth Amendment. But, however exasperating the conduct of the Southern states was, or however unwise their course may have been in rejecting the plan of reconciliation offered in the Fourteenth Amendment, Congress did them an unpardonable injury by hastening to reconstruct them on the basis of negro suffrage. The South would never have cherished resentment against the North for the defeat of 1861–1865 on the fair field of battle; but all the years that have passed since the death of Abraham Lincoln have hardly seen the extinction of the bitter passion roused in the hearts of the men, women, and children of the South against their fellow countrymen of the North, for the "crime of Reconstruction."

---

[1] In the presidential election of 1868, for example, six of the eight states of the secession which took part in the election voted for the Republican candidate, General Grant! Such a result could have been accomplished only by the enfranchisement of the negroes and the disfranchisement of the whites. Virginia, Mississippi, and Texas were not restored to their place in the Union until 1870; and as a condition they were obliged to ratify the Fifteenth Amendment (adopted in 1870), which forbids the nation or any state to disfranchise a person on account of "race, color, or previous condition of servitude."

The Aftermath of the War

552. The Civil War a Turning Point in American History. The Civil War was a turning point in our history. It settled political and moral questions which had been vexing the American people for nearly half a century, and it opened other questions, industrial and economic, which have been increasingly absorbing the attention of our country. It cleared the way for the development of the great free West through the renewed migration of the farmer, the miner, and the ranchman,— a migration which was promoted by the liberal distribution of public lands to Western settlers and the completion of the railway to the Pacific coast. It changed the scene and the setting of our national stage, bringing on the railroad magnate, the corporation promoter, the capitalist legislator, the socialist agitator, in place of the old champion of "free speech, free soil, free men," and the old defender of the Constitution and the Union.

553. A Land of Freedom. The first and most important question settled by the war was that this reunited country should be free soil from sea to sea. Westward expansion has been the most continuous and influential factor in our national development. From the days when the colonial pioneers first pushed across the ridges of the Alleghenies, almost all our great political problems had been intimately connected with the growth of our country and the development of its vast natural resources. The great outburst of national enthusiasm which followed the War of 1812 and which was encouraged by the invention of the reaper, the steam railway, and the electric telegraph would have led undoubtedly to the rapid extension of our population and our industry to the Far West had not the slavery question cast its sinister shadow across the path of the pioneer. The broad fields of Kansas, which now produce a hundred million bushels of corn, were destined first to be fertilized by the blood of civil strife. The triumph of the cause of freedom brought the assurance that our immense Western domain was to be filled not by hostile factions wrangling over the constitutional and moral right of the white man to hold the negro in slavery, but by fellow Americans competing in the generous rivalry of developing a common heritage and building a new empire of industry.

554. The Supremacy of the Nation. In the second place, the war decided the supremacy of the national government over the states. From the days of the ratification of the Constitution down to the secession of South Carolina, there had been widely divergent opinions as to the amount of power the states had "delegated" or resigned to the national government. The states, both North and South, had frequently claimed the right to suspend or annul an act of Congress which they judged to be a violation of the Constitution; and in some instances they had even threatened to secede from the Union unless such offensive acts were repealed.[1] But the appeal to arms in 1861–1865 not only put to rest the idea of a separate Southern Confederacy; it stimulated the national government to the exercise of great and unusual powers. The President had suspended the regular process of the courts in the arrest and trial of men for treason; he had recognized loyal minorities in some of the Southern states as the true state governments; he had, by proclamation, emancipated the slaves of all men in rebellion against the United States. Congress had imposed direct taxes, had created a national banking system, had borrowed huge sums of money, had put into circulation paper currency, had admitted the loyal counties of Virginia to the Union as the new state of West Virginia, and, finally, had proposed an amendment to the Constitution (the thirteenth) abolishing slavery in every part of the country. When the war was over, therefore, national supremacy was firmly established; and it has grown stronger rather than weaker in the years that have followed.

555. New Problems created by the War. It was inevitable, however, that the long, severe war should bring in its train perplexing problems. A huge national debt had been incurred; trade and industry had been unduly stimulated by the government's immediate demand for munitions, clothing, food, and supplies of every kind; our relations with foreign countries had been disturbed; and our country was in a state of feverish unrest at home. The problem before our statesmen was how to restore political and economic equilibrium.

556. The Impeachment of President Johnson. Congress had generously indorsed Lincoln's exercise of war powers, but when peace came the pendulum swung to the other extreme. We have seen how

---

[1] The student will recall the protest of Virginia and Kentucky against the Alien and Sedition laws in 1798, of the Hartford Convention against the War of 1812, and of South Carolina against the tariff acts of 1828 and 1832 (pp. 172, 189, 230).

Congress antagonized Johnson, overriding his vetoes with mocking haste and depriving him of his constitutional control of the army. On March 2, 1867, Congress passed a law called the Tenure of Office Act, which forbade the president to remove officers of the government without the consent of the Senate and made the tenure of cabinet officers extend through the term of the president by whom they were appointed. This was an invasion of the privilege which the president had always enjoyed of removing his cabinet officers at will. The purpose of the act was to keep Stanton, who was in thorough sympathy with the radical leaders of Congress, at the head of the Department of War. President Johnson violated the Tenure of Office Act, as Congress hoped he would, and removed Stanton. The House impeached him, February 24, 1868, and the Senate assembled the next month under the presidency of Chief Justice Chase to try the case (Constitution, Article I, section 3, par. 6). To the chagrin of the radical Republicans the Senate failed by one vote of the two-thirds majority necessary to convict the President, seven Republicans voting with the Democrats for his acquittal (May 16, 1868).[1] Johnson finished out his term, openly despised and flouted by the Republican leaders, and was succeeded on March 4, 1869, by General U. S. Grant.

557. President Grant. As a soldier Grant had been superb; as a statesman he was untrained. He knew nothing about the administration of a political office. He had simply been rewarded for his services in the war by the presidency of the United States, as a hero might be rewarded by a gold medal or a gift of money. He was so simple, direct, and innocent himself that he failed to understand the duplicity and fraud that were practiced under his very nose. Unfortunately his early struggle with poverty and his own failure in business had led him to set too high a valuation on mere pecuniary success, making him unduly susceptible to the influence of men who had made millions. He was easily managed by the astute

---

[1] The condemnation of President Johnson would have been a gross injustice. The Tenure of Office Act was passed only to set a trap for him. His veto of acts of Congress in 1866–1867 had been entirely within his rights by the Constitution, and his abuse of the congressional leaders in public speeches, while a personal insult, could not be called a political crime. In a desperate attempt, therefore, to find grounds ("high crimes or misdemeanors") on which they could impeach the President, the radical congressmen passed a most unfair law which they were pretty sure Johnson would violate.

Republican politicians in Congress, who could, by their plausible arguments, make the worse cause appear to him to be the better.[1] In his treatment of the South, for example, Grant was changed by his radical Republican associates, like Benjamin F. Butler, from a generous conqueror into a narrow partisan. "He dwindled from the leader of the people," says Dunning, "to the figurehead of a party." At Appomattox he had been noble. In a visit to the Southern states, a few months after the close of the war, he had become convinced, as he wrote, that "the mass of thinking men at the South accepted in good faith" the outcome of the struggle. Yet as president he upheld the disgraceful negro governments of the Reconstruction Act and constantly furnished troops to keep the carpetbag and scalawag officials in power in the South, in order to provide Republican votes for congressmen and presidential electors.[2]

558. The Low Tone of Public Morality. Probably the tone of public morality was never so low in all our country's history, before or since, as it was in the years of Grant's administration (1869–1877), although a more honest president never sat in the White House. The unsettled condition of the country during the Civil War and the era of Reconstruction furnished a great opportunity for dishonesty. Men grew rich on fraudulent deeds. Our state legislatures and municipal governments fell into the hands of corrupt "rings." The notorious "Boss" Tweed robbed the city of New York of millions of dollars before he closed his career in the Ludlow Street jail in 1878. Secretary of War Belknap resigned in order to escape impeachment for sharing the graft from the dishonest management of army posts in the West. The President's private secretary, Babcock, was implicated in frauds which robbed the government of its revenue tax on whisky. Western stagecoach lines, in league with

---

[1] The contemporary criticism of Grant by men of the highest political wisdom was one of pity rather than censure. George William Curtis wrote to a friend in 1870, "I think the warmest friends of Grant feel that he has failed terribly as a president, but not from want of honesty." James Russell Lowell wrote, "I liked Grant, and was struck by the pathos of his face; a puzzled pathos as of a man with a problem before him of which he does not understand the terms."

[2] Congress, by the "Force Bill" of February, 1871, established federal supervision over elections for the House of Representatives. From 1870 to 1878 the United States spent from $60,000 to $100,000 on each congressional election. In the presidential contest of 1876, which cost the government $275,000, the polling places in the Southern states were supervised by 7000 deputy marshals of the United States.

corrupt post-office officials, made false returns of the amount of business done along their routes and secured large appropriations from Congress for carrying the mails. Some of these "pet routes," or "star routes," cost the government thousands of dollars annually and carried less than a dozen letters a week. Members of Congress so far lost their sense of official propriety as to accept large amounts of railroad stock as "a present" from men who wanted legislative favors for their roads.

559. The Reform Movement. Before Grant's first term was over, a reform movement was started in the Republican party as a protest against corruption in national, state, and municipal government. Among the leaders of the movement were Carl Schurz, a refugee from the German Revolution of 1848, Charles Francis Adams, our minister to England during the Civil War, and George William Curtis, editor of *Harper's Weekly*. The chief policies advocated by the new party were first, civil service reform, by which appointments to office should be made on the basis of the merit and not of the political "pull" of the candidates; second, tariff reform, by which the highly protective war duties, which were enriching a few manufacturers at the cost of the mass of the people, should be reduced; third, the complete cessation of Federal military intervention to support the carpetbag governments of the South.

560. Defeat of the Liberal Republicans. Had the reform party shown the same wisdom in the choice of a candidate and the management of their campaign as they did in the making of their platform, they might have defeated Grant in 1872 and put an end to the corrupt partisan government which he was powerless to control. But dissensions in their own camp (always the curse of reform movements in politics) prevented the delegates to the new party's convention in Cincinnati, May, 1872, from nominating a strong candidate. They finally united on Horace Greeley, editor of the New York *Tribune*, a vehement, irritable man, who had no qualifications for the high office of president and whose only real point of agreement with the reformers was a desire to see the Southern states delivered from the radical Reconstruction governments. The Democrats accepted Greeley, but his defeat was overwhelming. He carried only six states, with 66 electoral votes, while thirty-one states, with 286 votes, went for Grant.

TWENTY YEARS OF REPUBLICAN SUPREMACY

561. Maximilian in Mexico. Meanwhile the administrations of Johnson and Grant were witnessing important negotiations with foreign countries, rising out of the conditions of the war. We have already noticed how both England and France favored the Southern cause and how eager the agents of the Confederacy were to get substantial aid from these countries (p. 343). Napoleon III, emperor of France, thought the moment of civil strife in America favorable for the expansion of French interests in the Western Hemisphere. He prevailed upon Archduke Maximilian, brother of the Emperor of Austria, to accept the "throne of Mexico" and sent an army of 35,000 Frenchmen to uphold his dynasty. Maximilian, with his French army, easily made himself master of Mexico; but when our Civil War was over, Secretary Seward politely informed the Emperor of the French that the United States could not allow the Monroe Doctrine to be thus infringed and that no part of this Western Hemisphere was open to the encroachment of European powers. At the same time General Grant, acting on the President's orders, sent General Sheridan with an army to the Mexican border (1865). Napoleon, realizing that his position was untenable, withdrew his troops from Mexico. The unfortunate archduke, refusing to give up his precarious throne, was taken by the Mexicans, court-martialed, and shot (June, 1867).

HORACE GREELEY

562. The *Alabama* Claims. The British government entertained no such wild scheme as Napoleon's of setting up an empire in the Western Hemisphere, but its offense against the United States was more direct and serious. In spite of warnings from our minister, Charles Francis Adams, the British Foreign Secretary, Lord Russell, allowed warships built for the Confederacy to leave the ports of England to prey on the commerce of the United States. The *Florida* sailed in March, 1862, and the famous *Alabama* slipped away from Liverpool in July. The next summer two ironclad rams were ready to leave Laird's shipyards, when they were stopped by Lord Russell, to whom Adams wrote curtly, "It would be superfluous in me to point out to your Lordship that this is war." The damage done to the commerce of the United States by the *Alabama* and the other cruisers built in England for the Confederacy was immense.[1] Not only did they destroy some $20,000,000 worth of our merchant ships and cargoes on the high seas but their encouragement of the Confederate cause prolonged the war perhaps for many months.

563. The Geneva Tribunal. Charles Sumner, the chairman of the Senate committee on foreign relations, made the extravagant demand that the British government should pay $200,000,000 damages and give up all its colonies on the mainland of America (Canada, Honduras, Guiana). On May 8, 1871, British and American commissioners signed a treaty at Washington adjusting some points of dispute in the perennial boundary and fishery questions and agreeing that the claims of the United States for damage done her commerce by the *Alabama* and the other offending cruisers should be settled by an international arbitration tribunal to meet at Geneva in Switzerland. Besides the British representative (Lord Cockburn) and the American (Charles Francis Adams), the tribunal contained a distinguished statesman from each of the countries of Switzerland, Italy, and Brazil. The tribunal decided that Great Britain had been guilty of a breach of the neutrality laws in allowing the cruisers to sail from her ports and awarded the United States damages to the amount of $15,500,000 in gold (September, 1872).[2]

564. The Purchase of Alaska. The government of the Russian Czar, Alexander II, had been in sympathy with the Union cause during the war. Therefore, when Russia asked us to buy Alaska of her, we were favorably disposed toward the negotiation. The distant arctic region had apparently little value except for its seal fisheries, but Secretary Seward closed the bargain for its purchase, March 30, 1867. The price paid Russia for 577,390 square miles of frozen territory was $7,200,000, or about two cents an acre. It

---

[1] After destroying about sixty Northern merchant vessels, the *Alabama* was sunk by the Union warship *Kearsarge*, Captain Winslow, in a spectacular battle off the coast of Cherbourg, France, June 19, 1864. The *Shenandoah*, another swift commerce destroyer in the Confederate navy, was still cruising in the Pacific when the news reached her, several weeks after the surrender of Lee and Johnston, that the Civil War was over.

[2] A few years later the United States was condemned to pay Great Britain about $5,500,000 for violating the fisheries treaty of 1818.

has proved an exceptionally good purchase, the gold taken in the last twenty years from the Yukon valley alone being worth very many times the $7,200,000 paid for the territory.

565. Secretaries Seward and Fish. It was fortunate for the country that we had two such able and judicious men as Seward and Hamilton Fish at the head of the State Department during the troubled administrations of Johnson and Grant. Fish rendered the country great services besides his negotiations with Great Britain

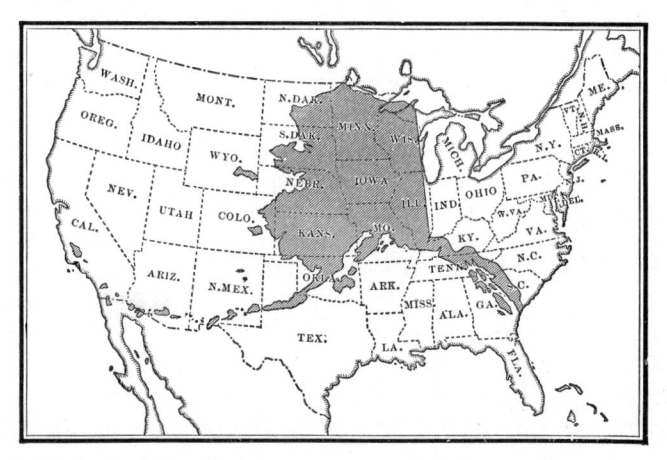

MAP OF ALASKA SUPERIMPOSED ON THE UNITED STATES

in the treaty of Washington and the *Alabama* claims. He kept President Grant from hastily recognizing the Cubans as belligerents in their revolt against Spanish authority in the island in the summer of 1869; and four years later prevented our going to war with Spain over the execution of nine American citizens of the crew of the *Virginius*—a vessel captured while carrying arms and ammunition to the insurgent Cubans.[1] He restrained the President in his desire to purchase and annex the republic of Santo Domingo through a treaty negotiated by his private secretary. Had our congressional leaders during this period been men of the stamp of Seward and Fish,

---

[1] The Spanish authorities returned the *Virginius* and the surviving members of her crew to the United States; but it was soon proved that the vessel was sailing under a false registry and hence fraudulently flying the American flag. This made her crew pirates, justly subject to execution.

instead of the violent, vindictive Stevens, the unspeakable demagogue Butler, the visionary Sumner, and the proud, uncompromising partisan Conkling, American history would have been spared many humiliating pages.

566. The Economic Results of the War. While the war left the South prostrate, impoverished by the strict blockade and wasted by the invading armies, it served rather as a stimulus to business in the North. Capital was abundant and was freely invested. During the decade 1860–1870 the employees in factories increased over 50 per cent and their productions over 100 per cent. The rush to the mines and ranches of the Far West led to the creation of the territories of Nevada (1861), Dakota (1861), and Arizona (1863). In 1862 Congress approved several projects for building railroads to the Pacific to replace the overland and the pony expresses, and in the same year, by the Homestead Act, bestowed quarter sections (160 acres) of land on Western pioneers who should cultivate their farms for five years. In 1863 Secretary Chase established the system of national banks. In 1864 the value of the oil products of the Pittsburgh region alone reached $15,000,000.

567. Railroad Building after the War. The extension of the railroad is the best index of this post-bellum prosperity. Between 1865 and 1873 the total mileage in the United States increased from 35,000 to 70,000, and from 819 miles of new tracks to 7439 miles. Between 1869 and 1873 the New York Central, the Hudson River, and the Lake Shore roads were joined to make through connections between New York and Chicago under a single management. By 1875 there were five trunk lines from the Great Lakes to the Atlantic seaboard. The generosity of Congress to the Pacific railroad companies was almost unlimited. It granted them over 100,000,000 acres of land along the proposed routes, and loans in government bonds amounting to $60,000,000. The 47,000,000 acres granted to the Northern Pacific alone were estimated by a high official in the railroad business to be valuable enough "to build the entire railroad to Puget Sound, to fit out a fleet of sailing vessels and steamers for the China and India trade, and leave a surplus that would roll up into the millions."

568. The Union Pacific and the Crédit Mobilier. Rail communication between the Atlantic and Pacific coasts was completed when the Union Pacific starting westward from Omaha and the Central Pacific starting eastward from San Francisco met at Ogden, Utah, in May, 1869. A golden spike was driven to celebrate the event. But even this great engineering feat of laying iron bands for 1800 miles from the Missouri to the Pacific, over yawning chasms and precipitous ledges, through long deserts where the only signs of life were the black herds of buffaloes or the hostile bands of Sioux and Cheyennes, was not accomplished without the taint of that corruption which seemed to pervade every field of public activity during

DRIVING THE LAST SPIKE IN THE UNION PACIFIC RAILROAD

Grant's administration. Some leading directors of the Union Pacific formed a construction company called the Crédit Mobilier, and in their capacity as directors awarded to themselves as builders huge contracts at enormous profits. To secure favors from Congress and ward off investigation, they distributed shares of the Crédit Mobilier stock where they would "do the most good." That honest men, like Vice President Colfax and James A. Garfield, accepted this stock without investigating its origin only proves how low was the general moral tone of public life.

569. The Panic of 1873. A too rapid and optimistic expansion of business and the conversion of too large a part of the resources of the country into "fixed capital" in railroads and factories brought on a severe panic in 1873, sending up the price of living and causing great misery among the working classes. Strikes occurred on the railroads and in the mines. Labor congresses, held in our largest cities, made public the demands of the working classes for an eight-hour day, for the exclusion of Chinese laborers from the country, for the government inspection of mines and factories, for the direct issue of money by the government instead of by the banks, for the cessation of land grants to railroads or corporations, for the regulation of railroad rates, a tax on incomes, and the establishment of a national Department of Labor at Washington.

570. The Challenge to the Republican Party. Sobered by the panic and warned by the contemporaneous reform movement which we have already noticed (p. 394), the Republicans began to set their house in order. The capture of the House of Representatives by the Democrats in 1874 (for the first time since 1856) warned the Grant administration that the time was past when the Republican party could appeal to the voters on the old issue of the "crime of rebellion" and, on the plea of having saved the country, could rule it as they pleased. New questions—of currency, of transportation, of the tariff, of immigration, of civil service reform, of monopolies, of capital and labor—were coming to the fore. In 1872 a national labor party was in the field with demands for an eight-hour working day and free public education at the nation's expense. In 1876 the farmers of the West were demanding national regulation of the railroads and the issue of large amounts of paper currency not based upon the security of gold, silver, and government bonds.

571. The Hayes-Tilden Campaign. In the national convention of 1876, therefore, the Republicans rejected the brilliant but somewhat discredited Speaker of the House, James G. Blaine of Maine,[1] and nominated a man of sterling honesty and conciliatory views on the Southern question, General Rutherford B. Hayes, governor of Ohio. The Democrats nominated Governor Samuel J. Tilden of New York, who had won a national reputation for his good work in the exposure of the rascality of the Tweed Ring. The result of the Hayes-Tilden campaign was of little importance, for the election of

---

[1] Blaine was one of the most brilliant men in the history of American politics. In his personal charm, his splendid oratory, his keenness in debate, his hold on the affections of his followers, he resembled his great predecessor in the chair of the House, Henry Clay. But Blaine was far inferior to Clay in moral stature. He was involved in dealings with Western railroads which even his highly dramatic speech of self-defense in the House could not make seem regular and honest to his countrymen. We shall meet his name later in these pages.

either man meant the inauguration of a new era in our politics,—the end of the carpetbag rule in the South and of the tyranny of Congress. But the election itself was the most exciting in our history. Late in the evening of election day (November 7) it was almost certain that Tilden had carried enough states to give him 184 electoral votes. Only 185 votes were necessary for a choice. A double set of returns came from the four states of South Carolina, Florida, Louisiana, and Oregon.[1] A single vote from any of these states, therefore, would give Tilden the election. The Hayes managers claimed all the disputed votes; but there was no provision made in the Constitution or in any law of Congress to decide which set of returns was legal. The Constitution (Amendment XII) simply states: "The President of the Senate shall, in the presence of the Senate and House of Representatives, open all the certificates and the votes shall then be counted."

572. The Electoral Commission. Excitement ran high as the winter of 1876–1877 passed and the possibility presented itself of the country's being without a president on March 4, 1877. As a compromise an Electoral Commission of 15 members was created by act of Congress, to consist of 5 senators (3 Republicans, 2 Democrats), 5 representatives (3 Democrats, 2 Republicans), and 5 justices of the Supreme Court (2 Republicans, 2 Democrats, and 1 to be elected by these 4). The fifteenth member, Justice Bradley, voted with the Republicans on every question. By a vote of 8 to 7 the Republican certificates were accepted from all the states in dispute, and Hayes was declared president by an electoral vote of 185 to 184. The decision was reached on the eve of inauguration day, and the new President took the oath of office in perfect security and tranquillity. That the inauguration of a man whom more than half the country believed to have been fairly defeated on election day could take place without a sign of civil commotion is perhaps the most striking proof in our history of the moderate and law-abiding character of the American people.

---

[1] The double set of returns from the three Southern states was due to the fact that the carpetbag governments which were still in control there rejected the votes of some districts on the ground that there had been fraud and intimidation at the polls. In Oregon one of the Republican electors chosen was disqualified by the fact that he held a federal office in the state, and the Democrats insisted that the man with the next highest vote on the list (a Democrat) should replace him.

A New Industrial Age

573. The Centennial Exposition at Philadelphia. The closing year of Grant's presidency (1876) was the centennial of American independence. The event was celebrated by a great world's fair at Philadelphia, the birthplace of the republic. Ten million visitors to the exposition grounds caught the inspiration of the wonderful achievements in science and invention which the years of peace were bringing forth. The Centennial Exposition was a pledge of the recovery of our nation from the political, industrial, and financial difficulties brought on it by the Civil War. Already the rule of the stranger was passing in the Southern states, and a Mississippi congressman had pronounced a eulogy over the body of Charles Sumner, exhorting his fellow countrymen to know one another that they might love one another (1874). Already the United States had passed a law pledging the payment of every dollar of its war debt in the precious metals of gold and silver (1875). Already a national convention had declared in its platform that "the United States of America is a nation, not a mere league" (1876). It had taken a full hundred years and cost a long and bloody war to decide that point. The century had seen the rounding out of our national domain. The railroad ran from the Atlantic to the Pacific, and all the area between had been organized into states or territories. The country was ready for new tasks, and the belted wheels, the giant shafts, the splendid specimen products of the farms, gardens, and wheat fields of the land, and the thousands of drawings and models of new inventions in implements and machinery, which were displayed at the Centennial Exposition of 1876, were all a witness and a prophecy of the new era of industrial expansion on which we were entering.

574. Growth of our Productions, Manufacture, and Trade. Whatever chapter of the census reports we open for the decade following the war, we read the same story. Our coal output increased fivefold and our steel output a hundredfold in the period from 1865 to 1875. The wheat crop in Dakota alone increased from 1000 bushels in 1860 to 3,000,000 in 1880, and the corn crop in Kansas from 6,000,000 to over 100,000,000 bushels. When the Civil War opened we were producing about $50,000,000 worth of precious metals annually; twenty years later the single state of Colorado was taking from its mines over $1,000,000 worth of gold, lead, and silver per month. Nevada, which was a mining camp of less than 7000 inhabitants in 1860, had grown by 1870 into a state of the Union with a population of 42,000. In the decade preceding the war the value of our manufactures increased 85 per cent; in the decade following they increased 125 per cent. The year of Hayes's election marks the permanent change in favor of the United States in the statistics of foreign trade. From the middle of the century to 1876 our exports had exceeded our imports in but three years (1857, 1862, 1874); since 1876 there have been but three years (1888, 1889, 1898) in which our imports have exceeded our exports.

575. Our Wealth and Population. The wealth of the country grew from $16,000,000,000 to $43,000,000,000 between 1860 and 1880, and the deposits in our savings banks (the best index of a nation's prosperity) increased 600 per cent. During the same period our population grew from 30,000,000 to 50,000,000, while the liberal homestead laws and the development of the Western railroads attracted an unprecedented number of Irish, German, and Scandinavian immigrants to the fertile farm lands beyond the Mississippi. Between 1860 and 1870 Arizona, Colorado, Dakota, Idaho, Montana, and Wyoming were organized as territories, and Kansas, Nebraska, and Nevada were admitted as states of the Union. Edmund Burke, in his famous "Speech on Conciliation with America," delivered in Parliament in 1775, had exclaimed, "Such is the strength with which population shoots in that part of the world that, state the numbers as high as we will, while the dispute continues the exaggeration ends." It seemed in 1875 as though the orator's enthusiastic language of a century earlier were fulfilled in sober fact.

576. Effects of the Industrial Boom. With the recovery from the panic of 1873 our industries entered on a period of unprecedented expansion. New inventions followed each other in rapid succession — the electric light and trolley, the telephone, the phonograph, the bicycle, the typewriter. The elevated railroad began to appear in our cities; through trains to the West were operated with increasingly luxurious equipment; steel bridges were thrown across our rivers. Immigration, which had fallen to 70,000 during the war, almost reached the half-million mark by 1880. More and more the mills and factories, the commercial houses and the big shops, gathered the population into cities. When the first census was taken only 3.4 per cent of our people lived in communities of 8000 or over; by the census of 1880 the proportion had increased to 22.6 per cent. Already organized labor was facing organized capital with the consciousness of its interests as a class. Railway engineers, conductors, and firemen, bricklayers, cigar-makers, ironworkers, were gathered into unions, to oppose capital's "right to own and control labor for its own greedy and selfish ends." The Knights of Labor, a loose federation of workers with the motto "The injury of one is the concern of all," had nearly 150,000 members through the country. The Grangers, or Patrons of Husbandry, championed the cause of the farmer in the West and passed laws in the grain states (notably Wisconsin, Illinois, and Minnesota) regulating the freight rates on the railroads. The miners were demanding shorter hours and higher pay.

RUTHERFORD B. HAYES

577. The Difficult Position of President Hayes. It was high time for our government to have done with the old questions of the war and reconstruction, with petty partisan politics and sectional animosities, and to face seriously the great problems of the new industrial age. None realized this better than President Hayes, but he was hampered at every step. A Democratic House opposed him during his entire administration, and a Democratic Senate also during the last two years of it. For this opposition party he was a "usurper," occupying the seat rightfully belonging to Tilden. Nor was he the choice of the leaders of the Republican party. He had been nominated in the convention of 1876 only because the deadlock between the supporters of Blaine and the supporters of Grant could not be broken. His face appeared in the Democratic press with the word "fraud" written across his brow, while the men of his own party who were still devoted to the methods of "machine politics" sneered at his efforts for reform, called him a "goody-goody," a hypocrite, and a "Granny Hayes." Upright, industrious, and public-spirited, he lacked the genial and winsome traits of character which could conciliate political opponents; and, like John Quincy Adams, he pursued his lonely path of duty, confiding to his diary the rectitude of his conduct.

578. His Excellent Administration. In spite of personal unpopularity, and in the face of political and economic turmoil, Hayes gave the country one of the cleanest and most courageous administrations in its history. He immediately withdrew the Federal troops that were still upholding the negro Republican governments in Louisiana and South Carolina, letting these states revert to the Democratic column. He still further incurred the wrath of the Republican machine by dismissing from their important offices Chester A. Arthur (collector of the port of New York) and Alonzo B. Cornell (naval officer), who with Thomas Platt and Roscoe Conkling made up the "big four" who ruled the politics of New York State. He sent a commission to China to prepare the way for the negotiation of a treaty which would protect the workers of our Pacific coast against the invasion of cheap Mongolian labor.[1] He strove earnestly to repair the faith of the nation in the eyes of the Indian tribes of the Far West, who had been fed on rotten rations, deceived by false promises, robbed by unscrupulous agents, and goaded into uprisings that had cost our government over $22,000,000 and the lives of nearly 600 men since the Civil War.[2]

579. The Railroad Strikes of 1877. Hayes had been in office but a few months when railroad strikes of unprecedented violence

---

[1] Between 1850 and 1860 the Chinese immigrants to our shores had increased from 10,000 to 40,000. The work on the western end of the Union Pacific Railroad attracted tens of thousands more in the next decade. As these Chinese laborers lived on a few cents a day and were content with dirty quarters and poor food, they were a menace to the American laborer of the Pacific coast, who demanded "four dollars a day and roast beef." Mobs in California and Oregon organized to "run out of town" the Chinese coolies, in spite of the fact that our government, by the Burlingame Treaty of 1868, had guaranteed the Chinese visiting our shores protection in trade, religion, and free travel. In 1879 Congress repealed parts of the Burlingame Treaty, but Hayes vetoed the bill. Finally, through the efforts of the Hayes commission, an arrangement was made with China by which that country agreed to our regulation of labor immigration from her shores.

[2] The most disastrous of these Indian uprisings was the resistance of the Sioux, under their chief Sitting Bull, to the orders of the government bidding them leave their hunting grounds in southern Montana and move further west. The gallant Colonel George A. Custer, with a force of 262 men, trying to surprise Sitting Bull at the Little Big Horn River, was defeated and killed with every soul of his little army, June 25, 1876.

broke out. The trouble started with a 10 per cent reduction in the wages of the trainmen on the Baltimore and Ohio and the laying off of train crews on the Pennsylvania. By midsummer of 1877 a number of roads in the states from the Atlantic coast to the Missouri River were tied up by strikes, and the anthracite mining region of eastern Pennsylvania was terrorized by lawless mobs. Chicago, Baltimore, Reading, Scranton, and Pittsburgh were the scenes of riots and bloodshed. The President was forced to call on the militia of several states and even to dispatch United States troops to certain points to quell the disorder. In Pittsburgh, where the rioting was at its worst, $10,000,000 worth of property in cars, buildings, and freight was destroyed and over 50 men were killed or wounded before order was restored.

580. Financial Measures of Hayes's Administration. Two financial measures of importance were carried in Hayes's mid-term,— the Bland-Allison Act for the coinage of silver and the bill for resumption of specie payments. From Washington's administration till long after the close of the Civil War comparatively little silver had been coined into money at the United States mints. The business of the country was not large enough to demand more currency for its transactions than the supply of gold could furnish. The government stood ready to receive silver bullion at its mints for coinage at the established rate of fifteen ounces of silver to one ounce of gold before 1834 and approximately sixteen ounces of silver to one ounce of gold after that date. But such was the comparative scarcity of silver in the middle years of the century that the mine owners could sell it to the jewelers and artisans at a higher price than the government paid. Between 1850 and 1873, therefore, almost no silver was brought to the mints, and in the latter year Congress quietly passed a law stopping the coinage of silver dollars.[1] Just at that moment enormous deposits of silver were discovered in our Western states. One mine, whose product in 1873 was worth but $645,000, increased its output to $16,000,000 in two years. The

---

[1] This law simply recognized the state of affairs which existed. Since the amount of silver which went into a silver dollar could be sold to the silversmiths for $1.02 in 1873, the mine owners naturally disposed of their product in the market where it brought the highest price. It was they, and not the government, that discontinued silver coinage. In later years the advocates of the free coinage of silver spoke of this act as the "crime of 1873,"— as if the government had repudiated silver and cheapened it by refusing to coin it.

famous Comstock lode in Nevada yielded $42,000,000 in three years. Our total production of silver, which was $1,000,000 annually in 1861, rose to $20,000,000 in 1875. The market was flooded. The price of silver fell, and the mine owners were anxious again to have their product coined at the old rate. In 1874, for the first time in a generation, the silver in a dollar was worth more than the same weight of silver in a napkin ring or an umbrella handle. The mine owners, therefore, clamored for the repeal of the law of 1873 and the resumption of silver coinage. They were joined in their demand by the large class of Western farmers, who, being obliged to borrow money for the development of their farms and the transportation of their crops, had to pay high rates of interest to the bankers of the East, who controlled the nation's gold.

581. The Bland-Allison Act. Representative Richard P. Bland of Missouri therefore introduced into Hayes's first Congress a bill for the unlimited, or "free," coinage of silver at the old rate of approximately 16 to 1. The bill was modified in the Senate by Allison of Iowa. Instead of accepting unlimited amounts of silver presented at its mints for coinage, the government was to agree, by the Allison Amendment, to purchase, for coining into silver dollars, not less than $2,000,000 worth nor more than $4,000,000 worth of silver a month. In this form the bill passed both Houses of Congress in February, 1878, and, although wisely vetoed by President Hayes, commanded the necessary two-thirds vote to override his veto. By the Bland-Allison Act, then, our government pledged itself to take from the mine owners at least $24,000,000 worth of silver every year to coin into "dollars" which were worth, in 1878, less than ninety cents apiece. We shall see in a later chapter some of the results of this policy of trying, simply by stamping the United States eagle upon coins, to make them more valuable than the worth of the metal they contain.

582. The Resumption of Specie Payments. The other financial measure of the Hayes administration was the resumption of specie payments, that is, the decision of the United States to pay its obligations in "specie," or coin. The "greenbacks," or legal-tender notes issued to the amount of about $450,000,000 during the Civil War, were simply pieces of paper on which were printed the government's promise to pay the bearer the amount specified. When the government began to "redeem," or cancel, these notes the debtor classes in the West protested and even asked that more greenbacks be issued. They had borrowed paper money and did not want to have to pay back their debts in gold. But Congress refused to heed their demand. In order to maintain the honor of the government and uphold its credit in the eyes of foreign nations, Congress passed a law in 1875, fixing January 1, 1879, as the date when the Treasury of the United States would redeem in coin[1] all the outstanding greenbacks (about $347,000,000). During the years 1877–1878, John Sherman, Hayes's able Secretary of the Treasury, had accumulated some $140,000,000 worth of gold by the sale of bonds at home and abroad; and when resumption day came, so perfect was the faith of the people in the credit of the government that greenbacks to the amount of only about $135,000 were presented at the Treasury to be exchanged for gold.

583. The Republican Convention of 1880. No president ever deserved a second term more than Hayes. But the shadow cast on his title in 1876, combined with his uncompromising independence of the leaders of the party, and his failure, through a certain aloofness of manner, to appeal to the popular imagination, made his nomination in 1880 out of the question. General Grant had just returned from a world-circling tour in which he had been received with royal honors by the sovereigns of Europe and Asia. A branch of the Republican party, called the "stalwarts,"[2] led by Senator Roscoe Conkling of New York, boomed Grant for a third term, chiefly with the hope of reëstablishing under the cover of his popularity the rule of the Republican machine, which had been somewhat damaged by President Hayes. Grant's chief rivals in the convention were Senator James G. Blaine of Maine and Hayes's Secretary of the Treasury, John Sherman of Ohio. After the convention had balloted thirty-five times without giving the necessary majority vote to either Grant or Blaine, the Wisconsin delegation led a "stampede"

---

[1] Since the government practically recognized gold as the standard "coin" in 1875, by demanding gold in payment of customs dues and paying in gold the interest on its bonds, specie payment was taken to mean gold payment.

[2] The "stalwarts," in opposition to the reforming "half-breeds," stood for uncompromising partisan rule, for a high protective tariff, for distribution of offices as spoils of political victory, for the assessment of officeholders for party contributions, and for the continued use of federal troops to coerce the Southern states and of federal inspectors to guard the polling places.

to General James A. Garfield[1] of Ohio, who had been sent to the convention to work in the interests of Sherman. Chester A. Arthur of New York, a "stalwart," was nominated for vice president to appease the Conkling faction. The Democrats nominated General Winfield S. Hancock, the hero of the battle of Gettysburg.

584. The Election of Garfield. Garfield was elected by 214 votes to 155, and at the same time the Republicans regained the majority in the House of Representatives, which they had lost in 1874. It was the first presidential election since 1860 in which all the states of the Union took part, with the opportunity of expressing freely their choice; for even after the Civil War was over and the states of the secession were nominally restored to their places in the Union, the presence of federal troops at the polls in the reconstructed states made a fair election impossible (see p. 393, note 2). The South, embittered against the Republican party for its harsh policy of Reconstruction, cast a solid Democratic vote, even though the candidate of that party was the victor of Gettysburg; and for a quarter of a century thereafter the "solid South" was found in the Democratic column at every presidential election.

JAMES A. GARFIELD

585. Garfield's Assassination. The choice of Garfield was a bitter disappointment to the machine politicians. Though a strict Republican, the new President elect belonged to that reform wing of the party which the "stalwarts" contemptuously called "half-breeds." Even before his inauguration he showed such independence of the "stalwart" leaders in his selections for cabinet positions and high federal offices that the party was hopelessly split. At the earnest request of Grant, Conkling had taken the stump in the campaign

---

[1] Garfield was one of the best examples of our self-made men of the West. He had worked his way up from the towpath to a college presidency and then to a seat in the state senate of Ohio. He had distinguished himself for gallant conduct in the famous corps of General Thomas at Chickamauga. In the winter of 1863 he had been elected to the House of Representatives, where he served with great distinction until his promotion to the presidency in 1880.

and contributed not a little to Garfield's election. Yet Garfield made Blaine, Conkling's bitter enemy, Secretary of State, and refused to consider the wishes of the New York senator in his appointments. Stung by this "ingratitude," Conkling and his colleague from New York, Thomas C. Platt, resigned their seats in the United States Senate.[1] Factional spirit ran high and culminated in a dastardly crime. A few weeks after the resignation of the New York senators, as President Garfield, accompanied by Secretary Blaine, entered the Baltimore and Potomac station at Washington, Charles Guiteau, a "stalwart" fanatic, crept up to the President and fired a bullet into his back. He did it, he said, to rid the country of a "traitor" and seat the "stalwart" Arthur in the presidential chair. After lingering through the hot weeks of summer in dreadful agony, President Garfield died at Elberon, New Jersey, September 19, 1881.

586. Civil Service Reform. Guiteau's pistol shot roused the whole country to the disgraceful state of the public service. Political offices were the prize of intriguing politicians and wirepullers. Crowds of anxious placemen thronged the capital for weeks after the inauguration, pestering the President for appointments in post offices, customhouses, and federal courts. Republicans and Democrats brought against each other the charge of "insatiable lust for office,"— and both were right. One politician, when taken to task for not working in his office, cynically replied, "Work! why, I worked to get here!" "Voluntary contributions," or assessments, equal to 2 per cent of their salary, were levied on officeholders for campaign expenses, and the funds so raised were used shamelessly to buy votes. At the very close of the Civil War thoughtful men had attacked this corrupt "spoils system," which had prevailed since Jackson's day. For seven years in succession Congressman Jenckes of Rhode Island introduced a bill into the House "for the regulation of the civil

---

[1] The quarrel between Conkling and Garfield led to a most dramatic scene. Conkling, accompanied by Platt and Arthur, called on Garfield at his room in the Riggs House shortly after his arrival in Washington, and for two hours stormed up and down the floor, pouring out the vials of his sarcastic wrath upon the President elect, who sat unmoved on the edge of his bed. Neither Platt nor Conkling was returned to the Senate by the legislature of New York. The latter retired from politics and a few years later lost his life through exposure in the great blizzard which swept New York City in 1888. Platt returned to the Senate in 1897, where he served two terms, being replaced by Elihu Root in 1909.

service,"[1] until in March, 1871, a law was passed authorizing the president to appoint a commission to ascertain the fitness of candidates for office in the federal civil service and prescribe rules for their conduct. The commission advocated what was later called by Theodore Roosevelt "the merit system," that is, the selection of candidates by competitive examination rather than their appointment for party services, on the sound principle that a man's political opinions have little to do with his capacity for a clerkship. The low tone of public morality prevailing during Grant's administration discouraged reform of the civil service, and in 1875 Congress discontinued the commission by failing to make any appropriation for its labors. President Hayes encouraged the merit system wherever he could. During his administration civil service leagues were formed in over thirty states of the Union, and the movement resulted in the establishment of the National Civil Service League at Newport in 1881.

587. The Pendleton Act. Under pressure from this national league a bill was introduced into the Senate by George Pendleton of Ohio in 1882, which was passed in both Houses of Congress by large majorities and signed by President Arthur in January, 1883. The Pendleton Act provided for the reëstablishment of the Civil Service Commission and for the extension of the "merit system" as far as the president saw fit. It forbade the assessment of federal servants for campaign purposes or the discharge of a competent clerk on account of his political opinions. Under its wise provisions about 14,000 officials in the post-office and customs departments were immediately protected against the partisan revenge of victorious political bosses.

588. The Attitude of the "Stalwarts." The passage of the Pendleton Act was a tardy and rather desperate concession to the reform idea on the part of the "stalwart" Republicans. For ten years they had seen a reform movement going on in their ranks and had met that movement with indifference or scorn, ridiculing the civil service as "snivel service," and had maintained the high tariff which was enriching the few protected manufacturers at the expense of the many consumers and was piling up in the Treasury of the United States a surplus of money which ought to have been circulating in business among the people. The boom in trade which had

---

[1] By the civil service is meant the great number of clerks and assistants in the executive department of the government.

followed the panic of 1873 was beginning to slacken in 1881 and "hard times" came on. In the congressional elections of 1882 the Republican majority of 19 in the House was changed to a Democratic majority of 82, and the Republican party, thoroughly alarmed, began to consider how it should save its supremacy of a quarter of a century in the approaching presidential election of 1884.

589. James G. Blaine. By far the most prominent man in the Republican party was James G. Blaine, whom we have already met as candidate for the presidential nomination in 1876 and 1880. As Secretary of State for a few months in Garfield's cabinet Blaine had heightened his immense popularity with that large portion of our population which loves a display of energy in its public servants. He had intervened in a quarrel between Peru and Chile with language which implied the right of the United States to settle the disputes of her weaker sister republics of South and Central America. He had negotiated (but failed to persuade the Senate to ratify) a number of commercial treaties with these republics on the principle of "reciprocity," or the admission into each country, free of duty, of goods which were not produced in that country. He had assumed a lofty tone toward Great Britain in a controversy over the control of a canal to be cut through the Isthmus of Panama. His foreign dispatches were written in the nervous, confident, assertive style of the editorial page of a popular journal rather than in the guarded, deliberative language of diplomacy.

JAMES G. BLAINE

590. The Mugwump Opposition to Blaine. But in spite of Blaine's impetuous assertions of patriotism and his great personal "magnetism," the reproach of shady dealings with Western railroads and land schemes, which had prevented his nomination in 1876, still clung to his name. And as the time for the national convention of 1884 drew near, those same reformers whom he had sarcastically dubbed "the unco guid,"[1] "pharisaical, not practical," began the

[1] A Scotch phrase meaning " goody-goody."

movement to prevent his nomination at Chicago. They were ridiculed in the New York *Sun* as "Mugwumps"—an Indian name meaning "big chief"—because they affected superiority to the rest of their party. When Blaine's great popularity secured him the nomination over his rivals, President Arthur and Senator Edmunds of Vermont (the candidate of the New England reformers), the Mugwumps, or Independent Republicans, organized a league at New York under the leadership of George William Curtis, the chairman of the original Civil Service Commission of 1871. They protested against the nomination of a man "wholly disqualified for the high office of president of the United States" by his alliance with the most unscrupulous men of the party and his stubborn opposition to all reform; and they called upon the Democrats to nominate an honest, independent candidate for whom truly public-spirited citizens could conscientiously vote.[1]

591. Grover Cleveland. The Democrats responded to this invitation by nominating Grover Cleveland, governor of New York. Cleveland was the son of a poor Presbyterian minister. He had grown up in western New York, supporting himself as best he could by tending a country store, teaching in an asylum for the blind, and acting as clerk in a lawyer's office in Buffalo. Here he studied law, was admitted to the bar, and, entering local politics, served as assistant district attorney, then as sheriff of Erie County, and in 1881, in his forty-fifth year, was elected mayor of Buffalo on an independent ticket. His administration of the office was so honest, able, and courageous that it brought him the Democratic nomination for the governorship of New York the next year. He carried the state by the unprecedented plurality of 192,000 votes. In the governor's chair he showed the same fearless independence which had won him the name of the "veto mayor" in Buffalo. He was, like Lincoln and Garfield, a "self-made man."

592. Cleveland and Blaine compared. By nature and training Cleveland was the direct antithesis of his rival for the presidential election. Blaine was brilliant, genial, daring, and unreliable; Cleveland was deliberate, patient, plodding, but firm as a rock when he had

---

[1] Several influential Republican newspapers, like the *New York Times* and the *Springfield Republican*, advised voting for Cleveland. "The defeat of Blaine," wrote one, "will be the salvation of the Republican party."

once reached his decision. Blaine, after a college training and ten years' experience as teacher and journalist, had entered the Maine legislature and from there had gone to the national Congress, where he served fourteen years in the House of Representatives (as its Speaker from 1869 to 1875) and four years in the Senate, whence he was called by Garfield in 1881 to the first place in the cabinet. Cleveland had had absolutely no experience in national affairs, had never been a member of a legislative body of any sort, and had only the political training obtained in the executive offices of sheriff, mayor, and governor.

593. The Campaign of 1884. The campaign was perhaps the most bitter and disgraceful of all our history, conducted, as the *Nation* remarked, "in a spirit worthy of the stairways of a tenement house." Being unable to revive the issues of the Civil War for a generation of voters who had grown up since the surrender at Appomattox, and having no ground for criticism of Cleveland's public record in the state of New York, the Republican campaign orators attacked the private life of the Democratic candidate, ransacking every page of it for occasion of slander or traces of scandal. The Democrats in turn revived the whole miserable story of Blaine's railroad bonds and the famous Mulligan letters.[1] It was clear on election night that the result hung on the state of New York, but several days of intense excitement passed before it was definitely known that Cleveland had carried the state by the slim majority of 1149 votes out of 1,167,169.[2]

594. The Party Revolution of 1884. Cleveland's election was the first Democratic victory since the campaign of 1856. For the

[1] These were letters which Blaine had written to the railroad manipulators, and which he himself thought so damaging to his chances for nomination that he had "borrowed" them from Mulligan and refused to return them — though he later in a very dramatic scene read them to the House, "inviting the confidence of 44,000,000 of his fellow citizens." The sharp-tongued Conkling, being invited to take the stump for Blaine in 1884, replied, "Thank you, I don't engage in criminal practice."

[2] The vote throughout the country (except in the "solid South") was very close, Cleveland receiving 4,874,986 to 4,851,981 for Blaine. Many people believe that Blaine lost New York, and consequently the election, on account of a remark made near the end of the campaign by a certain Dr. Burchard at a meeting of the ministers of New York, which had been called to congratulate Blaine and wish him success. On that occasion Dr. Burchard referred to the Democratic party as the party of "Rum, Romanism, and Rebellion." The insulting phrase, which implied that Roman Catholics were in a class with drunkards, and that both were in sympathy with "rebels," was taken up as a campaign cry all over the land and doubtless cost Blaine thousands of votes.

quarter of a century since the Confederate mortars had opened their fire on Fort Sumter the Republicans had held control of the executive branch of our government, with the tens of thousands of offices in its patronage. For only one term of Congress during that period had the Republicans lost control of the Senate, and they had a majority in the House in all but four terms. This long tenure of power was the reward the country paid the Republican party for its services in preserving the Union and abolishing the curse of slavery. Those services were great, but the uses to which the reward was put were unworthy. Considerations of public welfare, even of common honesty, were often set aside for party ends. Confident in their majorities, the Republican leaders defied the growing demand for reform in the conduct of the government offices. They sneered at the civil-service rules. They tried, by waving the "bloody shirt," to keep alive the savage desire to coerce the South. They hampered and hectored their "reform president," Hayes. They cynically reduced the tariff 3 per cent (by an act of 1883), when their own expert commission recommended a reduction of 20 per cent. They refused to take warning by the gathering of the reform forces in 1872. In the opinion of half the country they had "stolen" the election of 1876 and were generally accused of having "bought" the election of 1880. Consequently, in 1884, they were deposed from their long supremacy by the votes of the reformers in their own party, to whose entreaties and remonstrances they had turned a deaf ear for more than a decade.

References

Reconstruction: W. A. Dunning, *Reconstruction, Political and Economic* (American Nation Series), chaps. i–v; also *Military Government during Reconstruction* and *The Process of Reconstruction* (*Essays on the Civil War and Reconstruction*); W. L. Fleming, *The Sequel of Appomattox* (Chronicles, Vol. XXXII); *Documentary History of Reconstruction*, Vol. I, chaps. ii–v; J. W. Burgess, *Reconstruction and the Constitution*, chaps. i–viii; J. G. Blaine, *Twenty Years of Congress*, Vol. II, chaps. i–xii; F. L. Paxson, *The New Nation* (Riverside History), chap. iii; William MacDonald, *Select Documents of United States History, 1861–1898*, Nos. 42–44, 50–52, 56–62; A. B. Hart, *American History told by Contemporaries*, Vol. IV, Nos. 145–153; Hugh McCulloch, *Men and Measures of Half a Century*, chaps. xxv–xxvii; J. F. Rhodes, *History of the United States from the Compromise of 1850*, Vol. V, chap. xxx; Vol. VI, chaps. xxxi, xxxii; series of articles on Reconstruction in the *Atlantic Monthly*, Vol. LXXXVII, pp. 1–15, 145–157, 354–365, 473–484.

The Aftermath of War: DUNNING (Am. Nation), chaps. v–xxi; also *The Impeachment and Trial of President Johnson* (*Essays on the Civil War and Reconstruction*); E. B. ANDREWS, *The United States in our own Time*, chaps. i–xiv; PAXSON, chaps. iv, v; RHODES, Vol. VI, chaps. xxxiii–xxxix; HART, Vol. IV, Nos. 159, 174–176; MOORFIELD STOREY, *Life of Charles Sumner*, chaps. xix–xxiv; HAMLIN GARLAND, *Ulysses Grant: his Life and Character*, chaps. xxxix–l; FREDERIC BANCROFT, *The Life of William H. Seward*, Vol. II, chaps. xl–xliii; E. L. BOGART, *Economic History of the United States*, chaps. xx, xxii, xxv; EDWARD STANWOOD, *History of the Presidency*, chaps. xxiii–xxv; P. L. HAWORTH, *The Hayes-Tilden Election*.

A New Industrial Age: CARROLL D. WRIGHT, *Industrial Evolution of the United States*, chaps. xiii, xiv, xxii, xxiii; BOGART, chaps. xx, xxii, xxv; N. S. SHALER (ed.), *The United States*, Vol. I, chap. vii; Vol. II, chaps. i, ii, xii; E. E. SPARKS, *National Development* (Am. Nation), chaps. i–v, xviii; D. A. WELLS, *Recent Economic Changes*, chap. ii; HART, Vol. IV, Nos. 162, 163, 165, 168, 169; ANDREWS, chaps. ix–xiv; JOHN SHERMAN, *Recollections of Forty Years*, chaps. xxii–xxvii, xxix–xxxvii; ALBERT SHAW, *Political Problems of American Development*, chaps. vi–viii; D. R. DEWEY, *Financial History of the United States*, chaps. xiv–xvii; A. D. NOYES, *Forty Years of American Finance*, chaps. ii, iii; JOHN MITCHELL, *Organized Labor*, chap. viii; JAMES BRYCE, *The American Commonwealth*, Vol. II, chap. xlv; J. F. RHODES, *History of the United States from Hayes to McKinley*, chaps. i–x; CARL R. FISH, *The Civil Service and the Patronage*.

TOPICS FOR SPECIAL REPORTS

1. **The Ku-Klux Klans:** HART, Vol. IV, No. 156; RHODES, Vol. VI, pp. 180–191, 306–320; FLEMING, *Documentary History of Reconstruction*, Vol. II, pp. 327–377; W. G. BROWN, *The Lower South in American History*, pp. 191–225; J. W. GARNER, *Reconstruction in Mississippi*, pp. 338–353; D. L. WILSON, *The Ku-Klux Klans* (*Century Magazine*, Vol. VI, pp. 398–410); MRS. M. L. AVARY, *Dixie after the War*, pp. 268–278.

2. **The Treaty of Washington:** C. F. ADAMS, *Lee at Appomattox and Other Papers*, pp. 31–198; RHODES, Vol. VI, pp. 335–341, 360–376; ANDREWS, pp. 87–92; W. H. SEWARD, *Diplomatic History of the War for the Union*, pp. 446–481; BANCROFT, Vol. II, pp. 382–399, 492–500; STOREY, pp. 340–350.

3. **The Homestead Acts:** J. N. LARNED, *History for Ready Reference and Topical Reading*, Vol. V, pp. 3463–3464; S. SATO, *The Land Question in the United States* (*Johns Hopkins University Studies*, Vol. IV, pp. 411–427); THOMAS DONALDSON, *The Public Domain*, pp. 332–356; J. B. SANBORN, *Some Political Aspects of Homestead Legislation* (*American Historical Review*, Vol. VI, pp. 19–37); A. B. HART, *The Land Policy of the United States* (in *Essays on Practical Government*).

4. **The Granger Movement:** ANDREWS, pp. 281–284; A. T. HADLEY, *Railroad Transportation, its History and Laws*, pp. 129–139; E. W. MARTIN, *History of the Grange Movement*; C. F. ADAMS, JR., *The Granger Movement* (*North American Review*, Vol. CXX, pp. 394–410); C. W. PREISEN, *Outcome of the Granger Movement* (*Popular Science Monthly*, Vol. XXXII, pp. 201–214).

5. **Civil Service Reform:** FISH, pp. 209–245; ANDREWS, pp. 230–235, 336–342; E. BIE K. FOLTZ, *The Federal Civil Service*, pp. 38–82; SPARKS, pp. 182–201; HART, Vol. IV, No. 199; DORMAN B. EATON (articles in J. J. LALOR's *Cyclopædia of Political Science*, Vol. I, pp. 153, 472, 478; Vol. II, p. 640; Vol. III, pp. 19, 139, 565, 782, 895).

6. **The Movement for a Third Term for Grant:** SPARKS, pp. 165–172; STANWOOD, *James G. Blaine*, pp. 225–231; ANDREWS, pp. 307–312; SHERMAN, pp. 766–774; A. BADEAU, *Grant in Peace*, pp. 319 ff.; series of articles for and against a third term, by G. S. BOUTWELL, J. S. BLACK, E. W. SLAUGHTER, and TIMOTHY HOWE (*North American Review*, Vol. CXXX, pp. 116, 197, 224, 370).

CHAPTER XVIII

THE CLEVELAND DEMOCRACY

A People's President

595. Cleveland's Idea of the Presidency. In a book of essays called "Presidential Problems," written in 1904, some years after his retirement from public life, Mr. Cleveland spoke of the presidency as "preëminently the people's office." His administration of that office during the two terms 1885–1889 and 1893–1897 proved the sincerity of his remark, for he acted always as the head of the nation, even when such action threatened to cost him the leadership of his party. He did not believe that the people, in choosing a president, simply designated a man to sit at his desk in the White House and sign the bills which Congress passed up to him and make the appointments to office which the managers of the party dictated to him. Cleveland's exalted view of the independence and responsibility of the president was partly a result of his directness and decision of character and partly due to the fact that his political career had been occupied solely with executive duties — as sheriff, mayor, and governor.

596. His Quarrel with the Senate. It was inevitable that President Cleveland should come into conflict with Congress. The Democratic House which had been chosen in the election of 1884 expected him to sweep the Republicans out of all the offices which they had held for a quarter of a century; while the Republican Senate, whose consent was necessary for all the President's appointments, reminded him that the Mugwump vote, which had elected him, had been cast by Republicans who believed him an unpartisan reformer of the tariff and the civil service. When the President chose two cabinet members[1] from states of the lower South and divided the chief foreign missions and consulships between the North and the South,

---

[1] These were L. Q. C. Lamar of Mississippi, Secretary of the Interior, and Augustus H. Garland of Arkansas, Attorney-General.

as a pledge of the cessation of sectional bitterness, he was assailed for intrusting the offices of government to "ex-Confederate brigadier generals." When his sense of justice led him to remove several federal officers, especially postmasters, who had used their office unblushingly for campaign purposes, he was accused of going back on his public profession of devotion to the principles of civil service reform. The Senate made a direct issue with the President early in 1886 over the removal of District Attorney Duskin of Alabama. Invoking the Tenure of Office Act of 1867 (p. 392), the Senate refused to confirm the nomination of Duskin's successor and called on the President, through Attorney-General Garland, for the papers relating to the dismissal. Cleveland, believing that the Tenure of Office Act was unconstitutional, replied that his power of removal was absolute, refused to furnish the papers, and added that "no threat of the Senate was sufficient to discourage or deter" him from following the course which he believed led to "government for the people." A bitter fight followed in the Senate, during which Cleveland was roundly abused and his Attorney-General formally censured. But the President won and had the satisfaction of seeing the Tenure of Office Act repealed by Congress (March 3, 1887).

GROVER CLEVELAND

597. The Presidential Succession Act. In the same year the Presidential Succession Act was passed, providing that in case of the death or disability of both president and vice president the succession should go to the officers of the cabinet in the order of the creation of their departments (State, Treasury, War, etc.), instead of to the president *pro tempore* of the Senate and after him to the Speaker of the House, who might both be of the opposite party to the president. Vice President Hendricks had died in

November, 1885, and the Senate had chosen John Sherman as president *pro tempore*, thus putting a prominent Republican in line for the presidency, under the old law of 1792, in case of Cleveland's death or disability.

598. The Problem of the Surplus. Important as Cleveland regarded his contest for the restoration of the independence and dignity of the executive office,— so completely overshadowed by Congress since the Civil War,— he felt that his chief duty was the protection of the public purse by the strictest administration of the government's finances. The unexampled prosperity of our country after the recovery from the panic of 1873 had created so much wealth at home and stimulated such a volume of foreign trade that the tariff duties and revenue taxes brought into the Treasury every year far more than enough money to run the government. From $102,000,000 in 1870 the surplus grew to $145,000,000 in 1882, and in the three years following the government rolled up balances totaling $300,000,000. This large surplus was an evil in itself because it withdrew millions of dollars from the channels of business to lie idle in the vaults of the Treasury; and it was also the proof of a greater evil still, the excessive taxation of the people. Now the accumulation of a surplus could be remedied in either of two ways,— the government might increase its expenses or it might decrease its revenues. Obviously, only the latter way would lessen the burden of taxation.

599. Ways of reducing the Surplus. It would seem as if the most natural thing for the government to do with its surplus would be to pay off its debts, as an honest man would do. But the matter was not so simple as an individual transaction would be. The government's debt was largely in the shape of bonds, which were held as safe investments by people at home and abroad and which, on account of our general prosperity, were selling at a high figure. For the government to step into the market and buy back its own bonds from the public at a premium would not only mean considerable loss to the Treasury but would deprive the public of one of its best forms of investment as well. Besides, as the bonds were the security on which the notes of the national banks were issued (p. 359), to call in and cancel the bonds would mean to reduce the circulation of bank notes, just at a time, too, when more currency was needed for the volume of the country's trade.[1] There were other ways in which the surplus might be spent besides extinguishing the national debt. Congress might appropriate large sums for the improvement of rivers and harbors, for coast defenses and a new navy, for education in the South, or for increased pensions to veterans of the Civil War. This idea of the public Treasury, however, as a bountiful source of wealth for encouraging the development of our country — the old "American system" of Henry Clay and the Whigs — was opposed to all the tradition and practice of the Democratic party. Cleveland phrased the matter neatly in one of his epigrams, "The people must support the government, but the government must not support the people."

600. Cleveland's Fight for Tariff Reform. The best remedy, then, for the disposal of the surplus, the remedy which would both relieve the people of undue taxation and remove from Congress the temptation to squander the people's money, was the reduction of the tariff. To this end Cleveland devoted the chief energies of his administration. He began the attack on the protective tariff in his first annual message to Congress (December, 1885), but the House refused by a vote of 157 to 140 to consider any bill for revision. In December, 1886, the President returned to the attack, pointing to a surplus of $93,956,588 for the fiscal year and calling the protective tariff a "ruthless extortion" of the people's money. The next year he so far departed from precedent as to devote his *entire* annual message (December, 1887) to the tariff situation. He declared that it was not a time for the nice discussion of theories of free trade and protection. It might, or might not, be true that a protective tariff made American wages higher, kept our money in our own country, built up a market for American manufactures, and made us independent of foreign nations for the necessities of life. He did not advocate free trade. He only insisted that the people were being overtaxed by a tariff that was "vicious, illegal, and inequitable," and that the surplus must be reduced at once. "It is a condition that confronts us, and not a theory," he wrote.

---

[1] In spite of these considerations the government bought bonds to the value of $50,000,000 in 1886, $125,000,000 in 1887, and $130,000,000 in 1888. The bank-note circulation was reduced $126,000,000 between 1886 and 1890. This lack of notes, however, was largely remedied in 1886 by the issue of silver certificates by the Treasury in denominations of $1, $2, and $5.

601. Defeat of the Mills Bill. By dint of much persuasion Cleveland got the House to pass a tariff bill, framed by Roger Q. Mills of Texas, reducing the duties by some 7 or 8 per cent. But the Republican Senate refused to agree, and the rates remained as they were under President Arthur. Cleveland had spent his entire term fighting for a reduction of the tariff, and lost. His daring message of 1887, written in spite of the protests of the manufacturing interests in the Democratic party, was taken up by the Republican campaign orators and pamphleteers and attacked as a free-trade document which showed hostility to the prosperity of American industry and indifference to the welfare of the American wage earner. The presidential campaign of 1888 was waged entirely on the issue of the tariff, in the very days when the Mills Bill was before Congress. The Republican platform declared, "We favor the entire repeal of internal taxes rather than the surrender of any part of our protective system." On this platform they won. In the four revisions of the tariff made previous to the Underwood Bill of 1913 (the McKinley Bill of 1890, the Wilson-Gorman Bill of 1894, the Dingley Bill of 1897, and the Payne-Aldrich Bill of 1909) the duties were kept at figures averaging nearly 50 per cent,— the highest duties in our history.

602. The Tariff and the Trusts. Had Cleveland's fight for the reduction of the tariff come ten years earlier, it would have had a better chance for success. But in the decade which had followed the election of Hayes a process had been going on which gave great strength to the protectionist policy. This was the consolidation of business interests into large corporations, or "trusts."[1] By the end of Cleveland's first administration the great "coal roads" of Pennsylvania (the Erie, the Lehigh Valley, the Pennsylvania, the Lackawanna) had got control of practically all the anthracite-coal beds in the country. The lumber men, the whisky distillers, the oil, lead, and sugar refiners, the rope makers, the iron smelters, with many other "captains of industry," were consolidated into great

---

[1] The "trust" (or board of trustees) was originally a body of men holding in trust the certificates of stock of various companies included in a combine. This form of consolidation was declared illegal in the eighties, but the great industrial and transportation companies still continued, through the purchase of the majority of the stock of the smaller companies, or through management of them by identical boards of directors, to control business and prices as before. The name "trust" is commonly applied to any combination large and wealthy enough to tend to monopolize the production and distribution of any commodity.

trusts. These trusts by no means created the policy of high protection, which had been advocated for decades by the manufacturers of the North, but they exerted an influence in Congress against the reduction of the tariff.

603. The Demands of Labor. The consolidation of capital in great corporations was attended in the same epoch by combinations of laborers for the securing of adequate wages, a fair working day, humane treatment in case of sickness or disability, and protection against unmerited discharge. The workers demanded "full enjoyment of the wealth they create and sufficient leisure to develop their intellectual, moral, and social faculties, to share in the gains and honors of advancing civilization." For the accomplishment of these ends they asked the state and national governments for laws guaranteeing health and safety in mines and factories, prohibiting the employment of children, enforcing arbitration of disputes between capital and labor, laying a graduated tax on incomes, forbidding the importation of foreign labor or the employment of convict labor, and securing the "nationalizing" (that is, the taking over by the government) of the telegraphs, the telephones, and the railroads.[1] At the same time, with growing numbers and influence, united labor was itself guilty of arbitrary and unjust acts, such as the limitation of output and the denial of the "right to labor" to nonunion workers.

604. Labor and the Government. The strife between capital and labor was very bitter in Cleveland's first term. Over 500 labor disputes, chiefly over wages and hours of work, were reported in the early months of 1886; and the number of strikes for that year was double the number of any previous year.[2] President Cleveland was

---

[1] The labor movement became prominent in politics and literature in the year 1886, when Henry George, the author of "Progress and Poverty" and an advocate of the "single tax" (a tax on land only and not on industry or commerce), ran for mayor of New York on the labor platform. A widely read novel of Edward Bellamy, entitled "Looking Backward," pictured the utopian state of society in the year 2000, when complete coöperation should have taken the place of competition and wage struggles.

[2] The number of strikes tabulated by Adams and Sumner's "Labor Problems" (p. 180), is as follows: 1884, 485; 1885, 695; 1886, 1572; 1887, 1505; 1888, 946. The most serious of the strikes of 1886 culminated in a deed of horror. An open-air meeting in Haymarket Square, Chicago, called by anarchists to protest against the forcible repression of the strike in the McCormick Reaper Works and to demand an eight-hour day, was ordered by the police to disperse. When the police charged, a dynamite bomb was thrown into the midst of the squad, instantly killing 7 men and wounding 60 more. With intrepid step the police closed their ranks and dispersed the meeting. The ringleaders of the anarchists were arrested, and the next year four of them were hanged.

greatly concerned over these labor troubles. In the spring of 1886 he sent to Congress a special message on the subject,— the first presidential message on labor in our history. The House had already appointed a standing committee on labor, and had created (1884) a national Bureau of Labor in the Department of the Interior for collecting statistics on the condition of wage earners. Cleveland now recommended the creation of a national commission of labor, to consist of three persons who should have power to hear and settle controversies between capital and labor. Congress failed to adopt this important recommendation, but several of the states (including Massachusetts and New York) passed laws providing for the settlement of labor disputes by arbitration.

605. The Railroad Problem. The most serious trouble was with the railroads. We have already seen in the Granger movement the hostility of the Western farmers to the railroads in the early seventies (p. 404). As the great wheat and corn fields, the ranches, and the mines west of the Mississippi were developed, and the cities of the Middle West grew into busy manufacturing and distributing centers, the problem of freight transportation became of increasing importance. The railways, except for some slight competition on the Great Lakes and the Mississippi, had a monopoly of this transportation, and their charges were regarded as a tax on the producer and the manufacturer,— a tax which the roads could regulate at their own good pleasure. Now in matters of taxation the public objects both to excessive rates and to a difference in rates for different persons,— to extortion and to discrimination. It felt that the railroads were guilty of the former offense, and knew that they were guilty of the latter. It saw their power and wealth rapidly increasing.[1] It saw their influence extending into state legislatures and the national Congress. It saw them allying themselves with trusts, like the Standard Oil Company, to crush out competition and ruin the small producer. It saw them cutting their rates on through hauls from Chicago or St. Louis to New York, where there was competition with other trunk lines, and making up the loss by charging high freights to shippers who depended on one road alone for getting their products to the markets.

---

[1] The railroad mileage doubled in the decade 1870-1880, growing from 53,000 to 100,000 miles. During the years 1879-1884 the mileage increased four times as fast as the population of the United States.

606. The Granger Laws and the Wabash Case. In all this the public, too prone to forget the good which the railroads had done in developing the great vacant tracts of the West, judged the railroads to be guilty of gross injustice and ingratitude. They had been granted charters by the states as public benefactors; they had been the recipients of large grants of public lands; they had been accorded privileges of tax exemption; they had been allowed to take private property when necessary for the construction of their lines; they had had their bonds guaranteed by the state legislatures. Their obvious duty in return for these favors was to give the public the best possible service consistent with a fair interest on the actual capital invested in their construction and operation. Some of the state legislatures, responding to the outcry against the railroads, passed so-called Granger Laws, fixing the maximum of rates which the roads could charge for freight and storage and compelling equality of treatment for all shippers. But when a decision in the United States court (Wabash Railroad *vs.* the State of Illinois) ruled in 1886 that no state law could apply to commerce carried on between two or more states, the Granger Laws were seen to be utterly ineffective, for no railroad of any importance had its traffic confined to a single state.

607. The Interstate Commerce Act. Now the Constitution (Article I, sect. 8, par. 3) gives Congress power "to regulate commerce with foreign nations, and *among the several states.*" By virtue of this power Congress passed the famous Interstate Commerce Act (or Cullom Act) in February, 1887. The act provided for a commission of five men, with power to investigate the books of railroads doing interstate business and to call the managers of the roads to hearings. It forbade any discrimination in rates and required the roads to file their tariffs for public inspection. It prohibited the "pooling" of traffic[1] and the charging of a higher rate on a short haul than on a long haul. The commission had no power of jurisdiction, but only of investigation; that is, each case against a railroad had to be tried in a federal court. The influence of the railroads with the courts and the skill of shrewd corporation lawyers in "interpreting" the rather vague language of the statute reduced the Interstate

---

[1] By "pooling" is meant dividing the traffic by amicable agreement among the various roads which would naturally compete for it. The total profits are then put into a common treasury and divided according to the business assigned to each road. It is a device to kill competition between the roads.

Commerce Act to a "useless piece of legislation," in the opinion of Justice Harlan of the Supreme Court. Yet, for all its failure to control the railroads adequately, the act was of great importance. It taught the people that our government could and would exert its power in the sphere of private industries. It made the railroads open their books and publish their rates.[1] Most important of all, it created a precedent for the government regulation of railroads and other corporations and made the more effective legislation that followed in the twentieth century seem like the natural extension of a policy already firmly established by the government.

608. Cleveland defeated by Harrison in 1888. President Cleveland came out of the trying circumstances of his first administration indisputably the leading man of the Democratic party. Even his enemies in the party were obliged to concede his "unflinching integrity and robust common sense." He was renominated by acclamation in the Democratic national convention held at St. Louis in June, 1888. Blaine, his rival in 1884, was absent in Europe on an extended trip. He would undoubtedly have been the choice of the Republican convention at Chicago had he not written from Florence, and again cabled from Paris, his unconditional refusal to take the nomination. The convention, passing over the more prominent candidate, John Sherman, selected, at Blaine's suggestion,[2] General Benjamin Harrison, United States senator from Indiana, an able lawyer and an honored veteran of the Civil War, the grandson of the old Whig hero and president, William Henry Harrison. Cleveland's famous tariff message of 1887 was denounced as a free-trade document by Republican orators, and the benefits of a protective tariff were lauded in a long cablegram from Blaine, congratulating the American workman on his advantages over his European brother. Cleveland lost the support of the veterans of the Civil War by his veto of a great number of pension bills[3] and by his executive order

---

[1] During 1887 and 1888 about 270,000 freight tariffs were filed. At one time they were received by the commission at the rate of 500 a day.

[2] After the fifth ballot had been cast a cable message was sent by the convention leaders to Blaine, who was visiting Andrew Carnegie at his country seat, Skibo Castle, in Scotland, asking him to change his mind and accept the nomination. The answer came: "Too late. Blaine immovable. Take Harrison and Phelps." The convention took Harrison and Morton.

[3] In 1885 nearly three times as many persons were receiving pensions from the government as at the close of the Civil War. In 1866 our pension charge was $15,000,000; by 1885 it had grown to $56,000,000. Pensions were obtained by swindling agents on absurd claims.

directing that the Confederate flags stored in the War Building at Washington be restored to the Southern states from whose regiments they had been captured.[1] And, finally, in the pivotal state of New York, the defection from Cleveland on the national issue of the tariff was sufficient to cause his defeat, although the Democratic candidate for governor, David B. Hill, was elected in a campaign involving state issues and engendering much bitterness within the party. The state went Republican by 12,000 in a total of 1,300,000 votes, giving Harrison the presidency. Cleveland's popular vote throughout the country, however, exceeded Harrison's by over 100,000 — more than double the popular plurality of any successful presidential candidate since 1872. Grover Cleveland returned to private life with this splendid indorsement of his policies by his fellow citizens.

A Billion-Dollar Country

609. The Republican Reaction. Although the election of 1888 gave the Republicans only a narrow majority in Congress and actually registered a popular triumph for Cleveland, the Republicans proceeded as though they had been swept into office by a tidal wave like Jackson's victory of 1828 or the Whig revolution of 1840. They reversed the entire policy of the Cleveland administration, advocating large expenditures in the place of public economy, increase in tariff rates rather than reduction, a bold, aggressive foreign policy to replace the cautious diplomacy carried on by Cleveland's State Department. The new President was a complete contrast to his predecessor. He was a party man, willing to receive and respect the warning sent him just after his election by the leader of the Senate, John Sherman: "The President should have no policy distinct from that of his party, and this is better represented in Congress than in the executive." Courtesy required that Harrison should offer the highest position in his patronage to the man who had made him the choice of the party. Blaine accepted the portfolio of State and throughout

---

Hundreds of pension bills were passed at a single sitting of the Senate. Cleveland insisted on investigating each case thoroughly and vetoed 233 out of the 747 pension bills passed in his first term. Only one was passed over his veto.

[1] This so-called "Rebel Flag Order" was a blunder on the part of the President. He had no authority to restore the flags, which were national property; and he revoked the order when he saw his mistake. In 1905 a Republican Congress passed a bill restoring the "rebel flags" to their states, and the bill was signed by a Republican president.

the administration completely overshadowed his nominal chief in the White House. The Speaker of the House, Thomas B. Reed of Maine, was also a masterful, conspicuous figure in the administration. He ran the House in such dictatorial fashion that he was nicknamed "Czar Reed." When the Democrats sought to prevent a quorum by refusing to answer to the roll call, Speaker Reed counted as "present" all members on the floor of the House. He refused to recognize speakers or put motions whose evident intent was to delay the business of the House. In a word, he made Congress a perfect machine for the dispatch of the Republican program and elevated the Speaker to a position of autocratic power which he held unimpaired up to the year 1910.[1]

610. Public Works and Pensions. The Republican Congress of 1889–1891, approving the remark of General Grant's son that "a surplus is easier to handle than a deficit," began immediately to reduce the surplus by generous appropriations. It increased the number of steel vessels in the navy from three vessels in 1889 to twenty-two in 1893, putting the United States among the half-dozen greatest naval powers of the world. It spent large sums on coast defenses, lighthouses, and harbors. It repaid the state treasuries some $15,000,000 of the direct taxes levied at the beginning of the Civil War. In the matter of pensions it was more than liberal. During the campaign, Harrison, referring to Cleveland's careful examination of all applications for pensions, remarked that it was "no time to be weighing the claims of the old soldiers with an apothecary's scales." Congress now proceeded

BENJAMIN HARRISON

---

[1] The immense power of the Speaker consisted in the fact that he appointed all the committees of the House, that as presiding officer he could recognize, or not, as he pleased, the member who rose to speak, and that he was ex officio a member of the Rules Committee, which arranges the whole calendar of the House and can keep any bill from "coming up" as long as it chooses to. In the spring of 1910 a body of Republican insurgents, with the help of Democratic votes, passed a resolution depriving the Speaker (Joseph G. Cannon) of some of his power. For example, he was "deposed" from the Rules Committee, which was hereafter to be enlarged to fifteen members and elected by the House.

to grant them pensions sometimes without weighing their claims at all. The disbursements for pensions rose during Harrison's term from $88,000,000 to $159,000,000 annually,—a sum greater than the cost of the army and navy of the United States in any year of peace during the nineteenth century.

611. Our Billion-Dollar Country. Altogether the appropriations of Harrison's first Congress reached the $1,000,000,000 mark. When the Democrats cried out against "the raid on the Treasury" and the extravagance of a billion-dollar Congress, Speaker Reed quietly replied that it was "a billion-dollar country." If there was some carelessness in expenditure it is also true that there was wise and patriotic forethought in the Republican program, especially in the creation of the nucleus of our magnificent navy. We were rapidly growing to be a power of the first magnitude, and our government recognized that it must keep abreast with the development of the country. The eleventh census (1890), compiled in 25 volumes, revealed the astonishing prosperity of the United States at the end of the first century of its existence under the Constitution.[1] Our population was 62,500,000 and our wealth $65,000,000,000. Especially noticeable was the concentration of our people in cities. The number of cities of over 8000 inhabitants doubled in the decade 1880–1890, and by the latter year such cities contained fully one half the population of New England, New York, New Jersey, and Pennsylvania.

612. Progress of the South. The census showed also that the South was recovering from the ravages of the Civil War and the Reconstruction period and was beginning that marvelous career of industrial prosperity which has been the feature of our growth in the present generation. Encouraged by Northern capital, the South was building mills for spinning her own cotton, improving her transportation lines by land and water, exploiting the splendid forests of the Carolinas and Georgia, and opening the rich deposits of coal and iron which stretched in an unbroken line of over 500 miles through the highlands from West Virginia to Alabama. By 1890 the latter state ranked third in the Union in the production of iron, and the South as a whole was producing more coal and iron than the whole country had mined twenty years earlier.

---

[1] A few weeks after his inauguration Mr. Harrison had been the central figure in an imposing pageant in New York City in celebration of the one hundredth anniversary of the inauguration of George Washington (April 30, 1789).

613. New States in the Northwest. In the Far Northwest the tier of territories extending from Minnesota to Oregon were filling rapidly with farmers, ranchmen, lumbermen, and miners. The Indian frontier had largely disappeared. The reservations were an obstacle to the Pacific railroads, and had to go. The government tried to break up the tribal organization of the Indians by the Dawes Bill of 1887, which granted each head of an Indian family 160 acres of

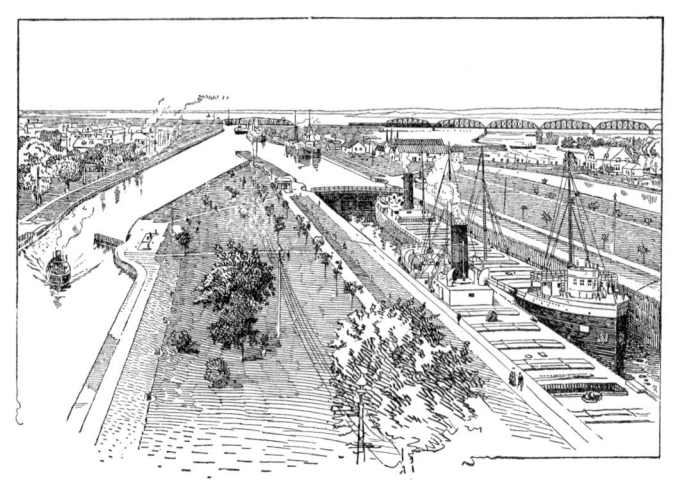

THE LOCKS IN THE "SOO"

The Sault Sainte Marie Canal at the outlet of Lake Superior, through which over $40,000,000 worth of merchandise passes annually

land and American citizenship. The next year some 15,000 Indian youths were in government schools, where it was hoped that they would be weaned by the industry and science of the white man from the shiftless, roaming, cruel life of the tribe. With the stubborn but vain resistance of the Sioux of Dakota, in 1890, to the advancing tide of civilization our great Indian wars were at an end. By that date the territories of the Northwest had already become states of the Union. On November 2, 1889, President Harrison proclaimed the admission of North and South Dakota, Montana, and Washington, and the next year Idaho and Wyoming were added. An unbroken tier of states reached from the Atlantic to the Pacific.[1] Politics also figured in the admission to statehood of the six territories of the Northwest. The Republicans counted on a majority in all of them except Montana, as they had been largely settled by pioneers from the stanch Republican states of Iowa, Wisconsin, Minnesota, and Illinois. As states they were expected to contribute 10 senators and 5 or 6 representatives to the slim Republican majority in Congress, besides adding about 15 electoral votes to the Republican column in the next presidential year.

614. The Federal Election Bill. There was no doubt that the Southern states were violating both the Fifteenth and the Fourteenth Amendment. They were depriving the negro of his vote by fraud, force, or intimidation; and they were still enjoying a representation in Congress based on their total population, black and white. At the time of Harrison's election they had over twenty congressmen and presidential electors more than the strict enforcement of the second section of the Fourteenth Amendment would entitle them to. Accordingly, the Republican House of 1890 passed the Federal Election Bill (called by the Democrats the "Force Bill"), providing that, on the petition of 500 voters, federal agents should supervise the national elections in any district. In the more conservative Senate the bill, which would have fanned into flame again the dying embers of sectional bitterness, was fortunately defeated, and the attempts of the North to compel the South to allow the negro to vote ceased.[2]

[1] The government purchased from the Indians the district of Oklahoma ("the beautiful land") in Indian Territory and opened it for settlement at noon, April 22, 1889. A horde of pioneers, who had been waiting anxiously on the borders, swarmed into the coveted territory, and before night several "cities" were staked out. In 1890 the only territories that remained within the limits of the United States were Utah, Oklahoma, Indian Territory, Arizona, and New Mexico. Utah was entitled to statehood by its population, but the existence of the Mormon institution of polygamy prevented its admission until the Mormon Church promised to abolish polygamy (1895). Oklahoma and Indian Territory were combined and admitted as the state of Oklahoma in 1907. In 1912 New Mexico and Arizona were admitted to statehood after a long controversy over the proposed union of the territories. With the admission of New Mexico and Arizona we have a solid band of forty-eight states from ocean to ocean, and our only territories (Alaska, Hawaii, Porto Rico) are rather of the nature of foreign colonies.

[2] Most of the Southern states have framed constitutions since 1890 containing clauses which practically disqualify the negro, for a while at least. For example, in the Louisiana Constitution of 1898 the famous "grandfather clause" restricts the suffrage to those who have certain educational and property qualifications or who are sons or grandsons of the legal voters of January 1, 1867. Under this clause the negro registration was reduced in

615. The McKinley Tariff Bill. The Republican platform of 1888 pledged the party to a high protective tariff. In the spring of 1890, therefore, William McKinley of Ohio, chairman of the Committee on Ways and Means, introduced into the House the tariff bill which bears his name. Duties were increased on almost all articles of household consumption,— food, carpets, clothing, tools, coal, wood, tinware, linen, thread. Prices rose immediately. Wage earners felt the pinch throughout the country. The opponents of protection claimed that the tariff benefited the trusts alone; that the increased American capital due to the tariff went into the pockets of the manufacturers as profits, not to the workers as wages.

616. The Sherman Silver Act. So perfect was the Republican control of the House under the Reed rules that the important McKinley Bill was passed in less than two weeks. In the Senate, however, it was held up for four months. Seventeen of the forty-seven Republican senators came from farming and mining states west of the Mississippi. They were not much interested in high protection, but some of them were very much interested in silver mining. They thought Congress ought to "protect" silver as an American product just as much as wool or iron. This could not be done by any kind of tariff legislation, but the government might purchase enough silver to keep the price of the metal from falling in the general market. Although by the Bland-Allison Act of 1878 (p. 407) the government had for twelve years been purchasing silver at the rate of $2,000,000 a month, the price of the metal declined steadily. The silver miners clamored for the government to buy still more, even to take all the silver that should be brought to the mints. In order to win the Western votes for the tariff and also to "do something for silver" as an American product, Congress in 1890 passed the Sherman Silver Purchase Act, by which it pledged the government to buy 4,500,000 ounces of silver every month at the market price (at that time about a dollar an ounce), and issue legal-tender

---

Louisiana from 127,000 in 1896 to 5300 in 1900. The Supreme Court has refused to pronounce on the constitutionality of such proceedings,— in other words, has "let the South alone," which is all that it asks. The cause for this complacency on the part of the North is probably chiefly the large investments of Northern capital in Southern industries, and the consequent desire to have business undisturbed by political wranglings. It may be that the idea of a tardy reparation for the injuries done the South in the Reconstruction days also influences the Northern attitude.

treasury notes to the full amount of the silver purchased. The silver itself, constantly shrinking in value, accumulated in the treasury.[1]

617. The "Tidal Wave" of 1890. The congressional election of 1890 resulted, as mid-term elections very frequently do, in the defeat of the party in power. Charging the Republicans with extravagance (pension bills), sectionalism ("Force Bill"), and surrender to the trusts (McKinley Bill), the Democrats called on the country to rebuke the administration. And the country, influenced mainly by the high prices following the new tariff act, returned 235 Democrats to Congress against 88 Republicans. For the remaining two years of Harrison's term nothing in the way of legislation could be accomplished. The large Democratic majority in the House frustrated the administration's plans, while the Senate, with its Republican majority of six, kept the House from repealing the high tariff legislation. All interest in these years centers in the foreign policy of the country, where the executive and the Senate could act unhampered by the House.

618. Pan-Americanism and Reciprocity. It will be remembered that Blaine, during his few months of vigorous service as Secretary of State in Garfield's cabinet (1881), had tried to increase our influence in Central and South America by securing control of the Isthmian Canal route and by negotiating reciprocity treaties of commerce between the United States and the Latin-American republics (p. 412). In Harrison's cabinet Blaine resumed his active policy. A Pan-American Congress (already proposed in 1881) met at Washington in October, 1889. It was composed of delegates from nineteen countries of Latin America. The subjects discussed were mutual trade regulations, a uniform standard of weights and measures, a common currency, and a code for the arbitration of the frequent quarrels among the Latin republics. A Bureau of the American Republics was founded at Washington to keep us informed of the fortunes of our sister states in the tropics. By using his personal influence with members of Congress, Blaine finally got his reciprocity doctrine incorporated into the McKinley Tariff Bill.

619. The Samoan Islands. Diplomatic quarrels with Germany, Great Britain, Italy, and Chile brought us at times to the verge of

[1] In the same year (1890) Congress passed the Sherman Anti-Trust Act, which was aimed against the restraint of foreign or interstate trade by the trusts. But the act was so vague that it was easily evaded, and remained for many years ineffective.

war during Harrison's administration. The Samoan Islands in the Pacific Ocean were occupied on a "tripartite" agreement between Great Britain, Germany, and the United States. Prince Bismarck, the German chancellor, was anxious to build up a large colonial empire to rival Great Britain's. Acting under his orders the German consul in Samoa schemed to oust the British and Americans. He raised the German flag over Apia, the chief town of the islands, set up his own "king," declared war on the rightful king in the name of his Majesty the German emperor, and prepared to shell the villages which resisted him. American warships were hurried to Apia, and the decks were cleared for action, when a terrific typhoon struck the harbor (March 16, 1889), capsizing the German and American ships or dashing them on the beach and the coral reefs. A conference followed at Berlin the next month, in which the chancellor recognized the neutrality of the islands and the full rights of England and the United States in the protectorate over the native king. It was the first conspicuous participation of our country in "world politics," and it was also a spur to the construction of an adequate navy. By the end of the following year Congress had appropriated $40,000,000 for the building of new warships, and before the end of Harrison's administration we had risen from the twelfth to the fifth place among the naval powers.

620. The Seal Fisheries in Bering Sea. Blaine had inherited from the Cleveland administration a dispute with Great Britain over the seal fisheries in Bering Sea. He contended that Bering Sea was a *mare clausum* ("closed sea"), appertaining entirely to Alaska, and hence within the sole jurisdiction of the United States. The British claimed that it was the "high sea" and that our jurisdiction extended only to the ordinary three-mile limit from shore. Under executive orders our revenue cutters seized eight British sealing vessels during the summer of 1889, all outside the three-mile limit, and Blaine addressed the British premier, Lord Salisbury, in language which drew in reply a virtual threat of war (June, 1890). On sober reflection our government receded from its dictatorial position and agreed to submit the whole matter to arbitration. The tribunal, which met at Paris in 1893, decided every point against us. Bering Sea was declared open, and we were forced to pay damages for the seizure of the British vessels.

621. Quarrels with Italy and Chile. Serious quarrels with Italy and Chile also disturbed the Harrison administration. In the former case the Italian government, not understanding that our federal administration has no concern with the criminal jurisdiction of any state, demanded that our State Department investigate the lynching of some Italians in New Orleans and bring to punishment the guilty men. Finally, after diplomatic relations had already been severed between Washington and Rome, the Italian government accepted as reparation a vote of $25,000 by Congress for the families of the murdered men. The trouble in Chile was caused by our minister's partiality for the dictator Balmaceda, whom a successful revolution of the Congressional party had overthrown. It looked like certain war with Chile when, in the autumn of 1891, an American sailor from the cruiser *Baltimore* was killed in the streets of Valparaiso, and the Chilean foreign minister publicly characterized President Harrison's protest to Congress as an "erroneous or deliberately incorrect" statement. But the firm attitude of our government, coupled with patience and considerateness in the negotiations, brought Chile to offer the apologies which closed the incident.

622. The Resignation and Death of Blaine. Blaine's popularity was enhanced by his vigorous administration of the Department of State. In 1891 there were rumors of his nomination for the presidency the next year. Blaine himself gave no support to the movement and even declared early in 1892 that he was not a candidate. However, three days before the Republican convention met at Minneapolis (June 4, 1892), Blaine suddenly resigned his cabinet position in a curt note. His motives have never been fully known. Illness, tedium of the cares of office, lack of sympathy with his chief, an eleventh-hour desire for nomination for the presidency, have all been advanced as the causes for his resignation. At any rate, he received only 182 votes in the convention to 535 for Harrison and retired, much broken in health, to his Maine home. He died the following January. Blaine's character is one of the hardest to estimate in all our history. He was brilliant, able, genial, and brave, but with all his powers of intellect, gift of leadership, and charm of personality he never succeeded in winning the full confidence of the American people. He could be mercilessly clear in his exposure of other men, but in his revelation of himself there was always a suggestion of fog. On the whole, he was our most prominent political leader between Lincoln and Roosevelt.

623. The Populist Party. As the presidential campaign of 1892 approached, it was evident that a new factor of great importance had entered our national politics. We have already noticed the activity of the Grangers and the Knights of Labor in the seventies and the eighties. About 1890 these organizations (expanded already into the Farmers' Alliance and the American Federation of Labor) united to make a compact political party. They held a national convention at Cincinnati in May, 1891, with over 1400 delegates from 32 states. They adopted the title of People's party (familiarly "Populists") and drew up a radical platform demanding, among other reforms, the free coinage of silver, the abolition of the national banks, a graduated income tax, the government ownership of railroads, steamship lines, telegraph and telephone service, and the election of United States senators by popular vote. The next year they assembled at Omaha and nominated James B. Weaver of Iowa for president.

624. Cleveland reëlected in 1892. Meanwhile the Democrats were in a quandary. Cleveland was their strongest man, but he had enemies among the machine politicians of the East, like Governor David B. Hill of New York, while his fearless condemnation of free silver made him an impossible candidate in the eyes of the Democratic managers in the West. But the very qualities which disqualified Cleveland in the eyes of the politicians commended him to the people. He had been a people's president in 1885; he became the people's nominee in 1892. In spite of the efforts of the Democratic machine politicians to secure anti-Cleveland delegates to the convention, the tide of popular feeling set stronger and stronger toward the ex-President as the day of the convention approached. He was nominated on the first ballot, and the following November was elected over Harrison by 277 votes to 145, with a popular plurality of about 400,000. A Democratic House was reëlected, and the Republicans lost their long hold in the Senate. For the first time since Buchanan's day a Democratic administration had a majority in both branches of Congress. For the first time also since the election of 1860 a third party figured in the electoral column. Weaver, the Populist candidate, carried the four states of Colorado, Idaho, Kansas, and Nevada, receiving 22 electoral votes and polling over

1,000,000 popular votes. The significance for the Democratic party of this radical movement in the West will appear when we study the presidential campaign of 1896.

Problems of Cleveland's Second Term

625. Difficulties confronting President Cleveland. It is doubtful if any other American president in times of peace had ever had to contend with such harassing problems as confronted Grover Cleveland when he was inaugurated for a second time, March 4, 1893. The Treasury was nearly empty. The gold reserve, maintained by the government to protect its paper money in circulation, had sunk to the danger limit. Throughout the country there was serious industrial depression, due to uncertainty as to how a solid Democratic Congress would treat the tariff and to apprehension lest the radical Populists of the West should capture the Democratic party. Thousands of laborers were thrown out of employment just at the time when the high prices following the McKinley tariff made their living most precarious; and agitators were ready to organize the discontented into a crusade against the great capitalist interests, the railroads, and the protected trusts.

626. The Gold Famine. The most immediate problem that confronted the President was the condition of the Treasury. Ever since the resumption of specie payments, in 1879, it had been the policy of the government (confirmed by an act of Congress in 1882) to keep a reserve of at least $100,000,000 in gold for the redemption of any of the $346,000,000 in greenbacks still in circulation. By the Sherman Silver Act of 1890 the government was steadily increasing the volume of its paper money by issuing legal tender to the value of the silver purchased. The greenbacks and notes in circulation in 1893 amounted to nearly $500,000,000, all of which the Treasury considered itself bound to redeem in gold if the demand were made. Now it is a well-known economic law that when currency of different grades of value exists in a country, the cheaper kind drives the other out of circulation. This means simply that if a man has his choice between paying a bill with dollars that he knows will always and everywhere be worth 100 cents and dollars which he suspects may sometime or somewhere be worth only 50 cents, he will part with the latter and save the former. In spite of our government's efforts to maintain a "parity," or a constant ratio, between silver and gold, silver steadily declined in price, and the value of the silver dollar consequently shrank. Banks and individuals then began to hoard their gold. The yellow metal threatened to disappear from circulation. Just before the passage of the Sherman Act the government was receiving 85 per cent of its customs duties in gold; two years later less than 20 per cent of these payments were made in gold. To make matters worse, the uncertainty and depression in business made foreigners unwilling to invest in our securities, and we had to ship large quantities of gold abroad to pay unfavorable trade balances.

627. The Repeal of the Sherman Act. Two immediate duties were before President Cleveland,—to stop the further purchase of silver and to replenish the Treasury with gold. To accomplish the first of these duties Cleveland called an extra session of Congress in the summer of 1893 and asked it to repeal the Sherman Act. The repeal passed the House readily, but the senators of the seven "silver states" of the West (which contained less than 2 per cent of the population of the country) fought the bill for several weeks before they yielded.

628. The Bond Transactions. The replenishment of the gold supply, however, proved a more difficult task, which occupied the entire administration. Twice during the year 1894 the Secretary of the Treasury sold $50,000,000 worth of bonds for gold, without helping matters much. For the buyers of the bonds simply presented greenbacks at the Treasury for redemption, to get the gold to pay for the bonds. They thus took out of the Treasury with one hand the gold they put in with the other. Determined to stop this "endless-chain" process of the withdrawal and the restoration of the same millions continually, Cleveland early in 1895 summoned to the White House Mr. J. Pierpont Morgan, the most powerful financial figure in America. Mr. Morgan arranged with the President to furnish the Treasury some $62,000,000 in gold in return for the government's 4 per cent bonds. The price Mr. Morgan charged for the gold secured him the bonds at a considerably lower figure than the public were paying for them at the time, and a cry went up from the Western Democrats and Populists that Cleveland had entered into an unholy alliance with the money lenders and was squandering the country's resources to enrich the bankers of New York and London. If Mr. Morgan did drive a hard bargain with the government, he at least secured an actual supply of gold for the Treasury (one half the amount being obtained from foreign bankers) and went to considerable expense to prevent the shipment of gold abroad. The President defended himself for entering into this private bargaining for gold on the ground that the state of the Treasury was desperate and that the people had twice within a year given proof of their unwillingness to part with their gold hoardings to strengthen the credit of the government.[1] Altogether during Cleveland's administration the government issued bonds to the amount of $262,000,000 in order to attract enough gold to keep the reserve up to the $100,000,000 mark. The election of 1896, which was fought on the currency issue, resulted in the defeat of silver, and gold came out of hiding.

J. PIERPONT MORGAN
Copyright, Pach Brothers

629. The Wilson-Gorman Tariff. Although Cleveland was elected in 1892 chiefly on the tariff issue, his efforts to get from Congress a purely revenue tariff were no more successful than they had been in 1888 (p. 422). William L. Wilson of West Virginia introduced a bill in December, 1893, providing for the removal of duties on raw materials (wool, iron ore, coal, lumber, sugar) and a considerable reduction in the duties on manufactured articles (china, glass, silk, cotton and woolen goods). The bill promptly passed the House by 182 votes to 106, but when it reached the Senate it was "held up." It made no difference that the Senate was Democratic. The "coal senators"

[1] Opinion will always be divided on the wisdom of Cleveland's action. It cost him the bitter hostility of the West, but it satisfied his own conscience. He concludes the chapter on The Bond Issues in his "Presidential Problems" (1904) with the words, "Though Mr. Morgan and Mr. Belmont and scores of others who were accessories in these transactions may be steeped in destructive propensities and may be constantly busy in sinful schemes, I shall always recall with satisfaction and self-congratulation my association with them at a time when our country sorely needed their aid."

of West Virginia, the "iron senators" of Alabama, the "sugar senators" of Louisiana, the "lumber senators" of Montana, all fought for the protection of their "interests." Under the lead of the Democratic Senator Gorman of Maryland (heavily interested in the sugar trust) the Wilson Bill was "mutilated" beyond recognition by over 600 amendments. Only wool, copper, and lumber were left on the free list, and the average of the duties was as high as under the Republican bill of 1883. It was still a "protective" tariff. The House reluctantly yielded, to save a deadlock, but President Cleveland refused to sign the bill, which he called a piece of "party perfidy and dishonor." It became a law (August, 1894) without his signature.

630. The Income Tax Decision. To make up for an anticipated loss of some $50,000,000 in tariff duties, the Wilson Bill contained a provision for a tax of 2 per cent on incomes exceeding $4000. An income tax ranging from 3 per cent to 10 per cent had been imposed by the federal government during the years 1861 to 1872, to help meet the tremendous cost of the Civil War; but the income tax in time of peace was resisted as unconstitutional and inquisitorial by the wealthy classes, on whom its burden would fall. In May, 1895, the Supreme Court decided, by a vote of 5 to 4 (reversing its decision of 1870), that the income tax was a direct tax and hence could be levied only by apportionment among the states according to population (Constitution, Art. I, sect. 2, par. 3). Such apportionment would be impossible, as the wealth of the states bore no fair ratio to their population. This decision exempted the wealth obtained from rents, stocks, and bonds from contributing to the support of the government, while almost every article of consumption of the poor laborer was taxed by the tariff. It still further stirred the radical temper of the West. The Supreme Court was decried as the rich man's ally, and the revocation of its power to pronounce laws of Congress unconstitutional was demanded.

631. Coxey's Army. With the financial and tariff policy of the country at sixes and sevens, the administration was still further harassed by serious labor troubles. The industrial depression of 1893 brought failures, strikes, and lockouts in its train. The winter was attended with great suffering throughout the country, and tramps and vagrants swarmed over the land. An "army" of the unemployed, led by one Jacob Coxey, marched from Ohio to Washington to demand that Congress issue $500,000,000 in irredeemable paper currency, to be spent in furnishing work for the idle by improving the highways all over the Union. The "invasion" of Washington by "Coxey's army" ended in a farce. As the men marched across the lawn of the Capitol on May-day morning their leaders were arrested for "walking on the grass," and the men straggled away to be lost in the motley city crowd.

632. The Pullman Strike. There was nothing farcical, however, in the conflict between capital and labor which broke out in Chicago that same month of May. The Pullman Palace Car Company, whose business had been seriously injured by the hard times of 1893, discharged a number of employees for whom it had no immediate use and cut the wages of the rest. But in view of the fact that the company was paying 7 per cent dividends, that it had accumulated a surplus of $25,000,000 on a capital of $36,000,000, the workers could not see that the company was suffering, and a committee of the docked men waited on Mr. Pullman to remonstrate. For this "impertinence" three men on the committee were discharged. Then nearly all the employees struck. About 4000 of the Pullman employees were members of the powerful American Railway Union, an organization founded in 1893 under the presidency of Eugene V. Debs. The union took up the matter at its June meeting in 1894 and demanded that the company submit the question of wages to arbitration. This Mr. Pullman refused to do. The union then forbade its men to "handle" the Pullman cars. The boycott extended to 27 states and territories, affecting the railroads from Ohio to California. But the dire conflict came in Chicago. Early in July only 6 of the 23 railroads entering the city were unobstructed. United States mail trains carrying Pullman cars were not allowed to move. President Cleveland ordered troops to the seat of disturbance, and an injunction was issued by the federal court ordering the strikers to cease obstructing the United States mails. The reading of the injunction was received with hoots and jeers. Debs had appealed to the strikers to refrain from violence and the destruction of property, but they could not be restrained.[1] Trains were ditched, freight

---

[1] Especially as their number was swelled by thousands of vagrant ruffians and "bums," who had been attracted to Chicago by the great Columbian Exposition of the preceding summer. This so-called "World's Fair" of 1893, in celebration of the four-hundredth anniversary of the discovery of America, was a veritable fairyland of dazzling white buildings, softened by fountains and lagoons. The Exposition cost about $30,000,000 and was visited by over 12,000,000 people.

cars destroyed, buildings burned and looted. At one or two points it became necessary for the federal troops to fire on the mob to protect their own lives. Debs and his chief associates were arrested and imprisoned for contempt of court in not obeying the injunction.

633. Consequences of the Strike. The strike was broken by the prompt action of the government, but it left ugly consequences. For the first time in our history federal troops had fired upon American citizens to preserve order. Governor Altgeld of Illinois, who

COURT OF HONOR, COLUMBIAN EXPOSITION

had pardoned the anarchists of the Haymarket riot (p. 423, note 2), took the President severely to task for sending troops into the state, declaring that "Illinois was able to take care of herself"; and he was generally supported by the Populist element of the West, while even among the conservatives of the East there was grave complaint of the injustice and danger of "government by injunction."[1] The discontent of the radicals with the administration was still further increased when the Supreme Court handed down a unanimous decision upholding the sentence of the Chicago federal judge against Debs, just

---

[1] By an "injunction" a judge "enjoins" certain persons not to commit an act which he has defined in advance as punishable. If the person disobeys the judge's order, he is fined or even committed to prison for "contempt of court," instead of being duly tried and sentenced for the act itself. The judge by this procedure becomes both the accuser and the punisher

one week after its condemnation of the income tax provision of the Wilson-Gorman Act as unconstitutional (May 27, 1895).

634. The Discontent of the Radicals. On March 4, 1895, a call went out from some "insurgent" congressmen, addressed to the Democrats of the nation, declaring that the policy of the administration was not that of the majority of the party and urging the radicals of the West to organize and take control of the Democratic party. The crusaders were ready,— radical Democrats, Populists, National Silverites; it needed only a leader to unite them into a compact army against the "money lords" of Wall Street, who, they believed, had loaded their farms with mortgages and purchased legislatures and courts to thwart the people's will. But before we describe the great battle between the East and the West in the election of 1896 we must turn for a moment to foreign affairs in Cleveland's second administration.

635. Our Intervention in Hawaii. The little kingdom of the Hawaiian Islands in the mid-Pacific had for many years harbored American residents, who came first as missionaries, then as planters and merchants to exploit the coffee and sugar farms. The American residents enjoyed rights of citizenship in Hawaii, with the franchise, and occupied high offices. Ever since 1854 there had been talk of annexation. Early in 1893 the new Queen Liliuokalani, a bitter enemy of the whites in the Islands, was deposed for attempting to overthrow the Constitution. A provisional government was set up by the white inhabitants, and the United States minister, John L. Stevens, protected the new government by a detachment of troops landed from the cruiser *Boston*. The Islands were declared a "protectorate" of the United States, and the American flag was raised over the government buildings. A few days later a treaty of annexation was sent by President Harrison to the Senate for ratification (February 15, 1893). The United States was to assume the Hawaiian debt of $2,000,000 and pay the deposed queen a pension of $20,000 a year. But before the treaty was ratified Congress expired, and Cleveland succeeded Harrison in the White House (March 4, 1893). Cleveland withdrew the treaty from the Senate, and after satisfying himself through a special commissioner to Hawaii that Stevens had acted too zealously in the January revolution, he ordered the flag to be lowered from the state buildings and offered to restore Queen

Liliuokalani to her throne on condition that she should pardon all the Americans concerned in the revolution. When the queen refused to abandon her cherished plans of vengeance, President Cleveland dropped the whole matter. He was abused roundly for "hauling down the American flag" in Hawaii, but he had followed the century-old tradition of our Republic in refusing to seize by force the distant possessions of weaker nations on the plea of "civilizing" them.[1]

636. The Venezuelan Boundary Dispute. That the President lacked neither force nor courage in dealing with foreign nations, however, was amply proved in a serious controversy with Great Britain over the validity of the Monroe Doctrine. The South American republic of Venezuela borders on the British colony of Guiana (see map, p. 503). A chronic boundary dispute between the two nations assumed acute form in 1886, when Great Britain maintained that the line of her frontier included some 23,000 square miles of territory, containing rich mineral deposits. Venezuela complained of the rapacity of her powerful neighbor, and diplomatic relations between the countries were broken off (February, 1887). The United States, by the Monroe Doctrine of 1823, had guaranteed the integrity of the Latin-American republics by declaring that the western continent was closed to any further extension of the European colonial system. Our State Department offered its friendly offices to Great Britain in arbitrating the disputed boundary line, but the British government rejected the offer. Lord Salisbury regarded the Monroe Doctrine as an antiquated piece of American bravado and declined to view the United States as an interested party in the dispute. Importuned by Venezuela, our State Department again and again begged Great Britain to arbitrate her claims. In February, 1895, Congress took up the matter, and by a joint resolution urged the same policy. Still Lord Salisbury remained obdurate; and when Secretary Olney in a rather sharp dispatch (July 20, 1895) declared that the United States was "practically sovereign on this continent," and that it would "resent and resist any sequestration of Venezuelan soil by Great Britain," the British prime minister again replied in polite terms that the dispute was none of our business.

[1] The provisional government maintained itself without much difficulty until the Republican administration which followed Cleveland annexed the Hawaiian Islands to the United States, by a joint resolution of Congress (July, 1898), and later made them a fully organized territory with United States citizenship (April, 1900).

THE CLEVELAND DEMOCRACY 445

637. The Monroe Doctrine upheld. But the American people believed that the maintenance of the Monroe Doctrine *was* their business. In December, 1895, President Cleveland sent a message to Congress recommending that we take the decision of the boundary between Guiana and Venezuela into our own hands, "fully alive to the responsibility incurred and keenly realizing all the consequences that may follow," — in other words, even at the risk of war with Great Britain. Both Houses of Congress immediately adopted the recommendation by a unanimous vote, appropriating $100,000 for the expenses of a boundary commission. The President's message and the action of Congress took the British people by storm. A wave of protest against war with their American kindred swept over the country. Three hundred and fifty members of Parliament rebuked Lord Salisbury's stubborn attitude by sending a petition to the President and Congress of the United States that all disputes between the two nations be settled by arbitration. The prime minister gave way and consented courteously to furnish the American boundary commission with all the papers it needed. In January, 1897, a treaty was signed at Washington, by which Great Britain agreed to submit her entire claim to arbitration; and on October 3, 1899, a tribunal at Paris gave the verdict (favorable on the whole to Great Britain), fixing the line which had been in dispute for nearly sixty years.

638. Dissension in the Democratic Ranks. The defense of the Monroe Doctrine in the Venezuelan controversy was the only official action of President Cleveland's second administration (with the exception of the opening of the World's Fair at Chicago) that had the general approbation of the country. Denounced by the capitalists and corporations of the East for his attempt to lower the tariff, and by the Populist farmers of the West for his determination to maintain the gold reserve, berated by the labor unions for his prompt preservation of law and order at Chicago, and threatened with impeachment for hauling down the flag which he believed was unjustly raised in the islands of the Pacific, Cleveland must have felt relieved as the time of his deliverance from the cares of office drew near.

639. Bryan nominated at Chicago. The convention of the Democratic party, which met at Chicago, July 7, 1896, proved to be entirely in the hands of the radicals of the West. They rejected by a majority of 150 votes the resolution of the Eastern "moderates" commending the administration of Grover Cleveland. They wrote a platform demanding the free and unlimited coinage of silver at the ratio to gold of 16 to 1 "without waiting for the aid or consent of any other nations." They condemned the issue of bonds in time of peace, denounced government by injunction, and demanded enlarged powers of the federal government in dealing with the trusts. The choice of a prominent Eastern candidate for nomination, like Senator Hill of New York, or ex-Governor Russell of Massachusetts, was impossible from the first. Among the free silverites Richard P. Bland of Missouri, author of the Silver Law of 1878, seemed to be the most promising candidate until William Jennings Bryan of Nebraska swept the convention off its feet by an oration filled with the enthusiasm of a crusader in a holy cause. The silverites made him the man of the hour, "the savior of Democracy," "the new Lincoln." He was nominated on the fifth ballot amid scenes of the wildest enthusiasm.

WILLIAM JENNINGS BRYAN

640. Bryan and McKinley. Mr. Bryan, born in 1860, had hardly more than reached the legal age of eligibility for the presidency. He was a self-made man, of Spartan simplicity of tastes and unimpeachable personal habits. As a rising young lawyer in Nebraska he had made a remarkable campaign for a seat in Congress, turning a Republican majority of 3000 in his district in 1888 into a Democratic majority of nearly 7000 in 1890. He served two terms in Congress, then returned to the West to devote himself to writing and speaking in the cause of free silver. His opponent in the presidential race of 1896 was Major William McKinley of Ohio, one of the most admirable and amiable characters in our history. McKinley could oppose to Bryan's four short years of public service a well-rounded career, including meritorious service in the Civil War, fourteen years in Congress, and two terms as governor of Ohio. McKinley's nomination was secured and his campaign managed by his devoted friend Marcus A. Hanna, a prominent business man of Ohio, the very incarnation of that spirit of commercial enterprise which we have seen creating the great trusts of the last years of the nineteenth century.

641. The Free Coinage of Silver. The campaign was fought on the issue of free silver. The radical Democrats demanded that the government should take all the silver presented at its mints and coin it into legal currency at the ratio of sixteen ounces of silver to one ounce of gold. As sixteen ounces of silver were worth in the open market only about $11 in 1896, while one ounce of gold was uniformly worth $20.67, the silverites demanded that our government should maintain in circulation dollars that were worth intrinsically only about 50 cents.[1] Their arguments for this apparent folly were that the United States was strong and independent and rich enough to use whatever metal it pleased

WILLIAM McKINLEY

for money, without regard to what England, France, or Germany did; that the supply of gold did not furnish sufficient currency for the business of the country anyway, and that what there was of it was in the hands of bankers, who hoarded it to increase its value; that the farmers and small traders consequently were forced to pay an ever-increasing tax in the fruits of their labor to meet the interest (reckoned in gold values) on their mortgaged farms and shops; that the Eastern bankers, who alone had the gold to buy government bonds, could control the volume of currency, which (since the repeal of the Sherman Act in 1893) was based increasingly on the national bonds. The unlimited coinage of silver would, they thought, break up this monopoly of the nation's money held by a few rich bankers on the Atlantic seaboard.

---

[1] The value of the silver "dollar" of $371\frac{1}{4}$ grains sank as follows: 1873, $1.004; 1875, $0.96; 1885, $0.82; 1893, $0.60; 1894, $0.49 (due to the suspension of silver coinage in India in 1893).

642. Bimetallism. The Republicans and the "sound-money" Democrats were willing to admit that we needed more currency and favored "international bimetallism," or the use of both gold and silver by agreement with the leading commercial nations of the world. The Republican platform pledged the party to work for such an agreement.[1] But for the United States alone to adopt the double gold and silver standard would be to make us the dumping ground for the silver of the world and so ruin our credit that we should not be able to sell a dollar's worth of our securities abroad.

643. The Campaign of 1896. It was a bitter battle between the Western plowholder and the Eastern bondholder. Bryan made a whirlwind campaign, traveling 18,000 miles in fourteen weeks, making 600 speeches, which it is estimated were heard by 5,000,000 Americans. He won thousands of converts to the doctrine of free silver, but was not able to carry the country in November. In a presidential vote of 13,600,000 McKinley won by a plurality of about 600,000. Even in McKinley's home state Bryan polled 477,000 votes to his opponent's 525,000. The electoral vote was 271 to 176. The election of 1896 was of tremendous importance in our history. It split the Democratic party into two irreconcilable camps.[2] It signalized the victory in the Republican party of the business "power behind the throne" of government. Many thousands of Americans were ready in 1896 to support a platform which advocated a sane opposition to the growing power of the trusts, to the monopoly of coal, oil, and lumber lands, to the nurture of highly prosperous industries by a protective tariff which taxed the poor man's food and clothing, and to the growing influence of railroads, express companies, and other corporations with our legislatures. But neither of the great parties offered such a platform. The Democrats, led astray by the glittering oratory of the silver champion, rallied to a call that was intensely sectional, to a doctrine that was economically unsound, and to a leader who was immature and

---

[1] Even this concession could not keep the ranks of the Republicans intact. Several silver delegates from Colorado, Utah, Idaho, Nevada, South Dakota, and Wyoming, including four United States senators and two congressmen, seceded from the convention under the leadership of Senator Teller of Colorado, who had "been at the birth of the Republican party," and voted for every one of its candidates from Frémont to Harrison.

[2] Late in the summer the "gold Democrats" held a convention and nominated General John M. Palmer for president. He polled only 134,645 votes.

untried. "Lunacy dictated the platform," said a Democratic paper in New York, "and hysteria evolved the candidate." The election of McKinley undoubtedly strengthened the influence of the big business interests on our government, but the election of Bryan would have opened the way to the repudiation of our financial honor in the eyes of the world and to the reign of untempered radicalism at home. Confronted with this alternative at the polls, a majority of the voters who hesitated were convinced that the choice of McKinley was at least the safer course.

References

A People's President: D. R. Dewey, *National Problems* (American Nation Series), chaps. ii–viii; H. J. Ford, *The Cleveland Era* (Chronicles, Vol. XLIV), chaps. iv–vii; E. L. Bogart, *Economic History of the United States*, chaps. xxvii, xxix; A. B. Hart, *American History told by Contemporaries*, Vol. IV, Nos. 164, 165; H. T. Peck, *Twenty Years of the Republic*, chaps. i, ii, iv; Grover Cleveland, *Presidential Problems*, chap. i; J. F. Rhodes, *History of the United States from Hayes to McKinley*, chaps. xi–xiii; F. L. Paxson, *The New Nation* (Riverside History), chaps. viii–ix; E. B. Andrews, *The United States in our Own Time*, chaps. xvii, xviii; J. W. Jenks, *The Trust Problem*, chaps. x–xii; Adams and Sumner, *Labor Problems*, chaps. vi–viii; Edward Stanwood, *History of the Presidency*, chaps. xxvii, xxviii; C. D. Wright, *Industrial Evolution of the United States*, chaps. xxiv, xxvi; William MacDonald, *Select Statutes of United States History, 1861–1898*, Nos. 111, 115.

A Billion-Dollar Country: Dewey, chaps. i, ix–xv; Ford, chap. viii; Bogart, chap. xxvi; Hart, Vol. IV, Nos. 166, 170, 178; Peck, chap. v; Andrews, chaps. xix, xx; Rhodes, chaps. xiv–xvii; Paxson, chaps. x–xiii; Stanwood, chap. xxix; *James G. Blaine*, chaps. x–xi; *American Tariff Controversies in the Nineteenth Century*, chap. xvi; MacDonald, Nos. 120, 129; J. D. Long, *The New American Navy*, Vol. I, chap. i; Francis Curtis, *The Republican Party*, chaps. ix–x; R. T. Ely, *Monopolies and Trusts*, chap. vi; James Bryce, *The American Commonwealth* (enlarged edition of 1911), Vol. II, chap. xciii.

Problems of Cleveland's Second Term: Dewey, chaps. xvi–xx; *Financial History of the United States*, chap. xix; Ford, chaps. ix–x; Hart, Vol. IV, Nos. 171, 179, 194; Peck, chaps. vii–xi; Andrews, chaps. xxi–xxvi; Rhodes, chaps. xviii–xx; Paxson, chaps. xiv, xv; Cleveland, chaps. ii–iv; Stanwood, *Presidency*, chaps. xxx, xxxi; *Tariff Controversies*, chap. xvii; MacDonald, Nos. 98, 100, 102, 103, 117, 125, 126, 130; F. W. Taussig, *The Silver Situation in the United States* (Publications of the American Economic Association, Vol. VII, pp. 1–118); J. W. Foster, *American Diplomacy in the Orient*, chap. xi; W. J. Bryan, *The First Battle*, chaps. ix–xi, xlix–l; F. J. Stimson, *The Modern Use of Injunctions* (Political Science Quarterly, Vol. X, pp. 189–202); W. H. Harvey, *Coin's Financial School*.

Topics for Special Reports

1. **The Formation of the Trusts:** R. T. Ely, *Labor Movement in America*, pp. 1–38; H. D. Lloyd, *Wealth against Commonwealth*, pp. 373–388; Henry Seager, *Introduction to Economics*, pp. 476–509; Bogart, pp. 400–416; Dewey, *National Problems*, pp. 188–202; Burton Hendrick, *The Age of Big Business* (Chronicles, Vol. XXXIX).

2. **"Czar" Reed:** Dewey, pp. 152–156; Peck, pp. 198–201; Andrews, pp. 562–564; M. P. Follett, *The Speaker of the House of Representatives*, pp. 185–214; articles for and against Reed's methods, in the *North American Review*, Vol. CLI, pp. 90–111, 237–250; T. B. Reed, *A Deliberative Body* (a defense in the *North American Review*, Vol. CLII, pp. 148–156).

3. **The New South:** Paxson, pp. 192–207; Bryce (ed. of 1911), pp. 491–511; E. S. Murphy, *Problems of the Present South*, pp. 11–27, 97–103; Hart, *The Southern South*, pp. 218–277; editorials in the *Outlook*, Vol. LXXXVIII, pp. 760–761; Vol. XCII, pp. 626–629; the *Review of Reviews*, Vol. XXXIII, pp. 177–190; series of articles, with interesting illustrations, in the *World's Work*, Vol. XIV (the Southern number, June, 1907).

4. **The Knights of Labor:** Ely, *Labor Movement*, pp. 75–88; Wright, pp. 245–263; *Reports of the United States Industrial Commission*, Vol. XVII, pp. 3–24; T. V. Powderly, *Thirty Years of Labor*, pp. 186–196; *The Organization of Labor* (*North American Review*, Vol. CXXXV, pp. 118–126).

5. **The Venezuelan Controversy:** J. B. Henderson, *American Diplomatic Questions*, pp. 411–442; Cleveland, pp. 173–281; Peck, pp. 412–436; MacDonald, No. 126; Hart, *Contemporaries*, Vol. IV, No. 179; A. D. White, *Autobiography*, Vol. II, pp. 117–126.

CHAPTER XIX

ENTERING THE TWENTIETH CENTURY

The Spanish War and the Philippines

644. The Island of Cuba. Thrusting its western end between the two great peninsulas of Florida and Yucatan, which guard the entrance to the Gulf of Mexico, lies the island of Cuba, "the pearl of the Antilles." From the time of its discovery by Columbus down to the very close of the nineteenth century Cuba belonged to the crown of Spain. Corrupt officials squandered its revenues, raised by heavy taxation, and Spanish soldiery ruthlessly quelled the least movement of rebellion. The fate of Cuba was a matter of great concern to the United States, both because the island lay close to our shores and because its possession by a strong or hostile power would threaten our interests in the Gulf of Mexico. In the prosperous decades following the Civil War, large amounts of American capital were invested in the sugar and tobacco plantations of the island. Many Cubans were naturalized in the United States, where they established centers of agitation for Cuban liberty. And many others, after naturalization, returned to the island under the protection of their American citizenship, to aid their brother Cubans in throwing off the Spanish yoke.

645. The Insurrection of 1895–1898. An especially severe insurrection broke out in 1895. The insurgents quickly overran nearly all the open country, and the Spanish leader, General Weyler, unable to bring them to face his 150,000 troops in regular battle, resorted to the cruel method of the "reconcentration camps." He gathered the noncombatants—old men, women, and children—from the country into certain fortified towns and herded them in wretched prison pens under cruel officers, where tens of thousands died of hunger and disease. The cries of the Cuban sufferers reached our shores. Scores of American citizens in the island were also being thrust into prison, and millions of American capital were destroyed.

646. Our Intervention in Cuba. Prudence and humanity alike forbade the continuance of these horrible conditions at our very doors. The platforms of both the great parties in 1896 expressed sympathy for the Cuban insurgents, and both Houses of Congress passed resolutions for the recognition of Cuban independence. President McKinley labored hard to get Spain to grant the island some degree of self-government and spoke in a hopeful tone in his message to Congress of December, 1897. But in the early weeks of 1898 events occurred which roused public indignation to a pitch where it drowned the voices of diplomacy. On February 9 a New York paper published the facsimile of a private letter written by the Spanish minister at Washington, Señor de Lome. The letter characterized President McKinley as a "cheap politician who truckled to the masses." The country was still nursing its indignation over this insult to its chief executive when it was horrified by the news that on the evening of February 15 the battleship *Maine*, on a friendly visit in the harbor of Havana, had been sunk by a terrific explosion, carrying two officers and 266 men to the bottom. The Spanish government immediately accepted the resignation of Señor de Lome and expressed its sorrow over the "accident" to the American warship. But the conviction that the *Maine* had been blown up from the outside seized on our people with uncontrollable force. Flags, pins, and buttons, with the motto "Remember the *Maine!*" appeared all over the land. The spirit of revenge was nurtured by the "yellow journals." Congress was waiting eagerly to declare war.

647. War with Spain. After a last appeal to the Spanish government had been met with the evasive reply that the Cubans would be granted "all the liberty they could expect," McKinley transferred the responsibility of the Cuban situation to Congress in his message of April 11. Eight days later, on the anniversary of the battle of Lexington and of the first bloodshed of the Civil War, Congress adopted a resolution recognizing the independence of Cuba, demanding the immediate withdrawal of Spain from the island, and authorizing the President to use the military and naval forces of the United States, if necessary, to carry out the resolution. Congress further pledged the United States, by the Teller Resolution, "to leave the government and control of the island of Cuba to its own people" when its pacification should be accomplished. The resolutions of April 19, 1898, were a virtual declaration of war against Spain.

648. Dewey's Victory at Manila. Our Navy Department, under the vigorous administration of Secretary Long and Assistant Secretary Roosevelt, was thoroughly prepared for the crisis. The Far Eastern fleet had been gathered, under Commodore George Dewey, at the British station of Hongkong on the Chinese coast. Scarcely a week after the war resolutions had been passed, Dewey's ships in their drab war paint were on their way across the 600 miles of the China Sea that separate Hongkong from the Spanish colonial group of the Philippine islands. The last night of April, with a bravery like that of his old commander, Farragut, at New Orleans, Dewey ran his fleet of armored cruisers and gunboats, under fire, through the fortified passage of Boca Grande into Manila Bay; and early on May-day

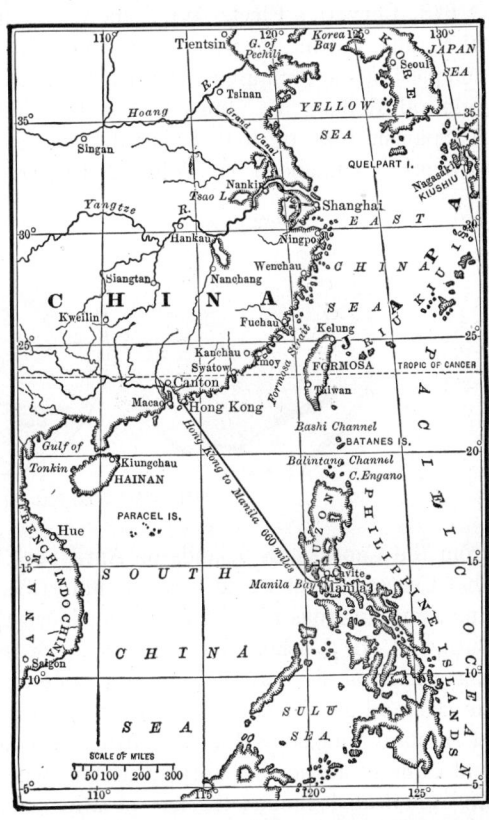

EASTERN ASIA AND THE PHILIPPINE ISLANDS

morning he opened fire on the Spanish fleet anchored off Cavite. Five times Dewey led his squadron up and down the line of Spanish ships, pouring into them an accurate and deadly fire, then drew out of range to give his grimed and hungry gunners their breakfast. He returned a few hours later to complete the work of destruction. By noon the entire Spanish fleet of ten ships was sunk or in flames, the land batteries of Cavite were silenced, and the city of Manila lay at the mercy of Dewey's guns. The Spanish had lost 634 men and officers. On the American side, in spite of the constant fire of the Spaniards, not a ship was hurt nor a life lost. It was the most complete naval victory in our history.

649. Cervera's Fleet. While the victorious fleet lay in the harbor of Manila, waiting for troops from the United States to complete the conquest of the Philippines, the Atlantic squadron, acting under Rear Admiral William T. Sampson, was blockading the coast of Cuba. A Spanish fleet of four armored cruisers and three torpedo destroyers, commanded by Admiral Cervera, had sailed westward

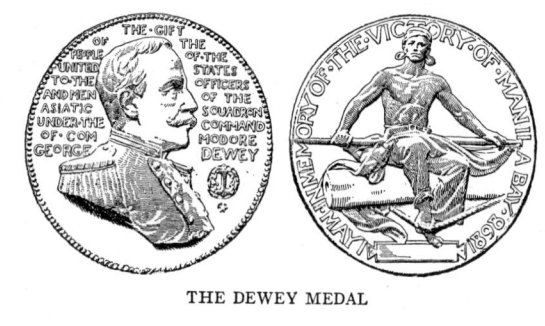

THE DEWEY MEDAL

from the Cape Verde Islands on April 29. There were wild stories that Cervera's fleet would shell the unfortified cities along our coast, and some timorous families even abandoned their customary summer outing at the seashore for fear of the Spanish guns. But experts knew that the fleet would put in at some Spanish West Indian port for coal and provisions after its journey across the Atlantic. In spite of Admiral Sampson's diligent patrol, Cervera's fleet slipped by him and came to anchor in Santiago harbor, where it was discovered by the American lookouts, the last of May, and immediately "bottled up" by Sampson's blockading squadron.[1]

650. The Land Campaign in Cuba. Meanwhile about 16,000 troops had been sent from the American camps in Florida to invade

---

[1] The fleet included Commodore Schley's "flying squadron" (the cruiser *Brooklyn* and the battleships *Massachusetts*, *Texas*, and *Iowa*) with Admiral Sampson's own squadron (the cruiser *New York*, which was his flagship, and the battleships *Indiana* and *Oregon*). The *Oregon* had just completed a marvelous voyage of 14,000 miles in 66 days, from San Francisco to Florida, around Cape Horn. She arrived and joined the blockading squadron as fresh as if she were just from the docks, "not a bolt nor a rivet out of place."

Cuba, under the command of Major General Shafter. The most picturesque division of this army was the volunteer cavalry regiment, popularly known as the "Rough Riders," commanded by Colonel Leonard Wood, made up of Western cowboys, ranchmen, hunters, and Indians, with a sprinkling of Harvard and Yale graduates. Theodore Roosevelt resigned his position as Assistant Secretary of the Navy to become the lieutenant colonel of the Rough Riders. In a spirited attack, through tangled jungles and over rough fields strung with wire fences, the American troops charged up the heights of San Juan and El Caney in the face of a galling fire from the Spanish Mauser rifles and intrenched themselves on the hills to the east of Santiago (July 1, 2). But General Shafter found the defenses of the city too strong and notified Washington that he should need reënforcements to drive General Toral from Santiago. It was a critical position in which the little American army found itself Sunday morning, July 3, on the hills above Santiago. Reënforcements would be weeks in reaching them. Their supplies were inadequate and bad.[1] The

THE BLOCKHOUSE AT EL CANEY, RIDDLED WITH BULLETS

dreaded fever had already broken out among them. And Cervera's fleet in the harbor below could easily drive them from the heights by a well-directed fire.

651. The Battle of Santiago. But fortune favored our cause. That same Sunday morning the Spanish ships steamed out of the harbor and started to run westward along the southern shore of Cuba, the flagship *Maria Theresa* leading and the *Vizcaya*, the *Colón*, the *Oquendo*, and the destroyers following. Admiral Sampson, with his flagship, the *New York*, was absent for the moment conferring with General Shafter on the critical situation of the American army.

[1] The inadequacy of the War Department, under Secretary Alger, was a striking contrast to the efficiency of the Navy Department. The soldiers were supplied with heavy clothing for the hot Cuban campaign and with inferior canned meats, which General Miles called "embalmed beef."

Commodore Schley, on the *Brooklyn*, was left as ranking officer. Following Sampson's orders, the American ships closed in on the Spaniards and followed them in a wild chase along the coast, pouring a deadly fire into them all the while. The Spaniards replied, as at Manila, with a rapid but ineffectual discharge. One by one the Spanish cruisers, disabled or in flames, turned and headed for the breakers, until the last of them, the *Cristóbal Colón*, bearing the proud name of the man who four centuries earlier had discovered for Spain the western world whose last remnants were now slipping from her grasp, was beached by the relentless fire of the *Brooklyn* and the *Oregon*, forty-five miles west of the harbor of Santiago. Only one man was killed and one seriously wounded in the American fleet, while less than $10,000 repaired all the damage done by the Spanish guns. But the enemy's fleet was completely destroyed, over 500 officers and men were killed, wounded, or drowned, and 1700 taken prisoners. The Spanish loss would have been far greater had not the American sailors rescued hundreds of their foemen, including the brave Admiral Cervera himself, from the burning decks and the wreck-strewn waters. A few days later General Toral surrendered the city of Santiago, now at the mercy of Sampson's guns, and turned over his army as prisoners of war to General Shafter (July 17).

652. The Capture of Manila. The total loss of two fleets and an army brought Spain to sue for terms. The preliminaries for the treaty of peace were signed in Washington and hostilities were suspended August 12. News of the peace reached Porto Rico just in time to stop General Miles's advance against the Spanish forces, and the governor of Porto Rico immediately surrendered the island to the American army. But before the news of peace reached the distant Philippines an event of great importance had occurred there. Three "relief expeditions," comprising over 10,000 troops, had reached the Philippines from San Francisco by the end of July, and on August 13 these troops, supported by Dewey's squadron, took the city of Manila and raised the American flag over the governor's palace.

653. Emilio Aguinaldo. Then the situation began to grow complicated. The Filipinos had been in revolt against Spain at the same time as the Cubans. In 1897 the Spaniards had bought off the leaders of the revolt, including one Emilio Aguinaldo, with a promise of $1,000,000. Aguinaldo had retired to Singapore. While at Hongkong, Dewey had welcomed Aguinaldo as an ally, and later had him conveyed back to the Philippines on an American ship and furnished him with arms from the arsenal at Cavite. The Filipino troops had entered Manila with the Americans on August 13. Aguinaldo now claimed that Dewey had promised to turn the Philippines over to him when the power of Spain was crushed, but there is no evidence that Dewey ever made such a promise. Forced to withdraw from the city of Manila (September 15), Aguinaldo organized a Filipino republic, had himself proclaimed dictator, and prepared to maintain his position by force of arms.

654. Peace with Spain. So the American and the Filipino troops were facing each other in ill-concealed hostility near Manila when the terms of peace between Spain and the United States were signed at Paris, December 10, 1898. Spain agreed to withdraw from Cuba and to cede Porto Rico, Guam, and the Philippine Islands to the United States. As the war had been begun for the liberation of Cuba, and as the city of Manila had not been taken until the day after the peace preliminaries were signed and hostilities suspended, the Spanish commissioners at Paris were unwilling to have the Philippines included in the peace negotiations at all. But President McKinley and his advisers were unwilling to leave the Islands a prey to internal wars or European domination, and Spain consented finally to give them up for an indemnity of $20,000,000.

655. The Philippine Insurrection. Before the treaty was ratified by the United States Senate or the Spanish Cortes, President McKinley ordered General Otis, commanding at Manila, to extend the authority of the United States over all the island of Luzón, and the Filipino Congress replied by authorizing Aguinaldo to make war on the American troops. It came to a battle before Manila on February 4, 1899. The superior quality and training of the American army made victory over the Filipinos in the open field of battle very easy; but when the Filipinos took to a guerrilla warfare among their native swamps and jungles, the wearying task of subjugating them dragged on for more than two years. Even the tricky seizure of Aguinaldo himself in his mountain retreat by a party of American scouts disguised as insurgents (February, 1901), and his proclamation two months later acknowledging American sovereignty in the

Islands, did not end the insurrection. It was not until April, 1902, that the last insurgent leader surrendered and the Philippines were officially declared "pacified."

656. The Anti-Imperialists. The war in the Philippines was carried on against the vigorous protest of the "anti-imperialists" in America, who saw in the acquisition of tropical colonies which could never become states of the Union, and in the war to "subjugate" the native inhabitants of those colonies, the abandonment of the principles of freedom and self-government on which our Republic was founded. President McKinley was invested by Congress (March 2, 1901) with "all the military, civil, and judicial powers necessary to govern the Philippine Islands,"—an "authority like that of a Roman emperor rather than of the president of a free republic." Our army was rapidly increased fivefold in the Islands (from 10,000 troops in August, 1898, to 54,000 in May, 1900), and during the severest period of the insurrection (May, 1900–June, 1901) there were 1026 "contacts," or petty battles, with a loss to the Americans of about 1000 men killed, wounded, and missing. Moreover, the exasperating method of guerrilla fighting practiced by the Filipinos, with its barbarous details of ambush, murder, treachery, and torture, tempted the American soldiers to resort at times to undue cruelty. The whole business was sickening, even to those who believed that it had to be done with all the unrelenting firmness that our generals displayed; while the anti-imperialists taunted the administration with having converted the war, which was begun as a noble crusade for the liberation of the Cuban, into a diabolical campaign for the enslavement of the Filipino.

657. The Administration Indorsed. For all that, the country at large supported the policy of the McKinley administration. The election of 1900, held during the insurrection, was fought chiefly on the issue of "imperialism." At the Democratic national convention at Kansas City large placards were displayed with the inscription: "Lincoln abolished slavery; McKinley has restored it." A huge American flag was floated from the roof girders of the convention hall, edged with the motto, "The flag of the republic forever, of an empire never." McKinley defeated Bryan by 292 electoral votes to 155, with a popular majority of nearly 1,000,000. The vote was the verdict of the American people that the situation in the Philippines must be accepted as our "manifest destiny," or, in the words of Senator Spooner, as "one of the bitter fruits of war."

658. Our Government of the Philippines. President McKinley used his extraordinary powers of government in the Philippines with admirable moderation and wisdom. As soon as the force of the insurrection was broken, he appointed Judge William H. Taft as civil governor (June 21, 1901), with a commission of four other experts, to administer the departments of commerce, public works, justice,

AN OLD STREET IN A PHILIPPINE TOWN

finance, and education in the Islands.[1] Native Filipinos were given a share in the local government of the provinces, and three Filipino members were soon added to the commission. Under Governor Taft's strong and sympathetic administration the Islands recovered rapidly from the effects of the war. Roads and bridges were built, harbors and rivers improved, modern methods of agriculture introduced, commerce and industry stimulated.[2] The American government

[1] A commission had been appointed in 1899 with President J. G. Schurman of Cornell at its head, to study the political, social, and economic condition of the Philippines. Its report (1901) in four volumes contains the best information on the Islands.

[2] Secretary of War Root estimated that the cost of the Philippines (1898–1902) was $169,853,512, exclusive of the $20,000,000 purchase money. Mr. Edward Atkinson, an authority on economics and the leader of the anti-imperialists, claimed that $1,000,000,000 was not too high an estimate of the cost of the Islands up to 1904.

purchased of the friars some 400,000 acres of Church lands for $7,200,000, which it sold to the natives on easy terms; and sent hundreds of teachers to the Philippines to organize a system of modern education. A census of the Islands was completed in 1905, showing a population of 7,635,426, of whom 647,740 belonged to savage, or "head-hunting," tribes. Two years after the census was taken, an election was held for a Philippine National Assembly, to share in the government of the Islands, as a lower House, with the commission appointed by the President. The Assembly convened in October, 1907, ex-Governor Taft (then Secretary of War) visiting the Orient to assist at the inaugural ceremonies. The professed policy of our government ever since the Spanish War has been to give the Filipinos their independence "when they are fit for it"; but as yet we have been unwilling to part with so rich and populous a domain as the Philippine Islands or abandon so fine a strategic post in the Far East.

659. The Organization of the Cuban Republic. The reorganization of Cuba proceeded more smoothly. On January 1, 1899, Spain withdrew her civil and military authority from the island, leaving it under a military governor appointed by President McKinley. In November, 1900, a convention of Cubans drew up a constitution for a republic, closely patterned on that of the United States. Congress established a mild sort of "protectorate" over Cuba by compelling the convention to incorporate in the constitution certain clauses known as the "Platt Amendment." They provided (1) that Cuba should never permit any foreign power to colonize or control any part of the island, or impair in any way its independence; (2) that Cuba should not incur any debt which the ordinary revenues of the island could not carry; (3) that Cuba should sell or lease certain coaling stations to the United States; and (4) that we might intervene in Cuba, if necessary, to maintain a government adequate for the protection of life, property, and individual liberty. When the Platt Amendment was duly adopted, the Cubans were allowed to proceed with their elections. On May 20, 1902, General Leonard Wood turned the government of the island over to its first president, Estrada Palma, and Cuba took her place among the republics of the world.[1]

---

[1] Under the Platt Amendment we were obliged to take temporary charge of the government of Cuba from 1906 to 1909 on account of factional strife in the island and the

660. Porto Rico a Colonial Territory. Porto Rico was organized (April, 1900) as a sort of compromise between a colony and a territory of the United States. A governor and a council of 11 (including 5 Porto Ricans) were appointed by the President, and a legislature of 35 members was elected by the natives. The council had full charge of the administration of the island and sitting as an upper House could veto the acts of the native legislature. The island was put under the protection of our laws and formed a customs district of the United States. On March 2, 1917, President Wilson signed the Porto Rican Civil Government Bill granting United States citizenship to the Porto Ricans and replacing the appointive council by a senate elected by the people of the island.

661. The Constitution does not "follow the Flag." While our flag was raised in the West Indies and in the distant islands of the Pacific, our Constitution was not extended in full force to the new possessions. Congress, as we have seen, turned the administration of the Philippines over absolutely to President McKinley and devised a new form of government for Porto Rico. Furthermore, by the famous "Insular Cases" of May, 1901, the Supreme Court decided that Congress might impose a tariff duty on the products coming from those possessions, thus treating them as foreign countries.

662. The Spanish War an Epoch in our History. The Spanish War, with the resultant acquisition of colonial possessions in the tropics, marks a momentous epoch in our history. During the twenty-five years preceding the McKinley administration our State Department played but a minor rôle. The question of the seal fisheries in Bering Sea, or of the control of a half-civilized king in the Samoan Islands, on which Blaine exercised his vigorous ability, seem rather petty now; and even the serious Venezuelan boundary dispute with Great Britain was only an episode in the great absorbing questions of finance, the tariff, and labor agitation, which filled the second administration of Grover Cleveland. But with the closing years of the century the nation turned to new fields. Our army and navy became conspicuous and began to absorb appropriations reaching into the hundreds of millions of dollars annually.

resignation of President Palma. We have rendered inestimable services to Cuba in the way of education and sanitation. Yellow fever, formerly the scourge of the island, has been stamped out, and Havana has been converted from one of the filthiest and deadliest cities of the Western Hemisphere to one of the cleanest and most sanitary. We spent over $10,000,000 in the sanitation of Cuba.

Our attention was drawn to the interests of colonizing nations, the trade of distant lands, and the fate of the old empires of the East. Our new possessions in the Pacific and our concern in the Orient gave great impetus to the development of our western coast and made imperative the immediate construction of the long-planned canal through the Isthmus of Panama. England had been our traditional enemy since the days of the Revolutionary War, but her cordial support of our cause in the war with Spain, when all the other nations of western Europe desired and predicted a Spanish victory,[1] won our hearty friendship and roused in the breasts of statesmen of both countries the prophetic hope that the two great English-speaking nations should henceforth be united in their efforts for the maintenance of world peace.

663. Our Influence in the Far East. Only a few months after the ratification of the treaty with Spain there came a striking proof of our new position in the affairs of the world. An association of men in China known as the "Boxers," resenting the growth of foreign influence in their country, gained control of the territory about Peking in the summer of 1900 and, with the secret sympathy of the Empress Dowager of China and many of the high officials, inaugurated a reign of terror. The foreign legations were cut off, and the German minister was murdered in broad daylight in the street. The rest of the foreign diplomats, with their staffs and their families, to the number of four hundred, took refuge in the British legation, where they were besieged for two months by a force of several thousand armed men, including troops from the imperial army. Sixty-five of the besieged party were killed and 135 wounded before the relief army, composed of American, British, French, German, Russian, and Japanese troops, fought its way up from the coast and captured the city of Peking. We were in a position, by virtue of our occupation of the Philippines, to furnish 5000 troops promptly and to take a leading part in the rescue of the legations at Peking; and when our able Secretary of State, John Hay, took the

[1] The friendly spirit of England was especially shown in the conduct of the fleets in Manila Bay. The German admiral, Von Diederich threatened Dewey by unfriendly demonstrations and would have effected a combination of the European warships to attempt to drive Dewey from the bay or to frustrate his bombardment of Manila had not the British admiral openly declared his sympathy for the American cause. When the news of Dewey's victory reached London, American flags were hung in the streets and "The Star Spangled Banner" was played in the theaters and music halls.

initiative in dealing with the question of the adjustment of the outrage and the punishment of China, he won the respectful coöperation of the courts of Europe.[1]

664. Adjustment of Domestic Problems. At the same time that they opened these new vistas of our national destiny the closing years of the century seemed to settle many of the domestic problems which had vexed us since the Civil War. The Dingley Tariff Bill of 1897 quickly and quietly restored even the slight reduction made by the Wilson-Gorman Act of 1894 and fixed our tariff for a dozen years. The discovery of large deposits of gold in the Klondike region of Alaska in August, 1896 (at the very moment when Mr. Bryan was making his whirlwind campaign for free silver), together with the opening of new gold mines in South Africa, expanded the volume of the world's currency sufficiently to make silver coinage a dead issue. A marvelous burst of industrial activity following the Spanish War, combined with abundant corn and wheat crops, gave employment to thousands who were out of work and enabled the farmers of the West in many cases to pay off their mortgages and have a balance left for comforts and luxuries. Finally, the Spanish War healed the last traces of ill feeling between North and South, when the men from Dixie and the men from Yankeeland fought shoulder to shoulder under Colonel Roosevelt of New York or "little Joe" Wheeler of Alabama.

665. The United States among the World Powers. For better or worse we had begun a new policy of expansion and entered into the race for colonial supremacy and world trade. After warning the nations of Europe away from the Western Hemisphere for nearly a century, we had now ourselves seized on possessions in the Eastern Hemisphere. We had inaugurated governments strange to the letter and the spirit of our Constitution. We had voted down by large majorities the counsel of the men who urged us to return to the old order and had accepted as the call of our "manifest destiny" the

[1] The aged senator John Sherman was made Secretary of State by McKinley to make a place in the Senate for Marcus A. Hanna. Sherman was unable to manage the trying negotiations with Spain and gave way to Judge Day, who in turn resigned, to head the Peace Commission in Paris, December, 1898. John Hay, our ambassador to England, succeeded him and proved to be one of the ablest, if not the ablest, of our Secretaries of State. His wisdom and tact preserved the integrity of the Chinese Empire, with the principle of the "open door," or equal trade privileges for all nations, at a time when the European powers were ready in anger and revenge to break up the empire and unchain war in the East.

summons to "enlarge the place of our habitation." We had no longer the choice whether or not we should play a great part in the events of the world. The only question was, in the words of Theodore Roosevelt, "whether we should play that part well or ill."

THE ROOSEVELT POLICIES

666. The United States at the Opening of the Twentieth Century. When President McKinley was inaugurated a second time, on March 4, 1901, the country was at the flood tide of prosperity. Capital, which was timidly hoarded during the uncertain years of Cleveland's administration, had come out of hiding at the call of Hanna and the other "advance agents of prosperity." The alliance between politics and business was cemented. Trusts were organized with amazing rapidity and on an enormous scale. Up to the Spanish War there were only about 60 of these great combinations with a capital ranging generally from $1,000,000 to $5,000,000, but the years 1899–1901 saw the formation of 183 new trusts with a total capitalization of $4,000,000,000,—an amount of money equal to one twentieth of the total wealth of the United States and four times the combined capital of all the corporations organized between the Civil War and Cleveland's second administration. The statistics published from year to year by our Census and Treasury Bureaus revealed such gains in population, production, and commerce that the imagination was taxed to grasp the figures, and even the most sanguine prophecies of prosperity were in a few months surpassed by the facts. From the inauguration of Washington to the inauguration of McKinley the excess of our exports over our imports was $356,000,000, but in a single year of McKinley's administration the excess reached $664,000,000. By the end of the nineteenth century we were mining 230,000,000 of the 720,000,000 tons of the world's coal, 25,000,000 of its 79,000,000 tons of iron, and 257,000 of its 470,000 tons of copper, and were steadily increasing our lead over all other countries in the production and export of wheat, corn, and cotton. During the whole of the nineteenth century we had been a debtor nation, inviting the capital of Europe to aid in the development of our great domain and paying our obligations abroad from the yield of our Western fields; but now our land was occupied, our resources exploited, and our industrial position assured. We began to export great quantities of manufactured goods and to seek new markets in the far corners of the earth. We bought the bonds of China and Japan. We sold millions of dollars' worth of our industrial stocks to Europe. The king of England received more money annually in interest from his private investments in American securities at the beginning of the twentieth century than George the Third had hoped to wring from the thirteen colonies by taxation.

667. The Assassination of McKinley. The progress of the United States and her sister republics of Central and South America was celebrated by a Pan-American Exposition held at Buffalo in the summer of 1901. President McKinley attended the exposition and in a noble speech, on the fifth of September, outlined the policy of friendly trade and reciprocal good will which we should cultivate with the nations of the world. It was his last public utterance. The next day, as he was holding a reception, he was shot by a miserable anarchist named Czolgosz, whose brain had been inflamed by reading the tirades of the "yellow press"

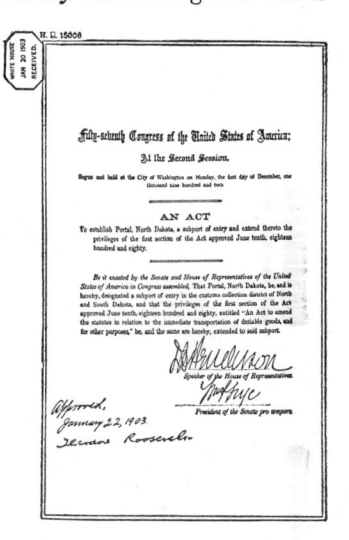

FACSIMILE OF THE TITLE-PAGE OF AN ACT OF CONGRESS

against "Czar McKinley." After a week of patient suffering the President died,— the third victim of the assassin's bullet since the Civil War.

668. Theodore Roosevelt. The lamented McKinley was succeeded in the presidency by a man who filled the stage of our public life more completely and conspicuously than any other American and who became probably the best-known man of the civilized world. Theodore Roosevelt was born in New York City, October 27, 1858, of sturdy Dutch stock. After graduating at Harvard in the class of 1880 he entered the legislature of his state. He was a delegate to the famous Republican national convention of 1884, where he opposed the nomination of James G. Blaine, but he did not "bolt" the ticket with the Mugwumps to vote for Cleveland. The next two years he spent on a ranch in North Dakota, strengthening his rather feeble health, satisfying his longing for the free, vigorous life of the plains and his intense love of nature, and at the same time gaining that appreciation of the value of our great Western domain which so conspicuously influenced his public administration. He was appointed to the Civil Service Commission by President Harrison in 1889, where he showed his devotion to clean and honest politics by greatly enlarging the "merit system" of appointment to office.[1] We have already seen how he resigned his assistant secretaryship of the navy in 1898 to accept the lieutenant-colonelcy of the Rough Riders in the Spanish War. Returning to New York with the popularity of a military hero he was chosen governor of the Empire State in the November election. As governor Mr. Roosevelt set too high a standard of official morality to please the leaders of the Republican machine, and they craftily planned to "shelve" him by "promoting" him to the vice presidency, an office of practically no influence or responsibility. Against his determined protest up to the very eve of the nomination, the Philadelphia convention of 1900, by a unanimous vote, placed his name on the presidential ticket with

Copyright by Harris & Ewing

THEODORE ROOSEVELT

---

[1] During Roosevelt's six years on the commission (1889–1895) the offices under the classified civil service were increased from 14,000 to 40,000. A great part of the voluminous annual reports of the commission (VI–XI) was written by Roosevelt, besides numerous magazine articles in support of the merit system. When he resigned his office in 1895 to become president of the New York police board, President Cleveland congratulated him on "the extent and permanence of the reform methods" he had brought about in the civil service.

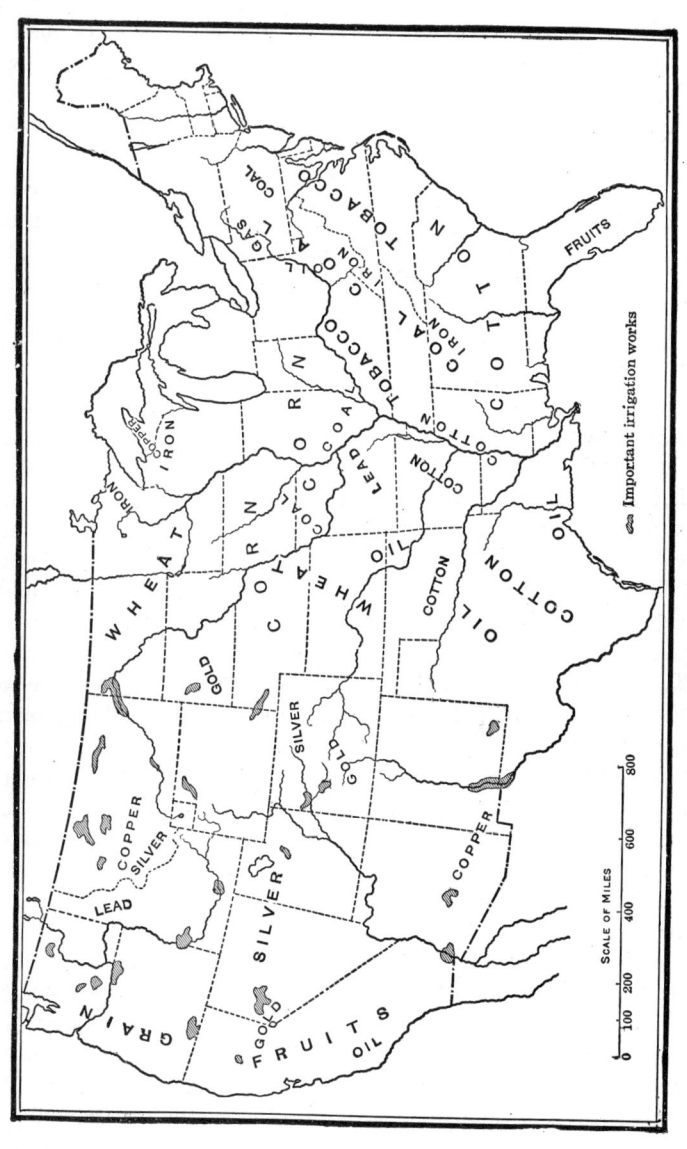

MAP SHOWING THE PRODUCTS OF THE UNITED STATES

McKinley's. The politicians of New York considered Governor Roosevelt "laid in his political grave." But his resurrection was speedy. Less than a year after his election to the vice presidency he was called on to take the oath as president of the United States (September 14, 1901).

669. Roosevelt's Conception of the Presidency. On the day of his inauguration President Roosevelt announced his intention of carrying out the policies of his predecessor, and gave an earnest of his statement by requesting the cabinet officers to retain their portfolios. But the seasoned old politicians at Washington and the shrewd bankers in Wall Street were apprehensive lest "this young man" of forty-two, with his self-assurance, his independence, his dauntless courage, and his unquenchable idealism, should disturb the well-oiled machinery of the "business man's government" and play havoc with the stock market. They soon discovered that they had in Roosevelt a president who, like Grover Cleveland, interpreted his oath to "preserve, protect, and defend the Constitution of the United States" to mean not waiting docilely in the White House for bills to come from the Capitol, but initiating, directing, and restraining the legislation of Congress, in the name and interest of the great American people, whose representative he was.

670. Roosevelt's First Annual Message. In his first message to Congress, December 3, 1901, — a very long and very able state paper, — Roosevelt demanded more than a dozen important "reform" measures and sounded the keynote of his entire administration. He recommended that the federal government assume power of supervision and regulation over all corporations doing an interstate business; that a new Department of Commerce be created, with a Secretary in the president's cabinet; that the Interstate Commerce Act be amended so as to prevent shippers from receiving special rates from the railroads; that the Cuban tariff be lowered; that the president be given power to transfer public lands to the Department of Agriculture, to be held as forest reserves; that the navy be strengthened by several new battleships and heavy-armored cruisers; that the civil service be extended to all offices in the District of Columbia; and that the federal government inaugurate, at the public expense, a huge system of reservoirs and canals for the irrigation of our arid lands in the West. Besides making these specific recommendations, President Roosevelt discussed "anarchy," the trusts, the labor question, immigration, the tariff, our merchant marine, the Monroe Doctrine, civil-service reform, and our duty toward our new possessions.

671. Roosevelt's Popularity. The energetic President traveled through the various states, emphasizing his policies in many public speeches and winning immense popularity in every section of the country. He spoke in plain, vigorous language on all subjects in which he himself, as a virile, courageous, democratic American citizen, was interested, from the government of our foreign colonies and the control of our domestic industries to the choice of an occupation and the training of a family. He popularized the expressions, "the criminal rich," "the square deal," "clean as a hound's tooth," and made the rare adjective "strenuous" one of the commonest in our vocabulary. He showed little regard for precedent or the staid decorum of official propriety when it was a question of performing what he regarded as a fair or useful act. In spite of the hostile criticism of almost the entire South, he appointed an efficient colored man collector of the port of Charleston. When a severe strike in the anthracite mines of Pennsylvania brought on a coal famine in the summer of 1902, and threatened to cause untold suffering during the following winter, the President called together representatives of the miners and of the owners of the coal fields, in a conference at the White House, and prevailed upon them to submit their dispute to the arbitration of a commission which he appointed. There is no phrase in the Constitution of the United States, in the definition of the president's powers and duties, that could be interpreted as giving him the right to intervene in a dispute between capital and labor. But he did intervene for the relief of millions of his anxious fellow countrymen; and no public act ever brought him a greater or more deserved reward of praise.

672. His Attitude toward the Great Corporations. Recognizing that great combinations of capital were inevitable, and that the corporation, or trust, was a necessary instrument of modern industry, he repeatedly declared that no honest business had anything to fear from his administration. At the same time he insisted that those corporations which practically monopolized such necessities of life as coal, oil, beef, and sugar, or, like the railroads, had received invaluable public franchises in return for services to be rendered to the public, should not be allowed to reap fabulous profits by charging exorbitant prices or by securing illegal privileges through the bribery of legislatures, but should be subject to proper regulation by the government. Therefore he directed his attorney-general to commence over forty suits against railroads or industrial corporations during his administration. The government won only a few of these actions, but the indirect effect of what was popularly called "busting

THE ROOSEVELT DAM, ARIZONA

A monument of the conservation policy

the trusts" was highly beneficial. It aroused public sentiment on the most important economic problem confronting our nation.

673. His Attitude toward Labor. Toward labor President Roosevelt was sympathetic. He had great respect for the men who go down into the mines or drive the locomotive across the plains of the West. He believed in the right of labor to organize in unions for the sake of preserving the quality of its output and of making its demands on the employer more effective by collective bargaining. He recognized the justice of the strike when no other form of action

ENTERING THE TWENTIETH CENTURY 471

was able to secure a "square deal" for the worker. He declared that the injunction without notice was an unjust restraint against organized labor.[1] But violence or wanton destruction of property or interference with the liberty of any man to work where and when he chose, he condemned as a violation of the law; and lawlessness he considered just as intolerable in the strikers who burned freight cars as in the directors who doctored freight rates.

674. His Conservation Policy. In his first message to Congress President Roosevelt spoke with the eloquence of a true lover of nature of the need of preserving our forest domain. It was, in his opinion, "the most vital internal question of the United States." We have seen (p. 398) how lavishly our government disposed of its unoccupied lands in the days when they were believed to be inexhaustible. Andrew Johnson soberly calculated that it would take six hundred years for our great West to "fill in"; but twenty-two years after he left the presidential chair the menace of the exhaustion of our forest domains from reckless and wasteful cutting was so great that Congress authorized the president, at his discretion, to withdraw timberlands from entry for public sale (1891). Roosevelt got Congress to extend the same authorization to mineral lands, and withdrew from sale over 100,000 acres of coal fields in Alaska. Altogether Roosevelt's proclamation brought the area of our reserved forest and mineral lands up to more than 180,000,000 acres,—a tract larger than France and the Netherlands combined. Had our government adopted this wise policy a generation earlier, it would have been able in Roosevelt's day to draw from its sales of timber and water power, its leases of coal and oil lands, a revenue sufficient to run the federal government without the imposition of a tariff, which hampered foreign trade, taxed the laboring man on almost every necessity of life, and by its protective clauses enriched the corporations which had seized on the natural resources of our opulent country.[2] President Roosevelt put the crowning stone on his splendid

---

[1] See note, p. 442.

[2] The iron deposits of Michigan, Wisconsin, and Minnesota alone, which furnish 88 per cent of the ore of the country, are estimated by the United States Steel Corporation, whose property they are, to be worth over $1,000,000,000. By the census of 1900, of the 800,000,000 cultivable acres of the United States 200,000,000 were owned by 47,000 people,—the population of a fourth-rate Eastern city. The mineral output of the country is worth over $2,000,000,000 a year. A government royalty of 15 per cent on this sum would yield a revenue equal to that collected from our tariff.

work for the conservation of our natural resources when he invited the governors of all the states to a conference at the White House, in May, 1908, to outline a uniform policy of preservation.

675. The Irrigation of the Arid West. For his irrigation policy the President secured, in June, 1902, the passage of a Reclamation Act, by which the proceeds from the sale of public lands in sixteen mining and grazing states and territories of the West (the so-called "cowboy states") should go into a special irrigation fund instead of into the public treasury. The irrigated lands were to be sold to

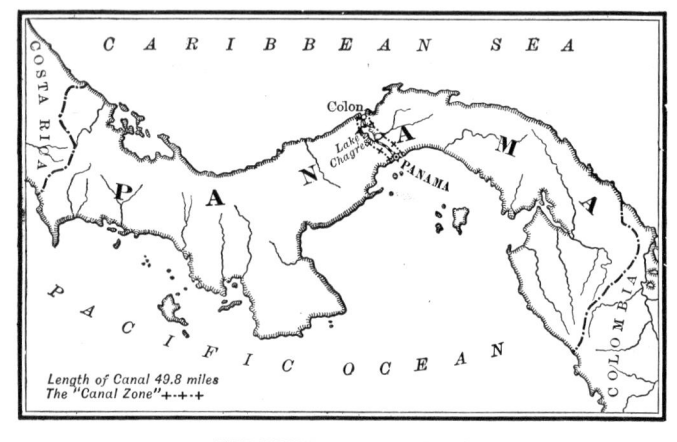

THE REPUBLIC OF PANAMA

settlers at moderate prices, on a ten-year installment plan, the proceeds going constantly to renew the fund. Under the beneficial operation of this law large tracts of land, formerly worth only a cent or two an acre for cattle grazing, have already become worth several hundred dollars an acre for agriculture; and one may see in the Eastern markets apples, four or five inches in diameter, grown on Arizona farms which, twenty years ago, were sandy wastes covered with coarse, scrubby grass or "sagebrush." It is not unlikely that future generations, looking back on Theodore Roosevelt's work, will rank his part in the conservation and redemption of our Western lands as his greatest service to the American Republic.

676. The Panama Canal. Under the Roosevelt administration work was begun on the greatest piece of engineering ever undertaken

ENTERING THE TWENTIETH CENTURY

in America,—the Panama Canal. Since the Clayton-Bulwer Treaty of 1850, the piercing of the Isthmus of Panama had been contemplated; and after a French company, organized by the successful builder of the Suez Canal, Ferdinand de Lesseps, had begun work at Panama (1881), various American companies began to make estimates for a route across Nicaragua. The Spanish War, with its serious lesson of the 14,000-mile voyage that had to be taken by the *Oregon* to get from one side of our country to the other, and with the new responsibilities which it brought by the acquisition of colonies in the Pacific Ocean and the West Indies, showed the immediate necessity for a canal. Secretary Hay, in December, 1901, by the Hay-Pauncefote Treaty secured from the friendly British government the abrogation of the Clayton-Bulwer Treaty, thereby allowing the United States to build and control an Isthmian canal alone. At the same time a commission which had been appointed to investigate the relative advantages of routes through Nicaragua and Panama reported in favor of the former. The French Panama Company, however, had failed as a result of scandalous mismanagement and thieving and was anxious to sell its rights and apparatus at Panama to the United States. After a warm fight over the two routes Congress voted, in June, 1902, that the canal should go through Panama if the President could

ROUTE OF THE PANAMA CANAL

secure the route "within a reasonable time"; if he failed to do so, the canal should go through Nicaragua.

677. The Revolution in Panama. President Roosevelt had no difficulty in buying out the French Panama Company for $40,000,000. But when he tried to negotiate with Colombia (of which Panama was a province) for the right to build the canal, offering Colombia $10,000,000 down and a rental of $250,000 a year for the control of a strip of land six miles wide across the Isthmus (the Hay-Herran

A STEAM SHOVEL AT WORK ON THE CANAL

Treaty), the Colombian Senate rejected the treaty (August 12, 1903). Both the United States and the province of Panama were exasperated by this attempt of Colombia to hold back the world's progress by barring the route across the Isthmus. Some rather high-handed diplomacy was conducted at Washington by secret agents from Panama, and when the Colombian Senate adjourned at the end of October without having reconsidered its refusal, United States gunboats were already hovering about the Isthmus with orders to let no armed force land on its soil. On the evening of November 3 a "quiet uprising" took place in Panama, under the protection of

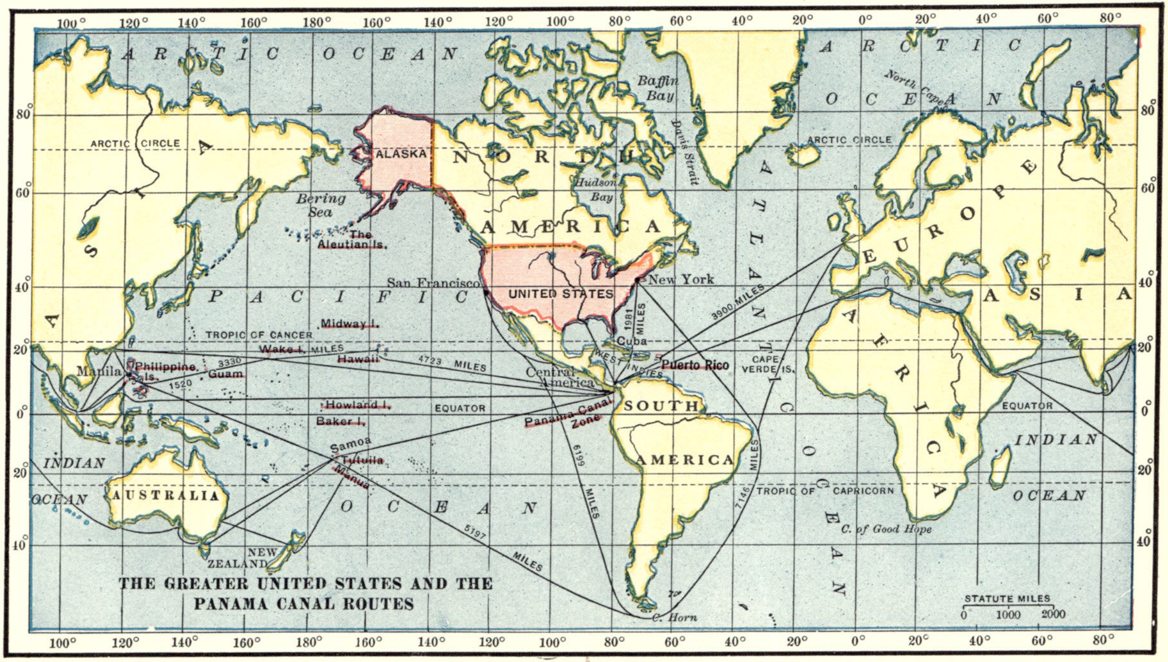

THE GREATER UNITED STATES AND THE PANAMA CANAL ROUTES

our marines, and the Colombian authorities were politely shown from the province. Within a week the new republic of Panama had its accredited representative, Bunau-Varilla, in Washington, who resumed immediately the negotiations for the construction of the canal. The Hay-Bunau-Varilla Treaty, of November 18, 1903, with Panama was essentially the old Hay-Herran Treaty rejected by Colombia the preceding August, except that we bought a ten-mile strip outright from Panama.[1]

678. The Construction of the Canal. The route decided on and the treaty secured, the work of excavation began in May, 1904. But there were many difficult problems to meet at Panama,— the sanitation of the Isthmus, the importation of efficient laborers who could dig in the tropical climate, dissensions in the Canal Commission, the decision between a lock or a sea-level canal, the testing of the soil for the locks and the big dam at Gatun, and the question of letting out the work by private contract or intrusting it to government engineers. In June, 1906, Congress determined on the high-level lock canal, and the next spring, after securing the bids of several contractors, the President decided for government construction. The canal was ready for ships in the summer of 1914. The tremendous advantages resulting from the opening of the canal to the world's traffic may be judged from the following table of distances:[2]

From	To	Distance via Cape Horn or Suez	Distance via Panama Canal	Miles Saved
New York	San Francisco	13,000	5,300	7,700
New York	Yokohama	13,000	9,700	3,300
New York	Panama	10,800	2,000	8,800
New York	Manila	13,000	9,000	4,000
Havana	San Francisco	11,000	5,000	6,000
San Francisco	London	16,000	9,000	7,000

[1] The encouragement of the secession of Panama from Colombia has been called an "ineffaceable blot of dishonor" on the Roosevelt administration. The government at Washington was, of course, aware of the impending revolution in Panama, but Roosevelt consistently maintained to the end of his life that he had done nothing to foment the revolution and that the action of our marines in Panama was no more than the fulfillment of our pledge by the treaty of 1846 with Colombia to maintain the "free transit" across the Isthmus.

[2] The Suez Canal, which was completed in 1869, was entirely paid for by the fees of vessels passing through in the first seven years. In 1904 over 4000 vessels paid fees of $20,000,000. The shares which the British government bought in 1875 for $20,000,000 are now worth over $150,000,000. The Panama Canal was very expensive, costing about $375,000,000. In 1926 the tolls ($22,391,055) exceeded the operating expenses by about $17,340,000.

679. Our Relations with South America. The influence upon the republics of Central and South America of our presence at Panama and in the West Indies will be increasingly felt. Till very recent years our attitude toward those republics has been generally that of cold and distant friendship. Because we have been essentially a food-producing country like Brazil and Argentina and Chile, we have let England, France, and Germany have their trade.[1] Of the $500,000,000 worth of goods that the South American republics imported in 1900, the United States, their nearest and richest neighbor, sold them but $41,000,000 worth. But now that we have become a great manufacturing country we need the growing markets of these southern republics for our agricultural implements, our electrical machinery, our steel rails and locomotives, our cotton, woolen, and leather goods. We have revived Blaine's fertile idea of the Pan-American congresses,[2] and a Bureau of American Republics has been organized at Washington to facilitate our cordial relations with the other American republics.

680. Roosevelt's Extension of the Monroe Doctrine. Coincident with this revival of interest in the Latin republics of America came a very significant extension of the Monroe Doctrine by President Roosevelt, when, in order to satisfy the European creditors of Santo Domingo, he appointed a receiver to manage its bankrupt treasury. Heretofore we had only forbidden Europe to step into the republics of the New World; now, at the request of Europe, we stepped in ourselves. If this principle is followed out, it may mean a virtual protectorate of the United States over all the weaker republics of the South,—a move which many "expansionists" have long regarded as the logical and desirable outcome of the Monroe Doctrine.

681. The Election of 1904. President Roosevelt's independence of sanctioned forms, his attack on the evils of the corporations, his

---

[1] Elihu Root, when Secretary of State, returning from a Pan-American Congress at Rio Janeiro in the autumn of 1906, reported that the previous year there were seen in the harbor of that great Brazilian seaport 1785 ships flying the flag of Great Britain, 657 with the German flag, 349 with the French, 142 with the Norwegian, and *seven* sailing vessels (two of which were in distress) flying the Stars and Stripes.

[2] Such conferences were held in Mexico in 1901, in Rio Janeiro in 1906, and in Buenos Aires in 1910. Of this last congress Professor Shepherd of Columbia, its secretary, said: "The Conference will attempt to standardize certain customs and sanitary regulations, and to agree on uniform patent, trade-mark, and copyright laws. It will do all it can to cement friendly relations, and perhaps arrange for exchanges of professorships and scholarships similar to the Roosevelt exchange professorship with Germany."

insistence on larger powers for the regulation of the railroads by the Interstate Commerce Commission, roused a good deal of opposition in Congress, and especially in the Senate. The Senate had been "scolded" by Roosevelt for not ratifying some reciprocity tariff treaties which he had negotiated in accord with the policy of McKinley, and as the presidential year of 1904 approached, a movement was started to supplant him by Senator Hanna. But with the death of Hanna in February, 1904, the opposition collapsed, and Roosevelt was unanimously nominated for what was practically a second term. The Democratic convention at St. Louis came again into the hands of the conservatives, who had been beaten at Chicago eight years before. It nominated Alton B. Parker, chief judge of the New York Court of Appeals, who immediately made it clear by a telegram to St. Louis that he was inalterably pledged to the gold standard. His views were accepted by the convention, in spite of Bryan's protest. Judge Parker was a man of the highest character and unquestioned ability, but he proved a veritable man of straw against Theodore Roosevelt. The Republicans won by the largest majority in the popular vote (2,541,734) until the election of Harding in 1920. Roosevelt carried every state north of Mason and Dixon's line, and even invaded the "solid South" by winning Missouri and Maryland. The electoral vote was 336 to 140. Roosevelt announced on the evening of his victory that he would not be a candidate for renomination.

682. Measures of Roosevelt's Second Term. After the popular indorsement of 1904 President Roosevelt intensified rather than relaxed his strenuous program. He secured the passage of the Hepburn Rate Bill (1906), enlarging the control of the Interstate Commerce Commission over the railroads by giving it important powers of rate regulation, started suits against several trusts which were guilty of law-breaking, set on foot a thorough investigation of the meat-packing houses in Chicago, Omaha, and Kansas City, secured the passage of a pure food and drugs bill through Congress (1906), greatly improved the consular service, pushed the work on the Panama Canal, urged the admission to statehood of the territories of Oklahoma, Arizona, and New Mexico, and waged a continual fight for the conservation of our forests and the redemption of our waste plains.

683. Roosevelt's Foreign Influence. Roosevelt's prestige was acknowledged abroad as well as at home. At his suggestion a dispute over the right of European nations to collect their debts by force from the South American republics was referred to the Hague Court.[1] On his initiative Russia and Japan, who were engaged in a bloody war

THE PEACE PALACE AT THE HAGUE

Given by Andrew Carnegie

for the possession of the ports of Manchuria and Korea, were tendered the friendly offices of the United States and brought to conclude peace at Portsmouth, New Hampshire (September, 1905). In January, 1907, President Roosevelt received the Nobel prize[2] for his services in the cause of international peace.

[1] On the motion of the Czar of Russia all the nations in diplomatic relations with the Russian court were invited to attend a conference at The Hague, Holland, in 1899, for the purpose of discussing the reduction of armaments, the humanizing of warfare, and the settlement of international disputes by arbitration. As a result a permanent Court of Arbitration was established, to which many cases of international dispute were referred for settlement. In 1904 President Roosevelt suggested a second Hague conference, but it was postponed on account of the Russo-Japanese War until the summer of 1907, when it met in a splendid new hall built by Andrew Carnegie, an ardent apostle of universal peace.

[2] In 1896 Alfred Nobel, a Swedish scientist, left a large fortune, the income of which was to be devoted to prizes to be awarded annually to men who had made conspicuous contributions to science, letters, and the cause of international peace. Roosevelt devoted his prize of $36,743 to establishing a commission to work for industrial peace in our country.

684. Taft Elected in 1908. Roosevelt had declared immediately after his election in 1904 that he would not be a candidate for reelection. His recommendation of his Secretary of War, William H. Taft, as his successor was equivalent to a nomination — as Jackson's recommendation of Van Buren had been, seventy years before. Taft was nominated on the first ballot in the Republican convention at Chicago, June 18, 1908, and easily defeated his opponent, Bryan, by 321 electoral votes to 162, in a campaign devoid of any special interest. The old issues of silver and imperialism, on which Bryan had run in 1896 and 1900, were dead. Both parties in 1908 pledged themselves to tariff revision, and Roosevelt had given his administration so democratic a character by his prosecution of the trusts that he had stolen most of Bryan's thunder. The Republicans maintained their invasion of the "solid South" by again carrying the state of Missouri, together with all the Northern and Western states except Nebraska, Colorado, and Nevada.

WILLIAM H. TAFT

685. Ex-President Roosevelt. Immediately after the close of his term of office, Colonel Roosevelt went to East Africa on a long hunting trip to procure specimens of rare game for the Smithsonian Institution at Washington. When he "emerged from the jungle," in the spring of 1910, he at once became the center of observation of the whole Western world. His trip from Egypt through Italy, Austria, France, Germany, Holland, and England was a continuous ovation, such as no private citizen had ever received. Emperors, kings, princes, presidents, and ministers all received him with the highest marks of honor. He delivered addresses at the University of Cairo, at the Sorbonne, at the University of Berlin, and at Oxford University. He represented the United States at the funeral of King Edward VII in London. When he landed at New York, on June 18,

480   THE REPUBLIC SINCE THE CIVIL WAR

1910, he was welcomed with an enthusiastic demonstration. In reply to the Mayor's greetings, before an enormous crowd at the Battery, he said: "I am glad to be back among the people I love. And I am ready and eager to do my part, so far as I am able, in helping solve problems which must be solved if we of this, the greatest democratic republic on which the sun has ever shone, are to see its destinies rise to the high level of our hopes and its opportunities."

THE RETURN OF THE DEMOCRATS

686. "Big Business." Roosevelt's words were not empty rhetoric. The country to which he returned in the summer of 1910 was in the midst of a political agitation such as it had not known since the free-silver campaign of 1896. The Republican party, which he had led to triumphant victory in 1904, was split into warring factions. On the one side were a group of reformers who were demanding that the will of the people should find more complete expression in the government. On the other side were the conservatives ("standpatters") who insisted that prosperity and order should not be endangered by rash experiments in politics. The cause of the controversy lay chiefly in the development of "big business" since the Spanish War. Railroad magnates, like E. H. Harriman, W. H. Vanderbilt, and J. J. Hill, had added thousands of miles of track to their "systems," until they controlled the transportation of areas comprising a quarter or even a third of the United States. Copper, sugar, oil, lumber, whisky, cordage, rubber, coal, and steel were monopolized by huge trusts which regulated output, dictated prices, fixed conditions of labor, and influenced legislation.

687. Remedies Proposed. For some years before the election of Taft there was a growing conviction in the country that big business had a sinister influence on the government, which could be remedied only by a larger participation of the public in practical politics. A group of men in Congress, especially senators from the Middle West (Cummins and Dolliver of Iowa, La Follette of Wisconsin, Clapp of Minnesota, Bristow of Kansas, Beveridge of Indiana) led the movement. Roosevelt himself, though not opposed to the trusts as such, had, by his insistence that rich and poor alike should obey the law and by his prosecution of the "bad" trusts,

ENTERING THE TWENTIETH CENTURY 481

given aid and comfort to the reform movement; while his frequent moral exhortations in messages, speeches, and articles had encouraged a higher tone of business and political ethics. A number of popular magazines, like *Collier's*, the *Outlook*, the *American*, *McClure's*, *Everybody's*, and the *Cosmopolitan*, took up the task of exposing crookedness in big business and wickedness in high places — "muck-raking," as it was called. The program of the reformers contained many innovations in politics, such as the nomination of officials by the people in direct primaries, the initiative, and referendum, and recall,[1] the stringent regulation of business by the government, and the popular election of senators and judges.

688. The Payne-Aldrich Tariff. President Taft had been in office but a few weeks when the conflict between the reformers and the stand-patters broke out. According to the preëlection pledge of his party, Taft called Congress in extra session (March 15, 1909) for the purpose of "revising the tariff downward." The bill brought in by the Committee of Ways and Means (Sereno E. Payne, of New York, chairman) and passed by the House contained substantial reductions. But the Senate, under the lead of Nelson W. Aldrich, of Rhode Island, restored the protective features, so that the Payne-Aldrich Bill, as finally passed in August and signed by the President, differed but slightly from the existing Dingley tariff of 1897. Seven Republican senators and twenty members of the House voted against it. These "insurgents" joined with the Democrats in denouncing the Republican party for its broken pledge. When President Taft, in a speech in Minnesota, praised the Payne-Aldrich tariff as the best in our history, he was charged with putting himself squarely on the side of the stand-patters. Taft's sturdy support of his Secretary of the Interior, Richard A. Ballinger, who was accused of unduly favoring the big business interests in his management of the timberlands of the Northwest, still further discredited him in the eyes of the insurgents.

689. President Taft. Taft was not a reactionary. Many of his measures showed a genuine sympathy with progressive ideas. He

[1] By the "initiative" is meant the right of the people to initiate legislation. On the petition of a certain small percentage of the voters of the state, a proposed law must be printed on the ballot of the next election to be voted on by the people. The "referendum" provides that laws passed by the legislature must, upon petition of a percentage of the voters of the state, be "referred" to the people for indorsement or rejection. The "recall" is the power of dismissing an official or a legislator before his term of office expires.

added over 10,000 positions to the classified list of the Civil Service, as against 9000 added by McKinley. He favored the extension of the powers of the Interstate Commerce Commission in his railroad bill of 1910. He instructed his Attorney-General, George W. Wickersham, to bring 45 suits against the trusts, where Roosevelt's attorneys had brought 25. He encouraged his Secretary of State, Philander C. Knox, to negotiate treaties of arbitration and reciprocity.[1] But in spite of this record, he failed to win confidence and popularity. His ability, his ample equipment, his high character, were acknowledged, but the qualities of leadership were lacking. After seven and a half years of Theodore Roosevelt he seemed tame and uninspired. His long years on the bench had bred in him a judicial attitude of mind, which made it impossible for him to ride at the head of a movement like a dashing knight. He was conservative by nature, and his rejection by the radicals made him seem more closely allied to the reactionaries than he really was. He wanted the country to walk toward reform with something of his own dignified and measured pace, while the insurgents were spurring it to a gallop.

690. The Election of 1910. Not being able to hurry President Taft, the insurgents ignored him and concentrated their attack on the machine to which they claimed he had become a slave. In the spring of 1910 they combined with the Democrats to depose the stand-pat Speaker of the House, Joseph G. Cannon, from his chairmanship of the powerful Committee on Rules, which controlled the whole procedure of legislation. They doubled the size of the committee and provided for its election by ballot. The following November the country pronounced against the administration by electing Democratic governors in a number of Republican states (Massachusetts, Ohio, New York, Connecticut, New Jersey) and turning a Republican majority of 47 in the House to a Democratic majority of 54. It was the first time since 1892 that the Democrats had got control of either branch of Congress. Their opposition made impossible any effective legislation during the second half of President Taft's term.

---

[1] Chief among these measures were a reciprocity treaty with Canada which the Canadians rejected by turning out their government in September, 1911; and an arbitration treaty with England which our Senate amended out of existence.

ENTERING THE TWENTIETH CENTURY

691. Senator La Follette. On January 21, 1911, the insurgent senators and representatives met at La Follette's house in Washington to lay plans for capturing the Republican party in the presidential campaign of the next year. They formed the National Progressive Republican League for the "promotion of popular government." A few months later they selected La Follette as their leader, and in a conference held at Chicago, in October, they recommended the Wisconsin senator to the country as "the logical candidate for the presidency" in 1912. La Follette, before his entrance into the Senate in 1906, had been governor of Wisconsin for three terms. His public life had been one of persistent championship of radical measures in economics and politics. He had fought the railroads in Wisconsin, eliminating their agents from the control of the legislature and reducing their fares to two cents a mile. He had secured the adoption of the direct primary, a graduated income tax, and important labor laws, and during his administration kept the record of the Wisconsin congressmen at Washington before the people of the state.

692. Roosevelt supplants La Follette as Progressive Leader. The laurels of Roosevelt, however, troubled the ambitions of La Follette. The ex-President did not join the Progressive League, though he had preached its doctrines months before its formation, in a famous speech on "The New Nationalism," at Ossawatomie, Kansas (August 31, 1910). In spite of Roosevelt's declaration in 1904 that he would "under no circumstances" be a candidate for a third term, the Progressive forces in the East turned to him more and more, fearing La Follette's excessive radicalism and doubting his ability to fill the presidential office. La Follette assailed Roosevelt bitterly, contending that his record had been no whit better than Taft's on the trusts or the tariff and ridiculing his "rhetorical radicalism" and "mock heroics" now as the device of insatiable ambition to return to office. In spite of his protests and denunciations, however, La Follette saw his support steadily going to Roosevelt. When seven Progressive governors joined, early in 1912, in an appeal to the ex-President to accept the leadership of the movement, Roosevelt yielded. On February 24, 1912, he entered the presidential race with the declaration that his "hat was in the ring."

693. Formation of the Progressive Party. When the Republican convention was opened at Chicago, June 18, 1912, a battle royal ensued between the Progressives and the administration. Roosevelt had the overwhelming support of the delegates who had been chosen by popular vote in the dozen states which had direct primaries — showing that he was the people's choice in so far as that choice could express itself. But Taft had control of the administration machinery and through the support of officeholders secured the delegations from the Southern states, which were fully represented in the convention though they did not contribute electoral votes to the Republican ticket. When the seats of more than 250 of the Taft delegates were contested, the convention (including the challenged delegates themselves) voted the Roosevelt claimants down. The administration forces elected their chairman by the close vote of 558 to 502. Thereupon Roosevelt bolted the convention, hurling against it the defiant manifesto that "any man nominated by the convention as now constituted would be merely the beneficiary of a successful fraud," and would have "no claim to the support of Republican voters." By Roosevelt's advice the Progressive delegates returned to their states, organized a new party, and reconvened in a national convention at Chicago, August 5. Two thousand enthusiastic delegates came. The platform adopted included the radical political program of the insurgents with pledges of social and industrial reforms. With the religious fervor of crusaders, interrupting their cheers with stanzas of "Onward, Christian Soldiers," the delegates of the new Progressive party unanimously nominated Theodore Roosevelt for president and Governor Hiram Johnson of California for vice president.

694. The Election of Woodrow Wilson. Meanwhile the Democratic convention had met at Baltimore (June 25), and after an exciting week's contest between Speaker Champ Clark of Missouri and Governor Woodrow Wilson of New Jersey, had nominated the latter (chiefly through the influence of William J. Bryan). Wilson conducted his campaign in a dignified manner, commending progressive ideas in admirable speeches of somewhat cautious enthusiasm; while Roosevelt and Taft, lately bosom friends, exhibited the unedifying spectacle of a campaign of mutual abuse. The election in November resulted in a decisive victory for Wilson, though his popular vote was 2,000,000 less than the combined vote for his opponents. The Democrats got control of both Houses of Congress

Copyright by Harris & Ewing

WOODROW WILSON

(Senate 51 to 45, House 291 to 144), an advantage which they had held in only one session (1893-1895) since the presidency of James Buchanan.[1] The figures of the election are as follows:

Candidate	Party	Popular Vote	Electoral	States carried
Wilson	Dem.	6,298,857	435	All except
Roosevelt	Prog.	4,124,597	88	Cal., Mich., Minn., Pa., S. Dak. Wash.,
Taft	Rep.	3,484,960	8	Utah., Vermont
Debs	Soc.	901,725		

695. Wilson's Inaugural Address. On the fourth of March, 1913, Woodrow Wilson delivered his brief inaugural address as twenty-seventh president of the United States to an immense and enthusiastic throng gathered before the east front of the Capitol at Washington. He spoke of the abundant forces, material and moral, in American life, of the evil that had come in with the good, the inexcusable waste amid the unparalleled riches. He characterized the task of the new day as the elevation of all that concerns our national life to the high plane of the enlightened individual conscience. He abjured all spirit of partisanship, and in words recalling Abraham Lincoln's immortal speech at Gettysburg he declared, "This is not a day of triumph; it is a day of dedication." He summoned "all patriotic forward-looking men" to his side, and promised not to fail them if they would but counsel and sustain him. The address was distinguished for its spirit of reasonableness joined with lofty idealism, of firm conviction without a trace of partisanship, all expressed in language well-nigh faultless.

696. The New President. Practical politicians had some misgivings as to how this "scholar in politics," this "theorist" and "schoolmaster," would manage men at the Capitol.[1] Cartoonists pictured him in cap and gown shaking his ruler at Congress. He had broken up the machine in New Jersey, to be sure, but he would find Washington a far different place from Trenton. Little by little, however, the "scholar," with a quiet confidence and unruffled tenacity, established his power over cabinet, Senate, House, and lobby, and

---

[1] For many years before his election as governor of New Jersey (in 1910) Wilson had been connected with Princeton University as professor of politics and, since 1902, as president. He is the author of several books on American politics and history.

before six months were past made himself the most complete master of Congress since the days of Thomas Jefferson. Foreign observers anticipated a "fair and just order of things under his wise, gifted leadership." "He is a man of fresh, virile, original mind," wrote the London *Chronicle*, "who should leave his name and work deeply impressed in history."

697. The Cabinet. The chief place in the cabinet was given to William J. Bryan, whose influence in the Baltimore convention had secured Wilson's nomination. Lindley M. Garrison of New Jersey was made Secretary of War, and Franklin K. Lane of California, Secretary of the Interior, both exceptionally strong men. William G. McAdoo, soon to become the President's son-in-law, was made Secretary of the Treasury. William B. Wilson, closely affiliated with the labor unions, was Secretary of Labor. James C. McReynolds (Attorney-General), Josephus Daniels (Navy), Albert S. Burleson (Postmaster-General), D. F. Houston (Agriculture), and William C. Redfield (Commerce) completed the cabinet.[1]

698. "The New Freedom." Wilson, like Jackson, Lincoln, Cleveland, and Roosevelt, considered the presidency a great popular trust and conceived his duty to be the leadership of the American democracy. At the moment of his assumption of office he published his program in a volume entitled "The New Freedom," made up of the most constructive passages of his campaign speeches. It was a kind of expanded inaugural address to the whole American people, advocating the return to free competition in industry and full publicity for public affairs. "I take my stand absolutely, where every progressive ought to take his stand," he said, "on the proposition that private monopoly is indefensible and intolerable." "You are willing to act *for* the people, but you are not willing to act *through* the people," was his challenge to the leaders of the invisible government of special privilege; "now we propose to act for ourselves." It was an economic Declaration of Independence.

---

[1] Bryan resigned the Secretaryship of State in the midsummer of 1915 because he thought Wilson's tone to Germany in the second *Lusitania* note (p. 499) too belligerent. He was succeeded by Robert Lansing of New York. Garrison resigned the war portfolio in February, 1916, for the opposite reason: he wanted a strong national army in place of the militia system. He was replaced by Newton D. Baker of Ohio. James C. McReynolds of Tennessee, the Attorney-General, was promoted to the Supreme Bench in August, 1914, and his place taken by Thomas W. Gregory of Texas. The other cabinet officers remained unchanged through Wilson's first administration.

ENTERING THE TWENTIETH CENTURY

699. The Underwood Tariff Bill. On April 7 President Wilson called Congress together in extra session for the revision of the tariff. Believing that the relations between the executive and the legislative should be close and harmonious, Wilson revived the custom, in abeyance since the days of John Adams, of appearing in person to read his "messages" to Congress. In this first brief address of April 8, 1913, he spoke of the revision of the tariff alone. He declared that we must abolish everything that had "even the semblance of privilege or artificial advantage" and make our business men and producers "better workers and masters than any in the world" by constantly sharpening American wits in competition with the wits of the rest of the world. The tariff bill, bearing the name of Oscar Underwood of Alabama, Chairman of the Ways and Means Committee, passed the House, May 8, by a vote of 281 to 139, and the Senate, in the following September, by a vote of 44 to 37, the Louisiana senators standing out against it for its provision for free sugar after three years. Wilson signed the bill with great satisfaction, declaring that "a fight for the people and for free business, which had lasted a long generation through, had at last been won handsomely and completely." The Underwood Bill reduced the average of duties to 26 per cent, from 39.4 per cent under the Wilson-Gorman Act of 1894, and 40.12 per cent under the Payne-Aldrich Act of 1909. Luxuries like diamonds, furs, ivory, silks, perfumes, wines, tobacco, automobiles, were either put on the taxed list or left there unchanged; but a great number of necessaries and comforts, including food, farm implements, wool, sugar, lumber, coal, cottons, cattle, eggs, were either put on the free list or greatly reduced. To make up for the loss in revenue from these objects, an income tax was levied (see Amendment XVI). Net incomes above $3000 for a single person, or $4000 for a married couple, were subject to a tax of 1 per cent up to $20,000, 2 per cent from $20,000 to $50,000, and so on by degrees until the additional tax reached 6 per cent on incomes above $500,000. How the Underwood tariff as a whole would have affected business and prices in America under normal conditions it is impossible to say. The advent of the World War in Europe the year after the bill was passed created an unprecedented demand for American foodstuffs and manufactures, sending our foreign trade from about $4,500,000,000 in 1913 up to over $10,000,000,000 in 1919.

700. The Banking and Currency Problem. Second only to the tariff in the President's mind was the reform of our currency and banking system. Every year of the rapid development of our agriculture and manufactures that followed the Spanish War revealed the inadequacy both of the volume and of the flexibility of our currency to meet the business needs of the country. Most of the business of the country is done on credit, and the extent to which the banks could furnish credit was limited by the fact that they could issue currency only on the basis of government bonds (see p. 359). Periods of prosperity and business expansion, when the demand for credit at the banks was greatest, were naturally just the periods in which the government bonds stood highest and offered the least attractive investment for the banks. The difficulty, under these conditions, of securing credit for the legitimate business enterprises of the country led to the charge of a "money trust" or "credit trust," monopolizing the fluid capital of the country. A committee of the House (the Pujo Committee), appointed to investigate this charge, reported just at the close of the Taft administration, finding evidence of such a trust; but the bankers replied by a circular, published by Mr. Morgan, attributing the evils to "a clumsy and outgrown banking system" rather than to "the schemes of men."

701. The Glass-Owen Bill. Various remedies were proposed for this "outgrown system" dating from the Civil War. The Aldrich-Vreeland Act was passed, May 30, 1908, creating "national currency associations," which were allowed to issue emergency currency in times of need, based on other securities than national bonds, but the scheme did not work smoothly or satisfactorily. In the midsummer of 1913 Carter Glass of Virginia introduced a Currency and Banking Bill into the House, on which he had been working for a year and in which President Wilson and Secretaries McAdoo and Bryan had a part. Senator Owen of Oklahoma took charge of the measure in the Upper House. The Glass-Owen Bill, known as the Federal Reserve Act, was passed by substantial majorities in both Houses, and signed by President Wilson, December 23, 1913. It divides the United States into twelve federal districts, in each of which is a central city with a federal reserve bank. Every national bank of the district is obliged to enter the federal reserve system, subscribing 6 per cent of its capital and surplus to form the capital of

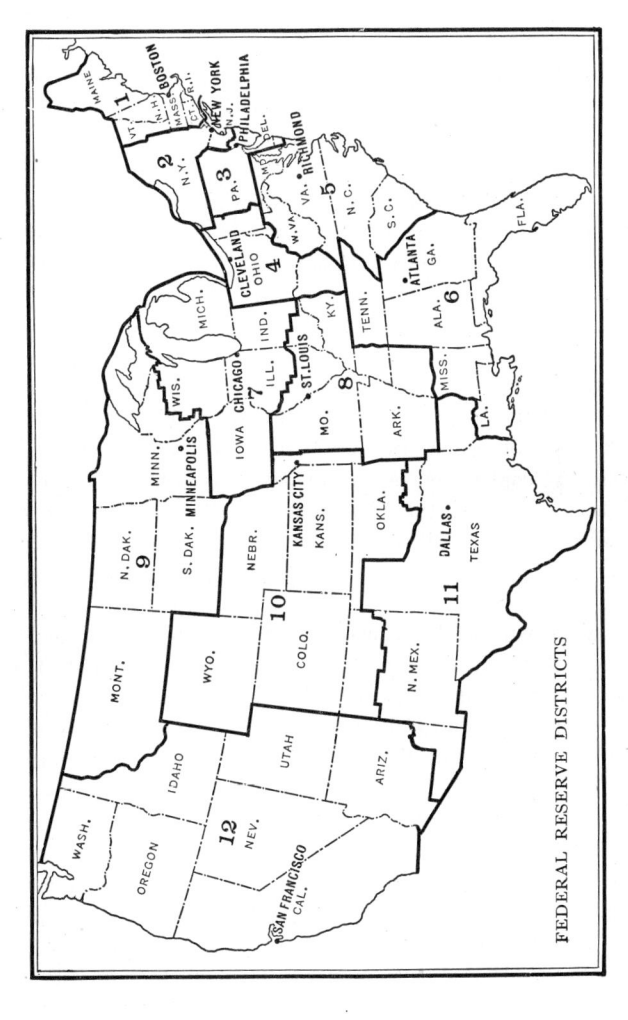

FEDERAL RESERVE DISTRICTS

On January 1, 1924, the Treasury reported the total stock of money in the country as $8,977,466,356, or a per capita amount of $82.10. Nearly half of the money ($4,005,062,279) was in the Treasury, mostly in the form of gold coin and bullion ($3,553,932,238). The amount of money in circulation (nearly $5,000,000,000, or $44.22 per capita of the population) was in the following forms: Federal Reserve notes, $2,230,000,000; national bank notes, $713,000,000; gold coin, $415,000,000; silver coin, $320,000,000; gold certificates, $582,000,000; silver certificates, $375,000,000; greenbacks, $307,000,000.

the Federal Reserve Bank. These subscribing banks are called "member banks." The management of the Federal Reserve Banks is vested in a central committee, called the Federal Reserve Board, consisting of the Secretary of the Treasury, the Comptroller of the Currency, and five other members appointed by the President.[1] The powers of the board are ample, including the inspection of the Federal Reserve Banks, the determination of what kinds of "paper" the member banks may discount, the transfer of funds from one district to another, the establishment of branches in foreign countries, and the fixing of rates of interest on loans. The system prevented panics until the depression of the early 1930's.

702. The Clayton Anti-Trust Act. The extra session of Congress called by Wilson in April, 1913, lasted through the summer and autumn and merged into the regular session of December, before the Glass-Owen Bill was signed; still the President kept Congress at work like a "schoolmaster" for another eight months without interruption. In the continuous session of 567 days, whose reported debates fill 18,000 pages of the *Congressional Record*, many important bills were put through besides the major acts of the tariff and the currency. The Clayton Anti-Trust Bill, signed in October, 1914, consolidated a number of amendments and additions to the industrial legislation which had been put on the statute books since the passage of the Sherman Anti-Trust Act of 1890 (p. 433, note). It prohibited "interlocking directorates" (that is, the appearance of the same men on several boards of directors) for banks and trust companies whose deposits, capital, surplus, and profits amounted to $5,000,000, forbade price discriminations in favor of dealers who agreed not to use the goods of a rival company, and forbade the use of injunctions in labor disputes over questions of the terms of employment, "unless necessary to prevent irreparable injury to property rights for which there was no remedy at law." The radicals called the Clayton Act "a dough-bullet bill," because it failed to give the Interstate Commerce Commission the right to regulate the issues of stocks and bonds by corporations doing an interstate business;

---

[1] The board, with Charles S. Hamlin of Massachusetts as president, took office August 10, 1914, and the reserve banks were opened November 16. The World War had broken out early in August, so that the new system came just in time to help steady the finances of the country, which were much disturbed by the war.

ENTERING THE TWENTIETH CENTURY

while the conservatives called it "a muddle and a sham" whose only effect would be to disturb the business of the country.

703. Other Measures of the 63d Congress. Other important measures of the 63d Congress, which President Wilson in a speech at Indianapolis, January 8, 1915, called "the most remarkable Congress since the Civil War," were the creation of a Federal Trade Commission to investigate the conduct of "big business" and advise the Departments of Commerce and the Interior in its regulation; the Smith-Lever Act, granting federal aid to establish farm bureaus; an Industrial Employers' Arbitration Act; a Ship Registry Act, for the transfer of foreign ships to the American flag; an Alaskan Railway Act; a Philippine Act, replacing the appointive Commission by a Senate elected by the Filipinos; and the repeal of the Panama Canal Tolls Act.

704. The Repeal of the Panama Canal Tolls Act. The last-named act deserves some comment. In August, 1912, the Democratic House and the Republican Senate had concurred in passing a bill exempting coastwise American vessels from paying tolls through the Panama Canal, which was rapidly nearing completion. The third clause of the Hay-Pauncefote Treaty of 1901 with Great Britain (see p. 473) reads: "The canal shall be free and open to the vessels of commerce and of war of all nations . . . on terms of entire equality, so that there shall be no discrimination against any such nation . . . in respect of the conditions or charges of traffic or otherwise." The British government protested that the act of August, 1912, was a violation of this clause; while the Taft administration maintained that the phrase "open to all nations on terms of entire equality" meant to all *foreign* nations. The United States, as sole builder and owner of the canal, was bound by the treaty not to "discriminate against any nation," but was not bound to refuse a favor to her own vessels engaged in a purely domestic trade. We had a treaty of arbitration with Great Britain, negotiated under Roosevelt in 1908, which pledged us to arbitrate the dispute. But in the first week of March, 1914, President Wilson came before Congress, and in a speech of less than three minutes' duration urged, almost commanded, the repeal of the act. "I ask this of you," he said, "in support of the foreign policy of the Administration. I shall not know how to deal with other matters of even greater delicacy and nearer consequence, if you do not grant it to me in ungrudging measure." Without asking what the "President's secret" was, Congress repealed the act.

705. The Panama Canal Opened. The canal was opened for world traffic in August, 1914, when the American steamer *Ancon* went through the locks with her decks thronged with officials and distinguished guests of the American and Panama governments. The tonnage passing through the canal in the first few years was rather small, owing both to the World War and to the need for closing the canal for some months at a time in order to remove "slides." In 1916, 4,931,911 tons passed through, paying tolls of $3,673,233, while the cost of operation and repairs was almost $7,000,000. But by the end of 1919 the tonnage had increased to about 8,000,000 a year. The traffic has not yet paid 2 per cent on the investment, but under peace conditions and with the rapid development of our South American trade, the canal will become a very profitable investment. In January, 1914, Colonel George W. Goethals, "the prophet engineer" who had completed this greatest work on the western continent, was made the first governor of the Panama Canal Zone. Percy MacKaye wrote the ode in honor of the occasion:

> A man went down to Panama
> Where many a man had died,
> To slit the sliding mountains
> And lift the eternal tide.
> A man stood up in Panama,
> And the mountains stood aside.

706. The Elections of 1914. The mid-term elections, which followed only ten days after the adjournment of the long session of the 63d Congress, resulted, as usual, in a reaction against the Administration. Republican governors were chosen in New York, Connecticut, Pennsylvania, and several other states, while the Democratic majority in Congress was reduced to 31 in the House. The tariff and trust legislation offered many points for criticism. Bryan's conduct of the State Department was severely censured. A terrible strike war had been raging for nearly a year in the mining regions of Colorado, which neither the state militia furnished by Governor Ammons nor the six troops of cavalry sent by President Wilson had been able to quell. And, finally, the policy of the Administration in

U.S.S. *NEW MEXICO* IN GATUN LOCKS, PANAMA CANAL

ENTERING THE TWENTIETH CENTURY 493

regard to Mexico was branded by its opponents as vacillating, stupid, arbitrary, and cowardly all at once.

707. The Mexican Revolution. Seldom has a president of the United States inherited a more difficult problem than that which confronted Wilson in the Mexican situation. On the last Saturday of February, 1913, President Madero of Mexico was murdered and a week of turmoil followed, with fierce fighting in the very streets and squares of the Mexican capital. A ruthless, dissipated, revolutionary general, with Indian blood in his veins, fought his way to power—Victoriano Huerta, the reputed murderer of Madero. Although twenty-six foreign nations recognized Huerta, and our ambassador to Mexico, Henry Lane Wilson, advised the Administration at Washington to follow suit, President Wilson refused to do so. He sent John Lind of Minnesota as his special agent to Mexico to propose terms for the settlement of the anarchy reigning there. The United States promised to recognize the Mexican government after a general and free election should be held, in which Huerta should not be a candidate. Huerta replied that he had the allegiance of twenty-two of the twenty-seven states of Mexico with an army of 80,000 men, and that he could easily put down the rebellion. He asked the United States to ignore the disturbances and to send an ambassador to his government. Huerta's real character came out, however, when on October 10, two weeks before the general elections in Mexico, he invaded the Assembly with an armed force, arrested and imprisoned a hundred deputies, and proclaimed himself dictator. England, France, and Germany, recognizing America's paramount interests in Mexico and respecting the Monroe Doctrine, urged this country to act in safeguarding foreign lives and property across our southern border.

708. Our Intervention in Mexico. Wilson's policy of "watchful waiting" until Mexico should straighten out her own tangled affairs grew more and more difficult to maintain. An embargo on the export of arms to Mexico had been laid in 1912, which Wilson raised in February, 1914, in behalf of General Carranza, who was fighting to overthrow Huerta. The murder of an Englishman named Benton, about the same time, increased the pressure put on our government to restore order in Mexico. On April 9, 1914, a boatload of American sailors from the launch *Dolphin* landed at Tampico to buy gasoline. The launch was flying the American flag, but one of Huerta's officers seized the entire party and started to carry them off to jail amid the jeers of the crowd. Rear Admiral Mayo demanded the release of the sailors and an apology for the insult in the shape of a formal salute to our flag. Huerta disavowed the act of his officer, released the men, but refused to salute the flag. Eleven warships and three cruisers of the Atlantic fleet were ordered to Tampico. On April 20, President Wilson came before Congress, asking permission to use force against Huerta "to maintain the dignity and authority of the United States." The vote was 337 to 37. On the same day our forces were ordered to occupy Vera Cruz on the Gulf of Mexico. Admiral Fletcher landed a detachment of marines and seized the customs house, while the battleships *Utah* and *Florida* shelled the arsenal from the harbor. Seventeen American lives were lost before Fletcher had control of the seaport.

709. Carranza and Villa. To avert war between Mexico and the United States, the greater republics of South America now offered their mediation. Representatives from Argentina, Brazil, and Chile (the "A B C powers") met the delegates of Huerta and the United States at Niagara Falls, Canada, in May, and urged Huerta to resign. He departed from Mexico on the German cruiser *Dresden* in July, and in September President Wilson withdrew our forces from Vera Cruz and returned to his policy of "watchful waiting," declaring that it was none of our business how Mexico settled her own troubles. But anarchy continued in Mexico while Carranza slowly fought his way to power against the bandit Villa. Carranza made himself master of the capital in July, 1915, and as his fortunes improved, his antagonist Villa grew more desperate. Finally, on March 10, 1916, Villa's ruffians crossed our border with cries of "Death to Americans!" and raided the town of Columbus, New Mexico, killing seven soldiers and twelve civilians, and wounding a score of others. We were obliged to send a punitive force into Mexico (with Carranza's permission) in pursuit of Villa. But the clever bandit eluded our soldiers, and before long Carranza, charging us with designs on his power, demanded our withdrawal. The troops came back from their wild-goose chase over the hot plains of northern Mexico without Villa and with little glory. Carranza's power grew slowly but steadily in the distracted land, until he was able to

ENTERING THE TWENTIETH CENTURY

summon a constitutional convention and get himself elected the first president of the Mexican Republic under the new constitution for a term of four years (March, 1917).

President Wilson asked nothing more than to be allowed to go on with the program of social and industrial reform which he outlined in his speech to Congress in December, 1914. But the World War was already under way in Europe, which, in spite of our declaration of strict neutrality, was affecting our commerce, arousing our sympathies and protests, and absorbing our attention to the exclusion of all other interests. It almost monopolized the labors of our government during the remainder of Wilson's first term of office, and at the opening of his second term drew us into its angry vortex (April 6, 1917).

REFERENCES

The Spanish War and the Philippines: J. H. LATANÉ, *America as a World Power* (American Nation Series), chaps. i-x; A. C. COOLIDGE, *The United States as a World Power*, chaps. v-viii; J. W. FOSTER, *American Diplomacy in the Orient*, chap. xiii; J. G. SCHURMAN, *Philippine Affairs*; D. C. WORCESTER, *The Philippines, Past and Present*; E. E. SPARKS, *The Expansion of the American People*, chap. xxxvi; C. R. FISH, *The Path of Empire* (Chronicles, Vol. XLVI), chaps. ii-v; J. D. LONG, *The New American Navy*, chaps. v-xii; H. T. PECK, *Twenty Years of the Republic*, chaps. xii-xiv; A. B. HART, *American History told by Contemporaries*, Vol. IV, Nos. 180-196; *The Obvious Orient*, chaps. xxiv-xxvi; E. B. ANDREWS, *The United States in our Own Time*, chaps. xxvii, xxviii; JAMES BRYCE, *The American Commonwealth* (enlarged edition of 1911), Vol. II, chap. xcvii; Histories of the Spanish War by H. C. Lodge, R. A. ALGER, and HENRY WATTERSON.

The Roosevelt Policies: THEODORE ROOSEVELT, *Autobiography*; LATANÉ, chaps. xii-xvi; PECK, chap. xv; COOLIDGE, chaps. xv-xix; J. W. FOSTER, *A Century of American Diplomacy*, chap. xii; E. L. BOGART, *Economic History of the United States*, chap. xxx; H. C. LODGE (ed.), *Addresses and Presidential Messages of Theodore Roosevelt, 1902-1904*; GIFFORD PINCHOT, *The Fight for Conservation*; FRANCIS CURTIS, *The Republican Party*, chaps xvi-xviii; F. W. HOLLS, *The Peace Conference at The Hague*, chaps. i, ii, viii; W. F. JOHNSON, *Four Centuries of the Panama Canal*, chaps. viii-xii; JOHN MITCHELL, *Organized Labor*, chaps. xvii, xviii; biographies of Roosevelt by J. A. RIIS, WM. D. LEWIS, WM. R. THAYER, CHAS. G. WASHBURN, and LAWRENCE ABBOTT.

The Return of the Democrats: F. A. OGG, *National Progress* (American Nation Series), chaps. i-xvi; E. D. DURAND, *The Trust Problem*; IDA M. TARBELL, *The Tariff in our Times*; W. H. TAFT, *Presidential Addresses and State Papers* (New York, 1910); W. WILSON, *Presidential Addresses and State Papers* (New York, 1917), *The New Freedom*; R. M. LA FOLLETTE, *Autobiography*; F. W. TAUSSIG, *The Tariff Act of 1913* (*Quarterly Journal of Economics*, Vol. XXVIII, 1-30); H. P. WILLIS, *The Federal Reserve*; C. W. BARRON,

The Mexican Problem; E. R. JOHNSON, *The Panama Canal and Commerce*; H. CROLY, *The Promise of American Life and Progressive Democracy*; biographies of Wilson by H. J. FORD, WM. B. HALE, and H. W. HARRIS (an Englishman).

TOPICS FOR SPECIAL REPORTS

1. **The Hague Peace Conference of 1899:** HOLLS, pp. 1–35, 365–372; LATANÉ, pp. 242–254; A. D. WHITE, *Autobiography*, Vol. II, pp. 250–354; J. W. FOSTER, *Arbitration and the Hague Court*.

2. **Anti-Imperialism:** COOLIDGE, pp. 148–171; PECK, pp. 610–612; ANDREWS, pp. 853–858; G. F. HOAR, *Autobiography of Seventy Years*, Vol. II, pp. 304–329; EDWARD ATKINSON, *The Cost of War and Warfare from 1898 to 1904*; MOORFIELD STOREY, *What shall we do with our Dependencies?*

3. **The Convention of the Progressive Party at Chicago:** E. STANWOOD, *History of the Presidency*, Vol. II, pp. 288–298; *Review of Reviews*, Vol. XLVI, pp. 310 ff.; W. R. THAYER, *Theodore Roosevelt*, pp. 350–375; W. D. LEWIS, *Life of Theodore Roosevelt*, pp. 370–380.

4. **Were we Unjust to Colombia?** ROOSEVELT, *The Panama Blackmail Treaty* (*Metropolitan Magazine*, Vol. XLI, p. 8); THAYER, *John Hay and the Panama Republic* (*Harper's Magazine*, Vol. CXXXI, 167–175); ABBOTT, *Impressions of Theodore Roosevelt*, pp. 137–141; CHAMBERLAIN, *A Chapter of National Dishonor* (*North American Review*, Vol. CXCV, pp. 145–174).

5. **Oregon's Experiments in Direct Democracy:** J. D. BARNETT, *Operation of the Initiative, Referendum, and Recall in Oregon*, pp. 189–218; DICKEY, *The Presidential Primary in Oregon* (*Political Science Quarterly*, Vol. XXXI, pp. 81–104); HAYNES, *People's Rule in Oregon* (*Political Science Quarterly*, Vol. XXVI, pp. 32–62).

CHAPTER XX

THE WORLD WAR AND AFTER

Neutrality

710. The Origin of the War. On the 28th of June, 1914, the heir to the Austrian throne was assassinated in the Bosnian capital of Serajevo by a Serbian youth named Princip. Holding the anti-Teutonic propaganda of Serbian revolutionary societies responsible for the murder, Austria, backed by her powerful ally Germany, started to punish Serbia by invading her territory and bombarding her capital. The Czar of Russia mobilized his troops on the Austrian border to protect his fellow Slavs in the Balkans and check the German "push to the east" (*Drang nach Osten*). France was Russia's ally, and Great Britain was on the friendliest terms (*Entente*) with France. When, therefore, Germany ordered Russia to demobilize within twelve hours, it looked as though all the great powers of Europe would be drawn into the Austro-Serbian quarrel over the assassination of a prince. In vain did the foreign ministers in the great capitals of Europe labor to avert the terrible catastrophe of a general war, in the last week of July, 1914. In vain did they plead for time, for the submission of the dispute to the Hague Tribunal or to the arbitration of the four great powers of Great Britain, France, Germany, and Italy. Germany had for years been nourishing the belief that England, France, and Russia were hemming her in with an iron ring of jealous hatred, to crush her industrial and commercial expansion. She had prepared the most mighty military engine the world has ever seen and determined now to strike before she was struck. Self-defense was her plea, but to the majority of the nations her action looked like a deliberate piece of aggression to win "a place in the sun" for her colonial ambitions and to impose her "Kultur" on Europe by force of arms. Her first military move, the ruthless invasion of Belgium, whose neutrality Prussia had guaranteed with the other great powers in the Treaty of 1839, provoked a storm of protest on both sides of the Atlantic.[1]

711. The Submarine Peril. The United States government declared its strict neutrality, but the people of the United States were not neutral. Their sympathies were overwhelmingly on the side of the Entente Allies (Great Britain, France, Russia, Belgium, Serbia) against the Central Powers (Germany and Austria-Hungary). The pressure of public opinion naturally affected our policy. When, for example, Great Britain, mistress of the seas, blockaded the coasts of Germany by mines sown in the North Sea, arbitrarily extended the list of contraband goods, seized our vessels and cargoes, the protests from Washington were so friendly that the German government accused us of being virtually England's ally. When Germany, on the other hand, resorted to the submarine and drew a "war zone" around the British Isles in order to starve them into submission, we insisted on maintaining the freedom of the high seas. Germany's offense against neutral rights was incomparably more serious than England's, because whereas England seized property only, Germany destroyed lives. The submarine is a frail instrument of defense, being easily rammed by a powerful ship or destroyed by a single shot from a moderate-sized gun. Hence it will not expose itself to destruction by observing the rules of visit and search. It has no way of placing in safety the crew and passengers of a ship carrying contraband, before destroying ship and cargo. It strikes quickly, sending its torpedo on its swift and secret mission of death. It has been called the stiletto of the seas. The British seizures of ships and cargoes violated the rules of international law, but the German destruction of neutral and noncombatant lives outraged the dictates of humanity. For the former there could be redress and indemnity after the war; for the latter there was no reparation.

712. The *Lusitania* torpedoed. It was inevitable that American lives should be lost if Germany persisted in submarine warfare,

---

[1] Von Bethmann-Hollweg, the German Chancellor, confessed in a speech to the Reichstag that the invasion of Belgium was "contrary to the dictates of international law" and promised to make reparation for the wrong when the German "military object" was obtained. "Necessity knows no law" was his plea. The "necessity" in this case was the rapid march on Paris by the most favorable route. He found the Treaty of 1839 only "a scrap of paper" in the way.

unless American citizens renounced their privilege of traveling on the high seas and American ships remained moored to their wharves as in the days of Jefferson's embargo. Our government dispatched a note to Germany immediately after the war zone was traced (February 10, 1915), declaring that we should hold the Imperial Government to a "strict accountability" if an American vessel or the lives of American citizens were destroyed. Germany replied that it was not her intention to harm neutrals but that the destruction of England was necessary. She "expressly declined all responsibility for such consequences" as might follow if neutral vessels entered the zone. On May 7, 1915, the civilized world was horrified by the news that the magnificent Cunarder *Lusitania* had been torpedoed off the Irish coast without warning and sent to the bottom with the loss of nearly 1200 lives, including 114 Americans. Germany defended this shocking act on the ground that the *Lusitania* had hidden guns below decks, was listed in the British navy, and was carrying thousands of tons of ammunition. The German government expressed regret that American lives were lost, but insisted that their blood was on England's head.[1] It refused to disavow the sinking of the *Lusitania*, declaring that "the German government has no guilt therein."

713. The *Sussex* Pledge. President Wilson labored to keep the peace, expostulating with Germany in note after note, while public opinion in this country turned more and more to questions of military preparedness and national defense. Scattered cases of unprovoked attacks on merchant ships, in which American lives were lost, added to the tension. When on March 24, 1916, a German submarine torpedoed the French Channel steamer *Sussex* (on which it was thought Earl Kitchener was crossing to France), with the loss of American lives, President Wilson served an ultimatum on Germany. He recalled the patience of the American government, which had "hoped against hope that it would prove possible for the

---

[1] In further extenuation of the sacrifice of American lives the German government called attention to the warning which the German embassy at Washington had published in the American newspapers against neutrals sailing to the war zone on ships of Great Britain or her allies. This action was a gross breach of diplomatic courtesy. "A foreign minister is here," says John Bassett Moore, "to correspond with the Secretary of State.... He has no authority to communicate his sentiments to the people by publication, and any attempt to do so is contempt of this government" ("Digest of International Law," Vol. IV, p. 68).

Imperial Government so to order and control the acts of its naval commanders as to square its policy with the recognized principles of humanity." That hope proving vain, there was but one course to pursue: "Unless the Imperial Government should now immediately declare and effect an abandonment of its present methods of submarine warfare against passenger and freight-carrying vessels, the United States can have no choice but to sever diplomatic relations with the German Empire altogether." President Wilson was congratulated for having at last by patience won a diplomatic victory when Germany replied that she was "prepared to confine the operations of the war for the rest of its duration to the fighting forces of the belligerents" and promised that "merchant vessels . . . should not be sunk without warning and without saving lives, unless the ship attempted to escape or offer resistance." At the same time Germany disavowed the act of the naval commander who sank the *Sussex*, and offered indemnity for the loss of American lives. It was hoped that the *Sussex* pledge had removed the danger of war between the United States and Germany.

714. Our Aversion to War. Meanwhile the mass of the American people were coming to realize that the black cloud of war which hung over Europe threatened to reach our own shores. Our attachment to peace was strong. The warnings of Washington, Jefferson, and Monroe to keep this western republic out of the quarrels of European nations had been the basis of our foreign policy for over a century. Our country was the land of the immigrant: fully a third of our 100,000,000 inhabitants were foreign born or of foreign parentage, and these people represented all the belligerent nations, with the preponderance largely on the side of the German and Austro-Hungarian Empires. The farmers of the West and the manufacturers of the middle states, made prosperous by the large demands of Europe for our wheat, beef, steel, and iron, were slower than the merchants and bankers of the Atlantic coast to realize the danger to our land should the great naval power of England be destroyed by the German submarines. To the many thousands of pacifists, who abhorred war on principle, were added other thousands who advocated peace for the sake of profits. For after the first shock of war, which had closed European markets and led to financial panics, the Entente countries began to place huge orders in the United States.

We fell heir to a large part of Germany's commerce with Asia, Africa, and South America. Neutral powers, like Denmark, Holland, Norway, and Sweden, bought from five to ten times their ordinary purchases of American commodities. A great part of these purchases undoubtedly went across the frontier lines and the Baltic into Germany and Austria-Hungary. The excess of our exports over our imports was $691,000,000 in 1913; in 1915 it jumped to $1,768,000,000, and for the first ten months of 1916 to $2,490,000,000.

715. Germany's Acts of Provocation. But against all arguments, idealistic or materialistic, for neutrality were working the forces which month by month brought us closer to the decision of arms. As nation after nation joined the war, and the aims of Germany for world dominion became more and more evident, it was clear that the struggle was not merely a European fray but a world-decision between the ideals of autocracy and democracy. Every tradition of American history and every fiber of American sympathy was on the side of democracy. It seemed shameful that America should be content to grow fat on her prosperity, when all that could make prosperity a blessing in her land and in the world was threatened. Moreover, every month brought revelations of German and Austrian intrigues in our country, which made neutrality harder to maintain. Failing to gain their unreasonable demand that we should forbid the shipment of munitions because only their enemies could carry them,[1] the Central Powers began a campaign of *sabotage* in the United States to hinder the manufacture and exportation of munitions. They promoted strikes in factories, set on fire and blew up plants, put bombs on British and French vessels in our harbors, and even encouraged a plot in Mexico to invade the United States. In September, 1915, Dr. Dumba, the Austrian ambassador, was dismissed for his part in inciting the workers of the Bethlehem Steel Company to strike; and in December the recall of Captains Von Papen and Boy-Ed, the German military and naval attachés at Washington, was demanded on account of similar "improper activities."

[1] In reply to notes from Berlin and Vienna in the spring of 1915, protesting against the sale of American munitions to the Entente Allies, our Secretary of State replied that not only was such sale sanctioned by international law but that Germany herself had freely sold munitions to the belligerent nations in the Boer War, the Russo-Japanese War, and the Balkan Wars.

716. Preparedness. The advocates of military preparedness in America were active from the beginning of the war. A nonpartisan National Security League was formed in 1914 to promote universal military training and service. The next summer, largely through the labors of General Leonard Wood, an officers' training camp was established at Plattsburg, N. Y. Since a strong navy had been for years a cherished American policy (our navy in 1914 being inferior to England's and Germany's alone) it was easy for Secretary Daniels, in 1916, to get Congress to adopt a three-year naval program, calling for the expenditure of $600,000,000 for new ships alone. But the nation was averse to much enlargement of its army of less than 100,000 men. Participation in European wars was unthinkable, and for the defense of our country Secretary Bryan said that we could "raise a million men between sunrise and sunset." President Wilson in his message of December 8, 1914, deplored a large standing army and declared that we must depend in times of peril "on a citizenry trained and accustomed to arms"—that is, to a militia. The next December, however, he recommended a standing army of 142,000 and a reserve force of 400,000. In January, 1916, he made a tour of the Middle West, recommending military preparation "as effective and prompt as possible," without "losing a day." Yet on his return to Washington, he refused to support Secretary Garrison's plan to enlarge the regular army to 400,000. Whereupon Secretary Garrison resigned (February 10, 1916) and was succeeded by Newton D. Baker of Ohio, a lawyer with pacifist leanings. During the spring months of 1916 Congress wrangled over the army bill, each party trying to make capital for the approaching presidential campaign. The National Defense Act which resulted, June 3, was a poor makeshift by which the federal government assumed the expense of training the citizen armies in the states, without authority to federalize this militia or incorporate it into the regular army.

717. Our Interests in the Caribbean. Problems raised by the great war occupied the attention of our government and people, almost to the exclusion of other matters.[1] In normal times a lively

[1] The most important bills of the 64th Congress (1915-1917) were a Federal Child Labor Act, forbidding the entry into interstate commerce of products of mines and quarries in which children under sixteen were employed, or factories and canneries in which children under fourteen worked; a Federal Workman's Compensation Act; a Federal Farm Loan Act; the repeal of the free-sugar clause in the Underwood Tariff (continuing a revenue of

controversy would have been waged in the nation over the extension of our power in the region of the Caribbean Sea. In September, 1915, we concluded an arrangement with Haiti by which the control of the revenues and the police of that republic passed into our hands. In the other half of the island, Santo Domingo, we had exercised a financial protectorate since Roosevelt's day, but did not interfere in the politics of the state until the spring of 1916, when we landed

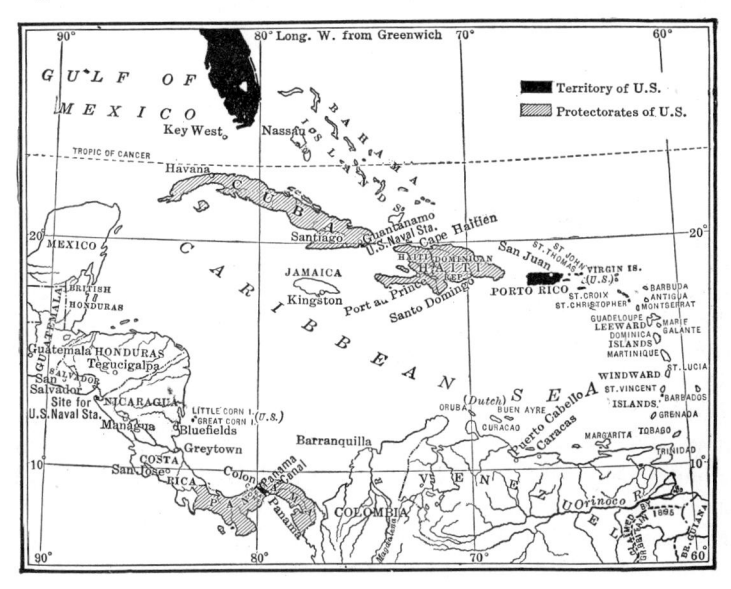

THE UNITED STATES IN THE CARIBBEAN

marines and proclaimed a military government on the island till the elections of the following January should be completed. In July, 1916, we made a treaty with Nicaragua, securing us the right to construct an interoceanic canal across her territory, and granting us the permit for ninety-nine years to establish naval bases on Corn Island and "in the territory of Nicaragua bordering Fonseca Bay." Early in 1917 we gave citizenship to the inhabitants of Porto Rico and purchased for $25,000,000 the Danish islands of St. Thomas, St. John,

$40,000,000); a Philippine Government Act, enlarging the electorate and abolishing the Commission for a Senate; and the Adamson Act, providing for an eight-hour day for railroad employees.

and St. Croix (the Virgin Islands). Little by little, through the intervention of special agents, the dispatch of warships and marines, formal treaties, and purchase, we had, by the close of Wilson's first administration, made ourselves the controlling power in the Caribbean. If Wilson's policy here, as well as in South America and China, was less obviously for the support of big-business interests than Taft's so-called "dollar diplomacy,"[1] it was nevertheless a steady enlargement of America's power.

718. The Presidential Campaign of 1916. Though the Democratic platform of 1912 had declared against a second term, there was no thought of replacing Wilson. When the campaign of 1916 approached there were several aspirants for the Republican nomination, including Senator La Follette, Henry Ford (the millionaire automobile manufacturer who had financed the "Peace Ship"—a Utopian expedition to the neutral countries in the late autumn of 1915 to get the soldiers "out of the trenches by Christmas"), Charles E. Hughes (a justice of the Supreme Court), and Theodore Roosevelt. For although the latter had not formally severed his connection with the Progressive party, he had been for some time drawing closer to the regular Republican organization. The Progressives, who held their convention in Chicago in the same June days of 1916 as the Republicans, nominated Roosevelt only a few minutes before the Republicans nominated Hughes. Roosevelt immediately sent a telegram from Oyster Bay, refusing to accept the Progressive nomination until he knew "the attitude of the candidate of the Republican party on the vital questions of the day," which meant that he would support Hughes if he was strong enough on preparedness and the assertion of American rights. The "defection" of Roosevelt made the Progressives withdraw from the presidential race. Hughes was a strong man with an enviable record. As governor of New York from 1907 to 1910 he had devoted his administration with great energy to liberal measures, breaking up the monopoly of private interests, fighting for open primaries against the party machine, and urging the creation of public service boards for the control of public utilities. He had resigned in the last year of his second

[1] For example, the Taft administration was in favor of asking American bankers to join with the financial powers of Europe in a great loan to China (the "six-power loan"), with the privilege of supervising China's policy so as to secure the payment of the interest. But when Wilson came into power he withdrew from the project.

term as governor to accept an appointment by President Taft to the Supreme Court, and in his six years of service on that high tribunal he had written over one hundred and fifty opinions, all noteworthy for their sound legal knowledge and judicial temper. Former Vice President Charles W. Fairbanks was named as his running mate.

719. "Americanism" the Issue. The campaign was waged almost wholly on the issue of "Americanism." Hughes toured the country, urging a stronger national defense, a policy of firmness and consistency in Mexico, and the insistence of full American rights on the high seas. He sounded the keynote of his campaign in his speech of acceptance in Carnegie Hall, New York, July 31, 1916: "An America conscious of its power, awake to its obligations, erect in self-respect, prepared for every emergency." He was somewhat of a disappointment as a campaign orator, lacking in the very vigor which he made his text. His friends attributed this to his six years of quiet on the Supreme Bench, while his enemies found the explanation in the lack of any real material for criticism in the Wilson administration. Wilson remained at his "summer capital" of "Shadow Lawn" at Long Branch, New Jersey, receiving delegations of pilgrims every Saturday afternoon from September 23 to the end of the campaign. The Democrats pointed with pride to Wilson's record, commending him for keeping the country out of war; while the Republicans asserted that he had sacrificed the honor of the nation to preserve peace. "The election of Wilson," said Theodore Roosevelt, "means that we are ready to accept any insult, even the murder of our women and children, if only we make money." Hughes was criticized for "sullying the ermine" by descending from the dignity of the Supreme Court into the arena of politics.

720. The Reëlection of Wilson. The election proved to be one of the closest in our history. Before midnight of election day it was known that Hughes had carried the eastern states, together with Indiana, Illinois, Michigan, and Wisconsin. Telegrams of congratulation began to pour in on him, and he retired, confident of his election. The *New York Times*, a strong Wilson paper, appeared in its earliest morning edition on November 8 with large headlines conceding a "sweeping victory" for Hughes. But as the day advanced and the returns from the country districts were counted, Wilson's fortunes grew brighter. One after another, states that had been assigned to Hughes were transferred to the Wilson column. Thursday night it became certain that Wilson had carried California, and with it the election. The electoral vote was 277 for Wilson and 254 for Hughes; and the popular vote, 9,129,606 to 8,538,221. The Socialist candidate Benson received 585,113 votes, the Prohibitionist candidate Hanly, 220,506, and the Socialist Labor candidate Reimer, 13,403.

721. Wilson defines the Peace Terms which America will Sanction. A single topic absorbed the country during the remaining months of Wilson's first term; namely, our relations to the World War in Europe. On December 12, 1916, the German government, speaking in the tone of a victor to the vanquished, offered to meet the Entente Allies in a conference to discuss peace. But the Allies rejected the offer as a "sham proposal" intended only to divide them and strengthen the patriotic war sentiment in Germany. President Wilson attempted a mild form of mediation between the warring groups when he sent an identic note to all the belligerent powers, on December 18, asking them to state their terms for ending the war and guaranteeing the world against its renewal. A month later (January 22, 1917) Wilson addressed the Senate in a remarkable speech, declaring the conditions on which America would give "its formal and solemn adherence to a league of peace." It must be, he said, a peace that should satisfy the whole world; a peace secured by the "organized major force of mankind"; a peace guaranteeing the freedom of the seas and the security of small and weak nations; and a peace based on the principle that "governments derive their just powers from the consent of the governed." "These are American principles, American policies," he declared. "We can stand for no others. And they are also the principles of forward-looking men and women everywhere, of every modern nation, of every enlightened community. They are the principles of mankind, and must prevail."

722. The Break with Germany. Indignant at the reply of the Entente to her proposals of December 16, and ignoring President Wilson's appeals, Germany issued a proclamation on January 31, 1917, enlarging the war zone and removing all former restrictions on her submarine warfare. She offered to let the United States send one passenger ship a week (very plainly marked on hull and funnels) through a narrow lane of safety to the English coast. This breach of the *Sussex* pledge President Wilson met on February 3, 1917, by breaking off diplomatic relations with Germany. "We do not desire any conflict with the German government," he said. "We are the sincere friends of the German people, and earnestly desire to remain at peace with the government which speaks for them. We shall not

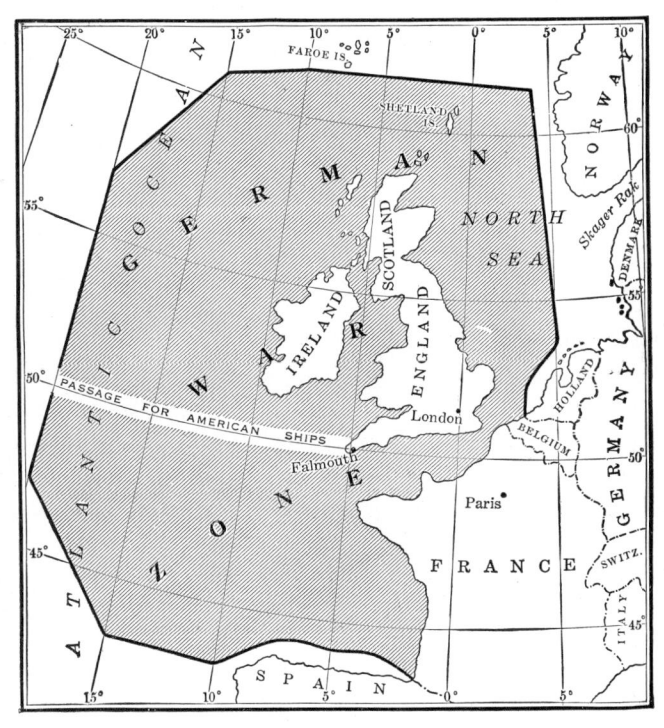

GERMAN WAR ZONE OF JANUARY 31, 1917

believe that they are hostile to us until we are obliged to believe it, and we purpose nothing more than the reasonable defense of the undoubted rights of our people."

723. The Arming of American Merchantmen. During the month of February, 1917, the German submarines sank 200 ships, of which 51 were neutrals, with a tonnage of 456,000. To send American vessels unarmed to meet such risk as these figures show would have been sheer folly. Wilson therefore asked Congress on February 26, 1917, for the power to arm American merchant vessels. The House readily passed the bill by a vote of 403 to 13, but eleven senators, taking advantage of the Senate rule which allows unlimited debate, refused to let the bill come to a vote before the expiration of Congress at noon on March 4, 1917. In spite of this resistance of "a little group of willful men," the President, relying on the advice of his Attorney-General and Secretary of State, proceeded to arm

AMERICAN ARMED LINER SAILING FOR THE WAR ZONE

the ships. The American liner *St. Louis* soon afterwards left New York with guns fore and aft, and safely traversed the danger zone.

724. The Declaration of War with Germany. President Wilson had called the 65th Congress to meet in extra session April 16, to consider the pressing questions of national defense. But the continued aggressions of the U-boats, as the submarines were called, coupled with the popular protest roused by the revelations of an intercepted dispatch of the German foreign minister Zimmermann to the German minister in Mexico, suggesting an alliance of Germany, Mexico, and Japan against the United States in case our country entered the war, and offering Mexico as her reward the recovery of her "lost provinces" of Texas and New Mexico, determined Wilson to advance the date of meeting by two weeks. On the evening of April 2, 1917, the President appeared before Congress to deliver one of the most momentous messages in the history of our country. Declaring that the "irresponsible German government" had "cast aside all considerations of humanity" and was "running amuck" among the nations, he asked Congress to recognize that the course of the German government was "nothing less than war against the people and government of the United States," and to accept formally the status of belligerent which had been forced upon us. "We have no quarrel with the German people," said the President, "but only with the military despotism of Germany. *The world must be*

PRESIDENT WILSON READING THE WAR MESSAGE

made safe for democracy. . . . We desire no conquest of dominion. . . . We are but one of the champions of the rights of mankind. We shall be satisfied when these rights have been made as secure as the faith and the freedom of nations can make them."

A resolution declaring a state of war with Germany and empowering the President to carry on war with all the power of our nation was passed through the Senate by a vote of 86 to 6 on the fourth of April and was adopted by the House (373 to 50), after a sixteen-hour debate, early in the morning of Good Friday, April 6, 1917. For the first time in over a century we were at war with a first-class foreign power.

Participation

725. Why Neutrality was Ended. President Wilson in his Flag Day address at Washington, June 14, 1917, summed up the reasons why our neutrality, maintained with increasing difficulty for thirty-two months, finally came to an end. "It is plain enough how we were forced into the war. The extraordinary insults and aggressions of the Imperial German Government left us no self-respecting choice but to take up arms in defense of our rights as a free people and of our honor as a sovereign government. The military masters of Germany denied us the right to be neutral. They filled our unsuspecting communities with vicious spies and conspirators, and sought to corrupt the public opinion of our people in their own behalf. When they found that they could not do that, their agents diligently spread sedition amongst us and sought to draw our citizens from their allegiance. . . . They sought by violence to destroy our industries and arrest our commerce. They tried to incite Mexico to take up arms against us and to draw Japan into a hostile alliance with her. They impudently denied us the use of the high seas, and repeatedly executed their threat that they would send to their death any of our people who ventured to approach the coasts of Europe. . . . What nation, in such circumstances, would not have taken up arms? . . . The flag under which we serve would have been dishonored had we withheld our hand."

726. America's War Aims. But however numerous and varied the offenses of Germany which finally drove us into war, we accepted the challenge with a single aim and purpose. Again and again — in his war message to Congress of April 2, 1917; in his Flag Day address of June 14, 1917; in his reply to the Pope of August 27, 1917; in his enumeration of the "Fourteen Points" of January 8, 1918; in his Baltimore address of April 6, 1918; in his speech at Washington's tomb of July 4, 1918; in his speech at the New York Metropolitan Opera House of September 27, 1918 — President Wilson reiterated the simple truth that we were fighting only to overthrow the hateful system of Prussian military autocracy and to establish government by the consent of the governed throughout the civilized world. "The great fact," he said, "that stands out above all the rest is that this is a peoples' war, a war for freedom and justice ... a war to make the world safe for the peoples who live in it and who have made it their own." In these statements the President had the enthusiastic approval of the press and the people of our country. In the heat of this noble purpose the feeling of vengeance for the insults and injuries which Germany had heaped upon us was fused into the pure passion of a crusade for humanity.

Canadian Official War Photograph

RUINS OF THE CLOTH HALL TOWER, YPRES, BELGIUM

Destroyed by the Germans

727. Europe's Need. Our task was immense. The Allied nations, which for two and a half years had borne the brunt of the apparently inexhaustible attack of the German military machine, were in sore need of munitions, money, food, men, and ships. In the very month when the United States entered the war the German submarine attack reached its peak. That month 800,000 tons of shipping, mostly British, were sent to the bottom of the ocean, and the German press was boasting a destruction of 1,000,000 tons a month, which was to bring Great Britain to her knees before summer. France was "bled white." Her rich regions of coal and iron, her vineyards and factories, were in the hands of the invaders. One out of every six of her population had been called to the colors. The exhausted men on the battlefields of Flanders and Champagne needed all the supplies that our wealth could furnish, needed our surgeons and nurses and ambulances, needed most of all the presence of American troops — the visible proof that a new, fresh, and powerful nation had come to their aid. Immediately after our entrance into the war, the British and French governments sent missions to this country to place their information and experience at the disposal of our government and to advise how our aid could best be organized. The British mission, headed by the Foreign Secretary, Arthur J. Balfour, and the French mission, headed by Marshal Joffre, the hero of the Marne, and René Viviani, the eloquent Minister of Justice, received an enthusiastic welcome, which was later extended to Belgian, Italian, and Russian missions.

728. The Task of Congress. The Congress which had been called in extra session, April 2, to receive the President's war message, immediately set to work to raise and equip our armies, to enlarge our shipping, to stimulate our agriculture and our manufactures, and to provide the huge sums of money necessary to make our weight felt as soon as possible as a decisive factor in the war; while the President began to assume the great powers intrusted to our executive as commander in chief of the army and navy of the United States.

729. Raising an Army. Our army numbered only a little over 200,000 men. We needed millions. Congress passed the Selective Service Act, May 18, requiring all men between the ages of twenty-one and thirty inclusive to register for military service. On June 5 some 9,500,000 were thus enrolled. Six weeks later numbers were drawn by lot in Washington, each number drawn calling into the service the man of the corresponding registration number in each of the 4557 local boards of the country. After careful physical examination and the consideration of causes for exemption, the 687,000 men retained for the service were distributed among sixteen cantonments in as many states; while the national guard, a militia called into federal service, were sent to sixteen other camps. These thirty-two training camps, with all their apparatus of barracks, hospitals, shops, lighting and heating plants, water supply, and sewage systems, were built in a few months' time at a cost of $200,000,000.

AMERICA AND THE WORLD WAR

730. Pershing in France. On the same day that the Selective Service Act was passed, President Wilson announced that Major-General John J. Pershing would command the American Expeditionary Force in France. General Pershing and his staff reached Paris on June 13 and were received with tumultuous demonstrations of welcome. A dramatic incident of Pershing's arrival was his visit to the grave of Lafayette, on which he deposited a wreath of flowers. The debt of gratitude which we had owed to France for one hundred and forty years was to be paid. The first American soldiers landed in France towards the end of June, after two encounters with submarines, and month by month they continued to arrive, passing first into camps for intensive training before they went to the "quiet sector" assigned to them at the front. President Wilson wrote to them: "The eyes of all the world will be upon you, because you are in some special sense the soldiers of freedom. Let it be your pride, therefore, to show all men everywhere what good soldiers you are but also what good men you are. Keep yourselves fit and straight in everything and pure and clean through and through."

GENERAL PERSHING

From a painting by J. F. Bouchor, Official Painter to the French Armies

731. Our Navy. The navy, better prepared than the army, through the generous appropriations of former Congresses, was mobilized on the day war was declared, and 87 ships of the German merchant marine in our ports were taken over. A fleet of our destroyers reached European waters on May 4 to coöperate with the British and French in hunting the submarines. Battleships and cruisers followed in June and took their place in the line of the British Grand Fleet which was bottling up the German warships in the harbor of Kiel. The Emergency Fleet Corporation made provisions for the rapid construction of supply ships and troopships.

When we entered the war we had only 13 of these service ships, with a weight of 94,000 tons. By the end of the war our fleet had increased to 2113 ships with a tonnage of over 5,000,000. The cost of our navy and auxiliary ships in the two years 1917 and 1918 ($3,833,000,000) was about equal to their entire cost from 1794 to 1916. We carried to French ports alone, during the war, 7,500,000 tons of cargo, including locomotives, freight cars, automobiles, trucks, rails, and food supplies, of which only 1.6 per cent was lost in transit. The transports, especially the great *Leviathan* taken over from the Germans, with its capacity for 11,000 troops, plied back and forth with the regularity of a ferry, carrying over 2,000,000 soldiers to France. More than half these men were carried in British and French ships, but America furnished over 82 per cent of the naval convoys. Only a single troopship, the *Tuscania*, was sunk by submarines on its eastern voyage.

732. The Air Service. All former wars had been waged on land or on the surface of the sea, but the World War was carried on beneath the seas and in the air as well. The airplane was an American invention, like the submarine, but in spite of an appropriation by Congress of $614,000,000 for the air service, our contribution to that branch of the war was slight at first. We had but two small aviation fields and about 300 second-rate planes in April, 1917, so that our aviators were trained mostly in French, English, Italian, and Canadian schools. We sent millions of feet of spruce from the forests of our Northwest to help build planes abroad, but it was not till the spring of 1918 that our airmen were flying over the German lines. As in every department of the war, our help in the air service grew marvelously during the summer of 1918. We had over 50,000 men abroad in the air service, though few actually flying on the front, at the signing of the armistice, and we were producing 1500 planes and 5000 motors a month. Over sixty of our airmen won the distinction of "aces"—that is, fliers who had brought down at least five enemy planes. The prospect of a host of American aviators on the front in the near future surely hastened the day of Germany's surrender.

733. Food Conservation. Of no less importance than these direct military contributions to the war was the part played by America in feeding the armies and the civilian population of the Allies. On May 15, 1917, Herbert C. Hoover, whose splendid management of the Belgian Relief Commission had kept the people of Belgium and the devastated portions of France from starvation, was appointed Food Administratoi of the United States, with large powers of control over the conservation and distribution of food supplies. A thoroughgoing Food Control Act was signed by the President, August 10, forbidding the raising of prices or the restriction of supply, punishing hoarding, and authorizing the President to fix the price of wheat. "Food will win the war—don't waste it!" was the slogan. Meatless and wheatless days were prescribed. The people of the country responded with hearty coöperation. Farmers planted a larger acreage. Hotels and restaurants saved wheat and sugar. Families pledged themselves to eat corn bread and drink unsweetened coffee. Even the children planted "war gardens." The Food Administration, served by an army of volunteer workers, was handling the purchase and distribution of foodstuffs to the value of $300,000,000 per month at the close of the war. Some idea of the magnitude of the conservation movement may be gained from the following figures of our exports in 1917–1918, as compared with the average of the three-year period before the war. Exports of beef increased from $186,000,000 to $565,000,000; of pork, from 996,000,000 to 1,691,000,000 pounds; of grain, from 183,000,000 to 349,000,000 bushels; of sugar, from 621,000,000 to 2,149,000,000 pounds; of dairy products, from 26,000,000 to 590,000,000 pounds. The total value of our food contributions to Europe in 1918 was over $2,000,000,000.

WILLIAM G. McADOO

734. Control of Transportation and Fuel. The production and conservation of food and the manufacture of munitions, however, would have been to no purpose if these supplies could not reach their destination in Europe. In order to move them to the great shipping ports and to carry them overseas the government had to take control of the transportation system and coal production of the country. Priority orders gave coal and iron, wheat and meat, preference over private shipments on freight lines. A fuel administrator was appointed in August, 1917, whose representatives were sent to every mining region of the country to stimulate production. On December 27, 1917, President Wilson took over the railroads of the United States, assuring the owners that their interests would be "as scrupulously looked after by the government as they could be by the directors of the several railways systems." Secretary of the Treasury McAdoo was made Director-General of the railroads, which were to be returned to their owners within twenty-one months after the close of the war. They were to receive a yearly rental from the United States based on their average annual earnings from June, 1914, to June, 1917. The Director-General authorized the expenditure of $938,000,000 for improvements and equipment during 1918 and increased the wages of the railroad men that year by $300,000,000. Owing to the increase of wages and the rise in the price of material of all sorts, the railroads lost hundreds of millions of dollars under government management. The large express companies also were merged into a single concern to handle the government's shipments, and the telephone and telegraph lines passed under the control of the Postmaster-General. To conserve fuel, heatless days and lightless nights were observed, illuminated advertising signs were extinguished, and the time was advanced an hour during the spring and summer months to "save daylight." When 250 laden ships were detained at our ports in January, 1918, for lack of coal in their bunkers, the fuel administrator shut down for a period of five days all the manufacturing plants of the country east of the Mississippi River.

735. America's Generosity. No finer example of patriotism was ever offered than the ready self-denial with which the people of the country supported the government in these measures. Labor agreed to waive its right to strike during the war. Thousands of men left highly paid positions to place their expert knowledge at the service of the government for a dollar a year. Newspapers and magazines gave space freely to help the cause of public and private charities. A nation accustomed to lavish spending dispensed with its luxuries to aid the various welfare organizations. The Red Cross, the Salvation

Army, the Knights of Columbus, the Jewish Welfare Board, the Y. M. C. A., the War Camp Community Service asked for hundreds of millions of dollars, and never asked in vain. "It is estimated," says Mrs. Florence Kelly in her stirring book "What America Did," "that the American people contributed to these several welfare purposes close to $4,000,000,000." And this was all a free-will offering over and above the heavy taxes imposed by the government and the subscription to five loans aggregating $21,448,000,000.

736. War Taxes and Liberty Loans. It was the policy of the government to meet approximately one third of its war expenses by taxation. During the summer of 1917 a War Revenue Bill for raising $2,000,000,000 was debated in Congress. As finally passed in October it provided for an increased income tax, excess profits taxes ranging from 20 to 60 per cent, increase in postal rates, and a variety of taxes on amusements, luxuries, transportation, and business transactions. But these taxes were trivial as compared with the revenue bill introduced into the House in the autumn of 1918 and signed by the President the following February. It called for over $6,000,000,000, the largest sum ever levied by a government on its people at one time. Most of the money came from the incomes of rich individuals and corporations. The normal rate on incomes above $4000 was raised to 12 per cent, with graded surtaxes reaching 65 per cent on incomes above $1,000,000. Until our entrance into the World War our government had not been accustomed to ask the people to come directly to its support by the purchase of its bonds. But in May, 1917, the first Liberty Loan of $2,000,000,000 was offered for popular subscription in bonds ranging from $50 to $10,000 each. It was followed by three other Liberty Loans before the signing of the armistice, each larger than its predecessor and each oversubscribed by enormous amounts:

Number of Loan[1]	Date	Amount Asked	Rate of Interest	Amount Subscribed	Number of Subscribers
First	May, 1917	$2,000,000,000	3½	$3,035,000,000	4,000,000
Second	Oct., 1917	3,000,000,000	4	4,617,000,000	9,400,000
Third	April, 1918	3,000,000,000	4¼	4,176,000,000	18,300,000
Fourth	Oct., 1918	6,000,000,000	4¼	6,988,000,000	21,000,000

[1] A fifth loan, the Victory Loan, was announced by the Treasury, April, 1919. It called for $4,500,000,000 at 4¾ per cent interest, and was taken by 15,000,000 subscribers.

In addition to financing our own war expenses and raising billions of dollars for private relief and welfare work, we loaned nearly $10,000,000,000 to the allied governments of Great Britain, France, Italy, Belgium, and Serbia.

737. Opposition to the War. Though there was considerable activity among the confirmed advocates of peace to keep us out of the war up to the very eve of our decision, when that decision was once made opposition ceased, except for some aliens and that small and disloyal part of our citizens made up of I. W. W. agitators, certain sections of the Socialists,[1] and the partisans or paid agents of Germany and Austria. To counteract the work of enemy aliens in obstructing the draft, destroying property, and advocating treason to the United States, a severe Espionage Act was signed by President Wilson on June 15, 1917. Conscientious objectors to war were allowed to perform noncombatant service in the medical, the quartermaster's, and the engineering corps. Those drafted men whose conscience would not permit them to serve in military uniform were allowed to work on farms under surveillance of the War Department. Less than 500 men refused to comply with the military laws of the country. They were imprisoned, along with those who obstructed the draft or plotted disloyal acts.

738. Conditions of Peace Defined. The German government affected at first to feel no concern over the entrance of the United States into the war. They despised our "undisciplined" army and believed that their submarines would bring the war to a victorious close before we could render any military aid to the Allies. But as the summer wore on and the submarine sinkings diminished, while the American contingents began to land in France, the Germans changed their tone. The Pope, prompted by a desire to end the slaughter in Europe, suggested peace negotiations on August 11, to which President Wilson replied a fortnight later, stating emphatically that we could not "take the word of the present rulers of Germany as a guaranty of anything that is to endure, unless explicitly supported by such conclusive evidence of the will and purpose

---

[1] On July 7, 1917, the Socialists condemned our entrance into the war by a referendum vote of 21,639 to 2752, showing that the party was dominated by German sympathizers. Whereupon a number of prominent Socialists, including John Spargo, William E. Walling, J. G. Phelps Stokes, Upton Sinclair, and Allan Benson (the presidential candidate in 1916), withdrew from the party.

of the German people themselves as the other peoples of the world would be justified in accepting." The German Reichstag disclaimed any purpose of annexing territory or exacting indemnities, and the kaiser talked much of his love of peace. But as the Reichstag was powerless in the face of the military authorities, and as the kaiser continued to maintain the preposterous falsehood that he was fighting on the defensive against a group of bloodthirsty nations that had attacked Germany, there was little hope for peaceful negotiations. On January 5, 1918, Premier Lloyd George, in a speech to the British Trades Unions Congress, declared that peace could come only on the basis of the sanctity of treaties, of complete restoration and reparation by Germany, of a territorial settlement secured by the consent of the governed, and of "some international organization to limit the burden of armaments and diminish the probabilities of war." Three days later President Wilson laid before Congress his famous "Fourteen Points"—a detailed program for world peace. They included open diplomacy, the freedom of the seas, the removal of economic barriers, the reduction of armaments, the reparation of wrongs committed in the war, the principle of self-determination, and a league of nations.

CANTIGNY

Cartoon by Cassel, *The World*, New York

739. The Great German Drives. Meanwhile American military plans were being pushed with vigor. By the end of October, 1917, we had sent over 100,000 men to France, and on November 3 our troops had their baptism of fire at the front. In a desperate attempt to win the victory before the immense resources of America should be thrown into the scale against them, the Germans, on March 21, 1918, launched the first of a series of five tremendous attacks on the British and French armies, driving great wedges, or "salients," into the Allied line.[1] Mile by mile they pushed the British and French back, until at the beginning of June they were at the Marne again, only forty miles from Paris, with 45,000 prisoners in their hands. It was at this crisis that the fresh American troops came to the support of the sorely tried Allied armies who were fighting "with their backs to the wall." On May 28 American soldiers in France captured their first town of Cantigny. During June the American marines,

"YANKS" BRINGING IN GERMAN PRISONERS

in a series of irresistible attacks, drove the Germans out of Belleau Wood, which was rechristened, by order of the French general in command, "The Wood of the Marine Brigade."

740. Americans on the Battlefield. Ferdinand Foch, the most brilliant of the French strategists, was made generalissimo of the Allied forces in March, 1918, and General Pershing put all the

[1] The German army was greatly reënforced for these drives by fresh troops from the Eastern front, relieved by the utter collapse of the Russian army. The Russians had overthrown the despotism of the Czar in March, 1917, but the moderate revolutionists, under Kerensky, were not able to maintain themselves. The government fell into the hands of the Bolshevist leaders, Lenine and Trotzky, who in the spring of 1918 concluded the disgraceful peace of Brest-Litovsk with Germany, deserting their Allies and sacrificing the integrity of their country.

THE BRIDGE AT CHÂTEAU-THIERRY

At this point American and French troops stopped the German advance in the Second Battle of the Marne. The Germans reached the right side of the river, as shown in this picture, but could get no farther

American troops at his disposal.[1] Foch began his counterdrive against the Germans in July. Assigned to a distinct sector near Verdun and the Argonne Forest, the American troops, in their first independent offensive early in September, brilliantly wiped out the salient of St. Mihiel, which the Germans had maintained for four

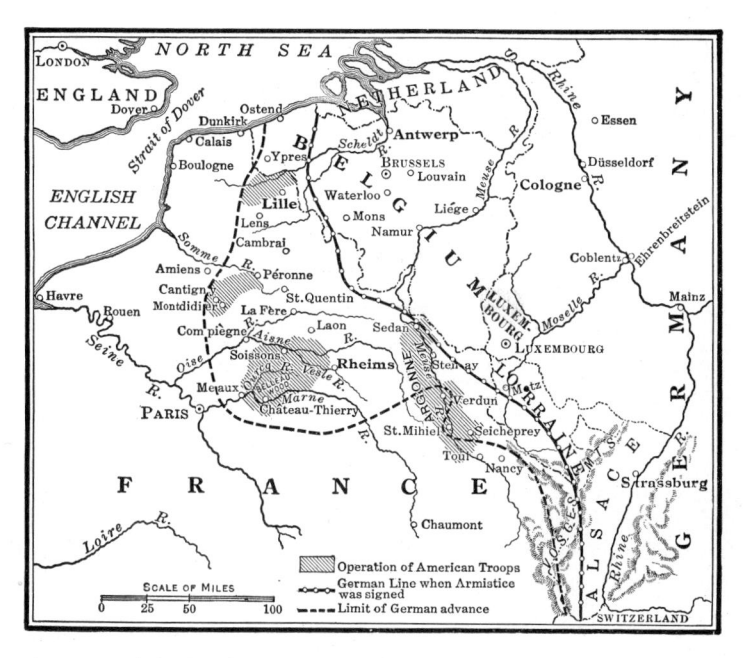

MAP SHOWING AMERICAN OPERATIONS IN EUROPE

years. Further north two American divisions, coöperating with the British army, broke the proud Hindenburg line in the face of a terrific artillery and machine-gun fire. The crowning work of the American troops was the magnificent Argonne-Meuse drive (September–November, 1918). Twenty-one divisions, comprising 1,200,000 men, many of whom had never been in battle before, faced forty divisions of trained German troops. The scene of the conflict was

[1] The Americans were arriving rapidly by midsummer, 1918. In March 83,811 reached France; in April, 117,222; in May, 244,345; in June, 276,372.

the Argonne Forest, which no army had ever tried to penetrate before, and which the French officers declared impregnable. "Day after day the American troops moved slowly forward, over rugged, difficult ground, broken by ravines and steep hills, through dense underbrush, in the face of deadly fire from artillery and nests of machine guns hidden in every vantage point, through incessant rain and mud and fog and penetrating cold, pushing the enemy steadily back, until they reached Sedan, cut the German army's most important line of communication, and so brought the end of the war in sight." In that wonderful movement the Americans advanced 25 miles and

	IN DOLLARS	MEN KILLED IN BATTLE
Germany	39,000,000,000	1,600,000
British Empire	38,000,000,000	900,000
France	26,000,000,000	1,385,000
United States	22,000,000,000	49,000
Austria	21,000,000,000	800,000
Russia	18,000,000,000	1,700,000
Italy	13,000,000,000	462,000

COMPARATIVE COST OF THE WAR TO SEVEN CHIEF BELLIGERENTS

captured 26,000 prisoners (some of them of the kaiser's crack regiments), with 490 guns. Marshal Foch's laconic comment on the drive was, "The American soldiers are superb!"

741. The Armistice. Driven back at every point from France and Belgium, and practically deserted by her allies,[1] Germany realized that the game was up. The new Chancellor, Prince Max of Baden, an avowed peace man, asked President Wilson (October 4) to invite all the belligerent countries to send envoys to a conference to negotiate peace terms on the basis of the Fourteen Points. After a brief exchange of notes with the Central Powers, the Allied War Council

---

[1] Bulgaria was brought to an unconditional surrender by the French General d'Espérey on September 30. The British General Allenby, who had restored Jerusalem to Christian hands after nearly seven centuries of uninterrupted Turkish rule, conquered the whole of Palestine. The Italian troops, aided by British and French units, had driven the Austrians back behind the Piave River and repaired the losses of the disastrous rout of Caporetto. Bulgaria was thus already beyond help, and it was clear that the other two allies of Germany could not hold out much longer.

INDEPENDENCE DAY. AMERICAN SOLDIERS SALUTING THE STATUE OF WASHINGTON, PARIS, JULY 4, 1918

From a painting by J. F. Bouchor, Official Painter to the French Armies

at Versailles arranged the terms for an armistice. On November 3 the Austro-Hungarian government signed the terms, and on November 11, two days after the kaiser had abdicated and fled to Holland, the plenipotentiaries of the new German Republic signed. Hostilities ceased at 11 A. M. on November 11, 1918. The Germans agreed to the immediate evacuation of the territory of France, Belgium, Alsace-Lorraine, and Luxembourg. German armies were also to be withdrawn from all German territory on the left bank of the Rhine, and from a strip ten kilometers wide on the right bank, extending from the frontier of Holland to the frontier of Switzerland. Allied and American troops were to occupy the left bank and to garrison the three great centers of Mayence, Coblentz, and Cologne. Furthermore the Germans were to surrender all their submarines, 50 destroyers, and 24 warships; to hand over vast stores of cannon, machine guns, airplanes, locomotives, freight cars, and motor trucks; to repatriate all prisoners and exiles, to make reparation for the damage done by their invading armies, and to pay for the upkeep of the Allied armies of occupation.

742. The End of the War. The signing of the armistice was hailed with wild demonstrations of joy in the United States. Our losses in battle were trivial as compared with those of the nations who for years had borne the brunt of war in the field. Less than 50,000 Americans were killed, somewhat over 50,000 died of disease, and of the 240,000 wounded five sixths were restored for duty again. The loss in the navy was 10,000. Thousands of families mourned their valiant dead, but to millions of families the cessation of hostilities meant the lifting of a great weight of anxiety and apprehension. For we were planning to have between 4,000,000 and 5,000,000 men on the battlefields of Europe by midsummer of 1919. Our great adventure was crowned with success. "The vision for which we fought" was won. "It will now be our fortunate duty," said President Wilson in a proclamation to his fellow citizens on the morning the armistice was signed, "to assist by example, by sober friendly council, and by material aid, in the establishment of just democracy throughout the world."

Problems of Peace

743. America Mobilized. When the order came to cease firing on the Western front we were just getting into our war stride. Soldiers were flowing from American camps to France at the rate of 10,000 a day. Seventy-five thousand tons of supplies were sent over in October, 1918, as against 16,000 tons in June, 1917. A fleet of 431 troopships and cargo ships were plying across the ocean ferry, while 386,000 men were at work in our shipyards on a program of construction laid out by our Emergency Fleet Corporation, calling for 13,000,000 tons of shipping. The Man Power Act of August 31, 1918, called into the service all men between the ages of 18 and 45. Over 13,000,000 were registered under it on September 12, and provision was made for enrolling the younger men as Students' Army Training Corps (the S. A. T. C.) at government expense in some 500 colleges and technical schools. The government's mobilization of industry was complete. A number of administrative boards (Shipping, War Trade, War Industries, Labor, Censorship, Food Administration, Fuel Administration, Railroad Administration, Employment Service, Industrial Housing, War Finance Corporation, etc.) had taken out of private hands practically all the business of the country that had any bearing on the conduct of the war. Factories and foundries had been converted into munitions plants. An Alien Property Custodian[1] had

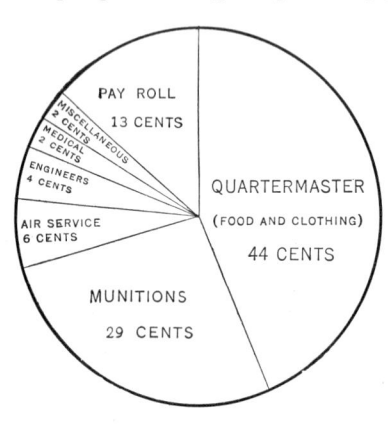

HOW THE AMERICAN DOLLAR WAS SPENT IN THE WAR

PAY ROLL 13 CENTS
MISCELLANEOUS 2 CENTS
MEDICAL 2 CENTS
ENGINEERS 4 CENTS
AIR SERVICE 6 CENTS
QUARTERMASTER (FOOD AND CLOTHING) 44 CENTS
MUNITIONS 29 CENTS

---

[1] A. Mitchell Palmer of Pennsylvania, who succeeded Secretary Gregory as Attorney-General on March 4, 1919. Other changes in Wilson's cabinet since the war have been the replacement of William G. McAdoo in the Treasury by Carter Glass (December 5, 1918), who in turn resigned in January, 1920, to take the place in the United States Senate vacated by the death of T. S. Martin of Virginia. He was succeeded by the Secretary of Agriculture, D. F. Houston, whose place was filled in turn by E. T. Meredith of Iowa. In December, 1919, J. W. Alexander, of Missouri, succeeded William C. Redfield as Secretary of Commerce. Early in 1920 Franklin Lane resigned from the Department of the Interior, and

taken over German and Austrian industries in the United States to the value of $700,000,000. Millions of people were working for the government, millions more were creditors of the government. Through the War Risk Bureau $40,000,000,000 of insurance was issued to soldiers and sailors. Never had our government come into such intimate relations with its citizens. Demobilization meant not only getting our men back from France, and into civil employments, but also the restoration of our political and industrial life to a peace basis.

744. Tasks for the Peace Council. Naturally the first task was the conclusion of a treaty of peace. The European governments were chiefly interested in the settlement of specific questions, like the adjustment of boundaries, the restoration of territory, the reparation for damages, the rebuilding of shattered industries, the disposal of Germany's colonies, the limitation of her economic growth, the destruction of her military and naval power, and the guaranty of new states like Poland, Czechoslovakia, and Jugoslavia. President Wilson's primary interest was in the establishment of a League of Nations, which should make war less probable in the future and transfer from the diplomats and military leaders to the people the control of the destinies of states. "As I see it," he said in an address in New York, September 27, 1918, "the constitution of that League of Nations and a clear definition of its objects must be a part, and in a sense the most essential part, of the peace settlement itself."

745. President Wilson goes to Paris. As the champion of this idea, President Wilson believed that his presence at the Peace Conference at Paris was necessary. He appointed as his colleagues Colonel Edward M. House, his intimate friend and adviser, Secretary of State Lansing, General Tasker H. Bliss, and Henry M. White, former ambassador to France. Immediately after sending his message to the final session of the 65th Congress, he sailed for France, December 4, accompanied by a large staff of expert advisers. The peace conference held its opening session January 18, 1919. Thirty-two nations were represented in the plenary council, but the important

his place was taken by John B. Payne of Chicago, chairman of the United States Shipping Board. The whole country was surprised when President Wilson asked for the resignation of Secretary of State Lansing (February 7, 1920) on the ground that he had "usurped" the president's prerogative by holding meetings of the cabinet during the president's illness. On February 25 Wilson nominated as Lansing's successor Bainbridge Colby, a lawyer of New York, who had been a supporter of Roosevelt in the Progressive campaign. The Senate delayed Mr. Colby's confirmation for about three weeks.

decisions were made by a Supreme Council, comprised of the chairmen of the delegations of the five leading powers—the United States, Great Britain, France, Italy, and Japan. Later the council was narrowed to four members—President Wilson and Prime Ministers Lloyd George, Clemenceau, and Orlando.

746. The League of Nations. A covenant of a League of Nations prepared by a committee of ten was reported to the conference by President Wilson in February and in slightly amended form was incorporated into the peace treaty. The chief provisions of its 26 articles concern the reduction of armaments, the publicity of treaties, the arbitration of international disputes, and the punishment of nations that go to war in defiance of the covenant. The famous Article X declares that "the members of the league undertake to respect and preserve as against external aggression the territorial integrity and existing political independence of all members of the league." Article XVI gives the council the right to recommend to the various governments what military and naval forces they shall contribute to enforce obedience to the covenant. The executive power of the League was intrusted to a council of nine members, of whom five were to be always representatives of the United States, Great Britain, France, Italy, and Japan. As soon as the provisions of the covenant were known in America more than one third of the Senate (that is, enough to defeat the treaty) signed a round robin declaring their opposition to the document "in the form now proposed," and advocating making peace with Germany first and then discussing plans for a League of Nations. But Wilson insisted on the immediate establishment of the league. On the eve of his return to Paris in March, 1919 (after a brief visit to the United States), he said, "When the treaty comes back, gentlemen on this side will find the covenant not only in it, but so many threads of the treaty tied to the covenant that you cannot dissect it from the treaty without destroying the whole vital structure."

747. Opposition to Wilson in the Senate. The peace treaty was signed at Versailles on June 28, 1919, and the President immediately brought it home to lay before the Senate for ratification. Opposition was strong from the beginning. In the first place the 66th Congress, which Wilson had called in extra session by cable from Paris (May 19, 1919), was Republican in both Houses. Wilson had made the mistake of appealing to the public just before the autumn elections of 1918 to return a Democratic Congress—after having said in a message six months earlier, "politics is adjourned." The result of the President's partisan appeal was a Republican majority of 45 in the House and 2 in the Senate. Furthermore, the Senate had not been taken into the President's confidence in the negotiation of the treaty. Not a senator was appointed on the peace commission and it was only as guests at informal luncheons at the White House, during the President's brief "vacation" in America (February–March, 1919), that some of the leading senators were acquainted with his plans. The President later sent word from Paris that he did not want the treaty discussed until he returned to America. The treaty was published in Europe, and copies reached private citizens here before the official copy was presented to the Senate.

748. Criticism of the League of Nations. But aside from any feeling of resentment that they had been "ignored" by the President, many senators were opposed to various articles in the treaty and especially in the covenant of the League of Nations. The points of complaint were that the sovereignty of the United States was sacrificed, that we were pledged to make war at the bidding of the council of the league, that we would be eternally embroiled in the quarrels of Europe, that purely domestic questions like immigration laws and the tariff were subjected to the interference of other nations, that Great Britain was represented by six times as many votes in the assembly of the league as we were. About a dozen senators, led by Borah of Idaho, were opposed to the treaty altogether; but the majority, led by Henry Cabot Lodge of Massachusetts, chairman of the Foreign Relations Committee, were in favor of ratifying with certain amendments or reservations. The administration senators, obeying the behest of the President, insisted that the treaty must be ratified without any modifications. The amendments and reservations proposed would, said Wilson, "take the teeth out of the treaty."

749. The Treaty Rejected. In September President Wilson started on a tour across the country to explain the treaty to the people at large and create a public sentiment which should force the Senate to ratify. In the midst of the trip the President suffered a severe physical breakdown, due to many months of mental overstrain, and was hurried back to Washington, where he was completely removed from public business. His spokesman in the Senate, Mr. Hitchcock of Nebraska, carried on the fight for unconditional ratification. Neither side would budge. When the vote was finally taken (November 19, 1919) on the treaty with fifteen Lodge reservations attached, it was defeated by a vote of 39 to 55.[1] The extra session came to an end the same day, with each party in the Senate throwing on the other the blame for the deadlock. When the first regular session of the 66th Congress convened on December 1, President Wilson announced from his sick room that he would not resubmit the treaty to the Senate, but would shift the responsibility for its adoption to the shoulders of his countrymen. In other words, unless the Senate should choose to reconsider its position, the treaty might become the issue of the presidential election of 1920. The Senate again took up the treaty, the debate centering chiefly on Article X. Both Mr. Lodge and the administration senators seemed more anxious to arrive at a compromise; but again (March 19, 1920) the treaty was rejected by a vote of 49 in favor to 35 against.

750. The Railroad Situation. Although discussion of the treaty and the League of Nations was the most absorbing topic of the nation after the signing of the armistice, and occupied the attention of the Senate almost to the exclusion of other business, nevertheless grave problems connected with our return to a peace basis were pressing for solution. The telegraph, telephone, and cable lines were restored to private ownership in the summer of 1919, but the opening of the new year saw the railroads still in the hands of the government and no plan agreed on for their return.[2] The two years of government operation had been far from successful. For 1918 the deficit was $200,000,000, and in the first ten months of 1919 it mounted up to $192,000,000 more. While the revenues increased 40 per cent, the expenses increased over 80 per cent, due to the high price of all materials and to advances in wages amounting to $580,000,000. As the roads had been taken over by the government with the assurance

[1] A number of previous votes showed that the majority of the Senate favored some form or other of amendment or reservation. On November 7 Lodge's "preamble," requiring three other great powers to accept our changes before the treaty became valid, passed by a vote of 48 to 40. On November 15 ten other reservations were adopted by about the same vote. Senator Underwood's motion that the treaty be adopted "without the dotting of an *i* or the crossing of a *t*" was defeated by 53 votes to 38.

[2] On December 24 President Wilson issued a proclamation fixing March 1, 1920, as the date of the return of the railroads to their owners.

that their interests would be scrupulously looked after, it would have been unfair to hand them back to their owners burdened with an enormous deficit and with 39 per cent of their stock paying no dividends.

751. Conflicting Plans for the Solution of the Railroad Problem. Many plans were proposed for the disposition of the roads. The railway executives recommended private ownership and management under federal regulation, with the legal prohibition of strikes and lockouts and the settlement of labor disputes by the government. The stockholders wanted the government to guarantee 6 per cent on their invested capital, while any profits above this sum should be distributed equally between the employees, the owners, and a fund for improvements. Mr. Glen E. Plumb, counsel for the railroad brotherhoods, advocated a plan of public ownership. The government should buy the roads and operate them through a corporation composed one third of railroad employees, one third of managers, and one third of members appointed by the president. The government should receive a rental of 5 per cent out of the revenues from the roads, and half of any excess should go to the employees. If a deficit resulted instead of a surplus, it should be made up by public taxation. Labor disputes were to be settled by wage boards. On November 17, 1919, the elaborate Esch Bill, over 80 pages long, was passed by the House. Its main provisions were (1) immediate return of the roads to private ownership, (2) deduction of the $775,000,000 spent by the government from the rental due the companies, (3) advancement to the companies of public capital for five years at 6 per cent interest, (4) settlement of labor disputes by boards of adjustment. Finally, in December, 1919, the Senate passed the Cummins Bill, providing for the division of the country into railroad "regions" and the merging of the roads into 18 or 20 systems. The revenues were to be pooled in each region, the successful roads paying for the losses of the unsuccessful ones. The Esch Bill and the Cummins Bill were so far apart that it seemed hardly possible that a compromise could be arrived at by the two Houses before the date (March 1, 1920) set by the President for the relinquishment of government management.

752. The Cummins-Esch Bill. By dint of hard labor, however, the conflicting views were reconciled in the Cummins-Esch Bill, or

Transportation Act of 1920, which was adopted (February 21) by the House by a vote of 250 to 150, and by the Senate (February 23) by a vote of 47 to 17. President Wilson, in spite of the protests of the railway workers and the Farmers' National Council that the bill was flagrantly unfair to labor, signed the bill on February 28, and two days later the railroads reverted to their former owners. The main provisions of the bill were (1) the enlargement of the powers of the Interstate Commerce Commission (increased to eleven members), which should fix rates so as to yield a return of $5\frac{1}{2}$ per cent on the estimated valuation of the railroads and could control the issue of securities; (2) the creation of a Railway Labor Board of nine members appointed by the President—three from the railroad workers, three from the owners, and three from the public—to settle labor disputes; (3) the appropriation of $200,000,000 to aid the roads to get back to their prewar status, and of $300,000,000 as a "revolving fund" out of which loans to the roads should be made; (4) the prohibition of any increase in rates or decrease in wages before September 1, 1920; (5) the provision that no man should serve as officer or director of more than one road after December 31, 1921.

753. Industrial Unrest. The relations of capital and labor have been the gravest problem of the country since the signing of the armistice. During the war there was a truce in the long struggle between these two economic rivals. Labor, under the lead of Samuel Gompers, president of the American Federation of Labor, proved its patriotism and thorough Americanism by refraining from any strikes that would interfere with war production. Over 1000 cases of dispute, involving 500,000 employees, were submitted to the War Labor Board, and most of them settled quickly and peaceably. But after the cessation of hostilities industrial strife broke out again in a perfect epidemic of strikes. Dockmen, shiphands, firemen, garment workers, textile workers, silk makers, carpenters, builders, miners, telegraph operators, street-car men, steel workers, expressmen, policemen, hotel waiters, barbers, followed each other out of their jobs, until it seemed as if the industry of the country were completely demoralized. Many causes contributed to this industrial unrest in the country: the return of the soldiers to civil life, the rapidly mounting war prices, which labor charged to the greed of profiteers and capital charged to the outrageous demands of the wage earner. "No one who has observed the march of events in the last year," said the President in his message of December, 1919, to Congress, "can fail to note the absolute need of a definite program to bring about an improvement in the conditions of labor. There can be no settled conditions leading to increased production and a reduction in the cost of living, if labor and capital are to be antagonists instead of partners. . . . The only way to keep men from agitating against grievances is to remove the grievances. . . . The unwilling workman is not a profitable servant. . . . We are a partnership or nothing that is worth while. We are a democracy where the majority are the masters, or all the hopes and purposes of the men who founded this government have been defeated or forgotten." But a conference, composed of representatives of capital, labor, and the public, which President Wilson called together at Washington in October to devise methods for better industrial relations, broke up in discord.

754. The Great Coal Strike. The most serious of the many strikes of 1919 was inaugurated on November 1, when, in spite of Wilson's plea for the maintenance of a full supply of fuel for the world's need, 400,000 men in the bituminous coal fields laid down their tools to enforce their demands for a 60 per cent increase in wages and the guaranty of a minimum of thirty hours of work a week. As we were still technically at war with Germany, the Lever Act of 1917, giving the President the power to regulate the fuel supply, was still in force. H. A. Garfield, fuel administrator under its provisions, resumed his activities. On November 8 a federal judge of Indianapolis enjoined the officers of the United Mine Workers to end the strike before November 11, on pain of punishment for "rebellion against the government in time of war." Mr. John L. Lewis, acting president of the union, complied with the order, remarking, "We are Americans, we cannot fight against the government." Though the strike was called off, the men were slow in returning to work. The cold days of December came on with only about 40 per cent of the normal production of coal. The governors of some states took over the coal mines within their borders, and volunteers came forward to work them. Meanwhile the fuel administrator, the Secretary of Labor, and the mine operators and workers were seeking to arrive at a satisfactory settlement.

Garfield proposed a 14 per cent increase in wages, Secretary Wilson a 31 per cent increase; but the miners declared both inadequate. Finally, on December 11, the miners agreed to return to work on Garfield's terms, pending a final adjustment of wages and hours. The operators quarreled with the administration, on the ground that Secretary Wilson arranged terms with the miners over their heads, and threatened to raise the price of coal if Garfield's terms were altered. Garfield himself resigned. The strike was over, but it was not till the end of March, 1920, that a settlement was made on the basis of a wage increase of 27 per cent. The strike had cost $125,000,000, of which nearly half was in loss of wages.

755. The "Reds" in America. A sinister element in the labor situation was the presence of a number of radical agitators, whose confessed object was not the attainment of reasonable demands for better conditions and higher wages through peaceful negotiation but the overthrow of the industrial system of the country and the appropriation of all its wealth by the laborers. These apostles of "direct action" were the Industrial Workers of the World (the I. W. W.), organized in 1904 in America. For ten years they had comparatively little influence in our labor world, but with the disordered conditions brought on by the World War, and especially with the triumph of the Bolshevists in Russia, their power grew. They entered the unions with the purpose of "boring from within," stirring discontent where it had not existed before, and preaching revolution as the remedy. Their violent methods recommended the wrecking of property and the destruction of life. The red flag was their banner; bombs were their weapons; revolution was their aim. Many of them were aliens from the desperate classes in Europe. In the autumn of 1919 a round-up of these men was made by the agents of the Department of Labor in many of the cities of the country, and on December 22 over 200 of them were deported to Russia on the "Red Ark," as the United States transport *Buford* was called. President Wilson in his December message to Congress said: "With the free expression of opinion and with the advocacy of orderly political change, however fundamental, there must be no interference; but towards passion and malevolence tending to incite crime and insurrection under the guise of political evolution there should be no leniency. . . . The instrument of all reform in America is the straight road of justice.

THE WORLD WAR AND AFTER

... Let those beware who would take the shorter road of disorder and revolution." The American Federation of Labor, in a conference representing 119 unions at Washington, in December, 1919, repudiated the doctrines of the I. W. W., and adopted by an overwhelming vote the resolution that the Federation was "an American institution believing in American principles and ideals."

756. The Eighteenth Amendment. A movement in favor of the prohibition of the manufacture and sale of intoxicating liquors, which for some years had been carrying state after state into the "dry" column, culminated in December, 1917, with the passage through Congress of an Eighteenth Amendment to the Constitution, providing for nation-wide prohibition to go into effect one year after the ratification of the amendment. With Nebraska's ratification, January 16, 1919, the assent of the necessary 36 states was obtained, and the amendment went into effect on January 16, 1920. Meanwhile, as a war measure for the conservation of grain, the Food Production Bill of November 21, 1918, forbade the manufacture of intoxicating liquors after July 1, 1919, until the "completion of demobilization." This law was not strictly obeyed, but when the "wet" interests sought to get relief from the courts, in order that they might dispose of their large stocks of liquor before the constitutional amendment went into effect, their hopes were dashed by a unanimous decision of the Supreme Court, December 15, 1919, upholding the law. Thus the year of grace given to the liquor interests by the amendment was denied them by the war-time prohibition.

757. Woman Suffrage. The House passed the Nineteenth Amendment, granting woman suffrage, in January, 1918, but, in spite of President Wilson's repeated recommendations, it was not until eighteen months later that the necessary two-thirds majority was secured in the Senate by the narrow margin of 56 to 25 votes. By the close of 1919 only 22 states had ratified the amendment; but the National Woman Suffrage Association was determined that the necessary 36 states should be secured before the opening of the presidential campaign of the following summer. Their untiring zeal won state after state, until Tennessee, on August 28, 1920, completed the list. The adoption of nation-wide woman suffrage resulted in the enlargement of the electorate by some 8,000,000 voters in the presidential contest of 1920.

758. The Republican Landslide. The Republican nominating convention met at Chicago on June 8, 1920. When it became evident that neither of the two leading contestants for the nomination, General Leonard Wood, the political heir of Roosevelt, and Frank O. Lowden, the conservative governor of Illinois, could command a majority of the votes of the convention, Senator Warren G. Harding of Ohio was chosen on the tenth ballot. Harding's nomination came as a surprise to the country, for his career in national politics was confined to a single term in the United States Senate, where he had been a rather inconspicuous member of the Lodge group. The vice-presidential nomination went on the first ballot to Governor Calvin Coolidge of Massachusetts, who had come into national prominence in connection with the suppression of a strike of the Boston policemen in the autumn of 1919. The Democrats, meeting at San Francisco (June 28), after a long contest between William G. McAdoo, President Wilson's son-in-law, and Attorney-General A. Mitchell Palmer, finally nominated Governor James M. Cox of Ohio on the forty-fourth ballot. Eugene V. Debs, who was serving a prison term for the violation of the Espionage Act, was nominated by the Socialists, and P. P. Christensen of Utah, by the new Farmer-Labor party. The Democrats attempted to make America's duty to ratify the Treaty of Versailles and enter the League of Nations the chief issue of the campaign, but it is doubtful whether that issue influenced the voters as strongly as did certain domestic questions—burdensome taxation, the high cost of living, industrial unrest, and a general reaction against the policies of President Wilson. Harding and Coolidge carried the entire North and West, with all the border states except Kentucky, and even invaded the "solid South" by capturing Tennessee. The electoral vote was 404 to 127, and the popular vote 16,152,220 to 9,147,553.

WARREN G. HARDING
© Baker Art Gallery

THE WORLD WAR AND AFTER 535

The Republicans also retained their control of both Houses of Congress by greatly increased majorities (309 to 132 in the House and 59 to 37 in the Senate). "It was not a landslide," said Mr. Tumulty; "it was an earthquake."

759. The New Administration. President Harding's choice of official advisers was generally approved, especially the selection of Charles E. Hughes of New York as Secretary of State, Andrew W. Mellon of Pennsylvania as Secretary of the Treasury, and Herbert C. Hoover of California as Secretary of Commerce.[1] While protesting our readiness to "associate ourselves with the nations of the world, great and small, for conference and counsel, for the suggestion of plans of mediation, conciliation, and arbitration," the President made it clear that we would not join the League of Nations. He concluded a separate peace with Germany (and later with Austria and Hungary), and on January 1, 1922, we resumed diplomatic relations with Berlin. Domestic questions occupied the chief place in the President's mind —the readjustment of taxation, the reduction of prices, the retrenchment of expenditures, the restriction of immigration, the restoration of the high tariff, the removal of industrial and agrarian discontent: in short, as he phrased it, "the return to normalcy."

760. The Sixty-Seventh Congress. The road back to normal conditions, however, was a slow and difficult one. There was much discontent among the farmers, because the price of their products fell to prewar levels much faster than the products of manufacture, which were protected by the tariff. Strikes of unusual severity in the coal fields and on the railroads vexed the country and interfered with the pacific program of the administration. The American Legion was conducting a campaign for a soldiers' bonus which would cost the Treasury hundreds of millions of dollars. Though the 67th Congress met in extra session in April, 1921, and continued, with only a few days' recess, for a year and a half, it showed no such zeal and unanimity in carrying out the President's recommendations as the first Congress of Woodrow Wilson had done. To be sure, it passed the

---

[1] The other cabinet appointments were Harry M. Daugherty of Ohio, Attorney-General; John W. Weeks of Massachusetts, Secretary of War; Will H. Hays of Indiana, Postmaster-General; Edwin F. Denby of Michigan, Secretary of the Navy; Albert B. Fall of New Mexico, Secretary of the Interior; Henry C. Wallace of Iowa, Secretary of Agriculture; and James J. Davis of Indiana, Secretary of Labor. Daugherty was criticized from the first as a purely political appointee, not equal to his position.

Fordney-McCumber tariff (September, 1922), restoring the high rates of the Payne-Aldrich Act, created a national budget, gave some relief to the farmers in the Agricultural Credits Act, limited the immigration from any Old World country to the United States for the next thirteen months to 3 per cent of the nationals of that country living here by the census of 1910, and repealed some of the war taxes (excess profits, transportation). But Congress and the administration were not agreed in their general policy of financial legislation. Secretary Mellon, supported by the President, wanted a drastic reduction in the surtaxes of the income tax and was opposed to a soldiers' bonus. Congress, on the other hand, supported the view that the burden of taxation should still fall upon the large incomes, and held that we could pay the soldiers' bonus without interfering with a proper reduction of taxation. In March, 1922, the House passed the Bonus Bill by the enormous majority of 333 to 70, amid cheers from the crowded galleries, and the Senate concurred in August by a vote of 47 to 22. President Harding vetoed the bill. The House immediately overrode the veto, but the Senate fell four votes short of the two-thirds majority (44 to 28).

761. The Washington Conference. Although the United States had rejected the League of Nations and the Treaty of Versailles, the country at large approved when Senator Borah, a bitter opponent of the League and the treaty, moved as an amendment to the naval appropriation bill of $494,000,000 that the President be asked to invite the two great naval powers of the Old World, England and Japan, to a conference to consider the limitation of naval armaments and the "pacification of the Pacific." More than two years had passed since the Armistice, and yet there was war in many quarters, and the nations were staggering under the weight not only of tremendous war debts but of military and naval preparations for "the next war." The United States had inaugurated a program of shipbuilding under Secretary Daniels which would have made it by 1924 the strongest naval power of the world.

It was with eager satisfaction, therefore, that the foreign governments accepted President Harding's invitation. France and Italy were included, as important naval powers, and China, the Netherlands, Belgium, and Portugal, as nations with large interests in the Far East. Delegates from eight European and Asiatic powers, therefore, assembled at Washington for the opening of the conference on

November 12, 1921. Secretary of State Hughes, the chairman, fairly electrified the great assembly when he frankly proposed a "naval holiday" for ten years, and offered on the part of the United States to sacrifice 30 battleships and cruisers (15 in process of construction), totaling 845,740 tons. He asked Great Britain to scrap 23 ships of 585,375 tons, and Japan 13 ships of 448,928 tons—a total reduction of about 2,000,000 tons of the world's navies. He proposed a naval ratio of 5:5:3 for the three powers (525,856 tons for the United States,

THE WASHINGTON CONFERENCE

582,959 for Great Britain, and 313,300 for Japan). France and Italy agreed to an allotment of 175,000 tons each of capital ships. Great Britain thus abandoned her policy of maintaining a navy equal to the combined fleets of her two strongest possible rivals.

Besides this most important treaty of the five powers on the limitations of naval armaments, the conference produced several other agreements, namely: three four-power treaties (the United States, Great Britain, France, Japan) guaranteeing the peace of the Pacific and terminating the Anglo-Japanese alliance, two nine-power treaties safeguarding the interests of China, and a five-power treaty regulating the use of submarines and poison gas in warfare. The conference adjourned in February, 1922, and the treaties were ratified by the Senate in the next few weeks.

762. The Mid-Term Elections. The prestige of the Washington conference could not save the administration from rebuke at the polls in the autumn elections of 1922. The coal strike had just been settled, but the railroad strike was in full swing. To industrial discontent was added the growing disaffection of the farmers, who were far from satisfied with the relief furnished them by the extension of farm loans. The new tariff act was denounced as a device for imposing a burden of $400,000,000 a year upon the American consumer. Secretary Mellon was accused of running the Treasury Department in the interests of the rich. The voters who had put their faith in the Republican manifesto of 1920, that the best way to secure our participation in the association of nations was to elect Mr. Harding, were disappointed at the administration's continued hostility to the League. The Republican majority in the House was reduced from 177 to 14 in the November election, and the administration was left with the slim margin of eight votes in the Senate. Even these meager majorities were illusory, for a number of nominal Republicans belonged to the so-called "farm bloc," which was not in sympathy with President Harding's policy.

763. Coolidge succeeds to the Presidency. The trying task of facing this divided Congress, however, did not fall to Mr. Harding. In the midsummer of 1923 the President, with Mrs. Harding and a party of sixty-five, made a visit to Alaska. He was taken ill with ptomaine poisoning just before the return trip, and died at San Francisco on August 2. The news reached Vice President Coolidge at his boyhood home in Vermont soon after midnight, where, by the light of the kerosene "parlor" lamp, the oath of office was administered to him by his father. The new president entered upon his duties without ceremony. He showed himself simple in tastes, laconic in speech, and thoroughly absorbed in his job. He requested all the members of the Harding cabinet to remain in office and announced the policy of continuing the work of his predecessor. But his relations with the 68th Congress were strained. Even the Republican leaders refused to heed his voice. He vetoed the revived Bonus Bill in May, 1924, but both Houses passed it over the veto by wide margins. He urged the Mellon plan for the reduction of surtaxes, but Congress rejected the proposal. He tried in vain to persuade the legislators to approve the project of our entrance into the World Court at the Hague. He asked Con-

THE PRESIDENT AND MRS. COOLIDGE AT THE WHITE HOUSE

gress to modify the new immigration bill[1] so as not to offend the sensibilities of the Japanese, but his request went unheeded.

764. The Presidential Campaign of 1924. It was evident, however, that President Coolidge stood better with his party and the country than with Congress. At the Republican convention, which met at Cleveland, June 10, he was nominated on the first ballot, with 1065 votes to 34 for La Follette and 10 for Hiram Johnson. Governor Lowden of Illinois was nominated for vice president, but he declined, and Brigadier General Charles G. Dawes[2] was named in his place. The Democrats met at Madison Square Garden, New York, on June 24, where the partisans of William G. McAdoo and Governor Alfred E. Smith of New York battled for more than a fortnight in the sweltering heat. At last the wearied convention turned to John W. Davis of West Virginia, who was nominated on the one-hundred-and-third ballot. Davis was a former ambassador to England and an able corporation lawyer. To satisfy the more radical elements of the party Governor Charles W. Bryan of Nebraska, the brother of William J. Bryan, was named as Davis's running mate. On the adjournment of the Cleveland convention Senator La Follette repudiated the Republican nominee, declaring that President Coolidge had "literally turned his back upon the farmer." On July 4 an independent progressive party was launched at Cleveland, and La Follette was indorsed for the presidency. Burton K. Wheeler, the Democratic senator of Montana, was the vice-presidential candidate. The national convention of the Socialist party immediately indorsed the candidacy of La Follette by a vote of 106 to 17. The Democrats attacked the Republican administration at every point—the tariff, foreign policy, the treatment of the veterans, and especially the management of the government's oil-reserve lands.[3] They also believed that La Follette

---

[1] The Johnson-Lodge Immigration Bill of May, 1924, amended the bill of 1921 by reducing the quota percentage to 2 per cent, based on the census of 1890, and barred all aliens ineligible to citizenship. It was the latter clause which offended the Japanese.

[2] General Dawes had been the American agent for the purchase of supplies for the Allies in France during the war, and the first Director of the Budget under President Harding. In the early spring of 1924 he had been chairman of the commission which worked out the Dawes Plan for the payment of the German reparations. The acceptance of the Dawes Plan in Europe was a great asset to the Republicans in the campaign.

[3] In the spring of 1924 the former Secretary of the Interior, Albert B. Fall (who had resigned from the cabinet the year before), was indicted for bribery and conspiracy in leasing the oil field of Teapot Dome in Wyoming to the Sinclair interests. The revelation of the oil scandals caused the resignation of Secretary of the Navy Denby, who was replaced

would carry several Western states which were normally Republican, and that Mr. Coolidge, even if he led the poll, would not secure a majority in the electoral college. But the election of November 2 completely disappointed the hopes of the Democrats and the radicals. Davis carried only 12 states, all south of Mason and Dixon's line, with 136 electoral votes. La Follette won only his own state of Wisconsin (13 votes). Coolidge carried the other 35 states of the Union, with 382 electoral votes. The popular vote was 15,718,789 for Coolidge, 8,378,962 for Davis, and 4,822,319 for La Follette. Thus Calvin Coolidge was chosen "President in his own right" for the term 1925-1929 by a verdict as decisive as that given to Harding in 1920.

The Coolidge and Hoover Administrations

765. The Coolidge Policies. In his inaugural address, which was heard by millions of his fellow countrymen over the radio, President Coolidge declared that the election showed unmistakably that the American people did not approve such radical measures as the government ownership of railroads and electrical utilities or the modification of the authority of the Supreme Court. He commended the tariff and immigration laws, advocated tax reduction and economy, emphasized obedience to the law as "the first rule of citizenship," and favored our coöperation with the nations of the world in the promotion of peace and prosperity, without, however, sacrificing "our position of detachment and independence." In addresses to the New York Chamber of Commerce (November 19, 1925) and the Chicago convention of the American Farm Bureau (December 7), he reiterated his opposition to "needless government regulation of business" in general, and in regard to agriculture declared against the government's "directly or indirectly fixing prices or buying or selling farm products." By the encouragement of agricultural education, the extension of credit facilities, the construction of good roads, and financial aid to marketing associations, the government should help the farmers to help themselves, but should not itself go into the marketing business as the advocates of the McNary-Haugen bill demanded. When a strike broke out in the

by Curtis D. Wilbur of California. About the same time the pressure of adverse criticism forced the resignation of Attorney-General Daugherty, and President Coolidge appointed Dean Harlan F. Stone of the Columbia Law School to fill the vacancy. The Democrats asserted that the administration had completely broken down in demoralization and corruption.

anthracite coal region of Pennsylvania, which lasted over five months during the autumn and winter of 1925–1926 and entailed a loss of $150,000,000 in wages and a reduction of 35,000,000 tons of coal, President Coolidge refused to intervene as President Roosevelt had done in 1902 and President Harding in 1922, though the Senate adopted a resolution asking him to call a conference between the operators and the miners. He was in favor of leasing to private operators the great government war plant established at Muscle Shoals on the Tennessee River for the manufacture of nitrates and fertilizers. He wanted the government to sell the merchant marine which had been taken over from Germany or constructed at home during the World War.[1]

766. The President and Congress. President Coolidge met determined resistance in Congress both in his domestic and in his foreign policies. The Senate refused to ratify a number of his appointments, including the nomination of Charles B. Warren as Attorney-General — the first rejection of a cabinet nomination since the days of President Grant (1868). In both Houses the administration's plans for tax revision and prohibition enforcement, the funding of the European debts, railroad consolidation, the naval program, and intervention in Nicaragua encountered bitter hostility. The mid-term elections of 1926 saw the Republican majority of 16 wiped out in the Senate, with the return of 48 Republicans, 47 Democrats, and 1 Farmer-Laborite, and reduced from 60 to 36 in the House. In the face of disappointments and rebuffs, however, the President pursued the even tenor of his way. He neither scolded Congress nor whined to the people. He abstained equally from the biting sarcasm of Cleveland, the spectacular self-justification of Roosevelt, and the thinly veiled contempt of Wilson. With characteristic silence and undeviating regularity he worked through the scheduled hours of each day, and won

---

[1] In June, 1923, five of these freight and passenger ships of the "President" class had been purchased by the Dollar Line. In May, 1928, the Jones-White Act reluctantly continued the policy of maintaining the merchant marine through federal aid by the appropriation of a $250,000,000 loan fund for the construction of new vessels. The most attractive bid for the United States ships came on January 16, 1929, in response to the invitation of the Shipping Board, when the P. W. Chapman Company of New York offered $6,782,000 for the *Leviathan*, $2,000,000 each for the *George Washington* and the *America*, $1,000,000 each for the *Republic*, the *President Harding*, and the *President Roosevelt*, and $460,000 each for the five vessels of the American Merchant Line — a total of $16,082,000 for eleven ships. The Chapman Company also agreed to build two new vessels "superior in type and speed to the *Leviathan*."

increasing popularity with a people that respects above all else the example of "work done squarely and unwasted days."

767. National Finances. The years 1925–1928 were a period of unprecedented prosperity in the United States. In spite of substantial reductions in federal taxes and continuous payments on the national debt (which stood at $17,604,290,563 on June 30, 1928, as against about $26,000,000,000 at the close of the World War), the Treasury showed a large surplus at the end of each fiscal year. The cut in the income-tax rates in 1924 did not result in a decrease of revenue from that source, and at the end of the next fiscal year there was a surplus of over $370,000,000, inviting further tax reduction. The new bill signed by Coolidge in February, 1926, besides abolishing certain "nuisance" taxes, lowered the normal rates on incomes from 2 per cent to $1\frac{1}{2}$ per cent on the first $4000, from 4 per cent to 3 per cent on the next $4000, and from 6 per cent to 5 per cent on the excess of $8000. It also raised the exemption from $1000 to $1500 for a single person and from $2500 to $3500 for a married couple. Further reduction of taxes became improbable as President Coolidge's term drew to a close, because of extraordinary expenses anticipated for the construction of the Boulder Canyon dam on the Colorado River ($165,000,000), the building of fifteen cruisers and an airplane-carrier for the navy ($274,000,000), and federal engineering works for the prevention of floods in the Mississippi Valley ($325,000,000), the lower states of which suffered an appalling loss of life and property by an inundation in the spring of 1927.

768. The Problem of Farm Relief. The one conspicuous exception to the general prosperity of the country during the Coolidge administration was the condition of the farmers. They had grown poorer while the rest of the country was growing richer. In the five-year period 1922–1927 it was estimated that over 1,000,000 people had left the farms for the cities and that the value of farm capital had decreased from $79,000,000,000 to $59,000,000,000. The net income of the farmer was rated at less than $800 a year, against $1300 for the school teacher, $1650 for the government employee, and $1675 for the preacher—all poorly paid professions. The farmers constituted 22 per cent of the working population of the country and received less than 10 per cent of the income. While the American people paid $22,500,000,000 for 17 food products in 1928, the farmers received but one third ($7,500,000,000) of this sum, the other two thirds going to the middlemen. Furthermore, the steady rise of state and local taxes since the World War imposed an increasing burden upon the farmer, while the prices which he had to pay for farm implements were kept high by the tariff. His mortgage indebtedness grew from $1,762,000,000 in 1914 to over $4,500,000,000 in 1929. We have already seen how the "farm bloc" in Congress attempted from the beginning of the Harding administration to get legislation passed which would give the farmers some favors equivalent to those which the protective tariff gave to the manufacturers, and how President Coolidge vetoed the McNary-Haugen bill in February, 1927. The 70th Congress passed a second McNary-Haugen bill in the spring of 1928, by votes of 53 to 23 in the Senate (April 13) and 204 to 121 in the House (May 3). But as the new bill would still "put the government into the farming business" by requiring it to purchase the farmers' surplus of grain, cotton, live stock, and tobacco, and sell it abroad for what it would bring in the world market, recouping itself by the so-called "equalization fee,"[1] President Coolidge again vetoed the bill (May 23, 1928). These vetoes of the farm relief measures aroused a good deal of resentment in the West and led to prophecies that the great agricultural states of the Mississippi Valley and the Northwest would refuse to support for the Republican nomination for the presidency any candidate but a "friend of the farmer," like ex-Governor Lowden of Illinois or Senator Norris of Nebraska.

[1] The purpose of this was to give the farmer the benefit of the tariff, which he could not enjoy as long as he had to sell his crop at the price which the surplus part of it would bring in the world market. To illustrate: There is now a duty of 42 cents a bushel on wheat imported into this country. Suppose the wheat crop of America to be 750,000,000 bushels, of which the American people consume 650,000,000 bushels. The remaining 100,000,000 bushels have to be sold abroad. If the price of wheat in the world market is $1.00 a bushel, obviously the farmer can get only $1.00 a bushel for his whole crop — for a producer must sell all his crop for the highest price which he can get for any of it. Therefore the farmers would receive $750,000,000 for their 750,000,000 bushels. Now if the farmers could sell their whole crop *within* the country, they would have the advantage of the 42 cents tariff, and could charge at least $1.40 a bushel. This would give them $1,050,000,000 for the crop. But the government, having bought the farmers' 100,000,000 surplus bushels at $1.40 a bushel and being obliged to sell them abroad at $1.00, would lose $40,000,000. The "equalization fee" proposed to assess this loss on the producers of the wheat, which would mean a tax of $5\frac{1}{3}$ cents a bushel on the crop of 750,000,000 bushels. This would reduce the net sale price to the farmers from $1.40 to $1.34\frac{2}{3}$ a bushel, or $1,010,000,000 for the total crop. Comparing this price with the $750,000,000 which they would receive without the tariff protection, we see that the farmers would be better off by $260,000,000.

769. Relations with Mexico and Nicaragua. Friction with Mexico over her legislation to put into effect the articles of the Constitution of 1917 regulating alien exploitation of agricultural and mineral lands was constant during the first two years of the Coolidge administration. However, when the President sent his old Amherst classmate, Dwight W. Morrow of the firm of J. P. Morgan, as ambassador to Mexico in September, 1927, the difficulties with President Calles were cleared up in a few months by the extraordinary tact and good will of the new ambassador. The renewed friendship between the two countries was greatly strengthened when Colonel Charles Lindbergh, after a non-stop flight of 2200 miles from Washington, landed at Mexico City (December 14, 1927) as an "American ambassador of good will."[1] However vexing our controversy with Mexico was to the Americans who had mining, oil, or ranching interests there, the American public as a whole was much more concerned over the administration's policy in Nicaragua. Hardly had our marines been withdrawn from Nicaragua in 1925 when a new revolution broke out and we again sent troops (eventually more than 5000) to establish neutral zones for the protection of American lives and property. In the spring of 1927 President Coolidge dispatched Colonel H. L. Stimson to Nicaragua with an ultimatum to both parties to lay down

THE BIG SNOWSTORM

[1] Colonel Lindbergh continued his tour of good will, flying over each of the republics of Central America, Colombia, Venezuela, and the West Indies, returning in a non-stop flight from Havana to St. Louis on February 14, 1928. He flew 10,000 miles over mountain, sea, and jungle, through fog, rain, and sunshine, without an accident, and was the object of the wildest demonstrations of enthusiasm in all the sixteen countries that he visited.

their arms, on pain of our starting military operations against them, but the Liberal rebel leader Sandino continued a guerrilla warfare against the United States marines for several months, during which more than twenty of our men were killed and fifty wounded. Protests against the administration's policy in Nicaragua were constant. Petitions came from the American Federation of Labor, peace societies, and various committees of clergymen, educators, and publicists. Senators Borah, Heflin, Reed, and Wheeler flayed the administration, and a resolution was proposed in both Houses to prevent the President from using the army or navy of the United States without permission of Congress, except to protect American lives actually in danger. Senator Wheeler declared in a speech at Cleveland (February 11, 1928) that war was "being waged in Nicaragua by Calvin Coolidge privately in defiance of the Constitution," and that Nicaragua had been "reduced from a sovereign state to a Wall Street protectorate." When Sandino was finally overcome, both factions agreed to abide by a fair election, which was held in November, 1928, under the supervision of Brigadier-General Frank R. McCoy with a large force of American inspectors and a constabulary of two thousand marines. But it was not till the close of 1932 that the last detachment of our bluejackets was withdrawn from the Nicaraguan capital.

770. The Sixth Pan-American Congress. While American marines were hunting out nests of Sandino rebels in Nicaragua, the sixth in the series of Pan-American congresses inaugurated by Secretary Blaine in 1889 met at Havana, Cuba (January 16, 1928). About one hundred and fifty prominent men from the twenty Latin-American countries attended as delegates, and the six-week session produced a mass of resolutions and agreements concerning the nature and functions of the Pan-American Union, international law, aviation, trade, immigration, education, copyrights, and so forth. Charles E. Hughes headed the American delegation. President Coolidge went to Havana to open the Congress with a message of good will to our sister republics. "All the nations here represented," said he, "stand on an exact footing of equality." Mr. Hughes renewed his oft-repeated assurances of the disinterested friendship of the United States: "We have no policy of aggression. Nothing could be happier for the United States than that all the countries in the region of the Caribbean should be strong and self-sufficient . . . settling their problems with peace at home and the fulfillment of their obligations abroad." With great skill Mr. Hughes kept the Congress clear of political questions, such as intervention and the scope of the Monroe Doctrine. One of the resolutions provided for the negotiation of arbitration treaties between the Latin-American states, and provision was made for a supplementary Pan-American Conference to meet at Washington in December, 1928, to draw up such treaties. The Washington conference completed (January 5, 1929) a set of arbitration treaties which Secretary Kellogg called "the most advanced ever adopted by the nations of the world," but which, unfortunately, have not prevented the Latin-American republics from resorting to several wars since.

771. The Briand-Kellogg Peace Pact. On April 6, 1927, the tenth anniversary of the entrance of the United States into the World War, M. Aristide Briand, the French Minister of Foreign Affairs, and a noble champion of the cause of peace among the nations, approached our government with the proposal that the United States and France should sign a pact outlawing war "as an instrument of national policy," and agreeing to find a pacific means for settling "all disputes or conflicts of whatever nature" that might arise between them. Secretary Kellogg was in favor of extending the pact to the other nations of the world, and on April 13, 1928, he sent identical copies of a multilateral treaty for the outlawry of war to the governments of Great Britain, Italy, Germany, and Japan—all of which accepted the idea. On August 27, 1928, the representatives of fifteen nations met at Paris and signed the Briand-Kellogg Peace Pact, to which some sixty governments (practically the whole civilized world) have given their assent. On January 15, 1929, the pact was ratified by the Senate of the United States by the overwhelming vote of 85 to 1, Senator Blaine of Wisconsin being the only one to vote "nay." Many senators, however, expressed their misgivings of the efficacy of the pact, because it was interpreted as excepting from outlawry any *war of defense*, each nation being "free at all times to defend itself" and being "the sole judge of what constitutes self-defense and the necessity and extent of the same." Since every nation that went to war in 1914 did so in what it regarded its own necessary defense, critics of the Briand-Kellogg Peace Pact failed to see how it would prevent future wars. Nor has it, in fact, prevented signatory governments in the Far East and South America from resorting to "war as an instrument of national policy."

772. Our Naval Policy. On February 10, 1927, President Coolidge sent an identic note to Great Britain, France, Italy, and Japan, asking them to empower their delegates to the Geneva Preparatory Conference on Disarmament, which was to assemble in May, to negotiate a treaty with the United States limiting the construction of cruisers, submarines, and destroyers—types of war vessels which had not been covered by the provisions of the Washington conference of 1921–1922. But France and Italy declined his invitation outright, and while Japan and England accepted, the latter power made a demand for about double the cruiser tonnage proposed by the United States, which meant, in President Coolidge's words, "not a limitation but an extension of war fleets." Disappointed by the failure of the conference, the President committed himself more openly to the cause of naval preparedness on our own part. In an address at Washington on Armistice Day, November 11, 1928, he said that while America had made and would continue to make "every reasonable effort" in the direction of international peace, she was also "committed to a policy of adequate national defense." Secretary of the Navy Wilbur had proposed a five-year building program calling for seventy-one new vessels, to cost about $800,000,000. This extravagant program was cut down to fifteen cruisers and one aircraft-carrier, estimated to cost $274,000,000, and a bill stipulating the construction of these sixteen vessels in three years was passed by the House on March 17, 1928, by a vote of 287 to 58. After prolonged discussion the Senate accepted the bill, with the provision that five new cruisers should be begun in each of the years 1929, 1930, and 1931. President Coolidge signed the cruiser bill on February 5, 1929—just three weeks after the Senate had ratified the pact which outlawed "war as an instrument of national policy"!

773. The Conquest of the Air. In the field of industry and invention America has made enormous progress in the last few years. The automobile industry, for example, which was not considered of enough importance to find mention in the census of 1910, has now become our leading industry, with billions of dollars invested and an annual output of between 4,000,000 and 5,000,000 motor vehicles. The greatest triumph of invention has been the conquest of the air, both as a medium of instantaneous communication of sound and even of photography by radio, and as a path of travel for dirigibles and airplanes. Though the first successful flight in a heavier-than-air machine was made by Wilbur and Orville Wright at Kittyhawk, North Carolina, in December, 1903, little progress in aviation was made until the World War. Now, not only has the air service become an indispensable and expanding branch of national defense in both the army and the navy, but the Post Office Department lets contracts for the transportation of many tons of mail a day by planes flying more than a hundred thousand miles over seventy-five routes in the United States. The postal routes are lighted for night flying by beacons of 2,000,000 candle power at ten-mile intervals, while huge beacons of 500,000,000 candle power light the regular landing fields on the transcontinental route. Air-mail routes have recently been extended to Montreal, Mexico City, the Canal Zone, the West Indies, and other points in Latin-American countries. In 1932 the Department of Commerce reported 97 air routes for the transportation of merchandise, and 105 for passenger travel. Of the 1,163,171 passengers carried from July 1, 1931, to July 1, 1932, only 152 lost their lives. Since Lindbergh thrilled the world by his daring non-stop flight from New York to Paris in the *Spirit of St. Louis* in May, 1927, several successful attempts (but more that were fatal) have been made to cross the ocean by air. The first successful flight from Europe to America was made by Captain Koehl and Major Fitzmaurice in the Junkers monoplane *Bremen*, April 12-13, 1928. The *Bremen* landed on a little island off the coast of Labrador, with injuries which made further flight impossible. But an American plane hastened from Detroit to the rescue, and the aviators were brought in triumph to New York and Washington. A most romantic chapter in the conquest of the air has been written in the recent polar expeditions. When Lieutenant Peary, in 1909, left his ice-bound ship in the Arctic to make his dash with dogs and sleds for the north pole, he and his companions were lost to civilization for several months. But when the Amundsen-Ellsworth-Nobile party, in the dirigible *Norge*, cruising 2000 miles from Spitzbergen to Point Barrow, Alaska, passed over the north pole on May 12, 1926, they sent a radio message (the first message from "the top of the world") which was published a few hours later by the *New York Times*. Commander Richard E. Byrd and Floyd Bennett had made the flight from Spitzbergen to the north pole and back in sixteen hours in a plane only two days before the *Norge* started. In May, 1928, General Umberto Nobile, after cruising across the pole in the dirigible *Italia*, met with disaster.[1] The latest of the polar expeditions, and by far the most elaborate, left New Zealand, under the command of the intrepid Byrd, for the exploration of the Antarctic, and reached its base at the Ross Ice Barrier on Christmas Day, 1928. The Byrd expedition of some thirty men, provided with four airplanes, one hundred dogs, ice tractors, radio equipment, and moving-picture apparatus, at an expense of over $860,000, spent two years making a detailed study of the great Antarctic continent which surrounds the south pole. The whole country was thrilled by the moving pictures of the expedition which were shown on Byrd's return.

774. The Campaign of 1928. Whether or not President Coolidge would stand for reëlection in 1928 was a question discussed by the politicians and the public, but the President himself gave no hint of his intentions until August 2, 1927, when he issued the ten-word statement from his vacation camp near Rapid City, South Dakota: "I do not choose to run for president in 1928." Mr. Hughes, perhaps next to the President the most influential man in the party, announced definitely that he would not be a candidate. The withdrawal of these two men left Herbert C. Hoover, the efficient Secretary of Commerce, as the most likely choice of the party. It was understood that he was favored by the administration, although the President gave him no public support until the very eve of the election. Alfred E. Smith, who had steadily gained in popularity since the election of 1924, and who was serving his fourth term as governor of New York, with an excellent record in political and social administration, was evidently the strongest contestant in the Democratic party. His nomination was made almost certain by the withdrawal in September, 1927, of William G. McAdoo, his opponent in the Madison Square convention of 1924. A veritable epidemic of presidential fever seemed to invade the Senate. Curtis of Kansas, Norris of Nebraska, Goff of West Virginia, Willis of Ohio (who died suddenly on March 30, 1928), and Watson

[1] Nobile and his crew were rescued from the Arctic ice in an exhausted condition. The great polar explorer Amundsen, who had been the first to reach the south pole (1911), was one of those who responded to the S O S of the *Italia*. He left Tromsö, Norway, in a seaplane on June 18, 1928, to save his companion of the *Norge* cruise of 1926, but was never heard from again.

AIRWAYS OF THE UNITED STATES

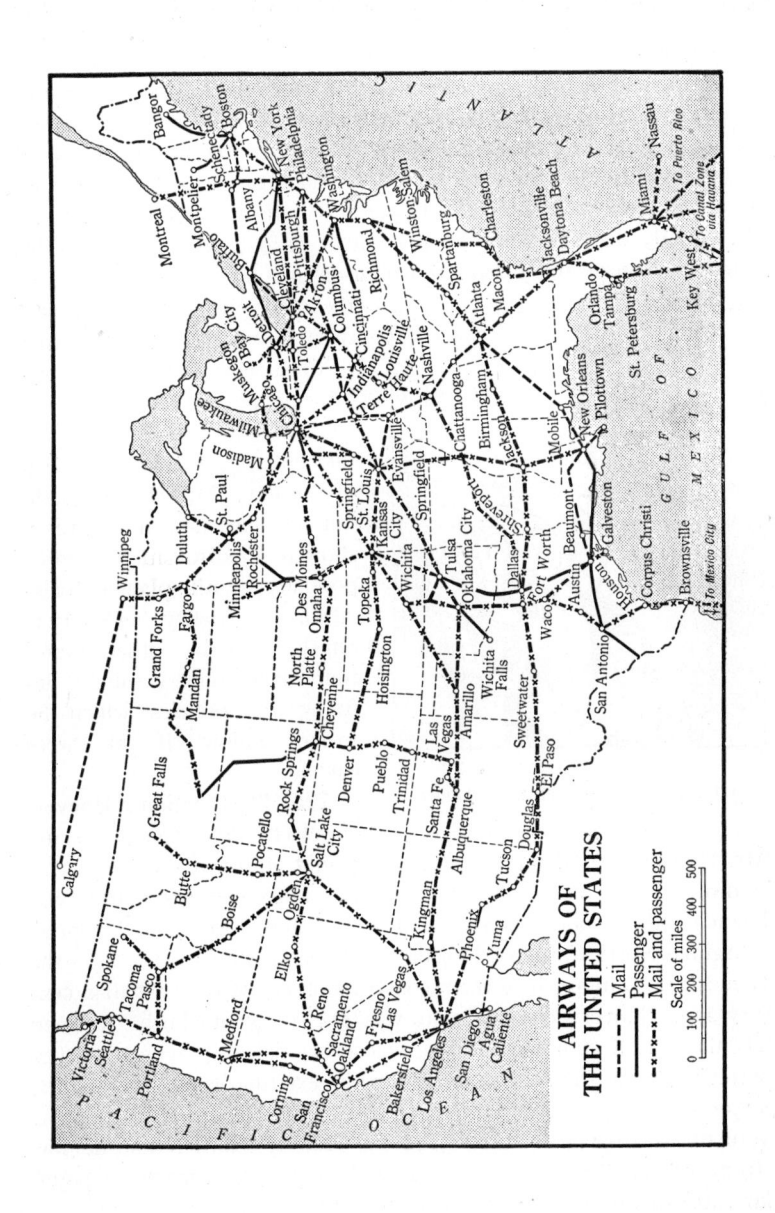

Mail — — —
Passenger ———
Mail and passenger —×—×—

Scale of miles
0 100 200 300 400 500

of Indiana on the Republican side, and Walsh of Montana, Reed of Missouri, and George of Georgia on the Democratic side announced their candidacies. The Republican convention met at Kansas City, Missouri, on June 12, and nominated Hoover on the first ballot, with 837 votes out of a total of 1088. The Democrats, meeting at Houston, Texas, on June 26, nominated Governor Smith on the first ballot, by the equally decisive vote of $849\frac{2}{3}$ out of 1100. Senators Charles E. Curtis of Kansas and Joseph T. Robinson of Arkansas were named as the respective vice-presidential candidates. Both platforms pledged their parties to the enforcement of the prohibition legislation and the relief of the farmers, the two burning issues of the day. Mr. Hoover made but few speeches, and in them showed no disposition to propose any definite plans of legislation or policy. Governor Smith, on the other hand, toured the country widely, defining the policies which he would follow if he were elected.

"BUT THE RAVEN — STILL IS SITTING"
Sioux City Tribune

775. The Election of Hoover.

On election day (November 6) Mr. Hoover carried forty of the forty-eight states of the Union, including all the West and North (except Massachusetts and Rhode Island), all the border states, and four states of the "solid South" (Virginia, North Carolina, Florida, and Texas) which had been in the Democratic column since the reconstruction era of over a half a century ago. Hoover's electoral vote was 444 to 87 for Smith. Norman Thomas, the Socialist candidate, whose campaign speeches deserved better attention than they received in the exciting battle between the major parties, polled only 267,835 votes. Governor Smith's popular vote of 15,016,443 to 21,392,190 for Hoover showed that he was stronger than either Davis in 1924 (with only 33 per cent of the popular vote) or Cox in 1920 (with 39 per cent). Still, Smith lost his own

HERBERT C. HOOVER

state of New York, where for the first time he ran behind his ticket, the Democratic candidates for governor and United States senator, Franklin D. Roosevelt and Dr. Royal S. Copeland, respectively, defeating their Republican opponents, Albert Ottinger and Alanson B. Houghton. The congressional elections insured substantial Republican majorities in both Houses of the 71st Congress—269 Republicans to 165 Democrats in the House and 55 Republicans to 39 Democrats in the Senate. Mr. Hoover's extraordinary victory, especially his invasion of the "solid South," was attributed by the Democrats to the prejudice against Governor Smith as a Roman Catholic, a "wet," and a Tammany man. The Republicans, on the other hand, maintained that it was a nation-wide recognition of Mr. Hoover's great ability as an executive with wide experience, and attributed the victories below Mason and Dixon's line to the fact that the South, with its increasing industrial development, was turning toward the Republican policies of high protection and the encouragement of big business. Soon after the election Mr. Hoover sailed from San Pedro, California, on the United States battleship *Maryland* for a visit to the Central and South American republics, his object being, as he said at a state banquet in Peru, to "better prepare himself for the task of reënforcing the peace and friendship" between North America and Latin America "by a widened knowledge of the men and problems of our sister republics." The president-elect's tour was both a graceful gesture of international courtesy and a practical recognition of the importance of first-hand acquaintance with a region in which our investments had grown from less than $1,500,000,000 in 1913 to over $5,000,000,000 in 1928, and with which our trade had passed the $1,000,000,000 mark. Mr. Hoover visited Honduras, Nicaragua, Costa Rica, Ecuador, Peru, Chile, Argentina, Uruguay, and Brazil, sailing from Rio de Janeiro for home on the battleship *Utah* on December 21, 1928.

776. The New Administration Installed. While the short, "lame-duck" session of the 70th Congress was debating the Briand-Kellogg Peace Pact and the cruiser bill, Mr. Hoover was studying the problems which would confront him after the fourth of March. On March 2 the names of the cabinet were given to the public. The only members of the Coolidge cabinet to be retained were Secretary of the Treasury Mellon and Secretary of Labor Davis. Secretary of State Kellogg consented to remain for a few weeks, until Colonel Henry L.

Stimson of New York should arrive from his post at Manila as Governor-General of the Philippine Islands to take the first place in the new cabinet. The other cabinet portfolios were assigned as follows: Secretary of War, James W. Good of Iowa; Attorney-General, William D. Mitchell of Minnesota; Postmaster-General, Walter F. Brown of Ohio; Secretary of the Navy, Charles Francis Adams of Massachusetts; Secretary of the Interior, Ray Lyman Wilbur of California, a brother of the retiring Secretary of the Navy; Secretary of Agriculture, Arthur M. Hyde of Missouri; Secretary of Commerce, Robert P. Lamont of Illinois.[1] None of the four states of the "solid South" that voted for Mr. Hoover were represented in the original cabinet. In the late morning of March 4 President Coolidge and President-elect Hoover rode together through the crowded streets of Washington from the White House to the Capitol, where Chief Justice Taft administered the oath of office to Mr. Hoover before a vast crowd of citizens standing in the cold, drizzling rain, and the new President read his inaugural address, which was carried by radio to the ends of the land. He emphasized first of all and as "the most sore necessity of our times" the vigorous enforcement of the laws, and recommended the "reform, reorganization, and strengthening of our whole judicial system." He pledged the coöperation of the government in the work of education, public health, agricultural relief, and general business prosperity. He expressed the hope that the United States would enter the World Court, and declared that he coveted for his administration "a record of having further contributed to advance the cause of peace." He closed with a jubilant confession of optimism: "Ours is a land rich in resources, stimulating in its glorious beauty, filled with millions of happy homes, blessed with comfort and opportunity. In no nation are the institutions of progress more advanced. In no nation are the fruits of accomplishment more secure. In no nation is the government more worthy of respect. No country is more loved by its people. I have an abiding faith in

[1] Secretary Good died in November and was succeeded by Patrick J. Hurley of Oklahoma. In 1930 William N. Doak of Virginia replaced Secretary of Labor Davis, who resigned to run for the Senate. Early in 1932 Secretary Mellon left the Treasury department (in which he had served longer than any other Secretary except Albert Gallatin) to become Ambassador to Great Britain, and his place was taken by the Under-Secretary, Ogden L. Mills. Lamont was succeeded in the Department of Commerce by Roy D. Chapin of Michigan in the same year. The other six secretaries retained their portfolios during the whole of the Hoover administration.

their capacity, integrity, and high purpose. I have no fears for the future of our country; it is bright with hope."

777. The Brief Day of Promise. President Hoover had had a wonderful career. Born in comparative poverty on an Iowa farm in 1874, an orphan at the age of ten, he had been cared for by an uncle in Oregon. After working his way through Leland Stanford Junior University at Palo Alto, California, and securing a degree in engineering, he had amassed a fortune in the promotion of mining companies in Australia, China, Russia, South Africa, Central America, and other parts of the world. His work as head of the commission for the relief of the starving population of Belgium (1914–1917), and as food administrator in America after we entered the war, had brought him international renown and the gratitude of millions of hungry people in central and eastern Europe. Appointed Secretary of Commerce by President Harding in 1921, he had raised that hitherto insignificant department to one of major importance by his energetic and scientific methods. His election to the presidency was hailed as the guaranty of continuing and increasing prosperity. Poverty was to disappear under the scientific management of the "great engineer." Prices of stocks were soaring in the "Hoover bull market." Our foreign and our domestic trade were booming. Our debt was being steadily reduced, and surpluses in the Treasury had warranted several reductions in the federal taxes since the close of the war. Money was abundant for the purchase of securities at home and loans abroad. The 71st Congress, which Hoover called in extra session on April 15, had a Republican majority of 103 in the House and 14 in the Senate. To help the farmers it created a Federal Farm Board provided with a fund of $500,000,000 from which to make loans at not over 4 per cent to farmers' "coöperative associations" in the marketing of their grain, cotton, fruit, dairy products, and live stock; and to aid the manufacturers the House, on May 28, passed the Hawley Tariff Bill, raising the duties on a great number of articles. On the same day President Hoover met at the White House a commission of eleven distinguished citizens, including ex-Attorney-General Wickersham, Newton D. Baker, and Dean Pound of the Harvard Law School, whom he had appointed to study what he called "the dominant national problem," namely, the observance and enforcement of law in the United States.

778. The Eclipse of Prosperity. But soon the "bright hopes" of which President Hoover had spoken in his inaugural address were clouded over. Billions of dollars which should have gone into the industries of the country had been absorbed by Wall Street in the wild orgy of speculation. A terrific crash in the stock market in October ruined thousands of investors in all ranks of life who had put their savings and borrowings into securities which they expected to sell on the morrow at higher prices. At first the men in high political office, from the President down, gave cheering assurances that the market crash was only a temporary reaction and that business was "fundamentally sound"; but as the months passed it became evident that we were facing a severe depression. Factories and mills were closing, the numbers of the unemployed were mounting rapidly, banks were failing, prices of wheat, cotton, oil, copper, and other commodities were steadily falling, exports were declining, and mortgages were being foreclosed all over the land. Moreover, the measures of Congress proved ineffective. Though the Farm Board, contrary to the President's wishes, purchased large amounts of wheat and cotton, it failed to keep the prices of these commodities from sagging. And when the Senate, dominated by the high protectionist Grundy of Pennsylvania, had finished with the tariff in the summer of 1930, it presented a bill with such high rates as to elicit protest from consumers and economists all over the country. President Hoover, in spite of the remonstrances, signed the Hawley-Smoot bill. Able as he was in managing subordinates, he was showing a lack of the tact, persuasiveness, and conciliation necessary to deal with Congress, and especially with a jealous, powerful Senate which contained a "bloc" of Republicans opposed to his farm and tariff policies.

779. The Plight of the Government. The distress of the country, increased by a prolonged drought which destroyed the crops and live stock in a dozen of the Southern and Western states, resulted in the election of a Democratic Congress (219 to 214) in November, 1930. This made impossible the harmony between the White House and the Capitol which was necessary for measures of relief, and made the last two years of Hoover's term as trying as a president in peace times has ever had to face. The revenues of the government were drying up. Customs duties, in spite of the high tariff, were reduced 47 per cent when our imports dropped from $4,399,000,000 in 1929 to $2,089,000,000 in 1931. The yield from internal revenue (chiefly income taxes) fell from $2,939,000,000 to $1,558,000,000 between 1929 and 1932. At the same time the expenses of the government were increasing, and various groups, the farmers, the bankers, the veterans, were asking for aid from the public treasury. Some clamored for the issue of paper money to relieve the debtor by decreasing the value of the dollar he owed. Others would have the government undertake a great program of public works, involving billions of dollars, in order to provide labor for the unemployed. The ex-service men demanded the immediate payment of their certificates in cash (paper money if necessary) as an aid to the buying power of the country. This item alone would have cost the Treasury $2,000,000,000, which was almost equal to the *total* income of the government in 1932. The national deficit for that year reached the enormous total of $2,885,000,000. It was evident that Congress would have to cut down expenditures and find new sources of revenue if the budget were to be balanced and the government saved from bankruptcy. But there was no disposition on the part of Congress to exercise economy, nor was there agreement on the subject of new taxes. The more radical members were in favor of "soaking the rich" by greatly increased income, corporation, and inheritance taxes, and resented the creation of the Reconstruction Finance Corporation (January, 1932), which furnished $2,000,000,000 for loans to banks, railroads, insurance companies, building-and-loan associations, and other capitalistic organizations. The administration favored a general sales tax which it estimated would yield $600,000,000. It was rejected by the House. Finally, on June 6, 1932, a revenue bill was signed by the President which increased the income rates and laid taxes on a variety of objects (automobiles, telephone and telegraph messages, stock transfers, bank checks, etc.). The new taxes were estimated to produce $1,118,500,000, but the yield actually fell far below that figure, and the national budget, instead of being balanced, threatened to show a deficit of over $1,700,000,000 for the year 1932–1933.

780. The London Naval Treaty. Meanwhile President Hoover was eager to continue the policy of his predecessors in the reduction of naval armaments. The Washington conference of 1921–1922 had not set any limit on the building of cruisers, destroyers, and submarines, and after the failure of Coolidge's effort at Geneva in 1927, competi-

ESTIMATED RECEIPTS, 1932–1933
$2,374,960,502

Income tax — $867,000,000
Customs receipts — $430,000,000
Internal revenue — $550,000,000
Payments on war debts — $269,976,571
Miscellaneous — $257,983,931

ESTIMATED DEFICIT, 1932–1933
$1,737,949,448

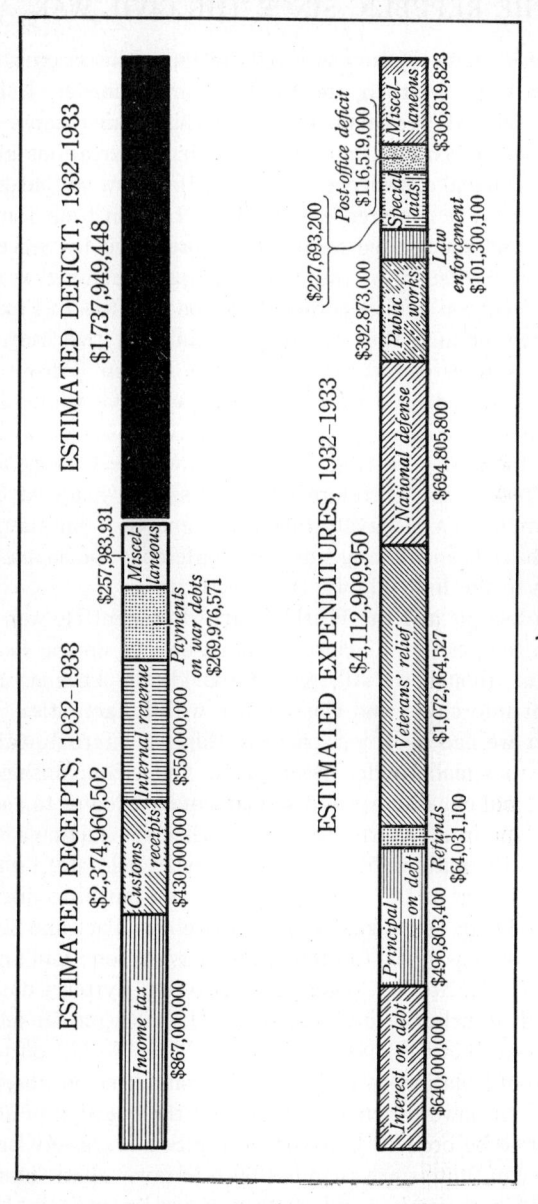

ESTIMATED EXPENDITURES, 1932–1933
$4,112,909,950

Interest on debt — $640,000,000
Principal on debt — $496,803,400
Refunds — $64,031,100
Veterans' relief — $1,072,064,527
National defense — $694,805,800
Public works — $392,873,000
Special aids — $227,693,200
Post-office deficit — $116,519,000
Law enforcement — $101,300,100
Miscellaneous — $306,819,823

UNCLE SAM'S BALANCE SHEET

tive building in these types of war vessels (especially in cruisers) was rampant. In October, 1929, the British Prime Minister, J. Ramsay MacDonald, visited President Hoover at his fishing camp on the Rapidan River in Virginia, and out of their conversations grew the plan for a new naval conference of the same five powers that had met in Washington. The conference was held in London from January to April, 1930, and the United States was represented by Secretary of State Stimson, Secretary of the Navy Adams, Ambassadors Dawes, Morrow, and Gibson, and Senators Robinson and Reed. France and Italy withdrew because they failed to obtain what they regarded as necessary guaranties of security. But Great Britain, Japan, and the United States agreed on a ratio for the types of vessels under consideration. We established the principle of naval "parity" with Great Britain, but the parity, instead of scaling down the tonnage allowed, actually increased it. Therefore no progress was made at London toward the reduction of naval armaments, and the "big navy" men in America have been working since the conference for increasing our naval forces to the limit allowed by the treaty.

781. The League and the World Court. President Hoover did not depart from the position of Harding and Coolidge on the League of Nations. But, though we still remain outside the League, we have been brought into closer and closer touch with its activities. By the close of 1931 we had become a party to thirteen international agreements or treaties made under its auspices. Our championship of the Kellogg Pact and our interest in disarmament have led us to coöperate with the League in its efforts for peace. When the Japanese invaded Manchuria in the autumn of 1931, an American delegate, Prentiss B. Gilbert, actually sat at the table of the League Council to discuss the obligation of Japan as a signatory of the Kellogg Pact and the nine-power Pacific treaty of the Conference of Washington; and an American general, F. R. McCoy, was a member of the Lytton Commission which visited Manchuria to investigate and report on the situation. The only reason that we have not yet joined the World Court is that a little group of isolationists in the Senate Committee on Foreign Relations has been powerful enough to prevent the question of adhering to the Court to be brought to a vote in the Senate. Every president and Secretary of State since 1920 has been in favor of our joining the Court. The Senate itself voted (with only 17 "nays") in January,

1926, to join if certain changes were made in the constitution of the Court. Those changes were made to the satisfaction of the administration, and in December, 1930, President Hoover submitted our treaty of adherence to the Senate for ratification. As far more than two thirds of that body are ready to ratify and the Committee finally (May 12, 1932) reported the treaty to the Senate for a vote, it is likely that we shall become a member of the Court before the new Democratic administration is many months old.

782. The War Debts. Toward the close of President Hoover's administration there came a crisis in a situation which had been embarrassing to our government ever since the close of the war. We had loaned about 20 European countries over $10,000,000,000 before and after the armistice of 1918, the money being raised by Liberty Bonds sold to the people of the United States. Our European debtors agreed at the time they borrowed the money to pay it back with interest at the rate borne by the bonds. From 1923 to 1930 practically all these countries made "funding agreements" with the United States, specifying the semiannual installments of principle and interest which they were to pay. So long as they received payments of reparations imposed on Germany as a war penalty, and so long as Germany could borrow the money (chiefly in the United States) to pay the reparations, the scheme worked fairly well. But when the depression put an end to our lending abroad, and Germany threatened to collapse financially, President Hoover, in June, 1931, declared a "moratorium" stopping the payment of *all* intergovernmental debts for a year. In the autumn Premier Laval of France and Foreign Minister Grandi of Italy came here to talk over the whole situation with President Hoover, who gave the former to understand that if the European creditors would take the initiative in relieving Germany, we would reconsider the matter of their debts to us. In doing so the President departed from the position which our government had held ever since the war, that the German reparations and the war debts were not to be coupled together. In July, 1932, the European powers at Lausanne cut Germany's reparation bill down to $714,000,000, and expected in return that we would reduce or postpone their December 15th payments to us. When we declined to do this, Great Britain paid under protest, but France, Belgium, and two or three other countries failed to send their installments. It will remain for President Roosevelt and the new Congress to decide whether to cancel, revise, or attempt to collect the debts. Legally the countries are bound to pay; but most American economists believe that it would be more profitable for us to have a friendly and prosperous Europe to trade with than to attempt to collect a few hundred millions annually from our debtors.

783. The Election of 1932. The Republican convention, meeting at Chicago on June 14, renominated Hoover and Curtis on the first ballot, as was expected. The Democrats met in the same building on June 27. Governor Franklin D. Roosevelt of New York, who had been Assistant Secretary of the Navy under Wilson and vice-presidential candidate with J. M. Cox in 1920, had a majority of the delegates pledged to him, but not the 770 (or two-thirds) necessary for nomination. He was opposed by ex-Governor Alfred E. Smith of New York. The Speaker of the House, J. N. Garner of Texas, and five other "favorite sons" of various states were put in nomination. Roosevelt led on the first ballot with $666\frac{1}{4}$ votes to $201\frac{3}{4}$ for Smith and $90\frac{1}{4}$ for Garner. On the fourth ballot William G. McAdoo, who had been supporting Garner, threw the California delegation to Roosevelt, Garner released his delegates, and state after state declared for the New York Governor, who was nominated with 945 of the 1154 votes. He immediately flew out to Chicago to deliver his acceptance speech to the convention in session. Speaker Garner was named for vice president. Roosevelt's strength grew as the campaign progressed. He toured the country widely and by his vigorous speeches had little difficulty in convincing the people, who were suffering from the widespread depression, that all their ills were due to the Republican administration. He promised "a new deal." Aroused by the evident drift towards Roosevelt, President Hoover in the last month of the campaign made heroic efforts to stem the tide, leaving Washington four times to speak to large audiences in the Western cities. But he failed to convince the electorate that the advent of a Democratic administration would be a calamity for the country.[1] On election day, November 8,

---

[1] The Hoover administration, besides having to bear the burden of the depression with its 10,000,000 of unemployed, was troubled by movements of discontent and protest during the summer of 1932. Late in May groups of men, eventually reaching an "army" of over 10,000, began to march on Washington to demand the full cash payment of the soldiers' bonus. They camped on the grounds of the Capitol and in shacks and tents along Pennsylvania Avenue and the river banks, and when sanitary conditions necessitated their removal, there were clashes with the police resulting in three deaths. The government had finally to use troops and tanks to dislodge the "Bonus Expeditionary Force." In August a thousand

Governor Roosevelt carried 42 of the 48 states (all but Maine, New Hampshire, Vermont, Connecticut, Pennsylvania, and Delaware), with 472 electoral votes to 59 for Hoover, and had a popular majority of over 6,000,000. The Socialist candidate, Norman Thomas of New York, who was expected to poll an exceptionally large vote on account of the depression, fell far below Debs's figure of 920,000 in 1920. The Democrats elected 313 Representatives to the 73d Congress, as against 117 Republicans and 5 Farmer-Laborites, and changed a Republican majority of 1 in the Senate to a Democratic majority of 22. Many old members of the Senate, like Moses of New Hampshire, Smoot of Utah, Watson of Indiana, and Shortridge of California were retired to private life. President-elect Roosevelt immediately began preparing for his arduous task by consultations with President Hoover, members of Congress, and various experts in political and economic science.

784. The New Administration. On March 4, 1933, Franklin D. Roosevelt took the oath of office at the hands of Chief Justice Charles Evans Hughes, and delivered a brief and inspiring inaugural address in which he bade the American people lay aside fear and coöperate with him in the restoration of prosperity. His cabinet choices were promptly ratified by the Senate. Senator Cordell Hull of Tennessee was given the portfolio of State. William B. Woodin of Pennsylvania was assigned the difficult task of administering the Treasury. Senator Thomas J. Walsh of Montana, noted for his investigation of the oil scandals in the Harding administration, had been chosen for Attorney-General, but he died suddenly a few days before the inauguration and was replaced by Homer S. Cummings of Connecticut, like Hull a former chairman of the National Democratic Committee. The other cabinet members were Governor George H. Dern of Utah (War), Senator Claude A. Swanson of Virginia (Navy), Harold L. Ickes of Illinois (Interior), James A. Farley of New York (Postmaster-General), Henry A. Wallace of Iowa (Agriculture), Daniel C. Roper of Washington, D.C. (Commerce), and Miss Frances Perkins of the New York State Industrial Commission (Labor), the first woman in

---

farmers in Iowa picketed the roads to prevent the delivery of farm products to the cities at prices which did not pay for raising the grain and live stock. On the other hand, the threatened rift in the Democratic ranks was healed when ex-Governor Smith came to the hearty support of Roosevelt, and Mayor James J. Walker, by resigning in the face of charges, removed what might have been a bitter quarrel between the Governor and Tammany Hall.

our history to sit in a cabinet. The 73d Congress was called in extra session on March 9 to cope with the acute financial problem which had already forced the new President to declare a nation-wide bank holiday for four days (March 6 to 9 inclusive). By large majorities Congress, bowing to the emergency and recognizing the unanimous confidence of the nation in the courageous, indefatigable new President, passed bill after bill conferring upon Mr. Roosevelt powers scarcely inferior to those of a dictator: bills for the reorganization of our banking system, for the saving of over a half a billion dollars by reducing veterans' payments and official salaries, for the legalizing of 3.2 per cent beer to increase the federal revenue. Other measures for farm relief, federal aid to the states, and the stimulation of employment by a program of reforestation and public works were recommended to Congress. Republicans and Democrats alike rallied to the support of President Roosevelt in his fight for the recovery of the American people from a long and dismal period of depression.

785. The Strength of America. The fourth decade of the twentieth century finds the United States facing problems of immense difficulty in the adjustment of its political, industrial, and social life, but strong and confident to meet them. Enormous as the cost of the war had been, increasing our debt twenty-fold, the expense had been met by willing payment of taxes and by enthusiastic oversubscription to the nation's bonds. While the debt of some of the belligerent countries mounted to nearly 50 per cent of their national wealth, and in the case of Italy to nearly 80 per cent, the interest on our own debt amounted in 1932 to but $559,277,000, or about $1\frac{1}{2}$ per cent of our national income of $39,000,000,000. Our country was spared both the devastation of its territory and the decimation of its man power in the war. Production of every kind was stimulated. More wheat and live stock were raised, more steel and textiles manufactured, than ever before in our history. Markets were clamoring for our goods in all parts of the world. Our foreign trade, increasing 500 per cent over the prewar figures, reached a total for the year 1919 of $10,079,888,111 (exports, $7,074,011,529; imports, $3,005,876,582) — "a figure never approached in the commerce of any nation in the world." It is true that the United States has felt the full force of the world depression since 1930 in the decline of its trade, the paralyzing of its industries, the unemployment of its workers, and the consequent decline of its

HAIL AND FAREWELL! PRESIDENT HOOVER GREETS PRESIDENT-ELECT ROOSEVELT
AS THEY START FOR THE INAUGURATION

© Harris & Ewing

buying power. But we still have enormous wealth, which, if more equitably distributed, can bring security and comfort to all our people.

786. The New American State. The American state is taking on new functions and new powers year by year. A generation ago the government was thought of primarily as a police power. Its attitude toward business and social problems was chiefly negative. Now it is interested, through administrative boards and by copious legislation, in a thousand and one concerns of production and distribution, of industrial regulation, of social betterment, of international coöperation. Aggressive presidents like Roosevelt and Wilson have brought the government close to the people. The Congresses of other days sat for a few months of the year, and their rather perfunctory acts were scantily noticed by the press and the public. From the entrance of America into the World War to the close of the year 1919 Congress was in session for twenty-eight out of thirty-three months, and its debates were conducted before a forum of 100,000,000 citizens. The nation's business tends every year to become of more concern to the people at large.

787. The Problems of American Democracy. The war came like a great searchlight to reveal both the latent powers and the hidden dangers of our new democracy. Disloyalty and greed, ignorance and violence, appeared, as well as courage, patriotism, sacrifice, and devotion. We have a serious race problem on our hands in the just treatment and constructive education of 12,000,000 American negroes. We have to make our schools adequate for the training of citizens and to wipe out illiteracy in our land. We have to assimilate the aliens who come to our shores. Merely taking out naturalization papers will not make them Americans. Herded in the slums of our cities or driven in gangs of laborers to the mills and mines, these people can escape the evil influence of the preachers of disloyalty, lawlessness, and class hatred only by being taught the basal principles of American democracy—respect for law, the responsibilities of freedom, and the duty of each citizen to make himself as capable as possible of participating in the common task of securing social justice. The day of the heartless exploitation of human lives for the sake of profits must cease. The little children, "the seed-corn of the nation," must not be taken from the school and from the sunlight to toil in the cigar factories, the canning sheds, the cotton mills, and the coal

THE WORLD WAR AND AFTER

breakers. We must have healthy parents and happy homes; for the home is the ultimate life-cell of our society, conditioning its soundness or its decay.

788. American Idealism. America has often been called "the land of the dollar," as if we cared for nothing but sordid material gain. The history of the last few years has proved how false that judgment is. When the clear call came for the defense of an ideal, Americans, rich and poor, high and low, rallied to the banners with the fervor of the crusaders of old. They poured out their money like water; they gave their lives with joy. Their presence on the battlefields of Europe was an inspiration like the breath of a new morning. And when our own prosperity suffered shock, and the specter of starvation stalked before the eyes of anxious millions, our public and private agencies of relief responded to the call of suffering as nobly as the people had responded to the call of sacrifice. There never has been a moment in our history when the welfare of the whole American people has been so sincere a concern of statesmen, business men, laborers, educators, and even pessimistic critics as it is today.

References

Neutrality: F. A. OGG, *National Progress* (American Nation Series), chaps. xiv, xv, xvii, xxi; BERTRAM BENEDICT, *A History of the Great War*, Vol. I, pp. 169–281; J. B. MCMASTER, *The United States in the World War*, Vol. I, chaps. i–xiii; ROBINSON and WEST, *The Foreign Policy of Woodrow Wilson*; A. MAURICE LOW, *Woodrow Wilson, an Interpretation*, chaps. vii–ix; WOODROW WILSON, *Presidential Addresses and State Papers* (1917); C. LLOYD JONES, *The Caribbean Interests of the United States*, chaps. ii, vii–x; American Academy of Political and Social Science, *Annals*, Vol. LX ("America's Interests as affected by the European War"), Vol. LXII ("America's Relation to the World Conflict").

Participation: MCMASTER, Vol. I (chaps. xiii–xvii), Vol. II; BENEDICT, Vol. I, pp. 282–412; FLORENCE F. KELLY, *What America Did*; FREDERICK PALMER, *America in France* and *Our Greatest Battle*; J. S. BASSETT, *Our War with Germany*; R. G. USHER, *The Story of the Great War*; JOSEPH HUSBAND, *A Year in the Navy*; J. C. WISE, *The Turn of the Tide*; H. P. DAVISON, *The American Red Cross in the Great War*; WALTER WEYL, *The End of the War*; DE CHAMBRUN and DE MARENCHES, *The American Army in the European Conflict*; G. J. HECHT, *The War in Cartoons*; ERNEST PEIXOTTO, *The American Front*; *The American Year Book* (1917, 1918); C. J. H. HAYES, *A Brief History of the Great War*, chaps. x–xv.

Problems of Peace: E. J. DILLON, *The Inside Story of the Peace Conference*; E. M. FRIEDMAN (ed.), *American Problems of Reconstruction*; ORDWAY TEAD,

The People's Part in Peace; E. L. BOGART, *The Direct and Indirect Costs of the Great World War*; NORMAN ANGELL, *America and the New World State*; J. G. BROOKS, *American Syndicalism, the I.W.W.*; E. J. CLAPP, *The Economic Aspects of the War*; T. W. VAN METRE (ed.), *Railroad Legislation* (Academy of Political Science, *Proceedings*, Vol. VIII); ADAMS and SUMNER, *Labor Problems*, Books II-V; NICHOLAS MURRAY BUTLER, *Is America Worth Saving?* E. A. STEINER, *Nationalizing America*.

TOPICS FOR SPECIAL REPORTS

1. **The Adamson Act:** OGG, pp. 353-363; E. J. CLAPP, in the *Yale Review*, Vol. VI, pp. 258-275; E. G. ROBBINS, *The Trainman's Eight-Hour Day* (*Political Science Quarterly*, Vol. XXXI, pp. 541-557); *The Review of Reviews*, Vol. LIV, pp. 389-393; T. R. POWELL, *The Supreme Court and the Adamson Law* (*The University of Pennsylvania Law Review*, Vol. LXV, pp. 3-27).

2. **National Defense:** OGG, pp. 384-390; BASSETT, pp. 71-79, 114-130; HAYES, pp. 219-224; HART and LOVEJOY, *Handbook of the War*, pp. 83-94 (with references appended); LANE and BAKER, *The Nation in Arms* (War Information Series, No. 2); GEORGE H. ALLEN and others, *The Great War*, Vol. IV, pp. 474-478; SAMUEL GOMPERS, *American Labor and the War*, pp. 50-68; *New York Times Current History of the European War*, Vol. III, pp. 18-22, 488-495, 685-687, 818, 1088-1092.

3. **Should Immigration be Restricted?** ADAMS and SUMNER, pp. 80-111; P. F. HALL, *Immigration*, pp. 309-323; R. MAYO-SMITH, *Emigration and Immigration*, pp. 266-302; JAMES BRYCE, *The American Commonwealth* (edition of 1911), Vol. II, pp. 469-490; FRANCIS WALKER, *Discussions in Economics and Statistics*, Vol. II, pp. 417-451.

4. **The American Army at St. Mihiel and in the Argonne:** BASSETT, pp. 229-282; HAYES, pp. 326-334; F. P. SIBLEY, *With the Yankee Division in France*, pp. 257-281; R. S. TOMPKINS, *The Story of the Rainbow Division*, pp. 102-144; *New York Times Current History*, Vol. IX, pp. 228-236, 526-539, and January, 1920, pp. 50-68 (General Pershing's Report).

5. **A League of Nations:** *New York Times Current History*, Vol. X, pp. 287-292 (text), pp. 87-108 (discussion); GOMPERS, pp. 69-82; BASSETT, 348-358; J. B. MOORE, *The Peace Problem* (*North American Review*, Vol. CCIV, pp. 74-89); TEAD, pp. 7-26; Pamphlets of the World Peace Foundation (Boston): *The Covenanter* (Letters on the League), No. 3, June, 1919; *Joint Debate on the Covenant of Paris* (by HENRY CABOT LODGE and A. LAWRENCE LOWELL), No. 2, April, 1919.

APPENDIX I

DECLARATION OF INDEPENDENCE[1]

IN CONGRESS, JULY 4, 1776

A DECLARATION BY THE REPRESENTATIVES OF THE UNITED STATES OF AMERICA, IN CONGRESS ASSEMBLED

WHEN, in the course of human events, it becomes necessary for one people to dissolve the political bands which have connected them with another, and to assume, among the powers of the earth, the separate and equal station to which the laws of nature and of nature's God entitle them, a decent respect to the opinions of mankind requires that they should declare the causes which impel them to the separation.

We hold these truths to be self-evident:—That all men are created equal; that they are endowed by their Creator with certain unalienable rights; that among these are life, liberty, and the pursuit of happiness. That, to secure these rights, governments are instituted among men, deriving their just powers from the consent of the governed; that, whenever any form of government becomes destructive of these ends, it is the right of the people to alter or to abolish it, and to institute a new government, laying its foundation on such principles, and organizing its powers in such form, as to them shall seem most likely to effect their safety and happiness. Prudence, indeed, will dictate, that governments long established should not be changed for light and transient causes; and accordingly all experience hath shown that mankind are more disposed to suffer while evils are sufferable, than to right themselves by abolishing the forms to which they are accustomed. But when a long train of abuses and usurpations, pursuing invariably the same object, evinces a design to reduce them under absolute despotism, it is their right, it is their duty, to throw off such government, and to provide new guards for their future security. Such has been the patient sufferance of these colonies; and such is now the necessity which constrains them to alter their former systems of government. The history of the present King of Great Britain is

---

[1] The original copy of the Declaration of Independence is kept in the Library of Congress in Washington. The Declaration was adopted July 4, 1776, and was signed by the members representing the thirteen states August 2, 1776. John Hancock, whose name appears first among the signers, was president of the Congress.

APPENDIX I

a history of repeated injuries and usurpations, all having in direct object the establishment of an absolute tyranny over these states. To prove this, let facts be submitted to a candid world.

He has refused his assent to laws the most wholesome and necessary for the public good.

He has forbidden his governors to pass laws of immediate and pressing importance, unless suspended in their operation till his assent should be obtained; and when so suspended, he has utterly neglected to attend to them.

He has refused to pass other laws for the accommodation of large districts of people, unless those people would relinquish the right of representation in the legislature — a right inestimable to them, and formidable to tyrants only.

He has called together legislative bodies at places unusual, uncomfortable, and distant from the depository of their public records, for the sole purpose of fatiguing them into compliance with his measure.

He has dissolved representative houses repeatedly, for opposing, with manly firmness, his invasions on the rights of the people.

He has refused, for a long time after such dissolutions, to cause others to be elected, whereby the legislative powers, incapable of annihilation, have returned to the people at large for their exercise; the State remaining, in the mean time, exposed to all the dangers of invasions from without, and convulsions within.

He has endeavored to prevent the population of these States; for that purpose obstructing the laws for the naturalization of foreigners; refusing to pass others to encourage their migration hither, and raising the conditions of new appropriations of lands.

He has obstructed the administration of justice, by refusing his assent to laws for establishing judiciary powers.

He has made judges dependent on his will alone for the tenure of their offices, and the amount and payment of their salaries.

He has erected a multitude of new offices, and sent hither swarms of officers to harass our people and eat out their substance.

He has kept among us in times of peace, standing armies, without the consent of our legislatures.

He has affected to render the military independent of, and superior to, the civil power.

He has combined with others to subject us to a jurisdiction foreign to our constitutions, and unacknowledged by our laws; giving his assent to their acts of pretended legislation:

For quartering large bodies of armed troops among us;

For protecting them, by a mock trial, from punishment for any murders which they should commit on the inhabitants of these States;

For cutting off our trade with all parts of the world;

For imposing taxes on us without our consent;

For depriving us, in many cases, of the benefits of trial by jury;

For transporting us beyond seas, to be tried for pretended offences;

For abolishing the free system of English laws in a neighboring province, establishing therein an arbitrary government, and enlarging its boundaries, so as to render it at once an example and fit instrument for introducing the same absolute rule into these colonies;

For taking away our charters, abolishing our most valuable laws, and altering, fundamentally, the forms of our governments;

For suspending our own legislatures, and declaring themselves invested with power to legislate for us in all cases whatsoever.

He has abdicated government here, by declaring us out of his protection, and waging war against us.

He has plundered our seas, ravaged our coasts, burned our towns, and destroyed the lives of our people.

He is at this time transporting large armies of foreign mercenaries to complete the works of death, desolation and tyranny, already begun with circumstances of cruelty and perfidy scarcely paralleled in the most barbarous ages, and totally unworthy the head of a civilized nation.

He has constrained our fellow-citizens, taken captive on the high seas, to bear arms against their country, to become the executioners of their friends and brethren, or to fall themselves by their hands.

He has excited domestic insurrection among us, and has endeavored to bring on the inhabitants of our frontiers the merciless Indian savages, whose known rule of warfare is an undistinguished destruction of all ages, sexes, and conditions.

In every stage of these oppressions we have petitioned for redress in the most humble terms; our repeated petitions have been answered only by repeated injury. A prince whose character is thus marked by every act which may define a tyrant, is unfit to be the ruler of a free people.

Nor have we been wanting in our attentions to our British brethren. We have warned them, from time to time, of attempts by their legislature to extend an unwarrantable jurisdiction over us. We have reminded them of the circumstances of our emigration and settlement here. We have appealed to their native justice and magnanimity; and we have conjured them, by the ties of our common kindred, to disavow these usurpations, which would inevitably interrupt our connections and correspondence. They, too, have been deaf to the voice of justice and consanguinity. We must, therefore, acquiesce in the necessity which denounces our separation, and hold them, as we hold the rest of mankind, enemies in war, in peace friends.

We, therefore, the Representatives of the United States of America, in General Congress assembled, appealing to the Supreme Judge of the world for the rectitude of our intentions, do, in the name and by the authority of the good people of these colonies, solemnly publish and declare, That these united Colonies are, and of right ought to be, free and independent states; that they are absolved from all allegiance to the British crown, and that all

APPENDIX I

political connection between them and the state of Great Britain is, and ought to be, totally dissolved; and that, as free and independent states, they have full power to levy war, conclude peace, contract alliances, establish commerce, and do all other acts and things which independent states may of right do. And, for the support of this declaration, with a firm reliance on the protection of Divine Providence, we mutually pledge to each other our lives, our fortunes, and our sacred honor.

The foregoing Declaration was, by order of Congress, engrossed, and signed by the following members:

JOHN HANCOCK

NEW HAMPSHIRE
Josiah Bartlett
William Whipple
Matthew Thornton

MASSACHUSETTS BAY
Samuel Adams
John Adams
Robert Treat Paine
Elbridge Gerry

RHODE ISLAND
Stephen Hopkins
William Ellery

CONNECTICUT
Roger Sherman
Samuel Huntington
William Williams
Oliver Wolcott

NEW YORK
William Floyd
Philip Livingston
Francis Lewis
Lewis Morris

NEW JERSEY
Richard Stockton
John Witherspoon
Francis Hopkinson
John Hart
Abraham Clark

PENNSYLVANIA
Robert Morris
Benjamin Rush
Benjamin Franklin
John Morton
George Clymer
James Smith
George Taylor
James Wilson
George Ross

DELAWARE
Cæsar Rodney
George Read
Thomas M'Kean

MARYLAND
Samuel Chase
William Paca
Thomas Stone

Charles Carroll, of Carrollton

VIRGINIA
George Wythe
Richard Henry Lee
Thomas Jefferson
Benjamin Harrison
Thomas Nelson, Jr.
Francis Lightfoot Lee
Carter Braxton

NORTH CAROLINA
William Hooper
Joseph Hewes
John Penn

SOUTH CAROLINA
Edward Rutledge
Thomas Hayward, Jr.
Thomas Lynch, Jr.
Arthur Middleton

GEORGIA
Button Gwinnett
Lyman Hall
George Walton

Resolved, That copies of the Declaration be sent to the several assemblies, conventions, and committees, or councils of safety, and to the several commanding officers of the continental troops; that it be proclaimed in each of the United States, at the head of the army.

APPENDIX II

CONSTITUTION OF THE UNITED STATES

Preamble

WE, the people of the United States, in order to form a more perfect union, establish justice, insure domestic tranquillity, provide for the common defense, promote the general welfare, and secure the blessings of liberty to ourselves and our posterity, do ordain and establish this CONSTITUTION for the United States of America.

ARTICLE I. LEGISLATIVE DEPARTMENT

Section 1. Congress

All legislative powers herein granted shall be vested in a Congress of the United States, which shall consist of a Senate and House of Representatives.[1]

Section 2. House of Representatives

Election of Members. The House of Representatives shall be composed of members chosen every second year by the people of the several States, and the electors in each State shall have the qualifications requisite for electors of the most numerous branch of the State Legislature.

Qualifications. No person shall be a representative who shall not have attained to the age of twenty-five years, and been seven years a citizen of the United States, and who shall not, when elected, be an inhabitant of that State in which he shall be chosen.

Apportionment. Representatives and direct taxes shall be apportioned among the several States which may be included within this Union, according to their respective numbers,[2] which shall be determined by adding to the whole number of free persons, including those bound to service for a term of years, and excluding Indians not taxed, three-fifths of all other persons.[3] The actual

---

[1] The term of each Congress is two years. Under the twentieth amendment to the Constitution, ratified in 1933, Congress assembles at noon of the third day of January of each year.

[2] The apportionment under the census of 1910 is one representative for every 212,407 persons.

[3] The word "persons" refers to slaves. The word "slave" nowhere appears in the Constitution. This paragraph has been amended (Amendments XIII and XIV) and is no longer in force.

enumeration shall be made within three years after the first meeting of the Congress of the United States, and within every subsequent term of ten years, in such manner as they shall by law direct. The number of representatives shall not exceed one for every thirty thousand, but each State shall have at least one representative: and until such enumeration shall be made, the State of New Hampshire shall be entitled to choose three; Massachusetts, eight; Rhode Island and Providence Plantations, one; Connecticut, five; New York, six; New Jersey, four; Pennsylvania, eight; Delaware, one; Maryland, six; Virginia, ten; North Carolina, five; South Carolina, five; and Georgia, three.

Vacancies. When vacancies happen in the representation from any State, the executive authority[1] thereof shall issue writs of election to fill such vacancies.

Officers. Impeachment. The House of Representatives shall choose their Speaker[2] and other officers; and shall have the sole power of impeachment.

SECTION 3. SENATE

Number of Senators: Election. The Senate of the United States shall be composed of two senators from each State, chosen by the Legislature thereof, for six years; and each senator shall have one vote. [Repealed in 1913 by Amendment XVII.]

Classification. Immediately after they shall be assembled in consequence of the first election, they shall be divided as equally as may be into three classes. The seats of the senators of the first class shall be vacated at the expiration of the second year; of the second class, at the expiration of the fourth year; of the third class, at the expiration of the sixth year, so that one-third may be chosen every second year; and if vacancies happen by resignation, or otherwise, during the recess of the Legislature of any State, the executive[1] thereof may make temporary appointments until the next meeting of the Legislature, which shall then fill such vacancies. [Modified by Amendment XVII.]

Qualifications. No person shall be a senator who shall not have attained to the age of thirty years, and been nine years a citizen of the United States, and who shall not, when elected, be an inhabitant of that State for which he shall be chosen.

President of Senate. The Vice-President of the United States shall be president of the Senate, but shall have no vote, unless they be equally divided.

Officers. The Senate shall choose their other officers, and also a president *pro tempore*, in the absence of the Vice-President, or when he shall exercise the office of President of the United States.

Trials of Impeachment. The Senate shall have the sole power to try all impeachments: When sitting for that purpose, they shall be on oath or affirmation.

---

[1] Governor.

[2] The Speaker, who presides, is one of the representatives; the other officers — clerk, sergeant-at-arms, postmaster, chaplain, doorkeeper, etc. — are not.

CONSTITUTION OF THE UNITED STATES

When the President of the United States is tried, the Chief-Justice shall preside: and no person shall be convicted without the concurrence of two-thirds of the members present.

Judgment in Case of Conviction. Judgment in cases of impeachment shall not extend further than to removal from office, and disqualification to hold and enjoy any office of honor, trust, or profit under the United States; but the party convicted shall nevertheless be liable and subject to indictment, trial, judgment, and punishment, according to law.

SECTION 4. BOTH HOUSES

Manner of electing Members. The times, places, and manner of holding elections for senators and representatives shall be prescribed in each State by the Legislature thereof; but the Congress may at any time, by law, make or alter such regulations, except as to the places of choosing senators.[1]

Meetings of Congress. The Congress shall assemble at least once in every year, and such meeting shall be on the first Monday in December, unless they shall by law appoint a different day.

SECTION 5. THE HOUSES SEPARATELY

Organization. Each house shall be the judge of the elections, returns, and qualifications of its own members, and a majority of each shall constitute a quorum to do business; but a smaller number may adjourn from day to day, and may be authorized to compel the attendance of absent members, in such manner, and under such penalties, as each house may provide.

Rules. Each house may determine the rules of its proceedings, punish its members for disorderly behavior, and, with the concurrence of two-thirds, expel a member.

Journal. Each house shall keep a journal of its proceedings, and from time to time publish the same, excepting such parts as may in their judgment require secrecy, and the yeas and nays of the members of either house on any question shall, at the desire of one-fifth of those present, be entered on the journal.

Adjournment. Neither house, during the session of Congress, shall, without the consent of the other, adjourn for more than three days, nor to any other place than that in which the two houses shall be sitting.

SECTION 6. PRIVILEGES AND DISABILITIES OF MEMBERS

Pay and Privileges of Members. The senators and representatives shall receive a compensation for their services, to be ascertained by law, and paid out of the treasury of the United States. They shall in all cases, except treason, felony, and breach of the peace, be privileged from arrest during their

---

[1] This is to prevent Congress from fixing the places of meeting of the state legislatures.

attendance at the session of their respective houses, and in going to and returning from the same; and for any speech or debate in either house, they shall not be questioned in any other place.

Prohibitions on Members. No senator or representative shall, during the time for which he was elected, be appointed to any civil office under the authority of the United States, which shall have been created, or the emoluments whereof shall have been increased, during such time; and no person holding any office under the United States shall be a member of either house during his continuance in office.

SECTION 7. METHOD OF PASSING LAWS

Revenue Bills. All bills for raising revenue shall originate in the House of Representatives; but the Senate may propose or concur with amendments as on other bills.

How Bills become Laws. Every bill which shall have passed the House of Representatives and the Senate shall, before it become a law, be presented to the President of the United States; if he approve, he shall sign it, but if not, he shall return it, with his objections, to that house in which it shall have originated, who shall enter the objections at large on their journal, and proceed to reconsider it. If after such reconsideration, two-thirds of that house shall agree to pass the bill, it shall be sent, together with the objections, to the other house, by which it shall likewise be reconsidered, and if approved by two-thirds of that house, it shall become a law. But in all such cases the votes of both houses shall be determined by yeas and nays, and the names of the persons voting for and against the bill shall be entered on the journal of each house respectively. If any bill shall not be returned by the President within ten days (Sundays excepted) after it shall have been presented to him, the same shall be a law, in like manner as if he had signed it, unless the Congress by their adjournment prevent its return, in which case it shall not be a law.

Resolutions, etc. Every order, resolution, or vote to which the concurrence of the Senate and House of Representatives may be necessary (except on a question of adjournment) shall be presented to the President of the United States; and before the same shall take effect, shall be approved by him, or being disapproved by him, shall be repassed by two-thirds of the Senate and House of Representatives, according to the rules and limitations prescribed in the case of a bill.

SECTION 8. POWERS GRANTED TO CONGRESS

Powers of Congress. The Congress shall have power:

To lay and collect taxes, duties, imposts, and excises, to pay the debts and provide for the common defense and general welfare of the United States; but all duties, imposts, and excises shall be uniform throughout the United States;

To borrow money on the credit of the United States;

To regulate commerce with foreign nations, and among the several States, and with the Indian tribes;

To establish a uniform rule of naturalization, and uniform laws on the subject of bankruptcies throughout the United States;

To coin money, regulate the value thereof, and of foreign coin, and fix the standard of weights and measures;

To provide for the punishment of counterfeiting the securities and current coin of the United States;

To establish post-offices and post-roads;

To promote the progress of science and useful arts, by securing, for limited times, to authors and inventors the exclusive right to their respective writings and discoveries;

To constitute tribunals inferior to the Supreme Court;

To define and punish piracies and felonies committed on the high seas, and offenses against the law of nations;

To declare war, grant letters of marque and reprisal,[1] and make rules concerning captures on land and water;

To raise and support armies, but no appropriation of money to that use shall be for a longer term than two years;

To provide and maintain a navy;

To make rules for the government and regulation of the land and naval forces;

To provide for calling forth the militia to execute the laws of the Union, suppress insurrections and repel invasions;

To provide for organizing, arming, and disciplining the militia, and for governing such part of them as may be employed in the service of the United States, reserving to the States respectively the appointment of the officers, and the authority of training the militia according to the discipline prescribed by Congress;

To exercise exclusive legislation in all cases whatsoever over such district (not exceeding ten miles square) as may, by cession of particular States, and the acceptance of Congress, become the seat of the government of the United States,[2] and to exercise like authority over all places purchased by the consent of the Legislature of the State in which the same shall be, for the erection of forts, magazines, arsenals, dockyards, and other needful buildings;—And

Implied Powers. To make all laws which shall be necessary and proper for carrying into execution the foregoing powers, and all other powers vested by this Constitution in the government of the United States, or in any department or officer thereof.[3]

[1] Letters granted by the government to private citizens in time of war, authorizing them, under certain conditions, to capture the ships of the enemy.

[2] The District of Columbia.

[3] This is the famous elastic clause of the Constitution.

Section 9. Powers Forbidden to the United States

Absolute Prohibitions on Congress. The migration or importation of such persons as any of the States now existing shall think proper to admit, shall not be prohibited by the Congress prior to the year one thousand eight hundred and eight, but a tax or duty may be imposed on such importation, not exceeding ten dollars for each person.[1]

The privilege of the writ of habeas corpus[2] shall not be suspended, unless when in cases of rebellion or invasion the public safety may require it.

No bill of attainder[3] or ex-post-facto law[4] shall be passed.

No capitation or other direct tax shall be laid, unless in proportion to the census or enumeration hereinbefore directed to be taken. [Extended by Amendment XVI.]

No tax or duty shall be laid on articles exported from any State.

No preference shall be given by any regulation of commerce or revenue to the ports of one State over those of another; nor shall vessels bound to, or from, one State, be obliged to enter, clear, or pay duties in another.

No money shall be drawn from the treasury but in consequence of appropriations made by law; and a regular statement and account of the receipts and expenditures of all public money shall be published from time to time.

No title of nobility shall be granted by the United States: And no person holding any office of profit or trust under them, shall, without the consent of the Congress, accept of any present, emolument, office, or title, of any kind whatever, from any king, prince, or foreign state.

Section 10. Powers Forbidden to the States

Absolute Prohibitions on the States. No State shall enter into any treaty, alliance, or confederation; grant letters of marque and reprisal; coin money; emit bills of credit; make anything but gold and silver coin a tender in payment of debts; pass any bill of attainder, ex-post-facto law, or law impairing the obligation of contracts, or grant any title of nobility.

Conditional Prohibitions on the States. No State shall, without the consent of the Congress, lay any imposts or duties on imports or exports, except what may be absolutely necessary for executing its inspection laws; and the net produce of all duties and imposts, laid by any State on imports or exports,

---

[1] This refers to the foreign slave trade. "Persons" means "slaves." In 1808 Congress prohibited the importation of slaves. This clause is, of course, no longer in force.

[2] An official document requiring an accused person who is in prison awaiting trial to be brought into court to inquire whether he may be legally held.

[3] A special legislative act by which a person may be condemned to death or to outlawry or banishment without the opportunity of defending himself which he would have in a court of law.

[4] A law relating to the punishment of acts committed before the law was passed.

CONSTITUTION OF THE UNITED STATES

shall be for the use of the treasury of the United States; and all such laws shall be subject to the revision and control of the Congress.

No State shall, without the consent of Congress, lay any duty of tonnage, keep troops, or ships-of-war, in time of peace, enter into any agreement or compact with another State, or with a foreign power, or engage in war, unless actually invaded, or in such imminent danger as will not admit of delay.

ARTICLE II. EXECUTIVE DEPARTMENT

SECTION I. PRESIDENT AND VICE-PRESIDENT

Term. The executive power shall be vested in a President of the United States of America. He shall hold his office during the term of four years, and, together with the Vice-President, chosen for the same term, be elected, as follows:

Electors. Each State shall appoint, in such manner as the Legislature thereof may direct, a number of electors, equal to the whole number of senators and representatives to which the State may be entitled in the Congress: but no senator or representative, or person holding an office of trust or profit under the United States, shall be appointed an elector.

Proceedings of Electors and of Congress. [[1] The electors shall meet in their respective States, and vote by ballot for two persons, of whom one at least shall not be an inhabitant of the same State with themselves. And they shall make a list of all the persons voted for, and of the number of votes for each; which list they shall sign and certify and transmit sealed to the seat of the government of the United States, directed to the president of the Senate. The president of the Senate shall, in the presence of the Senate and House of Representatives, open all the certificates, and the votes shall then be counted. The person having the greatest number of votes shall be the President, if such number be a majority of the whole number of electors appointed; and if there be more than one who have such majority, and have an equal number of votes, then the House of Representatives shall immediately choose by ballot one of them for President; and if no person have a majority, then from the five highest on the list the said house shall, in like manner, choose the President. But in choosing the President, the votes shall be taken by States, the representation from each State having one vote; a quorum for this purpose shall consist of a member or members from two-thirds of the States, and a majority of all the States shall be necessary to a choice. In every case, after the choice of the President, the person having the greatest number of votes of the electors shall be the Vice-President. But if there should remain two or more who have equal votes, the Senate shall choose from them by ballot the Vice-President.]

---

[1] This paragraph in brackets has been superseded by the Twelfth Amendment.

Time of choosing Electors. The Congress may determine the time of choosing the electors, and the day on which they shall give their votes; which day shall be the same throughout the United States.[1]

Qualifications of President. No person except a natural born citizen, or a citizen of the United States at the time of the adoption of this Constitution, shall be eligible to the office of President; neither shall any person be eligible to that office who shall not have attained to the age of thirty-five years, and been fourteen years resident within the United States.

Vacancy. In case of the removal of the President from office, or of his death, resignation, or inability to discharge the powers and duties of the said office, the same shall devolve on the Vice-President, and the Congress may by law provide for the case of removal, death, resignation, or inability, both of the President and Vice-President, declaring what officer shall then act as President; and such officer shall act accordingly until the disability be removed, or a President shall be elected.[2]

Salary. The President shall, at stated times, receive for his services a compensation which shall neither be increased nor diminished during the period for which he shall have been elected, and he shall not receive within that period any other emolument from the United States, or any of them.

Oath. Before he enter on the execution of his office, he shall take the following oath or affirmation: — "I do solemnly swear (or affirm) that I will faithfully execute the office of President of the United States, and will, to the best of my ability, preserve, protect, and defend the Constitution of the United States."

SECTION 2. POWERS OF THE PRESIDENT

Military Powers; Reprieves and Pardons. The President shall be commander-in-chief of the army and navy of the United States, and of the militia of the several States, when called into the actual service of the United States; he may require the opinion, in writing, of the principal officer in each of the executive departments, upon any subject relating to the duties of their respective offices; and he shall have power to grant reprieves and pardons for offenses against the United States, except in cases of impeachment.

Treaties; Appointments. He shall have power, by and with the advice and consent of the Senate, to make treaties, provided two-thirds of the senators present concur; and he shall nominate, and by and with the advice and consent of the Senate shall appoint ambassadors, other public ministers and consuls, judges of the Supreme Court, and all other officers of the United

---

[1] The electors are chosen on the Tuesday next after the first Monday in November, preceding the expiration of a presidential term. They vote (by Act of Congress of February 3, 1887) on the second Monday in January for President and Vice-President. The votes are counted, and declared in Congress on the second Wednesday of the following February.

[2] This has now been provided for by the **Presidential Succession Act of 1886.**

States, whose appointments are not herein otherwise provided for, and which shall be established by law: but the Congress may by law vest the appointment of such inferior officers, as they think proper, in the President alone, in the courts of law, or in the heads of departments.

Filling of Vacancies. The President shall have power to fill up all vacancies that may happen during the recess of the Senate, by granting commissions which shall expire at the end of their next session.

SECTION 3. DUTIES OF THE PRESIDENT

Message; Convening of Congress. He shall from time to time give to the Congress information[1] of the state of the Union, and recommend to their consideration such measures as he shall judge necessary and expedient; he may, on extraordinary occasions, convene both houses, or either of them, and in case of disagreement between them with respect to the time of adjournment, he may adjourn them to such time as he shall think proper; he shall receive ambassadors and other public ministers; he shall take care that the laws be faithfully executed, and shall commission all the officers of the United States.

SECTION 4. IMPEACHMENT

Removal of Officers. The President, Vice-President, and all civil officers of the United States, shall be removed from office on impeachment for, and conviction of, treason, bribery, or other high crimes and misdemeanors.

ARTICLE III. JUDICIAL DEPARTMENT

SECTION 1. UNITED STATES COURTS

Courts established; Judges. The judicial power of the United States shall be vested in one Supreme Court, and in such inferior courts as the Congress may from time to time ordain and establish. The judges, both of the Supreme and inferior courts, shall hold their offices during good behavior, and shall, at stated times, receive for their services a compensation which shall not be diminished during their continuance in office.

SECTION 2. JURISDICTION OF UNITED STATES COURTS

Federal Courts in General. The judicial power shall extend to all cases, in law and equity, arising under this Constitution, the laws of the United States, and treaties made, or which shall be made, under their authority; — to all cases

---

[1] The president gives this information through a message to Congress at the opening of each session. Washington and John Adams read their messages in person to Congress. Jefferson, however, sent a written message to Congress. This method was followed until President Wilson returned to the earlier custom.

affecting ambassadors, other public ministers, and consuls; — to all cases of admiralty and maritime jurisdiction; — to controversies to which the United States shall be a party; — to controversies between two or more States; — between a State and citizens of another State;[1] — between citizens of different States; — between citizens of the same State claiming lands under grants of different States, and between a State, or the citizens thereof, and foreign states, citizens or subjects.

Supreme Court. In all cases affecting ambassadors, other public ministers and consuls, and those in which a State shall be party, the Supreme Court shall have original jurisdiction. In all other cases before mentioned, the Supreme Court shall have appellate jurisdiction, both as to law and fact, with such exceptions and under such regulations as the Congress shall make.

Trials. The trial of all crimes, except in cases of impeachment, shall be by jury; and such trial shall be held in the State where the said crimes shall have been committed; but when not committed within any State, the trial shall be at such place or places as the Congress may by law have directed.

Section 3. Treason

Treason defined. Treason against the United States shall consist only in levying war against them, or in adhering to their enemies, giving them aid and comfort.

No person shall be convicted of treason unless on the testimony of two witnesses to the same overt act, or on confession in open court.

Punishment. The Congress shall have power to declare the punishment of treason, but no attainder of treason shall work corruption of blood, or forfeiture, except during the life of the person attainted.

ARTICLE IV. RELATIONS OF THE STATES TO EACH OTHER

Section 1. Official Acts

Full faith and credit shall be given in each State to the public acts, records, and judicial proceedings of every other State. And the Congress may by general laws, prescribe the manner in which such acts, records, and proceedings shall be proved, and the effect thereof.

Section 2. Privileges of Citizens

The citizens of each State shall be entitled to all privileges and immunities of citizens in the several States.

Fugitives from Justice. A person charged in any State with treason, felony, or other crime, who shall flee from justice, and be found in another State,

---

[1] This has been modified by the Eleventh Amendment.

CONSTITUTION OF THE UNITED STATES xv

shall, on demand of the executive authority of the State from which he fled, be delivered up, to be removed to the State having jurisdiction of the crime.

Fugitive Slaves. No person [1] held to service or labor in one State, under the laws thereof, escaping into another, shall, in consequence of any law or regulation therein, be discharged from such service or labor, but shall be delivered up on claim of the party to whom such service or labor may be due.

Section 3. New States and Territories

Admission of States. New States may be admitted by the Congress into this Union; but no new State shall be formed or erected within the jurisdiction of any other State; nor any State be formed by the junction of two or more States, or parts of States, without the consent of the Legislatures of the States concerned as well as of the Congress.

Territory and Property of United States. The Congress shall have power to dispose of and make all needful rules and regulations respecting the territory or other property belonging to the United States; and nothing in this Constitution shall be so construed as to prejudice any claims of the United States, or of any particular State.

Section 4. Protection of the States

The United States shall guarantee to every State in this Union a republican form of government, and shall protect each of them against invasion, and on application of the Legislature, or of the Executive (when the Legislature cannot be convened) against domestic violence.

ARTICLE V. AMENDMENTS

How proposed; how ratified. The Congress, whenever two-thirds of both houses shall deem it necessary, shall propose amendments to this Constitution, or, on the application of the Legislatures of two-thirds of the several States, shall call a convention for proposing amendments, which, in either case, shall be valid to all intents and purposes, as part of this Constitution, when ratified by the Legislatures of three-fourths of the several States, or by conventions in three-fourths thereof, as the one or the other mode of ratification may be proposed by the Congress; provided that no amendment which

---

[1] "Person" here includes slave. This was the basis of the Fugitive Slave Laws of 1793 and 1850. It is now superseded by the Thirteenth Amendment, by which slavery is prohibited.

may be made prior to the year one thousand eight hundred and eight shall in any manner affect the first and fourth clauses in the ninth section of the first article; and that no State, without its consent, shall be deprived of its equal suffrage in the Senate.

ARTICLE VI. GENERAL PROVISIONS

Public Debt. All debts contracted, and engagements entered into, before the adoption of this Constitution, shall be as valid against the United States under this Constitution, as under the Confederation.

Supremacy of Constitution. This Constitution, and the laws of the United States which shall be made in pursuance thereof; and all treaties made, or which shall be made, under the authority of the United States, shall be the supreme law of the land; and the judges in every State shall be bound thereby, anything in the Constitution or laws of any State to the contrary notwithstanding.

Official Oath; Religious Test. The senators and representatives before mentioned, and the members of the several State Legislatures, and all executive and judicial officers, both of the United States and of the several States, shall be bound by oath or affirmation to support this Constitution; but no religious test shall ever be required as a qualification to any office or public trust under the United States.

ARTICLE VII. RATIFICATION OF THE CONSTITUTION

Ratification. The ratification of the Conventions of nine States shall be sufficient for the establishment of this Constitution between the States so ratifying the same.

> Done in convention, by the unanimous consent of the States present, the seventeenth day of September, in the year of our Lord one thousand seven hundred and eighty-seven, and of the independence of the United States of America the twelfth.
>
> In witness whereof, we have hereunto subscribed our names.[1]
>
> GEORGE WASHINGTON,
> *President, and Deputy from Virginia.*

---

[1] There were sixty-five delegates chosen to the convention: ten did not attend; sixteen declined or failed to sign; thirty-nine signed. Rhode Island sent no delegates.

CONSTITUTION OF THE UNITED STATES

NEW HAMPSHIRE	PENNSYLVANIA	VIRGINIA
John Langdon	Benjamin Franklin	John Blair
Nicholas Gilman	Thomas Mifflin	James Madison, Jr.
	Robert Morris	
MASSACHUSETTS	George Clymer	NORTH CAROLINA
Nathaniel Gorham	Thomas Fitzsimons	
Rufus King	Jared Ingersoll	William Blount
	James Wilson	Richard Dobbs Spaight
CONNECTICUT	Gouverneur Morris	Hugh Williamson
William Samuel Johnson	DELAWARE	
Roger Sherman	George Read	SOUTH CAROLINA
	Gunning Bedford, Jr.	John Rutledge
NEW YORK	John Dickinson	Charles C. Pinckney
Alexander Hamilton	Richard Bassett	Charles Pinckney
	Jacob Broom	Pierce Butler
NEW JERSEY	MARYLAND	
William Livingston	James M'Henry	GEORGIA
David Brearley	Daniel of St. Thomas Jenifer	
William Paterson		William Few
Jonathan Dayton	Daniel Carroll	Abraham Baldwin

Attest: WILLIAM JACKSON, *Secretary*

AMENDMENTS

Religion, Speech, Press, Assembly, Petition. ARTICLE I.[1] Congress shall make no law respecting an establishment of religion, or prohibiting the free exercise thereof; or abridging the freedom of speech, or of the press; or the right of the people peaceably to assemble, and to petition the government for redress of grievances.

Militia. ARTICLE II. A well-regulated militia being necessary to the security of a free State the right of the people to keep and bear arms shall not be infringed.

Soldiers. ARTICLE III. No soldier shall, in time of peace, be quartered in any house, without the consent of the owner; nor in time of war but in a manner to be prescribed by law.

Unreasonable Searches. ARTICLE IV. The right of the people to be secure in their persons, houses, papers, and effects, against unreasonable searches and seizures, shall not be violated, and no warrants shall issue, but upon

---

[1] These amendments were proposed by Congress and ratified by the legislatures of the several states, pursuant to the fifth article of the Constitution. The first ten were offered in 1789 and adopted before the close of 1791. They were for the most part the work of Madison. They are frequently called the Bill of Rights, as their purpose is to guard more efficiently the rights of the people and of the states.

probable cause, supported by oath or affirmation, and particularly describing the place to be searched, and the persons or things to be seized.

Criminal Prosecutions. ARTICLE V. No person shall be held to answer for a capital, or otherwise infamous crime, unless on a presentment or indictment of a grand jury, except in cases arising in the land or naval forces, or in the militia, when in actual service in time of war and public danger; nor shall any person be subject for the same offense to be twice put in jeopardy of life or limb; nor shall be compelled in any criminal case to be a witness against himself, nor to be deprived of life, liberty, or property, without due process of law; nor shall private property be taken for public use, without just compensation.

ARTICLE VI. In all criminal prosecutions, the accused shall enjoy the right to a speedy and public trial, by an impartial jury of the State and district wherein the crime shall have been committed, which district shall have been previously ascertained by law, and to be informed of the nature and cause of the accusation; to be confronted with the witnesses against him; to have compulsory process for obtaining witnesses in his favor, and to have the assistance of counsel for his defense.

Suits at Common Law. ARTICLE VII. In suits at common law, where the value in controversy shall exceed twenty dollars, the right of trial by jury shall be preserved, and no fact tried by a jury shall be otherwise reëxamined in any court of the United States than according to the rules of common law.

Bail, Punishments. ARTICLE VIII. Excessive bail shall not be required, nor excessive fines imposed, nor cruel and unusual punishments inflicted.

Reserved Rights and Powers. ARTICLE IX. The enumeration in the Constitution of certain rights shall not be construed to deny or disparage others retained by the people.

ARTICLE X. The powers not delegated to the United States by the Constitution, nor prohibited by it to the States, are reserved to the States respectively, or to the people.

Suits against States. ARTICLE XI.[1] The judicial power of the United States shall not be construed to extend to any suit in law or equity, commenced or prosecuted against any of the United States by citizens of another State, or by citizens or subjects of any foreign state.

Method of electing President and Vice-President. ARTICLE XII.[2] The electors shall meet in their respective States, and vote by ballot for President and Vice-President, one of whom, at least, shall not be an inhabitant of the same State with themselves; they shall name in their ballots the person voted for as President, and in distinct ballots the person voted for as Vice-President; and they shall make distinct lists of all persons voted for as President, and of all persons voted for as Vice-President, and of the number of votes for each, which list they shall sign and certify, and transmit sealed to the seat of the government of the United States, directed to the president of the Senate; —

[1] Proposed in 1794; adopted in 1798.   [2] Adopted in 1804.

CONSTITUTION OF THE UNITED STATES xix

the president of the Senate shall, in the presence of the Senate and House of Representatives, open all the certificates, and the votes shall then be counted; — the person having the greatest number of votes for President, shall be the President, if such number be a majority of the whole number of electors appointed; and if no person have such majority, then from the persons having the highest numbers not exceeding three on the list of those voted for as President, the House of Representatives shall choose immediately, by ballot, the President. But in choosing the President, the votes shall be taken by States, the representation from each State having one vote; a quorum for this purpose shall consist of a member or members from two-thirds of the States, and a majority of all the States shall be necessary to a choice. And if the House of Representatives shall not choose a President whenever the right of choice shall devolve upon them, before the fourth day of March next following, then the Vice-President shall act as President, as in the case of the death or other constitutional disability of the President. The person having the greatest number of votes as Vice-President, shall be the Vice-President, if such number be a majority of the whole number of electors appointed; and if no person have a majority, then from the two highest numbers on the list, the Senate shall choose the Vice-President; a quorum for the purpose shall consist of two-thirds of the whole number of senators, and a majority of the whole number shall be necessary to a choice. But no person constitutionally ineligible to the office of President shall be eligible to that of Vice-President of the United States.

Slavery abolished. ARTICLE XIII.[1] *Section 1.* Neither slavery nor involuntary servitude, except as a punishment for crime, whereof the party shall have been duly convicted, shall exist within the United States, or any place subject to their jurisdiction.

Section 2. Congress shall have power to enforce this article by appropriate legislation.

Negroes made Citizens. ARTICLE XIV.[2] *Section 1.* All persons born or naturalized in the United States, and subject to the jurisdiction thereof, are citizens of the United States and of the State wherein they reside. No State shall make or enforce any law which shall abridge the privileges or immunities of citizens of the United States; nor shall any State deprive any person of life, liberty, or property, without due process of law, nor deny to any person within its jurisdiction the equal protection of the laws.

Section 2. Representatives shall be apportioned among the several States according to their respective numbers, counting the whole number of persons in each State, excluding Indians not taxed. But when the right to vote at any election for the choice of electors for President and Vice-President of the United States, representatives in Congress, the executive or judicial officers of a State, or the members of the Legislature thereof, is denied to any of the male inhabitants of such State, being twenty-one years of age, and citizens of

[1] Adopted in 1865.   [2] Adopted in 1868.

the United States, or in any way abridged, except for participation in rebellion or other crime, the basis of representation therein shall be reduced in the proportion which the number of such male citizens shall bear to the whole number of male citizens twenty-one years of age in such State.

Section 3. No person shall be a senator or representative in Congress, or elector of President or Vice-President, or hold any office, civil or military, under the United States, or under any State, who having previously taken an oath as a member of Congress, or as an officer of the United States, or as a member of any State Legislature, or as an executive or judicial officer of any State, to support the Constitution of the United States, shall have engaged in insurrection or rebellion against the same, or given aid or comfort to the enemies thereof. But Congress may, by a vote of two-thirds of each house, remove such disability.

Section 4. The validity of the public debt of the United States, authorized by law, including debts incurred for payment of pensions and bounties for services in suppressing insurrection or rebellion, shall not be questioned. But neither the United States nor any State shall assume or pay any debt or obligation incurred in aid of insurrection or rebellion against the United States, or any claim for the loss or emancipation of any slave; but all such debts, obligations, and claims shall be held illegal and void.

Section 5. The Congress shall have power to enforce, by appropriate legislation, the provisions of this article.

Negroes made Voters. ARTICLE XV.[1] *Section 1.* The rights of citizens of the United States to vote shall not be denied or abridged by the United States, or by any State, on account of race, color, or previous condition of servitude.

Section 2. The Congress shall have power to enforce this article by appropriate legislation.

Income Tax. ARTICLE XVI.[2] The Congress shall have power to lay and collect taxes on incomes from whatever source derived, without apportionment among the several States, and without regard to any census or enumeration.

ARTICLE XVII.[2] The Senate of the United States shall be composed of two Senators from each State, elected by the people thereof for six years; and each Senator shall have one vote. The electors in each State shall have the qualifications requisite for electors of the most numerous branch of the State Legislatures.

Direct Election of Senators. When vacancies happen in the representation of any State in the Senate, the executive authority of such State shall issue writs of election to fill such vacancies: Provided, that the Legislature of any State may empower the Executive thereof to make temporary appointments until the people fill the vacancies by election as the Legislature may direct.

This amendment shall not be so construed as to affect the election or term of any Senator chosen before it becomes valid as part of the Constitution.

[1] Adopted in 1870.   [2] Ratified in 1913.

CONSTITUTION OF THE UNITED STATES

National Prohibition. ARTICLE XVIII.[1] *Section 1.* After one year from the ratification of this article the manufacture, sale, or transportation of intoxicating liquors within, the importation thereof into, or the exportation thereof from the United States and all territory subject to the jurisdiction thereof for beverage purposes is hereby prohibited.

Section 2. The Congress and the several States shall have concurrent power to enforce this article by appropriate legislation.

Section 3. This article shall be inoperative unless it shall have been ratified as an amendment to the Constitution by the Legislatures of the several States, as provided in the Constitution, within seven years from the date of the submission hereof to the States by the Congress.

Woman Suffrage. ARTICLE XIX.[2] *Section 1.* The right of citizens of the United States to vote shall not be denied or abridged by the United States or by any State on account of sex.

Section 2. Congress shall have power to enforce this article by appropriate legislation.

"Lame Duck" Amendment. ARTICLE XX.[3] *Section 1.* The terms of the President and Vice-President shall end at noon on the twentieth day of January, and the terms of senators and representatives at noon on the third day of January, of the years in which such terms would have ended if this article had not been ratified; and the terms of their successors shall then begin.

Section 2. The Congress shall assemble at least once in every year, and such meeting shall begin at noon on the third day of January, unless they shall by law appoint a different day.

Section 3. If, at the time fixed for the beginning of the term of the President, the President-elect shall have died, the Vice-President-elect shall become President. If a President shall not have been chosen before the time fixed for the beginning of his term, or if the President-elect shall have failed to qualify, then the Vice-President-elect shall act as President until a President shall have qualified; and the Congress may by law provide for the case wherein neither a President-elect nor a Vice-President-elect shall have qualified, declaring who shall then act as President, or the manner in which one who is to act shall be selected, and such person shall act accordingly until a President or Vice-President shall have qualified.

Section 4. The Congress may by law provide for the case of the death of any of the persons from whom the House of Representatives may choose a President whenever the right of choice shall have devolved upon them, and for the case of the death of any of the persons from whom the Senate may choose a Vice-President whenever the right of choice shall have devolved upon them.

Section 5. Sections 1 and 2 shall take effect upon the fifteenth day of October following the ratification of this article.

Section 6. This article shall be inoperative unless it shall have been ratified as an amendment to the Constitution by the Legislatures of three-fourths of the several States within seven years from the date of its submission.

[1] Ratified in 1919. In force in 1920.   [2] Ratified in 1920.   [3] Ratified in 1933.

The Repeal of Prohibition. ARTICLE XXI.[1] *Section 1.* The eighteenth amendment to the Constitution of the United States is hereby repealed.

Section 2. The transportation or importation into any State, Territory, or possession of the United States for delivery or use therein of intoxicating liquors, in violation of the laws thereof, is hereby prohibited.

Section 3. This article shall be inoperative unless it shall have been ratified as an amendment to the Constitution by conventions in the several States, as provided in the Constitution, within seven years from the date of the submission hereof to the States by the Congress.

APPENDIX III

MEMBERS OF THE SUPREME COURT, 1934

	APPOINTED BY PRESIDENT
CHIEF JUSTICE	
CHARLES E. HUGHES	HOOVER, 1930
ASSOCIATE JUSTICES	
WILLIS VAN DEVANTER	TAFT, 1910
JAMES C. MCREYNOLDS	WILSON, 1914
LOUIS D. BRANDEIS	WILSON, 1916
GEORGE SUTHERLAND	HARDING, 1922
PIERCE BUTLER	HARDING, 1922
HARLAN F. STONE	COOLIDGE, 1925
OWEN J. ROBERTS	HOOVER, 1930
BENJAMIN N. CARDOZO	HOOVER, 1932

[1] Ratified in 1933.

APPENDIX IV

THE STATES OF THE UNION

No.	State	Date of Admission	Population, 1930	Rank	Land Area	Capital	Largest City
1	Delaware	*Original States*	238,380	46	1,965	Dover	Wilmington
2	Pennsylvania		9,631,350	2	44,832	Harrisburg	Philadelphia
3	New Jersey		4,041,334	9	7,514	Trenton	Newark
4	Georgia		2,908,506	14	58,725	Atlanta	Atlanta
5	Connecticut		1,606,903	29	4,820	Hartford	Hartford
6	Massachusetts		4,249,614	8	8,039	Boston	Boston
7	Maryland		1,631,526	28	9,941	Annapolis	Baltimore
8	South Carolina		1,738,765	26	30,495	Columbia	Charleston
9	New Hampshire		465,283	41	9,031	Concord	Manchester
10	Virginia		2,421,851	20	40,262	Richmond	Richmond
11	New York		12,588,066	1	47,654	Albany	New York
12	North Carolina		3,170,276	12	48,740	Raleigh	Charlotte
13	Rhode Island		687,497	37	1,067	Providence	Providence
14	Vermont	1791	359,611	45	9,124	Montpelier	Burlington
15	Kentucky	1792	2,614,589	17	40,181	Frankfort	Louisville
16	Tennessee	1796	2,616,556	16	41,687	Nashville	Memphis
17	Ohio	1803	6,646,697	4	40,740	Columbus	Cleveland
18	Louisiana	1812	2,101,593	22	45,409	Baton Rouge	New Orleans
19	Indiana	1816	3,238,503	11	36,045	Indianapolis	Indianapolis
20	Mississippi	1817	2,009,821	23	46,362	Jackson	Jackson
21	Illinois	1818	7,630,654	3	56,043	Springfield	Chicago
22	Alabama	1819	2,646,248	15	51,279	Montgomery	Birmingham

THE STATES OF THE UNION (CONTINUED)

No.	State	Date of Admission	Population, 1930	Rank	Land Area	Capital	Largest City
23	Maine	1820	797,423	35	29,895	Augusta	Portland
24	Missouri	1821	3,629,367	10	68,727	Jefferson City	St. Louis
25	Arkansas	1836	1,854,482	25	52,525	Little Rock	Little Rock
26	Michigan	1837	4,842,325	7	57,480	Lansing	Detroit
27	Florida	1845	1,468,211	31	54,861	Tallahassee	Jacksonville
28	Texas	1845	5,824,715	5	262,398	Austin	Houston
29	Iowa	1846	2,470,939	19	55,586	Des Moines	Des Moines
30	Wisconsin	1848	2,939,006	13	55,256	Madison	Milwaukee
31	California	1850	5,677,251	6	155,652	Sacramento	Los Angeles
32	Minnesota	1858	2,563,953	18	80,858	St. Paul	Minneapolis
33	Oregon	1859	953,786	34	95,607	Salem	Portland
34	Kansas	1861	1,880,999	24	81,774	Topeka	Kansas City
35	West Virginia	1863	1,729,205	27	24,022	Charleston	Huntington
36	Nevada	1864	91,058	48	109,821	Carson City	Reno
37	Nebraska	1867	1,377,963	32	76,808	Lincoln	Omaha
38	Colorado	1876	1,035,791	33	103,658	Denver	Denver
39	North Dakota	1889	680,845	38	70,183	Bismarck	Fargo
40	South Dakota	1889	692,849	36	76,868	Pierre	Sioux Falls
41	Montana	1889	537,606	39	146,131	Helena	Butte
42	Washington	1889	1,563,396	30	66,836	Olympia	Seattle
43	Idaho	1890	445,032	42	83,354	Boise	Boise
44	Wyoming	1890	225,565	47	97,548	Cheyenne	Cheyenne
45	Utah	1896	507,847	40	82,184	Salt Lake City	Salt Lake City
46	Oklahoma	1907	2,396,040	21	69,414	Oklahoma City	Oklahoma City
47	New Mexico	1912	423,317	44	122,503	Santa Fe	Albuquerque
48	Arizona	1912	435,573	43	113,810	Phoenix	Phoenix

APPENDIX V

PRESIDENTS AND OTHER HIGH OFFICIALS

No.	Date	President	State	Vice President	Secretary of State	Secretary of Treasury
1	1789	George Washington	Virginia	John Adams	Thomas Jefferson	Alexander Hamilton
	1794				E. Randolph	
	1795				T. Pickering	O. Wolcott
2	1797	John Adams	Massachusetts	Thomas Jefferson		
	1800				John Marshall	S. Dexter
3	1801	Thomas Jefferson	Virginia	Aaron Burr	James Madison	A. Gallatin
	1805			George Clinton		
4	1809	James Madison	Virginia		Robert Smith	
	1811				James Monroe	
	1813			Elbridge Gerry		
	1814					G. Campbell
	1814					A. J. Dallas
	1816					W. H. Crawford
5	1817	James Monroe	Virginia	D. D. Tompkins	J. Q. Adams	
6	1825	J. Q. Adams	Massachusetts	J. C. Calhoun	Henry Clay	Richard Rush
7	1829	Andrew Jackson	Tennessee		M. Van Buren	S. D. Ingham
	1831				E. Livingston	L. McLane
	1833			M. Van Buren	L. McLane	W. J. Duane
	1833					R. B. Taney
	1834					L. Woodbury
8	1837	M. Van Buren	New York	R. M. Johnson	J. Forsyth	

APPENDIX V

PRESIDENTS AND OTHER HIGH OFFICIALS (CONTINUED)

No.	Date	President	State	Vice President	Secretary of State	Secretary of Treasury
9	1841	W. H. Harrison	Ohio	John Tyler	D. Webster	Thomas Ewing
10	1841	John Tyler	Virginia	—	{ H. S. Legaré	W. Forward
	1843				{ A. P. Upshur	J. C. Spencer
	1844				J. C. Calhoun	G. M. Bibb
11	1845	J. K. Polk	Tennessee	G. M. Dallas	J. Buchanan	R. J. Walker
12	1849	Zachary Taylor	Louisiana	M. Fillmore	J. M. Clayton	William Meredith
13	1850	M. Fillmore	New York	—	D. Webster	Thomas Corwin
	1852				Edward Everett	
14	1853	Franklin Pierce	New Hampshire	W. R. King	W. L. Marcy	James Guthrie
15	1857	James Buchanan	Pennsylvania	J. Breckinridge	Lewis Cass	Howell Cobb
	1860				J. S. Black	P. F. Thomas
	1860					John A. Dix
16	1861	Abraham Lincoln	Illinois	H. Hamlin	W. H. Seward	S. P. Chase
	1864					W. P. Fessenden
	1865			Andrew Johnson		H. McCulloch
17	1865	Andrew Johnson	Tennessee	—		
18	1869	U. S. Grant	Illinois	S. Colfax	{ E. B. Washburne	G. S. Boutwell
	1873			Henry Wilson	{ Hamilton Fish	W. Richardson
	1874					B. H. Bristow
	1876					L. M. Morrill
19	1877	R. B. Hayes	Ohio	W. A. Wheeler	W. M. Evarts	John Sherman
20	1881	J. A. Garfield	Ohio	C. A. Arthur	James G. Blaine	William Windom
21	1881	C. A. Arthur	New York		F. Frelinghuysen	C. J. Folger
	1884					W. Q. Gresham
	1884					H. McCulloch

PRESIDENTS AND OTHER HIGH OFFICIALS xxvii

No.	Date	President	State	Vice-President	Secretary of State	Secretary of Treasury
22	1885	Grover Cleveland	New York	T. A. Hendricks	T. F. Bayard	D. Manning
	1887					C. S. Fairchild
23	1889	Benjamin Harrison	Indiana	L. P. Morton	James G. Blaine	William Windom
	1891					Charles Foster
	1892				J. W. Foster	
24	1893	Grover Cleveland	New York	A. E. Stevenson	W. Q. Gresham	J. G. Carlisle
	1895				Richard Olney	
25	1897	William McKinley	Ohio	G. A. Hobart	John Sherman	L. J. Gage
	1898				William R. Day	
	1898				John Hay	
	1901			Theodore Roosevelt		
26	1901	Theodore Roosevelt	New York			
	1902					L. M. Shaw
	1905			C. W. Fairbanks		
	1907				Elihu Root	G. B. Cortelyou
	1909				Robert Bacon	
27	1909	W. H. Taft	Ohio	J. S. Sherman	P. C. Knox	F. MacVeagh
28	1913	Woodrow Wilson	New Jersey	T. R. Marshall	William J. Bryan	W. G. McAdoo
	1915				Robert Lansing	
	1918					Carter Glass
	1920				Bainbridge Colby	D. F. Houston
29	1921	Warren G. Harding	Ohio	Calvin Coolidge	Charles E. Hughes	Andrew W. Mellon
30	1923	Calvin Coolidge	Massachusetts			
	1925			Charles G. Dawes	Frank B. Kellogg	
31	1929	Herbert C. Hoover	California	Charles Curtis	Henry L. Stimson	
	1932					Ogden L. Mills
32	1933	Franklin D. Roosevelt	New York	John N. Garner	Cordell Hull	William B. Woodin

APPENDIX VI

MEMBERS OF CABINETS FROM WILSON TO ROOSEVELT, 1913–1933

WILSON, 1913–1921	HARDING, 1921–1923	COOLIDGE, 1923–1929	HOOVER, 1929–1933	ROOSEVELT, 1933–
Secretaries of State				
1913 W. J. Bryan 1915 Robert Lansing 1920 Bainbridge Colby	1921 C. E. Hughes	1923 C. E. Hughes 1925 F. B. Kellogg	1929 H. L. Stimson	1933 Cordell Hull
Secretaries of the Treasury				
1913 W. G. McAdoo 1918 Carter Glass 1920 D. F. Houston	1921 A. W. Mellon	1923 A. W. Mellon	1929 A. W. Mellon 1932 O. L. Mills	1933 W. B. Woodin 1934 Henry Morgenthau, Jr.
Secretaries of War				
1913 L. M. Garrison 1916 N. D. Baker	1921 J. W. Weeks	1923 J. W. Weeks 1925 D. F. Davis	1929 J. W. Good 1930 P. J. Hurley	1933 G. H. Dern
Attorneys-General				
1913 J. C. McReynolds 1914 T. W. Gregory 1919 A. M. Palmer	1921 H. M. Daugherty	1923 H. M. Daugherty 1924 H. F. Stone 1925 J. G. Sargent	1929 W. D. Mitchell	1933 H. S. Cummings

MEMBERS OF RECENT CABINETS (CONTINUED)

WILSON, 1913–1921	HARDING, 1921–1923	COOLIDGE, 1923–1929	HOOVER, 1929–1933	ROOSEVELT, 1933–
Secretaries of the Navy				
1913 Josephus Daniels	1921 Edwin Denby	1923 Edwin Denby 1924 C. D. Wilbur	1929 C. F. Adams	1933 C. A. Swanson
Postmasters-General				
1913 A. S. Burleson	1921 W. H. Hays 1922 Hubert Work 1923 H. S. New	1923 H. S. New	1929 W. F. Brown	1933 J. A. Farley
Secretaries of the Interior				
1913 F. K. Lane 1920 J. B. Payne	1921 A. B. Fall 1923 Hubert Work	1923 Hubert Work 1928 R. O. West	1929 R. L. Wilbur	1933 H. L. Ickes

MEMBERS OF RECENT CABINETS (CONTINUED)

WILSON, 1913–1921	HARDING, 1921–1923	COOLIDGE, 1923–1929	HOOVER, 1929–1933	ROOSEVELT, 1933–
Secretaries of Agriculture				
1913 D. F. Houston 1920 E. T. Meredith	1921 H. C. Wallace	1923 H. C. Wallace 1924 H. M. Gore 1925 W. M. Jardine	1929 A. M. Hyde	1933 H. A. Wallace
Secretaries of Commerce				
1913 W. C. Redfield 1919 J. W. Alexander	1921 H. C. Hoover	1923 H. C. Hoover 1928 W. F. Whiting	1929 R. P. Lamont 1932 R. D. Chapin	1933 D. C. Roper
Secretaries of Labor				
1913 W. B. Wilson	1921 J. J. Davis	1923 J. J. Davis	1929 J. J. Davis 1930 W. N. Doak	1933 Frances Perkins

INDEX

A B C powers, 494
Abolitionists, 255 f.; and South, 258 f.; and Congress, 259 f.; and mails, 260 f.; and Kansas, 304 f., 308 f.; sectional, 318; in 1860, 339 and n. 2
Abraham, Plains of, 87 f.
Acadia, 77, 79
Adams, Abigail, 174
Adams, Charles Francis, minister to England, 394 f.
Adams, Charles Francis, Secretary of the Navy, 555, 560
Adams, John, on Otis, 95 n.; in Continental Congress, 103; and "independency," 111; and Declaration of Independence, 114; on peace commission, 127; minister to England, 129, 142; a Federalist, 162; vice president, 167; and X Y Z affair, 170; war with France, 171; appoints "midnight judges," 173; appoints John Marshall, 198; ideal of government, 217
Adams, John Quincy, in election of 1820, 201; Secretary of State, 204 f.; character, 210 f.; in election of 1824, 215 f.; as president, 218 f.; signs tariff of 1828, 224; opinion on Missouri Compromise, 253; and gag resolution, 260; at Ghent, 260 n. 1; tries to buy Texas, 270; compared with Hayes, 405
Adams, Samuel, on resistance to rulers, 94; writes circular letter, 99; defies Governor Hutchinson, 100; in Continental Congress, 103; proscribed by King George, 105; opposes Constitution, 142, 146
Adamson Act, 502 n.
Aguinaldo, 456 f.
Air service, 514, 548 f., 551
Alabama, 194
Alabama claims, 395, 396 n. 1
Alamance, 113 n.
Alamo, 268 f.
Alaska, 201, 206, 396 f., 434, 463, 491

Albany, 48, 117
Albany plan of union, 82 f.
Aldrich, Nelson W., 481
Aldrich-Vreeland Act, 488
Alexander II, Czar, 396
Alexander VI, Pope, 8
Alexander, J. W., 524 n.
Alexandria, 382
Alger, Secretary, 455 n.
Algonquins, 71
Alien Property Custodian, 524 and n. 1
Alien and Sedition Acts, 171 f., 175
Allen, Ethan, 110
Allenby, General, 522 n.
Allied War Council, 522 f.
Allison, Senator, 407
Altgeld, Governor, 442
Amendments: I–X, 152; XII, 150 n., 216; XIII, 378 f., 383; XIV, 385 and n. 3, 386 and n. 1, 387; XV, 389 n.; XVI, 152; XVII, 152; XVIII, 152, 533; XIX, 153
Amendments, Crittenden, 329
America, name, 17
American army in France, 520 f.
American Association, 103 f.
American Expeditionary Force (A. E. F.), 513
American Federation of Labor, 436, 533
American policy, 219 f., 220 n.
American Revolution, 45, 90 f., 116 f.
American system, 241, 421
Americanization, 505, 535
Amerigo Vespucci, 10
Amherst, General, 87 f.
Anaconda Policy, 362
Anderson, Robert, 331 f., 373
André, Major, 122
Andros, Edmund, 43 f.
Anglican Church, 93 f.
Annapolis, convention at, 141 f.
Anne, Queen, 247
Antietam, 354, 376
Anti-imperialism, 458 f.
Antimasons, 240

xxxi

INDEX

Anti-Nebraska men, 307
Antislavery societies, 255, 259 n.
Apia, 434
"Appeal of the Independent Democrats," 302
Appomattox, 370
Aragon, 15
Argonne Forest, 521 f.
Aristotle, 5 n.
Arizona, 398, 431 n. 1
Arkansas, 260 n. 3
Armada, 15
Armistice, 522 f.
Army, American, 512 f.
Arnold, Benedict, 112, 118, 122, 302
Arthur, Chester A., 405, 413
Articles of Confederation, 136 f., 227
Ashburton, Lord, 271
Ashley River, 47
Assistants, 38
Assumption, policy of, 160 f.
Astor, John Jacob, 266
Astoria, 266
Atkinson, Edward, 459 n. 2
Atlanta, 365 f., 368
Austerlitz, battle of, 180
Australia, 107
Aztecs, 13, 19

Babcock, O. E., 393
Bacon, Nathaniel, 33
Bacon, Roger, 5 n.
Bahamas, 5 f.
Bainbridge, Commodore, 179
Baker, Newton D., 486 n., 502
Balboa, 12 n., 13
Balfour, A. J., 512
Ballinger, R. A., 481
Balmaceda, 435
Baltimore, Lord, 54
Baltimore, Md., 45, 53, 186 f., 323, 336
Bank, National, first, 161 f.; second, 197 f., 231 f.
Barbados, 91 f.
Barbary States, 138
Barry, John, 179
Bates, Edward, 324
Bay Psalm Book, 66
Beauregard, General P. G. T., 333, 347
Beecher, Henry Ward, 334
Belgian Relief Commission, 515
Belgium, invasion of, 497, 498 n.
Belknap, Secretary, 393
Bell, John, 324 f.
Bellamy, Edward, 423 n. 1

Belleau Wood, 520
Bellomont, Earl of, 62, 81
Benson, Allan, 506, 518 n.
Benton, Thomas Hart, 213 f., 218, 234, 266 f.
Bering Sea, 434
Berkeley, Lord, 52
Berkeley, Sir William, 33
Berlin Decree, 180
Bethmann-Hollweg, Von, 498 n.
Beveridge, Albert J., 480
Biddle, Nicholas, 233
"Big Business," 480 f.
Bill of Rights, 152
Bimetallism, 448
Binney, Horace, 262
Birney, James G., 261, 274, 330 n.
Bismarck, Otto von, 434
Black, Jeremiah, 329
Black codes, 383 f.
Black Republicans, 322, 342
Black Warrior affair, 298
Bladensburg, 186
Blaine, James G., 400 and n.; in campaign of 1880, 408; Secretary of State, 410, 412, 427 f.; nominated for presidency in 1884, 413; and Cleveland, 413 f.; and campaign of 1888, 426 and n. 2; Pan-American policy, 433, 476; resignation and death, 435; character, 435 f.
Bland, Richard P., 446
Bland-Allison Act, 406 f.
"Bleeding Kansas," 310 f.
Bliss, General T. H., 525
Blockade, in Civil War, 349; in World War, 498
Bolshevists, 520 n., 532
Bond transactions of 1895, 438, 439 n.
Bonhomme Richard, 119
Bonus Bill, of 1816–1817, 196 f.; of 1922, 536; of 1924, 538
Boone, Daniel, 124, 155
Booth, J. Wilkes, 373
Borah, Senator William E., 527
Border ruffians, 309
Boston, settlement, 37 f.; migration, 40; *News Letter*, 66; punishment of, 102 f.; siege of, 110; evacuation of, 115
Boston Massacre, 100 f.
Boston Tea Party, 100 f.
Boulder Canyon dam, 543
"Boxer" rebellion, 462
Boy-Ed, Captain, 501

INDEX

Braddock's defeat, 84, 86, 117
Bradford, Governor William, 35 f.
Bragg, General Braxton, 361 f.
Brandywine, battle of, 118
Breckinridge, John C., 323, 325
Brest-Litovsk, Treaty of, 520 n.
Briand-Kellogg Peace Pact, 547 f.
Bristow, Secretary Benjamin H., 480
Brooklyn Heights, battle of, 116
Brooks, Preston, 311 and n.
Brougham, Lord, 221
Brown, General Jacob, 186
Brown, John, 310, 321, 322 n.
Brown, Walter F., 555
Brown University, 65
Bryan, William J., in campaign of 1896, 446 f.; of 1900, 458; of 1908, 479; of 1912, 484; Secretary of State, 486, 492; resignation, 486 n.; and preparedness, 502
Bryant, William C., 200
Buchanan, James, and Ostend Manifesto, 298; and South, 303 n.; election to presidency, 312; and Lecompton Constitution, 315; in 1860, 328 f.; and forts at Charleston, 332 f.
Buell, General Don Carlos, 352, 361
Buena Vista, battle of, 277
Buford, 532
Bulgaria, 522 n.
Bull Run, battle of, first, 347; second, 354
Bulwer, Sir Henry Lytton, 297
Bunau-Varilla, 475
Bunker Hill, battle of, 111
Burchard, Reverend S. D., 414 n. 2
Bureau of Labor, 424
Burgesses, House of, 31
Burgoyne, General John, 116 f.
Burke, Edmund, 91, 105, 107, 403
Burleson, Secretary A. S., 486
Burlingame, Anson, 405 n. 1
Burnet, Governor, 81
Burns, Anthony, 305
Burnside, General Ambrose E., 354
Burr, Aaron, 172 f., 179
Bustamante, President of Mexico, 268
Bute, Lord, 107
Butler, General Benj. F., 353, 393, 398
Butler, Senator A. P., 311
Byrd, Commander Richard E., 549 f.

Cabeza de Vaca, 14
Cabinet, 149 and n.
Cabot, John, 8 f., 18, 28, 70
Cahokia, 126
Calhoun, John C., and Bonus Bill, 196; Secretary of War, 204; character, 213; "Exposition and Protest," 224; and Union, 230; and Missouri Compromise, 254; and abolition, 259; and slavery demands, 260 f.; and Texan treaty, 272 f.; on Compromise of 1850, 289
Calhoun-Davis theory, 284 and n.
California, 276 f., 279, 286 f., 291
Calles, President of Mexico, 545
Calvert, Cecil, 46
Calvert, George, 45
Camden, battle of, 120
Cameron, Simon, 324
Canada, 94, 107, 482 n.
Canal, *see* Panama
Canning, George, 206
Cannon, Joseph G., 428 n., 482
Cantigny, 519 f.
Cape Cod, 34 f.
Caporetto, 522 n.
Caribbean, our interest in, 502 f.
Carnegie, Andrew, 426 n. 2, 478 and n.
Carolinas, 47 f., 80, 120
"Carpetbaggers," 384 n.
Carranza, President of Mexico, 493, 495
Carteret, 52
Cartier, Jacques, 18, 71 f.
Cass, Lewis, 284 f., 292
Castile, 15
Cathay, 6 f., 13, 19
Caucus, 150 n. 2, 215 n.
Cavaliers, 32
Cavendish, Thomas, 18
Cavite, battle of, 453
Cecil, Lord, 19
Céleron de Bienville, 81 f.
Census, of 1860, 330; of 1880, 404; of 1890, 429
Centennial Exposition of 1876, 402
Cervera, Admiral, 454, 456
Champlain, battle of Lake, 186
Champlain, Samuel de, 71, 74, 77
Chancellorsville, battle of, 354 and n. 2
Chapin, Roy D., 555 n.
Chapultepec, storming of, 278
Charles I of England, 32, 36, 38 f.
Charles II of England, 40, 42 f., 45 n. 2, 48 f., 53, 57 f., 92
Charles V, Emperor, 15
Charleston, S. C., settlement, 47; courts, 64 n.; tea at, 101; captured by Brit-

ish, 120; and nullification, 231; and abolition, 260; convention of 1860, 323; convention of secession, 326; forts in harbor, 332 f.; celebration at, 1865, 373
Charlestown, 111
Chase, Salmon P., on Compromise of 1850, 290; on Kansas, 302; in campaign of 1860, 324; Secretary of Treasury, 332 n. 2; finances Civil War, 359; aspirant for presidency, 366 f.; and Lincoln, 367 n. 1; Chief Justice, 367 n. 1; at Johnson trial, 392; and national banks, 398
Château-Thierry, 520
Chatham, Earl, *see* Pitt
Chattanooga, battle of, 361 f., 363 and n.
Chesapeake affair, 182
Chickamauga, battle of, 362 f.
Child Labor Law, 502 n.
Chile, 14, 435
China, 18, 76; treaty with, 405 and n.; relations with, 462 f.; six-power loan, 504 n.
Chinese laborers, 296
Choate, Rufus, 292
Chowan River, 47
Cibola, cities of, 14
Cincinnati, 196
Circular letter of Massachusetts, 99 f.
Civil rights, 385 n. 2 and 3
Civil Rights Bill, 385 n. 2
Civil service, reform of, 410 f.; under Taft, 482
Civil Service Commission, National, 466 and n.
Civil Service League, 411
Civil War, 344 f.; in West, 350 f.; financing, 355, 359 f.; political effects, 390 f.; economic results, 398
Claiborne, William, 46
Claiborne, W. C. C., 203
Clark, Champ, 484
Clark, George Rogers, 126 f., 136
Clark, Jonas, 105
Clay, Henry, and the "War Hawks," 183 f.; and Spanish America, 205 f.; character, 214; in election of 1824, 215 f.; and compromise tariff of 1833, 231; and Bank, 233; nominated for presidency in 1832, 240; in election of 1844, 273; on Texas, 273; and Omnibus Bill, 287 f.; the "great Pacificator," 292; death, 294 n. 1; compared with Blaine, 400 n.

Clayton Act of 1914, 490
Clayton-Bulwer Treaty, 297
Cleveland, Grover, career of, 413 f.; elected president, 414 and n.; as president, 418 f.; and Senate, 418 f.; and surplus, 420 f.; and tariff, 421 f.; and labor, 423 f.; defeated in 1888, 426; vetoes pension bills, 426; re-elected in 1892, 436; problems of second term, 437 f.; repeal of Sherman Silver Act, 438; bond transactions, 439 n.; and Chicago strike, 441 f.; and Hawaii, 443; repudiated by Democrats in 1896, 445 f.; and Roosevelt, 466 n.
Clinton, De Witt, 212
Clinton, Sir Henry, 116, 120, 122
Coahuila, 268
Coal strike of 1902, 469; of 1919, 531
Cockburn, Lord, 396
Colbert, 77 f.
Colby, Bainbridge, 524 n.
Cold Harbor, battle of, 365 and n. 2
Colfax, Schuyler, 399
Colombia, 474 f.
Colonial implements, 65
Colonies, table of, 58; in 18th century, 56 f.; relation to Parliament, 92 f.; signs of revolt, 94
Colonization societies, 255 n.
Colorado, mining, 403
Columbia, S. C., convention at, 230
Columbia College, 65
Columbia River, 24
Columbus, Christopher, 4 f.
Columbus, N. Mex., raid on, 494
"Commemoration Ode," 374 and n.
Commerce, in Washington's day, 155 f.; after Civil War, 403; in World War, 487, 501; in 1919, 541; in 1928, 554
Committees of Safety, 105
"Common Sense," 113
Compromise of 1850, 303, 308
Concessions, New Jersey, 52
Concord, Mass., 105
Confederacy, Southern, 326, 335, 372 f.
Conkling, Roscoe, 398, 405, 408, 410
Connecticut, 39 f., 44, 56
Conscientious objectors, 518
Constitution, Confederate, 327
Constitution, Federal, 143 f., 146 f., 227
Constitutional Union Party, 324 f.
Continental Congress, first, 103 f.; second, 104 f., 110 f., 128
Contraband, slaves as, 374 f.

INDEX

Conventions, national nominating, 240
Coolidge, Calvin, vice president, 534; becomes president, 538; elected in 1924, 540 f.; policies, 541 f.; declines to run in 1928, 550
Cooper, J. Fenimore, 200 f.
Cooper, Thomas, 223
Cooper Union, 322 f.
"Copperheads," 384
Corn Islands, 503
Cornell, Alonzo B., 405
Cornstalk, Chief, 125
Cornwallis, General, 117, 122 f., 135
Coronado, 14
Cortez, Hernando, 13
Cost of World War, 522
Cotton, John, 37 f.
Cotton, production of, 193 f., 222, 296; and South, 343; and Civil War, 349
Cotton gin, 180, 194 n., 248
Council for New England, 36, 38
Coureurs de bois, 73
Cowpens, battle of, 120
Cox, Governor James M., 534
Coxey's army, 440 f.
Crawford, W. H., 198, 212 f., 215 f.
Creasy, Sir Edward, 118
Crédit Mobilier, 398 f.
"Crime of 1873," 406 n.
"Crime against Kansas," 311
"Critical period" of American history, 135 f.
Crittenden, Senator J. J., 329
Cromwell, Oliver, 127
Crown Point, 81
Cuba, discovery, 6; cultivation, 15; and Panama Congress, 219; desire of South for, 297 f.; insurrection in, 451 f.; our intervention, 452; abandoned by Spain, 457; organized as republic, 460
Cullom Act, 425 f.
Cummings, H. S., 563
Cummins, Albert B., 480
Cummins Bill, 529
Cummins-Esch Bill, 529 f.
Curtis, Charles, 550 f., 557, 562
Curtis, Geo. William, 393 n. 1, 394, 413
Custer, General Geo. A., 405 n. 2
Czolgosz, 465

Dakota, territory, 398
Dale, Governor, 31
Dallas, Secretary, 198
Daniels, Josephus, 486, 502, 536
Danish West Indies, 503
"Dark horse," 273 and n.
Dartmouth College Case, 199 f., 211
Daugherty, Harry M., 535 n., 541 n.
Davenport, John, 40
Davis, James J., 535 n., 554
Davis, Jefferson, on Oregon, 283; Secretary of War, 303 n.; and Kansas, 311; and Douglas, 318; and Pierce, 320; president of Confederacy, 327, 336 n. 1, 347 n., 360, 370, 372 n., 381 n.
Davis Resolutions, 323
Davis, John W., 540
Dawes, Gen. Charles G., 540 and n. 2, 560
Dawes Bill, 430
Day, William R., 463 n. 1
Dayton, William L., 312
Debs, Eugene V., 441 f., 485, 534
Debt, of U. S., in Revolution, 128, 138; in 1789, 160 f.; after World War, 541, 557 f.
Decatur, Stephen, 179
Declaration of Independence, 113 f.
De Grasse, Admiral Count, 122
De Kalb, Baron, 120 n.
Delaware ratifies Constitution, 144
De la Warre, Lord, 30
De Lesseps, Ferdinand, 473
De Lôme, Señor, 452
Demarcation line, 8
Democracy, Jacksonian, 218, 239 f.
Democratic party, 240 and n., 241; split, 318, 323 f.
Democratic-Republicans, 153 f.
Denby, Edwin F., 535 n., 540 n. 3
Dern, George N., 563
De Soto, Hernando, 14
De Tocqueville, Alexis, 146, 268 n., 339
Detroit, 76, 81, 126, 181
Dewey, Admiral George, 453 f., 456 f., 462 n.
Dias, Bartholomew, 4
Dickinson, John, 64, 103, 111, 136, 142, 144
"Diedrich Knickerbocker," 49 f.
Dieppe, 70
Dingley Bill, 463
Dinwiddie, Governor Robert, 82 f.
District of Columbia, creation, 174 n.; slave trade in, 288
Dixie, 339 and n.
Doak, William N., 555 n.
"Dollar diplomacy," 504 and n.

INDEX

Dolliver, Senator, 480
Domain, national, 137
Donelson, Fort, 352 n.
Dongan, Governor Thomas, 78
Doniphan, Colonel A. W., 277
Dorchester, Lord, 166 n.
Douglas, Stephen A., and Compromise of 1850, 292; and Kansas-Nebraska Bill, 301 f.; mistake of, 308; and campaign of 1856, 312; and Lecompton, 315 f.; and Dred Scott case, 315; and Lincoln, 316; private fortune, 316 n. 2; and South, 318; and convention of 1860, 323; in election of 1860, 325; and Sumter, 334
Dover, N. H., 79
Draft riots, 355
Drake, Sir Francis, 18
Drawbacks, 59
Dred Scott case, 313 f., 320, 322
Duke of York, 50, 77
Duke's Laws, 50
Dumba, Constantin, 501
Dunning, William A., 393
Duquesne, Fort, 83, 86
Dustin, District Attorney, 419
Dutch on Hudson, 40, 48

Early, General Jubal A., 368
East India Company, 101 f.
Edmunds, George F., 413
Education in colonies, 65 f.
Edward VII, funeral of, 479
"Elastic clause," 153
El Caney, battle of, 455
Election, of 1796, 170; of 1800, 172 f.; of 1804, 179; of 1812, 212; of 1816, 189; of 1820, 201, 210; of 1824, 215 f.; of 1828, 225; of 1832, 231, 232 n.; of 1836, 242; of 1840, 243 f.; of 1844, 273; of 1848, 285; of 1852, 294, 305, 307 n.; of 1856, 312 f.; of 1860, 325; of 1864, 366 f.; of 1868, 389 n.; of 1872, 394; of 1876, 400 f.; of 1880, 409; of 1884, 414; of 1888, 426 f.; of 1890, 433; of 1892, 436 f.; of 1896, 448 f.; of 1900, 458; of 1904, 476 f.; of 1908, 479; of 1910, 482; of 1912, 484 f.; of 1916, 504 f.; of 1920, 534; of 1922, 538; of 1924, 540 f.; of 1926, 542; of 1928, 550 f.; of 1932, 562 f.
Electoral College, 150
Electoral Commission, 401
Elizabeth, Queen, 15, 18, 45 n. 1

Ellsworth, Oliver, 142
Emancipation Proclamation, 376 f.
"Embalmed beef," 455 n.
Embargo Act, 182
Emergency Fleet Corporation, 513 f., 524
Emerson, Ralph Waldo, 322
Emery, Samuel, 62
Endicott, John, 42
English colonies in America, 26 f., 67 f.; liberties, 90 f.
Entail, 63
Enumerated commodities, 59
Episcopal Church, 44
"Equalization fee," 544 and n.
"Era of good feeling," 197
Ericsson, Captain John, 350
Erie Canal, 52, 212, 219
Erskine, British minister, 182
Erving, minister to Spain, 205
Esch-Cummins Bill, 529 f.
Espérey, General d', 522 n.
Espionage Act, 518
Ethnology, Bureau of, 22
Everett, Edward, 303, 324, 334
Executive department, 149 f.
Expansion to Pacific, 280
Exploration, early English, 18 f.; French, 18, 57, 70 f., 75; Spanish, 11 f.
"Exposition and Protest," 224

Fairbanks, Charles W., 505
Fall, Albert B., 535 n., 540 n. 3
Fallen Timbers, battle of, 166 n.
Falmouth, 112
Faneuil Hall, 131
Farewell Address, Washington's, 169 f., 207
Farley, James A., 563
Farm Loan Act, 502 n.
Farm relief, 543 f.
Farmer-Labor party, 534
Farmers' Alliance, 436
Farragut, Admiral David, 351 f., 352 f., 367, 453
Federal Election Law, 431
Federal Farm Board, 556
Federal ratio, 148
Federal Reserve Act, 488 f.
Federal Reserve banks, 490
Federal Reserve Board, 490 and n.
"Federalist, The," 146, 159
Federalist party, 162 f., 164 f., 172
Ferdinand and Isabella, 4
Ferguson, Colonel, 120

INDEX

"Fifty-four forty or fight," 274 f.
Fillmore, Millard, 290 f.
Finæus, map of, 16
Fish, Hamilton, 397
Fiske, John, 8
Fletcher, Admiral, 494
Fleuri, Cardinal, 80
Florida, 12 f., 192, 201 f., 205, 214
Floyd, John B., 331
Foch, General Ferdinand, 520 f., 522
Fonseca Bay, 503
Food, conservation, 514 f.; control act, 515; production bill, 533
Foote, Commodore A. H., 352
Foote, Senator H. S., 229
Force Bill, of 1833, 231; of 1871, 393 n. 2; of 1890, 431, 433
Ford, Henry, 504
Forks of the Ohio, 83
Forts: Marion, 15; Orange, 48; Louisburg, 80; Duquesne, 83, 86; Le Bœuf, 33; Necessity, 83; William Henry, 86; Ticonderoga, 110 f.; Vancouver, 267; Sumter, 331 f.; Donelson, 352 n.; Henry, 352
"Forty-niners," 286
"Fourteen Points," Wilson's, 519
Fox, Charles James, 105, 107
Fox, George, 522
Franklin, Benjamin, citizen of Pennsylvania, 54; on colonies, 64; postmaster, 65; and Albany Plan, 83; and Stamp Act, 96; loyalty to England, 111; friend of Paine, 113; and Declaration of Independence, 114; envoy to France, 119; peace commissioner, 127; Articles of Confederation, 136; in Constitutional Convention, 142, 144
Frederick the Great, 83 n.
Fredericksburg, battle of, 354
Freedman's Bureau, 384 n., 385 n. 2
Freeport Doctrine, 317 f.
Free-Soilers, 285, 287, 330 n.
Frémont, John C., 282 and n. 2, 312, 330 n., 375
French Alliance, 118 f., 128
French colonies in America, 72 f.
French and Indian War, 83 n., 85
French Revolution, 164 f.
Friends, 52 and n., 259 and n.
Frontenac, Count, 77, 79
Fugitive Slave Law, of 1793, 250; of 1850, 288, 291 f., 305 and n., 307, 322, 328

Fundamental Orders of Connecticut, 39
Fur posts, 138, 165, 167

Gadsden Purchase, 280 n.
Gag resolutions, 259 f.
Gage, General Thomas, 105 f., 111
Gallatin, Albert, 175, 212
Garfield, Harry A., 531 f.
Garfield, James A., 399, 409 and n., 410 and n.
Garland, A. H., 418 n.
Garner, John N., 562
Garrison, Lindley A., 486, 502
Garrison, William Lloyd, 255 f., 373
Gates, General Horatio, 118, 120
Geary, governor of Kansas, 312
"Generall Historie" of Smith, 30
Genêt, Edmond, 166 f.
Geneva Tribunal, 396
George, Henry, 423 n. 1
George I, 48, 93
George II, 55
George III, 100, 102, 107 f., 111, 116 f., 123, 127, 241, 248 and n., 465
Georgia, 27 n., 55, 105, 120, 220
Germaine, Lord George, 117
German drives, 519 f.
Germantown, 54, 118, 248
Germany, and World War, 497; destroys American lives, 499; plots of, 501
Gerry, Elbridge, 146, 170
Gettysburg, battle of, 356 f., 358
Ghent, Treaty of, 187
Gibraltar, 119, 127
Giddings, Joshua R., 261
Gilbert, Sir Humphrey, 18, 45 n. 1
Gist, Christopher, 82
Gladstone, William E., 360
Glass, Carter, 488, 524 n.
Glass-Owen Bill, 488
"Glorious Revolution," 44
Goethals, George W., 492
Gold in California, 285 f.
Gold Democrats, 448 n. 2
Gold famine of 1893, 437 f.
"Golden pills," 107
Goliad, 269
Gondomar, Spanish minister, 31
Good, James W., 555
Gorges, Sir Fernando, 33 f., 41 f.
Gorman, Senator A. P., 440
Governors, conference of 1908, 472
"Grand Model," 47
"Grandfather clause," 431 n. 2

INDEX

Grangers, 404, 424 f.
Grant, General U. S., victories in West, 351 f.; at Vicksburg, 356 f.; at Chattanooga, 363 f.; commander of armies, 364; in Virginia, 364 f.; and Lee, 370 f.; attempted assassination, 373 n. 1; elected in 1868, 389 n.; as president, 392 f.; reëlected, 394; and West Indies, 397; in campaign of 1880, 408 f.; third-term agitation, 408 f.
Gray, Captain Robert, 226
Great Britain, and Oregon, 274 f.; and Venezuela, 444 f.
Great Meadows, battle of, 83
Greeley, Horace, 305, 333 f., 376, 394
Green, J. R., 108
Greenbacks, 407 f.
Greene, General Nathanael, 120
Green Mountain Boys, 110
Greenville, treaty of, 166 n.
Gregory, Thomas W., 486 n.
Grenville, George, 94 f., 98, 103, 129
Guadalupe-Hidalgo, treaty of, 279
Guadeloupe, 94
Guam, 457
Guiana, British, 444 f.
Guilford, battle of, 120
Guiteau, Charles, 410

Hague Conferences, 478 n. 1
Hague Tribunal, 478, 497
"Hail, Columbia," 171
Haiti, 6, 13 f., 219, 255, 503
Hale, Edward Everett, 356 n. 1
Hale, John P., 330 n.
Half Moon, 48
"Half-breeds," 408 and n. 2
Halleck, General H. W., 352 f.
Hamilton, Alexander, at Annapolis Convention, 142; at Constitutional Convention, 142; and ratification of Constitution, 145; career, 159; Secretary of Treasury, 159 f., 175; and Jay Treaty, 168; major general, 171; opposition to Alien and Sedition Laws, 172; death, 179
Hamilton, Colonel, at Detroit, 126 f.
Hamilton, governor of S. C., 231
Hamlin, Charles S., 490 n.
Hampton, Indian school, 22
Hampton Roads, 350, 369
Hancock, John, 102, 105, 146
Hancock, General W. S., 357, 409
Hanna, Marcus A., 447, 463 n., 477

Hanover, House of, 55, 92 f.
Harding, Senator Warren G., elected president, 534 ff.
Harlan, J. M., 426
Harpers Ferry, 321
Harriman, E. H., 480
Harrison, Benjamin, 426 and n. 2, 427 f., 435 f., 443
Harrison, William H., 183, 188, 192, 242 f., 270
Hartford, 39
Hartford Convention, 189
Harvard College, 61, 65, 94
Havana, 88
Hawaii, 443, 444 n.
Hawkins, John, 18
Hay, John, 462, 463 n. 1
Hay-Bunau-Varilla Treaty, 475
Hay-Herran Treaty, 474 f.
Hay-Pauncefote Treaty, 473, 491
Hayes, Rutherford B., 400, 404 f., 407
Haymarket riot, 423 n. 2
Hayne, Robert, 224, 229 f.
Hays, Will H., 535 n.
Helper, Hinton R., 342
Hendricks, T. A., 419
Henry, Patrick, 96 and n., 100, 103, 108, 110, 126, 146
Henry, Prince of Portugal, 4
Henry VII, 8, 10
Henry VIII, 34
Henry of Navarre, 18
Hepburn Bill, 477
Hessians, 112, 117
Hicks, governor of Maryland, 336
Hill, David B., 427, 436, 446
Hill, James J., 480
Hindenburg line, 521
Hitchcock, Senator G. M., 528
Holland, 35, 49
Holy Alliance, 207
Homestead Act, 398
Hood, General John B., 366, 368 f.
Hooker, General Joseph, 354, 363
Hooker, Thomas, 39
Hoover, Herbert C., Food Administrator, 514 f.; Secretary of Commerce, 535; elected president in 1928, 550 f.; visits Latin America, 554; inauguration and cabinet, 554 f.; renominated, 562
Hopkins, Stephen, 103
House, Colonel E. M., 525
"House divided against itself," 317
Houston, D. F., 486, 524 n.

INDEX

xxxix

Houston, General Sam, 269
Howe, General William, 115 f., 130
Hudson, Henry, 48 f., 72
Hudson Bay, 77, 79
Hudson's Bay Company, 267
Huerta, General Victoriano, 493 f.
Hughes, Charles E., 504 f., 535, 537, 546, 550, 563
Huguenots, 60
Hull, Cordell, 563
Hull, General William, 186
Hundred Associates of Canada, 70, 73
Hungary, 296 n. 2
Hunter, General David, 375
Hurley, Patrick J., 555 n.
Huron Indians, 74
Hutchinson, Governor Thomas, 97 and n., 100, 105
Hyde, Arthur M., 555

Ickes, Harold L., 563
Idaho, 430
Idealism, American, 535
Illinois, 194
"Immemorial rights," 106
Immigration, 296, 403 f.
"Impending Crisis, The," 342
Impressment, 167, 181 f.
Income tax, 152, 359, 440, 487, 543, 558
Independence Hall, 131
Independent Treasury, 236
Independents, 34
India House, 14
Indiana, 194
Indians, American, 19 f., 165 f., 430, 431 n. 1
Indies, 3, 7
Industrial Employers' Arbitration Act, 491
Industrial Revolution, 156
Industrial unrest, 530
Industries, of 1860, 340, 341 n. 1; after Civil War, 402 f.; of 1900, 464 f.
Initiative, 481 n.
Injunction, 441, 442 n.
Insular cases, 461
Insurance, war, 525
"Insurgents," 443, 480 f.
Interstate Commerce Act, 425 f.
"Intolerable Acts," 102 f., 107
Iowa, 301
Ireland, 296
Iroquois Indians, 53, 77, 80, 137
Irrigation policy, 472

Irving, Washington, 200
Isthmus of Panama, 297, 412, 462 (see Panama)
Italy, quarrel with U. S., 435; victories in World War, 522 n.
I. W. W., 518, 532 f.

Jackson, Andrew, at New Orleans, 187 f.; and Florida, 192, 203 f.; character, 214 f., 329 n. 1; and election of 1824, 215 f.; elected in 1828, 225; and tariff, 225, 229; as president, 227 f.; era of, 227; and bank, 231 f.; censured, 234; and Texas, 270; on Mexico, 279
Jackson, General T. J. ("Stonewall"), 348 n. 2, 354 and notes
Jackson, governor of Missouri, 335
Jackson, Mich., 307
Jamaica, 15, 91 f., 119, 127
James I, 27 f., 34, 49, 92
James II, 43 f., 50
Jamestown, 29, 32 f., 35, 247
Japan, 478, 508, 510
Jay, John, 111, 127 f., 142, 146, 167
Jay Treaty, 167 f.
Jefferson, Thomas, home at Monticello, 63; writes Declaration of Independence, 114; supports G. R. Clark, 126; minister to France, 138, 142; and public lands, 157; Secretary of State, 158 f.; leader of Democrats, 162 f.; resigns from cabinet, 169; vice president, 170; and election of 1800, 172 f.; and Kentucky Resolutions, 172; political views, 174 f.; president, 174 f.; death, 197; and Monroe Doctrine, 206; and manufactures, 221; birthday dinner of 1830, 230; and slavery, 248 n., 249; and Missouri Compromise, 254; master of Congress, 486
Jenckes, 410
Jersey, 52
Jerusalem, capture, 522 n.
"Jesuit Relations," 74
Jesuits, 64, 74
Joffre, Marshal, 512
Johnson, Andrew, 352 n. 2, 381 f., 385 f., 387 n., 392 and n., 471
Johnson, Governor Hiram, 484
Johnson governments, 383
Johnston, General Albert S., 352
Johnston, General Joseph E., 347, 365
Joliet, map, 72, 76 f.

INDEX

Jones, John Paul, 119
Judicial department, 151

Kalm, Peter, 67, 94
Kanawha, battle of, 124
Kansas, 14, 308 f., 310 f., 316 n., 346 n. 2
Kansas-Nebraska Bill, 301 f.
Kaskaskia, 126
Kearny, General Stephen W., 276 f.
Keith, governor of Pa., 81
Kellogg, Frank B., 547, 554
Kelly, Mrs. Florence, 517
Kendall, Amos, 260
Kent Island, 46
"Kentucke," 124
Kentucky, 250
Kentucky Resolutions, 172
Kerensky, 520 n.
Key, Francis Scott, 186
King, Rufus, 189, 212
King George's War, 80 and n.
King William's War, 80 and n.
King's College (Columbia), 65
"King's Friends," 107, 127
King's Mountain, battle of, 120 f.
Kitson, H. H., 104
Klondike, 463
Knights of Labor, 404
Know-Nothing party, 307 n. 2
Knox, John, 171
Knox, P. C., 482
Knoxville convention, 218
Kosciusko, 120 n.
Kossuth, 296 n. 2
Ku-Klux Klans, 388

Labor, in the thirties, 238 f.; under Cleveland, 423 f.
Labor party, 400
Labrador, 8 n., 10
Lachine, 18, 71
Lafayette, 120 n., 122 f., 133
La Follette, 480, 483 f., 504, 540 f.
Lake Champlain, 78
Lake Erie, 71; battle of, 186
Lamar, L. Q. C., 418 n.
Lamont, Robert P., 555
Lane, F. K., 486, 524 n.
Lansing, Robert, 486 n., 524 n., 528
La Salle, Robert Cavelier, Sieur de, 74 f.
Lavoisier, 66
Lausanne Conference, 561
Lawrence, A. A., 309 n.
Lawrence, Kans., 309 and n., 311
League of Nations, 525 f., 534, 560 f.

Lear, Tobias, 66, 249 n.
Le Bœuf, Fort, 83
Lecky, W. E. H., 108
Leclerc, General, 177
Lecompton Constitution, 315
Lee, General Charles, 116, 120
Lee, Daniel, 267
Lee, Jason, 267
Lee, Richard Henry, 113 f., 146
Lee, Robert E., 213; at Harpers Ferry, 322; and Confederacy, 336; on secession, 344; and North, 354, 356 f.; surrender of, 370 f.; after war, 370 n.
Leif the Lucky, 8 n.
Leisler, Jacob, 50 n.
Lenine, 520 n.
Lenox globe, 16
Lever Act, 531
Lewis, John L., 531
Lewis and Clark expedition, 177, 266
Lexington, battle of, 104 f., 111, 125, 130, 182, 336, 452
Leyden, 36
Liberal Republicans, 394
Liberator, The, 256 f.
Liberty Loans, 517
Liberty party, 261, 285, 330 n.
Liliuokalani, Queen, 443
Lincoln, Abraham, and Jackson, 228; and Mrs. Stowe, 305 n.; and Douglas, 316 f.; Cooper Union speech, 322; nominations, 324, 367; election in 1860, 325; in 1864, 368; and South, 327, 328 n.; inaugural address, 331 f.; and Fort Sumter, 333; call for troops, 334; and capital, 336 f.; and war, 346; and *Trent* affair, 349; and Meade, 358 n. 2; on freeing of the Mississippi, 358; on war finance, 359; at Hampton Roads, 369; in Richmond, 370; assassination of, 373; on emancipation, 375 f.; to Greeley, 376 n.; plan of reconstruction, 382 and n.; on negro suffrage, 387 n.
Lind, Governor John, 493
Lindbergh, Colonel Charles A., 545 and n., 549
Lisbon, 7, 13
Literature, American, 200 f.
Little Big Horn, battle of, 405 n 2
Livingston, R. R., 114, 176 f.
Lloyd George, 519, 526
Locke, John, 47
Lodge, Senator H. C., 527 f.

INDEX

xli

Log Cabin campaign, 243 f.
London Company, 27, 33
London Naval Treaty, 558 f.
Lopez, Narcisso, 298
Louis XIV, 54, 60, 73 f., 82
Louisburg fort, 80, 86
Louisiana, 76, 80, 194, 203, 250, 265
Louisiana Purchase, 176 and n., 301
Lovejoy, Elijah, 261
Lowell, James Russell, 280, 330, 374 n., 393 n. 1
Loyalists (see Tories), 120
Lundy, Benjamin, 255 f.
Lusitania torpedoed, 498 f.
Luzon, 457
Lyons, Captain, 335
Lyons, Lord, 349
Lytton Commission, 560

McAdoo, W. G., 486, 516, 524 n., 534, 540
McClellan, General George B., 348 and n., 353, 354, 367 and n.
McCormick, Cyrus, 237
McCoy, General Frank R., 547, 560
McCulloch vs. Maryland, 199, 233
MacDonough, Thomas, 186
McDowell, General Irvin, 347
McHenry, Fort, 186
MacKaye, Percy, 492
McKinley, William, and tariff, 432 f.; election of, 446 f., 449; and Cuba, 452; and Philippines, 458 f.; assassinated, 465
McNary-Haugen bill, 541, 544
Macon's bill, 183
McPherson, General, 364
McReynolds, James M., 486
Madero, 493
Madison, James, 141; in Constitutional Convention, 142, 144; and "The Federalist," 146; and Virginia Resolutions, 172; as president, 182 f.; and internal improvements, 196; relations with Spain, 203 f.
Magellan, Ferdinand, 12 f.
Magna Carta, 68
Maine, 42, 45, 252, 253 n.
Maine, the, 452
Malvern Hill, battle of, 348
Man Power Act, 524
Manassas, battle of, 347
Manhattan, 48
"Manifest destiny," 459, 463
Manila, 88, 453 f., 456

March to the sea, Sherman's, 369 n.
Marcy, William M., 240, 298, 303 n.
Mare clausum, 434
Maritime science, 4
Marlborough, duke of, 79
Marne, battle of, 520
Marquette, Père, 76 f.
Marshall, John, 170, 172, 179, 198 f.
Martin, Senator T. S., 524 n.
Marye's Heights, battle of, 354
Maryland, 45 f., 136 f., 336
Mason, George, 142
Mason, John, 41 f.
Mason, John Y., 298, 349, 360 n.
Mason and Dixon's line, 53 n., 339 and n.
Massachusetts Bay Colony, 36 f., 42 f., 45, 102 f.
Max, Prince, of Baden, 522
Maximilian, Archduke, 395
Mayflower, 34 f., 39 n. 1
Mayo, Admiral, 494
Meade, General George, 356 f., 358 n. 2
Mecklenburg declaration, 113 n.
Mellon, Andrew W., 535 f., 538, 554
Mercantile theory of commerce, 57, 91
Mercator, 11 n., 17
Meredith, E. T., 524 n.
"Merit system," 411
Mexico, 13 f., 66, 267 f., 272, 275 f., 493 f.; war with, 276, 277 f., 279
Middle colonies, 64 f.
"Middle passage," 247 f.
"Midnight judges," 173
Milan Decree, 180
Miles, General Nelson A., 455 n., 456
Mills, Ogden L., 555 n.
Mills, Roger Q., 422
Miquelon, 88
Missionary Ridge, battle of, 363 and n.
Mississippi, 194
Mississippi River, 14, 70 f., 74, 543
Missouri, 194, 250 and n., 335
Missouri Compromise, 250 f., 252 f., 283, 302, 320, 329
Mitchell, William D., 554
Mobile, 203, 368
Mohawk valley, 52
Monitor, 349 f.
Monmouth, battle of, 120
Monroe, James, 176, 189, 197, 201, 253
Monroe Doctrine, 206 f., 210, 219, 395, 444 f., 493, 547
Montana, 430
Montcalm, General, 87 f.

Monterey, Calif., 286
Monterey, Mexico, 277
Montezuma, 13
Montgomery, Ala., 327, 333, 346
Montgomery, Richard, 112
Monticello, 63
Montreal, 18, 71, 88
Moore, John B., 499 n.
Morgan, General, 118, 120
Morgan, J. P., 438 f., 488
Mormons, 431 n. 1
Morris, Gouverneur, 138, 142, 174
Morris, Robert, 142
Morrow, Dwight W., 545, 560
Mount Vernon, convention at, 141, 163
"Muck-raking," 481
Mugwumps, 412 f.
Münster's map, 17
Murfreesboro, battle of, 361
Muscle Shoals, 542

Napoleon Bonaparte, 79, 88, 171, 175 f., 180 f., 184, 187, 203, 220
Napoleon III, 343, 360 n., 395
Nashville, battle of, 369
Nashville Convention, 292
National banks, 359 f.
National Defense Act, 502
Naturalization Act, 171
Navigation Acts, 57 f., 91 f., 94 f., 102, 106
Navy, American, 171, 185 f., 428 f., 434, 513 f., 548
Nebraska, 301 f.
Negro problem, 535
Nelson, Admiral, 180
Netherlands, 78
Neutrality in World War, 510
Nevada, 398, 403, 407
New Amsterdam, 41, 64
Newcastle, 53 n.
New England, 33 f., 61 f., 188 f., 200, 217, 223 f., 247 f.
New England Confederation, 42
New England Emigrant Aid Society, 309
Newfoundland, 18, 71, 79
New France, 70 f., 79 f., 82
"New Freedom, The," 486
New Granada, 297
New Hampshire, 42
New Haven, 40 f.
New Jersey, 52 f.
New Jersey plan, 142 f.
New Mexico, 276 f., 279, 431 n. 1

New Netherland, 42, 48 f., 50, 97
New Orleans, 76, 88, 138, 168, 176, 187 f., 214, 298, 352, 435
Newport, 139 and n.
Newspapers, colonial, 66 f.
New York, 12, 48 f., 77, 132, 137
Niagara, 81, 86
Nicaragua, 473 f., 503, 545 f.
Nicholson, Governor, of N. Y., 50
Nicolet, Jean, 74
Nobel, Alfred, 478 n. 2
Nonintercourse Act, 167, 182
North, resources in Civil War, 340 f.
North, Lord, 100, 107, 118, 127
North Carolina, 19, 47, 113 n., 145
North Dakota, 430
Northwest Ordinance, 140 f.
Northwest Territory, 126, 252
"Notes on Virginia," 249
Nullification, 229 f.

Obiter dictum, 314 n. 2
Ogden, 399
Oglethorpe, James, 55, 81
Ohio, 70 f., 250
Ohio Company, 82, 157
Ohio Valley, 81 f., 83
Oklahoma, 431 n. 1
Old Dominion, 32
Old South Church, 131
Oliver, 97
Olney, Richard, 444
Omnibus Bill, 287 f.
"Open door" in China, 463 n. 1
Orders in Council, 180 f.
Oregon, 177, 201, 266 f., 271 f., 274, 283, 401 and n.
Oregon, the, 454 n.
Oriskany, battle of, 117
Orlando, Signor, 526
Orleans, territory of, 178 n.
Ostend Manifesto, 303 n., 312
Oswego, 81
Otis, General, 457
Otis, James, 59, 95 n., 96 f., 102
Owen, Senator, 488

Pacific Ocean, 12
Pacific railways, 398 f.
Pacifism, 500 f., 518
Paine, Thomas, 113
Pakenham, British general, 187 f.
Palma, Estrada, 460
Palmer, A. Mitchell, 524 n., 534
Palmer, John M., 448 n. 2

INDEX

Palo Alto, battle of, 276
Palos, 4
Panama, 13; revolution in, 474 f.
Panama Canal, 472 f., 475, 491, 492
Panama Congress, 219
Pan-Americanism, 433, 465, 476 n. 2, 546
Panic, of 1837, 235, 236 n.; of 1857, 316 n. 2; of 1873, 399 f.; of 1929, 557 f.
Paris, Peace of: 1763, 88 f.; 1783, 127 f.; 1899, 457; 1919, 525
Parker, Alton B., 477
Parker, Captain John, 104 f.
Parker, Theodore, 322 n.
Parliament, authority of, in colonies, 90 f., 106 f.
"Parsons' Cause," 96 n.
Parties, political, 162 f., 240 and n.
Paternalism, French, 73
Paterson, William, of New Jersey, 143
Patrons of Husbandry, 404
Patroons, 48
Patterson, General, 347
Payne, John B., 524 n.
Payne-Aldrich Act, 481
Peking, relief of, 462
Pemberton, General, 357 f.
Pendleton, Louis, 342 n.
Pendleton Act, 411
Peninsular campaign, 348
Penn, William, 52 f.
Pennsylvania, 50, 52 f.
Pensacola, 203 f.
Pensions, 426 and n. 3, 428 f.
Pepperrell, Colonel, 80
Pequot Indians, 40
Percy, Lord, 105
Perkins, Frances, 563 f.
Perry, Captain O. H., 186
Perryville, battle of, 361
Pershing, General J. J., 513, 520
Personal Liberty Acts, 305
Peru, 14 f.
Petersburg, 370
Philadelphia, 54, 101, 103, 110, 119, 311 f., 402
Philip, King, 18, 36 and n. 1
Philip II, 15
Philippine Islands, 12, 453 f., 457 f., 459 f., 491
Piave, battle of, 522 n.
Pickens, Governor, of South Carolina, 333
Pickett's charge, 357

Pierce, Franklin, 293 f., 302, 303 n., 304, 311, 334
Pilgrim Fathers, 34 f., 71, 211
Pinckney, C. C., 170, 179
Pinckney, Thomas, 168
Pinzon, Martin, 6
Pitcairn, Major, 104 f.
Pitt, William (Earl of Chatham), 86, 93, 99, 107, 129
Pittsburgh, 87, 308, 406
Pizarro, 14
Platt, Orville C., 460 n.
Platt, Thomas, 405, 410 and n.
Plattsburg, camp at, 502
Plumb plan, 529
Plymouth Colony, 35 f.
Plymouth Company, 27, 33, 49
Poinsett, 231
Polk, James K., 273 f., 278 f., 284, 298
Ponce de Leon, 13
Pontiac, Chief, 95, 124
Pope, General John, 352 f.
Pope Benedict XV, 518
Popular sovereignty, 284, 311
Populists, 436
Port Hudson, 353, 358
Portland, 112
Porto Rico, 13, 15, 219, 456 f., 461, 503
Portsmouth, Treaty of, 478
Portuguese explorers, 3 f.
Post office, 64 f., 93
Pottawatomie, 310 f., 322 n.
Preble, Captain, 179
Pre-Columbian voyages, 8 n.
Preparedness, 502
President, powers of, 150 f.
Presidential Succession Act, 419 f.
Prigg vs. Pennsylvania, 293
Primogeniture, 63
Princeton College, 65
Printing press, 66 f.
Priority orders, 516
Proclamation Line of 1763, 123
Proclamation of neutrality of 1793, 165
Products of United States, 467
Progressive party, 483 f., 504
Prohibition, 152, 533
Proprietary colonies, 45 f.
Proprietary grants, map, 51
Protestants, 26 f., 46
Providence, 38
Ptolemy, 4, 11 n.
Public lands, 157, 200, 229, 235
Pueblos, 19

INDEX

Pujo Committee, 488
Pulaski, Count, 120 n.
Pullman strike, 441
Pure Food and Drugs Act, 477
Puritans, 36 n. 1, 61 f.

Quakers, 42, 52
Quebec, 71, 87 f., 112
Queen Anne's War, 80 n.
Quincy, Josiah, 265
Quitrents, 45

Railroads, 220 n., 237 f., 294 f., 398 f., 405 f., 424 f., 516, 528 f., 530
Raleigh, Sir Walter, 19, 34, 45 n. 1
Randolph, Edmund, 113, 142, 169
Randolph, Sir Edward, 43 and n.
Randolph, John, 184, 222, 249 and n.
Raphael, 11
"Rebel Flag Order," 427 and n.
Recall, 481 n.
Reciprocity, 433, 482 n.
Reconcentration camps, 451
Reconstruction, 381 f.
Reconstruction acts, 386 and n. 3
Reconstruction governments, 387, 388 n.
Reconstruction Finance Corporation, 558
Redfield, William C., 486, 524 n.
"Reds," 532 f.
Reed, Thomas B., 428 f.
Referendum, 481 n.
Reign of Terror, 165
Removal of deposits, 233 f.
Republican party, 307, 324 f.
Resaca da la Palma, battle of, 276
Resumption of specie payments, 407 f.
Revenues, national, in 1932, 558
Revere, Paul, 105, 130
Rhode Island, 38 f., 42, 56, 142, 145
Rhodes, James F., 304
Richelieu, Cardinal, 70, 73
Richmond, 346, 370
Rio Grande, 275 f.
Rio Janeiro, 476 n.
Ripon, Wisconsin, 307 n. 3
Rip van Winkle, 50
Roanoke, 19
Robertson, J., 124
Robinson, Charles, 310
"Rock of Chickamauga," 363
Rockingham, Lord, 98 f.
Roman Empire, 157
Roper, Daniel C., 563

Roosevelt, Franklin D., 554; elected president, 563; inauguration and cabinet, 563 f.; powers conferred upon, 564
Roosevelt, Theodore, on American Revolution, 94; and Jackson, 228; on civil service, 411; and "Rough Riders," 455; president, 465; career to 1901, 466; ideals, 468 f.; and corporations, 469; and labor, 470; and conservation, 471; and Panama, 475 n. 1; and Monroe Doctrine, 476; reëlected, 477; foreign influence, 478; ex-president, 479 f.; candidate in 1912, 483 f.; and the World War, 504 f.
Root, Elihu, 459 n. 2, 476 n. 1
Rosecrans, General, 361 f.
"Rough Riders," 455
Rules Committee, 428 n.
Rush, Richard, 206
Russell, Lord John, 395 f., 446
Russia, 396, 478 n. 1, 520 n.
Rutledge, John, 103

St. Augustine, 15
St. Clair, General Arthur, 166 n., 183
St. Croix, 504
St. John, island, 503
St. Lawrence River, 18, 70 f.
St. Leger, 117
St. Lusson, 74
St. Marks, 204
St. Marys, 46
St. Mihiel, 521
St. Pierre, 88
St. Thomas, 503
Salem, 38, 43, 105
Salisbury, Lord, 434, 444 f.
Samoa, 433 f.
Sampson, Admiral W. T., 454 f.
Sandford, John F., 313
San Diego, 277
Sandys, Sir Edwin, 31
San Ildefonso, 175 f., 178
San Jacinto, battle of, 269, 274 f.
San Juan Hill, battle of, 455
San Salvador, 16
Santa Anna, 269 f., 277
Santa Fé, 277
Santiago, battle of, 455 f.
Santo Domingo, 91 f., 397, 476, 503
Saratoga, 117 f.
Savannah, 120 and n., 369
"Scalawags," 384 n.

INDEX

Schenectady, 79
Schley, Admiral W. S., 454 n. 1, 456
Schofield, General J. M., 364
Schurman, Jacob G., 459 n. 1
Schurz, Carl, 394
Scioto Company, 157
Scotch-Irish, 60, 155
Scott, General Winfield, 277 f., 294, 307 n. 1, 346
Seal fisheries, 434
Secession, threats of, 312; ordinance of, 325 f.; right of, 330 f.; border states, 335
Selective Service Act, 512
Seminole Indians, 203 f.
Senatorial courtesy, 152
Separatists, 34 f.
Serajevo, 497
Serbia, 497
Seven Years' War, 83 n.
Seventh-of-March speech, 289 f.
Sevier, John, 124, 155
Seville, 14
Seward, William H., on Compromise of 1850, 290; and Kansas-Nebraska Act, 302 f.; and Dred Scott case, 314; and convention of 1860, 324 and n.; and *Trent* affair, 349; on victories, 368; at Hampton Roads, 369; attempted assassination, 371 n. 1; and emancipation, 376; and Maximilian, 395; purchases Alaska, 396 f.
Shafter, General W. R., 455 f.
Shakespeare, 32
Sharpsburg, battle of, 354
Shays's rebellion, 139
Shelburne, Lord, 127
Shenandoah Valley, 60, 81, 368
Shepherd, William R., 476 n. 2
Sheridan, General Philip H., 363 and n., 368, 395
Sherman, John, Secretary of Treasury, 408; president pro tempore of Senate, 420; in convention of 1888, 426; and Harrison, 427; Secretary of State, 463
Sherman, Roger, 103, 114, 142, 144
Sherman, General William T., at Vicksburg, 356; on war, 362; coöperates with Grant, 364; takes Atlanta, 366; march to sea, 368
Sherman Anti-Trust Act, 433 n., 490
Sherman Silver Purchase Act, 432, 437 f.
Shiloh, battle of, 352

Ship Registry Act, 491
Shirley, Governor, 82
Silver, free, 406 and n., 437 f., 446 f., 447 n.
Sinclair, Upton, 518
Sitting Bull, Chief, 505 n. 2
Slave labor, 296 n. 1
Slave trade, encouraged by English kings, 93; in Constitution, 144; in eighteenth century, 247 f.; prohibition, 249; reopened, 320 n., 321
Slavery, brought to Virginia, 31; excluded from Georgia, 55; in the Constitution, 144; amendments, 152; ominous in 1837, 244; in colonies, 247 f.; petitions for abolition of, 249; early favorable legislation, 250; in District of Columbia, 250; extension of, 252; and Missouri Compromise, 253; moral issue, 254 f.; restrictive laws, 257; apologies for, 261 f.; abolished in West Indies, 262; and West, 266; and Oregon, 283; in Mexican cession, 283 f.; status in 1850, 291; status in 1844–1854, 306; and Congress, 317 f.; fixed on South, 320; and Civil War, 330, 374; nature, 342; abolished in territories, 376
Slidell, John, 275, 343, 349, 360 n.
Sloat, Commodore John D., 276
Smith, Governor Alfred E., 540, 550 f., 562
Smith, Caleb, 324
Smith, John, 29 f., 34
Smith-Lever Act, 491
Socialists, 506, 518 and n., 540, 563
"Solid South," 409, 479, 554
"Soo" (Sault Sainte Marie), 430
Soulé, Pierre, 298
South, resources, 340 f.; disappointed hopes in 1861, 343 f.; progress after war, 429
South America, our relations with, 476, 554
South Carolina, 47; and nullification, 230 f.; secession of, 326 and n.
South Dakota, 430
South River, 49
South Sea, 12 n.
Southampton, Earl of, 32
Southampton massacre, 256 f.
Spain, possessions in 1815, 201; in America, 205 f.
Spanish boundary of 1819, 205 n.

INDEX

Spanish explorers, 13 f.; government in America, 14 f.
Spanish Succession, War of the, 79 n.
Spanish-American War, 452 f., 461 f.
Spargo, John, 518 n.
Speaker of House, 152, 428 and n.
Specie Circular, 235
Specie payments, 407 f.
Spoils system, 237
Squatter sovereignty, 284, 302
"Stalwarts," 408 and n. 2, 411
Stamp Act, 95 f., 98
Stamp Act Congress, 97
Stanton, Edwin M., 329, 348 n. 1, 374
"Star-Spangled Banner," 186
"Starving time" in Virginia, 30
State banks, 178
States, powers of, 148 f.
Stephens, Alexander H., 323, 327 f., 346, 369
Steuben, Baron von, 120 n.
Stevens, John L., 443
Stevens, Thaddeus, 385 and n. 1, 398
Stimson, Colonel Henry L., 545, 555, 560
Stokes, J. G. Phelps, 518 n.
Stone, Harlan F., 541 n.
Stowe, Harriet Beecher, 305 n.
Strict construction, 153
Strikes, under Cleveland, 423 and n. 2; coal, of 1919, 531
Stuart kings, 27 f., 78
Students' Army Training Corps (S. A. T. C.), 524
Stuyvesant, Peter, 48 f., 53
Submarines, 498, 507 f., 511 f.
Suez Canal, 475 n. 2
Suffrage, negro, 386 f., 431 n. 2; woman, 533
Sugar and Molasses Act, 91, 95
Sumner, Charles, and abolition, 258; assaulted, 311 and n.; and *Trent* affair, 349 and n.; character, 398, 402
Sumter, Fort, 331 f.
Supreme Council of Allies, 526
Supreme Court, 148, 151, 198 f., 233, 314, 317, 533
Surplus, in Cleveland's day, 420 f.; in Coolidge's day, 543
Susquehannock Indians, 77
Sussex pledge, 499 f.
Swanson, Claude A., 563
Sweden, colonies, 49 and n., 70
Symmes company, 157

Taft, William H., and Philippines, 459 f.; as president, 479 f.; in campaign of 1912, 484 f.; Chief Justice, 555
Talleyrand, Prince, 170, 176
Tallmadge, James, 251, 253
Tampico, 493
Taney, Roger B., 234 and n., 242, 314, 385 n. 3
Tariff, of 1789, 161 f.; of 1816, 221, 223; of 1824, 221; of 1828, 222 f.; of 1846, 313; of 1883, 415; and Cleveland, 421 f.; of 1890, 432 f.; in dependencies, 461; of 1897, 463; of 1909, 481; of 1913, 487; of 1922, 536; of 1929, 556; of 1930, 557
Taxation without representation, 94 f.
Taylor, General Zachary, at Rio Grande, 275; nominated for presidency, 284; election of, 285; death of, 290; at North, 341 n. 2
Teapot Dome, 540 n. 3
Tecumseh, Chief, 192
Teller, Henry M., 448 n. 1
Teller Resolution, 452
Ten per cent plan, 382
Tennessee, 250, 352 n. 2, 386
Tenure of Office Act, 392, 419
Texas, Spanish exploration of, 13; La Salle in, 76 n.; surrendered to Spain, 214 n.; expansion to, 265; in 1830, 267 f.; annexation of, 269 f., 274, 280; boundaries, 288; in Compromise of 1850, 288, 291
Thacher, Thomas, 66
Thames, battle of the, 186
Thayer, Eli, 308 f.
Thomas, General G. H., 362 f., 364, 369
Thomas, Senator, 253
Thompson, Secretary, 331
Three Lower Counties, 53
Three Rivers, 73
Thwaites, R. G., 74
Ticonderoga, 86
Tilden, Samuel J., 400
Tippecanoe, battle of, 183, 192, 244
Toleration Act, 46
Toombs, Robert, 287
Topeka Convention, 309
Toral, General, 455 f.
Tordesillas Treaty, 8
Tories (*see* Loyalists), 98 n., 111, 115, 118, 125, 129 f.
Toscanelli, 5
Townshend Acts, 99 f., 103, 129

Trade routes, early, 3
Trafalgar, battle of, 180
Transportation in 1789, 156 f.
Transportation Act of 1920, 530
Treaty, Tordesillas, 8; Utrecht, 60, 79; Paris (1763), 88; French (1778), 118 f., 136, 171; Paris (1783), 129; Greenville, 166 n.; Jay, 167 f.; Pinckney, 168; French (1800), 171; San Ildefonso, 175 f.; Ghent, 187; Webster-Ashburton, 271; Guadalupe-Hidalgo, 279; Gadsden, 294; Clayton-Bulwer, 297; Burlingame, 405 n. 1; Hay-Pauncefote, 473; Hay-Herran, 474; Hay-Bunau-Varilla, 475; Portsmouth, 478; Brest-Litovsk, 520 n.; Versailles, 527 f., 534
Trent affair, 349
Trenton, battle of, 117
Trevelyan, George O., 108
"Trewe Relaycion," 30
Tripoli, 179
Trist, Nicholas, 278 f.
Trotzky, 520 n.
Troup, Governor, 220
Trusts, 422 f., 464
Tryon, Governor, 112
Turks, 3 f.
Turner, Nat, 256 n.
Tuscania, 514
Tweed, William M. ("Boss"), 393
Tyler, John, 270, 274

"Uncle Tom's Cabin," 305 n.
"Unconditional Surrender" Grant, 352 n. 1
"Underground railroad," 292 f.
Underwood tariff, 487
Union Pacific Railroad, 398 f.
"Unwritten laws" of Constitution, 151 f.
Upshur, A. P., 271
Utah, 431 n. 1
Utrecht, treaty of, 60, 79

Vagrancy laws, 383
Vallandigham, Clement, 355, 356 n.
Valley Forge, 118, 130
Valparaiso, 435
Van Buren, Martin, in Jackson's cabinet, 228; succeeds Jackson, 236; in election of 1836, 242; and Texas, 270; Free-Soil candidate, 285, 330 n.
Vanderbilt, Cornelius, 297, 480
Vasco da Gama, 7

Venango, Fort, 83
Venezuela, 444 f.
Vera Cruz, 277, 494
Vergennes, 119, 128, 130, 140 n.
Vermont, 250
Verrazano, 18, 71
Vicksburg, convention at, 320; capture of, 356 f.; siege of, 358 n. 1; effect of fall of, 360; trenches of, 389
Victoria, Queen, 343
Victory Loan, 517 n.
Villa, General, 494
Vincennes, 126 f.
Virgin Islands, 504
Virginia, name of, 19; map, 28; settlement, 27 f.; courts, 64 n.; Civil War in, 345 f., 364 f.
Virginia plan, 142 f.
Virginia resolutions, 172
Virginia, the, 349 f.
Virginius affair, 397 and n.
Viviani, 512
Von Diederich, Admiral, 462 n.
Von Papen, Captain, 501

Wabash case, 425
Wade, Benjamin, 303
Wade-Davis Bill, 382 n.
Waldseemüller, Martin, 10
Walker, Robert J., 315, 334
Walker tariff, 313
Wallace, Henry A., 563
Walling, W. E., 518 n.
Walpole, Robert, 60, 80, 92 f.
Walsh, Thomas J., 563
War debts, 561 f.
"War Hawks," 183 f.
War Labor Board, 530
War Revenue Act, of 1917, 517; of 1918, 517
War Risk Bureau, 525
War zone, 506
Ward of Rhode Island, 112
Warren, General Joseph, 102
Warville, Brissot de, 139 n.
Washburne, E. B., 364
Washington, George, 55, 66; in French and Indian War, 83 f.; in House of Burgesses, 100; in Continental Congress, 103; commanding army, 110 f.; on Paine's "Common Sense," 113; proclaims Declaration of Independence to army, 115; conduct of Revolution, 116 f.; and Tories, 130; retirement from war, 130, 132;

INDEX

thanked by Congress, 140; proposes stronger government, 141; president of Constitutional Convention, 142; president of United States, 150; inauguration, 157 f.; policies, 157 f.; reëlected, 164; neutrality, 165 f.; Farewell Address, 169; abuse of, 170; commander, 171; and Monroe Doctrine, 207; and slavery, 249 and n.
Washington Conference, 534
Washington, city of, 174, 186, 336 f.
Washington, state, 430, 533
Watauga, battle on the, 124
"Watchful waiting," 493
Waterloo, 79
Wayne, General Anthony, 166 n.
Wealth, national, 403, 534
Weaver, James B., 436
Webster, Daniel, on Northwest Ordinance, 140; on Hamilton, 159 f.; on growth of West, 194; character of, 211; reply to Hayne, 229 f.; and abolition, 258; Ashburton treaty, 271; and Texas, 271; and Tyler, 271; on Compromise of 1850, 289 f., 292; death, 294 n.; Hülsemann letter, 296 n. 2; and Spain, 298; Secretary of State, 271, 296 n., 298
West, in Revolutionary War, 123 f.; growth after 1815, 191 f., 194; routes to, 195; pioneers, 217; expansion to, 264 f., 282
West Florida, 203
West India Company, Dutch, 48
West Indies, 91 f., 94, 123, 128, 138, 165 f., 180, 262
West Virginia, 344
Wethersfield, 39
Weyler, General Valeriano, 451
Wheeler, General Joseph, 463
Wheeler, Senator Burton K., 540
Whig party, 98 n., 240 and notes 1 and 2, 241 f., 305 f.
Whigs, English, 241
Whisky Rebellion, 170 and n.
White, H. M., 525
Whitman, Marcus, 267
Whitman, Walt, 373 n. 2
Whitney, Eli, 193, 194 n., 248
Whittier, John G., 309 n., 313
Wickersham, George W., 482
Wilbur, Curtis D., 541 n., 548
Wilbur, Ray Lyman, 555
Wildcat banks, 235 and n., 236
Wilderness campaign, 364 f.

Wilkes, Captain, 349
Wilkinson, General James, 179
William III, 44 f., 50, 57 n., 60, 78 and n.
Williams, Roger, 38 f., 47, 54
Williamsburg, 65
Wilmot Proviso, 283
Wilson, Henry L., 493
Wilson, James, 142
Wilson, William B., 486
Wilson, William L., 439
Wilson, Woodrow, 327 n.; and Porto Rico, 461; election of, 484 f.; policies, 485 f.; governor of New Jersey, 485 n.; and Panama, 491; and Mexico, 493 f.; and preparedness, 502; reëlection, 505 f.; on peace, 506; breaks with Germany, 506 f.; recommends war, 508; on war aims, 510 f.; to Pope, 518 f.; invites peace, 522; on armistice, 523; goes to Paris, 525; supports League of Nations, 526; illness, 527 f.; on law and order, 533; recommends woman suffrage, 534
Wilson-Gorman Act, 439
Winchester, battle of, 368
Windsor, 39
Winthrop, Governor John, 37 f., 42, 54
Wirt, William, 240
Wise, Governor H. A., 259, 312
Wolfe, General James, 87 n., 88
Wood, General Leonard, 460, 502, 534
"Wood of the Marine Brigade," 520
Woodin, William B., 563
Workmen's Compensation Act, 502 n.
World Court, 538, 557, 560 f.
World War, 208, 487, 490 n., 495, 497 ff.
World's Fair, 441
Wright, Orville, aviator, 549
Wright, Wilbur, aviator, 549
Writs of Assistance, 95 and n., 97, 99
Wyeth, Nathaniel, 267
Wyoming, 430

X Y Z affair, 170 f., 171 n.

Yale College, 65
Yancey, W. L., 323, 327
York, Duke of, 45 n. 2, 48
Yorktown, 122, 135
Yukon, 397

Zenger, Peter, 67
Zimmermann note, 508